THE HOME ✤ FRONT

THE HOME ✤ FRONT

REVOLUTIONARY HOUSEHOLDS, MILITARY OCCUPATION, AND THE MAKING OF AMERICAN INDEPENDENCE

LAUREN DUVAL

Published by the
OMOHUNDRO INSTITUTE OF
EARLY AMERICAN HISTORY AND CULTURE,
Williamsburg, Virginia,
and the
UNIVERSITY OF NORTH CAROLINA PRESS,
Chapel Hill

The Omohundro Institute of Early American History & Culture (OI) is an independent research organization sponsored by William & Mary and the Colonial Williamsburg Foundation. On November 15, 1996, the OI adopted the present name in honor of a bequest from Malvern H. Omohundro, Jr., and Elizabeth Omohundro.

Manufactured in the United States of America

Cover art: *Red Coat Soldiers Toasting the Ladies of the House,* by Howard Pyle. Courtesy Wikiart.org.

Complete Library of Congress Cataloging-in-Publication Data
is available at https://lccn.loc.gov/2025045837.
9781469690056 (cloth: alk. paper)
9781469690063 (epub)
9781469690070 (pdf)

For product safety concerns under the European Union's General Product Safety Regulation (EU GPSR), please contact gpsr@mare-nostrum.co.uk or write to the University of North Carolina Press and Mare Nostrum Group B.V., Mauritskade 21D, 1091 GC Amsterdam, The Netherlands.

for

KEVIN AND NELLE

CONTENTS

ILLUSTRATIONS

A NOTE ON LANGUAGE

This book is fundamentally a history of the household—an intimate, familiar, quotidian space that was deeply enmeshed in daily life. Inhabited by members of the same family and those that they employed and enslaved, households brought together occupants in close, sometimes forced, proximity. In crowded rooms, they navigated around and occasionally collided with one another; they shared living space and overheard one another's conversations. The household was a space of familiarity. Whether or not intimacy was desired, the routines and practices of daily life enacted in a shared living space fostered relationships among various household inhabitants. For these reasons, throughout this book, I primarily refer to members of revolutionary households by their first (or full) names. Doing so serves several purposes. Practically, this naming convention helps to avoid confusion among family members with the same last name. It also, importantly, underscores the intimacy of household life while attempting to counter both racial and gendered naming conventions that were embedded within household hierarchies. Too often, surnames are reserved for white men, while their wives and daughters are called by their first names; similarly, enslaved people often had no recorded family name. Rather than replicating these inequitable household relationships, my naming conventions seek to center the human dimension of occupation and convey the lived experience of war equally among diverse household occupants. To convey these varied voices, I have retained original spelling and punctuation—as words were often written phonetically—except where necessary for understanding.

THE HOME ❖ FRONT

PROLOGUE

An Englishman's House Is His Castle

The sound of shattering glass pierced the air, jolting Mary King awake. She reached across the bed for her husband, Richard. Her other arm cradled her swelling stomach in reassurance. She was near her time and unsteady on her feet; if danger lurked below, it was unlikely that she could run. Across the chamber, three small children stirred, their eyes bleary from sleep. Mary murmured soothing words, even as fear pulsed through her. Her mind raced to the other two children, sleeping above. Still clutching Richard's arm, Mary followed her husband as he opened the bedroom door and called out. There was "no humain voice in answer." Below, a raucous crowd of unsettlingly familiar faces filled the house, their features distorted by disguises. Wielding clubs and axes, they numbered somewhere between twenty and thirty; it was difficult to tell in the dark. Suddenly, a hatchet crashed through the bedroom window where the King family huddled. "Dashing the Glass about the[ir] Naked Bodys," the weapon "Scarce Miss'd their heads." Below, men were

"Thumping, Yelling, [and] Hooping." Mary felt faint. She faltered and sank to the floor, collapsing as the cries of her children filled her ears: "Father woant they kill me, Father Save me." Richard swept his wife's limp body up in his arms, terrified that her distress was fatal, and "Convey[ed] her back to her Bead to Die there."[1]

Mary King survived that March evening in 1766. Coming to, she awoke in the arms of a maid, a frosty chill seeping through the broken windows. A hatchet lay on the floor, surrounded by shards of glass. The smell of smoke lingered in the air. "Lord of Mercy where shall I go?" she murmured. The family's large two-story house was in ruins. The broad hall and winding staircase showed evidence of the evening's violence, the elegant wainscoting "hacked" and "defaced." Seven expensive windows were "broke and destoy'd." Shattered earthenware, brassware, utensils, and three dozen "bruised and ruin'd" pewter dishes littered the hall. Remains of smashed and charred furniture were strewn throughout the house. The mob had also ransacked Richard's nearby shop. They "burnt and destroy'd divers deeds, notes of hand bonds[,] and other papers" amounting to nearly £1,114 worth of debts owed to Richard King.[2]

Two days later, the Kings received a note from the Sons of Liberty, warning that any attempt to prosecute individuals "on account of the Riot" would result in "haveing their Houses and Barns Burnt and Consumed and themselves Cut in pices and burnt to Ashes." The perpetrators remained true to their word. The following year, after Richard initiated court proceedings, the mob attacked his "lately refitted" house, damaging it irreparably. After one of the participants was arrested, another mob burned the barn and shed; they killed two of his "best Calves" and "[hung] up a dead colt before" his house. Writing of these events, Richard recalled "a frish the Destress of a mother. Espessuuly upon hering her outcries Eccoed by one find [*fiend*] to another in the Neighbouring bushes. Here again the Cries of helples Children, Intreeting their pairents to flee as Expecting Every momentto be Surounded in flaims." "But flee wheather?" he asked; "Devowerers had Surrounded us, and were Yelling like finds of H—ll for their prey."[3]

Richard King was one of the wealthiest residents of Scarborough (now Maine), which at the time was part of the colony of Massachusetts. As dissension roiled the Bay Colony during the imperial crisis, he remained a political moderate, although neighbors suspected him of holding loyalist sympathies. Some of the men who participated in the March 1766 attack were motivated by the belief that he "was a favourer of [the Stamp Act], and had the Stamp papers in his house; and that it was probable if that Act took place, he would be Stamp Master for Scarborough." Others, many of them in arrears to King, resented his intention to call in his debts and simply thought "he deservd a good Whipping and to have his Ears cutt of."[4]

In the years after the riots, Richard King continued to seek justice and financial restitution, even as witnesses fled to the northern borderlands or refused to answer court summons. Finally, his case appeared before the Cumberland Superior Court in Falmouth (Maine) in July 1774. King left no record of his thoughts on the trial, but imagine his relief when he discovered that his attorney was none other than John Adams, the Boston lawyer who had infamously—and successfully—defended the British soldiers after the so-called Boston Massacre four years earlier. Here was a man who, despite his own revolutionary leanings, was firmly committed to the principle of equal justice under the law.[5]

Adams, for his part, was thrilled to be "engaged in a famous Cause." Writing to his wife, Abigail, John relayed the circumstances of the case: "A Mob . . . broke into his House, and rifled his Papers, and terrifyed him, his Wife, Children and Servants in the Night. The Terror, and Distress, the Distraction and Horror of this Family cannot be described by Words or painted upon Canvass. It is enough to move a Statue, to melt an Heart of Stone."[6]

Though he never said so explicitly, John Adams seemingly sympathized with his client, whose circumstances, in many ways, mirrored his own. Like Richard King, John had a young family at home; the Kings' situation echoed that of the Adams household during the 1770 Boston Massacre trials, which occurred when Abigail was six months pregnant with their son Charles. In fact, John recounted in his autobiography, after learning that soldiers had fired into a crowd of Bostonians, his first concern was for his family. Before proceeding to the Customs House, he took a quick detour to the Adams residence and "surveyed round" to ensure that Abigail and the children were safe. Returning home later that evening, John "was apprehensive of the Effect" that news of the shooting would have on his pregnant wife. His anxieties mounted in the coming months. In a decision that John felt "incurr[ed] a Clamour" and fueled "Suspicions and prejudices" from his neighbors, he agreed to serve as defense attorney for the British soldiers; before the trial convened, he was also elected as a representative to the Massachusetts legislature, positioning him squarely in the middle of the escalating conflict between colonists and royal officials. The confluence of events weighed on him. He was anxious that his choices had consigned his "family to ruin and myself to death."[7]

By the time that John traveled to Maine in the summer of 1774 to defend Richard King, the situation in Boston had only intensified. Following the

December 1773 Tea Party, additional troops had arrived to quell the restive population. John's departure from Boston in June 1774 coincided with the arrival of the Coercive Acts, which, among other measures, closed the port of Boston as punishment for the destruction of the tea. Later that same month, John learned he had been elected as a delegate to the First Continental Congress. "I feel unutterable Anxiety," he confided to his diary after his selection. He continued to ponder the situation as he made his way northward. Days later, on arriving at the court in Falmouth on July 3, 1774, John unburdened himself in a letter to Abigail. "I am much concerned for my Family," he confessed.[8]

In short, when John Adams stood before the court in Falmouth in the summer of 1774, he was deeply aware of how his political principles might endanger his family. He had spent the previous weeks ruminating on the implications of his actions for his loved ones. These concerns were at the forefront of his mind as he prepared his prosecution on behalf of Richard King. He must have contemplated whether a similar fate lay in store for his own wife and children. How was a man to defend his family when the civil contract appeared to be broken? Where else could a pregnant woman and her children be safe, if not in their own house? How was a man to reconcile himself to the knowledge that his actions had endangered the lives of those dearest to him?

John Adams's legal career is rightly marked by his defense of the accused soldiers in the Boston Massacre, but the lesser-known case of *King v. Stewart* deserves a place alongside it. For, in his closing argument, Adams invoked the principles that would come to undergird the American revolutionary project. Expounding on the rights of British subjects, he drew from common law precedent and the well-established maxim that "an Englishmans dwelling House is his Castle." "The Law has erected a Fortification round it," he proclaimed, and "every Member of Society has entered into a solemn Covenant with every other that he shall enjoy in his own dwelling House as compleat a security, safety and Peace and Tranquility as if it was surrounded with Walls of Brass, with Ramparts and Palisadoes and defended with a Garrison and Artillery." Legal training aside, Adams had recently been acquainted with the reality of the allusions he drew. Living in British-occupied Boston, he was intimately familiar with military defenses. He confronted armed troops and battlements on a daily basis as he walked through his city. British soldiers were a common sight in Boston's neighborhoods. Though himself no military man, Adams knew precisely what a military fortification looked like. Building his argument, Adams adopted the language of rhetorical slavery that saturated revolutionary pamphlets. "To deprive a Man of this Protection, this quiet and Security in the dead of Night, when himself and Family confiding in it are asleep, is treat[ing] him not like an Englishman not like a Freeman but like a Slave," Adams proclaimed. A man's sovereignty over his household and his family's security within embodied the principles of liberty and freedom; it was what separated a free man from a slave, who had no claim to property, even his own body. True liberty was found in domestic tranquility.[9]

Yet Adams's defense rested on more than legal principle and political rhetoric. In his closing argument, he made an overt appeal to the shared masculine prerogative of the jury, men who had "like Passions, feelings, Imaginations and Understandings." He asked them to contemplate "the Cruelty the Terror, the Horror of the whole dismal scene" and "the distresses of this innocent Family." He spoke to them as fathers, expounding on the danger of "Sudden Terror" on children's psyches, cautioning that "Habits of Fear . . . never can be cured," for "all the force of their Reason shall never be able to make them walk in the dark without fear." He entreated them as husbands, asking them to consider "the Danger, the real Damage and actual Cruelty" sustained by King's "amiable Wife . . . far gone in her Pregnancy." It was, Adams argued, a question of masculinity. "No Man who has a Soul, *who has the Spirit of a Man in him can ever after during his whole Life, ever forget such an Indignity,* tho he may forgive it. He can never think of it without Pain of Mind, without Impatience, Anger, Resentment, Shame and Grief." "If your Passions are not affected upon this Occasion, you will [not] be the Plaintiffs Peers," Adams reproved the jury.[10]

In a fervent plea, Adams implored the jurors to *"put yourself in his [King's] Place,* and be moved with his Passions," to "feel as he did." Drawing inspiration from one of Richard King's letters—and, it must be supposed, the anxieties and trepidations that had plagued him in previous weeks—Adams conjured an agonizing scene for the jury: a family sleeping peacefully, securely in their home as "the Darkness, the stillness the silence of Midnight" settled over the household. Suddenly, a mob shatters their tranquility. Breaking the windows, they burst into the house: "they Roar, they stamp, they Yell, they houl, they cutt break tear and burn all before them." Imagine, Adams encouraged the jury, the feelings of a husband and father in this moment—the jeers of an angry mob mingling with "the Cries of Distress" of his five "terrifyd" children as they cling to him; the grasp of his pregnant wife loosening on his arm as she collapses to the floor, "sinking fainting dying away in his Arms"; the shouts of his servants rising above the din. Going beyond the bounds of admissible argument, Adams spoke directly to the foreman of the jury: "What sum of

Money Mr. Foreman would tempt you, to be Mr. King, and to let your Wife undergo what Mrs. King underwent, and your Children what theirs did for one Night?"[11]

Asking the jury to envision their own families similarly threatened, Adams made his case on the basis of emotion. To be sure, there was a legal precedent for his argument, but Adams's appeal transcended mere academic rhetoric. He asked the jurors to instead consider what it meant to be a man, to consider the foundation of a man's liberties, his responsibilities, and the burdens that all men shared. A man's ability to defend and secure his household, Adams argued, was not only the root of liberty but the foundation of manhood. Drawing on his own position as a father and a husband, Adams was unequivocal: "I freely confess that the whole sum sued for would be no temptation to me, if there was no other Damage than this."[12]

Yet, Adams maintained, the damage extended beyond that fateful night. Indeed, he suggested, the trauma of household invasion would be a lifelong burden for Richard King. It would forever be a stain on his legacy, his duties to his wife, his patrimony to his children, his relationships with his neighbors. It would irrevocably alter the family and be a blemish on their domestic lives. For "how can the Impression of it be erased out of his Mind and hers and the Childrens?" Adams questioned. It could not, he reasoned. The memory of invasion might "lessen," but it would "frequently interrupt his Happiness." "As long as he lives," Adams insisted, "it will be a continual Sourse of Grief to him," an uncomfortable reminder of his failure to protect his family. It was horrible to contemplate. Richard King "might have killed em all and been justified," Adams avowed.[13]

Although never as secure in practice as in principle, many Anglo-American householders regarded the notion that a man's house was his castle not only as a settled legal principle but as an entrenched personal conviction that informed their perceptions of patriarchal obligations and political liberties. As one historian of early modern Britain has put it, "The threshold of the house was an ideological boundary of great power." Castle doctrine, according to Anglo-American jurisprudence, established male householders' legal authority over their families, laborers, and property and signified how the notions of masculine independence and wealth vested in households supported the larger patriarchal and political governing orders. "One of the most essential branches of English liberty, is the freedom of one's house," Boston lawyer James Otis proclaimed in 1761, as he condemned British writs of assistance that permitted searches of private property.[14]

As the political crisis deepened later that decade, the principle that a man's house was his castle intensified into a rallying cry for aggrieved American colonists. Denouncing the Townshend Acts, John Dickinson also drew on the metaphor in his widely read *Letters from a Farmer in Pennsylvania* (1768), insisting that under the common law a man's house was "a place of perfect security." The Townshend Acts—which, in addition to taxes, permitted customs searches of private homes—were, Dickinson declared, "utterly destructive" to American liberty. His rhetoric proved remarkably salient. Writing six years later from the outskirts of British-occupied Boston, Abigail Adams quoted the "admired Farmer." "Let these truths . . . be indelibly impressed on our Minds," she wrote, "that we cannot be happy without being free, that we cannot be free without being secure in our property, that we cannot be secure in our property if without our consent others may as by right take it away." Reverting to her own prose, Abigail declared, "We know too well the blessings of freedom, to tamely resign it." Two months later, shots rang out on Lexington Common, plunging the colonies into civil war.[15]

In many ways, John Adams's argument in *King v. Stewart* foreshadowed the domestic invasion, violence, and destruction that would define the American Revolution for many colonists. During the course of the war, American households came under assault on multiple fronts. No longer were debates about a man's control of his household theoretical. Americans faced invading armies at their doorsteps; they quartered British officers; and they found their valuable resources and supplies requisitioned for military use, regardless of their own needs or political dispositions. They withstood robberies, property destruction, and invasion. Most people encountered the violence of war, not on the battlefield, but in their households. This experience made clear to many Americans that their homes were not castles. Instead, they were vulnerable. The walls of the fortress had been irrevocably breached.

War gave new immediacy to questions of domestic control and the limits of arbitrary power. It compelled colonists to reassess their relationships to their households and produced a new awareness of the tenuousness of the households that undergirded their liberties. These circumstances convinced white men and women of the upper classes that to "secure the Blessings of Liberty to ourselves and our Posterity," they would first have to secure their households. The laws of the new nation erected legal fortifications around the private home, venerating domestic felicity as both the just reward for wartime sacrifice and the embodiment of masculine independence. Among those men who crafted the new Constitution in 1787 was a young Massachusetts politician named Rufus King. For King, like many Americans, the violence of war and the terror of household invasion were not abstract; these traumatic experiences were fundamental to how they experienced the long struggle for American independence. As an eleven-year-old in Scarborough, Maine, Rufus King had awakened in terror one evening in March 1766; he had huddled by his stepmother's limp body, fearing for his life while vengeful neighbors filled his home and threw a hatchet through his bedroom window, shattering his family's domestic tranquility.[16]

The story of the American Revolution is one that is deeply entwined with domestic life; households were politically resonant, yet intensely personal spaces. They mediated peoples' experiences and perceptions of war, even as they became sites of contestation over its meaning. Households therefore offer a valuable lens through which to consider how the war unfolded, what it meant to those who lived through it, and its legacies for the nation. Nowhere were these dynamics more apparent than in the six cities occupied by the British Army during the war: Boston, New York, Newport, Philadelphia, Savannah, and Charleston. Here, the line between home front and battlefront frequently blurred, drawing diverse civilians into the war's orbit and transforming households into critical fronts in the War for American Independence.

INTRODUCTION

All Our Worldly Comforts Are Now at Stake

Staring out the window in the early dawn hours of April 19, 1775, Hannah Winthrop dreaded "the rising Sun" and "the Bloody Carnage" that she knew it would illuminate. The sounds of war echoed across Concord's dew-covered fields: the staccato beat of drums. Church bells clanging in alarm. Musket fire resounding in the distance. Alarmed at the sight of British reinforcements marching past their house, Hannah and her husband, John, fled, "not knowing whither we went." Neighbors directed them to a house about a mile outside of town. There, they found an agonizing scene. The residence was overflowing with the anxious wives and crying children of the nearly eighty men who battled with British troops in the New England countryside. Sounds of "incessant fire" echoed in the distance, and Hannah glimpsed bayonets "glistening" in the sun. Day faded into night. The Winthrops spent a sleepless evening alongside the anguished families. Some of the women curled up on the floor beside their children; others nodded off to sleep in their chairs. They were, Hannah mourned, pitiable "monuments of that persecuting Barbarity of British Tyranny."[1]

The next morning, news of advancing British troops forced the families to evacuate their shelter. The Winthrops secured a chaise, squeezing in alongside three others. As they retreated deeper into the countryside, they witnessed the aftermath of the previous day's battle. Hannah spied a man, his cart overflowing with the "mangled" corpses of his neighbors, looking for his son among the dead. The "roads [were] filld with frighted women and children," Hannah noted, "Some in carts with their tallest furniture, others on foot fleeing into the woods." With the outbreak of civil war, panicked revolutionaries were fleeing British-occupied Boston, seeking refuge among family and like-minded neighbors in the surrounding regions. Some families drove the wagons themselves or carried their prized possessions carefully wrapped up in handkerchiefs. Others entrusted their valuables to enslaved laborers, who, unlike their enslavers, left no record of their feelings about fleeing Boston. A few of the exhausted refugees might have turned back for a glimpse of the residences they had abandoned. Others, like Bostonian Sarah Winslow Deming, gazed resolutely ahead. She would not yearn for the imperial ties that had been severed when shots erupted on Lexington Common. "We had got out of the city of destruction," Sarah remembered, but she "did not . . . look back [at Boston] after the similitude of Lots wife."[2]

Biblical metaphors also preoccupied Hannah Winthrop's mind as she fled into the Massachusetts countryside. Likening her situation to Eve's banishment from the Garden of Eden, Hannah mournfully quoted Milton's *Paradise Lost* as she recounted her flight to her friend, Boston author Mercy Otis Warren. "Methinks in that hour I felt the force of my Mother Eves Soliloquy on being driven out of Paradise," Hannah professed; "O unexpected stroke, worse than of death! / Must I thus Leave thee, Paradise?" Hannah feared that she would never again return "to that peacefull abode, that happy roof," where she and her husband had planned to live out the remainder of their days. "Since we were dispossest of our earthly enjoyments, all nature has seemd to be reversd," Hannah confessed, lamenting both the loss of her home and the security it represented, the calming normalcy of daily rituals and domestic comforts.[3]

Despite her anguish, Hannah acknowledged that her sufferings paled next to those who remained trapped in Boston. The city's harbor had been closed for nearly a year as retribution for the destruction of three shiploads of East India Company tea in December 1773. Supplies were scant in the beleaguered city—shortages that would only be exacerbated in the coming months as the New England militia and, after June 1775, a combined force including the newly formed Continental army lay siege to Boston. "I am ashamed that my inconvenience should have such an undue effect upon me," Hannah admitted.[4]

Reassuring Hannah that her feelings were justified, in her reply, Mercy Otis Warren conjured an evocative scene of the Winthrops being "driven from your own habitation, by an army of ruffians, though in the livery of a King." She lamented that the family's house, "once the residence of calm philosophy, [was] now occupied by the boisterous sons of Mars;- and instead of the music of the spheres, and the delightful harmony of nature, there is nothing now to be heard in this once happy retreat, but the din of arms, and the shrill clarion of war." As Mercy understood, the transformation of the Winthrop residence into a regimental barrack had destabilized Hannah's assumption of safety, and the emotional toll of fractured security amplified the loss of her home and property. The house remained standing, but its meaning had changed. It was no longer a pleasant drawing room, a treasured familial space, or a safe haven. The family was gone, replaced by "the noisy, turbulent mistress of war."[5]

Such scenes are rarely what come to mind when we think of the first hours of the American Revolution. Terrified families and weary refugees driving wagons overloaded with furniture offer seemingly mundane counternarratives to Paul Revere's daring midnight ride or minutemen hastening to their posts in the predawn hours. Yet the War for American Independence was, fundamentally, an eight-year military conflict fought in and around civilian communities, with devastating consequences for those who resided there. For civilian inhabitants, the Revolution introduced chaos and unprecedented violence into their lives. Domestic disruption, rather than being incidental to the war, defined how many people experienced the Revolution and understood its consequences for their families. As one Massachusetts woman lamented after the outbreak of war in 1775, "All our worldly comforts are now at stake."[6]

British-occupied cities and the surrounding regions offer especially vivid examples of these dynamics. Over the course of the eight-year war, American port cities were strategic strongholds for British forces reliant on overseas supply for reinforcements and resources. Every major city on the mainland Atlantic seaboard—Boston, New York, Newport, Philadelphia, Charleston,

FIGURE 1 Christian Remick, *A Prospective View of Part of the [Boston] Commons* (detail). 1768–1770. Watercolor. Concord Museum Collection, Gift of Mr. John Brown, Jr.; Pi409. Concord Museum, Concord, Mass.

Depicting the British Army drilling on Boston Common, this contemporary watercolor illustrates how fully war and military occupation infiltrated daily life as well as the diversity of civilians who came into contact with the army; note both the Black and white families in the foreground.

and Savannah—was occupied by the British Army during the war. As battles raged on city outskirts and civilians lived under martial law for extended periods, households throughout these regions became war zones, with differing consequences for their assorted residents. Integrating these varied, often contradictory wartime experiences, this study exposes the importance of the household as a site of wartime violence and as an additional front in the War for American Independence.[7]

The Home Front is a story about the domestic experience of war during the American Revolution. It argues that the experience of British occupation, in which Anglo-American men were disempowered within their households, represented an unprecedented threat to the patriarchal household as a financial investment, a sentimentalized cultural ideal, a projection of status and power, and the basic ordering unit of colonial society. After the Revolution, these deeply disorienting consequences of British occupation led white Americans to reify and reconsecrate the private home as a national symbol that epitomized masculine authority and the sacrifices of war. Reorienting the war around the household, *The Home Front* reshapes our understanding of the American Revolution and the founding of the nation as a fundamentally domestic story.[8]

British military occupation wrought havoc on the patriarchal households that undergirded and perpetuated the revolutionary social order. Inherited from British common law, the household was a legal construction that embodied the relations of power that structured colonial society, where authority was vested in the male head of household who functioned as the legal, social, and political representative for his assorted dependents, including his family, servants, and enslaved people. These paternalistic relationships, defined by bonds of mutual obligation between householders and those they were responsible for, upheld the hierarchies of race, gender, status, wealth, freedom, and political power that emanated from the household and that manifested in male householders' patriarchal authority, social power, political influence, and material wealth. Households—or "little monarch[ies]," as one historian has termed them—had real, lived implications for daily life, labor arrangements, family relationships, social communities, and financial transactions; they were familial, economic, and legal entities that functioned both as nexuses of emotional ties and power relations as well as centers of affective ties and family life. Moreover, as a consequence of the longer eighteenth-century emergence of idealized domesticity, by the time of the Revolution, households were increasingly foundational to the gendered, raced, and classed identities of free, primarily white people throughout the British Atlantic world, especially those of elite and middling status for whom domestic life functioned as a critical "site of self-fashioning and identity formation." British occupation unsettled these nascent identities and their accompanying power dynamics in alarming ways by threatening—at times violently—the financial, legal, and cultural underpinnings of the existing social order.[9]

Under British occupation American households faced military raids, invasion, property confiscation, and forced quartering; they became permeable, contested spaces. White Americans felt insecure in their property, and, in many instances, unable to exert power within their own houses. In resource-scarce garrisons, people, both enslaved and free, suffered from food shortages and the ravages of disease and destruction. Robbery, theft, and invasion were commonplace. Soldiers and civilians dismantled fences for firewood. Cannonballs burst through walls, and errant bullets slipped through windows, exposing civilians of all races and genders to new, frightening levels of violence. British officers demanded quarters in family residences, living alongside white women and children, servants, and enslaved laborers as they claimed civilian labor and resources for their own. For women of all races, large bodies of troops deepened the threat of sexual assault. These circumstances were exacerbated for enslaved people, some of whom became collateral damage in a war that was waged, not for their liberty, but for that of their enslavers. Legally classified as property, the enslaved were subject not only to the increased violence directed at civilians, they were also vulnerable to abduction and trafficking. Whether by choice or circumstance, civilians resided in military zones where fear—of illness, of death, of bloodshed, of starvation—stalked their daily activities with distinctive consequences for different household residents.

Within British garrisons, widespread destruction, violence, and limitations on the power of white revolutionaries strained household relationships in disorienting ways. Accustomed to unquestioned authority, white male heads of household were subjected to the scrutiny of commanding officers and British military policies that both intentionally and inadvertently constrained men's authority over both their property and their dependents. Within these reconfigured wartime households, white women, enslaved people, and domestic servants experienced heightened vulnerability. But the disruption to patriarchal governing structures also loosened oversight over their daily lives and labors, providing many people with new levels of autonomy that allowed them to determine the course of their lives or alter their circumstances. Domestic servants and enslaved laborers fled American households in large numbers, pursuing the promise of better lives behind

British lines. For various reasons, ranging from amusement to bids for survival, unmarried women of all races befriended, flirted, and socialized with British troops—much to the dismay of revolutionaries who felt that these women were forsaking their duties to their households and their obligations to the revolutionary cause.[10]

Whether decrying property damage, household disorder, personal discomfort, or, more broadly, the erosion of the patriarchal household and the social order it supported, critically, Anglo-American colonists conceived of their wartime losses and understood their implications for both individual families and the broader social order through the lens of domestic life. "Our Struggle has loosened the bands of Government every where," John Adams lamented in 1776. "We have been told," he reported, that "Children and Apprentices were disobedient—that schools and Colledges were grown turbulent—that Indians slighted their Guardians and Negroes grew insolent to their Masters" and that white women, a group "more numerous and powerfull than all the rest were grown discontented." He blamed this societal disorder, not on revolutionary ideals of liberty and equality, but on "wicked" British policies that had infiltrated the most intimate and private relationships and encouraged recalcitrance among household dependents—including his own wife.[11]

The wartime threat to white male property and authority had lasting consequences for the nation. To reclaim and fortify the power that they had lost during the war, in the early years of the Republic elite and middling white Americans reconceptualized the private home as a building block of the new nation and invested it with national significance. They erected stringent legal protections to ensure that their homes would never again face the invasion and terror of the war years. Postwar legal developments reinforced men's control over their households by safeguarding property and fortifying men's domestic power. Concurrently, shifting cultural ideas venerated the private home as an emblem of American independence—a shift that converged with the war's destabilization of organized religion to place the home firmly at the center of a new, secular national creed. The sanctification of the household was a critical feature of this new ethos, entwining the private home with the nation itself. No longer messy, dynamic home fronts characterized by rebellious household dependents, invaded wartime households came to signify masculine valor and American men's defense of home rule against British tyranny. This reframing of the home front obscured the dynamics of occupied households and domestic warfare that were defining features of many Americans' wartime experiences.[12]

British occupation draws these strands together in ways that illuminate the centrality of domestic life to the experience, meaning, and consequences of the American Revolution. The enhanced vulnerability of households in and around British garrisons introduced real danger to people's lives and destabilized the revolutionary social order in alarming ways—experiences that resonated throughout the colonies because of how households grounded nascent middle-class identities and intersected with other relations of power that undergirded revolutionary society. Indeed, the wartime endangerment to American households not only enhanced Anglo-Americans' attachment to domestic spaces—convincing many of the need to safeguard their households and the identities, wealth, and power embodied therein—but also hastened many colonists' disillusionment with Britain. Concurrently, the experience, and eventual outcome, of civil war dissolved any lingering notions that Anglo-Americans might have held about the metropole as home. Occurring at the moment of national creation, these twin processes had a lasting impact on the nation, entwining Americans' renewed reverence for domestic life with an emergent national identity. The domestic experience of war, *The Home Front* shows, helped to define the very meaning of American independence.[13]

CITIES INTO GARRISONS

This book examines Boston, New York, Newport, Philadelphia, Charleston, and Savannah, the six cities that the British Army occupied during the Revolution. Rather than a comparative approach, however, this study emphasizes the connections among these diverse locales. Such an analysis illuminates important threads that tell a bigger, national story about the experience of war and the founding of the United States.[14]

In accordance with the norms and strategies of European warfare, the British Army focused on capturing American ports, where they could more easily obtain supplies and reinforcements by sea and use the city as a base to launch excursions into surrounding regions. Although primarily an urban endeavor, British occupation nevertheless radiated out from metropolitan areas and affected large swaths of the American colonies. Urban civilians were more likely than rural inhabitants to interact with British forces and to reside under martial law; rural inhabitants were more likely to experience unrestrained violence and marauding. In both environments, British occupation introduced new levels of danger into civilian life, with varied consequences for the heterogeneous populations that resided in and around revolutionary cities.

Urban ports offer a critical venue to examine the consequences of the Revolution's domestic warfare and its influence on emergent national identities. The urban centers at the heart of the revolutionary conflict ranged in population from 3,500 in the relatively newer city of Savannah to 40,000 in the largest city, Philadelphia; New York (25,000), Boston (16,000), Charleston (12,000), and Newport (11,000) fell in between. Although representing only 10 percent of the population of mainland British North America, urban ports held outsized importance in revolutionary politics, cultures, and economies. These thriving commercial centers were vibrant, diverse hubs of fashion, culture, and trade that tethered the American colonies to the broader Atlantic world. Owing to these circumstances, urban ports were also, crucially, at the epicenter of the North American eighteenth-century consumer revolution, which progressively tied the nascent classed and racial identities of elite and middling Anglo-Americans—the same families who would go on to wield power in the early Republic—to commodities, households, and the material aspects of domestic life.[15]

Elite and middling American colonists were, in the words of one Hessian officer, "very house-proud." Houses varied by region and income: from the stately brick mansions that lined Charleston's rivers as well as the city's iconic single houses—long, narrow wooden buildings with spacious lawns to facilitate air circulation in the humid climate—to the tree-lined streets of Broadway and the elegant two-story houses of New York's merchants that overlooked the city's commercial district, to the orderly brick townhouses with white trim and classical architectural details of Philadelphia, to the plainer, wooden dwellings that lined the unpaved streets of Newport and Savannah. Yet, whatever the appearance, these residences served similar purposes. They projected the refinement and standing of their owners; they were places of familial life and sociability, of labor and enslavement, that undergirded family finances and ensured the transmission of wealth to future generations.[16]

Over the course of the eighteenth century, households became increasingly integral to the performance of status and identity among elite and middling Anglo-Americans throughout the Atlantic world, signaling the power, wealth, gentility, and emotional lives of their owners. The eighteenth-century consumer revolution made commodities more affordable, leading to the accumulation of luxury goods as markers of wealth, refinement, and status among affluent urbanites. Lush carpets, elegant drapery, marble fireplaces, and mahogany furniture adorned the houses of colonial elites. Gleaming silver ornaments, imported porcelain tea sets, and expensive portraits further conveyed families' wealth and status. Entertaining rooms reflected eighteenth-century European ideals about beauty and refined elegance, which were made manifest in the unblemished, shining, and polished surfaces of luxury goods—surfaces, especially in the southern colonies, that were polished by enslaved laborers whose presence, like the houses and the luxurious furnishings they contained, signified the wealth and power of their enslavers.[17]

Even so, city dwellers' lives were enmeshed with those of their neighbors. Houses often shared walls, and it was easy to peer into the windows of nearby residences, or to overhear conversations. This was especially true in impoverished neighborhoods, where communal childcare and shared resources were essential to survival. The houses of laboring and enslaved inhabitants illuminate the stark class differences within American cities. Scipio Handley, a free Black fisherman in Charleston, resided in a sparsely furnished residence with his mother, who might have owned the property. The Handleys possessed a couple of trunks, some linen, seven hogs, a quantity of spare cash, and a variety of furniture. Revealing the intersection of household goods, race, and status, Eleanor Lester, a white shopkeeper, recalled that "the furniture was good enough for Negroes." These meager circumstances nevertheless were significantly more comfortable than those of enslaved South Carolinians. Those in more rural areas, as one Hessian officer recounted, resided in "Wretched huts, made of logs placed one over the other." Some urban bondspeople slept in their enslavers' residences; more commonly, they lived on the second stories of outbuildings, such as kitchens and washhouses, located at the rear of the main houses—spaces designed to be surveilled. Though they were far from inviolable, these austere dwellings also could at times shelter family life, providing the enslaved with spaces where they could snatch moments of joy away from the probing eyes of their enslavers.[18]

During the American Revolution, these varied households became battlefronts. Active warfare was a novel experience for many urban Americans. Unlike borderlands inhabitants who were more accustomed to British regulars patrolling the backcountry and the omnipresent threat of danger from Native warfare, metropolitan ports had been sheltered from military conflict for much of the eighteenth century. Urban inhabitants supported British warfare with their taxes, fought in colonial militias, and attended balls to celebrate battlefield victories, but their homes and their cities remained remarkably free from military conflict.[19]

Still, British soldiers were not an unfamiliar presence in American ports. At varying points throughout the colonial period, most visibly during the Seven Years' War, British forces garrisoned in urban barracks along the

Atlantic seaboard. Likewise, the crown occasionally deployed regular troops to the colonies to keep public order, an official display of strength that functioned as a counterpoint to the boisterous street culture of Anglo-American politics. Operating within established methods of imperial governance, the presence of peacekeeping troops, in many ways, strengthened imperial ties: in addition to their official duties, British soldiers frequently integrated into civilian neighborhoods, laboring at odd jobs alongside colonists and building family connections and social networks, even as the military presence heightened tensions between soldiers and partisans. Such relationships endured, even after two regiments of British regulars arrived in Boston in 1768 to quell widespread discontent over the Townshend Acts, which culminated in the Boston Massacre in March 1770. Yet the British presence in Boston also prompted some of American colonists' earliest arguments against the British Army's invasion into their households. Citing the 1765 Mutiny Act, which prohibited the billeting of troops in private homes, Boston's selectmen challenged the army's right to quarter among the city's inhabitants, debates that showcase how fully cities and households in late eighteenth-century British North America were understood to be civilian spaces sheltered from war.[20]

Still, these prewar circumstances, however uncomfortable, differed from wartime occupation. Even after the 1774 Coercive Acts restricted Boston town meetings and King George III appointed British general Thomas Gage as the colony's governor, neither colonists nor soldiers saw themselves as existing in a state of occupation, despite their military governor. It was not until June 12, 1775—two months after the outbreak of war—that General Gage formally instituted military rule and Bostonians began to refer to themselves as residing under "marshall law." "There is no such thing as saying anything," Isaac Smith bemoaned, as he enumerated the Bostonians who had been jailed for seemingly innocuous comments that ranged from expressing support for the American rebels to a man who called out to his sister in the street. He was particularly incensed by the imprisonment of one man arrested for the crime of speaking his mind while "standing by his door." The English legal maxim that "a man's house was his castle" had been established for centuries, yet war threw these norms into disarray. Legal protections were the rights due to Englishmen—not enemies residing under martial law.[21]

According to the standards of eighteenth-century European warfare, civilians were ostensibly beyond the bounds of military conflict, so long as their actions did not undermine military aims. Influenced by Enlightenment thinkers, over the course of the eighteenth century, European armies adopted policies to encourage humane warfare and the honorable treatment of both military and civilian enemies. Emer de Vattel's *The Law of Nations,* published in 1758 and translated into English in 1760, was critical to this transformation. Outlining best practices for international relations, diplomacy, and warfare, Vattel encouraged moderation and exhorted soldiers to "never forget that our enemies are men." "If we are under the disagreeable necessity of prosecuting our right by force of arms," Vattel advised, "let us not destroy that charity which connects us with all mankind." Extreme measures such as violence against civilians, property destruction, and the razing of towns were only to be deployed when absolutely necessary.[22]

Yet these guidelines, however noble, were highly dependent on the disposition of commanding officers. It was widely accepted that punishing tactics were allowable to expedite victory or chastise enemies. The war effort was not to be sacrificed in the name of humanity. Officers' obligations to conquered civilian populations were similarly elastic. Women, children, the aged, and clergy were owed special consideration as "enemies who make no resistance," and soldiers were discouraged from using violence, imprisoning, or otherwise maltreating them—so long as their actions did not endanger military aims. Such customary "politeness, doubtless very commendable," Vattel acknowledged, was not, however, "in itself absolutely obligatory, and if a general thinks fit to supersede it, he cannot be justly accused of breaking the laws of war."[23]

The outbreak of war in 1775 thus fundamentally altered the relationship between British troops and American colonists. With the colonies in open rebellion, soldiers were no longer tasked with patrolling a discontented populace; they were acting to subdue an internal enemy. Military occupation transformed civilian spaces into urban battlefronts, broadening officers' control over civilian regions and granting them latitude in their dealings with inhabitants. Categorized as potential enemies, urban dwellers—especially white inhabitants of the upper classes—faced unprecedented threats to their persons and property as British forces attempted to reestablish control over the rebellious American colonies.

British occupation transformed American cities, unsettling the rhythms and patterns of urban life. Public buildings, warehouses, schools, and churches became quarters, stables, hospitals, prisons, guardhouses, and even riding academies for officers. Politics shaped these requisitions as much as necessity. Praising the conversion of Philadelphia's new State House—where the Declaration of Independence had been adopted only the previous year—into a prison, one British official relished the irony, observing, "This has been the Fate of some other public Buildings, wch were before employed in disseminating the Principles of Rebellion." To erect defensive fortifications, the army demolished houses and chopped down fruit trees. Civilian property became targets of requisition and plunder. Seeking to deprive revolutionaries of valuable labor and resources, the British offered freedom to enslaved people; over the course of the war, approximately twenty thousand enslaved refugees flooded the British lines. But others arrived there by force. Enslaved people were kidnapped and distributed as enlistment bonuses or rewards; they were conscripted to labor on public works projects, to perform domestic services, or to grow crops to feed the army. Elsewhere in occupied regions, aided by loyalists, the British identified, disarmed, and imprisoned those opposed to crown rule—measures typically, although not exclusively, aimed at Anglo-American men. Civilians' commercial activities came under increased scrutiny to ensure access to provisions and supplies. Curfews and mandatory passes restricted civilians' movement. Hostile surveillance became a constant in city dwellers lives.[24]

Visible, disruptive, and transformative, these policies affected every facet of urban life. In Philadelphia, six-year-old Molly Pemberton described the altered city in a letter to her grandfather. Wooden buildings were "in the Shambles," and there was "Scarce a fence or wood Standing." In the meal market, horses were stabled in the once vibrant stalls from which vendors hawked their wares. Wounded soldiers displaced the city's poor from the almshouse and the sick from the Pennsylvania Hospital. Congregations surrendered their places of worship. "The schools kept in the upper part of Esex Flours house pine Street meetinghouse hath been in danger to be taken for the sick," Molly worried. Troops drilled in the square outside her window, and she witnessed "a number [of] exercies" accompanied by "music of different Sorts Severals Times aday going round." Under the army's control, Philadelphia morphed from the vibrant commercial capital of the fledgling United States into a British military garrison—a transformation repeated in each city that the British Army occupied during the war.[25]

GENDER, HOUSEHOLDS, AND THE AMERICAN REVOLUTION

We cannot understand conversations about American independence apart from the daily domestic experiences within revolutionary households—the very households that colonists so vociferously defended in their prose and that they targeted in their calls to action. Revolutionaries argued that the security of property, which encompassed both proprietorship and the attendant rights of heads of households, was both a central feature of liberty and necessary to preserving that freedom. Such beliefs were, however, also deeply rooted in the affective and material aspects of domestic life. Alexander Hamilton explicitly drew this connection in 1774 as he exhorted colonists to resist Parliamentary taxation. "Perhaps before long, your tables, and chairs, and platters, and dishes, and knives and forks, and every thing else would be taxed," he warned; "Nay, I don't know but they would find means to tax you for every child you got, and for every kiss your daughters received from their sweet-hearts." For Hamilton, resistance was a matter of masculinity. "You would be a disgrace to your ancestors, and the bitterst enemies to yourselves and to your posterity, if you did not act like men, in protecting and defending those rights you have hitherto enjoyed," he proclaimed.[26]

Citing such rhetoric, scholars have long recognized property as an important feature of revolutionary rhetoric, resistance, and the waging of war during the American Revolution, although they have paid less attention to the lived experience of wartime households and the gendered dynamics to which Hamilton not so subtly alluded. Likewise, historians of women and gender have long insisted on the importance of domestic life—the household is a fixture in the historiography of women in the revolutionary era—but such studies typically focus on events far from the field of battle. Consequently, despite a shared recognition of the vital role of property and households in the revolutionary era, there have been surprisingly few attempts to bridge these historiographies and bring them into conversation with one another. Indeed, with a few notable exceptions, studies of war and studies of gender during the American Revolution have largely remained distinct from one another, siloed within their respective fields.[27]

Yet, as this study shows, the household can be an effective analytical tool to bridge these scholarly divides, resulting in a more holistic, interconnected examination of the Revolution that enhances our understanding of the conflict as a civil war with immense consequences for civilian communities. The warfare of the American Revolution was not contained to the battlefield; indeed, the Revolution—like all wars—was a societal experience that drew diverse people into its orbit, by both choice and by force. As battles raged in and around civilian communities, war invaded households, endangering property, individuals, and their families in ways that were deeply entangled with race and gender. Throughout the conflict, the household was simultaneously a nexus of emotional ties, financial interests, and race and gender relations that grounded the social order *and* a place of wartime violence, disruption, and chaos where people experienced fear and insecurity that had the potential to overturn the very stability that the household was supposed to represent. It is only by attending to the interplay of these dynamics that we can fully comprehend the scope of the military conflict and the vital role of gender and race to how people experienced the Revolution and understood the consequences of war for themselves, their families, and the nation.[28]

Since the publication of Elizabeth Ellet's three-volume *The Women of the American Revolution* (1848–1850), domestic life has been a prominent feature in histories of women and the Revolution. Over a century later, the 1980 publication of Mary Beth Norton's *Liberty's Daughters* and Linda K. Kerber's *Women of the Republic* reinvigorated the field by centering women's wartime experiences and intellectual lives. The Revolution, they showed, politicized the domestic sphere and endowed (primarily elite, white) women with a new conception of themselves and their roles, resulting in what Kerber termed "republican motherhood," or as Jan Lewis would later enlarge the concept, "republican wi[ves]." Within this framework, they demonstrated how women invested their postwar domestic roles with national, political significance. Subsequent historians have enlarged our understanding of the cultural and political meanings of independence for American women—what one historian has called "the ripple effects of the Revolution"—with studies that have enriched our knowledge of (primarily elite, white) women's lives. Their work has illuminated how women understood political rights and how they mobilized the Revolution's rhetoric of personal liberty and civic virtue to campaign for educational opportunities and engage in public advocacy, to exert increased control over their reproductive lives and partake in more companionate marriages, and to pursue financial possibilities and obtain easier access to divorce, even as coverture and the legal sublimation of wives to husbands persisted well into the early years of the nation.[29]

Deeply indebted to this pathbreaking scholarship, *The Home Front* differs from these studies in that it seeks to recenter the household in the history of the American Revolution, rather than examining the consequences of the Revolution on women's lives. Doing so allows us to consider the ramifications of this domestic, intimate experience for both individuals and the broader revolutionary society. Bridging the fields of war and gender, it asks not only how the war "unsettled domesticity" but how centering domestic life—as a lived experience for both men and women as well as an institution that reflected and embodied the interstices of power in early America—unsettles prevailing narratives of the experience, meaning, and consequences of the American Revolution and the founding of the nation. Because of this emphasis on the lived experience of war and imaginings of the household, this book is less concerned with questions about separate spheres or methods of household production that have dominated conversations about women, households, and domesticity. Rather, by making the household central to wartime experience, *The Home Front* examines the intensely personal as well as gendered, raced, and classed ways that people endured the war and exposes the lasting influence of these experiences as Americans rebuilt their lives and built a nation in the postwar years.[30]

Bringing the household to the fore also, crucially, accentuates the gendered contours of the military conflict—a topic that, with a few notable exceptions, has been sidelined within the broader scholarship on the American Revolution in which the home front is largely viewed as a space detached from war and under the province of women's history.[31] Often associated with the two world wars, the concept of the American home front typically refers to a civilian space where families support troops from afar and where patriotic women assume traditionally masculine responsibilities to compensate for men's wartime absences. Although there are certainly points of connection with home fronts in other wars, this is not the home front of the American Revolution. Over the course of the eight-year War for American Independence, American households were sites of battles, sieges, and violent conflict. Property destruction and invasion were rampant. Civilians were subject to varying levels of violence and vulnerability—although the extent to which wartime violence differed from prewar levels varied by race, gender, and class; for many people in colonial America, particularly those on the margins, households were places of brutality and fear, even before war invaded their lives. The war nevertheless introduced new forms of violence and widespread devastation that transformed American households and endangered their assorted inhabitants. As Holly A. Mayer has argued, "Warfare may be the essence of war, but war also happens to societies as it encompasses actions and peoples outside armed and uniformed ranks." An expansive approach to the study of war thus has the potential to illuminate new contours of the Revolution's military conflict and consequences that have hitherto been obscured.[32]

Examining the Revolution from the home front consequently broadens our understanding of where war occurred and the people who are relevant to that story. Here, the war looks messier, more complex, and more human; politics matter less. This was especially true in the six cities that the British Army captured and occupied over the course of the war, which were home to civilians of varying races, genders, and freedoms. Here, frequently, the home front and the battlefront blurred. In British-occupied regions, civilians experienced prolonged sieges, invasion, ongoing warfare, surveillance, property confiscation, the quartering of officers, and supply requisitions; they were riven by internal divisions, not only between soldiers and civilians, but between civilians themselves, as the Revolution eroded social norms and fractured the institutions that structured daily life. Yet, with a few notable exceptions, studies of occupation during the American Revolution have not wrestled substantively with issues of gender, instead focusing primarily on questions of loyalty or the failure of imperial authority.[33]

Occupied cities were, however, theaters of war fundamentally entangled in and shaped by race and gender. Because colonial politics limited political participation to white men of property, both gender and race were structural features of occupation as the British determined who was an enemy, who was permitted to move freely about the city, who was deserving of protection, and who was to be constrained by military authorities. Within this context, women of various races, statuses, and states of freedom acted to fill voids within their households and communities, wielding new levels of power and authority that made them prominent actors within the domestic, social, and military scenes of British garrisons. Still, women's experiences were hardly universal. Gender, race, class, marital status, and enslavement shaped individuals' responses to the new opportunities and dangers that the British Army introduced into urban life. Enslaved women's choices diverged significantly from those of free white domestic servants, which varied even more starkly from those of white women of the upper ranks. Occupation changed not only women's daily routines but also their relationships to one another and the households where they resided. Considering these interactions through the prism of the household therefore unites these diverse perspectives into a singular frame of reference, illustrating the varied, unpredictable, and contradictory experiences—as well as surprising points of connection—among the heterogeneous civilians who endured the American Revolution, often while residing in proximity to one another.[34]

Moreover, the view from the home front clarifies that household and family concerns were not the sole purview of women; domestic life grounded the identities of both men and women of the Anglo-American colonial elite. Among white men, the household was also a central feature of masculine identity and patriarchal power. As historian Karin Wulf observes, "The idea that men would rule over their households expressed, more than any other single concept, the basic premises that governed daily life." Reintegrating men into domestic life reveals how deeply disruptive war and military occupation was for them precisely because of how these experiences threatened the patriarchal and material power embedded within the household. Facing unexpected challenges from British soldiers, enslaved laborers, domestic servants, and their own wives and daughters, white men experienced unprecedented constraints on their domestic authority during the war. Such constraints had real emotional and financial consequences. Throughout the colonies, white men lamented that they were unable to care for their families; they worried that they were failing in their duties as fathers and husbands. Family concerns and the future financial security of their households—often, more so than political ideology—informed the choices that men made as they strategized how best to survive the war. Enslaved men similarly acted to protect their kin during the conflict, strategizing to safeguard their loved ones and secure their liberty. These practices of love and freedom were fundamentally at odds with the wartime aims of white enslavers, whose own domestic comfort and financial security were premised on the commodification of Black bodies and the erasure of their family ties.[35]

Collectively then, the view from the home front clarifies the inextricable relationship between gender, households, and warfare during the American Revolution. This insight has the potential to enrich our understanding not only of the war but also of household governance in the revolutionary and early national periods. The American Revolution has largely dropped out of studies of the American household. Scholars of household governance have minimized the Revolution's disruptive effects, citing postwar legal developments as evidence of continuities with the colonial period. Yet this narrow focus on legalities has overlooked the broader cultural and national meanings of the household in the revolutionary period—meanings, *The Home Front* argues, that were forged in the crucible of war. Historians have typically attributed Americans' reverence for domestic life in the 1780s and 1790s to political appeals to nurture the republican virtue that would sustain the Republic. Yet, by taking seriously the wartime endangerment to households and the power that they represented, *The Home Front* shows that these early national idealizations of domesticity also evolved out of the very real, messy, occasionally traumatic experiences of (primarily white) men and women who lived through eight years of civil war—a war that invaded their households, disrupted their finances, and subjected their families to fear, separation, and uncertainty. For these families, hopes for the nation's future existed alongside the very real memory of the Revolution's domestic warfare.[36]

A DOMESTIC HISTORY OF THE AMERICAN REVOLUTION

At the core of this book is a dedication to understanding the inner workings of the white, patriarchal households that became the foundation of the new American Republic. These households encompassed varied inhabitants: white husbands and wives, domestic servants, unmarried daughters, and enslaved families. Occasionally, their aims aligned; more often, they clashed. As these various household residents navigated wartime constraints, the pressures of military occupation, and the creation of a new nation, they did so within their households and in reaction to the behaviors of the other inhabitants. Narrating the war from inside these contested households, *The Home Front* endeavors "to recapture the way history felt" for the varied men and women who lived through the American Revolution, centering the quotidian, emotional dimensions of daily life in British-occupied cities to present a fresh perspective on the war that highlights the importance of domestic life for individuals and their families and the lasting influence of these wartime experiences on understandings of independence in the new nation.[37]

Occupation generated an enormous outpouring of documentation from both American civilians and British military officials detailing the use of household space and the minutiae of domestic life. White civilians corresponded with absent and anxious family members, who desperately sought information about their families and property. Inhabitants assured friends and relatives of their safety. They itemized property destruction. They catalogued stolen goods and enumerated household laborers—enslaved people as well as domestic servants—who fled to British lines. Runaway ads and testimonies before British tribunals further attest to these freedom-seeking efforts. Civilians described living with British officers, detailing how they shared household space and accomplished their daily routines alongside unfamiliar men. In their letters and diaries, civilians confided their fears and the anxieties that kept them awake at night.

Likewise, the private journals and correspondence of British and Hessian soldiers contain detailed impressions of American cities and inhabitants. The Quartermaster's Department recorded the houses and supplies commandeered from civilian inhabitants. Courts-martial proceedings illustrate how civilians of all races, genders, and classes challenged the British Army's use of their homes, labors, and bodies. Order books detail the destruction and repurposing of household materials as the British Army constructed fortifications around American cities. Petitions to commanding officers reveal the strategies that civilians deployed to protect their property. In the years after the war, loyalist exiles appealed to the Loyalist Claims Commission in London, detailing their losses. Even as the nineteenth century dawned, Americans continued to wrestle with the implications of wartime invasion; in novels and artwork, in schoolbooks and personal correspondence, in their memoirs, and in the laws of the new nation, Americans pondered the household and its place in the fledgling Republic.[38]

This archival record is tilted heavily toward the perspectives of elite and middling white families, whose households are better documented than those of their poorer neighbors of all races, the people they employed, or the people that they enslaved. Yet, by reading sources against and "along the bias grain," it is possible to gain insights into the experiences of those who did not leave written records. For instance, among those desperately fleeing Boston in April 1775 in the aftermath of the battles of Lexington and Concord was a woman named Lucinda, who had arrived in Boston several years earlier as a frightened seven-year-old, having survived the harrowing Atlantic crossing from Africa. The outbreak of war increased Lucinda's workload. Her enslaver, Sarah Winslow Deming, was not a healthy woman, and stress exacerbated her frailty; she refused to eat and barely slept—circumstances that deprived Lucinda of her own, much-needed rest. As the Demings prepared to flee, Lucinda spent hours caring for her trembling, anxious slaveowner, who appeared on the verge of fainting as she fretted about the house, volubly lamenting the impending danger. Lucinda helped her gather precious items, tying silver plate, jewels, money, and clothing into a handkerchief so that they could flee the minute that the roads out of the city were reopened. Amid this flurry of activity, possibly Lucinda managed to safeguard some of her own clothing or treasured keepsakes; a talented musician, perhaps she managed to tuck her pipe into one of the bundles.[39]

Later that afternoon, Lucinda clambered into one of two carriages that Captain John Deming had secured to transport his household out of the city. She rode alongside the Demings' niece Sally Winslow; the young woman looked as if she would "fall into hysterick fitts every minute." Lucinda left no account of her feelings about fleeing Boston. Perhaps, like Sally, Lucinda was scared. Maybe she turned back for a glimpse of the city. Possibly she kept her face turned out the window, searching the crowded streets for loved ones and friends that she was leaving behind. Or, perhaps, succumbing to the strain of the previous days, she closed her eyes and slept. Over the next several days, the Deming household retreated further into the countryside, crowding into hired carriages alongside other panicked refugees. Lucida often rode on the outside, exposed to the elements, while the two white women rode snugly ensconced in the coach. They lodged in eight different towns over the course of ten nights, dependent on the kindness of locals for food, shelter, and scraps of news, which often conveyed wild rumors of indiscriminate slaughter and torched cities.[40]

The onset of civil war upended Lucinda's life, saddling her with additional labor, an involuntary relocation, and the prospect of an indeterminate separation from loved ones. Undoubtedly, Lucinda found the early days of the war distressing. She would have been viscerally aware of how her race and gender not only exposed her to an enhanced risk of violence and sexual assault but also to kidnapping by looting soldiers. She might have feared that the cash-strapped Demings would hire her out on wages, subjecting her to the whims of an unknown, perhaps vicious, person. Or they could sell her. As enslaved property, Lucinda, was a productive, mobile form of wealth that the Demings relied on for financial security amidst the abandonment of their home and material goods. And yet, even as Lucinda worried for her safety, perhaps she did not share her enslavers' grief at the outbreak of civil war. In the previous months, she might have witnessed the half-dozen African drummers of the British Army's Twenty-Ninth Regiment marching through Boston's streets. She had likely heard whispered rumors that the British were promising emancipation to people like herself. Amid the fears that characterized these early hours of the war, might Lucinda have felt a glimmer of hope?[41]

For those, like Lucinda, who labored within elite and middling white households, both as domestic servants and as enslaved laborers, the War for American Independence was also about the pursuit of happiness—often beyond the confines and the reach of the white patriarchal household. Indeed, in many ways, their actions further destabilized the dynamics of wartime households already thrown into chaos by war, violence, and British occupation; many Anglo-American householders worried that the threat to their domestic security came not only from the British Army without but from discontented dependents within. This wartime domestic disruption brought into sharp relief the tangled, contradictory strands that undergirded both revolutionary households and revolutionary rhetoric: liberty, equality, safety, and domestic security were deeply entwined with the institution of the household, yet these notions did not mean the same thing to all household inhabitants—indeed, they often contradicted one another.[42]

To convey these varied experiences and underscore their entangled nature, each chapter of *The Home Front* narrates the war from the perspective of a different group of household inhabitants, both free and enslaved, who resided and labored within the households of the Anglo-American upper classes. Where possible, it broadens its analysis of domestic warfare to also include the households of ordinary white, free Black, and enslaved families in order to consider how men and women of various races, statuses, and states of freedom experienced the violence of war within familiar domestic realms.[43]

As an interpretive lens, the household thus frames this story in several distinct but interrelated ways, offering both deeply personal experiences of war and stretching beyond household walls to illuminate how domestic relations intersected with other institutions and forms of power that gave the household its meaning. Or, to put it another way: although this study traces the invasion of war into domestic spaces, it is not contained by them. Embracing the permeability of wartime households, *The Home Front* follows household residents into city streets and throughout British garrisons to consider how their wartime actions refracted back into domestic spaces and undermined the network of power relations contained therein. Like the households at the center of this book—institutions that structured daily life while also reflecting and reinforcing the power dynamics of Anglo-American society—*The Home Front* closely examines individual households while also widening its gaze to consider these experiences in relation to broader society, tracing the consequences of eight long years of war for both individuals and the nation.

The view from the home front clarifies how domestic life and ideas of home were integral to the American Revolution, reverberating throughout every aspect of the conflict: in the waging of battles, as the prism through which diverse individuals interpreted the costs and the possibilities of civil war and evaluated its consequences for their lives, in how white Americans envisioned independence and anticipated the fruits of victory, in how they imagined the nation, and in how they pursued happiness and domestic tranquility in the early Republic.

The Revolution looks different when viewed from the household. It looks messier, less cohesive, more contradictory. Revolutionary households were comprised of diverse inhabitants, including white men, women, and children, domestic servants, both Black and white, and enslaved families, each of whom had different priorities and divergent responses to the arrival of the British Army. The Revolution's domestic warfare threw all of their lives into disarray. And yet, because households were interstices of power relations that reflected and reinforced the broader social order, these deeply individualized and traumatic experiences held meanings that resonated beyond individual households and that became entwined with the founding of the United States. The Revolution's domestic warfare would come to define the very meaning of American independence in the new nation.

CHAPTER ONE

Fire and Sword Was Come amongst Us

Betsy Murray left church early on the afternoon of August 11, 1776. She was grateful that the service had concluded before Reverend Parker walked to the front of the congregation and read the Declaration of Independence aloud. News of the Declaration had reached Boston three weeks earlier, and people had gathered in King Street to hear the proclamation. Joyous crowds cheered at the orator's fervent cry, "God Save our American States," as guns and cannons fired in celebration. Much had changed in the five months since the British Army withdrew from Boston. Betsy's parents were now in Halifax, alongside other loyalist refugees who evacuated with the army in March 1776. The British officers she had flirted with were dispersed throughout North America. Betsy continued to correspond with some of the "Gentlemen of Genl: Howes Army," but letters were a faint substitute for the vibrant social scene of the British garrison. Earlier in the summer, she had even walked the streets of Boston in her "high heeled shoes," hoping for a glimpse of the British prisoners that remained in the city.[1]

Eager to escape the patriotic fervor, Betsy took a "solitary walk" to the house where she had resided with her loyalist parents when Boston was a British garrison. It was the anniversary of "a triffling scene" that had occurred there the previous summer, and she wanted to mark the occasion by returning to the property and reliving the moment "in imagination." Yet, as Betsy neared the dwelling, she saw that months of war and vacancy had wrought havoc on the happy home of her recollections. Even in the dim evening light, it was apparent that the house had fallen into disrepair. The windows were open, and the back door had been "torn of[f] the hinges." An elderly horse munched on the remains of her father's carefully cultivated garden. Approaching the abandoned house, Betsy considered going inside; the gaping doorway "seem'd . . . an invitation to enter." But she could not bring herself to cross the threshold. "My blood was already so chill'd with horror I had not resolution to proceed," Betsy explained, "especially as there was not even the footstep of a human Being to be heard." Unnerved, she abandoned her pursuit of memories and "retreated as precipitately as I could."[2]

Betsy Murray's harrowing homecoming suggests the deep material and emotional changes that British military occupation and the American Revolution's urban warfare wrought on American households. During the Revolution, for the first time in nearly two centuries, Anglo-American colonists found themselves the targets, rather than the perpetrators, of Britain's colonial warfare. The full might of the British Army was turned against, rather than acting to protect, their families and property. Their cities—Boston, New York, Newport, Philadelphia, Charleston, and Savannah, the six largest in British North America—were commandeered to support British military operations. Proximity to armies and battles exposed inhabitants to plunder, property destruction, assault, and other forms of violence. Demolition, material depredation, and outright theft altered family fortunes and enhanced feelings of precarity. War elevated the threat of rape, and fears of sexual assault loomed over daily life. Martial law and urban warfare upended the customary privileges of rank, representing an unprecedented threat to the livelihoods, safety, household security, and bodily autonomy of elite and middling Anglo-Americans. As vibrant metropolitan hubs morphed into military strongholds and urban battlefields, invasion, assault, and widespread destruction fractured civilians' sense of safety and remade their relationships to familiar spaces in terrifying ways.[3]

Such wartime realities were true for all civilians, regardless of their political leanings. We are accustomed to thinking of the Revolution as a political contest with distinct, opposing factions. In occupied regions, political divisions persisted, especially among the most zealous partisans, but, for most people, politics mattered far less than the daily struggle to ensure safety and survival amid civil war. Cannonballs did not differentiate between revolutionaries and loyalists; neither did the infectious diseases that stalked early modern armies. All civilian inhabitants of garrisoned cities were subject to martial law, including restrictive curfews, patrols, and surveillance measures. Soldiers and camp followers heightened the potential for violence. Premeditated assaults, certainly, were more likely to target revolutionaries, but it was improbable that opportunistic thieves or assailants inquired about political loyalties before attacking their victims. Thus, even among those whom contemporaries or historians might identify as loyalists, there were many people who distrusted British troops and feared the menace they posed to their communities.

These circumstances dramatically transformed both urban and domestic life. City dwellers in revolutionary America resided not only in their households but in vibrant, interdependent neighborhoods. Daily life was interwoven with the urban environment: in the crowded streets and bustling wharfs that characterized urban seaports, in the markets filled with vendors hawking their wares, and in the quiet churches and busy neighborhoods that urbanites relied on for both support and sociability. Rather than standing apart from this hubbub, revolutionary households were deeply enmeshed in urban life and represented just one of the many interconnected places where city dwellers lived, loved, and labored.[4]

Examining these varied spaces of urban life, this chapter employs an episodic approach to view occupation through the eyes of those who lived through it. Occupation occurred at different points in the war in different cities, but the process by which the British Army captured urban ports and transformed them into defensive garrisons was, with a few notable exceptions, essentially the same: bombardment, annexation, fortification, and the institution of martial law. Following these developments from afar, observers empathized with those who suffered under or were displaced by British occupation. But to personally experience these perils was something different altogether, especially for terrified civilians facing many of these conditions for the first time. For them, occupation was unpredictable and chaotic. It was a visceral, invasive experience that endangered their families, their safety, their property, and their lives. British occupation placed households and their inhabitants squarely in the crosshairs of the military conflict, with uneven consequences for civilians that were often delineated along lines of race, gender, and class. New Yorker Helen Kortright Brasher spoke for many people in occupied regions when she worried, "Where God can we fly from danger? All places appear equally precarious."[5]

Moving through the early weeks of occupation—from the macro city-level perspective to the micro intimate bodily experience of individuals—enables us to capture the chaos of occupation and how it reverberated through urban life. Such an approach also allows us to consider how people navigated the new threats that occupation introduced into their lives: from the fury of urban warfare, to the perils of streets flooded with soldiers, to the enhanced vulnerability of households in cities under occupation, to the heightened danger, especially for women, that large numbers of troops posed to their bodies. British occupation fundamentally altered the many overlapping and interconnected spaces where urban inhabitants resided. For many of them, this experience revealed with terrifying clarity that neither their status, their race, nor their Englishness could protect them, their families, or their property from the violence and destruction of civil war.

URBAN WARFARE: CHAOS, FEAR, AND VIOLENCE

The British Army's occupation of American port cities was a tactical strategy rooted in European warfare; urban ports were vital for British forces dependent on overseas supplies to subsist and reinforce troops. Although the British captured some cities more easily than others, each of the cities that the army occupied was the site of a major battle or a siege, either instigated by British forces attempting to seize control or Continental forces trying to oust them. Sometimes both. Throughout the war, civilian observers speculated on these military movements with interest. Ravaud Kearney, a lawyer residing in Perth Amboy, New Jersey, less than thirty miles from British-occupied New York City, routinely placed wagers of clothing, beaver hats, and boots on British troop movements and the fate of American cities.[6]

Inside urban centers, fears of impending invasions kept civilians in a state of constant anxiety. Warfare was a novel experience for many of the varied residents of colonial port cities, which had been remarkably free of military conflict in the decades preceding the Revolution. British regulars occasionally lodged in urban barracks, but warfare in the mid- to late eighteenth century was primarily waged in the contested backcountry, resulting in a consensus among colonists that cities were civilian spaces sheltered from combat. As one man lamented in the aftermath of the Battle of Bunker Hill, "It was a new and awful spectacle to us to have men carried through the streets groaning, bleeding, and dying."[7]

Rumors of advancing armies sent inhabitants scrambling, in the words of Philadelphian Sarah Logan Fisher, with "Waggons rattling, Horses Galoping, Women running, Children Crying . . . and all together the greatest consternation fright and terror that can be imagined." Those who could afford to leave frantically piled into carriages, clutching whatever valuables they could carry. Others made the journey on foot. As she ran through Newport's streets with her six children while warships fired "continually" overhead, loyalist Mary Gould Almy was alarmed by the distressed hordes of "shrieking" women and terrified "chilldren falling down crying." Recounting her own harried flight from Boston, Sarah Winslow Deming succinctly recalled the panic that characterized those hours: "Not knowing whither I might go—I fled for my life."[8]

Some inhabitants, such as Boston lawyer and revolutionary John Andrews, observed this flurry of activity with skepticism. Certain that his neighbors were overreacting, he characterized them in April 1775 as "either [affraid], mad, crazy or infatuated, which term you please . . . immagining to themselves that they shall be liable to every evil that can be enumerated, if they tarry in town." Andrews chose to remain in the city alongside the bulk of his property and investments. Two weeks later, with the Battles of Lexington and Concord occurring in the intervening time, he belatedly recognized the wisdom of those who had fled the city early, their wagons overloaded with furniture, clothing, and household effects. "If I can escape with the skin of my teeth, shall be glad," he wrote to his brother-in-law in dismay.[9]

Unlike their revolutionary neighbors, many loyalists rejoiced at the British Army's arrival. After the British captured New York City in 1776, two women tore down the rebel flag flying over the fort and "trampl[ed] . . . [it] under Foot with the most contemptuous indignation" before hoisting the royal standard in its place. Yet many urban residents were more ambivalent in their feelings. The army's presence offered a semblance of normalcy and order, but it also enhanced the potential for danger. Confronted with a formidable, occupying force in their homes, streets, and public spaces, many people, even those who favored peace, regarded British troops with nervous apprehension. "Gen. Howe intends its said to winter with us," Quaker Elizabeth Drinker worried in Philadelphia; "I hope he is a better man, than some people think him."[10]

Inhabitants who chose to remain, whether motivated by the desire to safeguard property, the inability to flee, or loyalist sympathies, endured new levels of violence as war descended upon their communities. Property-owning families scrambled to move their goods out of cannon range, hastily burying their china and secreting away precious linen and silver plate. They rushed to send their papers and accounts into the country for safekeeping. As Continental and allied French forces besieged Savannah in 1779, women and children crowded into barns as shells flew overhead and detachments of Cherokees and Creeks along with two hundred armed Black men stood guard. Elsewhere in Savannah, Ann Prévost, the wife of British major general Augustine Prévost, and her children spent the siege in a cellar lined with featherbeds to make it "bomb proof" while men stood outside with wet blankets to prevent the house from catching fire. Meanwhile, in Savannah's unpaved streets, enslaved children diffused unexploded shells by covering them with sand.[11]

In occupied regions throughout the colonies, civilians sheltered in their homes as cannon shot echoed "like thunder" and balls rained down "like haile." "The houses were riddled with the rain of cannon balls," Georgia loyalist Elizabeth Johnston recalled. Explosions shook the ground "like an Earth Quake," and guns fired at all hours of the day, often awakening inhabitants in the early morning hours, their heads pounding from the noise. Cannon shots broke through walls, destroying houses and civilians' sense of security. Even after the smoke cleared, rumors circulated that revolutionaries intended to set cities ablaze in defiance of occupying forces, causing loyalist volunteers to form patrols aimed at disrupting their plans. Shortly after the British assumed control of New York City in September 1776, a massive conflagration consumed large sections of the city. Rumored to be arson, the incident set a nerve-racking precedent for the remainder of the war.[12]

In addition to violence and property destruction, diseases such as smallpox, dysentery, and typhus flourished in military encampments. Contagions accompanied the British Army into American cities, embodying an invisible, yet terrifying, menace that further endangered and overwhelmed civilians. "My distress is not to be described," Sarah Winslow Deming declared, expressing her determination to get "out of Boston at almost any rate—away as far as possible from the infection of smallpox, and the din of drums and martial Musick as its call'd and the horrors of war."[13]

Although urban areas bore the brunt of occupation, British forces radiated out from metropolitan centers and affected large swaths of the American colonies. The British posted picquet guards on the outer limits of American cities, where skirmishes with the enemy were common. Civilians watched these maneuvers with interest, clambering up to city rooftops with spyglasses to watch British and American soldiers clash in the country estates of the urban elite, firing out of windows, barricading doors, and, in some cases, setting houses ablaze. Troops routinely launched forays into surrounding colonies. Foraging parties ventured beyond city limits to cut down trees, requisition hay, and commandeer livestock. Errant soldiers and camp followers plundered civilian residences in search of food, blankets, and valuables that could be sold for cash. Regions accessible by boat or within easy marching distance of garrisoned cities were especially susceptible to plunder and foraging expeditions. But parties of British troops also launched punitive raids to intimidate rebellious populations. New Jersey, laying between the British garrisons at New York and Philadelphia, was particularly devastated. With consequences ranging from inconvenient to life-threatening, the British Army's reach sprawled far beyond occupied cities, disrupting to varying degrees the livelihoods of diverse civilians who, whether by choice or coercion, were drawn into the army's orbit.[14]

In Connecticut, where the British routinely launched raids intended to terrorize inhabitants, one woman found the possibility of invasion so unnerving that it "banish'd sleep from my eye-lids." She became "so unwell" that she nearly fainted three times. After the British Army's arrival in Philadelphia, seven-year-old Molly Pemberton became "so frighted with the roaring of cannon" that she took to sleeping in her mother's bed, a comfort to both of them during the sleepless nights. Cannon fire resounded for miles. From her home in Braintree, Abigail Adams could hear firing around British-occupied Boston and observe the battles happening there. "The constant roar of the cannon is so {*illegible*} [distressing] that we can not Eat Drink or Sleep," she wrote to John during the Battle of Bunker Hill. The omnipresent threat of danger interrupted chores and disrupted daily routines. "We know not what a day will bring forth nor what distress one hour may throw us into," Abigail explained. One night, she recounted, she lay awake listening to cannons roar and feeling the house shudder around her: "I went to Bed after 12 but got no rest, the Cannon continued firing and my Heart Beat pace with them all night."[15]

In regions under British occupation, "the terror of constant alarms and the din of War" transformed urban communities, with frightening consequences for civilian populations. During the 1778 siege of Newport, loyalist Mary Gould Almy, whose husband fought as part of the Continental forces besieging the British garrison, recounted her "6 children hanging round me—the littel girls Crying out mamma will they kill us—the boys endeavour to put on an air of manliness and strove to assist, but step up to the Girls in a Whisper—who do you think will [hu]rt you—ant your Pappa coming with them." Witnessing her children's distress "cut me to the soul," Mary moaned. Anguished and unable to sleep, she lay awake the following evening, watching flies and mosquitoes buzz around the candle near her bed. "Nothing but frightfull dreams and broken slumbers," Mary confided to her diary. "To Attempt to describe the horrors of that night would pronounce me a fool—for no language could put it in it[s] Proper Coullours[.] fire and sword [was] com amongst us . . . and [the] Famine was not afar of."[16]

LIVING UNDER OCCUPATION: ALTERED CITIES, DANGEROUS STREETS

Once the battle had been won and British troops seized control of a city, they immediately set about securing urban garrisons. Soldiers demolished outlying buildings and constructed defensive ramparts. Officers implemented martial law, instituting surveillance regulations and issuing restrictions designed to bring city spaces, surrounding regions, and inhabitants under military supervision. These deliberate fortification measures, combined with the quotidian—and often dangerous—nuisances emanating from military encampments, reshaped the interrelated spaces of urban life and altered how civilians existed within them.

Widespread demolition and construction characterized the early weeks of occupation as the British Army remade urban ports into military strongholds. Within hours of taking Philadelphia in September 1777, engineers began constructing batteries along the Delaware River. Following the surrender of Charleston in May 1780, the British Army impressed large numbers of the city's enslaved population to repair damages from the three-month-long siege. Geography and defensive strategy determined the location of fortifications; troops destroyed anything that fell in the path of defensive lines or that could shelter enemy forces. The loyalties of individual property owners were subordinate to the security of urban garrisons, and houses belonging to civilians of all political stripes became collateral damage in these efforts.[17]

Approaching British-occupied Newport in August 1778 as part of the Continental forces besieging the city, Paul Revere was stunned by the altered landscape. The British Army had razed houses to the ground and hacked gardens down to stumps to create a barren perimeter that could be easily surveilled. Newport's once-bustling wharves had been repurposed as gun platforms, and the harbor was filled with sunken ships to deter enemy fleets. Fences and houses had been pulled down for firewood. "It does not look [like] the same Island," Paul wrote to his wife in astonishment; "some of the Inhabitants who left it, hardly know where to find their homes." The city, in the words of Ensign Thomas Hughes of the Fifty-Third Regiment, was "the picture of war and rapine."[18]

As American port cities morphed into British garrisons, the British Army's presence transformed urban environments. Fifes, drums, and the accompanying beat of marching boots became features of daily life. Early modern armies were loud; civilians could hear "the Noise of the Waggons, and rattling of the Cannon . . . at a great distance." British troops exercised in public spaces, and military encampments sprung up throughout American cities. On Boston Common, soldiers pitched threadbare tents, thin from overuse. In the encampment at Philadelphia, six-year-old Molly Pemberton observed that the tents were "as thickly Set as houses in roes like Streets." In Newport, civilians were shocked to see soldiers in various stages of undress bathing along the city's shoreline. Troops also made cities filthy. Charlestonians complained that "heaps of dirt and Rubbish" lined the streets, "owing to the total disregard of the soldiery, both British and Hessian." Grumbling about "the filth of the Streets," Savannah residents were alarmed by the army's usurpation of urban space, particularly "the indecent practice of burying dead bodies in various parts of the Town, and its environs."[19]

The sudden influx of troops created unfamiliar circumstances that altered the dynamics of urban life for men and women alike. Simply walking down the street brought civilians into close contact with soldiers who interrupted their daily chores and routines. Men chased one another through the streets, narrowly avoiding collisions with civilians. Rambunctious troops vandalized stores and overturned fruit carts. Soldiers stopped inhabitants on the street and demanded that they surrender their valuables. Without provocation, soldiers assaulted passersby, such as one British provost who caned an enslaved Boston man simply "for wheeling a barrow at the side of the street and not in the middle." Off-duty troops took to taverns, playhouses, and brothels. They also tended to travel in groups. One Charleston woman described officers walking in clusters of five or six, "hooking-arms." Elizabeth Hunter recounted an unknown sailor on the street grabbing her—twice—as she made her way to the Queen's Head Tavern in New York City. Resisting his advances, Elizabeth told him "to go about his business, that she did not know him, and wanted nothing to say to him." The sailor refused to relent, and the dispute only ended when another sailor intervened, running the man through with a sword.[20]

Holidays were particularly perilous, as intoxicated troops celebrated and caroused throughout the city. Drunken officers and soldiers regularly brawled with male civilians. In the wake of British victories and national holidays, civilians contended with jubilant soldiers crowding public spaces, loudly toasting King George III, and firing guns in celebration. Unilluminated residences were likely to have their windows broken. Similar atmospheres prevailed when the troops were in winter quarters, where, unfettered from the responsibilities of campaigning, soldiers indulged freely and frequently. "We daily hear of enormitys of one kind or other, being committed by those from whome, we ought to find protection," Elizabeth Drinker lamented from British-occupied Philadelphia in December 1777.[21]

Despite commanding officers' efforts to maintain discipline, troops often deliberately antagonized civilian populations. In March 1775, a fife and drum corps erected tents outside of the Harvard Meeting House and played "Yankee Doodle" on repeat during the morning services. Later that month, after disrupting commemorations for the Boston Massacre, British officers staged an election of a committee of seven mock selectmen from among the troops that culminated with an inflammatory public oration invoking "the most vile, profane, blackguard language" and heaping "scurrilous abuse upon the characters of the principal patriots." Bostonians derided officers' "childish play" in processing through the streets "with much greater courage . . . than they would face an enemy." Others scorned these actions as blatant hypocrisy. "Are not Riots raised and made by Armed Men, as bad as those by unarmed?" John Adams scoffed, as he lamented prevailing characterizations of military order and rabid colonial mobs.[22]

Alongside the troops, large communities of camp followers, including soldiers' wives and children, servants, loyalist refugees, and self-emancipated former slaves, crowded garrisoned cities. Lord Dunmore's proclamation in 1775 and Sir Henry Clinton's Philipsburg Proclamation in 1779 both offered freedom to people enslaved by American revolutionaries; throughout the war, approximately twenty thousand men, women, and children made their way to British lines, where they worked as laborers, drivers, street cleaners, cooks, laundresses, nurses, and personal servants. As tensions escalated and white loyalists were driven from their homes by rebellious neighbors, these families also sought refuge with the army, at times arriving with little more than the clothes on their backs. Military regulations strictly limited the number of women allowed to travel with each regiment, yet many families simply ignored these restrictions, especially as the war progressed and British soldiers gained American wives. Sex workers and merchants likewise flocked to British lines, seeking to ply their wares among the troops. Amplifying the army's disruptive effects, these groups further taxed the resources of urban garrisons and the surrounding regions. "Any place this horde approached was eaten clean, like an acre invaded by a swarm of locusts," Hessian captain Johann Ewald observed in 1781.[23]

Occupation transformed American cities. Widespread demolition and construction remade the landscape of American ports while the army's presence intensified the perils of urban life. As resources dwindled and inhabitants and troops eyed one another with suspicion, soldiers, their families, camp followers, prisoners of war, and refugees, both Black and white, introduced new pressures and strains into urban life, fundamentally altering how people existed within and moved through the cities they called home.

NEW RESTRICTIONS: SURVEILLANCE AND SCRUTINY

As commanding officers attempted to instill order among these diverse military and civilian communities, they implemented restrictive surveillance measures that upended privileges and restricted the mobility that many free white people took for granted. Officers mistrusted civilian populations and readily used their power under martial law to curtail civilians' ability to compromise the British war effort. Both disorienting and invasive, these circumstances were particularly galling for free white people of the upper ranks, exposing the precariousness of the bodily autonomy, privileges, and security of property to which their rank and their race had previously entitled them and subjecting them to levels of scrutiny and violence reminiscent of those that they themselves imposed on the people they employed and enslaved.

Upon entering Philadelphia in September 1777, Lieutenant John Peebles worried that many of the cheering inhabitants lining the city's streets were "by all accounts . . . publickly on the other side before our arrival." Contrary to popular myths of entrenched partisanship, many people were flexible in their allegiance and adapted their politics in an effort to safeguard their families and property. Although the most zealous partisans often refused to compromise their principles, either fleeing before the British Army's arrival or seeking refuge behind its lines, depending on their politics, such actions were atypical. More commonly, people stayed put and did what was necessary to survive. Americans, one British officer lamented, "swallow the Oaths of Allegiance to the King, and Congress, Alternately, with as much ease as [one] does poached Eggs."[24]

Throughout occupied cities, commanding officers implemented policies intended to target, identify, and punish rebellious inhabitants. "The town is full of [rebels] only they dare not show their feelings," one Hessian officer brooded in Philadelphia. Such qualms enflamed frictions in an already tense environment. Aided by local loyalists eager to endear themselves to occupying forces, troops typically disarmed and imprisoned revolutionaries upon taking control of a city. Soldiers demolished properties belonging to rebels to harvest building materials and confiscated revolutionaries' estates for military use. Such measures were an effective means of asserting brute power: silencing critics and demanding tacit obedience from restive civilian populations.[25]

Imprisonment was typically reserved for male inhabitants, but women could also be confined for too visibly expressing support for revolutionaries. In South Carolina, Eliza Wilkinson reported hearing that Charleston's "rebel ladies were obliged to compose their phizzes before they dared to venture in the streets." Anyone who complained, Wilkinson noted, was "insulted and laughed at; and upon the least suspicion imprisoned, ladies not excepted." Still, perhaps counterintuitively, women's gender, which marked them as nonpolitical and nonmilitary actors, emboldened some to antagonize British troops. Female Philadelphians, Lieutenant Loftus Cliffe of the Forty-Sixth Regiment observed, "ma[de] no Scruple of speaking their Sentiments"—remarks that led him to conclude with disgust that the city's residents were "all a damned set of rebels."[26]

The British Army's coercive governance measures were not exceptional during the war; revolutionary Committees of Safety likewise imprisoned and punished loyalist opponents. Even in peacetime, the urban inhabitants of British North America were accustomed to a degree of oversight on their daily life: night watchmen, sheriffs, and market regulation were regular features under the common law; and, just as in England, American colonists believed that public welfare often outweighed individual interests. Still, military governance diverged in significant ways from that typical of early modern cities. Martial law was not imposed from within; colonists had not consented to it, nor was it implemented by members of their own community. Rather, it was a coercive, intrusive regulation imposed by an outside authority.[27]

In regions under British military occupation, the free inhabitants of garrisoned cities thus experienced unprecedented levels of surveillance, and inhabitants of all races and genders faced new limits on their movement as

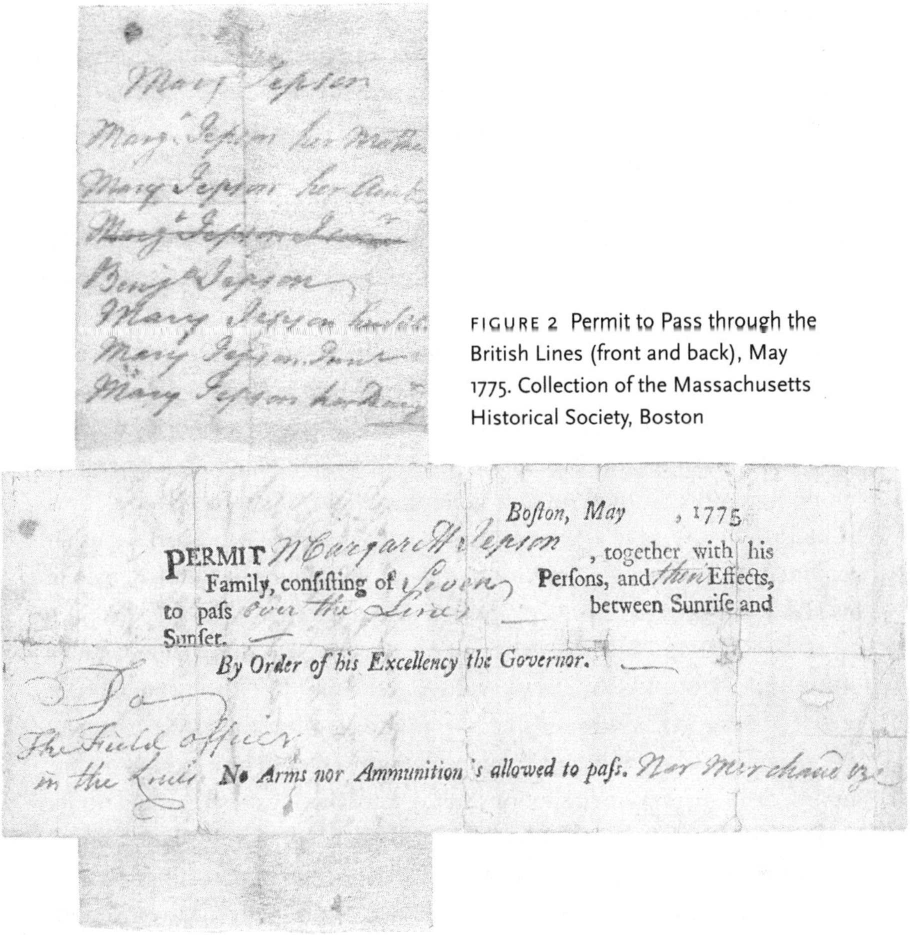

Boſton, May , 1775

PERMIT Margaret Jepson , together with his Family, conſiſting of Seven Perſons, and their Effects, to paſs over the Lines between Sunriſe and Sunſet.

By Order of his Excellency the Governor.

To
The Field officer
in the Lines

No Arms nor Ammunition is allowed to paſs. Nor Merchandize

FIGURE 2 Permit to Pass through the British Lines (front and back), May 1775. Collection of the Massachusetts Historical Society, Boston

the army instituted curfews and troops patrolled the streets. "We have been afraid to speak, to write, almost to think," Boston minister Andrew Eliot confessed. Enumerating what he termed "the usual Consequences of martial Law," Bostonian William Cheever recorded, "Press-Gangs parading the Streets . . . several Persons taken up and imprisoned" and "the Provost with his Band entering houses at his pleasure, stoping Gentlemen from enter:g their Warehouses and puting some under Guard." To prevent treasonous communications and deter espionage, officers closely monitored civilians' movements within garrisoned cities and limited their exchanges with the surrounding countryside. Passes were required to leave the city and were handed out only sparingly. Officers chaperoned meetings at the lines, even between family members, to monitor civilian communications and "be Eye and Ear Witness of all that passes." Observers speculated that the British kept civilians in Boston as a shield to prevent provincial forces from launching attacks on the city. In truth, both armies were hesitant to permit civilians to cross lines, fearing disease, espionage, and the loss of resources.[28]

The British Army's surveillance of white civilians created conditions that materially altered the circumstances of other inhabitants of occupied cities. As the army restricted white civilians' movement, many turned to enslaved laborers to run errands and carry letters, clothing, and supplies between family members separated by military lines. These practices, of course, predated occupation. Yet white civilians' hesitance to venture into the occupied city further facilitated bondspeople's mobility, as enslaved laborers became even more valuable assets because of how they extended the reach of white family networks within and across military lines. Some enslaved people turned these efforts to their own use, such as George, who had, whether genuinely or insincerely, "been a long time Complaining of a Violent pain in his Head and Eyes." In April 1781, he convinced his enslaver to dispatch him on an errand to the British garrison at Charleston, insisting that a "Change of Air and a jaunt to Chs. Town will recover him." In Charleston, George probably experienced greater freedom to move about the city, perhaps to visit friends and kin, to barter goods at the market, or to hire himself out for money. Still, there were limitations to this mobility. Just as they had under colonial regimes, enslaved laborers typically needed passes to move about British garrisons. Black refugees laboring for the army were required to wear marks identifying their department affiliation—although such restrictions were often unevenly enforced and dependent on individual officers. Still, the thousands of Black refugees flooding British garrisons and laboring for the army made it easier for enslaved people to evade systems of surveillance and move about occupied regions with a lesser degree of oversight than they had experienced under colonial legal regimes. As one Hessian officer observed in the Charleston garrison, "It was very easy, especially for Negroes, to pass between our picket."[29]

The necessity of running errands and managing family property during the war meant that white women also enjoyed comparatively greater freedom of movement within occupied regions than white men, so long as their actions did not hamper military aims. Commanding officers recognized that wartime conditions and British policies that restricted the mobility of male inhabitants necessitated women's increased management of family affairs and property. Although these efforts skewed toward the elite, enslaved women and domestic servants were often drawn into these endeavors and tasked with carrying messages or running errands. Women on both sides of the conflict seized on these gendered expectations to traffic intelligence and goods across military lines. Posing as peddlers, they infiltrated encampments to gather intelligence. They hid contraband under their skirts and braided scraps of paper into their hair, trusting that gender norms and propriety would protect them from close search. Indeed, both armies weaponized women's forays into enemy territory as a means of gathering intelligence.[30]

Nevertheless, these gendered privileges had limits, especially once commanding officers became more attuned to women's activities and began subjecting them to closer scrutiny, and, at times, outright intimidation. In Philadelphia, Joseph Galloway, the superintendent of police, coerced seventeen-year-old Mary Fygis into falsely confessing that she had trafficked intelligence—rather than family letters—across the lines, telling her that he had tracked her movements "from the first time that she came into Town" and that "a person had dogg'd her into every house that she had been at." Throughout British garrisons, searches of trunks and other items passing through the lines became commonplace the longer that an occupation lasted. "They are very Suspicious of Ladies," one Massachusetts woman reported en route to British headquarters in New York City. In Philadelphia, British sentries discovered two women attempting to smuggle salt and calfskin out of the occupied city to Valley Forge, where barefooted Continental troops were in dire need, by strapping the items to their abdomens and feigning pregnancy. "One cannot be too careful at the outposts," Hessian captain Johann Ewald cautioned after learning of the incident, "for who knows whether or not these women might have supplied the leather for shoes for an entire regiment of the enemy?"[31]

Designed to facilitate order and deter rebellion, British military policies exposed Anglo-Americans to hitherto unknown levels of surveillance by subjecting them to regulations that were typically reserved for the enslaved and others on the margins of colonial society. Echoing contemporary slave codes, curfews, patrols, mandatory passes, and restricted access to weapons placed new and unprecedented limitations on the movements and activities of Anglo-American colonists. Physical searches exposed white bodies to the probing fingers of authority in unfamiliar ways. It was, for many people, especially those of the middling and upper classes, a discomfiting change of circumstances—circumstances to which Black people, both free and enslaved, were well-accustomed. Occupation elevated the threat of racial violence and kidnapping, yet Black inhabitants' roles as laborers and messengers also allowed them greater freedom of movement within occupied regions. Indeed, Black residents often maneuvered city streets more easily than their white neighbors. A testament to these inverted dynamics, in November 1778, Connecticut loyalist William Bayard donned a "Disguise and Habbit of one of my own Slaves" to sneak into the New York garrison.[32]

PRIVATION AND DESPERATION: SUBSISTENCE IN OCCUPIED CITIES

In addition to heightened levels of surveillance, the Anglo-American inhabitants of occupied cities suffered from hunger and scarcity—uncomfortable and novel conditions for the urban elite that also trickled down and affected their less fortunate neighbors. As Philadelphian Sarah Logan Fisher observed in her diary in October 1777, "The Rich have not for themselves, nor have they it in their power to releive [*sic*] the cries of the poor." Inhabitants throughout British garrisons, especially those on the margins, thus turned to a well-established practice in urban life to feed themselves and their families: illicit markets. Although prohibited by commanding officers, a robust trade in secondhand provisions and plundered goods flourished in occupied regions. Military efforts to instill order were a minor deterrent to people facing hunger and cold, as well as those who sought to profit from these inequities. Yet, even as illicit exchanges could bring temporary relief, they also frequently landed civilian inhabitants before military justice, resulting in uncomfortable, often violent, and occasionally devastating consequences that further transformed urban life.[33]

Shortages were a regular occurrence within British garrisons, which were largely reliant on overseas shipping to supply their troops. Sieges and other military maneuvers intentionally interrupted resource chains. Some civilians were able to secure food through family networks that crisscrossed military lines, but many people were stranded in the middle as provisions dwindled and prices skyrocketed. Food shortages were especially dire among the urban poor, the majority of whom were single women and children who could not afford the escalating prices and who found traditional avenues of relief disrupted by the war. In Boston, meat that "formerly we would not have picked up in the street" sold for exorbitant prices. Some people resorted to eating rats. In British-occupied Philadelphia, Sarah Logan Fisher cracked open a barrel of "Ship Stuff" that her husband had purchased to feed their cow and was delighted to find that the contents were "sweet enough to make Bread of."

"How little did my dear Husband think . . . that we should be glad and rejoyc'd to make use of them for ourselves," she reflected in her diary.[34]

To lessen the effects of food shortages and ensure that troops had sufficient provisions, the British placed urban markets under military oversight. Civilians found their market activities regulated to ensure equitable distribution of supplies and prevent price gauging. These efforts were negligible at best and politicized at worst. Bakers in Charleston chafed against regulations prescribing the weight and size of their loaves. In Boston markets, only loyalists were allowed to purchase fresh meat. Many of the city's revolutionaries survived on salted provisions. "Pork and beans one day, and beans and pork another and fish when we can catch it," John Andrews wrote dejectedly. Meanwhile, in Philadelphia, women loudly proclaimed their willingness to "Starve for the good of their Country . . . provided the British Troops suffer with them."[35]

British officers nevertheless anticipated that civilians would soon tire of these shortages. Indeed, as circumstances worsened in British garrisons, many inhabitants professed loyalty to the crown in order to qualify for provisions. False loyalty, they reasoned, was preferable to genuine starvation. As one Newport woman observed, many inhabitants of the garrison, particularly those of the laboring classes, "care[d] not who was king, or who rebelled against him. it was enough for them to know, if somebody did not conquer soon, the[y] . . . must soon die."[36]

Food insecurity was a novel experience for the urban elite, a vulnerability that was exacerbated among enslaved and laboring populations. Under occupation, those on the margins of society often became more vulnerable. Unable to afford inflated market prices, impoverished inhabitants in the New York and Newport garrisons survived on soldiers' discarded salt provisions and ate "large quantities" of clams, which British physician Charles Blagden reported "are esteemed to make good soop." Although these people were among the most vulnerable behind British lines, many of them were also willing to work for the army in exchange for provisions, an arrangement that secured them varying levels of food, clothing, and wages, and, in the case of the enslaved, potentially freedom, while elite inhabitants starved. "I could not command a shilling—to provide myself a common fish dinner," Hannah Bancker moaned from the New York garrison in 1783, as she leveraged her furniture as security for overdue rent. Painstakingly counting the last of her remaining coin, Katherine Farnham Hay similarly feared the poverty that she foresaw "creeping into my pockets" in the New York garrison. "Good

God—what a change of circumstances," she bewailed; "I felt as if I shou'd dissolve into tears."[37]

Wartime deprivations fueled illicit trade between soldiers and civilians. Urban ports throughout the American colonies had vibrant informal economies that included extensive pawning and the trade of stolen and secondhand goods in which poor white women, free Black people, and enslaved laborers were vital participants. Wartime necessity ensured the persistence of these markets. Plunder was a common method by which soldiers in early modern armies supplemented rations; desperate inhabitants occasionally turned to robbery. Unregulated trade flourished between these groups. Lacking necessities, civilians purchased stolen goods from the troops, and soldiers' wives operated a lucrative and illegal trade in liquor. These practices, conducted in defiance of prohibitions on such exchanges, routinely frustrated commanding officers.[38]

Even so, such undertakings were not without risk. Throughout British garrisons, civilians were turned out of the lines, fined, or imprisoned for purchasing illegal goods. Anthony Cuff, a Black Philadelphian, was convicted and sentenced to a five-pound fine and six months imprisonment "for buying a Pair of Shoes from a Soldier of the 63d Regiment" in February 1778. With three children under the age of seven at home, Anthony and his wife, Ruth, were likely struggling to subsist their family in the resource-scarce garrison, circumstances that Anthony's imprisonment would only have exacerbated.[39]

In an effort to curb illicit activities, British officials sentenced offenders to public whippings and executions. Corporeal punishment became a regular occurrence on American streets. Although public punishments were common features of early modern justice, military officials imposed these sentences more frequently and more severely than civilian courts. All inhabitants of garrisoned cities, including soldiers, their families, and other members of the military community, along with civilian inhabitants, were subject to British military justice. Corporeal punishments were typically reserved for troops and their families, but civilian inhabitants—notably, Black inhabitants—were occasionally sentenced to public whippings, in addition to fines, imprisonment, exile, or impressment. Such punishments made an impression on civilians, particularly in the New England colonies, where the enslaved population was smaller and where white colonists were less inured to the brutality of whippings than those who resided in the South. "Its Shocking to conceive to what degree the Soldiers are punish'd . . . their ribs are laid quite bare, whereby their kidneys are so affected that they become incurable," one Boston man recounted to his brother-in-law in Philadelphia.

After witnessing one such punishment, Dorothy Murray wrote to her sister in horror of the "poor wretches whipt almost to death." "His back [was] as raw as a peice [*sic*] of Beef," she shuddered.[40]

Intended to impose authority and facilitate safety, public displays of military authority and the ubiquitous presence of soldiers on city streets also had the potential to intensify civilians' insecurities and exacerbate their fears. Quotidian violence, vocal jeers, the probing eyes and grasping hands of unfamiliar soldiers transformed city streets, exposing the civilian inhabitants of British garrisons to unnerving and at times invasive authorities and new levels of surveillance. These circumstances were unpleasant for all people, but they were particularly galling for Anglo-Americans of the upper classes, disrupting the privileges of autonomy and mobility to which many of them were accustomed. Hunger, scarcity, and deprivation compounded these unsettling feelings, contributing to a wider sense of instability that undergirded daily life within British garrisons. Faced with these circumstances, many inhabitants withdrew inside their residences, hoping that household walls might shield them against the chaos engulfing their cities. Yet, as the experience of occupation would prove, such hopes were a futile defense against the violence and terror that seeped from city streets and military encampments into civilian houses.

FRAGILE REFUGES: RETREATING INDOORS

As the British Army's transformation of American ports introduced new dangers to well-trodden streets, the unpredictability of war and the uncertainties of occupation tethered American civilians more closely to their homes. Feeling exposed among the troops, people withdrew from the streets swarming with unruly soldiers and the fetid encampments teeming with disease. Domestic spaces nevertheless offered uneven protections to those, both free and unfree, who resided within them. For many, particularly for the enslaved and other domestic servants, households had always been perilous places. Even so, diverse inhabitants throughout occupied regions, motivated both by a desire for safety and apprehensions of the unknown, retreated indoors—even as they recognized that war and occupation made those same households more porous, more precarious, more penetrable by troops and cannonballs alike. Households in occupied regions became at once more indispensable and more insecure.

"Ones own Home is and must be more comfortable than any other Place," Elizabeth Willing Powel wrote to her sister in April 1778 from

British-occupied Philadelphia, even as she lamented the damage the war had inflicted on her family's properties. Amid the devastation of war and occupation, households remained sites of family gathering that offered both the possibility of security and peace of mind amid the hazards in and near British garrisoned cities. Passing by large bodies of troops, even friendly ones, was daunting for any civilian, especially so for women used to traveling with male escorts. "I feel but little inclination to go into company," Abigail Adams admitted to Mercy Otis Warren, as she lamented her husband's absence. "I have no son big enough to accompany me," she wrote, and "I do not fancy riding thro [the Continental camp in] Roxbury with only a female partner." In the absence of male protectors, many white women living in occupied regions sought comfort from the normalcy of known spaces. Domestic seclusion, they hoped, would shield their families from the unknown dangers that lurked near military encampments.[41]

Domestic refuge was nevertheless a privilege of the elite, one made possible by the continued exposure of enslaved people, domestic servants, and other laborers to the hazards of the occupied city while their enslavers and employers remained ensconced indoors. Only the well-to-do could afford to task others with errands and the essential labors of daily survival. Many people throughout garrisoned cities had to undertake these responsibilities for themselves. Or on behalf of those that employed or enslaved them. Practically, domestic sanctuary was also more feasible in urban spaces than in the countryside, where it often fell to women to manage farms in their husbands' absence.[42]

When faced with the unknown challenges of wartime, anxious families withdrew into the spaces where they felt secure, where they felt they could best protect their loved ones: their houses. These sentiments recur throughout the letters of the wives of Philadelphia's Quaker exiles. In September 1777, with the British invasion of the capital imminent, the Pennsylvania Assembly, acting on orders from the Continental Congress, arrested twenty-two of the city's prominent men, primarily pacifist Quakers, for refusing to swear allegiance to the United States. The men's social standing and their desire for peace, Congress feared, would undermine the revolutionary cause once the city was in British hands. To prevent the Quakers' cooperation with the British, Congress forcibly removed the men before abandoning the city to the enemy. Following her husband's arrest, with the exception of attending meeting, Mary Pemberton "ha[d] not been over the Door sill . . . except once." Sarah Logan Fisher likewise found solace in her domestic refuge, professing disinterest in "what passes out of Doors." Neither Elizabeth Drinker nor her sister Mary Sandwith, who lived with the family, ventured out much in the five months after Henry Drinker's arrest. Mary had "not spent one Afternoon out" and Elizabeth "but few." Henry undoubtedly approved of his family's isolation: he advised his eldest son, William, to remain "at Home and within Doors" and devote his time to reading scripture in order to avoid "all rude and loose Company" and the other temptations lurking in the occupied city.[43]

For many people, indoor retreats represented a comforting notion of safety amid the unpredictability of wartime violence in and around British garrisons. Even so, many civilians were aware of the fragility of these refuges and were intensely conscious of their vulnerability. Such fears altered how they inhabited their houses. During the year that the British garrisoned in Boston, for instance, John Quincy Adams remembered, "My mother with her infant children dwelt, liable every hour of the day and of the night to be butchered in cold blood, or taken and carried into Boston as hostages, by any foraging or marauding detachment of men . . . [or] of being consumed . . . in a conflagration." Eager to avoid such a fate, thirteen-year-old Salem resident Susan Mason refused to take off her shoes for several days following the Battles of Lexington and Concord. Meanwhile, outside of Boston, Elizabeth Adams assured her husband, Samuel, that she had concocted an escape plan and was "in Readiness to Move at an Minute Warning," having pared her belongings down to only "a bed and a few Necessarys."[44]

Whether such threats materialized, the strain of exhaustion was wearing. "It is impossible for me to describe to you what I felt, while the British Army was on this side Ashley-Ferry," Mary Lucia Bull Guerard wrote from South Carolina; "we never went in to our beds at night, had Candles constantly burning and were alarmed at every noise that we heard." In Paramus, New Jersey, where Helen Kortright Brasher and her children fled after New York City fell to the British, she warily eyed the nearby Continental encampment, fearful that it would attract troops from the British garrison at New York. "This caused me to be on my guard," Helen recalled, and, "every night," before going to sleep, she gathered the family's unused apparel and secured their silver plate for safekeeping. British troops arrived in Paramus shortly after Helen implemented her nightly ritual. As she had feared, plundering parties ravaged the region, and the family received "two or three nocturnal visits" that "almost frightened us to death." For the remainder of the war, Helen was cautious whenever troops were in the vicinity. She continued to secure her valuables each night, even when neighbors "laughed" at her concerns and her family urged her to go to bed. Fearing nighttime invasion—the British "always surprised us in the dead of the night," she recalled—Helen urged her husband, a member of the state's provincial congress, "not to sleep at home" while on leave, for "if the enemy should come they undoubtedly would take him prisoner, and perhaps murder him."[45]

Similarly, outside of Charleston, Eliza Wilkinson "was always on the watch" for signs of danger and kept her "eyes fixed out of the window" for approaching soldiers. Complicating matters, troops, especially militia, were often indistinguishable from one another. When a party of soldiers arrived at Wilkinson's residence, she was uncertain whether the men were revolutionaries, loyalists, Britons, or Hessians. One officer's scarlet uniform and another's halting English convinced her that they were enemies. As it turned out, the men were Americans, and the soldier with the faltering speech was a French colonel. "O Major, that red! that hated scarlet . . . made me suspect you as a British officer," Eliza confessed, after realizing her error. Relieved to be among friends—for Wilkinson's distress had convinced the men she was a loyalist—the group collectively chuckled at their mistakes. The soldiers teased Eliza "that they really expected, by the time I had done wringing my hands, I would have no skin left upon them."[46]

Though spoken in jest, these observations contain a kernel of truth. The arrival of a group of unknown soldiers was terrifying for civilians, especially women. As Margaret Hill Morris explained after opening her door to six Continental soldiers and inquiring if they were Hessians, she had never seen a Hessian, "but they are *Men,* and you are Men and may be Hessians, for any thing I know." Margaret's confusion was feigned, a strategic delay to buy a loyalist neighbor concealed in her house time to hide. Indeed, women throughout the colonies recognized that strategic performances of defenselessness could facilitate their ability to secure assistance from both state governments and military officials by appealing to men's chivalric impulses. Yet, even as they did so, women nevertheless remained skeptical of soldiers' intentions, regardless of which side they supported. Confronted with strange and unknown occupying forces of both armies, uncertain of which troops offered protection and which posed harm, women were often only certain of one thing—that soldiers were men, and men brought the threat of danger and violence into their households and threatened their families.[47]

DOMESTIC INVASIONS: THEFT, PLUNDER, AND DEPREDATION

The experience of occupation proved that the security that civilians derived from domestic spaces was often fleeting. Throughout the war, civilian property was under constant threat from the depredations of both armies as well as noncombatants. The sheer numbers of soldiers, officers, camp followers, and livestock associated with the British Army taxed the resources of occupied cities and surrounding regions. Houses offered a ubiquitous source of food, shelter, firewood, and goods to be sold for profit. Civilians in occupied regions experienced an almost daily onslaught of plunder, theft, and marauding by soldiers, those affiliated with the army, other inhabitants, and common thieves. Camp followers and civilians alike scavenged dwellings in search of precious resources to sustain themselves and their families. Affluent residences, with their valuable commodities and surplus supplies, were more likely to be plundered; those owned by poorer residents, especially people of color, were perhaps less tempting targets, but their inhabitants were more likely to endure physical violence and rough handling. Within occupied regions and the surrounding areas, household invasion and material depredation eroded the sense of security that civilians derived from familiar spaces and routines. Enhancing feelings of vulnerability and intensifying insecurities, the relentless, ongoing contest to secure and protect household resources, quite literally, brought the war home for people throughout occupied regions.

Although officially discouraged under the norms of eighteenth-century European warfare, plunder was often tacitly condoned by commanding officers. Foraging, pilfering, gardening, and other "creative procurement," as one historian has termed it, were both a necessary and expected supplement to troops' paltry rations. Facing shortages, soldiers regularly destroyed fences, dismantled sheds and outbuildings, pilfered household valuables and foodstuffs, and commandeered livestock. They forced their way into civilian houses by breaking doors, shattering windows, or prying open cabinets with swords. In some instances, soldiers, sailors, and others associated with the army paid visits to neighbors under the guise of friendly relations in order to appraise potential targets. Such was the case for Philadelphia cabinetmaker Robert Black, who, after being visited by two mariners who "made several remarks upon [his] Cow," awoke the next morning to find the animal missing.[48]

Thieves often snuck in through open doors or unbolted gates. In search of rum and finding the back door of the Sharpe family's New York house ajar, Private William Gauble of the Coldstream Guards drunkenly crept up two flights of stairs and began rummaging through drawers. Interrupted by Mrs. Sharpe, Gauble pulled his bayonet on her, and she tumbled down the stairs. "Much alarmed" and fearing for her life, Mrs. Sharpe hobbled toward the kitchen crying for help. Private Gauble stumbled after her, bayonet still drawn, until a soldier quartered in the house, aided by the family's maid, apprehended him. Such incidents underscore the dangers of the occupied city. Unlocked doors, open gates—small, mindless mistakes—could have devastating consequences. "These are sad times for Thiveing and plundering," Elizabeth Drinker despaired in British-occupied Philadelphia; "tis hardly safe to leave the door open a minuet."[49]

Thieves targeted not only the goods and resources within civilian households but also the physical structures of the houses themselves. "Our very doors and window-shutters were taken from the house, and carried aboard the vessels which lay in the river," Eliza Wilkinson lamented in South Carolina. Fences, houses, and other buildings offered a ready source of firewood. By the end of the army's second winter in Newport, British troops had destroyed most of the region's natural resources. "Everyday here in Newport old buildings and unserviceable houses are torn down and the wood given to the regiments to burn," Hessian private Johann Conrad Döhla reported in December 1778. Often, troops utilized these resources themselves. But some enterprising soldiers sought to profit. In Philadelphia, several soldiers ventured outside the city "to bring in Fences etc. to sell to the Inhabitants," a practice that created circumstances in which wood-deprived inhabitants could potentially (and illegally) purchase their own fences from marauding British soldiers. Other inhabitants, unable to afford troops' inflated prices, survived frigid winters by turning to fuel sources typically utilized by the urban poor—a shocking change from the privileges to which the middling and urban elite were accustomed. "If you'll believe me Bill, I was necessitated to burn *horse dung,*" a Boston lawyer wrote in astonishment.[50]

Recognizing that genial relationships with colonists could stabilize British rule—especially among the elite whose residences were more likely to be plundered and whom officers more readily identified as members of their own class—commanding officers issued strict prohibitions against looting and stationed guards at empty houses. Plunder, General William Howe reproved the troops, was "Shameful and unsoldierlike" and "absolutely repugnant to all military Order and Discipline." Seeking to curtail predatory practices in Philadelphia, Howe ordered the provost martial "to execute upon the Spot any Soldier or Follower of the Army detected in pulling down Buildings or depredation of any kind." To further discourage plunder, British courts-martial imposed harsh sentences on soldiers and followers of the army caught ransacking civilian houses, including whipping, and occasionally death. Disciplinary threats and abstract ideals of honor were nevertheless ineffective deterrents for men facing hunger, cold, and dwindling provisions—and civilian houses offered a tempting source of relief.[51]

Plunder was often motivated by necessity, but it could also arise from soldiers' desire to assert dominance over civilian populations. Such undertakings were often violent and intentionally destructive: breaking valuable objects, demolishing furniture, and throwing cherished household furnishings into the yard. "Filth [is] deposited in them, make[s] the Houses so offensive, that it is a Penance to go into them," one of Admiral Richard Howe's secretaries observed with disgust. Lawns strewn with furniture, mirrors, portraits, and clocks—items too large to be easily concealed—were a common sight throughout occupied regions. Testifying about the condition of a plundered estate outside of Philadelphia, Lieutenant Edward Chandler of the Forty-Sixth Regiment conjured a scene of disarray: broken shutters and damaged doors, missing curtains, and feathers from two mattresses "thrown about the Room, and the ticking taken away." The liquor cabinet under the staircase had "the door broke open, and some of the Bottles broke, and others emptyed." Perhaps the soldiers, like some of their counterparts in Boston, "had revelling frolick in [the] parlour" before looting the rest of the house.[52]

Such attacks reveal what historian Stephen Conway has identified as widespread contempt among British forces for Americans, both military and civilian, whom they largely regarded as troublesome provincials. Disrespect translated into property destruction. By demolishing colonists' markers of elite status, soldiers—many of whom came from less affluent circumstances—both rejected colonists' claims to respectability and affirmed their own dominance. Many men felt as Sergeant John Crusard declared in defiance when a commanding officer ordered him to stop stealing fruit from a New York home: "'Dam them they are Rebels let us plunder them.'"[53]

For elite white women, rank and race could sometimes be an effective means of parrying these incursions. Trusting in soldiers' deference to their rank and gender, these women were, at times, able to defend their households and property by wielding their status as a shield. In South Carolina, for instance, Sarah Lowndes halted a raid on her family's plantation simply by rejecting the legitimacy of the soldiers' supposed orders to plunder and telling the troops "they should have nothing from me but what I gave them willingly." She served the men "breakfast and a plenty of drink" and "dismissed them."[54]

Women of color, by contrast, occupied a more precarious position within British garrisons, where their race and gender uniquely exposed them to the whims of individual soldiers—many of whom were well-aware that the mistreatment of Black inhabitants was less likely to be punished than crimes against white civilians. When a British patrol invaded her New York house in search of pilfered goods, a Mrs. Anderson was accosted by an officer who roughly twisted her arms behind her back and ordered a noose placed around her neck, threatening "that she should be immediately hanged, unless she" cooperated. Many Black women, however, were adept at using their ingenuity to distract and defend, a skill many of them had honed protecting their loved ones from the violence of slavery and the severe racial regimes of the American colonies. For instance, when British soldiers arrived to burn Stenton, a mansion outside of Philadelphia in November 1777, the quick thinking of Dinah, a free Black woman who resided at the property, saved the house from the flames. While the soldiers gathered kindling, an officer happened to arrive in search of deserters. Acting swiftly, Dinah informed him that "two such had just gone to secrete themselves in the Barn." Dinah's ingenuity saved Stenton, yet her actions also reveal a stark contrast with the strategies used by white women of the upper classes.[55]

Although status and race, in some instances, bolstered elite and middling inhabitants' ability to protect their property from the depredations of soldiers, the experience of household invasion was nevertheless deeply unnerving for people accustomed to the privileges of bodily autonomy and relative domestic security. Unlike the houses of their poorer neighbors, elite and middling residences were more likely to contain resources that soldiers coveted, circumstances that made them frequent targets and that further exacerbated civilians' feelings of insecurity. Writing from his home in Fairfield, Connecticut, only a short boat ride from British-occupied New York, Andrew Eliot, Jr., downplayed the disruptive effects of military raids. Nevertheless, he was worried. "Our Situation however is very precarious," he confided to his brother; "we are in frequent alarms as well as constant Uneasiness" from "maurading parties [of both armies] who pay us almost a weekly visit." It was harrowing, Andrew admitted; "we live—we sleep in constant fear."[56]

Thieves exposed the permeability of household boundaries and accentuated the vulnerability of the inhabitants within. One evening in December 1777, Ambrose Miles, a laborer who lived on the banks of the Schuylkill River in Philadelphia, awoke to the sound of voices in the street. Believing it to be a patrol, he "got out of bed and open'd the door." Five soldiers, one with a drawn cutlass and another wielding a bayonet, charged past him and began ransacking the house. The men ignored Ambrose's pleas, stuffing clothing "and several other small things" into a haversack. Realizing he was powerless to stop the invaders, Ambrose ran for the guard, presumably leaving his wife and children in the house. He returned with the patrol, and, by the end of the encounter, one of the robbers, a corporal, had been fatally shot.[57]

The incident must have been terrifying for the Miles family. Awaking in the middle of night to find armed men rummaging through their house, the family had no means of halting the men as they turned out drawers and ravaged through chests. For Mrs. Miles, along with any other women or girls who resided in the house, the invasion also held the threat of sexual violence, perhaps at the hands of multiple assailants. The arrival of the guard halted the robbery, but, even so, the ending was violent: a man shot to death by their back door. The Miles family—most likely Mrs. Miles, perhaps aided by her children, or servants, if the family could afford them—then had to tidy up the mess, reordering drawers and rehanging clothing, scrubbing muddy footprints from the floors, and washing away blood from the incident's grisly conclusion.

Invasion fundamentally altered the Miles household. Each evening, as the family prepared for bed, they must have wondered if they were secure, or if they would again be awakened in the middle of the night by armed men. Perhaps the Miles family, like Charleston widow Eliza Wilkinson, was anxious and weary after being plundered by British troops, haunted by memories of the encounter. "The thoughts of the vile men seemed worse (if possible) than their presence," Eliza recalled, as she described soldiers' raid on her home; "we could neither eat, drink, nor sleep in peace," and "the least noise alarmed us; up we would jump, expecting every moment to hear them demand admittance." Her family slept "in our clothes every night," ready to flee if necessary. Perhaps the Miles family, like Massachusetts loyalist Christian Barnes, who was held at gunpoint by a militiaman who invaded her house and threatened to "blow [her] brains out" unless she served him a meal, grew uneasy at the sound of troops. "I did not recover from my frieght for several days," Christian admitted; "the sound of drum, or the sight of a gun put me into such a tremor that I could not command myself." The notion of safety, once demolished, changed how families lived, moved, slept, and even dressed within their homes, irrevocably altering the domestic environment. As Benjamin Chew, Jr., reflected in Philadelphia, "The Remembrance of danger tho past will involuntarily excite Pain."[58]

One of the more terrifying aspects of household invasion was that it left families with few places to flee. In May 1781, Mary Heriot sat with her young children watching a departing British galley float down the Waccamaw River in Georgetown, South Carolina. An enslaved man named Gentry stood nearby. Suddenly, a boom echoed across the river. Balls exploded through the walls. Smoke and the acrid smell of burnt powder filled the air as glass shattered and heirlooms crashed to the floor. When the terror had subsided, Mary saw that, miraculously, the hall where she sat with her children was untouched by the damage. It was the only space in the house to be spared. Gentry had not been so fortunate; he later died from his injuries. Shaken, Mary put on a brave face as she recounted the incident to her husband. The peril had passed, she insisted, and it was better to "rejoice at our escape" than to dwell on what had transpired. Mary's cheerful outlook, however, masked deeper anxieties. Feeling exposed and vulnerable, she sensed "a damp on my spirits that I cannot get the better of." In search of safety, she retreated further into the wreckage of her destroyed home and resolved "to be seldom out of the Cellar." The family's brush with danger, she reflected, "affected me beyond any thing I have yet experienced."[59]

The invasion of domestic spaces not only physically destroyed the houses that civilians had carefully invested with both their time and money but also, chillingly, shattered civilians' sense of safety and the comfort that they derived from familiar spaces. Such losses were devastating for families. Passing through Fairfield, Connecticut, after it was attacked by the British, an unidentified woman described the wreckage. "There are scarcely a house left standing," she reported, "and in many of the cellars are to be seen the former possessor groveling among the ruins as if wedded to the spot that once contain'd his earthly treasure!" Amid the turmoil of civil war, the destruction of objects and spaces that anchored family life left civilians feeling adrift and exposed. This was true for families across the social spectrum. Plunder, martial law, urban warfare, and the Revolution's invasion into American households remade domestic spaces in ways that subjected inhabitants to uncertainty, danger, and insecurity.[60]

Civilians' emotional connection to their houses and the sense of security they engendered amplified the distress they felt at the loss of safe spaces. Reeling from the ruination of her family's estate on the southern banks of Philadelphia's Schuylkill River, a furious Elizabeth Willing Powel wrote to her sister Anne Francis, whose family estate was also wrecked by the troops, to commiserate over their shared losses at the hands of the British Army. "Tho' Christians are not allowed to have Idols yet I fear you and I . . . have transgressed," Elizabeth wrote, lamenting that the sisters' "terrestrial ones . . . have met the fate of those of old to be totally destroyed and torn down." Invoking the language of idolatry to underscore the depth of their losses, Elizabeth's metaphor conveyed the love and fervor that the women felt for their homes—their domestic idols—as if they were sacred spaces. "At first I was as much oppressed as I cou'd have been for the loss of my inanimate Thing but Rage soon succeeded Grief and I absolutely raved and ever shall when I speak on the Subject," Elizabeth avowed.[61]

RAPE AND SEXUAL ASSAULT

For many women in and around British garrisons, the war's incursion into civilian households offered an ominous reminder of the menace that British occupation posed to their personal safety. As they traversed altered streets and bolted their doors, the female inhabitants of occupied cities were intensely aware that the influx of thousands of potentially violent and hostile soldiers introduced an additional layer of peril into their daily lives: a heightened threat of rape and sexual assault.

In and around occupied regions, women encountered a spectrum of violence that ranged from unwanted touches to physical assault to sexual violence and, occasionally, death. These perils were not mutually exclusive. Deeply enmeshed within these other forms of violence, the increased risk of sexual assault in occupied regions altered women's relationships to city and household spaces. Although unevenly vulnerable, women of all races and statuses were acutely cognizant of the new dangers that an army introduced into urban life. Sexual assault was often situational, contingent on race and rank as well as the temperaments of individual soldiers. Rape could be premeditated; it could be random. But, for female civilians, it was an omnipresent threat. As in other wars, during the Revolution many women feared rape as a possible outcome of their interactions with soldiers of both armies. The looming menace of sexual assault influenced daily decisions about safety, about where to walk, whom to converse with, and how to answer their door. These anxieties were amplified in occupied regions, where the volume of troops and the frequency of soldiers' raids on civilian households elevated the potential for danger. Sexual consent and coercion in the early modern world existed on a continuum structured by intersections of gender, class, and race. Yet occupying forces wielded a different kind of power than men did in peacetime. The institutional culture of the military, combined with the violence of war and some soldiers' desires to force their enemies into submission, fostered a group mentality that emboldened some soldiers to assault civilian women.[62]

The norms of European warfare designated women as neutral noncombatants, so long as they "employ[ed] themselves in the occupations of their sex." In practice, such protections were at the discretion of commanding officers, and soldiers routinely flouted orders prohibiting violence against civilians. Race and status mattered, too. Widely regarded as ladies in need of defense, elite white women were more likely to benefit from military protection than poor white women or Black women of all statuses. Women of the laboring class, and Black women in particular, were especially at risk because their jobs more frequently exposed them to the caprices of individual soldiers. Typically responsible for running errands, these women were more likely to be alone in public spaces where they might encounter enlisted men, who did not adhere to the same code of gentlemanly honor that pervaded the British officer corps (not that officers always acted accordingly). Nor did they have the social status or connections to challenge men who legitimately or fraudulently presented themselves as military authorities.[63]

Such was the case for Catherine Stone and Isabella Mitchell, two Philadelphia servants who were stopped in the street one night by soldiers posing as the patrol. When the women expressed hesitation, the men "dragg'd them by force" and raped them outside the Southwark Theater. Both women managed to escape with their lives, but it was the men's assault on Catherine, a white woman, rather than Isabella, a Black woman, that sparked sympathy from their employer. The soldiers were arrested later that month, when Catherine glimpsed the men from her doorstep and alerted authorities. Convicted of "ill-using" the women, a lesser charge than rape, the assailants were sentenced to one thousand lashes before being drummed out of the lines. Although the men were punished for their crimes, their behavior in the days after the rapes nevertheless exhibits the sense of invincibility and masculine power that many soldiers believed their military status conveyed. As Catherine testified during the court-martial, "Some days afterwards . . . Upon seeing her" in the city, the soldiers "pointed at her and laughed."[64]

Women of all political affiliations were susceptible to sexual assault within garrisoned cities. Catherine Stone and Isabella Mitchell, for instance, were employed by a British officer. Politics offered little in the way of protection, but being labeled as an enemy made women more vulnerable to assault and amplified the danger that soldiers posed. Men on both sides of the war used political labels to justify violence, sexual or otherwise, against American women. Epithets of "rebel Bitch" and "yankee whore" recur throughout British courts-martial. Within and around British garrisons, soldiers cited the assumed rebellious politics of American women to rationalize their abuse. In New York, when charged with raping Elizabeth Johnstone in her home while her four-year-old daughter stood by crying, John Dunn and John Lusty nonchalantly responded "that she was a yankee whore or a yankee bitch, and it was no great matter."[65]

Although writing from Continental-occupied Newport, the experience of loyalist Catherine Dudley reveals the dangers lurking in the streets of any garrisoned city, particularly for women marked as political enemies. Walking home from the wharf in November 1775, Catherine encountered a group of about thirty men, two of whom "walk'd down to me watch'd me try'd to look under my Bonnet." The men's discomfiting behavior made Catherine feel exposed, their invasive stares offering both a subtle threat and an awareness of her own vulnerability. Unnerved and "a good deal frighten'd" by the encounter, Catherine was anxious to return home. As she "hurry'd thro'" the dark streets, she realized that one of the men was following her. "The fellow . . . was after me the whole way," she recalled, and she "expect'd every moment, they wou'd have seiz'd me." Fearful, Catherine sought shelter in a nearby house. "When I stop'd at Mr. P[ease]'s Door he said, Damn you; you bitch, you shall be mark'd as a Black Sheep, they were oblig'd to drag me in the Door, for I was unable to move Fear, Grief, Resentment, had got the better."[66]

Wartime sexual assault, as Sharon Block has argued, tended to be public, often with multiple assailants and victims, and frequently committed in the context of invasion and other marauding. Yet the threat of rape was not contained to the streets. Women's affidavits and the transcripts of British courts-martial indicate that sexual violence frequently occurred in domestic spaces during raids and plundering expeditions. Women residing in the paths of foraging armies were particularly vulnerable to these kinds of attacks. In 1777, the Continental Congress collected women's depositions detailing rape and other forms of violence at the hands of British soldiers. Several patterns emerge. Women were typically raped in their homes or dragged into nearby barns. Rape often occurred at the point of a bayonet, and bystanders, often family members, were helpless to stop them. A handful of the most egregious cases were prosecuted before British courts-martial, and guilty soldiers were sentenced to death or severe punishments. The army was, after all, invested in maintaining good relations with civilian populations. Moreover, rape prosecutions permitted British officers to exhibit paternalistic masculinity and martial honor by obtaining justice for vulnerable women. Commanding officers, however, retained full discretion in prosecuting cases. Underscoring the performative nature of these hearings, the defendants in all extant courts-martial for rape are either enlisted men or loyalists; no British officer was ever tried for the crime during the war.[67]

Although unrestrained pillaging was less common in urban environments, rape remained a potent threat to women's safety in occupied cities. Many assaults were opportunistic. Others were premeditated, committed, not by strangers in dark alleys, but by familiar faces. Anne Moore, a Boston woman who worked in the household of Dr. Trotter Hill, the regimental surgeon for the British Army's Fifty-Ninth Regiment of Foot, awoke in the middle of the night to Timothy Spillman, the doctor's servant, climbing into her bed naked "and taking hold of her." Anne recalled that he was irritated by "her resisting him, and refusing to gratify his desire." "He damned her, and said that she had disappointed him," and, when Anne attempted to get out of bed, Spillman "prevented her and knockt her head against the Window," breaking four panes of glass. He beat her until she fainted. When Anne regained consciousness, she "begg'd of him to let her alone, upon which he swore prodigiously, and at last left the room." Without pausing to grab a cloak or a blanket, Anne fled, groggy, injured, and frightened into the frigid predawn hours. Benjamin Hallowell, the Boston commissioner of customs, answered his door at five o'clock in the morning to find her standing in her shift, "cruelly beaten, and . . . almost perished with Cold." Her injuries, as regimental surgeons would later attest, were severe—they believed her life to be in danger—and were inflicted "by a Man's fist," not, as Private Spillman feebly suggested during the court-martial, by falling down the stairs.[68]

Neighbors occasionally intervened to stop assaults, but, when confronted with British bayonets, even those who were inclined to aid victims were often unable to do so, particularly if soldiers were in a group. Civilians had a far better chance of halting a single assailant, as in the case of Philadelphians Silver and Sarah Crispin and their neighbor Patty Brokington, who successfully intervened when they witnessed Mary O'Hara, the Crispins' servant, struggling with an officer on the street. Many people, however, also chose to look the other way in the interest of protecting themselves and their families. Men, in particular, were hesitant to intervene, in part because of the threat of imprisonment or impressment. When Sarah Willis was raped at knifepoint in her Brooklyn house by Thomas Gorman, a mariner who gained entrance to her house pretending to be a press gang, she cried out for help. The walls were thin. Peter Leary, a neighbor, heard Sarah say "several times . . . *Let me alone.*" Sarah even called out to him, "saying Leary; take this Man out of my house," pleading, "for God's sake, come to my assistance." But Leary, "imagining that there was a Press Gang in or about the house . . . was afraid to interfere." Likewise, William Anderson, another neighbor, testified that he had heard conversation and "a good deal of Scuffling on the floor, so much that it prevented him from Sleeping." Still, he declined to intervene, and "what was said or done, he does not know."[69]

Domestic invasion often subjected women to rough handling and unwanted physical contact, even when soldiers did not rape. To be at the mercy of the probing, violent hands of strangers was profoundly unsettling, both an implicit and an explicit reminder of soldiers' power under martial law and their ability to inflict harm. When an armed party comprised of British dragoons and Black men forced their way into the South Carolina house where Eliza Wilkinson and two other white women and several enslaved laborers had taken shelter, the dragoons lurched at the white women, swearing and "making as if they'd hew us to pieces with their swords." At least one enslaved Black woman, likely more, was also present during the raid, but Eliza failed to record her experiences, focusing only on the violations that the soldiers inflicted upon herself and the other elite white women. The soldiers yanked their caps from their heads; one of them forcibly wrenched the buckles from Eliza's shoes. The other white women in the house endured similar manhandling. A soldier pulled one woman's earrings from her lobes; another held the other woman at gunpoint until she surrendered her wedding ring. One of the men grabbed Eliza's arm so forcefully that bruises in the shape "of his thumb and three fingers" were visible "for several days after." Eliza was paralyzed with fear during the raid. "I seemed in amaze! Quite stupid!" she explained; "I cannot describe it." The soldiers did not rape the white women, but they made clear that they could have. Before departing, in a threat laden with foreboding, the dragoons informed the women "that they had favored us a great deal—that we might thank our stars it was no worse." After they departed, "I trembled so with terror, that I could not support myself," Eliza recalled.[70]

Among American revolutionaries, reports of rape by British and Hessian soldiers functioned as a powerful motivational tool, exhorting men to defend their female relations from the enemy's ravages. Indeed, revolutionary newspapers intentionally underreported rapes by Continental soldiers in favor of publicizing allegations against British troops. Similar to revolutionary rhetoric that decried the destruction of property, in public discourse, revolutionaries reinterpreted British assaults on women's bodies as evidence of the danger that British tyranny posed to masculine privilege, liberty, and autonomy.[71]

Within garrisoned regions, officers' use of sexualized political epithets to demean and humiliate male revolutionaries further underscored the connection between masculine and political independence. Bostonian John Leach, who was imprisoned on suspicion of being a rebel, watched helplessly as soldiers harassed his wife, Sarah, each time she entered the jail. "The Provost insulted her, by saying, I was a Damned Rebel, and my Family the Damnedest Rebel Family in the Country," he vented in his diary. The couple's young son endured similar taunts. According to another prisoner, the provost routinely "cursed" the child, and the boy "most always tremble[d]" when he came to visit or drop off food for his father. On one occasion, John overheard the provost muttering, "G--d Damn that Dog (meaning my Child) . . . that Dog deserves to be shot." Unable to protect his family, John bemoaned his predicament: "We are abused if we Don't complain of hard usage, and are abused if we do." He had learned, as Philadelphian Silver Crispin discovered when he was court-martialed for defending his wife's honor—Sarah "was no whore, but his Wife," he had chastised Lieutenant Benjamin White of the Twenty-Second Regiment, before tackling the officer into the snowy street—there were consequences to fighting back. Throughout the conflict, these actual and perceived attacks on men's honor and the accompanying sense of violation were essential to sustaining motivation for the war, especially among male revolutionaries.[72]

For female civilians throughout the colonies, however, rumors of rape by British soldiers offered chilling warnings that their bodies had become contested spaces in the midst of a brutal civil war. After reading a 1777 congressional report that included women's testimonies about being raped by British soldiers, an anxious Abigail Adams confessed that her advanced pregnancy compounded her fears of British troops. Approximately seven months pregnant and her movements cumbersome, she worried that if the British returned to Boston, "I should not dare to tarry here . . . nor yet know where to flee for safety; the recital of the inhumane and Brutal Treatment of those poor creatures who have fallen into their Hands, Freazes me with Horrour."[73]

For women throughout occupied regions, the threat of sexual assault was a ubiquitous aspect of the dangers that flooded city streets, that seeped into households, and that climbed into their beds. Their experiences reverberated among women throughout the colonies, who feared the elevated dangers that war brought to their own bodies and their own safety. But these accounts also resonated more broadly among people both inside and outside of British garrisons who understood rape as a particularly heinous manifestation of the vulnerabilities of civilians under military rule. Alongside widespread material depredation, property destruction, quotidian violence, scarcity, hunger, and urban warfare, sexual assault made clear to civilians, especially those whose lives had been relatively free of violence, privation, and fear, the tenuousness of these privileges and clarified the immediacy of the perils that they faced as war descended upon their communities.

Occupation transformed households on multiple levels, remaking domestic spaces and disabusing white families of the notion that their residences would be sheltered from war. Under British occupation, civilians found themselves subject to new, coercive authorities and surveillance measures that eroded the privileges and safeties to which they were accustomed. Material destruction and invasion contributed to a broader sense of vulnerability. Civilians regularly opened their doors to find men requisitioning provisions or soldiers demanding alcohol. Prized commodities that had once projected status now marked people as targets. Fences that had restrained livestock were torn down in the night; animals were stolen and slaughtered. Soldiers ventured into unlocked doors and accosted civilians in their beds. As Massachusetts loyalist Christian Barnes put it starkly, "No one knows where they are safest at this time."[74]

The close confines of city life meant that sounds carried, and neighbors were often aware of violence happening nearby, even if not within their own households. They saw thieves jumping over their neighbor's fences and men walking through darkened alleys. They heard women's frightened cries echoing in the street, and, from their windows, they witnessed altercations between soldiers and their neighbors. These circumstances eroded civilians' sense of safety, heightening feelings of unease and vulnerability. "Every noise now seems alarming, that happns in the Night," Elizabeth Drinker confessed from occupied Philadelphia. Awakened by her dog "bark[ing] voilently" one cold December evening, she confided to her diary, "I often feel afraid to go to Bed." The following evening, around eleven o'clock, Elizabeth spied two soldiers in the alley behind her house. Hoping to discourage unsavory intentions, Elizabeth "contriv[ed]" a deception. Venturing into the yard with her sister, Mary Sandwith, and Harry Catter, the stable boy, Elizabeth loudly inquired "if John and Tom were yet in Bed." Harry, confirming the existence of the fictional John and Tom, answered yes. But, in case the men's presence was an insufficient deterrent, before returning inside, Mary instructed Harry to "untye the Dog." As Harry and the women staged this elaborate scene, another servant, Jane Boon, watched from the upstairs window as the men disappeared into the night, carrying a "large Bundel," which, the family learned the next day, contained clothing stolen from the baker's wife next door.[75]

The increased wartime permeability of domestic boundaries altered how civilians existed within and regarded the spaces they inhabited. Rattling windowpanes, creaking gates, and nighttime shadows introduced new levels of fear and terrifying possibilities of violence into family homes. Warily eyeing their neighbors, servants, and enslaved laborers, white civilians viewed their surroundings with increased suspicion. They worried about unlatched doors and broken windows. They slept in their clothes, ready to flee, as cannons thundered overhead and the smoke from burning houses lingered in the air. They dreaded the sound of shattering glass and the heavy traipsing of boots on the stairs. As the rooms that had once hosted family dinners and festive gatherings became peppered with cannon shot, they huddled in fear in damp basements, drawing their loved ones close. Offering a fragile sense of security, the home became a feeble shield against the dangers of the occupied city. Even so, not all inhabitants felt equally safe within revolutionary households; the notion of domestic refuge, even amid wartime chaos, remained one that was deeply shaped by the privileges of race, class, gender, and freedom.

If British occupation exacerbated white civilians' sense of unease and precarity, it carried both the possibility of enhanced danger as well as potential opportunity for the enslaved, as later chapters will explore. Legally classified as property, bondspeople were seen as valuable commodities that could be kidnapped and sold for profit, or handed out as enlistment bounties. Yet raiding parties could also offer enslaved people an escape from bondage. South Carolina loyalist Jeremiah Savage lamented that twenty-five enslaved laborers "were all Lost to him by means of their being taken away by or of themselves joining the British Army." Maria, a twenty-two-year-old woman enslaved in South Carolina, "WENT OFF . . . with Lord Rawdon's Army" during the British occupation of Charleston. In Pennsylvania, Tony "RAN away the morning the British army left Philadelphia." Titus and Joe "absconded" from their South Carolina enslaver "just as the Fleet was about to part" and escaped on board British transport ships. Others, like Edinburgh, Simon, Cudjoe, York, Primus, Billy, Johnny, and Isaac, fled on foot and "followed the [British] army into Georgia."[76]

These defections unnerved enslavers. Slave revolts had long been a source of anxiety for white colonists; the notion that enslaved people might align themselves with invading British forces compounded these worries. Recounting an incident in which an enslaved woman guided British troops through the South Carolina Lowcountry to the house of a prominent revolutionary, Eliza Wilkinson alluded to these concerns, worrying that "private [enemies] were daily about." Frenzied rumors that enslaved people would seize on the disruption of battle to enact vengeance on their enslavers caused Phoebe Emerson—who resided alone in Concord, Massachusetts, with four small children and a handful of enslaved laborers—to faint at the sight of Frank, an enslaved man who rushed into her bedroom, carrying an axe, to warn her that "the Red Coats have come!" The British Army's threat to American households, white enslavers worried, was not only from without but also from within.[77]

In occupied regions, unpredictability, fear, and violence became the norm as diverse civilians struggled to defend themselves and safeguard their families and their property amid battles, plunder, home invasion, bodily violence, and property destruction. To counter these efforts, civilians adapted, using the resources at their disposal to protect their families. As people adjusted to the rules and rhythms of the occupied city, they became more comfortable negotiating with soldiers and bartering their resources to protect their families. They compromised with occupying forces and consented to the partial destruction of their fences and sheds in return for leaving their houses intact. They dismantled their fences and cut down trees, sharing the wood with neighbors. They sold household furnishings to supplement their income. They moved in with family members and offered their own houses for rent. Nevertheless, civilians could not forget that they resided in a city under martial law—the evidence was all around them. As American households became additional fronts in the war, British occupation not only physically transformed the spaces where civilians resided, it informed their every decision, as they evaluated their options and attempted to safeguard their families. The result was an omnipresent sense of vulnerability and peril that defined civilians' wartime experiences living under martial law.[78]

As the British Army settled into American cities, another threat to civilians' domestic security soon appeared on their doorsteps: scarlet-clad British officers demanding quarters.

FIGURE 3 *Silhouette of Elizabeth Drinker*, n.d. Society Portrait Collection. [V88 ID 129]. Collection of the Historical Society of Pennsylvania, Philadelphia

CHAPTER TWO

Our Family Is Somewhat Increased

Assessing the young Scottish officer standing before her, Elizabeth Drinker considered how to refuse his request. She had feared this might happen. People throughout Philadelphia had, in recent weeks, been obliged to quarter British or Hessian officers. Some of the men had been quite violent. In fact, earlier that week, one of her neighbors had been "dangerously wounded" by an officer who unsheathed his bayonet in the house. As Quakers, the Drinkers were pacifists who were opposed to war, and Elizabeth and her husband, Henry, had skillfully maintained their neutrality amid the fractious politics of the preceding decade. But three months ago, as the British advanced on Philadelphia in September 1777, the Continental Congress had exiled Henry for his refusal to swear allegiance to the new United States. Elizabeth was left alone in the British-occupied city with five children ranging in age from three to sixteen, along with two female servants, a stable boy, and her sister, Mary Sandwith. Religious convictions

FIGURE 4 *Silhouette of Henry Drinker,* n.d. David McNeely Stauffer Collection. [1095 ID 14034]. Collection of Historical Society of Pennsylvania, Philadelphia

aside, for her family's safety, she felt it was best to interact with the army as little as possible.[1]

In the months since the British Army had arrived in Philadelphia, Elizabeth had successfully deflected two requests to lodge officers in her house. But the young man before her was persistent. He could not be more than twenty-two or twenty-three, Elizabeth mused, only slightly older than her nephew, who had taken to sleeping in her house several nights a week in Henry's absence. And, unlike other soldiers she had encountered, he seemed polite. Sensing her hesitation, Major James Cramond insisted that "it was a necessary protiction at these times to have [a soldier] in the House" and urged her to consider his request. He would return tomorrow or the day after, he promised, to receive her answer.[2]

Like Elizabeth Drinker, urban inhabitants in occupied regions encountered the British Army, not on the battlefield, but on their doorsteps. Although quartering affected the lives of diverse civilians, it primarily unfolded in the residences of the middling and elite. Affluent urbanites lived in larger, more luxurious houses that had adequate room to accommodate officers' retinues and a level of affluence that made them suitable—coveted, even—lodgings. For these inhabitants, quartering, quite literally, brought the war home, posing an unprecedented threat to domestic life and the power enacted within and embodied by the institution of the household.[3]

By the late eighteenth century, households were increasingly entwined with the identities of free, primarily white, elite, and middling people throughout the British Atlantic as a symbol of their status and refinement. Although they did not enjoy equal power within household hierarchies, men and women of the upper classes were jointly invested in maintaining orderly households that structured their legal, financial, and social relationships and governing those household inhabitants under their authority, including not only their children but also domestic servants, apprentices, and enslaved laborers. Quartering upended these dynamics at both practical and ideological levels. With varying degrees of permission, officers—often complete and potentially violent strangers—claimed as their own the household space, furniture, and resources that undergirded affluent colonists' domestic identities. Quartering disrupted household routines, and officers, by their very presence, frequently undermined the traditional authority of householders over domestic spaces, laborers, and dependents. It was a deeply unsettling experience for those accustomed to wielding power in revolutionary society.[4]

Yet histories of quartering and the British Army during the Revolution often overlook both the experiential and ideological implications of these domestic arrangements. Instead, they tend to focus on debates between military commanders and local officials that occurred in official (masculine) spaces, as selectmen haggled over the costs, burden, and legalities of provisioning occupying forces. Often, they devote only cursory attention to the actual experience of quartering and the varied people for whom quartering unfolded, not in town halls, but in parlors and kitchens—people for whom quartering was, not an abstract legal question, but an intimate, lived experience that disrupted daily life and unsettled expectations of orderly household governance.[5]

Diaries and correspondence from the families of Philadelphia's Quaker exiles, twenty-two religious pacifists whom the Continental Congress banished to Virginia as the British advanced on the city in September 1777, offer exceptionally rich perspectives on the lived experience of quartering. Many people, understandably, were hesitant to commit words to paper about the British officers residing in their houses. But the extreme circumstances in which these families found themselves, navigating the simultaneous upheaval of men's banishment and the British Army's occupation of Philadelphia, mean that the correspondence of the Quaker exiles and their families describe quartering to an unusual degree. Of course, these sources represent a unique perspective; Quakers were pacifist neutrals who sought to avoid involvement in the war. But, when viewed from the household, the Quaker experience is also instructive. Elite and middling Quakers, just like their Anglo-American neighbors of similar rank and varied faiths, deeply valued family life and household order.[6]

Drawing primarily, but not exclusively, from the experiences of these Quaker households, this chapter examines the realities of quartering in households headed by white women of the upper classes, including women acting as provisional heads of household in their husbands' absences. Among this group, the Drinker family's ordeal is remarkably well-documented, a consequence of both Elizabeth's meticulous diary and her correspondence with her exiled husband, Henry. Reading these sources alongside British military regulations and other documents that detail officers' experiences and expectations, this chapter first gives an overview of official British quartering policies and the army's efforts to impose order on what was, in practice, often a frenzied and improvised process. It then outlines the risks and benefits of quartering for civilians and considers how white women of the upper classes navigated their roles as provisional heads of household in occupied regions. Lastly, it brings these perspectives together through a close examination of quartering in Elizabeth Drinker's household. Her case illuminates a more general experience about how white women wartime heads of household endured the possibilities, fears, and daily negotiations of cohabitation with billeted British officers—and what these encounters meant to both them and their absent husbands.[7]

These stories reframe our understanding of quartering in the American Revolution by illustrating the critical, often unacknowledged role that gender and status played in structuring quartering arrangements and, just as importantly, how these encounters tested prevailing ideologies of patriarchal household governance. As Chapter 3 will show, quartering in white male-headed households was often confrontational, as British officers and male civilians struggled to bend the other to their will. But, in wartime households headed by white women of the upper classes, quartering looked very different. Here, gendered performances of masculine honor, martial chivalry, and feminine dependency were crucial aspects of negotiations over quarters, as both British officers and elite female civilians both genuinely and performatively wielded gendered tropes in strategic efforts to secure advantageous situations for themselves.[8]

Operating within a shared worldview of elite gentility, these interactions, which in many ways were reminiscent of courtship, provided a recognizable gendered framework through which British officers and white women of the upper classes negotiated quartering arrangements. In female-headed households throughout occupied regions, a British military culture of chivalric honor converged with broader patriarchal gender norms (and intersected with other racial, class, and political identities) to grant white women of the upper classes a surprising amount of influence in negotiating and managing quartering arrangements. Yet, even as British officers and wartime female heads of household reached rapprochements, these living arrangements had the potential to destabilize patriarchal household governing ideologies. For absent American patriarchs witnessing these exchanges from afar, the notion of other men commandeering their residences, living alongside their wives and children, depleting their domestic resources, and ingratiating themselves into their households was a chilling violation of their rights as property owners, as heads of households, and as men.[9]

Attending to these gendered dynamics and the complicated personal relationships they produced enhances our perception of quartering during the Revolution. Contrary to how quartering has typically been portrayed in both conventional histories and popular understanding, it was not always a practice of forcible appropriation. Indeed, in households headed by white women of the upper classes, quartering was often an arrangement of flexible, negotiated cohabitation in which notions of gendered dependence and martial chivalry facilitated elite white women's ability to retain control over their households and the British officers residing within them—despite their husbands' fears.

QUARTERING THE TROOPS

For decades prior to the American Revolution, most notably during the English Civil War, English subjects had resisted billeting troops in their residences, decrying the practice as an infringement on their right as Englishmen to govern their own households and property. To assuage these concerns, over the course of the eighteenth century, British officials crafted policies that carefully outlined the regulations, responsibilities, and obligations of the army to householders and vice versa. In practice, however, these policies were somewhat flexible, especially in territories outside English borders, and dependent on officers' willingness to adhere to regulations and enforce compliance among the troops. For many Anglo-American colonists, the debates over quartering in the 1760s and early 1770s marked their first real experiences with billeting troops—experiences that reshaped colonists' understanding of their status as subjects and strengthened their notions that cities and houses were civilian spaces that should be protected from soldiers.[10]

During the prewar occupation of Boston (1768–1774), the British Army had adhered to the regulations outlined in the 1765 Mutiny Act. The act stipulated that American colonists should maintain barracks and contribute to troops' upkeep and provision but implicitly prohibited the quartering of soldiers in private residences. Indeed, citing the shortage of barracks and large public buildings in North America, commander in chief Thomas Gage lobbied for the billeting of soldiers in private homes in the American colonies—as the army did in Scotland, Ireland, and the borderlands of North America, including parts of Canada, Florida, and the western backcountry, where adequate accommodations were in short supply. Yet Parliament refused to take this step. Instead, the 1765 Mutiny Act directed that soldiers in North America were to be lodged, first, in existing or newly constructed barracks. If those accommodations proved insufficient, the army could utilize public buildings, inns, taverns, and stables. Private structures, including barns, outbuildings, and uninhabited houses were a last resort. Moreover, the Mutiny Act stipulated that if troops were billeted on individuals, it was to be at the direction of local civilian officials, not military authorities, and property owners were to be compensated for the use of their room and supplies. The 1774 Quartering Act loosened—but did not nullify—these restrictions in order to expedite the billeting of troops in private buildings when existing barracks proved inadequate. Even so, commanding officers largely abided by earlier iterations of the law, preferring to construct new barracks, renovate public spaces, or rent from business owners rather than force soldiers into civilian residences. "The Method of quartering troops in America, is in every particular totally different from what I have ever seen," Lieutenant Frederick Mackenzie grumbled from occupied Newport in 1778.[11]

The outbreak of war in 1775 and the arrival of additional regiments did little to alter these established practices, and British officers continued to replicate them in each subsequent city that the army conquered during the Revolution. Individual soldiers might have regarded Americans as enemies, but, as an institution, the army was committed to reintegrating the rebellious colonies into the British Empire, an objective that guaranteed the rights and protections of British subjecthood to the loyal inhabitants of garrisoned cities, including the security of their property. Clarifying his rationale for restricting officers' billets in New York City, General James Pattison explained, "Whilst I am desirous of accommodating Officers with proper Quarters, I cannot but attend to the Ease of the Citizens (who are equally under my Protection)."[12]

Limiting the space available for quarters, such policies complicated the army's efforts to house troops. Depending on the city, occupying forces numbered anywhere between thirty-five hundred soldiers in Savannah to approximately twenty-four thousand in New York. Camp followers, loyalist refugees, self-emancipated enslaved people, and Continental prisoners accompanied the troops, further overburdening accommodations. As one Hessian officer observed in Philadelphia, "With so little room in the desolate city . . . General Howe is probably worrying as much about the procurement of these necessities [quarters] as he is about the defense of the extensive banks of the Delaware and Schuylkill." Seeking to maximize available space, officials carefully catalogued civilian houses, numbering them with chalk and marking doors with the letters "G. R." (George Rex) to denote vacant and rebel properties that could be converted into barracks, officers' quarters, or storage. Army surveyors also noted households inhabited by women or property owners that expected compensation or insurance. The "very good House[s]" were earmarked for officers' lodgings. The barrack master then allotted quarters to each regiment.[13]

Politics mattered in this process. If private property had to be commandeered, the army reasoned, it should be troublesome revolutionaries, not loyal subjects, who bore the burden of these arrangements. Throughout British garrisons, enthusiastic loyalists accompanied the barrack master throughout town "pointing out Sons of Liberty's Houses" that could be appropriated for quarters. Eager to aid the army, many loyalists also opened their doors to occupying forces. Officially, the army did not force soldiers into inhabited residences, yet civilians were unable to opt out of inclusion in the army's report or contest chalk marks on their door that signaled available houseroom. Soldiers "have taken up part of several Houses, mark'd the Doors of others against their consent," Elizabeth Drinker bristled in Philadelphia.[14]

Urban quartering arrangements mirrored the social divisions of the army. Enlisted men resided in communal quarters assigned by the quartermaster, crowding into warehouses, schools, shops, public buildings, churches, almshouses, and existing barracks. Some fortunate regiments lodged in vacant houses; the less fortunate ones pitched tents in public squares and outlying orchards while they, aided by free and enslaved civilians, hastily constructed new lodgings with materials scavenged from city buildings. In Philadelphia, the new State House, where the Declaration of Independence was signed in 1776, served as a hospital and a prison for Continental soldiers and later housed the British regiment of Royal Artillery. "It makes a most excellent Barrack," General James Pattison enthused, as he reveled in the prospect of enforcing brigade discipline while all of his men resided under one roof. Enlisted soldiers in the Royal Artillery, however, were far less concerned with order and cleanliness; indeed, the political significance of their barrack might have encouraged misbehavior. Much to Pattison's dismay, the men routinely relieved themselves on the State House stairs and in the lower entryway.[15]

Unlike enlisted men, whose quarters were assigned by the quartermaster, officers were entitled to a choice of billet. Some elected to reside in barracks alongside their men, albeit in more spacious private rooms with access to stables and kitchens, but most opted to lodge in private residences designated as officers' quarters or to rent accommodations from civilians. In accordance with army regulations, only officers "billited on families." This policy was both an acknowledgement of officers' rank (and the gentlemanly status it implied) and a practical measure: most officers traveled with retinues consisting of servants, orderlies, livestock, and, occasionally, their wives and children, although the size of their retinue was commensurate with their stature. Field officers and captains typically had at least two orderlies and a personal servant or two, while subaltern officers might have one orderly and perhaps a servant or cook; it was also common for officers to pay other men's wives for domestic services. Nevertheless, not all officers' quarters were equal. Houses designated as officers' quarters could stretch for miles beyond the city, and higher-ranking officers inevitably snatched up accommodations in coveted central locations. "The Big wigs" lived in greater luxury than their subaltern counterparts. After dining with General James Grant in his quarters, Captain John Peebles observed, "The old fellow lives like a Prince."[16]

The residences of elite and middling civilians were among the most desirable billets. Many officers hailed from the European elite and were accustomed to a certain standard of comfort that was typically unattainable during active campaigns. "'Tis a hard unpleasant Life this of a Soldier's, which is passed in a little paltry Tent which will neither keep out Wind, or Rain, or Vermin," Admiral Lord Richard Howe's secretary Ambrose Serle remarked in 1776. Winter quarters offered a brief respite from this rough, nomadic existence, and many officers relished the domestic comforts they found in the homes of the urban elite. In Charleston, where many of the city's wealthiest inhabitants had vacated their town houses and fled to the country prior to the 1780 siege, Hessian captain Johann Ewald reveled in the rich furnishings and "beautiful mahogany furniture" in his "extremely well furnished" barrack. Writing from Philadelphia in the winter of 1778, Lieutenant Loftus Cliffe of the Forty-Sixth Regiment cherished his daily ritual of sharing a bottle of port with six other "Gentlemen of the Regt." in their communal "Mess Room," separate from their individual quarters. As the oldest of the men, Cliffe was the leader of the group. "I am myself Major Domo," he wrote contentedly, "having absolute Rule [of the mess] am as the Father of a Family." Cliffe's familial metaphors suggest the importance of these makeshift domestic spaces for military men, many of whom were far from their homes and loved ones.[17]

The process for distributing officers' quarters varied among regiments. Some men lucked into vacant dwellings that revolutionaries had hastily abandoned in the hours prior to the army's arrival. Others made personal appeals to inhabitants. Still others drew lots to divvy up regimental quarters designated as officers' billets on the barrack master's survey. Veteran officers who had fought in previous American campaigns occasionally relied on personal connections to obtain quarters from acquaintances. However quarters were acquired, once secured, officers marked their chosen property by posting their name on the door. The barrack master kept meticulous lists of officers' lodgings and the names of property owners; men were prohibited from exchanging or transferring their billet without authorization.[18]

Still, competition for quarters was fierce in crowded garrisons, as officers attempted to secure comfortable lodgings for themselves and their families. Ostensibly a voluntary arrangement, officers could and occasionally did obtain quarters by force. There were always men who ignored military regulations and acquired billets through intimidation or deceit. Some men hacked down doors or demanded billets at the point of a bayonet. One Philadelphia woman recalled an officer "as intent on gaining admission as he would have been of urging on the surrender of a fortress." Numerous civilians lodged grievances "against Officers and other Persons belonging to the Army for taking Possession of their Houses and Stables without any Sort of authority." Commanding officers likewise issued repeated exhortations that officers, soldiers, and other members of the army lodge in their allocated barracks. Taken together, these circumstances suggest that, in practice, the process of obtaining quarters was more disorganized and haphazard than regulations would suggest.[19]

NAVIGATING THE RISKS AND BENEFITS OF QUARTERING

When officers appeared on their doorstep requesting quarters, civilians faced a distressing choice and several, often inscrutable, questions: Should they accept the man or chance being incumbered with a worse lodger in the future? Might the billeted officer be a shield against the increased dangers of the occupied city? Or would his presence expose their households to disease, violence, and debauchery? The officer might be dangerous, or a nuisance. The man's associates, including his retinue and his social companions, opened their household to unknown men of varying characters. Might an officer's personal connections be beneficial in a resource-scare garrison, or would the man prove a drain on the family's valuable reserves? Although officers typically purchased their own provisions with cash supplied by the army, there was no guarantee that they would do so; theft abounded in occupied regions. Still, unlike their Continental counterparts, British officers paid rent for quarters, and rental income, certainly, was a welcome contribution to strained wartime budgets. Yet, even if the arrangement was cordial, might quartering an officer anger local partisans and mark the family for retribution after the army's departure? Or, of more immediate concern, would the officer become violent if rejected? Might refusal imply that the family were revolutionaries, begetting hardship and subjecting them to scrutiny for the indeterminate remainder of the occupation?[20]

There were compelling reasons to avoid quartering, and many people endeavored to do so. Still, space was at a premium in occupied regions, and circumstances often forced civilians into close contact with the army, whether or not they desired it. As the army moved into winter quarters, many householders reluctantly concluded that they would, eventually, be burdened with an officer. Some agreed to billet British officers out of fear of violence or of being identified as political enemies; in such instances, quartering was less of a negotiation and more of an obligatory acquiescence. Others opted to select their own lodger. Better to choose, they reasoned, than have one forced upon them. Indeed, realizing that quartering was inevitable in the British Army's overburdened New York headquarters, some inhabitants strategically requested known officers from the billet office. In such instances, officers might return to quarter with the same family intermittently throughout the war; both parties preferred the ease of familiarity.[21]

Voluntary arrangements, however begrudging, were preferable to forced ones. Outside Boston, with her house occupied by Continental forces, loyalist Elizabeth Inman described the troops patrolling her farm, the guards stationed in her parlor, and her closets transformed into munitions storage. "You know how fond I am of Grandure," she joked, "but never imagend I shou'd arrive at the Muckle honor of being a Generall." The circumstances of her letter nevertheless bely her lighthearted tone, even as she sustained the jest. Writing from her parlor at midnight, while soldiers slept in the adjacent room, she detailed the doors boarded over and nailed shut from the inside—ostensibly to "protect" the sleeping soldiers from harm. But, of course, in truth, the situation was reversed; unable to sleep, afraid to close her eyes, Elizabeth barricaded herself inside her parlor, warily watching the boarded-up doors of her sanctuary.[22]

In contrast, deliberate quartering arrangements could work to civilians' benefit. Selecting their own lodger not only provided families with a semblance of control—no small thing amid the chaos of war and occupation—it also held the potential to secure the favor of military men with the authority and the capability to protect their residence from other, potentially more dangerous, soldiers. As one Philadelphia woman explained, "Some of the Inhabitance have look'd out for Officers of reputation (if any such there be) to come into their Families, by way of protection, and to keep of[f] others." Such arrangements were appealing, even in households where men were present. The army collected civilian arms and munitions upon taking control of a city; any men wishing to retain their guns, even for hunting, required a permit. Lacking their own munitions, some civilians recognized that the presence of an armed officer could shield their vulnerable households.[23]

Quartering, although an inconvenience, could also forge unlikely alliances when military and civilian interests aligned. Agreeing to quarter officers could safeguard civilian property (and the status and comforts that it signified), as in the case of one Connecticut woman who, during a 1779 British raid, "sent immeditely to the Generals and beg'd them to put up at her house"; her residence was one of the few to survive the attack. Soldiers' wives could likewise offer security. In Philadelphia, Elizabeth Drinker and her sister Mary Sandwith reached an agreement with Janny Maxel, a soldier's wife who resided in the Drinker's Water Street property and who "promised to take care of the House." Although women like Janny Maxel are less visible in the sources than their military spouses, similar arrangements existed throughout occupied regions.[24]

Money was another persuasive incentive for civilians to permit their residence to be used as quarters. Unlike the Continental army, the British Army offered financial inducement to encourage inhabitants to accept officers into their houses. As General Nathanael Greene explained, the Continental army "made it a rule . . . not to pay any thing for Officers quartering with the inhabitants[.] The protection they give is always considered an equivalence for the inconveniences." The British, in contrast, required that the army compensate householders. British officers residing outside the barracks received an allowance for furniture and lodging expenses and were expected to pay a fair price for rent. As Lord Charles Cornwallis expressed in Charleston, he "thought it necessary, that the Proprietors of such Houses, as are occupied by Goverment, shou'd receive some Compensation for the same."[25]

With varying degrees of enthusiasm, civilians of diverse political loyalties opened their doors to British officers and their hard coin. Whether motivated by profit, necessity, genuine loyalism, or the desire to appear loyal, renting to the army offered civilians a reliable source of income in uncertain times. In Charleston, for instance, revolutionary Eliza Lucas Pinckney, whose two sons were officers in the Continental army, embarked on a "scheme" to "subsist" her family by leasing properties to British officers and others affiliated with the army. In Newport, Mary Wheatley agreed to quarter Captain John Peebles of the Forty-Second Regiment of Royal Highlanders. A widow who resided with her adult son and a Black servant, Mary occupied a five-room house on Pleasant Street capable of comfortably accommodating Peebles and his retinue. Seemingly, the two had a cordial relationship. They breakfasted together shortly after Peebles took up residence, and he noted that "the old lady [was] very kind to" his servant when the man fell ill. Yet Mary Wheatley's compassion might have been motivated more by self-interest than any personal regard for John Peebles. The protection of a friendly officer was a valuable asset for a widow in an occupied city, and rental income could offer financial stability in an indeterminate war. Captain Peebles certainly felt that she attempted to take advantage of him. As he settled his accounts in preparation for his departure from the city, he complained, "Tho I over paid her she did not seem to be satisfyed, greedy and cunning like the rest of the Yankees."[26]

Quartering could, nevertheless, inflict damages that far outweighed the benefit of rental income. Many officers took care to leave civilian residences in the condition that they found them. But regulations mandating the respectful treatment of civilian property were difficult to enforce, and many men disregarded these policies, especially when they lodged in revolutionaries' residences. Captain John André, for instance, infamous for his role in facilitating Benedict Arnold's treason, lodged in the absent Benjamin Franklin's Philadelphia house during the winter of 1777–1778. André and his "rapacious crew" pilfered books, musical instruments, Franklin's "electric Aparatus," and even a portrait of the doctor that hung in the dining room. On returning to their Charleston townhouse, which served as British headquarters during the occupation, the Motte family found a caricature of Sir Henry Clinton carved into the marble mantelpiece and a treasured family portrait gaping with bayonet holes. Other families returned to find peeling wallpaper and floors covered with mildew. Piles of dirt, coal, salt, or the remnants of poultry or rotting fish attested to soldiers' careless treatment of civilian property. "Nothing can exceed the Filthiness of the Houses which have been occupied by the Enemy," James Lovell reported from Philadelphia. Damages arose from both malicious intent and casual misuse. One unidentified Boston woman was astonished to witness General John Burgoyne's behavior in her neighbor's house, observing "raw meat cut and hacked upon her Mahogona Tables, and her superb damask curtain and cushings exposed to the rain as if they were of no value."[27]

In an effort to protect civilian property, military regulations outlined the obligations of both billeted officers and the residents who agreed to quarter them. An officer was forbidden from "molest[ing] the house he may be quartered upon, by taking up either more, or any other room, or rooms, than those specified in his billet." Inhabitants were "not obliged to furnish more room than is absolutely mentioned in the printed billeting instructions." If officers exceeded their allotted space, residents could lodge complaints at the billet office. These regulations were printed in newspapers so that civilians were aware of them. Still, whiteness was a critical, if unstated, element of these guidelines. When the army seized Black inhabitants' property, such as the case of New Yorker Thomas Farmer, whose house was appropriated by the barrack master, they had little means to contest these confiscations. With few alternatives, many dispossessed Black men, including Thomas Farmer, swallowed these injustices and turned to the army for employment.[28]

White civilians, moreover, retained various means of redress when officers overreached: they could petition military-installed civilian governing boards or appeal to commanding officers for assistance. Many civilians took advantage of these methods of recourse, although the success of suits was contingent on a variety of circumstances, including military needs, individual personalities, and local grudges. Any disputes that arose between officers and inhabitants were "settled . . . by the Appraisement of impartial Persons . . . except in Cases where the Property belongs to Persons disaffected to Government." Such limitations were, in the words of one historian, "powerful incentives" for male civilians to sign loyalty oaths and publicly side with the

REGULATIONS

For the BILLET-OFFICE at Charleſtown,

To be obſerved in future.

Reſpecting the iſſuing and receiving Billets for Quarters, regimental Store-Houſes, &c. &c.

1ſt. NO quarters for officers or ſoldiers; no regimental ſtore houſes, are to be occupied without a proper billet firſt obtained at the Billet Office.

2d. No billets are to be granted at the Billet-Office, without an order from Head-Quarters, or the Commandant.

3d. Officers, whether doing duty in garriſon, or detached, upon obtaining orders for billets, are to have quarters aſſigned them by the Billet-Maſter, ſuitable to their reſpective ranks, as mentioned in the rules and directions for the allotment of quarters, which muſt be particularly ſpecified in the body of the billet.

4th. No officer is, on any account, to moleſt the houſe he may be quartered upon, by taking up either more, or any other room, or rooms, than thoſe ſpecified in his billet, and marked for him by the Billet-Office.

5th. Officers vacating their quarters, regimental ſtore houſes, &c. are to give previous notice at the Billet-Office, where proper perſons attending will inſpect the ſame, and ſee that no damage has been wilfully or wantonly committed; as ſuch damage muſt be repaired at the expence of the Officers who occupied thoſe quarters; nor is an Officer, after having vacated his quarters in conſequence of being ordered on duty or detachment, to take poſſeſſion of it again without a freſh billet.

6th. If an entire houſe is vacated, the keys muſt be delivered up at the Billet-Office, where a proper receipt will be given for the ſame.

7th. No billets are to be transferred from one Officer to another, without referring ſuch change to the Billet-Office, and obtaining poſſeſſion through the proper authority.

8th. No vacated quarters ſhall be locked up with Officer's baggage when they are detached on duty; every corps being allowed a regimental ſtore in town, where ſuch baggage muſt be depoſited.—Officers infringing this regulation, will be liable to have the doors of ſuch quarters forced open, and their baggage removed.

9th. The Billet-Office is to keep an accurate regiſter of quarters, in order to aſcertain readily, at any time, the number and rank of quarters then vacant.

10th. In caſe of any diſputes between an Officer and an Inhabitant with whom he is billeted, upon complaint made to the Commandant, care will be taken to give due redreſs, and to puniſh whichever party may, on enquiry, be found to be in the wrong.

11th. And in order to prevent undue practices in the Billet Office, the Board of Police are required to be particularly attentive to enquire into and report upon all complaints that may be made to them of any oppreſſions or partial behaviour or other miſconduct of the Billet-Maſter, or ſuch as may be employed under his direction.

12th. No out-houſes, gardens or ſtables to be poſſeſſed by Officers without the particular conſent of the proprietors.

13th. All Inhabitants who have been billeted upon, are hereby ordered to report to the Billet-Maſter, within two days after their reſpective billets are vacated.

14th. The Billet-Maſter will iſſue a printed copy of theſe regulations with each billet he may deliver.

By Order of the COMMANDANT,

JOHN M'MAHON,

BARRACK-MASTER.

CHARLESTOWN, *December* 10, 1780.

FIGURE 5 "Regulations of the Billet-Office at Charlestown," *South-Carolina and American General Gazette* (Charlest[o]n, S.C.), Dec. 13, 1780, [3]

crown in order to access garrison services and safeguard their property. Still, not everyone was willing to embrace pragmatism. Unable or unwilling to pursue official recourse, other men resorted to informal retaliations against the officers billeted in their households—but, as the next chapter will show, such actions often landed them in front of a court-martial.[29]

In contrast, women of all political persuasions, as dependent, ostensibly apolitical, inhabitants, had more latitude to act to protect property in occupied regions. Indeed, as the British Army advanced on American ports, many women, recognizing this fact, strategically remained to guard family property while men fled for safety. Valuables, as Charlestonian Josiah Smith advised his cousin, were safest "in the care of some Faithful Female acquaintance, to prevent their becoming a Prey to any sudden maneuver of those now in, or that hereafter may be, in Power." These decisions had ripple effects that structured the experience of occupation and quartering: civilian populations in garrisoned cities were overwhelmingly female.[30]

WOMEN AS WARTIME HEADS OF HOUSEHOLD

The dual circumstances of British occupation and men's wartime absences, whether voluntary or forced, thrust many women into outwardly managerial roles at a time of immense uncertainty. Women throughout the colonies were already accustomed to managing large households consisting of not only their children, spouses, and extended families but also free and enslaved laborers. Many were also used to acting as "deputy husbands" in their spouses' absence, particularly in urban ports, where merchants often traveled for business, occasionally for weeks at a time. War, however, intensified and altered the context of these arrangements. To be a deputy husband in peacetime was a far different experience than being a provisional head of household in a city under military occupation. Even for unmarried women, who comprised a comparatively larger percentage of urban populations, life in a military garrison introduced new hardships and unprecedented dangers.[31]

Women's increased responsibilities on the revolutionary home front have been well-documented by historians. Some women welcomed these tasks; indeed, many thrived, embarking on wartime careers as *"farmeress[es],"* shopkeepers, speculators, and "wom[e]n of business." Others accepted these roles only out of necessity. As a heavily pregnant Sarah Logan Fisher worried in Philadelphia during the British occupation, "I have to think and provide every thing for my Family, at a time when it is so difficult to provide anything, at almost any price, and cares of many kinds to engage my attention." For many women, parenting amplified these burdens. Children inundated their mothers with questions about their fathers' return. Mothers fretted whenever their children played in proximity to troops; violence was a concern, but so, too, were the rampant diseases surrounding military camps. As one Massachusetts woman pondered, "In these perilous times I know not whether it [infertility] ought to be considerd as an infelicity, since they [child-free couples] are certainly freed, from the anxiety every parent must feel for their rising ofspring."[32]

Shouldering sole responsibility for the safety and supervision of the household could nevertheless be daunting for women accustomed to the protective presence of their husbands, fathers, sons, and brothers, especially when their assumption of these duties coincided with the unprecedented conditions that war and British occupation introduced into their lives. "The daily distresses that we hear and have at home on account of yr absence which in spite every other Circumstance is too oppressing for my spirits," Philadelphian Elizabeth Oswald Chew admitted to her husband during the occupation of Philadelphia. After her husband, Abraham, departed for the New York provincial assembly—what she dubbed his "declaration of independence"—Helen Kortright Brasher "felt as if God and man had forsake me." In what might be termed a declaration of dependence, in Abraham's absence, Helen "went to the apartment of my landlord and told him that I put my mother selfe and children under his protection and flattered myself he would be a father and a friend to us." Keenly missing the presence of their partners, many women also longed for the protection that their dependence bestowed. "I want you for my protector and justifier," Abigail Adams admitted to John in an uncharacteristic display of vulnerability following a contentious interaction with a tenant who obstructed her efforts to accommodate refugees from occupied Boston.[33]

Indeed, some married women adopted the language of widowhood to describe their wartime situations, a rhetorical device that not only conveyed the deep emotional toll of familial separation but that also gestured to the economic and legal power that many affluent white women wielded during the war. Classified as feme soles under British common law, widows enjoyed greater autonomy than married feme coverts, including ownership of property and the ability to conduct business and contract debts in their own names. Embracing the mantle of war widowhood provided many women in occupied regions with a recognizable, accepted form of feminine authority that affirmed their positions as provisional wartime heads of household. But, for women who missed their husbands and felt newly exposed to the dangers of war, metaphors of widowhood also conveyed a real sense of sadness and instability. Referring to herself and other women whose husbands were in exile as "women who are but half themselves," Elizabeth Drinker confessed she was greatly "distress'd by a seperation from him whome most I love." Such losses encompassed not only protection and companionship but also the physical aspects of these relationships: "I have been like a nun in a cloister ever since you went away," Abigail Adams wrote to John, hinting at her enforced celibacy in his absence.[34]

Adjusting to their status as provisional household heads with varying degrees of enthusiasm, married women in occupied regions were nevertheless largely united in their reluctance to quarter British or Hessian officers, even as they might have pondered the potential benefits of doing so. To admit a strange man (or men) into their household in their husband's absence and without his consent was a disconcerting proposition that placed women and their households in potentially risky situations. At a minimum, the man would claim family rooms and furniture for his own use. Likely he would open the residence to visitors, strange men of potentially dubious character and morals. Officers made households more permeable and exposed inhabitants to new potential dangers, including the threat of rape, robbery, and disease. Although theft was perhaps more of a concern among the elite, people of all classes, whether in their own households or laboring in another's, were susceptible to these perils.

Moreover, since the onset of war in 1775, American revolutionaries had loudly denounced the violent behavior of British forces, especially their Hessian, Indigenous, and Black allies, by circulating gruesome stories of invaded houses, violated women, and enslaved people stirred to vengeful rebellion. Whether they believed such propaganda, the diverse female inhabitants of British-occupied regions, although unevenly susceptible to wartime dangers, were mindful of the potential for gendered, sexualized, and racialized violence that accompanied soldiers. Such concerns were especially potent in female-headed households, and many women resolved to avoid quartering, a position that would prove increasingly untenable as troops moved into winter quarters in crowded garrisoned cities.[35]

NEGOTIATING QUARTERS: DEPENDENCY AND CHIVALRY

Throughout occupied regions, as female wartime heads of household and British officers engaged in negotiations over quarters, they did so within the context of a shared transatlantic culture premised upon gendered notions of masculine gallantry and feminine dependency. Both were deeply entangled with notions of whiteness and elevated status among the Anglo-American elite and middling ranks. Mirroring the dance of courtship, these gendered concepts were a critical aspect of quartering negotiations in female-headed households, as both affluent female civilians and British officers sought to influence the other by turning notions of chivalry and dependency to their advantage.[36]

Whether genuinely or performatively, many female heads of household embraced traditional gender roles in their interactions with officers, invoking their status as legal dependents as a defensive tactic to avoid quartering. Discrepancies always exist between law and practice, but, theoretically, the common law, which classified most Anglo-American women as dependent feme coverts, and the eighteenth-century laws of war, which identified women as noncombatants entitled to protections from violence, positioned white women as defenseless bystanders to the military conflict. Appealing to officers' sense of honor, many white women heads of household cited their vulnerability as reasons to be excused from quartering. It was not seemly, they insisted, to quarter officers in residences where only women and children resided.[37]

Such concerns were amplified among pacifist Quakers, who were morally opposed "to assist[ing], in any manner in matters of War." During the British occupation of Philadelphia from 1777–1778, the city's Quaker community rallied around the wives of the exiles, consulting with civilian administrators and lobbying military officials to keep the houses of those women "whose Husbands are gone . . . clear of the mellitary Gentlemen." In addition to these community efforts, Quaker women gathered intelligence and shared tactics with one another as they navigated both the unfamiliar military regime and their new positions as provisional heads of household. After the Battle of Mud Island in October 1777, for instance, Sarah Fisher borrowed a bed chair from Elizabeth Drinker to accommodate a wounded officer that was convalescing in her house. When an officer called at the Drinker house the next day with a similar request for quarters, Elizabeth successfully rebuffed the man with a prepared defense: "I put him off by saying that as my Husband was from me, I should be pleas'd if he could provide some other convenient place," Elizabeth recorded in her diary. Approached again three weeks later, Elizabeth again invoked her husband's absence, adding that she also had "a Number of Young Children round me" and would "be glad to be excus'd." Acquiescing, the man assured her, "as I desir'd it, it should be so."[38]

In part, this strategy is unsurprising. Accustomed to the protections that their dependence provided, many well-to-do women who became provisional wartime heads of household were genuinely uncomfortable with the prospect of quartering an officer, particularly in the absence of their husbands. Both sincerely and strategically, they cited their newly vulnerable situation and their domestic responsibilities as reasons to request exemptions from quartering—requests, they implied, to which any honorable gentleman would acquiesce. And, in many instances, they were successful. Mary Parker

Norris, for instance, successfully rebuffed Lord Charles Cornwallis's request to billet in her Philadelphia residence by citing her widowed state and her four children, insisting that these circumstances would make it "impossible . . . for her to stay in her own house with such a numerous train as composed his Lordship's establishment. He behaved with great politeness to her, said he should be sorry to give trouble, and would have other quarters looked out for him—they withdrew that very afternoon." Mary Pemberton, an elderly Philadelphia Quaker, avoided billeting by petitioning General William Howe, the commander of the British forces in Philadelphia. She cited her husband's absence, her advanced age, and that she held a Quaker meeting in her house—a consequence of the fact that the British Army had converted the Philadelphia almshouse into a barrack and relocated some of its inhabitants to the Fourth Street Meeting House. Perhaps she also subtly reminded General Howe of her coach, which he had personally commandeered upon taking control of Philadelphia. As these incidents suggest, even as they assumed heightened domestic and economic authority within their households, many female heads of household recognized that gendered rhetoric of dependency proved an effective shield to deny officers' solicitations for quarters.[39]

Yet, paradoxically, women's gendered defenses could also intensify officers' suits; officers could invoke gendered rhetoric, too. Among the British officer corps, performative generosity toward ladies—meaning white women of the upper classes—was foundational to the chivalric ideals and gentlemanly honor that undergirded British martial masculinity. Even as they waged war on American colonists, many officers felt that these chivalric obligations extended to women of diverse political loyalties, until given reason to act otherwise. Chivalry was a critical feature of late-eighteenth-century martial masculinity among British officers; it balanced battlefield prowess with an equally ardent adoration of the female sex. The courteous treatment of women of rank thus functioned as a critical vehicle for officers' performance of chivalric manhood; and prosperous white women heads of household, perhaps made newly vulnerable by the war, were ideal targets for officers' overtures.[40]

Throughout occupied regions, British officers in need of quarters presented themselves as honorable gentlemen dedicated to the protection of civilian households and the women who presided over them. Performatively invoking chivalric norms to bolster their attractiveness as lodgers, officers sought to turn women's desire for protection to their advantage by presenting themselves as defenders of civilian households. But status mattered, too. Introducing themselves as gentlemen, many officers insisted that their honor and their elevated rank made them uniquely suitable lodgers for female-headed households. American women received these applications with varying levels of patience. In South Carolina, a British colonel made a half-hearted attempt to secure quarters, advising a group of women disconcerted by the prospect of being invaded by "Indians and common Soldiers" that "we had better [s]ee him to stay with us, for he had good spirits, cou'd sing a good Song and had a deal of chitty-chatty." "Whether he said that to divert us, (for we were very dull) or whether he felt as little for our distress as he appeared to do, I will not undertake to say," one of the women wrote in annoyance.[41]

Throughout occupied regions, some female heads of household endeavored to turn officers' chivalric intentions to their advantage. Sarah Reeves Gibbes, for instance, strategically staged an elaborate tableau to greet British troops when they arrived at her South Carolina plantation. Instructing enslaved laborers to ready the household before dawn, she and her family, which included sixteen children and her wheelchair-bound husband, arranged themselves in the entryway. As the troops approached, she ordered enslaved laborers to open the doors to reveal the defenseless household. Shrewdly staging a scene of feminine distress and vulnerability, Sarah appealed to the soldiers' sense of honor. Her ruse worked. Although the troops briefly quartered in the house, confining the Gibbeses to the upper floor, they treated the family courteously. Female civilians' strategic performance of defenselessness intersected with class-based ideals of martial honor in ways that encouraged British officers to prioritize the safety of female civilians and their households. As political prisoner Josiah Smith wrote gratefully in Charleston, "instead of being plundered" during his absence, his family "were rather protected from the soldiery that lay about their Quarters, being kindly visited by many of the Officers and always supply'd with a Safe Guard when they desired."[42]

Even as female heads of household and British officers engaged in this dance of gendered negotiation, in most cases, women's efforts only delayed the inevitable. During campaigning season, when some regiments were absent from the city and the weather was mild enough to camp, troops could be more accommodating to civilian requests. But, as winter dawned, many women were dismayed to discover that their husbands' absence and the presence of children were not sufficient to excuse them from quartering. Housing troops was of utmost importance to the war effort, and military officials' commitment to mitigating women's discomfort had limits. The barracks department endeavored to ease women's circumstances, but often not to the extent that women wished. In May 1780, for instance, Catherine Buffleire petitioned for the removal of the twelve Anspach shoemakers quartered in her New York house, "as she was in distress for the room." Attempting to alleviate the situation, the commandant ordered the removal of four of the men. But, as an exasperated Buffleire explained, the gesture was ineffectual: "She would rather have the whole, than to have only four taken away, as they would have the same room in the house." Indeed, her appeal might have resulted in a net loss: with no solution to her space issues, the men's removal may very well have had the sole effect of reducing the income that she was able to generate from rent.[43]

NEGOTIATING QUARTERS IN THE DRINKER HOUSEHOLD

"The Oifficers and Soldiers are quartering upon the Families [Generaly]," Elizabeth Drinker reported from Philadelphia in December 1777, relating instances of two different women who were "in trouble on account of Oifficers who had been there and threatned to quarter themselves on them" and another neighbor who had agreed to billet an officer and his servant. Three days later, Major James Cramond of the Forty-Second Regiment, or the Royal Highlanders, appeared on her doorstep requesting quarters. Elizabeth's diary, which documents both her ensuing negotiations with Major Cramond and her ponderings about whether to accept his proposal, offers unparalleled insight into how white women heads of household navigated the question of quarters. Elizabeth's exchanges with Cramond gesture to the broader role of gender in how both female civilians and British officers approached negotiations over quarters.[44]

Major Cramond first requested lodgings in the Drinkers' Philadelphia residence in December 1777. Elizabeth equivocated, using the tactic that had successfully deterred two prospective billets in previous months: implying that she should be excused because of her husband's exile and the family's vulnerability in his absence. Such exemptions were, however, far less likely to be granted as the army transitioned from active campaigning and withdrew into crowded winter quarters. Cramond's reason for choosing the Drinker household is impossible to know with certainty. Most likely, the billet master allocated the residence as officers' quarters for the Forty-Second Regiment, and Cramond drew it as his billet; at various points throughout the war, officers in the regiment chose lots to apportion regimental lodgings. Indeed, a lottery would explain both the lack of competition for the Drinkers' elegant three-story house and Cramond's persistence in obtaining quarters there. Over the course of eleven days, Major James Cramond returned to the Drinker house four times to campaign for quarters. Invoking the chivalric rhetoric that officers deployed throughout occupied cities, Cramond presented himself as an honorable gentleman who would defend the Drinker household.[45]

It is also worth speculating how James Cramond's Scottish background might have influenced his efforts to obtain quarters. The rules, regulations, and customs around quartering differed north of the border, a consequence of the 1707 Acts of Union that integrated Scotland into the United Kingdom while preserving the Scottish legal system. Unlike in England, household quartering was permissible in Scotland for much of the eighteenth century; each household was liable to quarter two enlisted men. Scottish women, moreover, occupied a distinct status under Scottish law, which afforded them more equitable legal rights than Englishwomen enjoyed under British common law, particularly around issues of property. Unlike the informal system of deputy husbands that operated under the laws of coverture, married women in Scotland retained greater control over their own property, and Scots law permitted a husband to transfer his legal authority to his wife so that she could manage household affairs in his absence. Scottish officers like James Cramond were thus not only accustomed to residing in more intimate and domestic quarters alongside civilians, they also had well-established procedures for obtaining those lodgings in which negotiations with civilians, including female heads of household, were a critical component.[46]

The first encounter between James Cramond and Elizabeth Drinker followed a familiar script: the major presented himself as a protector for the household; Elizabeth "plead off," citing her husband's absence. Unlike her earlier exchanges with British officers, however, rather than graciously accepting her refusal, Major Cramond sought to turn her situation to his advantage. "It was a necessary protiction at these times," he insisted, for a woman "to have [a soldier] in the House." In truth, Elizabeth probably agreed that the occupied city held particular dangers for women. Throughout her husband's exile, she often arranged for her nephew or male neighbors to sleep in the house. Her diary is strewn with allusions to the noises and fears that disturbed her sleep. Yet, as her response to Cramond the following day made clear, an unknown officer taking up residence in a house full of women and children was also a risk—one that she was uncomfortable taking. "I expect'd that we who were at present 'lone women, would be excus'd," she demurred.[47]

Not to be deterred, Cramond then tried a different tactic: exploiting American fears of German auxiliary troops. "A great number of the Forign

FIGURE 6 *Bergschotten Officiere und Soldat* (Highland Officer and Soldier), 1800. Prints, Drawings, and Watercolors from the Anne S. K. Brown Military Collection. Brown Digital Repository. Courtesy of Brown University Library, Providence, R.I., https://repository.library.brown.edu/studio/item/bdr:228386/

Troops were to be quarterd in this Neighborhood," the major warned, and "he believ'd they might be troublesom." He was, almost certainly, fearmongering. Although Scottish, Cramond was affiliated with a Hessian regiment, and, later in the war, he would go on to serve as an aide-de-camp to General Wilhem von Knyphausen. Strategically distancing himself from the foreign troops among whom he served, Cramond invoked both his Britishness and his gentlemanly status to portray himself as a shield against an uncomfortable, possibly dangerous quartering situation. But Cramond's efforts at intimidation failed. Elizabeth knew from experience that the German auxiliaries were not fearsome as purported; a Hessian officer had been quartered in her neighbor's house for nearly a month, and she had successfully thwarted the man's attempts to lodge his horse in her stable.[48]

Inverting Cramond's premise, Elizabeth boldly retorted that British officers had been quite troublesome and enumerated "many . . . perticulars of their bad conduct that had come to my knowledge." The Drinkers had certainly experienced their share of frights during the occupation. Yet, in voicing qualms specifically about the conduct of British officers, Elizabeth strategically invoked a gendered rhetoric of vulnerability to regain control of the negotiation: if Major Cramond hoped to quarter among defenseless women and children, he would have to prove his integrity. Endeavoring to exhibit his honorable character, the major then engaged "a good deal of talk about the Mal Behaveour of the British officers," during which he condemned officers' misconduct and—in what was surely intended as a reassuring and self-serving gesture—confided to Elizabeth that "there was very few of the Officers he could recommend." Unlike his comrades, Cramond insisted, he was "a Man, who would suit in [the Drinker] Family," keeping "early hours and little Company."[49]

In Elizabeth's eyes, Major Cramond's gentlemanly status was perhaps the most persuasive argument in his favor. Recording the incident in her diary later that day, she mused, "I am straitend how to act, and yet determind . . . for this Man appears much of the Gentleman, but while I can keep clear of them, I intend so to do." Even as she resolved to deny his request, she regarded James Cramond as an honorable, trustworthy alternative to the other officers she had encountered in the city. The major's strategy had proven remarkably effective in securing Elizabeth's favorable impression. Later that week, as Elizabeth came to understand through conversations with friends that billeting was inevitable, this favorable impression proved pivotal in her decision to allow him to quarter in her house. She and her sister Mary Sandwith had consulted with other women who "had their Doors mark'd with respect to takin in Officers" to inquire how they "had manag'd the matter." Their accounts were disheartening. Resigning herself to the unavoidability of quartering, Elizabeth resolved to acquiesce to Cramond's billet. He seemed an honorable man, and, "as our House is large, we should not be excus'd," she reasoned; "I may be troubld with others much worse." When Cramond again appeared at the Drinker doorstep just over a week later, they "at last agreed on his coming to take up his aboud with us."[50]

The next day, Major Cramond moved into the Drinker household. Cramond's Scottish servant and his family secured quarters nearby in the neighborhood, but they, like the four Hessian orderlies that attended the major, spent many of their days in the Drinker kitchen. Cramond's three cows, three horses, two sheep, two turkeys, and assorted fowl resided in the

Drinkers' stable. The final member of Cramond's retinue, a Black servant named Damon, dwelt in the Drinker household alongside the major. Damon might have been free, or a self-emancipated refugee behind British lines, but he could have also been enslaved "booty" that Cramond had claimed during the war. Or perhaps Cramond had purchased Damon from an ad similar to one in New York that advertised the sale of "the smartest and most active negro boy in this town, almost 14 years old, well made and good tempered: he would best suit a single gentleman of the army." If Damon was indeed enslaved, his presence reinforces how occupation eroded civilians' control of their households: in 1776, the Philadelphia Yearly Meeting had prohibited enslaving among its members, decreeing that those who refused to manumit their slaves would be disowned by the meeting; Damon's presence in the Drinker household certainly violated the intent, if not the letter, of the edict. Perhaps tellingly, in a letter to her husband, Elizabeth omitted Damon from her list of Major Cramond's retinue.[51]

Although Elizabeth had agreed to Major Cramond's quartering in her house, she was clearly uncomfortable with the situation. "I hope it will be no great inconvenience, tho I have many fears," she admitted to her diary. Possibly at her request, Elizabeth's brother-in-law was present for Cramond's first evening in the house. The following evening, Elizabeth's nephew Henry and his friend slept in the house, something that Henry had not done for several weeks.[52]

Still, despite Elizabeth's worries, she exerted surprising control over the situation. She interviewed James Cramond on four different occasions before admitting him to her home—a process he willingly participated in and used as an opportunity to demonstrate his fitness as her lodger through his refined manners and his respect for her authority as a household head. Indeed, Elizabeth even characterized his demeanor as "complaisant." Exhibiting respect and consideration for Elizabeth as a provisional head of household, James Cramond adopted behavior that functioned as both a deliberate strategy to obtain quarters and a performative, if not genuine, chivalric gesture toward a woman he felt would benefit from his protection. But Elizabeth's actions were similarly purposeful. Negotiating from both a position of calculated defenselessness and a real desire to escape billeting, she employed hesitancy to force Major Cramond to negotiate on her terms in order to prove his honorable intentions and his respect for her domestic authority. Within the occupied city, where housing shortages and unruly officers abounded, Elizabeth Drinker assessed the situation and acted strategically to secure a lodger that suited the best interests of her family. As she explained to her husband in February, given the size of the house, she probably would have been compelled to quarter an officer. Echoing Cramond's rhetoric, she reasoned that it was better to accept a single lodger of "good carecter" than have "one or more in his place that would be more dissagreeable."[53]

LIVING TOGETHER

To be sure, civilians anticipated some level of disruption when an officer took up residence in their house—but to know something is not the same as experiencing it. Among affluent civilians, who were most likely to view their houses as refuges from the chaos of war and occupation, the disruption arising from quartering could be especially jarring. Even in the most collegial quartering arrangements, billeted officers altered household patterns and disturbed familial spaces. As one Hessian officer observed from Newport in 1776, "People feel the military presence is disrupting their normal lives." Living alongside strangers could be uncomfortable, existing along a spectrum that ranged from inconvenient to annoying to hostile—although the latter was most common in male-headed households. "You must be sensible . . . that they are not very agreeable neighbours," revolutionary John Andrews lamented in Boston. Yet, contrary to present-day popular understandings of forced, contentious quartering, officers in residences presided over by affluent white women frequently acceded to these women's domestic authority. Female heads of household may have strategically invoked a gendered rhetoric of helplessness in an effort to avoid quartering, but they were far from powerless. Accustomed to overseeing large households, many of these women were adept at managing the officers that resided under their roof, and officers' respect for women's household governance paved the way for cordial relations. Certainly, there were exceptions. But, when instances of misconduct arose, women did not hesitate to use both official and informal avenues of redress to manage recalcitrant officers. Far from being passive victims of occupation, female heads of household wielded gendered rhetoric to regulate officers' behavior and enforce the domestic boundaries that enabled them to retain control of their households and define the contours of officers' daily life, including where they slept, the rooms and supplies that they could access, and the hours they kept.[54]

These dynamics are evident in the ongoing domestic negotiations between Elizabeth Drinker and Major James Cramond, exchanges that persisted long after he took up residence in the Drinkers' Front Street house. Cramond's quartering profoundly altered daily life. Servants and orderlies rotated through the house as they carried goods and messages back and forth to headquarters. These flurries of activity unnerved Elizabeth, who worried that they portended impending military action or bad news. Although she could sometimes surmise the reason, the constant stream of soldiers passing through her house made the war tangible in a very different way from Henry's absence. Cramond's retinue also exposed the family to other dangers, especially the diseases that flourished in early modern army camps. On a snowy evening in early March 1778, two sick men died within hours of being lodged in the Wells house where Cramond's servants resided, circumstances that "alarm'd" both the Wells and Drinker families.[55]

The size of the Drinker house helped to diffuse any initial tensions that arose from shared living quarters. Capable of sleeping twenty-three people, the Drinker residence housed a mere eleven people during the winter of 1777–1778: Elizabeth; her sister Mary; her five children, Sally (16), Nancy (13), Billy (10), Henry (7), Molly (3); Jane Boon (a domestic servant); Harry Catter (the stable boy); Major Cramond; and Damon, Cramond's Black servant. The house was spacious enough that the major and the family could comfortably entertain their own guests without intruding—at least physically—on the other. Some days, the family and the major only crossed paths "en passant."[56]

Noise, of course, remained an issue. Sounds reverberated throughout the spacious rooms and lofty ceilings. From her upstairs chamber, Elizabeth could hear noises echoing below. Unlike her neighbor, the infamous Lydia Darragh, who spied on British officers meeting in her house, Elizabeth Drinker never engaged in espionage, as far as we know; any tidbits that she overheard were only useful to her insofar as they might help bring her exiled husband home. Nevertheless, she must have been acutely aware that these acoustics worked both ways. If she could hear Major Cramond, he could hear her. Elizabeth never voiced these fears, but her letters to her husband, which had to be sent unsealed for inspection at the lines, indicate that she was deeply uncomfortable with the surveillance of her intimate life. Admitting in February 1778 that "sentiments" did not "flow easyly from [her] Pen," Elizabeth resolved that if she could "say nothing that is servicable I must endeavour to avoid the reverse." Such caution also extended to her children. Although Henry lamented their lack of correspondence, Elizabeth was seemingly hesitant to encourage the children to write letters that could be left lying about the house or easily read by inquiring eyes. It was safer to apprise her husband of the family's welfare in carefully worded missives.[57]

As time progressed, the Drinkers and Major Cramond settled into a routine. They kept their supplies of wood and hay separate, which both parties believed to be a successful arrangement. Unlike some single officers who employed other men's wives to manage their housekeeping, James Cramond relied solely on his servants. To avoid confusion and crowding in the kitchen, Cramond's servants prepared his meals after the Drinkers had completed theirs, and the major, Elizabeth reported to her husband in February, "eats it in his own Room." All things considered, she concluded, the major "incommodes us as little as can be expected."[58]

James Cramond, did, however, slowly spread throughout the house. By the middle of January, he had moved his lodgings from "the bleu Chamber to the little front parlor," where he set up his camp bed. After this move, he had "the two front Parlors, a Chamber up two pair of stairs for his bagage, and the Stable wholly to himself, besides the use of the Kitchen." The front parlor, which Henry Drinker had occasionally used as office space, contained a desk in which he locked his business papers and other important documents. With a view of the street, it was also "much warmer and more lively than the back [parlor]," and, during the winter months, the family preferred to spend their time in "the little front parlor." Seven-year-old Henry also enjoyed watching carriages pass by the front window. Major Cramond's command of the front parlors thus not only deprived the family of one of the warmer rooms in the house during the cold winter months, it almost certainly made parenting more difficult.[59]

Despite his sprawl, Elizabeth was pleased that Major Cramond adhered to her conditions regarding his conduct while under her roof. He limited his business and entertaining to his private rooms. "There has not been any, excepting him who is with us further in the House then the front," Elizabeth reassured her husband, adding that Cramond shielded the family from these military visitors, "knowing it would be dissagreeable." The major also amended his late hours at Elizabeth's request. During his first few weeks in the house, Elizabeth consistently complained about Cramond's nocturnal activities. "I am out of all patience with our Major," she declared in February 1778; "he stays out so late almost every Night." Perturbed, Elizabeth dropped "some hints," which, to her great satisfaction, had the desired effect. In the weeks following this conversation, her diary entries about the major's nighttime outings dwindled, and Elizabeth mostly ceased complaining about his late hours—on a few notable occasions, she even applauded his early evenings. Cramond's willingness to acquiesce to these rules commended him to his host. "Our new Guest behaves unexceptionabley, and much like a gentleman," Elizabeth assured her husband.[60]

As Elizabeth Drinker's exchanges with Major Cramond indicate, gendered negotiations between officers and female heads of household did not cease once quartering commenced; rather, these exchanges simply evolved, as these women endeavored to enforce their conceptions of orderly households. By actively regulating officers' space within their homes and stipulating behavioral expectations, affluent white women were surprisingly successful in their efforts to convince officers to conform to their vision of household governance.

When informal conversations proved ineffective, however, many female heads of household did not hesitate to utilize military systems of redress to resolve disputes with the officers quartered in their houses. Philadelphian Mary Eddy balked at the presence of "a woman who he [the billeted officer] calls his Wife, but Mary thinks otherwise." As a widow and the mother of sixteen children, the youngest of whom were probably still residing at home, Mary was no stranger to managing a large household. The identities of the officer and his unnamed consort are lost, but the nature of Mary's suspicions suggests that the woman may have been one of the many American women, often from the lower ranks, who formed relationships with officers as a means of securing protection, shelter, and rations within British garrisons. Mary's indignation toward the couple may have stemmed from a sense of Quaker morality or a reluctance to expose her children to what she deemed a sinful arrangement. But the officer's "Insolence" was likely a determining factor in her decision to oust him from her home. According to a neighbor, the officer refused to let Mary and her family use the front door, instead requiring them to access the house from the alley, an entrance traditionally used by servants. Two days later, annoyed and suspicious of her tenants, Mary petitioned occupation officials for assistance remedying the situation.[61]

Phebe Pemberton, another Philadelphia Quaker, was also adept at navigating military justice systems and chivalric codes of honor to protect her property and regulate the officers quartered therein. Confronted with an intransigent officer at her family's country estate on the Schuylkill River, she conveyed her displeasure in a terse letter that, in an implicit threat, echoed the language of court-martial. She was disappointed, she informed Lord William Murray of the Forty-Second Regiment, to learn that he had "behave[d] himself in an ungentleman-like manner by abusing part of the affects on said place and also breaking open the doors of that part of the house occupied by my tennents and treating the famaly with barberious unbecoming behaviour very unworthy of a British Nobleman and officer." In addition to his mistreatment of her property and her tenants, Phebe warned Lord Murray that she was aware that, when "shewn General Howes Protection posted up in the house," he had responded by disparaging the commander in chief with "several expressions hily insulting to the Generals honour." Among the British officer corps, where honor formed the cornerstone of men's reputations, such slander could incur steep consequences. Making her threat explicit, Phebe warned the officer that if he failed to respond to her letter she would "enter a complaint at Head Quarters." Shortly thereafter, she conveyed her grievances to a friendly officer, who relayed them up the chain of command and assured her that the issue would "be punctually attended to" and "settled fully to her satisfaction." Lord Murray was gone within the month.[62]

Illustrative of civilians' awareness of military hierarchies and protocol, Phebe Pemberton's actions also exemplify how women could use the martial culture of honor and chivalry to their benefit. Her first overture to Lord Murray invoked the norms of elite sensibility and the language of honor in an effort to remedy the situation herself. When this approach failed, she elevated her complaint. Eager to exhibit his own chivalric conduct, Captain Lowther Pennington, second baron Muncaster, of the Coldstream Guards, swiftly came to her assistance by interceding with commanding officers to accelerate the case. As Phebe recognized, gendered appeals to officers' sense of honor, articulated in the shared language of genteel courtesy, could encourage officers to aid female household heads and defend their interests.[63]

The following month, Phebe again had reason to invoke these strategies. General James Pattison of the Royal Artillery requested to quarter in her "House upon the Banks of the Schuylkill." She responded in the language of genteel courtesy, assuring Pattison that "she shall ever esteem it a Happiness to oblige him in this or any other Instance in her power," and encouraged the general to assume lodgings "as Soon is as convenient to him." But there was a caveat. As Phebe explained, she "depended upon that Garden [at the house], for a supply of Vegetables for her Family." Staking claim to her garden and its yield, she acted from the implied assumption that the general would not tarnish his honor by depriving a lone woman and her children of vital sustenance in the resource-scarce garrison. Presuming the general's cooperation, she closed her letter with thanks for "reserv[ing] part of the Garden for her use."[64]

By limiting officers' access to certain rooms or property, female heads of household asserted their prerogative to set the terms of quartering arrangements in ways that best suited their households. Another Philadelphia Quaker, Sarah Logan Fisher, had little choice in selecting a lodger, noting in her diary that in December 1777 "an Officer came to desire and insist on taking up his Lodgings here which I was obliged to consent to." Begrudgingly admitting Lieutenant Charles Apthorpe of the Twenty-Third Regiment into her elegantly furnished house, Sarah made little effort to hide her misgivings about the arrangement. Limiting the officer to the front parlor, she "removd all my furniture up stairs, and gave some more ordinary." A small act of resistance, Sarah's actions reveal both a strategic attempt to protect her valuables and her apprehensions about the arrangement—fears which may have been exacerbated by reports circulating the city of British officers stealing furniture or, perhaps, her own experience of being forced to quarter Continental militia the previous year. The comparative sparseness of his quarters must have left little doubt in Charles Apthorpe's mind as to his host's feelings about his presence. Military authority had enabled Lieutenant Apthorpe to cross the Fishers' threshold, but, once he was inside, Sarah Logan Fisher made clear her power to shape the space in which the officer resided and her expectation that he would adhere to her household governance.[65]

Throughout British garrisons, the ability to make billets uncomfortable or unpleasant was one of civilians' most effective means of conveying their displeasure with quartering arrangements. Given the constraints of martial law and the necessity of subtlety, some of these efforts were rather creative. Some civilians exaggerated the dangers of North America to men, especially Germans, who were unfamiliar with its climate. Captain Johann Hinrichs of the Hessian Jaegers wrote home of the "abominable" rattlesnake. It "is twelve to sixteen feet long," he reported, and "kills with its glance." Such knowledge, he gravely asserted, he gained from the Philadelphia farmer in whose house he was quartered. In Long Island, Captain John Peebles of the Forty-Second Regiment observed that his "Landlady for this fortnight past has almost every day shown some signs of insanity." According to Peebles, the woman "was some years ago confin'd in the Madhouse at Philada."—but there was no way to verify the story. Perhaps the woman was mad; or perhaps she simply enjoyed making Peebles believe that she was. Peebles was, after all, quartered in the house of prominent revolutionaries, Reverend Samuel Sacket and his wife, Hannah, whose brother, Ebenezer Hazard, was postmaster general of the United States. During the war, the Sackets' sons enlisted in the Continental army. Their son Nathaniel helped to coordinate George Washington's spy ring in New York, and their daughter Hannah divorced her husband because of his loyalism. So, perhaps, the Sackets were not above making their lodger uncomfortable. Certainly, they did not go so far as one Philadelphia family who "continually made a noise over his [Captain Lowry of the Jaeger Corps] head so that he could get no rest" until Lowry petitioned to have his billet changed.[66]

Of course, officers could also be antagonistic. According to Continental veteran and historian Alexander Garden, in Charleston, Major George Hanger, fourth baron Coleraine, "introduce[ed] into the best apartments of the most respectable families, his cats, his dogs, and his monkeys, while revelling himself in every species of sensuality, under the eyes of the unprotected females on whom he was billetted." Lieutenant Colonel Banastre Tarleton, Garden related, similarly refused the Charleston woman whose house he was quartered in access to more than a single room, informing her "that the enemies of my country should not enjoy every convenience, that I hold it an act of propriety to retain the house in Broad-street, given me by the Commander in Chief for my sole accommodation."[67]

More commonly, however, throughout British garrisons, elite and middling female heads of household delineated the bounds of acceptable conduct in their house, rules to which officers were surprisingly amenable. "We have neither Swareing or Gameing under our Roof, that we know of," Elizabeth Drinker wrote to her husband of Major Cramond's conduct; "I believe he has given strict orders to his servants and we see very little of it in the Master." Even when he hosted company, Cramond abided by Elizabeth's rules. Captain John Peebles of the Forty-Second Regiment recorded dining with Cramond in mid-February 1778, on the same evening that Elizabeth noted in her diary that "our major had 8 or 10 to dine with him," remarking approvingly that "they broke up in good time." John Peebles was less satisfied with the evening, pronouncing it "a showy diner but not much drink." Respecting the boundaries that Elizabeth created within her household, James Cramond structured the dinner to minimize noise and the vices that she abhorred. When the meal concluded, the men departed to play whist—evidently Cramond upheld Elizabeth's strictures against gambling as well. His behavior is perhaps all the more notable because accounts from fellow officers suggest he was not an easy man to get along with. Although an excellent soldier and an "accomplish'd young man," James Cramond "had a pride a Vanity and a temper that prevented his being liked in the Regt. or esteem'd in the army."[68]

Shared status, of course, facilitated these relationships, but gender and age likely played a role in smoothing over any tensions that arose. Officers who might have felt compelled to put up a brave front for their comrades or make a show of masculine bravado may have acted quite differently when confronted with women who occupied more of a maternal role. The average soldier in the British Army was approximately thirty years old; most men joined the army around age twenty, although officers often purchased their commissions even younger in order to facilitate their advancement through the ranks. Major James Cramond was only twenty-two or twenty-three while he resided in the Drinker household. Similarly, Lieutenant Charles Apthorpe, who lodged with Sarah Logan Fisher, was "an agreable modest young man, is about 22 and is the oldest of 14 Children." Although the twenty-six-year-old Fisher was much closer in age to her lodger than the forty-two-year-old Drinker, she was already a mother to two children and had two younger brothers who were approximately Apthorpe's age. Especially for young soldiers, the familiar bustle and comforts of domestic life must have offered a respite from the boisterous barracks and austere military lifestyle. Notions of gentlemanly honor and chivalry, particularly officers' desire to accommodate women's needs and minimize their distress, might have further enhanced young officers' willingness to slip into established domestic routines.[69]

For women used to managing diverse households, a billeted officer, especially a young man who may have been of age with relatives, apprentices, clerks, or servants, might have simply represented another person to be integrated into family life. Indeed, Elizabeth Drinker even adopted familial language to describe the quartering arrangement. "J. Cramond who is now become one of our Family, appears to be a thoughtful sober young man," she wrote in her diary. During the early modern period, familial language typically referred to all household residents, not only blood relations. Her use of this language is nevertheless notable within the context of her diary. Various servants rotated through the Drinker household in the years surrounding the Revolution. Elizabeth carefully cataloged each arrival, using, not familial language, but the more neutral "came to live with us" or "came to work." Or, occasionally, she used the more transactional "purchased" or "came to hire."[70]

Elizabeth Drinker's use of the word *family* to describe a new household addition, however, is unusual. Perhaps she did so out of deference to Major Cramond's rank; his status was more aligned with that of the Drinkers than the hired help. Yet, in subsequent entries, she also referred to Cramond as "our Major" or "our officer," a possessive term of endearment that Elizabeth usually reserved for servants of whom she was particularly fond. That she asserted a similar rhetorical claim over Major Cramond suggests that she might have felt some semblance of maternal affection or protectiveness for the young man. At a minimum, Elizabeth viewed James Cramond as an occupant of her space who was dependent on her goodwill and could be evicted at her discretion. She understood their arrangement, not in terms of forceful occupation, but of negotiated cohabitation. As she explained to her husband, it was her choice to accept Major Cramond as a lodger. "Our Family is somewhat increas'd," Elizabeth informed Henry; "I made many efforts to be excused, but I am led to believe tis best to make a virtue of necessity, I have reason to think that I am quite as well of[f] as any of my neighbours, and find the matter much easyer than I expected." In the Drinker household, as in residences throughout occupied regions, officers' willingness to defer to the governance of female heads of household and uphold their rules eased the strains of cohabitation in ways that, occasionally, opened the door to cordial social relations.[71]

SOCIALIZATION AND COMPANIONSHIP

Shared social status and elite genteel sensibility provided common ground that allowed British officers and affluent female civilians to cultivate an easy camaraderie. Both parties benefited from these friendships, which not only offered sociability but also eased the tensions of cohabitation. For civilians, social relationships with British officers could be an asset in garrisoned cities. Officers provided news and gossip. They could intercede at headquarters on behalf of civilians. They could facilitate the movement of food and resources across military lines. They could even offer new and exciting experiences, proffering tickets to plays or excursions aboard warships. Officers similarly benefited from relationships with civilians; sociability was certainly attractive, but so was having a reliable and trustworthy source of local knowledge.[72]

Although many elite women were initially hesitant about officers' presence in their houses, as they became acquainted with their lodgers, relationships that began as intrusions occasionally morphed into friendly companionship. Shared politics facilitated this transition, but, as revolutionary Eliza Wilkinson noted in Charleston, so, too, did officers' manners. Writing of one "good-nature[d]" man who was billeted on an acquaintance, Eliza admitted that he approached them "so smilingly . . . that I could not find in my heart one spark of ill-nature towards him; so I smiled too." Despite many inhabitants' reservations about quartering, over time, officers integrated into household life. Shared living space and regular social interactions fostered collegial relations. According to Philadelphian Deborah Norris Logan, many officers felt "that living among the inhabitants, and speaking the same language, made them uneasy at the thought of acting as enemies." Officers' chivalrous treatment of white women of rank was not only vital to officers' own performance of gentlemanly honor and martial identity, it also, practically, helped them to endear themselves to their hosts. Such social courtship, as later chapters will explore, occurred in households and ballrooms throughout occupied regions, where officers, in pursuit of both personal companionship and political allegiance, wooed civilian women as part of the British Army's strategy to win civilians' hearts and minds. Such strategies were surprisingly effective. Deborah Norris Logan recounted the story of one family who initially "formed a terrible idea" of their "blustering inmate" but soon "became so pleased with him that 'Captain Scott' was quoted as authority by them upon every occasion."[73]

As these examples suggest, cohabitation and the resulting proximity could foster trust. By early March, three months after Major James Cramond's arrival, Elizabeth Drinker felt comfortable enough to retrieve her silver plate from her brother-in-law's house where she had hidden it for safety. This decision coincided with a rapid increase in their socialization. Throughout Philadelphia, elite and middling women found camaraderie with the officers quartered in and around their residences. Phebe Pemberton lent books to Captain Lowther Pennington of the Coldstream Guards. Hannah Pemberton regularly smoked her pipe with the officer billeted in her house. Sarah Logan Fisher's lodger, Lieutenant Charles Apthorpe, dined "by invitation" with her brother Charles. Mary Sandwith, Elizabeth Drinker's sister, invited an Anspach officer quartered in the neighborhood to tea.[74]

Throughout occupied regions, martial and civilian social networks slowly entangled to foster new social connections. Elizabeth Drinker and James Cramond regularly shared coffee or tea, often joined by various friends and neighbors. On at least one occasion, Cramond accompanied Elizabeth on her visiting rounds. Her friends approved of the officer. "Most of our acquaintance seems much taken with our Major," she noted in her diary with satisfaction. After an evening of socializing in the Drinker residence in early March 1778, Major Cramond walked Mary Pleasants home, suggesting that he not only became a valued acquaintance among Drinker's social circle but a surrogate male protector for the wives of the Quaker exiles in the occupied city. Elizabeth also became acquainted with some of Cramond's fellow officers, especially those quartered among her friends and neighbors. By the time that the British evacuated the city in June, Captain William Ford had become a fixture in the Drinkers' social circle, and he called on the family to pay his respects prior to his departure. And Elizabeth was on good enough terms with a Colonel Gordon that even after Cramond's departure, she did not hesitate to "ste[p] into" his quarters to ask his opinion on rumors circulating the city.[75]

The Drinker children left no recollections of living alongside Major Cramond. Perhaps, on meeting him the first time, Sally and Nancy Drinker behaved like their friend Sally Wistar, who "sh[oo]k with fear" upon her first encounter with a soldier. As Sally recounted in her journal, "My teeth rattled, and my hand shook like an aspen leaf." Perhaps James Cramond and his orderlies politely greeted the girls each morning, and such social niceties smoothed the way for friendly relations. Possibly the girls flirted with the soldiers or developed crushes. Although Quakers were expected to marry within their faith, other girls in the Drinkers' social circle enjoyed the attentions of soldiers and frankly assessed them as models of masculinity and the qualities they sought in future husbands. Perhaps Billy, like another Quaker teenager in occupied Philadelphia, enjoyed the flurry of activity that the occupation introduced and was eager to converse with the officers and observe their gentlemanly manners. Perhaps the Drinker children picked up "militaryish . . . talk." Possibly, Major Cramond, like other billeted officers, bestowed gifts on the Drinker children. Or, maybe, the Drinker children simply tried to stay as far away as possible.[76]

We only know that three-year-old Molly Drinker dreamed of a return to normalcy. "Mammy I seed Daddy last night, daddys come home," Molly squealed in excitement on awakening one cold February morning in 1778. "He did not laugh at me, nor hugg me, but he look'd at me," she insisted, as she relayed the strange homecoming to her mother. Pausing momentarily, confused, Molly reconsidered; "I belive it is a Story," she concluded. "The dear little creature had been dreaming," an amused Elizabeth recounted to her husband. Even so, perhaps Molly's dream was not as implausible as it seemed. At the time she had the dream, Major Cramond and his orderlies had resided in the Drinker house for approximately a month. Much to Elizabeth's annoyance, Cramond had not yet amended his late hours. Perhaps Molly heard the major come in. Or maybe she sleepily glanced him or one of his servants in the hallway. Perhaps the way he moved through the household recalled memories of her father. Maybe the child witnessed Cramond sitting at her father's desk or heard male voices emanating from the parlor. Whatever provoked Molly's dream, it is clear that for all the disruption that Major Cramond introduced, he had swiftly integrated into the daily life and routines of the Drinker household.[77]

WHO IS IT THAT COULD URGE TO BE RECEIVED INTO MY HOUSE?

Elite white women may have reached some level of accommodation with the officers residing in their households, but their absent husbands frequently had qualms about these arrangements. As the next chapter will explore in depth, men throughout occupied regions felt that quartering posed a fundamental threat to the paternal ideals that undergirded their household governance—yet these concerns were distinctively challenging for absent householders whose wives quartered British officers in their absence. Worrying about their families from afar, many men felt helpless as they imagined their households commandeered by British officers and their wives and children suffering in their absence. Concerns about quartering simultaneously reflected men's anxiety for their loved ones, their suspicion of soldiers, their apprehension about officers' behavior, and their indignation over what they understood as a violation of their rights as property-owning heads of household. Within this context, reports of officers' courteousness were a double-edged sword: on one hand, assurances of polite behavior eased absent men's fears about the dangers their families faced; yet, on the other hand, the thought of a genteel officer residing among their family and integrating into household life could also fuel concerns about how quartering compromised men's own paternal household governance. For many absent husbands and fathers, the real and imagined dangers that quartering posed to both their property and their families resonated on a visceral level.

These worries provide a glimpse into how quartering disrupted patriarchal governing ideologies in ways that were deeply disconcerting for men accustomed to presiding over their households. "I should be glad to know whether the Officer billoted on thee was yet with thee and how he conducted and that thou would be more explicit in some things," Quaker exile Thomas Fisher entreated his wife, Sarah. Reiterating his earlier qualms about "the Officer billoted" in his household alongside his wife and two young children, he admitted, "These things at best are hard to bear." On learning of Major James Cramond's billet in his absence, Henry Drinker wrote an urgent letter to his wife, Elizabeth, from his exile in Virginia demanding to know, "Who is it that could urge to be received into my House, after a proper representation of the situation the Master was in? How many of such intruders are there and what part of the House do they occupy, and do they demand Food, Firing etc. as well as House-Room?" Furious by what he saw as an inappropriate imposition and a plundering of his domestic resources in his absence, Henry's anxieties reveal both his own conception of the house as a wartime sanctuary and his feelings of violation, particularly as head of that household, that the refuge had been breached without his consent. He also worried about his children, urging Elizabeth to exercise "the strictest care" to prevent them from interacting or conversing with Major Cramond or any of his associates. "Did I not believe a Religious and watchful care was kept up in this matter, my distress of Mind would be great," Henry confessed.[78]

Undoubtedly expressing a real concern for the safety of their wives and children, these worries also reveal how many men's conceptions of themselves as fathers and husbands were tethered to domestic life and their responsibilities as patriarchal householders to provide for and protect their families. Already concerned that their wartime absence prevented them from fulfilling their domestic responsibilities, many men felt an increased sense of helplessness in the face of quartering that intensified their anxieties for the safety of their families and households. The inability to "alleviate" or "mitigate" his family's distresses, Thomas Fisher admitted, only compounded the worry that he felt for his wife and children in occupied Philadelphia. Many men felt, as an absent John Adams did when he envisioned his family near occupied Boston, that "the sound of Cannon, was not so terrible when I was at Braintree as it is here, tho I hear it at four hundred Miles Distance." Fathers with young children worried that their sons and daughters might forget them in their absence. "Does he retain any Idea of his Papa?" Miers Fisher inquired of his young son, "or has he forgot the sound at which he used to look pleas'd? I shall expect upon my Return that he will have been taught to respect the Person to whom the Name belongs." Wartime separation not only hampered men's ability to aid their families and ease their wartime burdens, their absence had the potential to erode the affective bonds that they desperately sought to protect.[79]

The letters of Philadelphia Quakers Sarah and Miers Fisher reveal the gulf between the expectations of absent husbands and the reality of wives' experiences under British occupation. Their correspondence exposes how daily domestic concerns—food, supplies, finances—could engender larger conflicts about domestic ideology, as couples struggled to navigate which spouse was best positioned to determine the course of action for their household. Short on cash as the price of necessities skyrocketed in the occupied city, Sarah considered leasing Miers's office to one of the many merchants who flocked to Philadelphia in search of profit. Alerted to his wife's plans by a relative, Miers wrote to quash the idea. "I have some Objections to it," he insisted. Nervous that the office's proximity to the rest of the house might endanger his family, Miers worried that "the Person who takes it will have the Command of the Front Door which will expose all the Stair Case and every Chamber Day and Night to great Danger. it is impossible to know the Characters of Persons so well as to be safe in admitting Inmates." Interpreting the rental as a threat to both his property and his family's security, Miers maintained that no amount of financial strain was worth the risk of letting an unknown man into the house. The consequences, he declared, "might [be] more Trouble than all the Rent was worth."[80]

As he attempted to protect his family from afar, Miers Fisher insisted on their isolation as the best means of safeguarding their interests. For absent patriarchs like Miers, who were often not in a position to provide concrete assistance to their families, abstract guidance intended to ensure their families' safety offered an accessible means of enacting their domestic responsibilities during wartime; it was more manageable to insist that their families isolate and wait for their return than it was to transmit food, money, or other necessities across military lines. Yet, in occupied regions, the realities of wartime circumstances had the potential to destabilize these patriarchal visions of household governance by underscoring the futility of men's efforts to protect their families.

Indeed, Miers's final argument suggests that part of his resistance to admitting a lodger was rooted in deeper anxieties about his inability to aid his family and, how, within this context, a lodger's presence might efface his own. Miers was already nervous that his young son would forget him, and he clearly longed to care for the infant born during his exile—as evidenced by the nearly half a page he wrote to his wife about proper nursing schedules, notwithstanding his assertion that "it is not my Business to interfere." He was not, as Sarah noted in a previous letter, taking the separation well. Worried and keenly missing his family, Miers's opposition to the rental agreement nevertheless hinged on a seemingly mundane matter: the papers that littered his office. "The removal of my Books and papers would in all Probability do me more Injury than double the Rent that could be had," Miers claimed, as he urged Sarah not to disturb them. "These Reasons *with others* induce me to wish it may not be let," he concluded. With his papers metaphorically staking his place in the house, Miers's insistence that the documents remain untouched, combined with his safety concerns and his fears of being forgotten, offer a glimpse into how disturbing the prospect of quartering could be for absent husbands who were deeply anxious about their ability to fulfill their domestic responsibilities in a time of great uncertainty and unprecedented danger. Even so, he trusted his wife—if the space was already rented, Miers assured Sarah, "Don't be uneasy; thou would do for the best and I will be content."[81]

Reflecting the almost universal concerns of family separation, such qualms also suggest how the experience of wartime households collided with revolutionary political ideology in ways that destabilized prevailing notions of patriarchal household governance, regardless of individuals' political affiliations. The household, in Anglo-American political thought, was envisioned as "a little monarchy"—a fitting metaphor for Englishmen who conceived of their houses as castles—whose structure replicated and reinforced that of the crown. As colonists severed their ties to Britain and denounced the legitimacy of monarchical rule, many Anglo-American men recognized the potential for revolutionary ideology to destabilize other patriarchal relationships. Quartering exacerbated these apprehensions. Billeted officers were a tangible manifestation of revolutionaries' fears that British rule would deprive American men of their property and endanger their families; and, in occupied regions, there was little that absent men could do to defend their households against this perceived assault on their rights.[82]

Consequently, some women actively tried to shield their absent male relatives from the knowledge of billeted officers' in their households in order to ease their worries or minimize the impact of quartering. Philadelphia teenager James Morton reported to his stepfather James Pemberton that "the Soldiery are quartering upon the Inhabitants, Grandmother Lloyd has 1 Officer, M Pemberton, and M Pleasants have 2 each—most of our Friends and neighbours have th[em]." And yet, when Hannah Lloyd wrote to her son-in-law just over a week later, despite detailing the army's seizure of the Fourth Street Meeting House and the uprooted congregation, she notably failed to mention the officer living under her roof. Several weeks later, James Morton's stepsister, Molly Pemberton, similarly wrote a letter to her father in which she mentioned that "Grandmammy and Sister Rachel, have both got officers quartered on them." Undoubtedly informed of the officer in his home from a letter such as this, John Pemberton, another Quaker exile, wrote to his wife, Hannah, surprised to "find my Dear has a Lodger imposed on her."[83]

Elizabeth Drinker took similar steps to reassure her exiled husband, Henry, that the family experienced no inconvenience from quartering, "unless we are inclin'd to make triffles such." Upon learning of Major James Cramond's presence in his house, Henry had implored Elizabeth for specifics, observing that other women "mention[ed] some of these particulars" in their letters to their absent husbands. When Elizabeth finally responded with details about "our new Guest," she assured her husband, "I need not tell thee, that I have as great objections to any of the Fraternity coming into our House as thee thyself can have." Yet, she maintained, the situation was surprisingly manageable; Major Cramond and his orderlies were respectful and well-mannered. Emphasizing the officer's courtesy, Elizabeth hoped, would mitigate some of Henry's fears about the strange man living in his house alongside his family. Her efforts display an additional facet of how the norms of genteel politeness functioned in quartering arrangements in middling and elite households. Having herself been persuaded by such arguments, Elizabeth echoed the language that Major Cramond had used to convince her of his suitability as a lodger in an effort to ease Henry's concerns and underscore the propriety of the arrangement. Although the major "some times has, (tho but Seldom) Company, in the front Parlor, they are at such a distance from us, that we see or hear but little of them, and they always break up timeously," Elizabeth assured him.[84]

Elizabeth's diary, however, offers a different perspective on life with Major Cramond. Her letter to Henry notably omitted her struggles over the officer's late hours. By the time she wrote the letter, Drinker had already confronted Cramond. Perhaps considering the situation resolved, she chose to omit the experience, believing that her exiled husband had enough worries without concerning himself with the minutiae of daily life. Either way, Elizabeth recognized that Henry was apprehensive about the officer's presence and the family's relationship with him. The day after Major Cramond took up residence, Elizabeth wrote to assure Henry that a male acquaintance was staying in the house. Given her own hesitations about the arrangement, the man's presence was likely a comfort to Elizabeth as well as Henry. Moreover, knowing that Henry "appear'd concern'd that any of them [soldiers] should be with us," Elizabeth reassured him that she was "perticular" in avoiding the major and that their relationship was akin to "neighbours fare." "Now and then [he] drinks a dish of Tea with us, which as he behaves like a Gentleman and and [*sic*] a man of sence, is not easily avoided," she wrote. Underscoring Cramond's elevated rank and polite behavior, Elizabeth hoped to assuage Henry's concerns by portraying her interactions with the major as civil, yet tiresome—a framing that suggests an intentional attempt to bolster her exiled husband's spirits, at once reassuring him as to the family's welfare while displaying her efforts to uphold Henry's vision for the Drinker household in his absence.[85]

Yet Elizabeth's representation of these interactions as tedious are more indicative of Henry Drinker's anxieties than her actual relationship with

James Cramond. Her diary reveals that she and Major Cramond socialized frequently, at some points drinking tea on an almost daily basis. The officer participated in social gatherings with Elizabeth and her friends. Her apparent lack of qualms about correcting Cramond's behavior suggests an intimacy to the relationship, and the frequency of their interactions indicates that she might not have minded them as much as she led her husband to believe. There is no evidence that anything untoward occurred between Elizabeth Drinker and James Cramond. But Elizabeth was lonely and worried, and she found unexpected companionship with the officer. Knowing that their camaraderie might exacerbate Henry's unease—he had, after all, been explicit in his wishes that his household interact with the officer as little as possible—she downplayed the full extent of her social interactions with Major Cramond when discussing him with her husband, instead simply emphasizing the young man's civility.[86]

Reports of Cramond's politeness might have eased Henry's concerns about his family's safety during his absence, but, in practice, the major's courteousness had ingratiated him into the household—over Henry's objections. In Henry's absence, and contrary to his wishes, James Cramond had become a valued member of the Drinker family's domestic circle. Indeed, the morning that the British evacuated Philadelphia, Elizabeth and her sister Mary Sandwith stayed up all night to say goodbye, and Cramond, who had dined with the family before departing, "was very dull at takeing leave." Standing at the doorway on "a fine moon-light Morning," the women watched the troops file out of the city. Cramond, Elizabeth recorded, "bid us adieu as they went by." Five days later, Elizabeth "wrote a few lines to J.C.," and the two maintained a casual correspondence until Cramond's death in 1781 from yellow fever. "Heard from New-York . . . of the Death of Js. Crammond," Elizabeth mourned in her diary, remembering fondly the "young Officer who had liv'd 6 months with us, while the British Troops were in this City, and Behav'd so in our Family as to gain our esteem."[87]

Returning from exile in April 1778, Henry Drinker resided alongside Major Cramond for approximately six weeks. The two were seemingly collegial. Elizabeth's diary mentions no overt conflicts, and, when Henry fell ill, he consulted an army doctor among Cramond's acquaintances. Unlike his wife, Henry left no record of his thoughts about the major. It is only from a small incident nearly three years later that we can guess at Henry's feelings. Following a January 1781 order to billet Pennsylvania troops among the city's Quakers, two French officers appeared at the Drinker doorstep to request quarters. In a carefully phrased sentence that conveyed a hint of disagreement, Elizabeth recounted that the men "behav'd very respectfully," but Henry, "resenting the impossition, as he thought it," denied their request. A billeted officer, no matter how polite, endangered Henry's ability to govern his own household, free from interference.[88]

Any number of factors might have influenced Henry Drinker's refusal, but almost certainly among his objections was a desire to avoid the uncomfortable experience of having another man living among his family and taking charge of household space. Henry had already endured those circumstances, first from afar, as he worried about Cramond's presence in his house. Then, on returning from his seven-month exile—during which time he himself had been quartered in a stranger's residence—Henry had been forced to live alongside the man. It was hardly the domestic bliss he had longed for during his imprisonment, when he envisioned his family sitting around a crackling fire: "Mammy a Sewing and Sister a Knitting—our precious Sal perhaps suddenly looks off from her employment. to impart some fresh thot. about Daddy, her dear Sister finds some inconsistency and gravely sets the matter forth in another way, William innocently shews he is not an unconcerned person by entering also into the prattle, which Henry shoots his Bolt artless and unpremeditated, and from pure nature perhaps hits the mark." Instead, Henry returned home to find nearly a quarter of the house inaccessible, the stable filled with strange livestock, and an officer sleeping in his own office as the sounds of concerts and dinners echoed through the halls.[89]

As a pacifist and a devout Quaker, Henry Drinker submitted to this arrangement. But, clearly, he had no desire to repeat the experience. Elsewhere, however, many male householders had no qualms about confronting the British officers lodged within their homes. An analogue to battlefield violence, contentious arguments over living arrangements erupted between American men and British officers, as each struggled to assert their patriarchal power and privilege by establishing control of their shared domestic space.[90]

CHAPTER 3

Very Improper Treatment to a Gentleman

The locked door was the final straw. For weeks, Captain William Demont of the King's American Rangers and his civilian landlord, tavern owner Silvester Fuller, had maintained an uneasy coexistence. Demont was convinced that the New Yorker was a rebel; he had even taken to keeping his door ajar in order to surveil his landlord's conversations. It was not only his duty as an officer, Demont believed, but also a matter of personal safety. Demont's vigilance was warranted. He had previously been a staff officer in the Fifth Pennsylvania Battalion, but he had deserted from the Continental army in 1776 and provided crucial intelligence that resulted in the British capture of Fort Washington, the final Continental holdout on Manhattan. Two years had passed since then, but, if Demont's suspicions about his landlord's allegiance were correct, Silvester Fuller not only had good reason to despise his lodger, he was in a prime position to inflict harm. But, at the moment, those concerns were less pressing than the issue at hand: William Demont had hired a woman to wash his clothes, but she was unable to do so because his disgruntled landlord had barred her from the kitchen and ordered his wife to lock the door.[1]

From Silvester Fuller's perspective, it was a simple household matter, a "domestic Squabble"—albeit, one precipitated by an officer that Fuller and his wife felt had been forcibly "imposed" on their household—that originated in Captain Demont's disrespect for Fuller's property. As he would later explain to an assembled court-martial, his "Quarrel was not with [Demont], *as an Officer,* It was with him as an acquaintance, who resenting too warmly the notice of injuries done to my family, by his." Over the previous weeks, several pewter spoons and earthen plates had vanished. The Fullers suspected "a Person who lives with Captain Demont had taken" them, but repeated requests for the missing items had been ignored. Locking the kitchen was no more than any man might do to protect his property, Fuller insisted. Besides, the captain only had use of the kitchen "on sufferance." As the property owner, Silvester Fuller had every right to revoke his access.[2]

Facing off outside the locked kitchen, the men began shouting at one another. Their voices echoed through the house and carried into neighboring apartments. Fuller shook his fist in the officer's face, calling him "a Scoundrel and a damned Rascal." Bristling at the insults, Demont responded with invectives "equally vilifying and abusive." As the confrontation escalated, it exposed underlying political resentments. Insisting that the tavern owner respect his military rank, Captain Demont declared that he would not tolerate "be[ing] called a Damned Scoundrel, as he was an Officer." Scoffing, Fuller retorted that the officer was little better than a common thief. "It was such people as he [Demont], that were sent over from England to take possession of peoples property, and preven[t] them from getting their living," Fuller sneered. Two days later, Silvester Fuller was arrested on trumped-up charges of inciting desertion, purchasing illegal beef, voicing rebellious sentiments, and "insulting Captain Dumont in his Quarters." A neighbor suspected that the captain had manufactured the accusations to evict the Fullers and claim their residence for himself.[3]

The conflict between Silvester Fuller and William Demont exposes the layered, multifaceted, and often overlapping challenges that white male heads of household faced in occupied regions. Throughout the war, British officers implemented policies intended to bring rebellious colonists to heel by targeting the property and livelihoods of male civilians. Troops disarmed and imprisoned anyone who contested these measures or otherwise proved offensive. Some of these practices, like quartering, served a practical need. Others, like property confiscation, were a calculated tactic intended to facilitate military rule and compel obedience among restive civilian populations by punishing those who resisted. Often, these policies had an outsized influence on men of the upper classes. This was deliberate on the part of the British Army. By targeting those men who wielded social and political power in colonial society, officers sought to compel leading citizens to allegiance in hopes that their example might persuade others.

Through such practices, however, British military officials destabilized three critical pillars of elite Anglo-American masculinity in occupied cities: men's ability to govern their households and dependents, men's control over their property, and men's expectations of deference to their elevated status. The three were, of course, related. In both the colonies and the metropole, propertied manhood, patriarchal power, and masculine honor were deeply entwined with the performance of genteel Anglo-American masculinity. In eighteenth-century British North America, becoming a head of household and acquiring the accompanying social status, civic and legal power, command of labor, and governance of household matters that the role conferred, was widely acknowledged as the marker of adult manhood. "Manly independence," in the words of historian Toby L. Ditz, "entailed control *over* others as well as freedom *from* social dependence."[4]

Occupation thus placed new pressures on the accepted customs and hierarchies that undergirded affluent white male colonists' patriarchal power, masculine independence, and elite status. For these men, the experience of occupation was, in all senses of the word, a household war. Occupation endangered their property; it destabilized their household governance; it insulted their honor; and it had the potential to draw their entire households into sustained confrontations with officers and their retinues. Many male householders resented how both military policies and the actions of individual officers relegated them to a subordinate position within the social and domestic hierarchies that they were accustomed to overseeing.

Exploring the interrelated ways in which British occupation both deliberately and inadvertently undermined white men's patriarchal power, this chapter illustrates how these household wars exposed contradictory notions of status, property, and honor, frequently engendering misunderstandings and exacerbating conflict in male-headed households. It does so, first, by considering how occupation eroded men's household governance in ways that diminished their ability to protect their female relations and deprived them of the benefit of women's domestic labors. Next, moving to Charleston, where the British Army instituted a formal system of property confiscation, it examines how the seizure of land, households, and enslaved laborers of men who actively promoted rebellion deliberately weakened the patriarchal system on which colonial society was built by dismantling the property rights and attendant privileges of white men throughout occupied regions. Finally, turning to billeting in male-headed households, it analyzes how, for many male civilians, quartering threatened long-standing Anglo-American legal and cultural precedents in which property, as a source of both wealth and self-sufficiency, undergirded white men's political rights and social privileges, securing their position at the head of both individual households and society. In male-headed residences, quartering frequently devolved into a contest of masculinities in which both male householders and British officers attempted to force one another to yield to what each believed was his superior authority. Together, these circumstances amounted to an unprecedented attack on the property rights, domestic prerogatives, and paternal identities of American men.

DOMESTIC DISTURBANCES

Once it became clear that the British would capture and occupy a city, male civilians faced a choice that affected not only themselves but their families, dependents, and property. British troops often required men to take loyalty oaths, occasionally demanded that they serve in the militia, frequently requisitioned supplies from their households, and routinely sought to billet officers in their houses. Unlike their female relations, who ostensibly stood outside of politics and thus could deploy gendered rhetoric to avoid such requests or defer quartering, men, as political actors, were expected to choose a side. They had limited ability to rebuff officers' requests: they could open their homes and prove their loyalty, or they could refuse, raising suspicions about their allegiance and marking their property for potential confiscation. Neither was an appealing option.

Still, many men chose to endure these ignominies in order to remain alongside their families, rather than leave their wives and children to endure occupation alone. They did so for a variety of reasons. Some were loyalists. Others were unable to flee, or they were unwilling to abandon their families and property. Some simply could not afford to relocate. In such cases, it was common for men to strategically adjust their allegiances. As one New York woman testified at a court-martial, her neighbor openly disparaged the men who administered the New York police, proclaiming that he "did not think an Oath made before them was binding, as they were only a set of old Women—that an Oath taken before the Rebel Congress, is of greater consequence." By taking an oath of allegiance to the crown, however insincere, men could protect their families and safeguard their property from confiscation. For many men, it was an easy choice to prioritize personal interests and familial obligations over political principles.[5]

Yet, whether for personal or political reasons, not all men were willing to embrace such pragmatism. Some committed revolutionaries absconded prior to the British Army's arrival in their city, choosing exile rather than imprisonment or professing false allegiance to the crown. According to family lore, Newport tavern keeper Walter Nichols simply abandoned his property, sneering at a British officer, "Take it all, sir, take it all. Do you think I would permit my family to live under the same roof with British soldiers?" The wealthiest men often had other properties to flee to, but many others lacked these resources. For the latter, as the experiences of New Yorker William Bayard suggest, exile was often painful and uncomfortable. "I was long a Fugitive from my own Family," Bayard lamented, enduring "unspeakable hardships" and often reduced to sleeping "in Barns, Lofts, Hovels, Swamps and Forrests suffering every concievable anxiety of Mind, as well as hunger and Cold."[6]

But flight introduced another, unprecedented set of complications for some American men: dependents who refused to accompany them into exile. Although family separation could be a calculated strategy to protect property—indeed, families throughout occupied regions employed this tactic to varying levels of success—it was not always so. Many men were surprised to discover that their female relations were unwilling to abandon their houses, families, and friends. As revolutionary Helen Kortright Brasher explained, "The zeal of my husband was so great, that his family which before had been his sole care and pleasure in which all his happiness centered, now became only a secondary object. He would often say, my country first and then my family. In this we differed. I thought a mans family should and ought to be his first object." Many women felt similarly. Some deliberately delayed their departure, prolonging their preparations and promising to follow at a later date. Others outright refused to leave. As the British Army descended upon American cities, with potentially calamitous consequences for male revolutionaries, many men had little choice but to acquiesce to women's choices to remain.[7]

Women's refusal to accompany their male family members into exile had the potential to not only make men's lives more uncomfortable but also to cause agitation and emotional distress, as men fretted about the safety of their female relations and their own inability to protect them. Revolutionary William Vernon fled Newport in 1776, mere hours before British warships arrived in the city's harbor. A prosperous slave trader, he brought three enslaved laborers, Barre, Accran, and Caesar, out of Newport with him, leaving Cadys, Belinda, and her child behind. Perhaps it was his choice to do so. Or perhaps Cadys and Belinda, like William's unmarried sister Esther, simply refused to leave Newport.[8]

Although not legally beholden to her brother as a wife would be, Esther had resided with William's family since his wife's death in 1762; she managed his household and, in many ways, acted as a surrogate spouse, including raising his sons. Eager to protect his sister as the British marched on Newport, William presumed that she would evacuate with him, an expectation that reflected his belief that, as head of household, he had both the responsibility and the right to act on her behalf to ensure reciprocal care and safety—while also preserving his own standard of living. The three enslaved laborers that William brought out of Newport surely added to his daily comfort while in exile. But, for fourteen years, he had also depended on his sister to administer his household, direct chores, and oversee labor. Undoubtedly, Esther's presence would have contributed to her brother's well-being by alleviating some of the labor of daily household management and maintaining the continuity of care to which he was accustomed. Contrary to William's expectations, however, Esther had different plans. "Aunt Esther I could not prevail with to leave Newport," William lamented to his son. As the British advanced on the city and her brother prepared to flee, Esther effectively resigned her position in William's household and moved in with their loyalist brother, Thomas. Perhaps she had loyalist leanings. Maybe she believed that she would be safer in a loyal household. Or possibly she simply did not want to leave. Whatever her motivation, Esther desired to remain in Newport, and her unmarried status afforded her the freedom to do so.[9]

Concerned about Esther and annoyed by how her declaration of independence from his household had upended his plans, William was nevertheless reluctant to accept her rejection of his domestic protection. Shortly after departing Newport, he wrote to his son Samuel—not his brother, with whom Esther now resided—and charged him with caring for Esther, asking him to "comfort your Aunt, whose obstinacy prevented her from" evacuating Newport. Effectively delegating his domestic authority to his son, William's request simultaneously reveals his concern for Esther and his hesitancy, both as a brother and as head of household, to relinquish responsibility for her. Obliquely criticizing Esther's decision and voicing the unease that it caused him, William admitted that his anxiety was enhanced by his isolation from his family and his inability to protect them from afar. "To be amongst enemies is disagreeable and such a feeling that I should not choose, and should be glad and rejoice if every part of my family was with me," he professed.[10]

Separation from their loved ones, and especially the women who managed their households, cooked their meals, and tended to their needs, introduced new levels of discomfort into the lives of male householders who were unaccustomed to living alone. "Hasten your way to Boston where we shall be happy," loyalist refugee Ralph Inman implored his wife, Elizabeth, who remained outside the British garrison on their Cambridge farm. "We have both gone thro many tryalls in this Life and all that I aim at, now is to make my latter days Easy[er]," he wrote. Knowing that his wife was concerned about protecting the couple's property, he urged her to abandon the endeavor. Property was of little importance, he insisted; he would rather have his wife by his side. "It never was any Inclination to be separated for a moment unless it was your own choice," he implored. Living apart "has wore me down," Ralph confessed, admitting, "I cannot continue long to be so much distrest, as I have Experienced since your Absence." Interspersed with professions of love, Ralph's letter reveals the havoc that British occupation had wrought on his domestic life. Eager for a return to normalcy, he beseeched Elizabeth to come to Boston, where her presence would "be a Comfort." He did not like living alone. And he was not above ultimatums: "This is my Only and last Request that you will come to Town with your Family and Servants for I cannot live in my present situation," he warned.[11]

Demurring, Elizabeth rejected this proposal, explaining to Ralph that joining him would be detrimental to the financial security of their household. He commanded only seventy pounds per year in the occupied city; the previous year, Elizabeth had spent more than four times that amount, supplemented by produce from the family's farm, to subsist their household. Even "the worst of provisions" would be insufficient, she calculated. Rather than stretching their budget and starving their servants, she suggested that it was prudent to harvest the crops on the couple's farm before joining her husband in Boston. "As we have sown it is a pitty not to reap," Elizabeth reasoned. Even so, she realized her actions would bruise her husband's pride and wrote to reassure him of her affection and her willingness to defer to his patriarchal authority—just not in this instance. "Be assured Dear Sir," she pledged, "If I did not see a fare prospect of saving your crop stock etc. etc. I woud immediately go to Town and convince you how ready I was to obey."[12]

Despite her soothing professions, Elizabeth's insistence on remaining outside the garrisoned city only aggravated her husband. Shortly thereafter, Ralph penned a petulant missive in which he threatened to go to London if she persisted in her plans. "Words cannot describe my astonishment when I recieved your message," Elizabeth responded angrily, as she enumerated Ralph's abandonment of his household responsibilities: his conflicting advice, fanciful financial proposals, and "cruel" willingness to starve their enslaved laborers and other servants for his own comfort. In short, she detailed his failures as a patriarch. Abandoning any pretense of subservience and reminding her husband of his financial dependence on her, Elizabeth sent him a money order for one hundred pounds and a letter dripping with sarcasm. "I beg you'll cast off your cares," she taunted; "anxiety is very bad for the health which you'll require a great share of as well as money and good spirits in seeing and being seen in England."[13]

Further south, Charlestonian Anne Hart similarly refused to join her husband in exile. A minister who fled South Carolina because of his rebellious politics, Oliver Hart eventually settled in New Jersey, where he intended that his wife would join him. But Anne had no desire to abandon her home or her adult children. "Is it worth the while . . . at my time of life to be removing from one Country to another[?]" she questioned; "I hardly think it is." Having witnessed the difficulties that other civilians encountered when departing the occupied city, she concluded, "The fatigue and trouble that all have to go thro' before they can get away wou'd be more than I cou'd bear." In her correspondence with her husband, Anne made repeated excuses as to why she could not leave South Carolina, citing illness, fatigue, familial responsibilities, financial impediments, and her fear of sea travel ("I shoul'd not like to Watry grave"). "Difficulties seem insurmountable at present," she determined; "my family Cannot come, to leave my Children and the little property I have, wont do neither."[14]

Motivated more by family concerns than political ideology, Anne refused to abandon her children and her property. And, as she made quite explicit, she was unwilling to undergo the inconvenience of crossing military lines simply because her husband had sided with the rebellion. To support herself in the occupied city, Anne opened a school, something she had previously done. "I must do something to keep me from want," she explained, so she returned to "this poor but not ungenteel way to get my living." A subtle critique of her husband's failure to provide for her, Anne's letter also suggests that she enjoyed teaching and was proud of her efforts. She encouraged Oliver to imagine her "with my little Tribe around me, endeavouring to lay the foundation for some Abler hand to raise the superstructure of education upon."[15]

Oliver was less impressed with Anne's newfound profession. "I can scarce bear the Thought that you should be fatigu'd with a School," he wrote, convinced that if she came to New Jersey she "might enjoy a Competency, with ease." In the privacy of his journal, Oliver worried whether he "could prevail on my Nancy to leave her Connexions and all behind." Still, he hoped that his "pretty little Farm" in New Jersey would be an enticement. "One Thing, only, is lacking, you only can supply that," he plead. Tellingly, as Oliver endeavored to persuade his wife to join him, his appeal exposed how completely he had come to depend on his wife's domestic labor (along with the unacknowledged labors of the people he enslaved). "Much rather" than envisioning Anne in her classroom, he confessed, "would I actually see you, on my Farm, busying yourself with your Poultry, traversing the Fields, admiring the Flocks and Herds, or within, managing the Dairy." Anne's labors, Oliver realized, were critical to his own comfort and happiness. He was relieved to once more have found "a Home of my own" in New Jersey but worried "if it may be proper to call it my Home, without having my dear Nancy in it." Anne's refusal to relocate to New Jersey was a devastating blow to Oliver's daily comfort and his vision of himself as a patriarch. He depended on his wife. And he was lonely without her. "No one to converse with, to amuse me my Thoughts therefore much employ'd about my Better-Half, O could I but have her [with] me I should have some of the best of Company, how sweetly would the Hours then glide away," he sighed.[16]

When Anne finally left Charleston, she did so neither because of Oliver's requests nor by her own choice; she was forced out by British authorities. In May 1781, Commandant Nisbet Balfour ordered that the wives and children of revolutionaries evacuate Charleston by the following August. As she contemplated her banishment, Anne received a peevish letter from her husband. Rebuking her for her hesitation in leaving Charleston, Oliver complained, "Some evil Demon sometimes whispers me in the ear, 'was her Affection equal to yours, she would break through every Obstacle, and fly to your arms to render you happy.'" He could hardly have picked a worse time to air his grievances. On the verge of being exiled because of Oliver's politics, Anne had little patience for his insinuations. She was well-acquainted with "this same Demon," she retorted, "for oft . . . Such thots as these fill'd my painfull breast."[17]

Voicing the emotions that she had long suppressed, Anne charged Oliver with failing to protect and provide for her, with abandoning her in the occupied city. She had often wondered, she confessed, "if my *once* loving Husband had not lost some of that Affection he once had for me"; otherwise, "he cou'd not, he wou'd not leave me Circumstanc'd as I am—certainly he cannot think a poor Weak Woman is hardy enough to bear more than he could—surely, he now himself regards not what becomes of her he once prized more than Rubies—left pennyless—friendless—almost—and if he is yet alive and at ease wou'd he not Contrive to fetch her to him, but to leave all for her to do—and now to Crown the Whole, she is liable to Banishment, to transportation for action not her own." Anne's outburst revealed very real concerns about the situation that her husband's politics had created. Clearly, life had been difficult. Facing Balfour's edict, she was about to be expelled from the city where she had fought for over a year to remain. "What must those Wives expect from their Husbands, for whom they will suffer so much, what can they render to recompense for the Trouble they give [?]" Anne lamented.[18]

Anne delayed in Charleston for the entire summer, even as hurricane season approached. Despite her fear of water travel, she was in no rush to leave the city she had called home for her entire life, and she was loath to abandon her family and property for the uncertainties of New Jersey. "I linger perhaps the longer because I think you are fix'd for life, and if I am once there no hopes to return," Anne confessed to Oliver; "I believe I shall come to you, but did not want to be hurried."[19]

In instances where husbands and wives differed in their political loyalties, the pressures of occupation further eroded men's control over their families and dependents. Like Anne Hart, many women refused to be bound by their husbands' politics and instead charted their own paths through the war. In an extreme illustration of this dynamic, Captain Benjamin Almy fought as part of the allied Continental, French, and militia forces besieging Newport in 1778 while his wife, Mary, an ardent loyalist, remained inside the city with their children. Recounting the battle in a letter to her husband, Mary warned him that it would be "don with Spirit—for my Dislike to the Nation that you call your freinds [*sic*] [page torn] Same as when you knew me."[20]

Remarkably, the Almys' marriage survived the war. But many others did not. In South Carolina, Elizabeth Dores, a "keen Loyalist" and British spy, "fled" her marriage because she and "Her Husband . . . did not agree about Politicks." Philadelphia loyalist Alexander Bartram evacuated to New York alongside the British Army in June 1778. His wife, Jane, remained behind. "Mrs. Bartram did not agree in Politicks," one man remembered, "and she lives in Philadelphia." Jane was more explicit in her 1782 petition to Pennsylvania authorities in which she presented herself as a dedicated revolutionary.

“Ever since the Arrival of the British at Philadelphia [Alexander had] used her grossly ill for her attachment to the cause of Liberty,” she asserted. Another Philadelphian, poet Elizabeth Graeme Fergusson, who “was very Zealous in the Cause of the Americans,” split from her husband, Henry, over political differences. According to one observer, as early as 1775, just three years into their marriage, politics had created friction between the couple. By 1786, when Henry applied to the Loyalist Claims Commission in London for support, the marriage was over. The couple’s “quarrel,” Elizabeth’s nephew, a lieutenant in the British Army’s Forty-Second Regiment testified, “originated in Politicks,” although intervening events, including Henry’s infidelity, had exacerbated the issue. “Their [*sic*] is no Probability of their living together again,” he vowed.[21]

As they navigated the challenges of occupation and endeavored to make decisions that would protect themselves, their property, and their loved ones, male civilians of all political stripes frequently found their patriarchal authority questioned—and criticized—by the very women whom they depended on for both companionship and domestic comforts. Unable to compel obedience or to reap the benefits of the labor of their female relations, men experienced frustration at the ripple effects of occupation’s destabilization of household life—frustrations that only worsened when men faced the loss of their property.

PROPERTY AS A TOOL OF RULE

Male householders in occupied cities swiftly comprehended how martial law and the presence of the British Army eroded their control over their property. “This Town is a Garrison—every face gathering paleness—all hurry and confusion,” Reverend Andrew Eliot reported from Boston in April 1775, mere days after the war broke out. Endeavoring to evacuate his wife, daughter, and enslaved laborers from the occupied city, he described the chaos unfolding around him. “Everything is distressing,” he worried; “all property is precarious or rather annihilated.” Shortly thereafter, Eliot was turned out of his Boston home to accommodate British troops. Lamenting the swift change in his situation, he mourned, “Last week I thought myself in comfortable circumstances. . . . Now, I am by a cruel necessity turned out of my house; must leave my books and all I possess, perhaps to be destroyed by a licentious soldiery; my beloved congregation dispersed, my dear wife retreating to a distant part of the country, my children wandering, not knowing whither to go, perhaps left to perish for want.” “My heart is wounded, deeply wounded, almost to death,” he grieved.[22]

Male civilians' loss of control over their property manifested in distinct, occasionally intersecting, and sometimes surprising ways. In addition to practical requirements like quartering and punitive measures such as property demolition and confiscation, some military policies aimed to promote the general welfare. Policies of this latter variety often required that civilians manage household spaces in ways that would promote the fitness of the British Army and protect its resources. To prevent fires, inhabitants had to keep their chimneys clean; to deter disease, inhabitants were instructed "to remove from their Houses all Kinds of Dirt; and to see that the Streets, in Front of their respective Lots of Land, are constantly kept Clean." "They will answer the contrary at their Peril," General Richard Prescott warned from Newport in 1777.[23]

Punitive policies, in contrast, intentionally sought to weaken male civilians' control over their property and deprive them of valuable resources, including both land and enslaved labor. Such measures had the dual benefit of disciplining intransigent colonists while furthering British war aims. In part, these policies were pragmatic—seizing rebel property and resources helped to outfit British troops who were otherwise dependent on overseas shipping for provisions. But they were also intended to remind American colonists of their position within the empire. As one British officer asserted in 1776, "America has grown rich at the Expence, and not to the Advantage of G. Britain . . . [and] a considerable Reduction . . . in the Strength and opulence . . . will render her the longer dependent upon G. Britain."[24]

The emotional and financial value of property made it an ideal target for British military policies: through the manipulation of property, commanding officers could both compel submission or inflict punishment. Both outcomes aided British efforts to reestablish control of American cities. This is not to suggest that loyalists did not experience property insecurity in occupied regions—they did. But, frequently, loyalists' property losses occurred as collateral damage to military strategies, such as the building of fortifications, rather than as the result of intentional efforts to subjugate them by divesting them of both the means and the symbols of their wealth, power, and status.[25]

To this end, punitive property policies exclusively targeted revolutionaries. As Boston schoolteacher John Leach discovered in December 1775, his reputation as a revolutionary marked his property for destruction and jeopardized his future security. Endeavoring to halt troops from destroying his wharf in December 1775, Leach appealed to a commanding officer "to prevent my Interest being torn to peices by the soldiers." But Leach, who had previously been imprisoned on suspicion of rebellious activities, found his entreaties rejected. The week after the wharf's demolition, Leach learned that his schoolhouse was also slated for destruction. After arguing with General William Howe for nearly forty-five minutes, Leach finally convinced the officer to intervene by invoking his rights as an English subject: "I told [General Howe] as an Englishman, and a Subject of the King's, I Claimed his protection of my property; and if my House was pulled down, I would follow him to England, or to China, for Satisfaction," Leach recorded in his diary.[26]

Leach's reprieve was short-lived, however. The next morning, he awoke to the news that word of General Howe's clemency had, rather suspiciously, failed to reach the officer tasked with dismantling the building. Running to the schoolhouse, Leach, "by dint of Resolution," temporarily halted the destruction. For three hours, he recalled, "[I] Stood by my Street Door," waiting for the commanding officer to obtain clarification from his superiors. The whole time, "the Soldiers never ceased abusing me," Leach wrote; they taunted him as a "d———d Rebel" and waved their axes as if "to Cut me down." Leach managed to save the schoolhouse, but his victory was not without consequences. Whenever he encountered one of the men involved in the incident, the man shot him "a malicious look, as if he thirsted for my Blood."[27]

As John Leach's experiences suggest, both the British Army and individual officers used property demolition and confiscation to coerce male civilians to allegiance by strategically limiting their access to resources and jeopardizing their future financial security. It was, indisputably, an effective means of subduing restive civilian populations; indeed, both sides confiscated their opponents' property. Both during and after the war, various state assemblies established commissions to seize loyalist estates; such measures were an effective means of raising funds and punishing political foes. Only the British Army, however, formalized confiscation as a military strategy. Nowhere was this more evident than in Charleston.[28]

CONFISCATION IN CHARLESTON

Upon the surrender of Charleston in May 1780, almost the entirety of the city's white male population—nearly six thousand men, including militia, Continental soldiers and officers, and civilians—became prisoners of war. Continental soldiers and officers remained prisoners for the duration of the occupation; however, the British Army initially paroled civilians, civil officers, and militiamen, effectively permitting them to remain neutral as long as they did not actively oppose British authority. Four months later, by September 1780, the British altered their policies and began confiscating the estates of those men who actively promoted the revolutionary cause and "who obstinately persist[ed] in their guilty and treasonable practices . . . in the service or acting under the authority of the Rebel Congress; or by abandoning their plantations, to join the enemies of Great-britain; or by open avowal of rebellious principles, and other notorious acts." These tactics, which envisioned confiscation as both a punitive measure and an enticement for loyalty, were part of a longer tradition that manipulated property to bolster British imperial rule. During the colonial period, land grants, headrights, and quitrents served as an effective means of ordering territory in British North America. Following eighteenth-century Jacobite rebellions in Scotland, and even earlier in Ireland, as well as during the English Civil Wars, the British used property confiscation as a disciplinary tool to punish political opponents and compel submission from an internal enemy. At the core of these policies was a metropolitan vision of patriarchal subjecthood that linked property ownership to both political loyalty and masculine authority. Property and its attendant patriarchal responsibilities were integral components of the ideas and practices of white masculine authority throughout the British Atlantic world.[29]

The British Army's leveraging of property for allegiance had particular resonance in Charleston's slave society. South Carolina's wealthy Anglicized planter class and majority enslaved population distinguished it from Britain's other mainland possessions. It was a society built on family patriarchy and racial slavery; the control of property was entwined with the performance of power. As historian Robert Olwell argues, South Carolina's "culture of power" derived from a system of white male domination over both enslaved laborers and dependents, including women and children. Plantations embodied and reflected this mastery, for they were "little kingdom[s]" that reinforced the patriarchal social order. Gender hierarchies formed the core of patriarchy, but property was an integral pillar of support; it bolstered white men's racial and gendered authority and served as a means for its display. As Olwell explains, "Patriarchs also had to have the economic and social resources that were expected of their station. A poor man was also a poor master."[30]

British sequestration policies, both deliberately and implicitly, disrupted this mastery and unsettled Charleston's racial and gender hierarchies. The transformation of the plantation under the British Army upended South Carolina's social order—the masters of plantations had always been the masters of society. Unseating male revolutionaries, the British Army proclaimed their mastery over the colony and its inhabitants through property seizure. If male civilians endorsed the crown's lawful authority, they regained their status and their property; if not, they remained prisoners, denied the rights of British subjects, their property sequestered, their families evicted, and their enslaved laborers put to work on confiscated plantations to produce crops for the British Army. American men's mastery became contingent on allegiance to the crown.[31]

For American officers, many of whom were elite men accustomed to the wealth and privileges of their status, their experience as prisoners during the occupation exposed an emerging tension between property and honor, both of which were intertwined with notions of masculinity and mastery in the revolutionary south. Paroled to Haddrell's Point, northeast of the city, Continental officers were accorded some conveniences befitting their military rank, but they were largely unable to manage their domestic or commercial affairs, as evidenced by many imprisoned officers' inability to halt the rampant flight of their servants and enslaved laborers from the barracks. Moreover, prisoners lost their rights as British subjects; they were disallowed from practicing business or bringing cases before the board of police. In effect, they were condemned to destitution and poverty—unless they swore fealty to the crown. In October 1780, after Charles Cotesworth Pinckney refused overtures to join the British Army, the commissioner of sequestered estates confiscated Pinckney's property and turned his wife and children out of their Charleston home. Later in the occupation, Charles expressed his helplessness, declaring, "Since I have been a prisoner it h< . . . > been impossible for me to look after my own affairs, or those of any body else." Suffering from a shattered leg bone, Major Thomas Pinckney (Charles's younger brother), was similarly despondent during his parole. Writing to his sister, he treated the matter lightly, joking, "If You enquire after my Leg I must still give you the lying in Lady's Answer." Although a wry attempt at humor, the joke reveals the potentially emasculating effects of parole. Likening his situation to pregnancy, Thomas suggested that his injury brought effeminizing dependence. Parole compounded these restrictions. As prisoners, men such as the Pinckneys, who were accustomed to wealth, independence, and the dual authority of both master and patriarch, found themselves in a position of enforced dependence, subject to the mercies of the British Army.[32]

For those men who were not in the Continental army, such hardship could be avoided if they embraced—however disingenuously—restored British rule. The British attempted to encourage allegiance by "indulg[ing] men who exhibit sincere prooffs of a return to their duty by admitting them to any greater degree of liberty, to the fullest enjoyment of their property." In May 1780, shortly after conquering the city, commander in chief Sir Henry

Clinton issued a proclamation reiterating that men who swore an oath of allegiance would receive "pardon and oblivion for their past offences" and regain both their property and their rights as British subjects. Conversely, he warned, those who promoted the rebellion or "hinder[ed] or intimidate[d]" the king's loyal subjects would have their estates "immediately seized." Surrender was an appealing option. As American general William Moultrie recalled, "the people quite harassed out and tired of war; their capital fallen, and their army prisoners, no place of safety for them to fly . . . the British troops in possession of their whole country, and no prospect of relief," many Charlestonians believed "resistance was useless" and surrendered in hopes of "remain[ing] peaceably and quietly at home with their families." By submitting to British rule and outwardly aligning their interests with the British Army, men could enjoy peace, property, and prosperity in the occupied city.[33]

For many men, the decision to accept British protection was therefore a practical one. Like the female heads of household who reluctantly agreed to quarter British officers, such decisions were often pragmatic choices that prioritized the immediate safety of family and property amid the uncertainties of an indeterminate occupation. Daniel Horry, a colonel in the South Carolina Light Dragoons, swore allegiance to the British crown upon the city's surrender in May 1780; in the postwar years, he insisted that the oath was "Nominal" and that he did not actively aid the occupying forces. Many Charleston men did the same, strategically trading their allegiance in order to safeguard their status, their households, and their property, including both real estate and enslaved laborers. Writing from exile in Saint Augustine, Josiah Smith criticized men who accepted British protection "thro' fear, or Self Interest" and praised "those Virtuous Citizens" who refused to submit and "risque[d] every inconvenience, [rather] than to be assisting towards the enslaving of their Country." Framing men's options as a stark choice between mastery and slavery, Smith's divisive rhetoric suggests the profound discomfort that many revolutionaries felt with their situation and their need to justify their choices. For Smith, who had elected to stand by—and suffer for—his political beliefs, men's decisions to subjugate ideology to personal affairs seemed a betrayal of the revolutionary cause. And yet, for many other men, operating under the contingencies and complexities of wartime, embracing restored British rule offered the most viable path to security in the occupied city. The reaction of Daniel Horry's brother-in-law Thomas Pinckney, a Continental officer who remained a prisoner, hints at the nuances of these decisions. Pinckney was both dismayed and reassured by Horry's actions. "Tho' I am sorry for the Step Col. Horrÿ has taken in one Sense," Pinckney wrote to his mother, "it can not but give me the greatest Pleasure to consider that you will have a Person with you to support and protect you."[34]

In his 1802 memoir, American general William Moultrie asserted that many Charleston revolutionaries accepted British protection "with the pleasing hopes" of preserving their property and "remaining neuter until the end of the war." Only through submission to occupying British forces could they retain a historically important form of masculine power and control, albeit at the cost of their political objectives. Charleston's revolutionaries were forced to decide where their loyalties lay: with their property or their politics. Put another way, they were forced to choose between domestic power and political independence. They could not have both.[35]

As a consequence of these dynamics, British policy evolved rapidly during the first month of the occupation. Fearing that many inhabitants had insincerely accepted British protection and were continuing to promote rebellion behind military lines, in early June 1780, British commander in chief Sir Henry Clinton invalidated all civilian and militia paroles and restored them to the rights of British subjects. No longer prisoners, these men were expected to "take an active part in settling and securing His Majesty's government, and delivering the country from . . . anarchy." This policy, Clinton explained, was intended to force "every man to declare and evince his principles." Some men willingly exchanged their paroles for militia service. Many others felt that Clinton had violated the terms of surrender and chose to instead take up arms against the British—a decision that effectively drove them underground. Clinton decreed that those who refused to adhere to the proclamation were to be "considered as enemies and rebels . . . and treated accordingly," subject to both harsh punishment and property confiscation and, in some instances, death. Country plantations offered temporary refuge, yet British patrols regularly scoured the region. As Gabriel Manigault reflected at the end of the occupation, for over a year, he was "obliged to take up my abode in some friends house, it having been unsafe, on account of the british Troops to remain at any plantation of my own." Charleston's propertied men—most of them slaveholders—therefore faced a choice: comply with British authority or abscond to the swamps, where they in effect emulated the resistance of their own enslaved people.[36]

Drawing on seventeenth- and eighteenth-century precedents, the sequestration of revolutionaries' estates, beginning in September 1780 under Commissioner of Sequestered Estates John Cruden, reinforced earlier policies that linked property to allegiance. Sequestration applied to three groups of men: those who had abandoned their plantations and joined the enemy, those who served in or acted under the authority of the Continental Congress, and those who openly avowed or acted to advance rebellious principles or sought to prevent the restoration of British government. Tasked with the "seizure, superintendance, care, custody and management of all property of whatever denomination" belonging to these men, Cruden's commission was both a disciplinary measure and a practical means of obtaining provisions. Attempting to reproduce South Carolina's plantation system, Cruden hired overseers for each estate and appointed men in each district to "superintend" the properties. He employed Black laborers "to the utmost advantage," producing crops to feed soldiers, enslaved laborers, and loyalist refugees, both Black and white. Property confiscation transformed American plantations, usurping their spaces, laborers, and resources to reinforce British military power. These policies aimed to subvert the seat of white revolutionaries' power by transforming the plantation from a marker of their authority to a symbol of their disobedience. "There is but one way of inducing the violent rebels to become our friends," Lord Charles Cornwallis asserted, "and that is by convincing them it is their interest to be so."[37]

British sequestration policies specifically targeted affluent white revolutionaries, who owned "many of the most valuable" and productive plantations in South Carolina. According to one observer, only one-third of Charleston's inhabitants, by which he presumably meant white men, were loyal to the British crown, "and these by no means the wealthiest." Sequestration thus sought not only to claim valuable resources but also, strategically, to garner influential allies among Charleston's slaveowning elite by encouraging prominent revolutionaries to side with Britain—an implicit endorsement of British authority that furthered the reestablishment of imperial rule. "If he is protected in the Enjoyment of his Property," James Simpson, intendant of the board of police, advised in regard to Brigadier General Andrew Williamson, "I think it will secure his Influence, which is considerable[,] to establish the King's Authority throughout the numerous and extensive District in which he resides." If revolutionaries could be convinced not only to submit but to deploy their mastery in service of the crown, their authority could be an effective means of subduing the colony. By subverting the power of Charleston's slave masters, the British Army could master Charleston.[38]

Cruden further articulated the importance of property to British strategy in a January 1782 plan in which he advocated arming enslaved men as a method of compelling white men's submission. "Striking at the root of all property, and making the Wealth and Riches of the Enemy the means of bringing them to obedience, must bring the most Violent to their senses," he asserted. The surest way to subdue Charleston's revolutionaries, Cruden advised, was to leverage the enslaved property that undergirded men's wealth, status, and authority. This tactic would dispossess the colony's elite revolutionaries of the economic underpinnings of their masculine and racial authority, but it would have only a marginal effect on southern loyalists, most of whom, Cruden explained, were merchants with "little property in Slaves." "I would not be surprized that those now most Violent, against us would be foremost in an application for Peace on our own Terms," Cruden predicted, because "Property all the World over is dear to Mankind and in this Country they are as much weded to it as in any other, and the Southern Provinces Men are great in proportion to the Number of their Slaves." The confiscation and arming of enslaved men—a deliberate attack on elite wealth and status—Cruden believed, would thus exploit revolutionaries' self-interest and align it with the British Army by appealing to their desire to protect their material and personal assets.[39]

Property sequestration intentionally destabilized the patriarchal vision of mastery that undergirded South Carolina's plantation system. For many of the men who faced confiscation, the experience could be uncomfortable, forcing them to choose between their political convictions, their self-image, and their patriarchal responsibilities to those who depended on them—their wives, their children, and the laborers, both enslaved and free, who resided within their households. But sequestration was not the only military practice that weakened white men's patriarchal clout in occupied regions. Quartering did so in ways that were both immediate and distressing. In a city under martial law, military men always outranked civilians. These dynamics were replicated in households headed by white men of the upper classes, where quartered British officers frequently ignored male householders' attempts to exert authority over household spaces and the officers who resided within them. Billeted officers, in effect, relegated men to inferior positions within their own households, upsetting the very hierarchies that embodied their genteel masculinity and anchored their status as patriarchs.

AN OFFICER AND A GENTLEMAN

As distressing as property confiscation was, perhaps no experience was as vexing for male household heads as quartering. British officers preferred to lodge in affluent and middling houses, billets that were not only more comfortable but that reflected the elevated social status that most officers, many of whom hailed from the British gentry, enjoyed in their personal lives. Indeed, recognizing officers' preference for luxurious dwellings, Isaac Winslow described how his loyalist father strategically rented a shabby former store for his family's residence in the British Army's New York headquarters. "Altogether it was but a sory habitation," he recalled, "but my father used to say, it was more comfortable to be in such a house, than where all the apartments but 2 or 3, might be taken by billets for the government officers . . . and the kitchen filled with officers servants." In his father's eyes, inconvenience was a small price to pay to avoid officers' infringing on his patriarchal rights and disrupting his household governance.[40]

Although never as complete in practice as in ideology, quartering blunted the domestic authority of male civilians. Housing a British officer subjected male householders to unprecedented scrutiny; it endangered (and often damaged) their property; and it had the potential to relegate them to a secondary position within the very households that formed a critical pillar of their identity. Households had long been foundational to Anglo-American men's patriarchal prerogatives and political rights, and, by the late eighteenth century, they were also deeply entwined with the masculine identity and class status of middling and elite Anglo-American men. These men carefully emulated elite manners and self-consciously fashioned both themselves and their households to signal elevated status; in their private lives, they were unaccustomed to answering to anyone besides themselves.[41]

To put it another way, quartering pitted colonists' presumptions about the inviolable rights of householders—sentiments epitomized by the legal maxim, "an Englishman's house is his castle"—against officers' expectations that colonists would defer to their martial and metropolitan superiority. Mindful of how martial law bolstered officers' power within the occupied city, some white male householders begrudgingly tolerated officers' insults and chose to avoid escalating confrontations that might result in injury, imprisonment, or death. But such pragmatism had limits, particularly when men felt that officers' actions threatened their property, endangered their families, or impugned their honor. Paternal responsibilities were central to white men's experience with quartering; both perceived and actual obstacles to household governance frequently strained their relationships with billeted officers. When white male householders felt that billeted officers impeded their ability to protect their wives and children, hindered their capacity to provide for their servants and enslaved laborers, or threatened the material markers of their status as household heads and patriarchs, men were more likely to challenge officers' actions and behavior within household spaces.[42]

Billeted households, in essence, had two heads—one military, one civilian—each responsible for his own dependents, including wives, children, and laborers, and each convinced that his claim to their shared domestic space was more pressing. The political contest and ongoing civil war intensified these dynamics, heightening suspicions, exacerbating feelings of injury, deepening both parties' perception of perceived slights, and amplifying fears of the potential dangers, both physical and ideological, posed by the other party. The result was sustained, often heated, and frequently violent struggles in which each man tried to force the other to recognize and defer to their respective domestic or martial authority in order to manage household inhabitants and domestic space as suited their needs and those of their families (or retinues).

Although ostensibly about the use of household space, clashes between British officers and their civilian landlords were deeply entwined with ideas about the privileges of rank, the defense of honor, and irreconcilable notions about who could legitimately claim gentlemanly status. Vigilance in defending one's reputation against slights and verbal attacks was a critical aspect of maintaining one's status as an honorable gentleman. Among civilians, gentlemanly status derived from social prestige and its attendant manifestation of power through property ownership, genteel manners, and one's position as a head of household as well as an adherence to a code of rituals, language, and behavior that could be used to enhance one's status or undermine one's foes. Such qualifications also existed among British officers, many of whom hailed from the British gentry, but military men also placed a heightened emphasis on martial chivalry and military rank, which contributed to a related, but distinctly soldierly, vision of honor.[43]

Honor, and its manifestation in these two iterations of genteel masculinity, therefore functions as an illustrative lens through which to analyze how the confluence of gender and status informed confrontations over property and quartering in male-headed households. Irreconcilable beliefs about the privileges of rank resulted in frequent, often volatile, disputes between white male householders and billeted officers that arose from contradictory expectations of the deference owed to them by the other party. Officers typically exhibited begrudging consideration toward affluent men whom they recognized as fellow, if provincial, gentlemen. In such instances, shared fluency in the language and rituals of honor culture could provide a path to resolution, echoing the dynamics of households where elite white women and billeted officers invoked honor and gendered norms to navigate quartering arrangements. But officers were more dismissive toward men of middling and lower ranks, often scoffing at their pretensions to status and, much to householders' fury, refusing to recognize their authority as property owners or to engage with them as peers. In such instances, quartering had the potential to foster resentment and precipitate explosive confrontations between civilian landlords and British officers that, although ostensibly about domestic life, were deeply rooted in contradictory, irreconcilable notions of status and the respect it conferred.[44]

Condescension toward the colonies was commonplace in the metropole, where people tended to view colonial subjects as rough and unsophisticated. Military status enhanced this cosmopolitan arrogance, particularly toward nonmilitary men. Their superiority over civilians, many officers felt, was indisputable. Many officers prided themselves on their martial honor and chivalry, their refined cosmopolitanism, and their genteel sensibility—all of which were piqued by prolonged interactions with, and at times dependence on, civilians who they deemed rude and unsophisticated. Exemplifying many officers' superior attitudes, Thomas Hughes, a British prisoner of war in Pepperell, Massachusetts, invoked racial stereotypes to disparage the white family that he lodged with, judging them "as ignorant as the Hottentots" owing to their lack of culture, decorum, and education. Particularly galling was the family's disregard for social hierarchy. "The people here have not the least idea of a gentleman," Hughes vented in his journal, grumbling that "servants are treated just like ourselves." With frustration, he recounted the family's daily invitation to his servants to join them at the table, a request that the servants always declined. The meals themselves also exhibited, in Hughes's eyes, a disturbing lack of propriety: "neither gentleman or lady use any ceremony—all hands in the dish at once." "If this is the kind of life the poets say so much of, and call Rural Happiness," he sighed, "I wish to my soul that they were here, and I in London."[45]

Contempt, however, could go both ways. Throughout occupied regions, many officers expressed irritation at what they perceived as civilians' contempt for social hierarchy. Particularly maddening was male civilians' stubborn refusal to concede to officers' superior status. Whether motivated by ideology, irritation, or ignorance, such behaviors on the part of American men clashed with officers' expectations of the respect owed them as both officers and gentlemen and illuminate how contradictory colonial and metropolitan notions of status, hierarchy, and propriety could exacerbate hostilities between military and civilian populations. Some frustrated officers resorted to violence. Major Harry Barry of the Fifty-Second Regiment, for instance, publicly struck Newport butcher Major Fairchild, whom neighbors identified as a revolutionary, "for not taking off his hat to a gentleman, as [Barry] styled himself." More common was the exasperation voiced by Captain John Bowater of the marines, who found the inhabitants in Newport "such a Levelling, underbred, Artfull, Race of people that we Cannot Associate with them." Recounting an interaction with a prominent Newporter, Bowater detailed how the man approached the door of the house where British general Lord Hugh Percy, second duke of Northumberland, quartered and asked to see Mr. Percy. "Thinking him ignorant" about the peerage, Bowater corrected the man "and told him again Lord Percy." But the omission had been intentional. Scoffing at the correction, the man avowed, "He knew no Lord but the Lord Jehovah." "Thus it is throughout America," Bowater fumed; "I frequently long to Shove a Soup ladle down their throat."[46]

The forced intimacy of quartering had the potential to exacerbate resentments between British officers and property-owning male civilians. In billeted households, British officers and male heads of household engaged in uneasy, daily negotiations over shared living spaces in which civilian property owners and British officers frequently felt that they had been disrespected by the other party. Over days, weeks, and months of cohabitation, small annoyances, minor aggravations, and daily slights accumulated on both sides. Still, the consequences of these confrontations varied widely, and their outcome was often contingent on the status of the civilian property owner. Aggrieved householders hailing from the upper echelons of colonial society often had far greater latitude than those of middling and lower rank to challenge officers' conduct and their use of household space.

"A slight altercation" in Charleston between Dr. Charles Drayton and Colonel Banastre Tarleton reveals the prominence of status-based notions of masculine honor in the progression and resolution of disagreements over quarters. When the British captured Charleston in 1780, Charles Drayton became a prisoner on parole, and Drayton Hall, his sprawling plantation on the Ashley River, was appropriated for Lord Charles Cornwallis's headquarters. According to one British officer who visited the property during the occupation, it was "one of the best houses I have seen in America." Built by English masons, Drayton Hall was "elaborately adorned with all the taste and skill which wealth could lavish upon it." The garden, in particular, was a point of pride. Meticulously maintained by enslaved gardeners, it abounded with "cultivated exotics and all the indigenous shrubs roses and sweet scented flowers perfuming the atmosphere with their fragrance." Ornamental statues and fountains adorned the garden, and "pebbled walks shaded by rows of superb Magnolias" wound through the greenery toward the river. Inscribing Drayton's status as an Anglo-American southern gentleman on the landscape, the garden was a visible manifestation of his wealth and taste and his familiarity with genteel English aesthetics.[47]

FIGURE 7 P. E. Du Simitiere, *Drayton Hall,* 1763. Watercolor. Private Collection of Jim Lockard. Courtesy of Drayton Hall, a Historic Site of the National Trust for Historic Preservation, Charleston, S.C.

Predictably, Dr. Drayton did not take kindly to Colonel Tarleton's insistence on pasturing his horses in his prized garden, where the animals trampled "allover [*sic*] it braking and devastating" everything within. Drayton's grandson remembered that when his grandfather first saw the horses in the garden while visiting the plantation on business, he instructed the enslaved gardener to remove the animals and convey his request that Tarleton cease pasturing them there, "for they destroyed every thing." Tensions mounted as Tarleton ignored this and a subsequent appeal to graze the horses elsewhere. Drayton threatened to crop the ears of Tarleton's prized horses; Tarleton threatened to kill him if he tried.[48]

Upon returning to the plantation a third time and finding the situation unchanged, Charles Drayton carried out his threat to crop the horses' ears. Ordering the gardener to convey the severed appendages to Colonel Tarleton "with his compliments," Drayton hastily retreated to his Charleston townhouse. On seeing his injured horses, Tarleton pursued the doctor back to the city, where he confronted him about the mutilation. "Did I not tell you to take them out of my garden, or I would?" Drayton retorted. Drayton's contemptuous response both conveyed his disdain for the officer and shifted responsibility for the horses' disfigurement onto Tarleton himself. It was Tarleton's selfishness and his disregard for Drayton's authority as a property owner, the

FIGURE 8 Charles Fraser, *Dr. Charles Drayton*, 1818. Watercolor on ivory. 3 5/8 in. x 3 in. Gift of Mrs. Leger Mitchell Courtesy of the Church Home Orphanage, York, S.C. Accession no. 1944.005.0001. Courtesy of the Gibbes Museum of Art/ Carolina Art Association, Charleston, S.C.

doctor suggested, that had made violence inevitable: he had simply acted to redress the insults perpetrated against him. Disrespecting a gentleman had consequences, Drayton implied, even in a city under martial law.[49]

A man's honor had indeed been sullied, Colonel Tarleton agreed; but it was he, not the doctor, whom he believed to be the injured party. Enraged by Drayton's nonchalance, Tarleton bellowed "defend yourself" as he unsheathed his sword and assumed a combat stance. Drayton, a prisoner on parole prohibited from carrying weapons, seized the poker from the fire.

FIGURE 9 Sir Joshua Reynolds, *Colonel [Banastre] Tarleton*, 1782. Oil on canvas. 236 c.m. x 145.5 c.m. Bequeathed by Mrs. Henrietta Charlotte Tarleton, 1951. NG5985. Courtesy of the National Gallery of the United Kingdom, London.

Eighteenth-century honor culture required that dueling weapons be equal. Observing the incongruence of their arms, Colonel Tarleton conceded, "Sir, you have the advantage of me no man fights with red hot weapons." Pointedly suggesting that it was not he but the officer who had acted dishonorably, Drayton reminded the colonel of his parole status. At a standoff, the two men relinquished their weapons and resumed their seats by the fire. But, before Tarleton departed, the men shared some wine and drank to each other's health.[50]

A somewhat bizarre episode, the incident between Colonel Banastre Tarleton and Dr. Charles Drayton suggests how elite status could facilitate the negotiation and resolution of civilian-military disputes over domestic spaces through mutual engagement in a transatlantic culture of genteel honor. Despite their political differences, Tarleton and Drayton operated within a worldview in which the genteel honor that grounded the masculine norms of both the colonial elite and the British officer corps needed to be vigorously safeguarded and slights swiftly, often violently, rebuked. Honor provided a common language, legible rituals, and mutual understanding; it offered both a means of recourse and a justification for violence that operated outside the bounds of the military conflict. Adhering to these norms, the men's confrontation signaled elite status and gentlemanly intentions in a way that, although initially exacerbating their conflict, also helped to defuse the situation. Dueling culture allowed the two men to identify one another as peers, thereby enabling them to engage in a ritualistic defense of their respective honor that afforded both men the opportunity to save face on terms of mutual respect. As a gentleman, Charles Drayton was permitted, within limits, to become emotional in defense of his property and indignant in remonstrating against his infringed liberties. Anger could be begrudgingly tolerated from social equals and resolved through mutual adherence to the customs of honor. This was, Tarleton tacitly acknowledged, how gentlemen responded to insults.[51]

Although divided by politics, shared notions of genteel masculine honor sometimes fostered surprising solidarity between affluent male civilians and the highborn British officers quartered in their homes. In a letter to Major Peter Traille of the Royal Artillery, Thomas Bee, one of South Carolina's delegates to the Continental Congress and a lieutenant governor of the state during the Revolution, articulated how a shared elite culture and expectations of honorable behavior had the potential to transcend political differences. During the occupation of Charleston, Traille lodged in the absent Bee's residence, where he, in some capacity, assisted the Bee family. After the British evacuated the city in 1782, Thomas Bee returned home for the first time in more than two years. He was astonished to find the house in perfect order, a situation that was in no small measure likely owing to the efforts of Peg Boden, a free Black woman who sought refuge with her husband in the Charleston garrison and whom Traille employed. In an effusive letter to the major, Bee expressed his "most sincere acknowledgements for your repeated acts of kindness and attention to my dear deceased Son, at a time it was out of my power to render him any myself—for your care of my House and other property whilst they were in your possession and for your very great exactness in leaveing every Article." "My gratitude for these favors, will be one of the last sentiments that dies with me," he avowed. Despite their opposing politics, Bee believed that the two men were connected through a shared commitment to masculine honor, patriarchal duty, and elite sensibility. "However we may differ in our Public Characters during the present unhappy contest," Bee acknowledged, "I flatter myself, for the honor of human nature, that as private Individuals we may be Friends."[52]

But the same notions of elite masculine honor that could facilitate respect among gentlemen, or encourage politeness toward white women of the upper classes, could also provoke violent confrontations—even among men aligned politically—when billeted officers and their civilian landlords were of unequal status. Just like their elite counterparts, civilian men of the middling and lower classes were vigilant in defending their property rights and jealously guarded their domestic prerogatives against military incursion. But many British officers were unwilling to tolerate opposition from men they deemed their inferiors; such insubordination, they felt, required a swift reprimand that firmly reasserted both social hierarchy and the superiority of military rule.

Political differences had the potential to prime men for conflict and compound the tensions of cohabitation, but examples from households throughout occupied regions suggest that status (and perceptions of status), more so than politics, frequently determined the tenor and experience of quartering in male-headed households. Such was the case for Newport apothecary Joseph Tweedy and Captain John Cambel of the Corps of Engineers, who quartered in Tweedy's house. Ostensibly a loyalist, Joseph Tweedy nevertheless maintained personal connections with several individuals "engaged in the heat of Rebellion," circumstances that caused both Captain Cambel and some of his neighbors to suspect that Tweedy's true sympathies lay with the revolutionaries and that his political conversion was a strategic move to protect his property and perhaps enhance his social status by collaborating with occupying forces.[53]

When hostilities erupted between Joseph Tweedy and John Cambel in August 1777, however, they were precipitated, not by politics, but by competing notions of domestic authority, status, and the associated privileges of gentlemanly honor. The dispute arose over the apothecary's treatment of Captain Cambel's enslaved servant, a young boy of about eight or nine years old. Joseph Tweedy insisted that he had playfully threatened to throw the child off the wharf and dipped his legs in the water. "He and the Captain had frequently amused themselves in doing this with the Boy," he claimed. Rejecting this explanation, Cambel contended that the apothecary's intentions had been far more malicious and that he had been attempting to drown or injure the child. When questioned about the incident, Joseph Tweedy brashly responded that he had terrorized the boy "to please my Fancy," thereby provoking Captain Cambel, who subsequently began beating the apothecary and threatened to send him to the provost.[54]

As the ensuing court-martial would reveal, Tweedy was frustrated by the quartering arrangement. He felt disrespected and disempowered in his own home. Although Tweedy insisted that he and Captain Cambel were on "intimate footing ever since his first quartering in the House," the relationship was not as cordial as he claimed. Both men confirmed that they had not spoken for several days prior to the incident. Their disagreement arose from the officer's behavior after the death of Tweedy's brother. Joseph Tweedy complained that the captain showed little sympathy, inviting company over to the house, playing music, and ignoring Tweedy when he saw him in the entryway. Captain Cambel, on the other hand, denied that the men were friendly. "Nay," they were "not even on speaking terms," he avowed. He accused the apothecary of exaggerating their intimacy in order to justify his harassment of the enslaved boy. Moreover, Cambel argued, he had done nothing wrong by entertaining company and playing music in his "own Quarters."[55]

These statements offer a glimpse of how each man regarded their shared domestic space. As the head of household, Joseph Tweedy expected his family's needs to take priority. He believed the billeted officer, as a temporary resident, should conduct himself in a manner that did not interfere with household life. His framing of the men's relationship as friendship, rather than a billet, suggests the importance of rank to this domestic negotiation: it was a subtle assertion of social equality in which Joseph Tweedy sought to establish his principal position within the household, implying that it was by his generosity, rather than military policy, that the officer quartered there. Captain John Cambel, conversely, was certainly aware that he inhabited Tweedy's space and could not have been oblivious to the family's loss. Yet, he insisted, he could do as he wished in his "own Quarters," indicating that he viewed his rooms as separate from the household. Furthermore, Cambel's refusal to acknowledge Tweedy's demands for gentlemanly satisfaction demonstrates that Captain Cambel did not consider him a peer, despite Tweedy's efforts to establish otherwise. Rather, he felt that his elevated class and his military rank excluded him from the apothecary's household governance.

Captain Cambel's court-martial clarified how perceptions of status informed this domestic power struggle. Charged with "beating and offering to send to the Guard Mr. Joseph Tweedy, a Gentleman of the Town of Newport; For Persisting he was right in what he had done: And for Declaring, let the Consequences be what they will, under the like Provocation, he would beat him again," Cambel invoked a surprising tactic to justify his actions. His primary defense was to argue that Joseph Tweedy was not, in fact, a gentleman—therefore, he had committed no crime.[56]

To prove the apothecary's inferior status, Cambel scrutinized Joseph Tweedy's attempts to initiate a duel. Earlier in the trial, Tweedy had testified that he "repeatedly demanded satisfaction, as a Gentleman," but that Captain Cambel had scorned his overtures and ordered the apothecary to hold his tongue. Countering this allegation, Cambel inquired whether Joseph Tweedy did "at any time, send me a Message, requiring satisfaction, and by whom?" Tweedy responded that he had not. "As Captain Cambel had denyed me Satisfaction when I requested it Verbally," Tweedy explained, he "Imagined . . . had I done such a thing he would have ordered the Guard to take me up." Tweedy instead lodged a complaint at headquarters, citing Cambel's "very improper treatment to a Gentleman." Cambel's line of questioning—as would have been abundantly clear to the assembled panel of officers—exposed Tweedy's ignorance of the rituals of honor, belying his supposed status as a gentleman. Duels were initiated by written letters of inquiry. Failing to properly demand satisfaction in writing, Tweedy instead snitched to the general. In so doing, he undercut the very claims to honor that he insisted Cambel had insulted. In declining to acknowledge Tweedy's demand for satisfaction as a legitimate request, Captain Cambel treated Tweedy as an inferior, rather than a fellow gentleman. As such, the apothecary was not entitled to make such requests; indeed, to engage with them was beneath Cambel's own status as a gentleman. Only gentlemen could demand honorable recourse.[57]

As the trial progressed, Captain Cambel's attacks on Joseph Tweedy's status intensified. Ironically, the very proximity that provoked the conflict provided the officer with his best defense. Owing to the forced intimacy of quartering, John Cambel knew Tweedy and his family, his profession and his connections. “The Charge of having beaten a Gentleman, is very singular, and very extraordinary,” he asserted. In a pointed rebuke that sharply underscored the apothecary’s opportunistic social ascent on the arrival of the British Army, Captain Cambel admonished, “I can hardly suppose that even a Gentleman of Nine Months Standing, would not be aware of this Novelty.” Building his defense, Cambel argued that his alleged crime rested “merely on the supposition” that Tweedy was a gentleman. Although Tweedy was “presented to [the Court] as a Gentleman, and in the most favorable appearance,” Cambel argued, he “but keeps an obscure Apothecarie’s Shop . . . [and] is, in fact the Son of a Transported Convict, an inveterate Rebel, and himself Notoriously reprobated.” In short, Cambel maintained, Tweedy had neither the lifestyle nor the lineage of a gentleman. He was simply a man of the middling sort—a rebel, at that—who had taken advantage of the occupation to better his social standing and pursue his self-interest. And John Cambel did not feel himself bound to respect such a man, even though he resided under his roof. Rather, he insisted, as a gentleman, he had been obligated to put a lowly rebel apothecary in his proper place.[58]

Transforming his trial into a referendum on Joseph Tweedy’s misrepresentation of himself, his household, and his politics, Captain Cambel insisted that the true issue at stake was, not whether he had assaulted the apothecary, but rather “the Consequence of admitting such a Man [as Tweedy], on any Account, to a situation he may abuse.” The policing of gentlemanly status was necessary to maintain the integrity of rank, Cambel argued. It was for the common good, he insisted, that strivers like Tweedy be excluded from the privileges of status. Implicit in Cambel’s argument was an assumption that genteel status and military rank entitled gentlemen officers to a certain degree of latitude in their interactions with male civilians, particularly those of the lower classes. The court’s verdict endorsed this position. Although the court found Cambel guilty of beating his landlord, the assembled officers chose not to punish him for the assault. Conceding that Cambel had overreacted in his use of violence, the court felt that, ultimately, the fault lay with Tweedy and his “very improper Behaviour and highly unmannerly reply” to the officer’s “Civil Message.” In a conspicuous omission, the court’s verdict avoided any reference to Joseph Tweedy as a gentleman.[59]

Contradictory perceptions of status and expectations of deference could lead to volatile conflicts, especially when well-to-do colonists felt that they had been disrespected by enlisted troops that they deemed their social inferiors. Many genteel civilians expected their inferiors to show a certain level of deference. But to their chagrin, occupying forces rarely regarded themselves as civilians' subordinates; martial law empowered military men of all ranks, even enlisted men who typically hailed from the lower classes. When these divergent expectations collided, they had the potential to provoke aggressive, inflammatory confrontations.

This dynamic is exemplified in the case of Virginia loyalist John Goodrich and his son James, both of whom were court-martialed in July 1781 after becoming embroiled in a physical altercation with James Susames and Barney Donally, the servants of the superintendent general of the British and foreign hospitals, Dr. John Nooth, who lodged next door to them in New York. According to the Goodriches, they and their enslaved laborers were on the beach with fishing nets loaded into their boats "waiting [for] the proper time of Tide" that would allow them to catch "the first and most valuable haul" from the cove "on [their] own Land" when they spied the doctor's servants, who had a permit to sell fish at the market, "coming around the Point from [Dr. Nooth's] house with the same intention." Not wanting to be outmaneuvered, John Goodrich directed his slaves to launch his boat and secure the better fishing position, a privilege that he felt that he, as the property owner and the first boat on the scene, was entitled to by both law and custom. Angered by these machinations, James Susames and Barney Donally bellowed "Vile Epithets" and maneuvered their boat to obstruct the Goodriches, intentionally tearing their line. Tempers flared. According to witnesses, "John Goodrich, ask'd Barney Donally, if he knew he was talking to a Gentleman." To which Donally replied "that he was no Gentleman, that no Gentleman would do as he had done, that he would be made to know better." In response to the disrespect shown his father, James Goodrich launched himself at the soldiers, kicking James Susames and punching Barney Donally in the face as he reprimanded him, saying, "You Rascal, how dare you talk so to a Gentleman." Shortly thereafter, his father joined the fray and whacked Barney Donally on the head "with a large Walking Stick" that "rendered him senseless" and cut so deeply that it exposed his skull.[60]

Standing before a court-martial the following month, John Goodrich maintained that he and his son had been in the right: "What I did was in the lawful defence of my Property, on which occasion, a Man does not always stop to consider the exact weight and strength of the force, which he is oblige[d] to exert." But, even as he framed his defense as a straightforward question of property rights, the privileges of status and conventions of gentlemanly honor formed a critical pillar of Goodrich's defense. The servants' "behaviour was expressive of a certain saucy contempt, which from people in their circumstances to a Man in my Station of Life is the highest of provocation," he expounded. "Thus provok'd—thus insulted—and thus injur'd—my Property torn to pieces before my face, was it born to put up with?" Goodrich thundered.[61]

John Goodrich's status as a loyalist refugee not only informed his defense, it might have strengthened his commitment to the privileges of rank. A prosperous merchant and one of the wealthiest landowners in Nansemond County, Virginia, in the prerevolutionary years, John Goodrich initially supported the rebellion in June 1775, but he switched sides shortly thereafter when British forces apprehended his son for smuggling gunpowder; he placed his merchant fleet at the crown's disposal and became a privateer. The Goodriches' loyalism made them a target for Virginia's revolutionary government and eventually forced the family to abandon the colony and take refuge at British headquarters in New York. Separated from his more than two-thousand-acre estate, John Goodrich clung to his status as a gentleman. "I hope [the court] will think that the head of a Family who left above Sixty thousand Pounds amongst the Rebels and whose private exertions have deprived the Enemy of above Three hundred Vessels and near Four thousand Prisoners, is intitled to at least common Civility," he remonstrated. Sacrifice, service, and gentlemanly status, Goodrich argued, elevated him and his needs above lowly servants, even those that wore military uniforms. The court disagreed. John and James Goodrich were each fined five pounds New York currency and ordered to give security of five hundred pounds of the same to ensure their good behavior for the next twelve months.[62]

Throughout garrisoned cities, irreconcilable beliefs about the privileges of rank—whether deriving from refined upbringing, military commissions, or property ownership—resulted in frequent disputes between civilian landlords and billeted officers that arose from contradictory expectations of deference. Excepting the most privileged gentlemen, male civilians in occupied regions found their efforts to defend their property, to protect their family, and to oversee household life were often stymied by the officers billeted in their houses. With limited recourse, male civilians often resorted to performative displays of anger in an effort to reclaim the status and domestic authority that they felt officers denied them. On occasion, these gambits worked, especially when officers and their landlords hailed from similar classes. More often, however, these confrontations turned combative. That disputes between men were frequently characterized by hostile belligerence, rather than being resolved over tea and polite negotiation, offers tantalizing glimpses into how status-based notions of masculinity structured quartering relationships in garrisoned cities.

But, as the examples of John and James Goodrich, of Charles Drayton, and of Joseph Tweedy show, such conflicts were rarely limited to the men themselves. Often, enslaved people were caught in the middle of these feuds. The men enslaved by the Goodriches, for instance, were the ones manning the boat, the ones that John Goodrich ordered to take actions that incurred the wrath of James Susames and Barney Donally. Charles Drayton's enslaved gardener was caught in the unfortunate position of intermediary between his enslaver and Colonel Banastre Tarleton and was primarily responsible for communicating escalating threats between the two white men. His precarious position reveals the liminal status of enslaved people within billeted households. Enslaved laborers' physical proximity to potentially violent officers and their roles as messengers made it likely that it would be they, and not intransigent slaveowners, who bore the brunt of officers' anger for white men's disobedience. Indeed, such was the case for the young boy enslaved by Captain John Cambel, who found himself manhandled by Joseph Tweedy as a consequence of the apothecary's efforts to rebuke the officer quartered in his house. Fundamentally, these incidents illustrate the perils that enslaved people faced when caught in the middle of power struggles between male civilians and billeted British officers.[63]

But enslaved laborers were not the only ones to become entangled in these quarrels. Often, entire households were drawn into these confrontations, as male householders and their military lodgers maneuvered to govern their shared lodgings, frequently marshalling their respective dependents in their efforts to antagonize one another and secure control of their shared domestic space.

HOUSEHOLD WARS

In residences where officers billeted, one of the ways that male heads of household attempted to enforce their vision of household governance while denying British officers' ability to do the same was by mobilizing their household against the officer. Within the context of daily life, quartering disputes often became proxy wars that dragged entire households and military retinues into the fray, as both male householders and British officers enlisted their respective dependents in their efforts to force the other man into submission. As British officers and male civilians attempted to control shared domestic spaces, they frequently invoked their elevated station to justify their behavior toward one another. Deeply tethered to status, these confrontations illustrate how both real and perceived disparities in rank escalated hostilities, often resulting in explosive household disputes.

Disagreements became especially volatile when they involved loyalist officers. Civilians seemingly felt more empowered to challenge their fellow countrymen, even when they wore an officer's uniform. Resenting this disparate treatment, loyalist officers responded aggressively to perceived disrespect. New York, which served as British headquarters throughout the war, was an incendiary environment. Overcrowded accommodations and the presence of large numbers of loyalist regiments led to more overt and sustained confrontations between officers and civilians.

The situation at 380 William Street in New York City epitomizes these dynamics. During the four months that they lived together, Dr. Daniel Kendrick, a loyalist and assistant surgeon in the army's general hospital, routinely clashed with Lieutenant Thomas Tomlins Pritchard of the Second Battalion of New Jersey Volunteers. The two men and their families lived in the same building and shared an entrance. Dr. Kendrick's family resided in the upper apartments; Lieutenant Pritchard's family occupied the lower floor. Although it is unclear whether Kendrick owned the building, his residency in the house predated the officer's billeting, and, from the quarrels that ensued, it is clear that the doctor felt that he had a superior claim to the dwelling. According to Kendrick, the officer routinely "illused me and my family, he has illused and abused Gentlemen that came to see me and struck some—even patients that came to me on business, have been insulted." Compounding these injuries, on multiple occasions, Lieutenant Pritchard threatened to shoot the doctor or run him through with a bayonet. He also spread rumors that "[Kendrick] was a Rebell and [his] Wife a Whore." The situation became so contentious, Dr. Kendrick testified, that he was "affraid to leave his family by themselves—for fear of" the loyalist officer.[64]

Pritchard countered that the doctor had been inconsiderate of their shared space. Attempting to undermine the man's credibility, Pritchard called witnesses who alleged that Kendrick was no gentleman, as evidenced by the fact that he regularly entertained "Women of very indifferent Characters" and "Masters of Vessels Sailors and Negroes [who] came to the House . . . and made a great deal of Noise, at all hours of the Night." Allowing that some of these visitors might have been patients, Pritchard was nevertheless annoyed by their presence. "This house was no public Hospital," he protested, insisting that patients ought "not disturb those, that had Quarters in the same house." Pritchard also detailed repeated verbal abuse at the hands of the Kendrick family. "Many other aggravating insults have been offered me," Pritchard testified, "such as taking away my Garden produce, killing my Cat, and such like." These circumstances, Pritchard confessed, were alarming. He took to sleeping with his firelock "laid at my bed side—that if any insult was intended me, I could defend myself."[65]

Weaponizing their shared living situation, both men manipulated the domestic environment and their roles as heads of household to make the other uncomfortable. According to one neighbor, the men "abuse[d] each other often." In one particularly evocative example, Dr. Kendrick accused Lieutenant Pritchard of filling the hallway with "heaps of Ordour . . . that it might be trail'd up by the Ladies Gowns." Denying the charge, Pritchard suggested that Mrs. Kendrick had in fact orchestrated the prank, citing "a Similar dirty transaction of hers" intended "to aggravate matters" within the household. Dr. Kendrick nevertheless used the incident as a pretext for retaliation, "stamping hard" in the hallway and on the stairs near Pritchard's rooms. On another occasion, he led horses through the house, rather than taking them around to the door by the garden. He was also in the habit of leaving the door by Pritchard's bedroom open to the street—especially in the winter—to "aggravate" his lodger. According to a neighbor, this instigated many of their fights. One night, Pritchard retaliated by bolting the door from the inside and locking the doctor out of the house. These confrontations routinely descended into shouting matches.[66]

The two men regularly sparred with one another, but, as Lieutenant Pritchard testified, it was also a proxy war that drew family members and household laborers into the fray. Dr. Kendrick encouraged his friends and patients to loiter on the stairs, lobbing insults at the lieutenant whenever he passed by. On another occasion, Mrs. Kendrick brandished her fist in the officer's face and insulted him with "very bad language." She and other women taunted Pritchard's wife. The Kendricks also encouraged impudence among their servants. One of the family's Black servants (of uncertain freedom) attempted to steal the rainwater that Pritchard's servant had gathered and struck the man when he refused to surrender it. Possibly the same servant, an enslaved person teased the Pritchard children and called them names. The most explosive confrontation occurred when the Kendrick family's maid threw dirt into the water that Mrs. Pritchard had lugged into the house to wash clothes. When confronted about it, the woman "answered that she would break Mrs. Pritchards head, if she spoke to her—during this altercation Mrs. Kendrick was in her Window encouraging her Maid to abuse Mrs. Pritchard." Fed up, Lieutenant Pritchard called for a file of men to arrest the maid. When she could not be found, he apprehended Mrs. Kendrick, declaring "one whore, must answer for the other."[67]

As the two men and their respective households fought over their shared domestic space, contradictory notions about the privileges of status—each man believing himself superior and expecting deference from the other—further exacerbated an already hostile situation. Lieutenant Pritchard was skeptical of the Kendrick family's associations with laborers, sailors, free and enslaved Black people, and women of perceived ill-repute. Attempting to discredit the Kendricks by linking them with these lower-status groups, Pritchard, who came from more humble origins, insisted that his loyalism and his military status elevated him above the family, whose disorderly and obnoxious household was not only indicative of their lack of decorum but also, he alleged, their supposed rebel politics. Dr. Kendrick, conversely, had little respect for Pritchard, whom he regarded as an insignificant man of mediocre status. Kendrick resented Lieutenant Pritchard's presence in the house and made clear that he viewed the officer as a social inferior, or a "Shitten puppy," as he put it on one occasion. Kendrick spread rumors of dubious origin, alleging that, prior to arriving in New York, the lieutenant had "been a common Vassall at Philadelphia, wheeling a wheelbarrow." Acknowledging that a military commission enhanced a man's status, Kendrick nevertheless asserted that loyalist officers, in large measure because of their lower-class status, were inferior to their counterparts in the regular army. Pritchard was "no more than an officer in a Provincial Corps," he scoffed. By contrast, the doctor "was a Gentleman, educated at College," who "could dine half a dozen Gentlemen at his Table at one time . . . that it was more, than [Pritchard] could do to dine one."[68]

The court-martial proceedings suggest that Dr. Kendrick might have been intentionally provoking his lodger. In fact, Lieutenant Pritchard suspected that the family sought to drive him from the house so that they could "appropriate the sole use of it to themselves." One neighborhood woman testified that the officer "always lived in good terms . . . with all the neighbours except Mr. Kendric[k]." Additionally, the barrack master's testimony revealed that the previous officer billeted in the Kendrick house had lodged complaints against the family "for keeping an irregular house . . . also that his looking Glass was broke, from dancing in the Rooms over his head." This behavior, however petulant, represented one of Dr. Kendrick's few avenues to protect his household in the British garrison. He might, as Pritchard suspected, have been a revolutionary who masked his politics as a means of survival in the British garrison. More likely, he was a genuine loyalist, as evidenced by his resettlement in Nova Scotia after the war—but one who was simply frustrated by the experience of quartering and who was unwilling to concede domestic power, however slight, to men he deemed his social inferiors.[69]

Although some households were more violent than others, these ongoing, pervasive contests over masculine authority and privilege present a vision of quartering that is fundamentally dissimilar from the courteous, gendered negotiations that unfolded in households governed by white women. A dispute that emerged between New Yorker William Maxwell and the Scottish officer billeted in his residence brings this distinction into sharper relief and clarifies how gender structured these arrangements. In January 1780, Maxwell lodged a complaint, substantiated by various reports from his servants, about the officer's behavior. The officer, he alleged, not only had a habit of "bringing dissolute women into his quarters, and retaining them there all night," he also "permitted his servants to treat Mrs. Maxwell with opprobrious speech, and threaten to kick her." Undertaken to protect his wife and reassert his authority over his household, William Maxwell's pursuit of justice was deeply entwined with his paternal responsibilities to his wife and other dependents, who he felt were endangered by the actions of the officer and his retinue.[70]

The accused officer, perhaps surprisingly, was none other than Lieutenant James Cramond of the Forty-Second Regiment—the very same officer quartered in Elizabeth Drinker's Philadelphia household two years previously. The same officer who had followed Elizabeth's rules, who had agreed not to drink, gamble, or swear in the household, who had promised that he would protect the family against unsavory billets. The very same officer whom she came to view as part of her family, whose polite behavior "gain[ed] our esteem," and with whom she maintained a correspondence for the remainder of his life.[71]

What then, had changed in New York? Such a stark transformation in behavior, although not impossible, was seemingly out of character for Cramond based on his experiences in the Drinker household. Offering a unique opportunity to compare the same officer billeted within a male-headed and female-headed household, this incident provides insight into the gendered dimensions of quartering. Of course, individual personalities mattered. James Cramond had almost certainly hired new servants or purchased additional slaves by the time he resided in New York, so the servants mistreating Mrs. Maxwell might not have been the same men who resided in the Drinker household. Cramond himself may also have changed; two additional years of war might have hardened his attitudes toward American civilians. He also, reportedly, had a temper, one that he might have felt less inclined to control when not residing in a household full of pacifist women and children.[72]

A court-martial would later vindicate Lieutenant Cramond, who vociferously contested these charges and lodged some of his own against William Maxwell. But the fact remains, while living under Maxwell's roof in 1780, Cramond engaged in far more contentious and routine confrontations with his civilian landlord than he did when he billeted with Elizabeth Drinker in 1778. Echoing patterns elsewhere in occupied regions, gender factored into how Lieutenant Cramond navigated and engaged with the civilians he lodged with; he was far more patient—more chivalrous—with women then he was with men.

To adjudicate the matter, New York commandant General James Pattison convened a board of examination comprised of three officers and the city magistrates. Each man had the opportunity to present his grievances; after hearing their testimonies, the board concluded that the allegations against Cramond were "totally unsupported by any proof." The charge that Cramond's servants had abused Mrs. Maxwell was seemingly rooted in fact, but, since she had never made Cramond aware of the issue, the board reasoned, the officer could not be held culpable. The brief published report of the trial omitted specifics, but the board noted that, although Maxwell offered "credible evidence" to support his other complaints, many of his allegations "appear[ed] of a frivolous nature." Cramond was cleared of all wrongdoing. As for William Maxwell, the board determined, his intentions had not been "malicious," but he had erred in "too credulously attend[ing] to the reports of servants." In two public apologies issued the following month—one on the city's grand parade and another published in the newspaper alongside the court's opinion—William Maxwell issued a perfunctory statement that failed to conceal his annoyance with the judgment. Likely contributing to Maxwell's begrudging tone was the fact that these public professions were actually his second attempt to make amends; Cramond had deemed his initial apology unsatisfactory.[73]

Clearly, all was not well in the Maxwell household. Whatever the motivation, tensions flared between the servants of both William Maxwell and James Cramond—so much so that the former's employees felt the need to report, and seemingly fabricate, stories about the officer in an effort to oust him from the house. Possibly these allegations were politically motivated; maybe they simply disliked the man. But they also, seemingly, contained a kernel of truth: Mrs. Maxwell suffered jeers and threats of physical violence at the hands of her military lodgers. And the household had risen to her defense.

The experiences of white male householders suggest the extent to which British occupation resulted in tangible, deeply uncomfortable consequences for American men. The circumstances many men found themselves in—from dislocation to the destruction and confiscation of property to the subordination of their place within domestic hierarchies as a result of quartering—eroded critical pillars of patriarchal power among elite men, loosening their grip over their households. Revolutionaries had long cautioned that Britain's threat to American property endangered colonists' liberty. As one Massachusetts woman declared as the British Army marched on Philadelphia, "If Men will not fight and defend their own perticuliar spot, if they will not drive the Enemy from their Doors, they deserve the slavery and subjection which awaits them." For many male civilians, quartering made this threat acutely, immediately tangible. Occurring in the politically resonant space of the household, quartering and householders' ensuing disputes with British officers exposed the limits of men's power and the fragility of the households that undergirded their social position and political rights. By accentuating the fragility of men's domestic authority, British occupation offered men new, immediate comprehension of how easily their customary rights and privileges could unravel, along with the status that property conferred. Indeed, for these reasons, quartering functioned as a potent metaphor for how the British infringed on American freedoms. Even now, more than two centuries later, Americans typically associate quartering with the British Army.[74]

Yet the Continental army quartered soldiers on civilian populations, too. And, as the example of one anonymous householder shows, Continental quartering also violated the domestic prerogatives of American men. Writing to George Washington in August 1776, the man enumerated grievances that summed up the feelings of white male householders who felt that military practices infringed on their property rights and threw their households into disarray. "My House is forcibly entered and possessed by officers and Soldiers without my Consent," the man complained, as he recounted the transformation of his home into a barrack and a hospital for nearly seventy soldiers. Protesting this treatment, he bemoaned that "the very chambers of my House which is ever considered a sanctuary to the owner, are not so to me, or my family." In addition to the damage to his property and possessions, he objected particularly to the discomfort that the arrangement inflicted on the women in his household. The soldiers' "want of Cleanliness" and their "rude manners" caused his daughters "unusual distress." Unable to shield his family from either the predations of soldiers or the diseases they carried, the man sent the women away—they were, the man lamented, "reduced by a lawless Invasion of every Avenue to their rooms, to fly from their Home, where they have not a friend to protect them."[75]

Infused with a sense of futility, the man's anger revealed his frustration at his inability to protect his property and his family and for the disrespect shown him as a property owner. Lamenting the inconsistency of American ideals and military practices, the man worried that the ideals of the Revolution—ideals that he had embraced and sacrificed for—might not apply to him. Comparing his disrupted and fractured household to one of his wealthier neighbors, the man condemned the discrepancies of status that he felt had subjected his property and his family to undue distress. Why, he inquired, was he forced to endure discomfort, privation, and the endangerment of his family "whilst my happier neighbor enjoys all his Enclosures, with that Sacred freedom from violation which is due to the words '*Peace, Liberty,* and Property.'—and for what Reason? Is it because he is powerful and my family weak and defenseless?" It was "intollerable," the man concluded: "Life is a Burthen and Death to myself and family would be a happy release from these troubles, if to be suffered longer." Quartering had trampled the man's rights, ruined his property, threatened his daughters, and made him long for death. Such sentiments were hardly a resounding endorsement for the revolutionary cause. Better that such injustices be forgotten, that the wrongs of quartering be laid at the feet of the British.[76]

Yet, even as Americans endeavored to forget Continental quartering and foist the experience on the British Army, the emotions that quartering provoked—the tensions, the conflicts, the destruction of property, how the violence of war intruded into households and interfered with daily life—remained deeply relatable for people on all sides of the conflict. Once the war was over, an awareness of how the conflict had complicated patriarchal responsibilities and endangered property rights frequently allowed men to communicate across classes and national allegiances, to articulate their grievances as property holders. As men. This shared language, together with how war clarified and concretized the need to defend their property and families, forged critical connections among white men from diverse social statuses, even among those with opposing political loyalties. As they set about building the nation, memories of the wartime threat to property and domestic life largely came to be seen as wrongs that the British had committed against American colonists. And, as later chapters will discuss, such narratives contributed to a collective, widespread aspiration for peace that was deeply entwined with idealized domestic prosperity. Independence offered an opportunity to reassert and reinforce white men's position at the head of both the household and society. For as the experience of war would demonstrate, it was not only the British Army but also dependent members of their own households whose wartime pursuits of happiness destabilized the patriarchal ideals embedded within domestic spaces.

FIGURE 10 Thomas Leitch, *A View of Charles-Town, the Capital of South Carolina*, June 3, 1776. Hand-colored line engraving. Accession no. 2017-287. Colonial Williamsburg Foundation Museum Purchase, The Friends of Colonial Williamsburg Collections Fund, Williamsburg, Va

CHAPTER FOUR

Maids Are Become Mistresses

Stepping off the boat, Elizabeth Anderson surveyed her new home. A humid breeze wafted off the water, the salty air mingled with the putrid odor of the British camp. Palmetto trees dotted the landscape. Beside the warships floating in the harbor, Black pilots skillfully navigated smaller boats through Charleston's shallow shoals. Unlike the unremarkable view of New York that had faded away on the horizon as she sailed south, Charleston was stunning from the waterfront. In the distance, a black steeple arose conspicuously above the city, the result of an ill-conceived plan to disguise Saint Michael's church from approaching British troops. Three-story buildings lined the broad, unpaved streets as far as the eye could see. Several of the houses were long and skinny, widening at the rear, with elegant piazzas along one side. Every house, it seemed, had a garden. One of them, perhaps, was her new residence.[1]

The past month had brought about a rapid change in Elizabeth's circumstances. Following the British Army's capture of Charleston in May 1780, her employer, Lieutenant Colonel Nisbet Balfour, had been appointed commandant of the city, and he had sent Elizabeth and a few other servants ahead to ready his quarters for his arrival. As commandant, Balfour would require the house to function not only as a living and working space but also as a place where he could entertain other officers and host dinners. Despite the novelty of her surroundings, Elizabeth's work as a servant in the commandant's household would be familiar enough.[2]

The move to Charleston nevertheless wrought significant changes in Elizabeth's daily life. "I never was harter [heartier] in my Life," she declared to her former landlady in New York, a Mrs. Morsey; "you would Skesley Beleave it if you seed me how I am oltred [altered]." Enthusing about the grandeur of the commandant's residence, Elizabeth continued, "Whe Have the handsomest House and Garden in town you might walk with pleshour all Day." Moreover, there were perks to her new position: "I have three Blak women to do the housework and wash," she reported. Of course, Elizabeth still had plenty of work herself, evidenced by the fact that she drafted her letter at four o'clock in the morning, when she was "amost asleep." Nevertheless, in assuming a supervisory role within the household, especially one over Black, likely enslaved laborers, she experienced a small taste of the power that elite and middling white women throughout the colonies wielded. Even so, her new position had not come without personal sacrifice. She was eager for news of her friends and neighbors in New York; she missed the Morseys' dog. And she had left a man behind in New York. "When you see hem give my Best Respects," she urged Mrs. Morsey, asking that the woman convey Elizabeth's hope that "maybe I may see him agane in New York."[3]

Free laboring women like Elizabeth Anderson experienced the American Revolution, first and foremost, not as a war for independence, but as a negotiation of their continued dependence. Within British garrisons, the sudden influx of officers and soldiers threw urban labor markets into disarray by increasing demands for women's domestic and sexual labor. Military men were eager for both companionship and domestic services. And they were willing to pay—often in precious hard coin, which was increasingly scarce as the war progressed and the value of paper money plummeted. Throughout occupied cities, many laboring women were able to turn these circumstances to their advantage and to procure employment that offered them higher wages or, perhaps, a path out of domestic service altogether.[4]

Military employment was nevertheless precarious. Officers typically shuffled between British posts, and, unlike Nisbet Balfour, they did not always take their servants with them. Indeed, the fact that Balfour moved Elizabeth

Anderson to Charleston suggests that she was very good at her job and had earned his trust, or perhaps that their relationship went beyond the professional. Far more typical was the fate of a Mrs. Clarridge, the British general James Pattison's New York housekeeper, whom he dismissed when his regiment relocated to Philadelphia in 1777 because "there can be no longer any Occasion for her remaining there." Neither did officers always make good on their promised wages. Some women struggled to secure backpay after the army moved on. Five years after she had performed "camp business" for "Gentlemen of the army," Philadelphian Amelia Taylor, for instance, had yet to be paid for her services.[5]

Even so, employment with individual officers offered at least the promise of steady income, access to food and other necessities, as well as useful contacts among the occupying forces—benefits that could temporarily permit poor and working women to survive, and even thrive, in war-torn and resource-scarce garrisons. Practicalities aside, for many young women, the prospect of working for an officer was exciting; it was an opportunity ripe with the promise of adventure, perhaps romance, and a welcome change from the doldrums of domestic service.

Free laboring women are often absent from histories of the American Revolution. With few exceptions, they have received comparatively little attention in histories of laboring people during the war. We know far more about the consequences of the Revolution for white working men—the shoemakers galvanized to civic responsibility, the apprentices who charted alternative paths to independence and manhood, the sailors and privateers who found their fortunes on the seas—than we do of those for working women. And what little we do know of them is often filtered through the perspectives of their employers, gleaned from asides in their diaries or newspaper advertisements or surfacing in wartime anecdotes documented in memoirs and family histories. It is rare to hear these women's voices, nearly impossible to fully comprehend their motivations.[6]

The circumstances of British occupation, however, allow us to better view these women. Working women, both white and Black, occupied a unique position in the social order of garrisoned cities. Female domestic servants existed within the household yet outside of the nuclear family. Working in kitchens and cellars, they came in close contact with quartered officers and soldiers, but they did so outside of the carefully supervised context of polite sociability. Servants were typically responsible for running household errands, chores that required them to traverse the city alone, often without the protection of a guardian. Their tasks made possible a degree of independence that many others lacked in this moment but also enhanced their vulnerability in British garrisons. Dependent on the income of their labor to survive, these women were forced by necessity to perform work that made them more susceptible to predation and assault. Attention from elite men seeking to exploit poor women was nothing new—women throughout the early modern world existed along a continuum of violence—but military rule and the sheer number of men in occupied cities added new weight and danger to these interactions, especially for laboring women who did not have the advantages of social connections with commanding officers. Soldiers emboldened by a combination of liquor, masculine bravado, and martial law made British garrisons potentially dangerous places for women of all races, but even more so for Black women, owing to their position at the bottom of the racial hierarchies that structured the British Atlantic world.[7]

Yet, despite the elevated risk, British occupation also created distinctive labor markets in which working women's services were uniquely in demand, resulting in new opportunities and unprecedented employment mobility. That so many laboring women elected to leverage their labor for military employment and the chance at a better life suggests the high stakes that British occupation created for female laborers, especially domestic servants. Within British garrisons, free women, both Black and white, were able—perhaps for the first time in their lives—to choose where and for whom they would labor, whether it be for an employer, a husband, a British officer or soldier, or the British Army as an institution.

The essence of women's labor, however, frequently did not change with military employment, even with higher wages earned in an officer's household. Many women, though not all, remained servants, although perhaps they found themselves elevated within household hierarchies. Most continued to wash clothes, scrub floors, and cook meals. Others engaged in sexual relations, both consensual and forced, with their military employers, just as they had in revolutionary households. The nature of these sexual relationships varied. Many were prearranged agreements; others developed over time; some were nonconsensual. Some women found love with British soldiers, occasionally formalizing these relationships with marriage. Others found themselves abandoned, perhaps pregnant, when the army moved on.

Whatever the eventual outcome, for the (often free and white) women who chose to abandon their positions in civilian households and pursue employment or sexual relationships with British officers or soldiers—acknowledging that the two often overlapped—it was a strategic, albeit risky, choice. One that many poor, working women hoped would offer a shield against the upheaval of war and, perhaps, would allow them to improve their future prospects. For these women, relationships with military men had the potential to be life-altering, for better or for worse.

NEW DANGERS, NEW RESPONSIBILITIES

Ann Bryan sighed as her employer's call pierced through the thundering cannon echoing overhead. It was nearing four o'clock, making it unlikely that she would be able to return to her bed before she had to begin her morning chores. Scrambling out of bed, she made her way to Phebe Pemberton's chamber, where her employer had been confined with illness the past several weeks. There, Ann found the cannon fire had awakened the whole house. Phebe was attempting to soothe her terrified stepdaughters; seven-year-old Molly was especially frightened. Concerned that cannons were "very near," Phebe directed Ann to climb "a top of the house to see where the fireing was." Making her way to the roof of the Pemberton's Philadelphia townhouse, Ann shivered in the November cold. In the distance, flames danced against the dark sky near Gloucester Point, the glow amplified by the water's reflection. "Sutch alight" was "the river that she thought there must be a grate many houses afire." But, on closer examination, it was clear that the conflagrations were contained to the river. Returning to the warm bedroom, Ann assured the family "that the fire was above the town." To her dismay, she was promptly sent back to the roof for further investigation. Peering into the distance, she counted the burning ships—nine—wanting to be sure that she had the number correct. She did not want to make a third trip.[8]

Writing to her father of the incident later that week, Molly Pemberton chastised him, claiming that "if dady had been at home mebey mamme and sisters would not a been so frighted." Perhaps. But, in James Pemberton's absence, it was Ann Bryan who comforted his wife and daughters, Ann Bryan who braved the Philadelphia cold and the windy rooftop, Ann Bryan who reassured the family of their safety. Ann left no record of her own thoughts about that evening—her fear, her annoyance, or perhaps her commiseration with the other women in the house—yet she was a critical part of the events that unfolded in the Pemberton household that November night.[9]

Like Ann Bryan, servants whom employers deemed trustworthy found themselves shouldering new responsibilities as white residents took steps to ensure their own safety in occupied regions. Elite white families routinely directed servants and enslaved people to inspect incoming visitors or investigate noises that disturbed them in the night. Such demands were not new, but the context of war and occupation was. In occupied regions, troops raised the frequency of these incidents and elevated the potential dangers that they posed. Jane Boon, another Philadelphia servant, was routinely waked by her employer to investigate nighttime noises in the months after the British captured the city. She must have been relieved that these nighttime summons dwindled after an officer was quartered in the house in December 1777. And yet, though Jane probably slept more soundly, the officer and his retinue altered her working environment and increased her daily chores. Men passed in and out of the house at all hours of the day, tracking mud and dirt through the hallways. Orderlies loitered in the kitchen, observing her as she went about her household duties. She shared kitchen space with the major's servants; although the men attempted to be courteous, they undoubtedly disrupted the rhythms and organization of the kitchen. Even if Jane did not serve the officer directly, his presence shaped her daily life and chores. Occupation upended the fundamental sinews of the household—sleeping, eating, cooking, cleaning—in ways that held particular resonance for women who labored as domestic servants.[10]

Because of their constant presence in revolutionary households, female servants throughout garrisoned cities were often the first line of defense and information gathering, especially if their employers were absent or otherwise occupied. Facing down soldiers and officers must have been exceedingly frightening. Such actions could result in threats of violence or retribution by soldiers or the possibility of punishment by disappointed employers. Even worse, servants could face discipline at the hands of a court-martial overseen by occupying forces. A child during the Revolution, Isaac Winslow recalled "the determined courage of an Irish maid servant" who prevented a Hessian officer from quartering himself in the family's rented New York house while his parents were out visiting. Entering the room where young Isaac and his brother Tom were already in bed, the officer ordered the boys "to clear out." Somehow, the unnamed woman managed to maneuver the man out of the bedroom that she shared with the two Winslow boys and then placed herself between the officer and the children, "standing guard at the door until" her employers returned. "She said she would not move for all the Sergeants in the army," Isaac recalled, as he remembered the woman's fierce defense of her room, her young charges, and her employer's house. Like the unnamed Irish woman, many free working women risked their safety and expended their efforts in defense of the elite households where they lived and labored as domestic servants.[11]

Sometimes, they did so involuntarily. Holiday Coggeshall, a free Black servant in Newport, was hauled in front of a court-martial in September 1778 after her employer learned that she had witnessed a British officer break into a cellar and steal a cask of rum. Acutely aware of both her position as a Black woman and the city's military hierarchies, Holiday had resolved not "to speak of it," fearing that to do so "might get me into trouble, an Officer being concerned." Nevertheless, she was unable to escape the incident. In the days after the theft, the officer's servant threatened Holiday, warning that if she "mentioned [the pilfering], I should get myself into trouble, and . . . not be Suffered to walk the streets." She was also under pressure from her employer; a witness at the court-martial implied that Holiday's testimony was given under duress and that her employer had threatened her with imprisonment if she did not corroborate his charges. Holiday's testimony, her employer recognized, could be an effective tool to secure renumeration for his damaged property. Trapped between these competing authorities, Holiday Coggeshall was in an impossible situation, one that she had tried her best to avoid. With limited options and dependent on others for her livelihood, she had little choice but to comply with her employer's demand to testify, fully aware of how doing so could endanger her well-being.[12]

British occupation therefore increased employers' demands of the free women who labored in elite and middling households, frequently exposing them to elevated levels of danger and the potential for violence at the hands of British forces. Yet, despite the new perils that British occupation introduced into the lives of laboring women, it also presented a moment of possibility. Throughout garrisoned cities, troops' demand for women's labor provided working women, if they so desired, with opportunities to change employers, perhaps to secure higher wages, or to otherwise benefit in the resource-scarce city by attaching themselves to individual soldiers and officers. Deserting civilian households in droves, many laboring women calculated that employment among the occupying British offered them the best chance to better their lives.

LABOR MARKETS IN OCCUPIED CITIES

Occupation created new demands for women's labor. Soldiers required cooking, cleaning, laundry, and housekeeping, and they desired sexual partners. The burgeoning market for women's labor in occupied regions allowed working women to exert an element of leverage previously unavailable to them, and many women seized on this unprecedented opportunity to alter their circumstances, choosing the unknown possibilities and uncertain dangers behind British lines over the familiar drudgery of laboring in the households of the urban elite.

FIGURE 11 *The Camp Laundry,* 1782. Prints, Drawings, and Watercolors from the Anne S. K. Brown Military Collection. Brown Digital Repository. Courtesy of Brown University Library, Providence, R.I., https://repository.library.brown.edu/studio/item/bdr:234304/

Women's labor was in high demand within British-occupied cities, where soldiers were eager for both their domestic and sexual services.

In December 1777, for instance, Margaret Taggart, an Irish apprentice in Philadelphia, ran away from her employer with four years remaining on her time. Advertising her escape in the newspaper, the man surmised that she was "lurking about the barracks." In a similar advertisement posted the following week, Ann Powell's employer echoed these sentiments, conjecturing that his servant was "gone with the army, as she was very fond of soldiers." Perhaps these women, like Nanny, a Boston servant, carefully planned their escape. Feigning illness, Nanny quietly removed her clothing and possessions from the house where she worked. Lulling her employers into a false sense of complacency, three days later she "appeared below stairs in perfect health" and "apparently contented"—until she slipped away later that week and "without provocation and without notice she disappeared."[13]

Typically, when domestic servants or cooks desired new employment, they applied to elite and middling women that they knew to be in need of staff. On occasion, established servants applied to their employer on behalf of their friends. If the initial meeting went well, the potential employer would write to the woman's current employer for a character reference. As *Poor Will's Almanack* cautioned readers in 1778, in regard to servants, "the fewer the better. Change is not good, therefore chuse well, and the rather because of your children . . . [for] if they [servants] are idle, wanton, ill examples, children are in great danger of being perverted. Let them therefore be sober, and such as are well recommended." Unless bound by indenture, working women had a certain element of choice in selecting and negotiating the conditions of their hire. Nevertheless, elite women shared social networks and class interests that could hinder working women's efforts to change employers. They might, for instance, refuse to hire a new servant until the former employer had found a replacement. As one Philadelphia woman protested after being accused of stealing another woman's cook, she abided by "an established Maxim . . . never to give the least Encouragement to Servants to leave a Place they were in," and, indeed, she had urged the cook "not to leave [her current employer] unprovided."[14]

Soldiers had no such compunction. "Wanted to live with two single gentlemen, YOUNG WOMAN to act in the capacity of housekeeper, and who can occasionally put her hand to any thing. Extravagant wages will be given, and no character required," a November 1777 notice advertised in occupied Philadelphia. Laden with sexual overtones, the advertisement illustrates the dual comforts that many soldiers sought from their female servants. After months on campaign, military men were eager for female companionship and labor—and they were willing to pay.[15]

WAnted to live with two ſingle gentlemen, a YOUNG WOMAN to act in the capacity of houſekeeper, and who can occaſionally put her hand to any thing. Extravagant wages will be given, and no character required. Any young woman who chooſes to offer, may be farther informed at the bar of the City Tavern.

FIGURE 12 "Wanted to Live with Two Single Gentlemen," *Pennsylvania Evening Post* (Philadelphia), Nov. 1, 1777, 527

This advertisement for a housekeeper in occupied Philadelphia showcases both the demand for women's domestic labor and the overtly sexual services that some men desired.

For many women, the decision to leave service positions was motivated by a combination of financial expediency and a desire to better their situations. The conditions of military occupation facilitated these shifts. Within occupied cities, absent male heads of household and white women's augmented wartime responsibilities meant that female servants faced less supervision at the same moment that a sudden influx of troops increased both the demand for and the value of their labors, both domestic and sexual. Recognizing the opportunities available to them in this moment, many laboring women seized on British occupation to alter or escape their circumstances. Others, recognizing the increased demand for their labor, demanded higher wages. "All the poor women here are rich in imagination, so that it was with difficulty one could be procured at any rate," one Pennsylvania man groused. In September 1778, nearly three months after the British evacuated Philadelphia, Elizabeth Drinker observed the drastic reduction in the availability of servants; many of them had departed the city alongside the British. The Drinkers had been "reduc'd from 5 Servants to one," and many other families fared similarly. "Good Servants are hard to be had," she despaired; "such a time was never known here, I beleive [*sic*] in that respect."[16]

One of the servants who left the Drinker household in favor of military employment was an Irishwoman named Ann Kelly. The British Army's capture of Philadelphia in the fall of 1777 coincided with Ann's two-year anniversary of working in the Drinker household. Recently arrived from Ireland, she was likely an indentured servant and was probably bound to the Drinkers for four years, the standard indenture during the revolutionary period. British occupation, however, presented Ann with an unexpected exit.[17]

For Ann Kelly, like many young women who resided in urban ports, the arrival of the British Army—for all of the potential dangers that it brought—could also portend an exciting change. The British Army intentionally recruited unmarried men; contemporary estimates suggest that five out of six soldiers in the British Army were single. Moreover, army regulations restricted the number of women who traveled with each regiment. The sudden influx of dashing young soldiers eager for female companionship offered a thrilling alternative to daily chores, tasks which had likely only increased in the weeks and months prior to the army's arrival to compensate for men's wartime absences. Soldiers brought the potential for entertainment, adventure, romance, or, at minimum, a welcome distraction from the hardship of wartime life. Perhaps Ann was simply looking for fun and flirtation. Perhaps she had family or acquaintances among the Irish troops, or hoped to ask after loved ones she had left behind in Ireland. Or perhaps she simply saw an opportunity to seize a different life. Eager to socialize with the soldiers, but likely forbidden to venture out into the city, Ann took to loitering by the front gate of the Drinkers' Front Street home, where she hoped to catch the attention of one of the many soldiers who were quartered in the neighborhood. Her actions exasperated her employer, who complained to her husband, "I have not been Able to keep [Ann] from the Gate . . . since the troops came in."[18]

Within two months, Ann had connected with a young officer whom her employer believed to be a Captain John Tape. One evening in late November 1777, Captain Tape hopped the Drinkers' fence to meet Ann in the Drinkers' "little House," a two-story outbuilding that contained the kitchen, washhouse, and servants' quarters and was connected to the main house by a narrow passage. Of course, soldiers regularly snuck into civilian households in search of food, drink, and other valuables. But Tape was a high-ranking officer; it is unlikely that theft was his aim. Moreover, given his status, it is also unlikely that it was a random action—if he wished to enter a house, he could simply knock on the door. His secretive arrival under the cover of darkness suggests that the meeting was prearranged. Perhaps Ann had agreed to go work for the captain and the two were discussing business arrangements. Yet it was also nine o'clock in the evening. And the officer was drunk.[19]

It is certainly possible that Ann Kelly and John Tape were in love; yet the vast difference in their statuses made any long-term relationship unlikely. The gulf between them also raises questions about how their relationship began. Clearly, Ann was not attending the balls and other social functions that British officers hosted for the city's elite. More likely, they encountered one another by the Drinkers' front gate. They might have struck up a conversation and become friendly, but for an officer of Tape's stature to befriend an indentured servant suggests that he had sex, rather than marriage, in mind.

Brothels were, of course, a regular feature of early modern cities. One Scottish officer praised Sal Leak for running her Newport "house of Pleasure . . . in a more decent and reputable manner than common." And, in Boston's red-light district—aptly located in a neighborhood near Mount Whoredom—John Andrews regaled a friend with the antics of fifteen British officers who "din'd at a housc . . . noted for their hospitality and kindness to Strangers, in admitting all comers to the *B–d* and *board*." "Towards eveng they [the officers] committed all manner of enormous indecencies, by exposing their anteriors, as well as their posteriors, at the open windows and doors, to the full view of people either men or women, that happen'd to pass by, with a great deal of opprobious language," he reported. Perhaps Captain Tape was seeking a less boisterous atmosphere, or perhaps he was in financial straits and could not afford the prices at Philadelphia's establishments. Or perhaps he sought the security of a stable relationship, one that, preferably, lowered his risk of contracting venereal disease and that allowed him to gain a housekeeper as part of the bargain. Officers' desires for such arrangements created a window of opportunity for women like Ann Kelly; indeed, Ann's choice to align herself with a high-ranking officer was also strategic. According to her employer she had numerous soldiers competing for her attentions, but Captain Tape promised a level of financial and material security unattainable among enlisted men.[20]

Throughout occupied cities, maids and other laboring women, perhaps out of desperation, perhaps out of desire, or perhaps out of love, engaged in sexual relations with soldiers, many of whom were single and eager for female companionship, owing to limitations on the number of women allowed in each regiment. In one notable instance in Newport in August 1779, a female civilian and a Hessian private stationed on guard duty were "caught in the act by an officer who visited the watch." More common, perhaps, was the situation of an unnamed Philadelphia maid in the house where Hessian lieutenant Heinrich Carl Philipp von Feilitzsch was billeted. The woman routinely entertained sailors and other men in her quarters. She "was not very pretty," the officer observed, "but she had lovers enough." The woman might simply have been participating in what historian Clare A. Lyons has identified as Philadelphia's "pleasure culture," but such relationships might also have been a means of securing money, food, or other favors amid the scarcity of the occupied city. For working women in British garrisons, relationships with soldiers—however brief—could provide real security in the uncertain months to come.[21]

Whatever Ann Kelly and Captain John Tape's motivations, their efforts at discretion failed. Another maid spied the pair speaking in the yard and alerted the household to the officer's presence. For Ann to invite an officer into the household without permission would have been a shocking challenge to her employer's household governance; conversely, if Tape was an unwanted visitor, Ann—and the rest of the household—were potentially in danger. By the time Mary Sandwith, the sister of Ann's employer, grabbed a candle and made her way to the yard to investigate, Ann and John had already gone into and then emerged from the "little House," suggesting that their encounter—sexual, business, or otherwise—was fairly brief and had been accomplished by the time that Mary confronted them. Mary demanded to know the officer's name. Irritated, Captain Tape retorted, "Whats that to you[?]" before recovering his manners and declaring that "he had mistaken the House."[22]

And yet, he refused to leave, following the women back to the kitchen. When the family, aided by a male neighbor, tried to oust the officer, John Tape responded by swearing at the man and shaking his sword at him. With a surprising deftness, the neighbor "twisted it [the sword] out of his Hands and Collor'd him," and Mary Sandwith grabbed the weapon and "lock'd it up in the draw in the parlor." More men arrived to help the Drinkers remove the unwelcome guest. Yet Captain Tape was persistent. He refused to leave without his sword, a marker not only of his military rank but also his gentlemanly status. To relinquish the sword, as generals did on surrender, would have been humiliating. An indication of his embarrassment, Captain Tape repeatedly insisted to the men that he was aware of the family's Quakerism (maybe Ann had told him) and that "he gave up his Sword on that account out of pure good natur[e]," rather than having it wrested from his grasp. The men escorted the captain to the door and returned his sword, expecting him to depart. Instead, he began wandering drunkenly throughout the house, cursing and pacing back and forth in front of the parlor where the Drinkers had locked themselves away, demanding that the family "let him in to drink a Glass of Wine." Perhaps he simply wanted a drink. Or maybe, if Captain Tape hoped to hire Ann for himself, he hoped that shared libations would permit him to broach the topic of Ann's employment. Unsuccessful in his efforts to obtain admittance to the parlor, Tape continued wandering throughout the house before eventually making his way into the alley. A servant locked the door behind him, but, ever persistent, Captain Tape continued to pound on the door until male neighbors finally convinced him to leave. Relieved,

Elizabeth Drinker secured the house and "had all the back doors boulted, the Gate and Front Door lock'd."[23]

Ann's whereabouts during this fracas are unclear. Perhaps, as the Drinkers cowered in the parlor, Ann was in her room, gathering clothing and essentials. For she was, as subsequent events would make apparent, determined to leave with Captain Tape. Less than ten minutes after the officer had been ejected from the residence and the doors bolted behind him, the man was back in the kitchen. Someone—Ann—must have readmitted him. But why? Ann could have conceivably played along with the captain's insistence that he had mistaken the house, claimed that the officer had surprised her in the yard. But, whether it was money, employment, sex, love, or some combination thereof, John Tape offered Ann something that she wanted. When Elizabeth Drinker and her children emerged from the parlor later that evening, they found "the Fellow was gone, and Ann with him."[24]

For Elizabeth Drinker and her family, the incident was alarming. Her "Children was never so frightend," and, even after she got them to sleep, Elizabeth could not relax; she stayed up past one o'clock in the morning recounting the incident in her diary. In the morning, she had not yet regained her equilibrium. "I have not yet got over last Nights fright," she confessed, "have been in a flutter all day." Invasion and violence were jarring, but Elizabeth also felt that she had been wronged. In conversation with another British officer the following month, she recounted "how I had been frightend by the Officer, that thief like stole my servant girl over the Fence." Placing the blame solely on Captain Tape, Elizabeth overlooked Ann's active role in that evening's events. Instead, positioning Ann as pilfered household property, like a candlestick or silver plate, Elizabeth reframed the incident as an attack on her household and positioned herself as the victim. In her eyes, that evening was not about a servant woman's bid for a better life; rather, it exemplified how British occupation had disrupted her household and endangered her family.[25]

But, for Ann Kelly, that November night held a very different meaning; it altered the trajectory of her life and offered her a means out of her indenture. Captain Tape was seemingly unwilling, or unable, to purchase her freedom. Perhaps he had promised Ann that he would buy her contract, but a combination of time, the captain's belief in his anonymity, or even outright deceit resulted in the debt remaining unpaid. Shortly after Ann's flight, she returned to Front Street and asked the stable boy to smuggle her some "Buckels etc." Unsuccessful, Ann nevertheless might have had some money stocked away, or perhaps she secured goods, legitimately or otherwise, that she pawned for cash—a risky endeavor given General William Howe's strictures against reselling stolen goods. Somehow, she amassed some money and returned the following day, "desereing to know" the Drinkers' price "for hir time" and promising that "she would bring the money in a minuit." Whether genuine or feigned, Ann's confidence, perhaps bolstered by her connections to the city's military authorities, revealed a sense of self-possession and a belief that she was beyond the Drinkers' reach. Unphased by threats of the workhouse, Ann admonished her former employers, "If you talk so, you shall neither have me nor the Money." Ann Kelly clearly felt that she had embarked on a new path: here was a woman taking care of business, tying up loose ends, and honoring her commitments before moving on to a better life. Ann's assurances were nevertheless premature. Disheartened by the twenty-pound sum that the Drinkers requested, she never returned to pay the balance of her contract.[26]

Ann Kelly's fate remains unknown. She might have continued as housekeeper to Captain Tape for the remainder of the occupation; perhaps she evacuated with him when the army moved on. But, two months after her flight, in early January 1778, Elizabeth Drinker happened to encounter Captain John Tape on the street. "If thee dont very soon pay me for my Servants time," she threatened, she would report his behavior to the "officers quarterd among Numbers of my acquaintance." Taken aback and "confus'd," Captain Tape insisted, "I han't got your Servant." His supposed ignorance about Ann's whereabouts might have been feigned, a strategy to protect her (or his pocketbook). Or, perhaps, Tape spoke the truth: the pair had parted ways. If this was the case, the experiences of other women suggest that hardship was the norm. Boston servant Betty Smith, for instance, fled domestic service to reside among the British Army. "No sooner was the 29th Regiment encamp'd upon the common but miss Betty took herself among them," Anna Green Winslow, the twelve-year-old daughter of Betty's employer, reported to her mother. While residing with the regiment, Betty was caught stealing; she was imprisoned and sentenced to public whipping. She attempted to rejoin the regiment, but she was turned away and briefly confined to the workhouse before she managed to escape. Shortly thereafter, Betty was reimprisoned for theft and engaged in a conspiracy to set the jail on fire. The women of the Boston jail, including soldiers' wives imprisoned for theft, were, according to a man confined there in 1775, "some of the Vilest Women . . . ; they acted such scenes as was shocking to Nature, and used Language, horrible to hear; as if it came from the very Suburbs of Hell." Perhaps Betty Smith was among them.[27]

For women like Betty Smith and Ann Kelly, the new labor markets and employment opportunities behind British lines combined with the broader wartime disruption of household governance in ways that offered them a moment of escape. It was not independence; it was almost always dependent on a soldier. Nor was it always successful. Indeed, many women faced hardship and deprivation behind British lines. Still, for women who labored as domestic servants, British occupation created conditions that could set them on the path toward a new life. Their flight, however, had consequences not only for themselves but also for the households that they had abandoned.

In occupied regions, the improved labor markets and elevated demand for working women's domestic services had ripple effects within civilian households, many of which suddenly found themselves at a loss for servants. For elite and middling Americans, these labor shortages were distressing, not only for how they disrupted household routines, but, more broadly, for how they assaulted their carefully cultivated sense of gentility by disrupting the homes, goods, and labor necessary to perform that status.

Just north of Philadelphia, Dr. Richard Farmar and his wife, Eliza, concocted a plan to safeguard their property as the British marched on Philadelphia in September 1777. The family remained in the house, a decision that undoubtedly saved their residence in the months that followed, but they endured constant plunder. Troops fired at one another outside the house. Soldiers pulled down their fences and destroyed their orchard. "And to compleat all," Eliza complained, the family was unable to retain a maid. As she wrote to her nephew, twice a week, "in the depth of winter . . . I was obliged to get up before day and dress by candle while Mr Farmar . . . got the chaise ready to go to Market otherwise we could get no Victuals." New Yorker Hannah Bancker would have empathized with the Farmars' situation. "I am still without a servant and have been so this day five weeks," she complained in May 1783. "I have been half distracted and am worn to a skeleton with fatigue and sorrow," she informed her husband, as she grumbled about the inattention of her sister, who had not "offer[ed] me the least assistance tho' she has got two servants." "See what a poor forsaken creature I am become," she moaned; "I am at present so bewildered that I seem more dead than alive."[28]

Writing from Lancaster, Pennsylvania, where he and his wife had fled from British-occupied Philadelphia and where servants were similarly scarce, Christopher Marshall encapsulated the conundrum that many families faced. "I and my wife . . . have our choice," he explained, "that is, either to do the necessaries or to leave them undone, as there is no person, white or black, male or female, old or young, to be had at any price, as we can find." "I must say that the little that I do really tires and fatigues me," he admitted. Acknowledging that his wife carried most of the burden of additional housework, at times rising before four in the morning to complete her expanded chores, Christopher also assumed new tasks around the house and the farm. Nevertheless, he confessed, it was "discouraging to have no help about us," especially for his wife. More so than the work, however, Christopher lamented how the lack of servants had altered his wife's emotional state and the atmosphere of the household, particularly after her cherished maidservant, Poll, ran off to Yorktown in May 1778. "Our house wears a quite different face when Miss Poll is in it," Christopher mused. Although he himself disliked the woman—at one point criticizing her as "a very ordinary lazy hussey"—he recognized that the maid's "presence gives pleasure to her mistress, this gives joy to all in the house, so that, in fact, [Poll] is the cause of peace or uneasiness in our house."[29]

As such accounts suggest, servants throughout occupied regions seized on the opportunities presented by wartime labor markets, and their actions had the potential to reverberate through civilian households in ways that were challenging for employers, both physically and emotionally. The loss of a valued servant and the labor that they provided could make life uncomfortable. But many employers also took these losses personally. "I do not know a greater, next to nearest kin, then the loss of a good and faithful Servant, one who makes ones interest their own, and to whom we can unbosom our selves," Massachusetts loyalist Margaret Mascarene Hutchinson reflected, declaring, "Such a servant is amoung the blessings of life."[30]

Even when white families managed to retain servants or successfully hire new ones, these arrangements did not always go as planned. Philadelphian Elizabeth Drinker struggled to replace the servants that she had lost during the British occupation of the city. In December 1778, she finally hired Betsy Stedman, her neighbor's former maid. To Elizabeth's shock, immediately after moving in, Betsy began hosting visitors and even "invited" one of them "to lodge with her, without asking leave." Perturbed by Betsy's presumptuous assertion of household space, Elizabeth resigned herself to the situation; she had few alternatives. "Times are much changed, and Maids are become mistresses," she observed with dismay.[31]

Gesturing to the disrupted dynamics of her own household, Elizabeth Drinker's comments nevertheless reveal an important factor that shaped many laboring women's wartime decisions: a relationship with a soldier offered a path out of domestic service and had the potential to make former servants mistresses of their own households. But, of course, not all relationships ended in marriage. In some instances, women became mistresses, rather than household mistresses.

SEXUAL RELATIONSHIPS WITH SOLDIERS

Throughout occupied cities, officers and soldiers from both the British and Hessian armies pursued romantic and sexual relationships with civilian women across the social spectrum. Of course, these relationships varied according to class, race, and age. Generally speaking, however, officers were more likely to socialize with the city's elite; common soldiers were more likely to engage with laboring populations. But, in occupied regions, just as in civil society, relationships between British troops and female civilians often blurred these lines, encompassing a wide variety of relations that ranged from employment to sex, from flirtation to marriage. Officers regarded elite white women as their social equals and companions; occasionally, they formed lasting unions. Yet many men also pursued sexual relations with domestic servants and enslaved women, encounters that often occurred within the context of employment or mutually agreed upon terms of sexual or domestic labor in exchange for protection, shelter, and rations. Alternatively, officers might pay for women's company, either in brothels or by renting enslaved women from their enslavers. Nor were officers the only soldiers who sought comfort and pleasure in women's company. Enlisted men, too, found love, pleasure, and companionship, typically with women who tended to labor for a living, whether as seamstresses, washerwomen, or domestic servants in elite households. Through employment, sex, flirtation, marriage, or some combination thereof, urban working women engaged in a variety of relationships with British soldiers and officers that formed a crucial facet of social and sexual relationships in occupied cities.[32]

Writing from Philadelphia in March 1778, Sarah Logan Fisher fretted over the "very bad accounts" circulating the city about "the licentiousness of the English Officers in deluding young Girls." And, certainly, there were duplicitous British soldiers who used deceit to obtain sex. Historian Sylvia Frey found in her study of British soldiers in the American Revolution that it was not uncommon for men to "marr[y] frequently and fraudulently." This was apparently the case for New Yorker Cornelia Bayeux, described by Hessian chaplain Georg C. Coester as "a pleasant young girl," who gave birth in September 1779 to a daughter fathered by a Hessian officer. According to the chaplain, who baptized the child, the officer "caused her downfall with a promise of marriage—nothing new in America, unfortunately."[33]

Such lurid accounts of deceit and seduction made for sensational stories, but, in practice, it was far more common for officers and female civilians to agree to temporary, mutually beneficial arrangements. One observer derisively characterized women who engaged in such relationships as "ammunition wi[ves]." Unlike enlisted men and noncommissioned officers, who required permission from their superiors to marry, commissioned officers had both the freedom and the wealth to form and support attachments with women of all races. Women who agreed to such arrangements were typically from the laboring or enslaved classes; they might be seamstresses or sex workers or maids fleeing domestic service. Informal agreements were nevertheless profoundly unequal, especially as they did not carry the legal protections of marriage and could easily go awry—with the consequences typically falling most harshly on women. The security that such arrangements conferred on women was tenuous, wholly dependent on both the whims and continued survival of the officers they attached themselves to. And, even within the military establishment, some people regarded these arrangements with skepticism. The New York garrison, according to the wife of a British officer, was filled with "libertines, and . . . women of doubtful character."[34]

Many urban working women, both free and enslaved, nevertheless wagered that a relationship with a soldier, especially an officer, had the potential to better their lives. For many of these women, such relationships functioned as a critical strategy of survival amid resource-scarce and war-torn cities. Mary Duché, a woman who lived with Captain James Murray of the Queen's Rangers, was, in the eyes of the regiment, "Captain Murray's girl" and a "kept" woman. Her experiences suggest that, even if poor women found security and protection with British officers, their positions remained precarious. When the Queen's Rangers were ordered on an expedition in March 1778, Mary remained behind in Captain Murray's Philadelphia quarters, and he arranged for her to draw victuals in his absence. Another member of the regiment, Lieutenant Nathaniel Fitzpatrick also stayed in Philadelphia to receive treatment for a "Violent Venereal Disorder." Details vary widely as to what happened next, but, at a minimum, the two flirted and had sex, at least once. Admitting a single sexual encounter, Mary Duché insisted that the two had previously maintained a cordial acquaintance but nothing more. Moreover, she testified, Nathaniel Fitzpatrick had failed to inform her of his condition; she only learned of it when he presented her with medicine after their rendezvous.[35]

In contrast, Ensign Edward Cotter of the Fifth Regiment of Foot recalled that the pair were intimate and that Mary Duché was "Frequently" in Lieutenant Fitzpatrick's rooms, "throwing her arms round his Neck and throwing him upon the bed with her." During the subsequent court-martial, in which Lieutenant Fitzpatrick was charged with "behaving in a Scandalous infamous manner" for having "disorder'd" Captain Murray through their shared relations with Mary Duché, three other officers also claimed to have slept with her, which she denied. Nevertheless, the men were united in their insistence that Mary, in the words of one of them, "enticed" the officers to her bed.[36]

It is possible, of course, that Mary Duché simply enjoyed male companionship; it is also possible that the officers lied, or that one or more of the men forced Mary into nonconsensual sex. Other courts-martial reveal that soldiers raped, murdered, and otherwise abused the women of the army. In late November 1780, Peggy McGuire, whose husband Patrick was in the Fifty-Seventh Regiment of Foot, was dancing and drinking with some other members of the regiment in their New York barrack. She was, according to witnesses, "much in Liquor" and stepped outside for a moment; two men followed her and attacked her in a nearby field, pulling her shoes from her feet, her handkerchief from her neck, and tearing "her Bed Gown open at the Breast" before her husband heard her cries and intervened.[37]

Most likely, however, is that Mary Duché was hedging her bets. Her circumstances suggest that she was a poor woman and that she had endured hardship during the war. In Captain James Murray, she found protection and security. At a minimum, he provided steady rations, a warm bed, and shelter in the barracks. Aware of the unpredictability of war and the fragility of a soldier's life, Mary's supposed flirtations (or otherwise) with the other officers—and notably, they were all officers—might have reflected a strategic effort to secure a landing pad if Captain Murray were to die or part ways with her. She sought to cultivate relationships with other officers in the captain's absence. Ensign Edward Cotter recalled that while the Queen's Rangers were on expedition, Mary often asked him to dine with her, as she was lonely and "wish'd that he . . . would come and keep her Company." More pointedly, Lieutenant William Atkinson of the Queen's Rangers accused Mary of "Inveigl[ing] Lieutenant Fitzpatrick knowing or at least hearing that he was then indisposed with a Venereal Complaint, to lay with her, and that she had taken the same pains with several others."[38]

Competing testimonies make it impossible to discern just how aware Mary Duché was of Nathaniel Fitzpatrick's condition when she slept with him. But if, as Atkinson suggested, she did so with the full knowledge that she was exposing herself to venereal disease, her actions take on a valence of desperation. In fact, in the days after Captain Murray ended their arrangement, Mary Duché supposedly slept with at least two other officers and moved in with another for a few days. None of those relationships lasted—in

FIGURE 13 Thomas Rowlandson, *English Barracks*, 1788. Prints, Drawings, and Watercolors from the Anne S. K. Brown Military Collection. Brown Digital Repository. Courtesy of Brown University Library, Providence, R.I., https://repository.library.brown.edu/studio/item/bdr:248561/

Women were an integral component of military life, including within the barracks, which were home to women and children as well as British troops.

part because the men learned of her connection with Lieutenant Fitzpatrick. Her options dwindling, while the court-martial was ongoing, Mary, twice over the course of a day, privately assured the provost martial that she had taken medicine and was "Cured" of her disorder. Such indelicate conversation could conceivably have emerged from the day's proceedings, yet Mary's persistent reassurances suggest that the two were discussing matters of a more personal nature. Indeed, recognizing just how fully Mary was grasping for a lifeboat, her protested ignorance about Lieutenant Fitzpatrick's condition and her denial of her alleged promiscuity—which might have been true—suggests a strategic staging of her own sexual virtue that she hoped might attract the interest of another officer. Such a relationship was essential to her survival and comfort within the occupied city, offering protection, lodging, and access to steady rations.[39]

Indeed, other women's experiences illustrate that prospects could be grim for women abandoned by soldiers, especially if they were pregnant. Philadelphian Suckey Johnson "Cohabited with a british officer and was left with Child." In April 1779, Johnson left her three-month-old child with Mary Thomas, "a Poor woman in Sugar Alley," and went off to New York, presumably to follow the army and find the father of her child. Such circumstances were not uncommon. In June 1777, loyalist Nicholas Cresswell and a friend stumbled across a woman in labor on the streets of occupied New York. Alone and desperate, the unnamed woman said that she was a soldier's widow and begged for assistance. The two men helped her into a neighboring house, despite the obvious displeasure of the owner, who "declar[ed] that he would not keep a lying-in Hospital for our W[hore]s." The woman might have been a widow, or, possibly, like Philadelphia seamstress Margaret Locke, she adopted the moniker after being abandoned by the father of her child as a means of claiming respectability and accessing systems of support for soldiers' widows. Many poor and laboring women with no families to advocate on their behalf and no material wealth to incentivize marriage found themselves abandoned, and perhaps pregnant, when the army moved on. As one Philadelphia woman warned, "These people have a wandering foot, that you cannot prosecute them under our laws when your daughters go too far with them. But bear in mind—to your own disgrace—that you must accept what they leave behind." Of course, such relationships were not limited to British soldiers. Writing from Reading, Massachusetts, in 1777, Sarah Bancroft regaled her husband with news of the numerous pregnancies that local women had sworn upon Continental soldiers and militiamen. "We wish you much joy upon the success of the soldiery in the service of her Majesty Venus, by which means the loss of men necessarily attending war is like abundantly to be compensated," she laughed.[40]

But, for the many women who had leveraged their sexuality in an effort to find security amid the precariousness of war, abandonment was no laughing matter. When they gambled their livelihoods on the tenuous promise of a better life with British soldiers, laboring women effectively severed their ties from the households and the associated social institutions that traditionally provided unmarried women with the means, or at least the possibility, to try to hold the fathers of their children accountable. There was, of course, no guarantee that these systems would work to a woman's benefit, or that employers would retain unwed mothers; indentured servants might even have their time extended if they became pregnant. But, broadly speaking, in their previous situations, many laboring women had had networks of social connections and access to legal or financial recourse that might have aided them with out-of-wedlock pregnancies. When soldiers abandoned them, especially if they did so after women had followed them to a different city, however, they often had to make their way on their own.[41]

Thus, although a relationship with a soldier could bring very real, if temporary, advantages for poor women, it also had the potential to introduce even more, life-altering instability into their lives. For no group was this more true than the Black women who risked not only their lives and safety but their freedom on relationships with British officers.

BLACK WOMEN AND BRITISH SOLDIERS

For Black women, especially enslaved refugees behind British lines, the protection of a British officer or soldier could not only offer security against the hardship of war, it could aid them in their quest for liberty. Such relationships were nevertheless precarious. Behind British lines, Black people continued to face racial discrimination and violence. Kidnapping and deceit were not uncommon. Soldiers might force women; they might break their promises of protection or freedom—and if they did so, Black women had little recourse to hold them to their word. Still, many Black women, whether by choice or circumstance, engaged in sexual relationships with British troops for reasons that overlapped with those of free white laboring women but that also diverged in important ways.

Relationships between Black women and British soldiers are less well-documented than those of white women, although certainly they occurred. Many enslaved women, such as thirty-two-year-old Rachel and nineteen-year-old Peg, absconded to British camps in pursuit of freedom. Although their enslaver hoped that the women would "weary of their acquaintance in the British army," he was, perhaps, overoptimistic. Behind British lines, historian Debra L. Newman asserts in her study of revolutionary Philadelphia, Black women led "an active social existence." Black women's presence in courts-martial and other testimonies, often as silent background actors, attests to their pervasive and visible presence in the military barracks. In fact, when Mary Basford, Mary Groves, and Elizabeth Jackson, three free Black New Yorkers, were accused of murdering another inhabitant by pushing him out of a window, the witnesses that they called to their defense were not their neighbors—who were eager to accuse the three women—but, rather, two soldiers, whose testimonies successfully acquitted them. The soldiers' willingness to appear in court on the women's behalf suggests that at least one of the women probably had a relationship with these men, although the nature of that relationship is unclear.[42]

Tantalizing archival glimpses of Black women's relationships with British officers and soldiers gesture to the pervasiveness of these arrangements, albeit with varying levels of consent. One white Charleston man asserted that "it was not uncommon for Persons to let out the Negro Girls to British Officers." These women, who had little choice in the matter, probably served as both housekeepers and sexual partners. Dinah, an enslaved New Yorker, might have been one of these women. In late December 1779, she absconded from Captain Paul Dayrell, who retired from the Fifty-Second Regiment in 1778 and settled in Brooklyn. Taking her infant son Jack with her, Dinah was "supposed to be gone on board the fleet" departing for Charleston, South Carolina, that same week. In stark contrast from the usually drab clothing of enslaved people, Dinah wore a "white cloth cloak with ermine round it."[43]

Ermine was expensive; white cloth was easily sullied—it was a cloak made for leisure and fashion, not for work. How then did Dinah come to have it? Possibly she scrimped and saved, investing her life earnings in a luxurious and portable form of wealth. She might have stolen the cloak, or perhaps she purchased it secondhand. It was common, Hessian captain Johann Ewald acknowledged, for enslaved refugees to clothe themselves in items "plundered [from] the wardrobes of their masters and mistresses." Alternatively, the cloak might also have been a gift from Captain Dayrell. British officers frequently engaged Black women as housekeepers and sexual companions, and, to slaveholders' ire, officers' Black consorts sometimes donned "the richest silks" and other fashionable attire. Nevertheless, a white ermine cloak would certainly draw attention, especially in a garrison where Black people, both enslaved and free, were regularly stopped by suspicious white inhabitants who suspected that they might be wearing pilfered clothes. Dinah's decision to wear the white ermine cloak at a moment when camouflage and discretion were of vital importance indicates, then, that it might have been something she wore regularly and therefore would not arouse suspicion, a suggestive, if speculative, indication of the nature of her relationship with Dayrell, who perhaps not only gifted her the cloak but might also have been the father of her child.[44]

Similarly, at five-foot-ten, light-skinned, and with a smooth, "likely face," Kate, a Black woman enslaved in New York, might have been what contemporaries termed a "fancy girl"—that is, a beautiful woman who often served as a sexual or social companion for her white male enslaver. Kate was fashionable. She styled "her hair very high and straight up, over a roll, with a great deal of pomatum" and owned "a variety of clothes," including a gorgeously detailed

"Callico Short Gown, with the figure of horses, carriages, and soldiers, in blue and yellow colours, particularly a row of the latter round the bottom of it." It was an unusual item of clothing, the martial details gesturing to her affiliation with the army and, perhaps also, her relationship with Ensign Richard Boyle, a "Gent[leman]" officer in the first battalion of General Oliver DeLancey's Provincial Corps.[45]

Whether Kate sought to catch the officer's eye, or whether Richard Boyle spied Kate in the garrison and initiated or compelled her into a relationship with him, the two formed an attachment, seemingly without the consent of Kate's enslaver. Gesturing to the intimacy of the pair's relationship, Kate assumed the officer's last name, introducing herself throughout the garrison as Kate Boyle. As the "ammunition wife" of an officer, Kate secured protection, received rations, and became part of the garrison's military community. She probably attended social events alongside Ensign Boyle. Beautiful, fashionable, and gregarious—her enslaver described her as "a great talker" with "a shrill voice," suggesting that she did not exhibit the social deference expected of enslaved laborers—Kate likely thrived in the garrison's active social scene. And, ultimately, Kate's relationship with Richard Boyle perhaps allowed her to escape bondage. In September 1783, the same week that the British provincial troops evacuated New York and embarked for Nova Scotia, Kate seized her freedom, possibly accompanying Richard Boyle to Nova Scotia, where in 1784 he received a grant of 550 acres in the parish of Woodstock in return for his service to the crown.[46]

For women like Kate, relationships with British soldiers were not only a means of obtaining shelter, sustenance, and social capital, they could also aid their efforts to secure freedom. But such arrangements were nevertheless risky, requiring women to trust that British soldiers would uphold their promises of protection. Inevitably, some men did not. In the New York garrison, Dorcas hired herself to a British officer, ostensibly "to wait on his Wife to London," but was instead shipped to Jamaica where she was "Sold—a Slave for Life." But, even for women who managed to avoid such overt duplicity, the simple fact of having fraternized with occupying forces could have lasting consequences on their reputations and future prospects. Whether she chose to remain behind, or was abandoned, Phillis, a Black Philadelphia woman, the *Pennsylvania Packet* reported in 1779, supposedly "staid in the city while the enemy possessed it, [and] had been seen too frequently in the company with British officers to be allowed to visit ladies of fair characters."[47]

For Black women, relationships with British troops held great risk but also great potential. Whether by choice or by force, Black women entered into these arrangements knowing that their relationships with British soldiers would never receive formal recognition, that any protections they earned would be at officers' discretion. Marriage was not a strategy that Black women could use to shore up their status in British garrisons. But that was not the case for white women of the laboring classes, whose relationships with British soldiers could very well result in matrimony. For these women, marriage endowed them with both legal protections and military benefits, vaulting them out of domestic service and into positions as soldiers' wives.

MARRIAGE TO A SOLDIER

The transactive, temporary relationships that working women, both Black and white, had with military men stand in stark contrast to those of white women domestic servants who married British soldiers in occupied cities. Unions between civilian women and British soldiers were, in the words of one historian, frequently "pragmatic" decisions between men and women of similar statuses that drew these women into military communities. Unlike officers, who sought temporary relationships, enlisted men were of working women's own class and thus viable candidates for marriage. For these men, marriage secured access to unpaid domestic and sexual labor at a time when both were precarious and expensive. For white women who worked as domestic servants, the disruption to household systems of oversight and the presence of large numbers of single men eager for their labor and companionship meant that British occupation presented them with both labor and marital opportunities that differed from peacetime. Along with the legal protections inherent in marriage, marrying into the military community also integrated women into established systems of rations, work, billets, and provisioning. Women's place within these systems was inconsistent and wholly dependent on the goodwill of commanding officers. Still, marriage to a soldier offered the promise of legal and financial security that could be life-changing for women accustomed to working for wages in the households of the urban elite.[48]

For many working women in occupied regions, marriage to a soldier offered companionship, perhaps love, and a path to personal and financial security. Many women eagerly seized the opportunity to escape domestic service and to embark on a new chapter. Jane, a Philadelphia servant who worked for the loyalist Stedman family, fell in love with the servant of a British officer during the occupation of the city from 1777–1778. Having spent five years in the army, the man had managed to save some money and was probably eager to settle down. Planning for the future, he and Jane envisioned a shared, self-sufficient life: he would leave the army, she would quit domestic service, and, together, they would "keep a Shop." Marriage offered Jane a start on a new life and improved her social position. Jane kept the arrangement secret from the Stedmans, suggesting that she did not intend to ask their permission but simply planned to leave when an opportunity presented itself.[49]

Servant women throughout British garrisons made similar plans. Two of Sarah Redwood Fisher's maids left her service to be married in February 1778. One of these women, whom Philadelphia diarist Sarah Logan Fisher referred to only as the daughter of her servant Betty, eloped without telling her mother. Three months later, Betty's daughter evacuated with the British Army to New York, leaving behind her family and her life as a domestic servant.[50]

There were also many couples among the troops who regarded themselves as married, even without a formal ceremony. Rhode Islander Barbara Rheider Dietzel, for instance, gave birth to her son Andreas in April 1780. The father was Lieutenant Dietzel of the Hessian Artillery. The couple, who also had an older son, considered themselves wed. As Barbara explained to the regimental chaplain who performed the baptism, "she calls herself Mrs. Dietzel, because . . . her marriage was made in Heaven." Such informal marital arrangements were common in colonial North America, especially among the laboring classes. Unwilling to sanction what the Dieztels considered to be a legitimate marriage, the clergyman was predictably skeptical of the couple's arrangement—feelings he made clear in a short couplet that he inscribed underneath Andreas's baptismal entry: "Take care and do not by fooled / By a man who promises to marry you."[51]

Reproving the Dieztels from a moral standpoint, the clergyman's skepticism nevertheless underscores an important point: formal marriage brought legal benefits and securities that could protect civilian women who engaged in relationships with soldiers. Soldiers' wives were quartered under the same guidelines as soldiers, whether in barracks, public buildings, or private homes. They earned wages while on the march or when they served as nurses in military hospitals, earning six pence per day, which was approximately 75 percent of a private's pay. They were also eligible for military rations, drawing about half the food allotted to their husbands. Still, such benefits were tenuous. When supplies were scarce, military women and children were often among the first groups to have their rations reduced; when troops were in garrison, women were frequently denied provisions, and formal opportunities to earn wages were scarce. Many women compensated by doing laundry and performing camp services for men in their husbands' regiments.[52]

The benefits allotted soldiers' wives were also highly contingent on the commanding officers who oversaw them. For instance, in the British garrison at Halifax during the Revolution, soldiers' families received smallpox inoculations, bedding, and firewood, and there was even a garrison school for the children. But not all commanding officers were so generous. To the contrary, many in the British high command were skeptical of soldiers' wives, viewing them as a source of chaos that could endanger the fitness of their troops and that introduced disobedience into the ranks. Indeed, for this reason, many commanding officers discouraged men from forming attachments and endeavored to limit the number of women who traveled with their regiments, especially women with children. Indicative of these suspicions is the example of Carolina Wetzler, a German woman who married Conrad Sackert of the Hessian Jaegers in Pennsylvania in September 1777. "Six days later," Georg C. Coester, the chaplain who performed the ceremony recorded in his diary, Carolina "was chased out of camp for being a prostitute." Many poor women turned to sex work to feed themselves during the war; perhaps Carolina was one of them. Perhaps she hoped that by marrying a soldier she could achieve a level of security that would permit her to abandon the trade. Instead, Carolina's marriage may have only resulted in a brief, temporary security before she might have been forced to return to sex work—perhaps with fewer clients, as she was no longer in the military encampment.[53]

For many women, marriage to a solider had the potential to substantially improve their situation. Such unions could, to varying degrees, be a shield against the hardship of war in occupied regions; they allowed women to establish their own families and expend their energies on their own behalf. This, for many women, was a compelling reason to consider such relationships, in spite of the pervasive violence and disease of military encampments and the scrutiny that soldiers' wives faced from suspicious commanding officers—although the degree to which these conditions differed from those of their previous employment also varied considerably. Moreover, in certain instances, marrying into the military establishment had real benefits for women. For example, Betty Smith, a Boston servant who fled domestic service in the Winslow household to join the Twenty-Ninth Regiment, was twice imprisoned for theft, but her marriage to a soldier might have spared her from the worst of the consequences. Gravely reporting the gossip circulating the city, twelve-year-old Anna Green Winslow informed her mother, "I heard somebody say that as she has some connections with the army no doubt but she would be cleared, and perhaps, have a pension into the bargain."[54]

To the dismay of both commanding officers and civilian employers, relationships between British soldiers and white working women flourished throughout British garrisons. Writing from Philadelphia in May 1778, General William von Knyphausen lamented the high rate of desertion among the Hessian and German troops, reporting, "desertions . . . caused by the dissolute womenfolk here do not cease." British general Richard Prescott was likewise concerned upon the army's evacuation of Newport that civilian women would entice men to desert. He ordered all of the houses locked and gave "the strictest orders . . . that no inhabitants, and especially no females, permitted themselves to be seen at any window or on the street, and should anyone show themselves, those who were on patrol to fire at them immediately."[55]

Fears that American women would entice soldiers to desert were not unfounded. While stationed in Philadelphia during the winter of 1777–1778, John Jefferies, a private in the First Regiment of Foot Guards, sought permission from his colonel to marry Mary Staiger, a Philadelphia woman. The colonel denied the request, but the couple—with or without another officer's permission—wed later that spring, and Mary evacuated the city with the British Army in June 1778. Just over a month later, Mary Jefferies found herself the subject of a court-martial in Brooklyn, accused of "having advised and persuaded" her husband to desert. A sergeant became skeptical of the couple along the march; they "always remained in the rear of the Company" and "made their Hut at a distance from the rest of the Men." Mary had expressed her desire to return to Philadelphia, and, when John, citing illness, requested permission to remain behind, the sergeant suspected that the couple was attempting to flee. John successfully deserted, but an officer apprehended Mary carrying a bundle of her clothes. Incredulous, Mary claimed that she had been doing laundry—hence, the bundle—and was ignorant of her husband's flight. It is possible, of course, that John Jeffries abandoned her. More likely, the couple planned to flee together; during the court-martial, the sergeant reported rumors that John had been seen in Philadelphia, where his wife's father lived. The prosecution was, however, unable to prove a conspiracy—indeed, they were unable to prove that Mary was not, in fact, doing laundry. She was acquitted of the charges and probably returned to Philadelphia in hopes of building a life together with her husband.[56]

There were any number of ways that working women might become acquainted with British soldiers, but quartering provided an unprecedented opportunity for such relationships to emerge. Servants of both civilian households and British officers lived in the same space and completed their chores side by side. Such was the case for Jane Boon, a maid in Elizabeth Drinker's

Philadelphia household, and Philip Sibal, a Hessian orderly who worked for Major James Cramond. In a letter to her husband, Elizabeth described Cramond's Hessian orderlies as "great Creatures" and "innofencive civel men" who "behave with Decorum." The men were in the habit of sitting in the Drinker kitchen while they awaited orders. As a domestic servant, Jane spent a great deal of time in and around the kitchen. Her daily chores provided her with numerous chances to interact, flirt, and socialize with Philip—and did so in ways that failed to attract Elizabeth's notice. Major Cramond resided in the Drinker household for nearly six months. During that time, there was plenty of opportunity for Philip and Jane to get acquainted.[57]

As the young couple's relationship developed, they also had ample time to snatch private moments together—especially during Elizabeth Drinker's almost month-long absence in April 1778, when she and four other women journeyed to Valley Forge and then on to the Supreme Executive Council of Pennsylvania in Lancaster to petition for the release of their exiled husbands. It seems that Jane might have become pregnant during this time. In late June, Jane spent several days "unwel with the Collick" and "vomitting." The Drinker children also fell ill at this time, but Elizabeth, a meticulous record keeper, never identified Jane's illness as the same flux. Just over a month later, in mid-August 1780, Jane left the Drinker household after almost four years of service to go live with her aunt in Wilmington. The excuse, while plausible, is also consistent with Elizabeth's response when Sally Brant, another of her domestic servants, became pregnant in 1794 and relocated to the country to bear her child. Jane's mysterious illness, seemingly different from that of the Drinker children, quite possibly was morning sickness.[58]

In early September 1778, a letter arrived at the Drinker house addressed to "Jane Sibal, formerly Boon," causing Elizabeth to surmise "that Janny is I suppose married to Philip one of the Majors orderly men." Later that month, Elizabeth listed Jane Sibal among her daily callers. Jane had not moved to Wilmington. To the contrary, Philip deserted from the army, and the couple married in late August or early September 1778, embarking on a new life together in Pennsylvania. In subsequent years, Jane continued to keep in touch with Elizabeth and occasionally visited, usually bringing one of her children along with her. In November 1795, Jane's son, Henry, called on the Drinkers, and Elizabeth recorded the meeting with fond memories, noting that his mother, Jane, "lived with us near four years . . . she married one of Major Crammonds Orderly Men Philip George Sibble an Anspach, he deserted from the troop when they left this City . . . he is now in business at Easttown as a Physician, sells medicine, and makes mony fast, German like."[59]

Jane's wartime circumstances, including both her single status and her labor in a billeted residence, shaped her response to the experience of occupation. Her decision to leave the Drinker household and marry a soldier irrevocably altered her life. She no longer labored as a servant; her domestic energies were expended for the good of her own family, not her employer's. Through her relationship with Philip, Jane built a life for herself amid the devastation and hardship of war. For white laboring women like Jane Sibal, the American Revolution was a moment of profound change and opportunity. Within occupied cities, the disruption of the household labor systems and alternative prospects behind British lines offered these women choices that had previously been unavailable to them.

But such choices were always negotiations of dependence—of labor, employment, or marriage—and their outcomes far from certain. Nevertheless, being young, childless, and unattached, many young servant women took a chance on relationships with soldiers, hoping that they might carve out a new life amid the uncertainties of war—a life far from the households where they would never be more than servants. Such choices were, fundamentally, a challenge to the household governance and paternal authority of their employers. Although inconvenienced and often frustrated by these decisions, white employers nevertheless understood these actions within an existing framework of labor relations in which servants often changed jobs or left service to marry. Many of them were wholly unprepared, however, to discover that not only their maids but their own daughters eagerly sought companionship, flirtation, and diversion in the arms of occupying British officers.

CHAPTER FIVE

A Shameful Scene of Dissipation

"The young Gentlemen of the army at present are much fonder of their pleasure than their duty," Captain John Peebles of the Forty-Second Regiment observed from winter quarters in Long Island in February 1779. Peebles himself had been an enthusiastic participant in the New York garrison's social scene, attending balls, dinners, and plays alongside both fellow officers and civilian women. But, he resolved, he needed to rein in his dissipation; his skin was showing the effects of his revelry. Determined to "clear my face of the pimples," Peebles declared his "intention to live soberly for some time." His resolution, however, was short-lived. For the remainder of his time in North America, John Peebles continued to dine, dance, golf, attend horse races and concerts, and otherwise enjoy the garrison social scene. Describing a particularly memorable ball in March 1781, he detailed a festive night. Dancing lasted until one o'clock in the morning, after which the company "sat down to the most elegant Supper ever I saw in this country." The women withdrew around three, but the officers "drank and sang" for several more hours. Finally, long after sunrise, "the remaining few retired to another room and got breakfast after which some went to bed, some to visit their partners, and some to the bawdy house."[1]

As John Peebles's description of life in occupied New York suggests, British garrisons had vibrant social scenes where officers and civilians gathered for entertainment and pleasure. Typically occurring during the winter months when campaigning slowed, these gatherings bolstered troop morale and satisfied officers' personal desires for diversion. But they also served a deeper purpose. Social engagements in occupied cities functioned as a form of social and political courtship that aimed to heal the breaches of civil war by promoting ties between British troops and American civilians.

Balls and other social events had long served a public function in British North America; they were sites of genteel sociability, where colonial elites and British officials gathered to celebrate royal birthdays, commemorate military victories, and nurture ties to the empire. Resurrecting these traditions in occupied cities—at times, mere weeks after their capture—British officers reinstated practices that had been essential to fostering a transatlantic sense of Britishness during the colonial era. In garrisons throughout the colonies, genteel officers attempted to win over hearts and minds in drawing rooms and ballrooms, endeavoring to secure colonists' political allegiance through social niceties and personal relationships. Deeply entwined with the military culture of honor and chivalry, these genteel, heterosocial entertainments formed an essential prong of Britain's campaign to return the colonies to the imperial fold.[2]

Elite young (and often single) white women were indispensable to garrison social events. They were the intended audience for officers' polite manners and chivalrous behavior. They hosted genteel dinners and attended balls. In ballrooms and household gatherings, they played cards, flirted, and danced with officers. They were social companions, romantic partners, and potential wives. Notwithstanding political allegiances, throughout British garrisons, many young white women of middling and elite rank socialized with British officers. Some simply sought diversion and a momentary escape from the hardship of wartime life; others sought marriage. Whereas their mothers and fathers might have viewed British officers as a potential threat to their household governance and the security of their property, many young white women who came of age during the war regarded officers as precisely the opposite: as opportunities for personal independence. A union with a British officer could permit a young woman to leave her parents' household and establish her own.[3]

The young women of the urban elite had various motivations for engaging in relationships with British officers, but they were not unique in doing so. As the war progressed and the British moved south, Black women, with varying degrees of choice and coercion, also served as social companions for officers. These pairings had the dual advantage of aiding enslaved women's pursuit of freedom and safety while also insulting white enslavers. Collectively, these women's experiences demonstrate how Britain's campaign of political and social courtship created conditions that endowed unmarried women—primarily, but not exclusively, white women of the upper classes—with unprecedented levels of leverage to both seize control over their own lives and exert influence over the social landscape of occupied cities.[4]

The context of civil war, however, heightened the political significance of these personal connections. Observers on both sides of the conflict understood young women's social and romantic choices as a referendum on the larger imperial contest and the men who waged it. The patriarchal connotations of both eighteenth-century heterosexual relationships and eighteenth-century slavery, with their embedded expectations of submission to white men's domestic and legal authority, meant that, in occupied regions, young women's participation in garrison social events not only functioned as a barometer of the British Army's success in the war for hearts and minds, it also implied a corresponding rejection of American men and the revolutionary cause. Adding insult to injury, garrison social engagements often transpired in the very households that embodied American men's patriarchal authority.[5]

Young women's romantic and social choices thus became central features in both British and American efforts to narrate occupation and define its significance. Entwining political, social, and personal courtship, these accounts were often tinged with subtle (and occasionally not-so-subtle) sexual undertones. Both sides frequently invoked gendered and racialized notions of sexuality—the supposed virtue of white women, the alleged promiscuity of Black women—in these efforts. British officers were well aware that their successful social and romantic courtship of young American women was an important symbolic victory and eagerly broadcast their conquests. Revolutionaries likewise grasped the import of these encounters, censuring the young unmarried women who socialized with the British and reproving them for forsaking their domestic and patriotic duties. In their eyes, unmarried women's promiscuous politics (and implied sexuality) exposed the precariousness of the patriarchal authority that formed a critical pillar of the revolutionary project.

These perspectives influenced the wartime narratives that emerged around young women's actions in occupied cities, narratives that, unsurprisingly, had the effect of obscuring the nuances of women's experiences and the rationale behind their choices. Young women had varied reasons for participating in garrison social events; politics determined some women's choices, but many others were guided by far more quotidian, mundane concerns. Analyzing young women's diverse motivations and the considerable power that Britain's campaign of social courtship imparted to them, this chapter considers not only how young women exerted this influence for their own ends but also how both British and American observers imbued these social activities with political and sexual connotations to aid their respective war efforts. These dynamics are exemplified by two balls, the 1778 Meschianza in Philadelphia, a military retirement party fabled for its extravagant costumes and elaborate stagecraft resembling a medieval joust, and the purported 1782 "Ethiopian Ball" in Charleston, a dance supposedly organized by three Black women for British officers and both enslaved and self-liberated Black women but that might not have actually occurred. Demonstrating how men on both sides of the conflict sexualized young women's relationships with British officers and infused them with political meaning, the conversations around these balls illustrate how social relationships between British officers and young women functioned as potent symbols through which men on both sides of the conflict meditated notions of their own masculine prowess and signaled the success of their respective political and military efforts. Effective propaganda, sexualized imagery could also function as an efficient shorthand to censure one's enemies, a tactic that revolutionaries in particular used to great avail. Indeed, as this and subsequent chapters will show, as the war progressed, this effort to narrate the war and its meaning would become a central preoccupation of American revolutionaries as they endeavored to reassert control over the spaces, civilians, and households that the British had claimed during the war.[6]

THIS REBELLION WILL OUTLAST MY YOUTH

Debby Norris lay aside her pen and quickly dressed to greet her unknown callers. Heading downstairs, the seventeen-year-old was delighted to find her friends Sally Jones and Molly Pleasants standing by the parlor window. As they explained, "they were contemplating the beauties of the grass lot—that the window commands a prospect off [*sic*]." Philadelphia was beautiful in April, its green squares and blossoming flowers heralding the end of winter,

FIGURE 14 *The Wishing Females*, 1781. European Cartoon Collection, box 4, folder 1. Courtesy of American Antiquarian Society, Worcester, Mass.

Throughout occupied cities, young women of the elite and middling ranks eyed British officers with great interest. Here, two women eagerly watch troops drilling from the safety of their home.

and the Norris' carefully cultivated garden was esteemed among the city's elite. Yet, perhaps the flowers were not all that the young women admired. The Norris house abutted the Philadelphia State House, its clock tower rising above the manicured gardens, where the Royal Artillery paraded in the front yard—that is, next to the Norris house—three times a day. Officers of the British Army and navy were also regular visitors to the Norris gardens.

Although the young Quakers, in accordance with their pacifist beliefs, were expected to marry within their faith and to avoid violence in all forms, including the handsome soldiers that filled Philadelphia's streets and common spaces, months of occupation had blurred these lines. Throughout the city, older women in Philadelphia's Quaker community befriended the officers quartered in their homes, leading to cordial social relations. A testament to the prevalence of these relationships, in January 1778, one Philadelphia woman admonished her meeting, expressing her dismay over the number of "women and girls . . . exchanging visits with these warriors" and "ma[king] so light of their shame that they stroll about with these people in broad daylight."[7]

Debby eagerly accepted her friends' invitation to walk, and the three girls set out to stroll and gossip in the streets of the bustling garrison. As spring blossomed in the following weeks, the girls' long walks became habitual. Wandering Philadelphia's streets, the young Quakers delighted in receiving soldiers' attentions. "We have not forgot our old fashion of pinching, when anything remarkable occurs[,] and we cannot conveniently speak," Debby wrote in a gossipy letter to an absent friend; "if . . . I happen to get a bow, at the same moment, I receive a smart pinch [from Sally] which often occasions me to return it—by the next opportunity." The young women were pleased one morning when they encountered an officer of their acquaintance on the street and he walked with them for several blocks. Of no relation, Lieutenant Norris had been introduced to the Norris family because of their shared surname; he was, according to Debby, "sociable, and Polite," and his accompanying them, she insisted, was simply owing to his good manners. Yet Sally Jones's determination to apprise the girls' absent friend of the encounter suggests that the young women enjoyed the officer's attentiveness and that at least one of them, perhaps, had developed a slight infatuation. "For further particulars," Debby discreetly directed the friend, "see my journal."[8]

Like Debby Norris and her friends, young white women of means delighted in capturing the attentions of soldiers and officers as they promenaded through the streets of British garrisons. In fact, some women sought them out. Eager to socialize with the troops, Betsy Murray gathered with friends at a house adjoining Boston's jail yard so that they could peek over the fence and eavesdrop on the British officers conversing within. Disappointed that they were unable to speak with the men, the women set out to walk about the city "in hopes of meeting more." Traveling in broad daylight with a group of similarly well-dressed white women signaled both their status and social power, insulating the young women, to a large degree, against the predations that female servants faced while running errands alone. Ensconced in the protections of their class and the respect due to them as ladies, young women of means had the privilege to embrace social diversions that eased, however briefly, the hardship of war and offered a semblance of normalcy—an illusion that was itself a privilege in occupied regions, where many starved and feared for their safety.[9]

Unlike free laboring women, many of whom gambled their livelihoods on the promise of a better life, young elite women's relationships with officers underscored their privileged status. Seeking a momentary escape from wartime hardship, loneliness, fear, and the cessation of mixed-gender social engagements as their male peers went off to war, elite young women welcomed the attentions of genteel officers. To be on the receiving end of such social niceties, however superficial, offered these women an opportunity to experience what war had deprived them of: to feel young, beautiful, and desired. Some women, fearing that the war was swallowing up their most marriageable years, certainly sought to find a husband among the troops. But many others recognized that the next few years of their life would bring marriage, motherhood, and the responsibilities of managing their own households. An evening of dancing and cards alongside dashing officers seemed innocent enough—indeed, it might be their only chance for a little fun during the long and indeterminate war. Reflecting on a friend's recent marriage, Elizabeth Cathcart, who herself married a British officer in 1779, acknowledged the carefree attitude that many women adopted toward these relationships: "I am sure I never believed her last winter when she used to talk so much about him," she admitted. Summing up the feelings of many young unmarried women, when confronted about her relationship with a paroled Continental officer in New York City, loyalist Elizabeth Shipton declared, this "Rebellion is not to last for ever . . . but I am a little of opinion it will outlast my youth."[10]

The resumption of social life was an enticing prospect for young women across the political spectrum. Throughout occupied cities, women of the upper classes flirted, socialized, and occasionally married British and Hessian officers. Loyalist women were, of course, most likely to do so. Yet political differences were not firm obstacles to socialization. Certainly, some committed revolutionaries snubbed occupying forces (actions, one Charleston woman proudly related, that "gives the proud conquerors the heart-burn"). But there were many, especially among younger women, who supported the rebellion's ideals whilst spurning its spartan ideology. Rejecting homespun in favor of high rolls and luscious silks, many young women of means refused to let politics dictate their social life and embraced the entertainments afforded them within occupied cities. Writing of the social exploits of her fellow Georgians alongside the British troops, Mary Clay, a seventeen-year-old revolutionary, commiserated with her sister that Savannah's women exhibited a lack of "patriotic spirit"—that they had pursued pleasure over politics, genteel socialization over principled seclusion. Yet, even as she levied these charges, Mary confessed that she was impatient to rejoin social events and dismayed by "the horrid idea that two months more of my youthful age must be devoted to solitude."[11]

Officers were similarly eager to socialize with female civilians. Cities full of young women marked a stark change from long, hard months on campaign. Entering a Philadelphia house in September 1777, Friedrich von Meunchhausen, aide-de-camp to General Sir William Howe, confessed that the "unexpected sight of seven very pretty ladies disconcerted me more than the bullets of the battle at Brandywine." In their letters and diaries, men frankly assessed women's beauty and detailed their efforts to court them. Stephan Popp, a twenty-three-year-old Hessian soldier stationed in Newport, declared the women there to be "almost like gods in attractiveness." "They have one fault," another soldier asserted, "they side with the rebels." Officers' motivations for engaging with young women varied. Some men sought companionship; other men simply sought fun. Scottish officer John Peebles, for instance, had no desire for a serious relationship. He regularly attended the theater "with a party of Ladies" but was cautious not to nurture any specific attachment. Still others found flirtation a pleasant way to pass the winter. An "agreeable and upright association with the fair sex caused me to make good progress in the English language," one Hessian officer happily reported from Philadelphia.[12]

Occupied cities had a vibrant social scene, especially once the British Army entered winter quarters for a period of rest between campaigning seasons. A welcome break from fighting, winter quarters allowed officers and soldiers to recover from the hardship of active warfare and bolstered troop morale. "I never was better for a Drawing Room in my Life," Lieutenant Loftus Cliffe declared from winter quarters in Philadelphia, admitting that he had "indulged too much of late in ease and Luxury." Concurring with his assessment, Hessian captain Johann Hinrichs laughed that "Assemblies, Concerts, Comedies, Clubs and the like make us forget there is any war, save that it is a capital joke." Dinners, concerts, and theatrical performances were regular features of social life in British garrisons, where men socialized with fellow soldiers and flirted with female civilians. These heterosocial events were full of boisterous—and often bawdy—fun. "But most women can bear

FIGURE 15 *A Visit to the Camp,* 1780. Prints, Drawings, and Watercolors from the Anne S. K. Brown Military Collection. Brown Digital Repository. Courtesy of Brown University Library, Providence, R.I., https://repository.library.brown.edu/studio/item/bdr:233818/

Elite women were integral to both garrison social events and British officers' performance of genteel martial masculinity. In this depiction of a British camp, note both the gentlemanly officer in the foreground, wooing the visiting woman, and the one in the tent, dining with a woman and young girl.

a little [lewdness] either very Publickly or very privately," Scottish officer John Peebles chortled.[13]

Offering amusement and companionship to men and women alike, garrison social events resurrected a semblance of normalcy. In occupied regions, British officers organized weekly subscription balls in coffee houses, taverns, and even the South Carolina State House. Balls, unlike the other entertainments available to officers and soldiers in occupied cities, required female participation; there could be no balls without women to dance with. White women's presence, in fact, was critical for the performance of officers' martial masculinity: to effectively demonstrate their chivalric manners and refined sensibilities, officers required social companions and dance partners. To encourage women's attendance, officers' contributions underwrote the cost of these "genteel Amusements," and "the ladies [we]re furnish'd with tickets gratis." Any officer who wanted to participate, "from the highest general down to the youngest ensign," contributed two days income in proportion to his status. Officers were nevertheless discerning in selecting dance partners. Disappointed at the turnout at a New York ball, Captain John Peebles of the Forty-Second Regiment complained that "none of [the women]" were "handsome," and "some [were] old ugly and fat." The company boasted "nothing very tempting to . . . spend your money for amusemt. to others," he concluded. Young, elite, and beautiful civilian women were thus crucial—and coveted—participants in the garrison social scene.[14]

Officers' demand for young, unmarried white women's presence at garrison social events endowed these women with an unprecedented level of power in occupied cities. Indeed, as Sarah Knott has argued in her exploration of female liberty during the Age of Revolutions, "sentimental gallantry"—an antipatriarchal assertion of liberty based in female sensibility and often tinged with sexual intrigue—offered elite women a means to challenge patriarchal conventions by asserting the primacy of "female feeling, not male prerogative, as the highest court of judgment." This insight is particularly useful for analyzing young unmarried women's actions within British garrisons: as sought-after social companions whose presence was integral to the success of many military entertainments, these young women wielded immense social power that permitted them to follow their own inclinations, at times, flouting the norms of social engagement. British occupation, in other words, created circumstances that encouraged young, unmarried women of the colonial elite to engage in the culture of "sentimental gallantry."[15]

"You can have no idea of the life of continued amusement I live in," Rebecca Franks enthused to a friend in 1778, "rakeing as much as you choose either at Plays, Balls Concerts or Assemblys." Her choice of words is revealing. In characterizing her activities as "rakeing," Franks claimed a method of social performance largely regarded as the preserve of elite men. Conventionally gendered male with sexualized undercurrents, a rake was dedicated to the pursuit of pleasure, someone who indulged in carefree, libertine habits; he was someone skilled at the art of seduction, someone used to taking, and getting, what he wanted. Yet, in occupied cities, Rebecca Franks suggested, it was young women who did the raking. After traveling to the New York garrison in 1781, she reported that it was not unusual "to hear a lady confess a partiality for a man" or to "single out her pet to lean almost in his arms at an Assembly or play-house." "'Tis the ladies and not the gentlmen, that shew a preference," Rebecca observed.[16]

As Rebecca Franks's forthright appraisal suggests, within British garrisons, the sudden influx of officers and their desire for female company inverted traditional gendered sociability in ways that translated into real power for the young, unmarried elite women that they sought to impress. Prior to the British Army's arrival, white women accounted for the majority of free wartime urban populations; many of the remaining men were those that were too old or too young to fight. Of course, there were exceptions to this trend, but the large numbers of officers and soldiers that made up occupying forces firmly reversed it.[17]

In occupied regions, suddenly, young women—especially those of the elite class—found themselves in the minority as gallant officers vied for their attentions. Two officers of the Sixty-Third Regiment went so far as to fight a duel over a young Boston woman. Describing a 1783 ball given in New York for the queen's birthday, Eleanor Jauncey reported that approximately "eighty Ladies" were in attendance but the "Gentlemen without number." There was "no loss for partners," Rebecca Franks wrote happily from Philadelphia in 1778. Three years later, she remained the belle of the ball. "Yesterday . . . this house swarm'd with beaux and some very smart ones," she enthused to her sister; "how the girls wou'd have envy'd me cou'd they have peep'd and seen how I was surrounded." Whether they sought marriage or simply fun and flirtation, to be the beneficiary of officers' ardent devotions was thrilling for many young women who had endured months, if not years, of wartime privations.[18]

Elite young women reveled in their newfound social power. Writing from the New York garrison, Eleanor Jauncey was pleased that her time spent among the troops "and being constantly in company" helped her to overcome her "awkwardness." Empowered by her experiences, in subsequent years, she continued to crave city life "and all the amusements that it affords." This transformation marked "a great change in her, as she was to a fault some years ago the contrary," Eleanor's stepmother remarked. Embracing a newfound confidence, one Philadelphia woman sat in the parlor, surrounded by officers, as she wrote a gossipy letter to her sister. "You may imagine what an indifferant I am to continue writing and beaux in the room," she observed, "but so it is—I am not what I was."[19]

Secure in their social position and certain of their desirability, young elite women were astutely aware of the power that they wielded within the garrison social scene. As attendees at balls and other social events, their presence could make or break the party, along with soldiers' morale. As hostesses, young women served as arbiters of social intercourse, presiding over mixed-gender gatherings of polite sociability, where they basked in the attentions of officers and displayed their feminine "cleverness." They organized card games and carefully guided the conversation to "entertain a large circle of both sexes." Flirtation was rampant, according to one observer, and many young women "decline[d] playing [cards] for the pleasure of making love." Returning to Philadelphia after the occupation, one man was shocked to find "the manners of the ladies . . . much changed." "They have really in great measure lost that native innocence which was their former characteristic and supplied its place with what they call an Easy behavior," he described.[20]

Social gatherings laid the foundation for mutually beneficial relationships between British and Hessian officers and American women—relationships that, crucially, extended young women's sway beyond the social arena in ways that had real consequences for other garrison inhabitants. Trading on their social connections with officers, women interceded on behalf of guilty parties in courts-martial. They secured pardons and paroles. They petitioned commanding officers for assistance and obtained valuable resources and favors for their families. They could also wreak havoc. Peter Edes, a Boston printer's apprentice who was imprisoned for his revolutionary sentiments, recorded that an elderly enslaved man was arrested and "unmercifully beat . . . to gratify a certain young woman."[21]

Gesturing to young women's influence, a poem printed in the *Newport Gazette* in April 1777 urged them to deploy their sexual appeal and "Charms, / (More pow'rful far than Caesar's Arms!)" in service of the British war effort. "Fair Maids!" the author beseeched, "Exert your Pow'rs—support the Laws":

And if she bids him rush to Arms,
Who would not bleed, to gain her Charms!

The tempting Lip—the sparkling Eye—
The rosy Cheek's soft blushing Die—
The gently-heaving snow white Breast,
And Love, in ev'ry Look express'd—
Who can resist? These must prevail,
When P——Y [British General Hugh Percy] and his Virtues fail.
Do then, ye Fair! reclaim our Youth!
Tell them, that Britain mourns their Stains,
With all a Mother's tender Pains;
That it again, in Duty's Sphere
They seek to move—she'll pour the Tear
On all their Woes—repress each angry Thought—
And in her Fondness, quite forget the Fault.[22]

By interweaving sexual desire, sentimental feeling, and political allegiance, the poem acknowledged the complementary aims of Britain's courtship of American colonists and American women and the power that it bestowed upon young women in occupied Newport. It was a power based in women's youth, their beauty, and their sexuality. Pleading with young women to use their allure to entice male civilians back to their allegiance and return to their place within the imperial family, the poem's anonymous author clearly stated what was implicit in much of the garrison's social entertainments: that young women were critical to winning the war for hearts and minds.

BY SONGS AND BALLS SECURE ALLEGIANCE

In British garrisons, war temporarily faded into the background as officers and elite women gathered for genteel dinners, polite conversation, and fashionable entertainments. "This is to be sure for young Ladies who love gaiety a most delightful place," one young woman observed of the New York garrison in 1782. In the course of a single week, Elizabeth Shipton recorded her social engagements "among the Gay ones and the Great," which included large numbers of British and Hessian officers, their families, and prominent New York loyalists. She danced at "a little Hop" on Thursday, visited on Saturday, dined with company on Sunday, attended a play on Monday as the guest of General William Phillips, and capped off the week with a party onboard the British warship *Fanny* on Tuesday. Such entertainments occurred throughout British garrisons. "There has been less thought and said for these two months past about Washington and his army in the City of Philadelphia than in any other city of His Majesty's Dominions," Lieutenant James Murray laughed in March 1778.[23]

The gaiety of the ballroom, however, concealed the larger political meaning of these gatherings. In the centuries preceding the Revolution, balls celebrating royal birthdays, holidays, and military victories had been critical tools of empire that reinforced British identity among colonial populations. Returning to these recognizable forms was a deliberate choice by British officials. By resurrecting these familiar practices, the military hoped to invoke nostalgia for imperial rule and sway inhabitants to the British cause. Throughout occupied cities, military settings, such as warships, regularly served as the backdrop for garrison social events. Such venues were a critical aspect of officers' efforts to conquer hearts and minds. Reminding inhabitants of the power of the British military establishment, balls and other ostentatious events marshalled pomp and spectacle to reinvigorate colonists' feelings of pride and connection to the mother country.[24]

The social nature of these gatherings also meant, however, that officers' efforts to coax elite civilians to allegiance were deeply entwined with the courtship of American women. In the ballrooms of occupied cities, British officers charmed, flattered, and courted young women of the urban elite with polished manners and witty banter—hallmarks of the transatlantic culture of genteel sociability that united the Anglo-American elite. Presenting themselves as refined gentlemen, officers professed that honor made no distinction between female loyalists and female revolutionaries, that chivalric norms eclipsed ideological divisions. Wartime context nevertheless infused these gendered social relations with symbolic political meaning that was legible to people on all sides of the conflict. As Connecticut lawyer and poet John Trumbull quipped, British officers sought to "By songs and balls secure allegiance, / And dance the ladies to obedience."[25]

As Trumbull's witticism suggests, British officers' courtship of young American women served several overlapping objectives: it satisfied officers' personal desire for female companionship, it flattered their own sense of masculinity, it boosted troop morale, and it facilitated an atmosphere of genteel sociability that provided entertainment while nurturing social connections and familial ties that would facilitate reconciliation once the war was won. And it humiliated their enemies. Revolutionary propaganda promised Continental soldiers that their wartime sacrifices would be rewarded with women's affections and that their "Sweethearts" would be dutifully waiting for them with a "Kiss" at war's end. "Go act the hero, every danger face, / *Love hates a coward's impotent embrace,*" one propaganda poem declared. Young women's participation in garrison entertainments—effectively submitting to Britain's military and cultural rule—wholly undermined this narrative, exhibiting a clear preference for British officers over their Continental counterparts. This partiality could have tangible consequences for the war, as women's romantic ties indicated which army was most likely to receive the benefit of their labor and support. For occupying British forces, American women's attendance at garrison social events was an important symbolic victory that was as much about perception as it was about personal desire.[26]

A ball hosted onboard the British warship *Roebuck* during the occupation of Philadelphia illustrates these intersecting aims. The event was a carefully orchestrated performance designed for public consumption. Docked at the wharf for the entirety of the event, the *Roebuck*—the evening's setting—manifested military might; the night's gaiety and festivity reinforced the social power of the British Army and the urban elite; and the affair's exclusivity accentuated the superiority of the British over their colonial counterparts. One Hessian officer recounted that the ship was entirely transformed: "chandeliers and candlesticks fixed in the wall, tapestries were fastened in front of the ropes, and high above the deck, and the mizzenmast was wound round with silk ribbon, so that the deck, which had so often been the scene of bloody fights, completely resembled a ball room." Fearful that covert revolutionaries might disrupt the evening by attempting to "set it [the *Roebuck*] on fire," male civilians were banned from the event and prohibited from even approaching the ship. Having thus secured their female guests' undivided attention, British officers spent the evening dancing and dining with them, courting them in full in view of the entire city.[27]

British officers' efforts to court the affections and allegiances of American women were effective not only because of how they marshalled colonial precedents and the power of the British military establishment, but, perhaps most persuasively for elite urbanites, because of how they operated within a recognizable transatlantic culture of Anglo-American genteel sociability. Identifying the young women of the colonial elite as their social equals, officers sought companionship and social connections with leading families in occupied regions—and vice versa. Mixed-gender socialization was a critical component of cosmopolitan elite sociability, and both officers and civilians were well-versed in the norms and manners that linked elite Euro-descended people around the Atlantic world.[28]

Shared fashions, entertainments, and etiquette meant that the city-dwelling elite often had more in common with aristocratic European officers than they did with the poorer inhabitants of their own cities or their rural

FIGURE 16 Major John André, *Self-Portrait*, 1780. Pen and brown ink. 4 in. x 5 1/8 in. (10.2 c.m. x 13 c.m.). Gift of Ebenezer Baldwin, B.A. 1808. Accession no. 1832.103. Courtesy of Yale University Art Gallery, New Haven, Conn.

In this self-portrait, Major John André appears a polished, refined gentleman—a styling that resonated among the urban elite and helped to forge critical social connections between civilian and military populations in occupied cities.

neighbors. "Certainly to a person of Taste the Dead is preferrable to any other than sensible well-bred People that have been accustomed to move in the same walks of Life with ourselves," Philadelphian Elizabeth Willing Powel avowed in 1778. Such disdain went both ways. Writing from the New Jersey countryside to her brother, a merchant in occupied Philadelphia, Rebecca Coxe declared that she and their cousins were unimpressed by his "account of the Amusements of the gay World" and that his description of garrison life "raised in us more astonishment than envy." Implicit in her response was an acknowledgment of the gulf between urban and rural enjoyments: if her sentiments and those of her cousins were known, she speculated, "we should be heartily laughed at by one half the Town at least . . . for three silly ignorant Country Girls." In contrast, eighteen-year-old Philadelphian Rebecca Franks delighted in the garrison's vibrant social scene. "I know you are as fond of a gay life as myself," she wrote in a letter encouraging a friend to visit. The fashion, she enthused, was "more ridiculous and pretty than anything that ever I saw." And she reveled in officers' attentions. "I've been but 3 evenings alone since we mov'd to town," she happily declared, and "scarce have a moment to myself."[29]

Through polite conversation and genteel manners, officers sought to counter revolutionary propaganda that villainized British troops as rapacious, violent, and bloodthirsty—what one officer referred to as an "intollerable delusion." "You will please acquaint the Ladies, who had abandoned their houses at the Savannah, that they have certainly been taught with other wild conceptions, to form the worst impression of British Officers," a disgruntled Lieutenant Colonel Archibald Campbell wrote from Savannah in 1779. Still, at least some women's notions of British officers might have been informed less by revolutionary propaganda than by exchanges that they witnessed with their own eyes. These officers were, after all, the same men who clashed with elite white male householders and who scoffed at the lower-status inhabitants in whose houses they billeted. The same men whose need for housekeepers lured domestic servants away from young women's households. The same men who hired poor women and enslaved women for sex, frequently abandoning their pregnant lovers. Indeed, some of the elite young women that officers courted were not unaware of this fact. Skeptical of officers' intentions in New York, poet Hannah Lawrence vehemently denounced garrison social life as "The scene of gay resort, / Here vice and folly hold their court, / Here all the martial band parade, / To vanquish—some unguarded Maid."[30]

Garrison entertainments strove to refute these perceptions by emphasizing the gallantry and romantic appeal of British officers. Deeply rooted in the military culture of honor, this characterization reflected a particularly martial strain of elite masculinity that regarded chivalrous behavior toward the female sex and battlefield valor as two sides of the same coin. Officers throughout British garrisons organized entertainments intended to portray the army, and especially officers, in a flattering light. A mix of political messaging and officers' own desires for female companionship, these presentations were accentuated by the proximity of actual men in uniform eager to capture the attentions of young female civilians. Indeed, the first play that "[General] Howe's strolling Company" hoped to perform in Philadelphia—a performance that was postponed because of the inability to locate a script—was Susanna Centlivre's bawdy romantic comedy *The Wonder: A Woman Keeps a Secret* in which a young woman elopes with a British officer. True love, the play suggested, was to be found among the troops—an apt message for the start of the winter social season.[31]

Other performances throughout British garrisons reinforced this idea. In a humorous poetic epilogue authored by General John Burgoyne, a British officer and playwright, and likely performed in the New York garrison, the speaker adopts the voice of a ten-year-old girl named Polly who desires to know, "What is a beau? Is that young Ensign one? / With ruby lips and chin so like my own, / With feather'd cap, and curling locks beneath, / Dear! How the pretty creature shews his teeth." Drawing comparisons between herself and the young ensign, Polly seemingly effeminizes the ensign, even as she is drawn to the officer's allure. Reprimanded by her grandmother for being too young and "too bold," Polly promises "to learn more sense, / And make these observations, three years hence." Beneath the jest, however, lay truth. Many women and girls *were* drawn to handsome men in uniform. As one woman joked from New York in 1781, women's fondness for British officers had "made the men so saucy that I sincerely believe the lowest Ensign thinks 'tis but ask, and have,—a red coat and smart epaulette is sufficient to secure a female heart." General Burgoyne's epilogue then, in situating a young, prepubescent ensign as the object of young Polly's affections, was also a reassertion of both masculine and military hierarchies: low-ranking officers possessed the appeal that characterized British martial masculinity, but they were boys, better fodder for girlish infatuations than the love of grown women. Winking at the audience, Burgoyne ribbed the ensigns who had become too bold while simultaneously encouraging American women to focus their attentions elsewhere, toward the higher-ranking and more manly experienced officers.[32]

Garrison entertainments emphasized the martial prowess and valor of British troops, especially in comparison with their American foes. At a dinner in New York City in August 1776, officers and female civilians gathered around Sir William Howe's table laughed at the handwriting and spelling in a note from Continental general Israel Putnam that was carried into the garrison by Margaret Moncrieff, the daughter of a British officer who had sheltered in the Putnam house during her father's absence. Aware of Margaret's affections for a Continental officer, General Putnam informed Major Moncrieff, "If you dont like hur send hur back and I will take cear [care] of hur and Provid hur a fine Whig husband." Interpreting the letter as bravado, General Howe read it aloud to the table, swapping the word *"twig* for *whig* husband"—a joke that "served as a fund of entertainment to the company." American men, General Howe laughed, were weak and would be easily broken.[33]

Conversations elsewhere reiterated these sentiments. At a ball in April 1780, British general William Philips teased New Yorker Elizabeth Shipton about the paroled Continental officer Aquila Giles who was courting the young loyalist. "How does the Pett do?" he inquired; "It is a Sparrow is it not?" "Dont let it fly away," he warned. The double entendre, referring both to the couple's courtship and to Giles's status as a prisoner, also, significantly diminutized the young Continental officer—whose name, Aquila, was the Latin word for *eagle*—rendering him, instead, a small, harmless songbird. It was a deliberate dig that served to both belittle the enemy while also exhibiting General Philips's wit before the assembled crowd. Meanwhile, at a 1781 dinner in Charleston to celebrate the British victory at Guilford Courthouse, the evening's entertainment consisted of a mock recruiting speech by a serjeant of the guards in which he proclaimed, "Trembling Yankeys all before us fled, / We came, we fought, we conquer'd and we bled." "Join with me," he urged the assembled crowd, "'Tis we enjoy the Sweets of Liberty; / . . . No cruel Master, nor no Scolding Wife; . . . / Our only labour and our hardest trade is, / To make our Quarters good and please the Ladies."[34]

Doubling as promotional campaigns, garrison entertainments, when combined with officers' gallant manners and the prevailing norms of polite society, could prove an effective tool to counter civilians' misgivings about British troops. Hesitant to allow her daughters to socialize with officers in the early months of the Philadelphia occupation, Elizabeth Oswald Chew finally relented after a friend "perswaded" her that the girls' absence "was particular and ~~much~~ thought a slight to Gentlemen who had made it a point to make every thing aggreable to the inhabitants." Yielding to the combined pressures of social norms, assurances of officers' gentlemanly manners, and presumably the entreaties of her daughters, whose close circle of friends were among officers' chosen companions, Elizabeth Chew permitted her daughters to join the garrison's vibrant social scene, where they quickly became favorites among the officers.[35]

Her apprehensions calmed by officers' gentlemanly behavior, Elizabeth was pleased by her daughters' enthusiastic reception among the aristocratic officer corps. "They [the girls] have been much noticed and by their Prudent Behavior gained many Friends their acquaintances are of the Chosen Gentlemen of worth and honor who visit and drink a dish of tea," she proudly informed her absent husband, Benjamin, the former chief justice of Pennsylvania. Assuring Benjamin of the propriety of both the garrison social events and the girls' conduct, Elizabeth "venture[d] to say that they all will behave with that becoming distant Civility you woud wish." "I don't doubt but you will hear various accounts of them," she wrote, "but depend upon it [I have] the Continual watch up all their motions and the truth shall come from me."[36]

Shared elite urban cosmopolitanism and the solidarity of rank were powerful counterweights to political differences within occupied cities. As Bostonian Katherine Farnham Hay explained to her sister, even though she was a "Rebel Lady," she enjoyed her time in a guard house at White Plains as she waited to be admitted into the New York garrison. It "w[as] truly diverting," she recounted, "as I had a Gentleman to take particular care of me, they were not a little Romantic and I confess I am yet a little Charm'd with [the] Novelty." Traveling as a lone woman, she was grateful for the protection of British officers, including one man who entertained her during the carriage ride to the garrison, "chating . . . Laughing . . . [and] shewing me the Forts and all the extroardinaries [*sic*] on the way." After securing her quarters, the young man—or "my Gallant" as Katherine referred to him—promised to return "the Next Day and know if I had any commands for he was ready to assist me all in his power."[37]

Still, within British garrisons, there nevertheless remained many young women who, despite officers' best efforts, rejected the premise of apolitical sociability and refused to conceal their political convictions. In April 1780, twenty-two-year-old New York poet Hannah Lawrence voiced her disapproval of the garrison social scene by excoriating British officers for their use of the walkway outside of Trinity Church as a promenade "to which the fair / In shining nightly throngs repair." To cultivate a romantic atmosphere, the "military gentlemen" had painted the walkway by the church green, installed railings and benches along the path, and hung "lamps fixed in the trees" so that "gentleman and ladies" could "walk and sit there in the evening" while being serenaded by a military band. A sentry stationed near the promenade ensured "that none of the common people may intrude" on their revelry. Channeling her anger into verse, Hannah drafted a searing indictment of officers' plans to widen the walkway by converting part of the burial ground. She left the anonymous poem on the church steps where it was found the following evening. "Of late . . . Belles and Beaux repair / In crowds to take the waning air, / Where riot, noise and joy prevail," she scorned. Ridiculing officers as "fools and knaves," she also mocked the women who joined them in these entertainments, suggesting that their actions had risen to the realm of sacrilege. "The female size, by hoops increast, / Demands a tomb or two at least" she sneered. In pursuing pleasure, she implied, these young women had forgotten their duty to the city's dead, including the Continental soldiers recently interred there. Anonymity allowed Hannah Lawrence to boldly proclaim her politics to the entire New York garrison, yet this was an avenue of expression that only few women could access.[38]

It was far more common for elite civilian women to cloak their political views in polite conversation. Viewing social interaction as a battlefield where she could contest British military authority with her wit, South Carolinian Eliza Wilkinson, an outspoken revolutionary, routinely engaged British officers on social terrain—exchanges that she characterized as "quarrel[s] with my enemies." Despite political differences, within occupied cities the norms of cosmopolitan sociability prevailed between elite civilians and British officers. "I despise them most cordially," Eliza assured a friend. Her deft political maneuvering is evident in a conversation between Eliza and a British officer posted at her South Carolina plantation. As she politely explained to the man, she had no interest in his invitation to attend the garrison "concerts assemblies, and other polite amusements, which ladies generally admire." Although she did not say so explicitly, Eliza's refusal was rooted, not in reticence, but in her sympathies for the rebellion. In previous years, she had regularly participated in Charleston's summer social season; however, at present, she preferred the swampy country—with its bugs, maladies, and sweltering heat—to British officers. "I would rather be where I am, than in Charlestown just now," Eliza demurred.[39]

When aired in social contexts and cloaked in the language of gentility, elite women were able to voice their opinions to officers' faces with surprising frankness. Eighteenth-century social norms viewed courtship as a delicate choreography of masculine pursuit and feminine submission; politically tinged banter fit naturally within this existing structure. Some officers even adopted political language in their romantic and social pursuits. And elite women responded in kind. Later in the occupation, Eliza Wilkinson reported visiting friends in Charleston, where she engaged in flirtatious banter with officers and shrouded her rebel politics in polite repartee. When an officer asked her to play the guitar, she demurred, insisting that she knew "nothing but rebel songs." On a separate occasion, she rejected a British officer's proffered arm, causing the man to joke, "You do not know what your condescension may do—I will turn rebel!"—to which she playfully replied, "Will you? . . . Turn rebel first, and then offer your arm." Recounting these interactions to a friend, Eliza expressed her surprise that officers had tolerated her impertinence. "I have often wondered . . . I was not packed off," she confessed, "for I was very saucy, and never disguised my sentiments."[40]

Although Eliza might not have realized it, officers' genteel manners, regardless of—indeed, in the face of—her rebellious politics represented not only a critical aspect of British officers' own performance of chivalric masculinity but a concerted tactic to foster personal connections that might smooth the path toward political reconciliation. Minimizing women's politics, officers insisted that gendered sociability, rather than ideological divisions, should dictate the tenor of their relationships. By sidestepping politics, they sought to convince young women to attend garrison social events by suggesting that ideological differences need not impede socialization. But doing so also represented a savvy political strategy. Even as officers minimized the significance of young women's politics within occupied cities, they recognized that, to outside observers, young women's attendance at garrison social events was an implicit endorsement of British officers and the British war effort. For precisely this reason, young women's attendance at balls and other garrison social events infuriated revolutionary leaders.

In British garrisons, social gatherings thus held meaning that reached far beyond entertainment. Certainly, there were women who, for reasons both personal and political, rejected officers' overtures. But there were also many others who were persuaded by officers' genteel manners and who eagerly joined the garrison social scene. With motivations ranging from impulse to deliberate calculation, the young women of the colonial elite engaged in whirlwind wartime romances with occupying British officers.

ROMANCE AND MARRIAGE

Within the inescapably politicized social environment of occupied cities, garrison social life nevertheless provided ample opportunities for romantic relationships to develop between officers and affluent young women. Balls, dinners, and plays were sites of polite, genteel sociability where young couples could fall in love. Observing young women's "great raptures . . . for the officers and soldiers" of the British Army—or lobsterbacks as they were derisively called because of their scarlet uniforms—one Massachusetts woman jokingly inquired of a young acquaintance "whether she has yet boiled her lobster." Although spoken in jest, the joke reveals an essential facet of life in British-occupied cities: garrisons were filled with young, single men and women of similar social status who were eager for fun and flirtation and for whom marriage was a real possibility, especially among officers seeking wealthy wives and well-to-do American women whose male acquaintances were displaced by the war. Indeed, even in British headquarters in New York, with its large loyalist refugee population, many elite young women exhibited a clear preference for military suitors. As one male loyalist lamented, "That female society which used to be the delight of my soul can be no otherwise enjoyed than by subjecting yourself to the feelings of Insignificance which the Lord's and Sir George's and dear Colonel's and etc frequently occasion, or by descending a step lower [in rank] than I would willingly do."[41]

The stakes of such relationships were, nevertheless, much higher for young women than their military beaus—armies moved on; men advanced in their careers; there would be more women in the next garrison. But, for young American women facing an indeterminate war, who felt that the conflict had delayed their entry into womanhood and who were eager to move out of their parents' houses and begin families of their own, prospects were less certain. Marriage to an officer provided a way to avoid, as one woman joked, "the horrid appellation of Old Maid" and the accompanying "pitty . . . from the Married part of our Sex." Like the laboring women who gambled that a relationship with a soldier might improve their lives, young women of means seized on the opportunities presented by wartime romances to launch themselves into matrimony and householding—frequently without the consent of their parents, many of whom felt that their daughters' actions posed yet another challenge to their embattled household governance in the occupied city. Writing of one such instance in New York, loyalist William Rawle reported, "A pretty Miss Griffiths of the age of fourteen finding marriages so very fashionable and thinking them very clever eloped with a Hessian officer for want of a better. Father and Mother, as usual, inconsolable."[42]

Still, impulsive marriages were not without risk. One unfortunate Boston bride, in an extreme illustration of these dynamics, discovered shortly after her 1777 marriage to "a Stranger" that, not only was her new husband an alcoholic, she "ha[d] the additional misery of finding herself the wife of a married Man and the Father of 5 children." In an era when divorce was rare and a wife's property, legal identity, and livelihood depended wholly on her husband, marriage was not a choice to be made lightly. As one woman cautioned in 1786, "A delicate mind must revolt at the idea of forming a Connection in which its happiness is so greatly dependant, so very precipitately, and with a Gentleman who was a perfect stranger, not only to herself and family, but to her Country." Even so, many young women such as seventeen-year-old Nabby Adams craved the excitement of romance, even as war raged around them. "I long to be in Love," she sighed, even as she worried that rash decisions that arose from "romantick sentiments of *Love* . . . are very daingerous I am told."[43]

Such desires, combined with the intoxicating atmosphere of British garrisons, accelerated elite young women's relationships with British, loyalist, and Hessian officers, leading to whirlwind wartime romances. "I am hurried on by an irresistable impulse to act in a manner that would shock those whose esteem is most dear to me, and astonish all those who ever heard [my] name," New York Quaker Hannah Lawrence—the same poet who so vehemently condemned the garrison's social scene—confided to a friend of her courtship by a loyalist officer. Although wary of Lieutenant Jacob Schieffelin's insistence on a quick marriage, Hannah was nevertheless tempted by his proposal, even though it would require her to renounce her Quaker faith and conflicted with her own sympathies for the rebellion. "I find the most extreme difficulty in . . . resisting the fervency of his entreaties," she confessed. Undeterred by Hannah's reluctance, in early August 1780, Jacob Schieffelin changed his quarters to the Lawrence household, where he continued to court the young woman and her family. The couple wed two weeks later, despite the objections of Hannah's brothers and her father's regret that the marriage would make the young woman a stranger to her family and the Quaker community. Nor was Hannah alone. Alluding to the mythological Greek god of marriage, Elizabeth Shipton reported from the New York garrison in 1780 that "Hymen we are told is to light the torch for several of our heros and fair ones." She was amused to discover among the prospective brides one woman who was "always pouring out bitter invectives against Matrimony, and vowd she would never subject herself to the Will of a tyrant husband."[44]

Romance aside, both officers and elite female civilians often approached wartime relationships with an element of practical financial calculation. Officers had more freedom to marry than enlisted men, whose marriages were subject to strict military oversight and required the approval of superior officers. Even so, as one New York woman observed in 1782, "marrying does not seem to be much the Fashion." Indeed, commanding officers actively discouraged men from forming serious attachments—unless the woman was rich. "I cannot conceal how much I should in general prefer, that the officers should entirely abandon all such intentions [of marriage], especially during the war and the continuance of the campaigns," the landgrave of Hesse expressed to General William von Knyphausen. Yet, he added, if an officer could obtain a wealthy American wife, such marriages were to be encouraged "with the hoped for and stipulated advantage that wife and fortune will follow the officer to Europe and Hesse without fail."[45]

As these comments suggest, wealth was a significant enticement for European officers to wed American women. In Newport, for example, Polly,

Elizabeth, and Ruth Wanton—the teenage daughters of Joseph Wanton, Jr., a prosperous merchant and son of the colony's royal governor—all married British officers, as did their stepmother, Sarah, after her husband's death. Wealth was, of course, not mutually exclusive with love. As Captain Johann Ewald of the Jaeger Corps professed to Jeannette Van Horne, the loyalist woman he was courting, "It is you upon whom depends my great happiness . . . you are the cause of my remaining in America after the peace, you are the foundation of my bright fortune." Although highborn, many officers were younger sons, whose inheritance would be minimal; a rich American wife would go a long way toward supplementing their pensions. Nor was this fact lost on civilians. Writing of one couple who eloped in the New York garrison, one woman tartly wondered, "You taste her lips—and how did you like them?—were they the sweeter for haveing twenty thousand Pounds hanging on them?" Female civilians also, however, frankly assessed the financial benefits of their military suitors. "I shou'd think the Din of Arms, and alarms of War, wou'd frighten away the God of soft delights and render the Temple of Hymen quite useless," Mary Murray mused in June 1775, after learning of the outbreak of war in Massachusetts. "But on the contrary I hear, Miss Day is about to enter the state, with a Mr. Butler an officer with £1600 a year. if this is a fact to be sure she is in the right . . . which I hope will be productive of lasting happiness to her."[46]

Despite the extenuating wartime circumstances, such attitudes toward marriage and courtship were, in many ways, normal, if intensified. In British garrisons, young men and women flirted, fell in love, weathered heartbreak, and dreamed of the future. Yet the backdrop of war subjected these relationships to new levels of critique and political polarization. Outside of British garrisons, revolutionary onlookers eyed these relationships with suspicion. For these critics, sociability between young unmarried women and British and Hessian officers functioned as a potent lens through which to critique British rule. Contrasting the actions of British troops with the supposed virtues of their Continental counterparts, revolutionaries alleged that British officers were seducing young women away from their proper roles, duties, and obligations—to the peril of the women themselves, their households, and, possibly, the entire revolutionary cause.

THE MESCHIANZA

Settling into her pose, Williamina Smith smoothed her white silk skirt, admiring the colorful, delicately embroidered bouquets of flowers (Figures 17 and 18). Reaching up to adjust the single strand of pearls that was artfully

Figure 17 Pierre Du Simitiere, *Pastel Portrait, Probably of Williamina Smith*, n.d. Du Simitiere, Drawings and Watercolors, 961.F.25a. Courtesy of the Library Company of Philadelphia

threaded through her dark hair, she thought back to the elegant gauze turban that had encircled her brown curls on the night of the Meschianza ball. The headpiece had been a work of art: decorated with pearls, a feather, and edged in gold, it included a veil that cascaded down her right side and ended below her waist, its delicate fabric brushing against the fringed sash that trailed down into her skirts, emphasizing her figure and marking her as a lady of the Burning Mountain (Figure 19). A bemused smile dancing on her lips, Williamina lifted her head to look directly at the Swiss portraitist, her gaze frank and aloof and her genteel posture embodying the elegance that had led the assembled British officers to laud her as "the Meschianza Queen" on the night of the ball.[47]

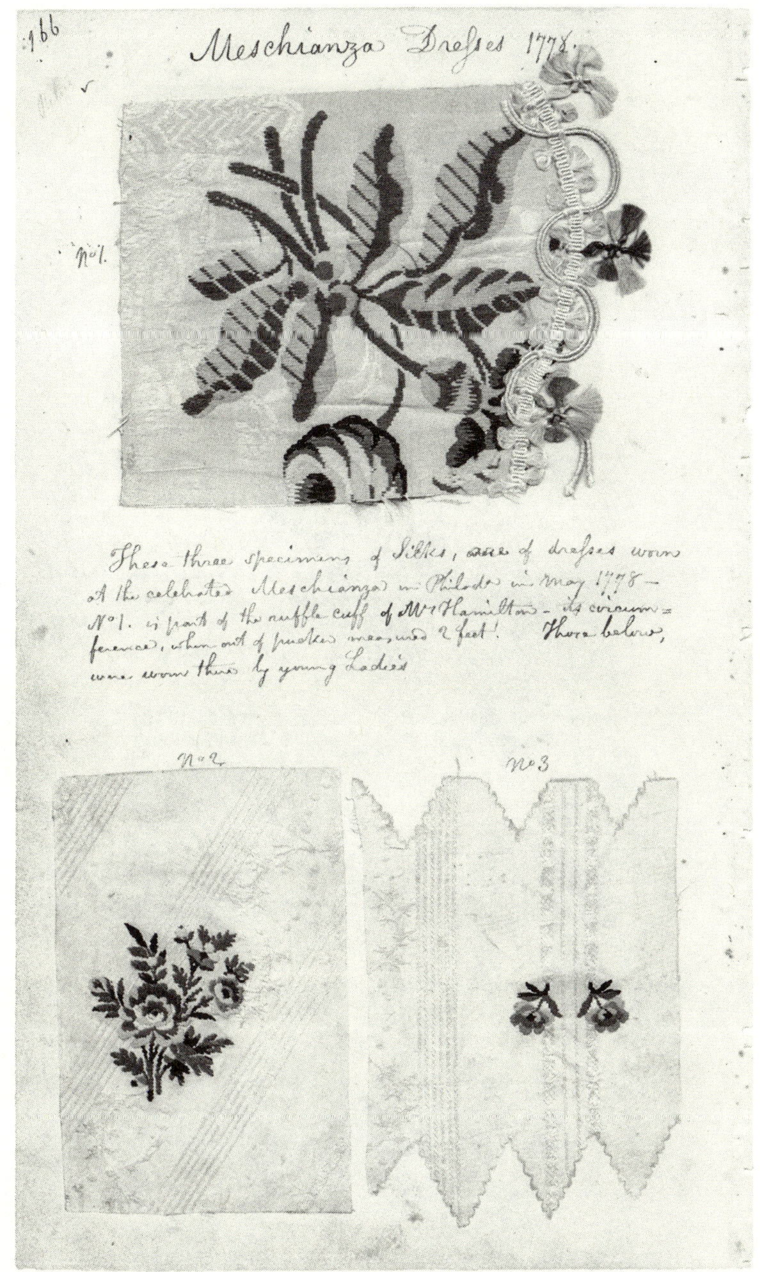

FIGURE 18 Meschianza Dresses, [1778]. Watson's Annals, Yi2 1609.F.163–166, the Library Company of Philadelphia. Photo by author

FIGURE 19 Major John André, *Sketch of a Meschianza Costume*, 1778. Watercolor. Gift of John Fanning Watson, 1830. Courtesy of the Library Company of Philadelphia

As the artist went about his work, Williamina's mind drifted back to that balmy May night, three weeks prior, when she, along with fourteen other young, unmarried Philadelphia women—who in the words of Captain John André were "the foremost in youth, beauty and fashion"—were at the center of the retirement celebrations for British commander in chief Sir William Howe. After several local inhabitants raised objections to the event, Williamina's father had not wanted her to attend, but she had convinced him. Escorted by the dashing dragoon Brigadier-Major Banastre Tarleton, who was handsomely adorned in black and orange silk, Williamina had donned her Turkish dress and turban, and, at half past three, she boarded a naval warship to enjoy a leisurely, three-hour sail down the Schuylkill River, surrounded by handsome officers and serenaded by military bands. Smaller boats surrounded each of the three galleys, and British warships with colors flying offered salutes as the regatta passed by. It was an elaborate staging, a spectacle for the city. Throngs of Philadelphians gathered along the river's banks, "crouding the wharfs, the shipping, the balconies, and the tops of the houses" to observe the procession.[48]

At seven o'clock the barges docked at the Wharton family mansion, Walnut Grove. Disembarking from the ship, Williamina "walked up between two files of Grenadiers" to take her seat on a "magnificent pavilion" on the lawn alongside the other fourteen similarly attired young women adorned in Turkish costumes. She settled in to watch the evening's main event: fourteen British officers attired in lavish silk costumes modeled on the court of Henry IV—divided into two opposing factions, the Knights of the Blended Rose (in red and white) and the Knights of the Burning Mountain (in black and orange)—engaging in a mock joust to defend the honor, wit, and beauty of their respective ladies. Charging at one another with spears and firing pistols, the knights engaged in hand-to-hand combat until, in a scripted intervention, the ladies called for a truce. Interrupting the swordfight, the women declared themselves "perfectly satisfied with the proofs of love, and the signal feats of valour given by their respective Knights; and commanded them, as they prized the future favours of their Mistresses, that they would instantly desist from further combat." Obeying instantly, the knights sheathed their swords and saluted the ladies before escorting them up the hill to the exquisitely decorated mansion. There, Williamina had enjoyed a lavish dinner served by twenty-four enslaved waiters dressed "in blue and white Turbans and sashes with bright bracelets and Collars," followed by hours of dancing, toasts, and other festivities as fireworks exploded overhead.[49]

FIGURE 20 Meschianza Ticket, 1778. Gift of Mrs. John Meredish Read, 1900. Courtesy of the Library Company of Philadelphia

The Meschianza, an invented Italian word meaning medley, was an elaborate undertaking organized by officers of the British Army in May 1778 to celebrate the retirement of General Sir William Howe. Held at an estate outside of Philadelphia, the event lasted eighteen hours, and festivities included a regatta, a mock jousting match, a ball, fireworks, and a feast. It was a fête champêtre, a popular contemporary outdoor entertainment characterized, in the words of one scholar, by "opulent stagecraft and the fancy dress of a masquerade ball." Even by contemporary standards, it was an extravagant affair. "Everything was as splendid and magnificent as possible," one participant

FIGURE 21 *Walnut Grove, the Residence of Joseph Wharton*, 1775. 2526.F.96 (Poulson), Walnut Grove Research File, the Library Company of Philadelphia. Photo by author

enthused, "and all, even those who have been in Paris or London, agree that they have never seen such a luxurious fete."[50]

For both contemporaries and historians, the Meschianza has symbolized the frivolity and dissipation of the British Army during the Revolution. Writing in her diary the night of the Meschianza, perhaps as fireworks exploded over the Schuylkill River, Elizabeth Drinker explicitly linked the suffering of the city's civilian inhabitants with her feelings toward the elaborate fete, lamenting the "Scenes of Folly and Vanity, promoted by the officers of the Army" while many inhabitants suffered. "How insensible do these people appear, while our Land is so greatly desolated, and Death and sore destruction has overtaken and impends over so many," she declared.[51]

When viewed within the context of the British Army's war for hearts and minds, it is evident that the Meschianza was more than a lavish retirement party, although it certainly was that, too. The event's organizers, scholars have shown, envisioned the Meschianza as a "precisely scripted" spectacle designed to exhibit the power of the British Empire, the valor of British military forces, and the polished, elite cosmopolitanism of British officers, whose

FIGURE 22 Major John André, *Meschianza Knight*, [1778]. Watercolor. Courtesy of Cliveden, a Historic Site of the National Trust for Historic Preservation, Philadelphia

chivalric feats secured the voluntary submission of their colonial subjects—embodied by fourteen young, unmarried elite white American women—to British authority. Indeed, the widespread publication of accounts of the ball after the fact make clear that the Meschianza was intended as an outward-facing projection of British power, even as local inhabitants expressed dismay over the event's extravagance.[52]

Epitomizing the British Army's strategy of intermingling personal and political courtship, the Meschianza illustrates the central role of young women in garrison social entertainments and the sexualized narratives that emerged around these events. Throughout occupied cities, this strategy was deeply entwined with the romantic courtship of young unmarried women. Military entertainments created spaces for these young women to wield a degree of social power that many women leveraged to alter their lives in tangible ways.

But, embedded within eighteenth-century notions of romantic courtship, and its more sinister form of seduction, were insinuations of women's eventual submission to their suitors, whether through marriage (with its notions of political and legal subordination) or sex. Thus, whether or not young unmarried women actually engaged in sexual relationships with British officers, the implication of sexual submission functioned as a potent weapon for both British officers and American revolutionaries to define the meaning of young women's participation in garrison social events. The Meschianza exemplifies these dynamics: insinuations of young women's sexual promiscuity and submission to British officers were evident in both the Meschianza's allegorical entertainments and the scorn that American observers directed toward the young women who attended the ball and partook in its pageantry.[53]

The Meschianza's sumptuous costumes were essential to conveying an overtly sexualized interpretation of the imperial relationship between Britain and the American colonies. The mottos emblazoned on the knights' shields, such as Captain John André's sigil of two gamecocks under the maxim "No Rival," brashly proclaimed the virility of British officers. Inspired by the Crusades, officers' neo-feudal garb and the women's Turkish costumes likewise conjured notions of European superiority and the subjugation of colonial peoples. The women's attire, in particular, buoyed this narrative. As historian Susan Klepp has argued, Turkish dress evoked "a sensualized, captive, nonmonogamous womanhood" that entwined women's social, political, and sexual loyalties. Seduced by the knights' gallant manners and martial prowess, the women's submission to British officers offered a satisfying narrative conclusion of British dominance and American capitulation whilst also flagrantly flaunting young women's preference for British rule and British officers over their Continental counterparts.[54]

Indeed, the Meschianza ladies' active role in the pageantry—bringing an end to the joust by promising to bestow their "future favours" to the knights—was critical to its symbolic significance. Alluding to the literal favors that the knights received in the next phase of the event, the promise of "future favours" conjured sexual connotations. It was an intentional choice of words. In his detailed account of the Meschianza published in the *Gentleman's Magazine* in August 1778, John André underscored the sexual nature of the young women's capitulation. Unfailingly referring to the female ball attendees as "ladies" throughout the piece, André notably altered his terminology only once: at the joust's conclusion, when the knights sheathed their swords in exchange for "the future favours of their Mistresses." The promise of favors, juxtaposed with Captain André's characterization of the young women as "Mistresses" and the subtle erotic imagery of sheathed swords, overtly sexualized this armistice. The young women's voluntary surrender to British officers, the Meschianza's carefully choreographed spectacle implied, signaled Britain's clear victory in the war for hearts and minds.[55]

The sexualized discourse surrounding the Meschianza is further evidenced in one of the evening's entertainments: the "Catalogue of Books." Attendees showcased their wit by devising fictional book titles (and, occasionally, real ones) that revealed characteristics of the purported author, typically other guests in attendance, but also well-known figures. The titles ranged from generic odes to women's beauty ("Miss in her Teens a pretty Pocket Volume . . . . . . Miss P. Ross"), to good-natured ribbing of women's elaborate hairstyles ("The Extravagance of Fashion or the portable Pyramid (a farce[)]. . . . Miss Stocker") to vilification of Continental officers and their French allies ("The Broken Parole a Moral Tale in french Ct. D'Estaing") to explicitly sexual jokes ("Frisky a la mode a Comedy second Hand worse for wear. . . . Mrs. Shaw"). The most overtly sexual titles—such as that for Mrs. Francis, "Calipaedia or Theory in Practice A Winter Nights Amusement. . . . To which is added a sensible and visible Appendix in Sheets. . . . by a British officer"—were reserved for married women. The lone exception to this trend was Rebecca Franks, renowned for her cutting wit, who was listed as the purported author of "The Secret History of Genl. Sir William Howe Knight of the Bath"—a sexualized double entendre of the general's title that might have alluded to Rebecca's ability to "undress" people with her sharp tongue but that nevertheless imbued the general's regular visits to the Franks household with sexual connotations. Titles for other unmarried women suggested their sexual inaccessibility, such as Miss Budden's "The Temptations of Tantalus," a reference to Greek mythology in which a parched and hungry Tantalus was condemned to spend eternity surrounded by water and low-hanging fruit that perpetually eluded his grasp. The catalogue also listed, however, a volume already sold, "The Counterfeit Virgin a Masque well stich'd in Sheets"—a sly innuendo which suggested that these unmarried women were perhaps not quite as innocent as they seemed.[56]

But implications of young elite Philadelphians' sexual submission to British officers resonated far beyond the entertainments of the Meschianza itself. Insinuations of these young women's implied sexual and political infidelity to the revolutionary cause are apparent in the vitriol that revolutionaries directed toward the women who socialized with British officers, both at the Meschianza and throughout the occupation.

The Meschianza occurred in a moment when the momentum of the war was shifting, making the ball an ideal target for exhilarated revolutionaries eager to humiliate their British foes. In February 1778, France had entered the war, signing a treaty of alliance with the United States. Indeed, in part motivated by the treaty, in June 1778—exactly one month after the Meschianza—the British evacuated Philadelphia and withdrew to British headquarters in New York City, taking many loyalists with them. Less than two weeks later, on a battlefield approximately sixty miles from Philadelphia, General George Washington demonstrated the success of his winter training regimen at Valley Forge when the Continental army defeated the British at the Battle of Monmouth. Jubilant revolutionaries celebrated their victory over the British forces who had spent the winter partaking in dancing and frivolity alongside Philadelphia's women. Touting their battlefield victory and their successful repossession of the capital city, revolutionaries set about reclaiming Philadelphia as their own following months of enemy occupation. Having occurred mere weeks before the Continental army's return to Philadelphia, the Meschianza loomed large in these efforts, functioning as a useful foil to illustrate the triumph of patriotic virtue over British indolence.

Fresh off victory at the Battle of Monmouth, in July 1778, Continental general Anthony Wayne dispatched a brief account of the engagement to the secretary of war. Invoking the Meschianza, Wayne boasted of his army's success: "Tell the Phil'a ladies that the heavenly, sweet, pretty red Coats—the accomplished Gent'n of the Guards and Grenadiers have humbled themselves on the plains of Monmouth[.]" "'The Knights of the Blended Rose' and 'Burning Mount'—have Resigned their Laurels to *Rebel* officers," Wayne crowed. Glorying in the Continental army's success, he proclaimed that "Numbers of the Richest blood of England" lay among the dead. Accentuating the status and gentility of British officers—their noble blood, handsome dress, and refined manners—and their demise at the hands of the more humble Continental forces, General Wayne's account reveals his pride in his troops and his eagerness to attest to their superiority. Yet the virulence that he directed at British officers' high class and the admiration it earned them with American women nevertheless echoed of bruised pride.[57]

General Wayne's malice toward the young women of Philadelphia, striking within the context of official military correspondence, reveals just how deeply young women's apparent preference for British officers reverberated among revolutionaries. Positioning cosmopolitan gendered sociability as the antithesis of virtuous patriotic domesticity, General Wayne vowed that his victorious troops would lay their trophies of war, that is, the laurels of the Meschianza knights, "at the feet of those Virtuous Daughters of America who cheerfully gave up ease and Affluence in a city for Liberty and peace of mind in a Cottage." Such revolutionary rhetoric intermingled notions of domestic and political virtue in ways that augmented the patriarchal power of American men over both their homes and their female dependents. Independence, in the minds of many revolutionaries, was entangled with the security of the patriarchal household and the varied, interconnected strands of power that it represented.[58]

Indeed, the domestic backdrop of elite young women's socialization with occupying British forces incurred the wrath of white revolutionaries throughout the colonies. Writing from Lancaster, Pennsylvania, in December 1777, where he and his wife had fled during the British occupation of Philadelphia, revolutionary Christopher Marshall expressed his disgust with those Philadelphians who cavorted with British troops and "revel[ed] in luxury, dissipation and drunkenness, without any feelings for the distress of their (once happy) bleeding country." The domestic setting of these social engagements exacerbated the offense. Condemning these entertainments, Marshall thundered against "our enemies revelling in balls, attended with every degree of luxury and excess in the City; rioting and wantonly using our houses, utensils and furniture."[59]

In British-occupied cities, then, social interactions between unmarried daughters and British officers in the very houses that grounded white men's patriarchal authority accentuated the limits of white men's domestic power and the fragility of the idealized household that represented that power. British officers could, and would, invade American homes to seduce young American women away from their duties, both politically and romantically. Heads of household recognized the temptation of handsome men in uniform: concerned about his "very young" and naïve (as he believed) wife home alone in Rhode Island, one Continental officer worried, "the Roads . . . are broad and hung with Alluring Ensigns to invite her astray."[60]

To the dismay of many revolutionaries, unmarried young women in occupied cities, including their daughters, domestic servants, and enslaved women, willingly yielded to officers' advances. These social and sexual relationships nevertheless posed a problem for revolutionaries, both personally and ideologically. As heads of household, white men were responsible for maintaining order, protecting their dependents, and ensuring virtuous behavior. Thus, precisely because of their dependent position within American households, young women's actions reflected back upon and were entangled with male revolutionaries' own sense of honor and patriarchal authority. From the war's outset, homespun clothing and patriotic boycotts made clear that domestic politics were entwined with formal ones. And such expectations intensified as the war progressed. For if a man could not retain control over his own household, how could he hope to contribute to the government of the new nation?

Furthermore, the sexualized connotations implied by young women's socialization with British officers at the Meschianza offered an explicit contrast to revolutionaries' emphasis on patriotic virtue, a deeply gendered concept that was, for white women, linked to sexual purity but that was broadly associated with notions of sacrifice, austerity, and morality. Within this context, revolutionaries frequently criticized fashion, with its gendered associations of imported metropolitan culture and goods, frivolity, and profligate extravagance, as a prime example of how British rule corrupted American virtue. During the early years of the imperial crisis, especially in urban centers like Philadelphia, fashion became a political flashpoint precisely because, much to revolutionaries' dismay, many young women refused to exchange their imported British silks for drab homespun—in direct opposition to revolutionaries' proscriptions. Philadelphia poet Hannah Griffitts articulated many women's sentiments when she rebuked Thomas Paine's prescriptions for female prudence in *The American Crisis* (1777): "Of female Manners,—never Scrible, / Nor with thy Rudeness wound our ear, / How'ere thy [Trimming] Pen may quibble—/ The Delicate is—'not Thy sphere.'" Women's refusal to sacrifice their fashion and their flagrant rejection of revolutionaries' proscriptions was worrying to many male supporters of the rebellion. Such behavior, they feared, signaled a troubling lack of virtue that had the potential to imperil the revolutionary cause by encouraging vice and bolstering imperial ties.[61]

The elaborate costumes and extravagance of the Meschianza confirmed these fears by positioning young women, adorned in the cloth and imagery of empire, at the center of the pageantry—as two historians have put it, as "trophies to be won"—a purposeful staging that flaunted young women's adoring (and implied sexual) submission to British officers. It was a resounding rejection of revolutionary principles. In the war for hearts and minds, the Meschianza suggested, young, elite American women had rejected upright minutemen and their quaint notions of sheltered, patriotic virtue in preference for the virile British officers, who offered them a central role in upholding the social and cultural fabric of Britain's cosmopolitan empire—virtue be damned.[62]

With this context, General Wayne's specific praise for the "Virtuous Daughters" of America takes on new weight. Domestic seclusion ensured that young women's virtue, both personal and political, was safeguarded against the predations of British officers. Praising young women who chose rural solitude over urban amusement, General Wayne lauded these daughters precisely because their obedience to revolutionary proscriptive behaviors buoyed the patriarchal authority of their fathers. He was not an impassive observer of this matter. Although his daughter was only eight years old at the time—far too young to socialize with British officers—Wayne proudly counted her among this group of virtuous American women. His daughter's behavior, General Wayne felt, was a key barometer of his own patriotism; her obedience testified to the strength of his domestic authority. Virtuous daughters were a point of pride for male revolutionaries, for whom their positions as fathers and heads of household were critical to how they conceived of and proved their identities as both patriots and patriarchs.[63]

"ROUGH MUSIC" AND RACIALIZED RETELLINGS

The sexualized discourse surrounding both the Meschianza and its southern counterpart, the so-called 1782 "Ethiopian Ball" in Charleston, which will be discussed later in this chapter, was also notable for the racialized notions of sexual impropriety that surfaced in the weeks, months, and years after the balls occurred. As the war progressed and Continental forces regained control of occupied regions, young women who had seized on the opportunities of occupation to challenge the status quo or pursue prospects outside of their households faced increasing backlash. But it was a delicate balance, especially once the headiness of victory dissipated and the need for political reconciliation became apparent. In such moments—for instance, when Philadelphia returned to Continental hands in 1778 and as peace appeared on the horizon in Charleston in 1782—revolutionaries subtly transferred their denunciations of young women's supposed infidelity to the revolutionary cause from the young, unmarried white women of the urban elite onto Black women, both free and enslaved. This rhetorical displacement served two interrelated purposes. First, it repaired the tarnished patriarchal authority of the male heads of household who had failed to contain and protect the virtue of their female relations. And secondly, it redeemed these young women in the eyes of American revolutionaries, transforming them from the scandalous consorts of British officers into virtuous republican women, who, though momentarily dazzled by British pageantry, would ultimately become the wives and mothers of future American citizens.

These dynamics are evident in an incident of "rough music" that occurred on July 4, 1778, the second anniversary of the Declaration of Independence. A mere three weeks after the British evacuated Philadelphia, a boisterous crowd paraded a dirty woman through city streets attired in finery and the elaborate headdress of the Meschianza ladies. The parade ended at the City Tavern, where weekly balls were held during the occupation. Writing of the episode in August 1778, New Hampshire delegate Josiah Bartlett asserted that the incident was sparked by loyalist women who "appeared in public" on the Fourth of July—a holiday to celebrate revolutionaries' military accomplishments and patriotic virtue—with their hair styled like "the Mistresses and wh[ore]s of the British officers." Once again conflating fashion and sexual promiscuity, Bartlett's scorn for elite women's sociability with the occupying forces suggests the extent to which these women's supposed sexual, social, and political infidelity, as epitomized through sartorial display, undermined the authority of male revolutionaries.[64]

As historian Susan Klepp has argued, the July Fourth 1778 street theater was intended as a gendered critique of elite Philadelphians' socialization with occupying forces that deliberately targeted the young women whose behavior had "corrupted revolutionary virtue." In mocking these young women, the episode of "rough music" endeavored to collectively mend male revolutionaries' damaged egos by disciplining the young women who had consorted with occupying forces. Infidelity, whether in politics, fashion, or sex, would not be tolerated. As revolutionary John Thaxter explained, the parade "was designed to ridicule" the ladies of Philadelphia. "The end was answered," he declared with satisfaction. Yet the young women who attended the Meschianza were not so easily chastened. Mere months after the Continental army regained control of Philadelphia, in the fall of 1778, Rebecca Franks gleefully recounted the cancellation of a ball that had been planned for the city's revolutionaries (presumably because the event would have violated prescriptions for patriotic austerity). In a cryptic comment that seemingly referred to the backlash against the Meschianza, she confessed, "I'm delighted that it came to nothing as they had the impudence to laugh at us."[65]

Significantly, however, the details of the rough music evolved in months after the incident. Increasingly, the woman at the center of the parade was referred to as a sex worker (she was, in the words of one observer, "a noted and infamous doxy"). And, by August 1778, when New Hampshire delegate

Josiah Bartlett wrote to his wife, Mary, he described the woman as "an old Negro wench." This interpretation held; nineteenth-century histories of the incident identified the woman as Black. This linguistic evolution signaled a crucial ideological shift. By displacing the sexualized womanhood embodied by the elite, white Meschianza ladies onto a Black sex worker, revolutionaries reaffirmed racialized conceptions of virtue and transferred their scorn from elite white daughters to Black working women.[66]

In Philadelphia, a city with comparatively few enslaved laborers, this revised interpretation endeavored to neutralize the threat that occupation had posed to male revolutionaries and their households: it removed the menace of seduction from their residences and onto the bodies of free Black women—women who were largely outside of the white patriarchal household structure. Black women's submission to British forces, redefined as prostitution, did not undermine the patriarchal rights of white American men; free Black women's actions did not reflect white American men's patriarchal failings in the same way as did those of elite white women and other dependents within the household. The street pageantry thus served the dual purpose of disciplining elite women and redeeming their virtue, consequently buttressing American men's domestic power by relocating the source of women's traitorous submission outside of the household and beyond the bounds of patriarchal authority. It was, to be sure, a performative exercise; no one truly believed that the Meschianza had been attended by Black women. Yet, by invoking racialized notions of sexuality, the street theater was intended to intimidate those women who had socialized with the British and to reassert the authority of male revolutionaries over their city, their households, and their female dependents. These efforts, which simultaneously disciplined young American women and redeemed their virtue, were critical steps in revising the narrative of the Meschianza in service of the revolutionary project.

This reinterpretation did not, however, gain traction immediately. The following year, in 1779, Philadelphia Quaker Hannah Griffitts wrote a scathing poem that mocked the Meschianza as "A shameful scene of dissipation / The Death of sense and Reputation." Declining to minimize the power that young unmarried white women of the upper classes had wielded within the occupied city, Griffitts instead emphasized their influence by placing these young women squarely at the center of the event. "Recollection's pained to know, / That *Ladies* joined the frantic show," she proclaimed, declaring, "When female Prudence thus can fail, / Tis time the Sex should wear the veil." Aiming her critiques at the female ball attendees, rather than the British officers who organized the event, Griffitts made clear that the women had not been deluded into attending; they had chosen to be there. Rebuking the Meschianza ladies for what Griffitts perceived as their infidelity to the revolutionary cause, Griffitts's poem—like the rough music that occurred on July 4, 1778—pointedly sexualized their betrayal, advising them to "wear the veil." Seclusion in a convent, and its requisite chastity, was the proper punishment for Philadelphia women's transgressive relationships with British officers.[67]

And yet, an alternative reading of the poem might also offer a prescription for what Griffitts saw as young, wayward women—one that offered a different path to redemption. Although bridal veils had largely fallen out of fashion in the eighteenth century, the practice dated back to ancient Rome, and Griffitts might have invoked the imagery of the veil as a metaphor for marriage, advising the Meschianza ladies to marry Continental soldiers. When viewed in conjunction with the rough music in Philadelphia on July 4, 1778, Griffitts's prescription gestures to a nascent logic of racialized redemption in which young white women's seemingly unchaste relationships with British officers could be redeemed through marriage to American patriots and honorable republican motherhood.[68]

The enduring legacies of this redemptive rhetoric are evident in John F. Watson's 1830 history, *The Annals of Philadelphia*. In his account, Watson reduced the Meschianza to fanciful, harmless fun; young women's attendance at the ball was simply the result of misguided youthful folly. "No offence was offered to the ladies afterwards for their acceptance of this instance of the enemy's hospitality," Watson explained, relating that the Meschianza ladies likewise attended a Continental ball in 1778, shortly after the British evacuation of Philadelphia. After the women danced with American officers and their French allies, he insisted, it was "as if nothing of jealousy had ever existed, and all umbrage was forgotten." The "rough music" of July Fourth 1778 is conspicuously absent from Watson's *Annals*. Instead, in Watson's hands, the Meschianza functions as a redemptive tale in which the Meschianza ladies, though briefly dazzled by British gallantry, are absolved of their youthful blunders by socializing with revolutionaries after the Continental army regained Philadelphia in June 1778.[69]

Emphasizing social reconciliation over discord, Watson's selective narration of the Meschianza as a tale of youthful folly reveals the success of efforts to rhetorically redeem the supposed traitorous sexuality of the young white women who would become the mothers of future American citizens. He excised contemporary allegations of sexual impropriety and dismissed the active role that young unmarried white women of the upper classes played in shaping the social atmosphere of occupied Philadelphia, along with the rancor that both incurred from revolutionaries. It was, Watson confessed, an intentional choice: after reading Hannah Griffitts's poem, he deliberately omitted the poem and its insinuations of impropriety from his *Annals*. "I cover it up to hide the apparent ill nature—to avoid offence to those who now survive and are deserving of my esteem," Watson explained.[70]

But such rosy reimaginings conceal the importance of these garrison social events and the power of the young women who attended them. For as the contemporary uproar surrounding the 1778 Meschianza and, further south, in reaction to a supposed 1782 ball between enslaved women and British officers suggests, the socialization of young women, both white and Black, with British officers was deeply entangled with notions of race, gender, and sexuality in ways that challenged the broader social order and the vision that revolutionaries had for their own independence. That revolutionaries endeavored to relocate, or in some instances, simply purge these relationships from their narratives of the war, only underscores how truly disruptive these relationships were.

THE "ETHIOPIAN BALL"

After 1779, the British Army pushed into the southern colonies, which were home to larger enslaved populations. Accordingly, the army adopted emancipatory policies, such as the 1779 Philipsburg Proclamation, that made strategic overtures to the enslaved in order to deprive revolutionaries of valuable laborers and financial resources. Reflecting these local contexts, racialized rhetoric about Black women's social and supposed sexual intercourse with British officers intensified in the south, an evolution that illustrates both the adaptability and the persistence of the dynamics on display in Philadelphia. Failing to acknowledge the often coercive nature of Black women's relationships with British officers, as the war moved to the south, revolutionaries increasingly associated treacherous socialization, not with the young unmarried women of the colonial elite, but with Black women.[71]

In South Carolina, these accusations contained a kernel of truth. By 1782, approximately a year and a half into the occupation of Charleston, the end of the war was on the horizon. Wary of facing reprisals from victorious revolutionaries, many white Charleston women were less inclined to socialize with British troops. Their hesitation, however, did not meaningfully impede officers' pursuit of revelry—they simply found other women to consort with. In occupied Charleston, where British officers routinely leased enslaved women from inhabitants and where large populations of freedom-seeking refugees crowded the garrison streets, British officers on at least one occasion in January 1782 appeared to have looked to these free and enslaved Black women for companionship.

Three months after Cornwallis's surrender at Yorktown—a defeat that presaged Britain's eventual loss of the war—the supposed January 1782 "Ethiopian Ball," as contemporaries called it, marked a stark reversal of the army's earlier tactics, in which officers hoped that elite sociability and genteel behavior would pave the way for political reunion. With the cessation of hostilities imminent, winning the allegiances of white civilians was no longer a priority. Consequently, by war's end, the social events that had once proved so integral to Britain's strategy of social and political courtship had morphed into a venue to insult the white colonists who rejected British rule and British officers. Only a single account of the ball, authored by a Continental officer, exists. Although it is impossible to determine the veracity of this account, or whether it was simply clever propaganda, it was built on a plausible foundation. The supposed ball highlights both the possibilities for Black women behind British lines and the dismay that their wartime actions engendered among white revolutionaries. It symbolizes how the control of Black women's bodies, rather than those of young, elite white women, similarly functioned as a proxy for the larger political contest that symbolized the maligned masculine authority and privileges of white American patriarchs.

According to the account, in early January 1782, three Black women, Hagar Roussell, Izabell Pinckney, and Mary Fraser, who were most likely formerly enslaved women behind British lines, organized a ball for "Officers of the Army" and "female Slaves, only." The women invited officers to the ball with calling cards, not unlike the ones used by Charleston's elite women. The event itself was held at 99 Meeting Street, "a very capital private House." Officers "dress'd [the women] up in taste, with the richest silks, and false rolls on their heads, powder'd up in the most pompous manner," and escorted them to the ball in carriages. It was an extravagant affair: "Supper cost not less than £80 Sterling," and the festivities lasted until four in the morning. In organizing and attending the ball, these women seized on the army's disruptive presence and the city's disordered patriarchal norms to claim new space and authority within Charleston's elite homes. As the British Army curtailed the power of slaveholding revolutionaries and denied them access to the houses that were markers of their status and prestige, enslaved women's transformation of these spaces and their functions—albeit temporarily—realigned power relations within Charleston's elite households and remade the domestic spaces within.[72]

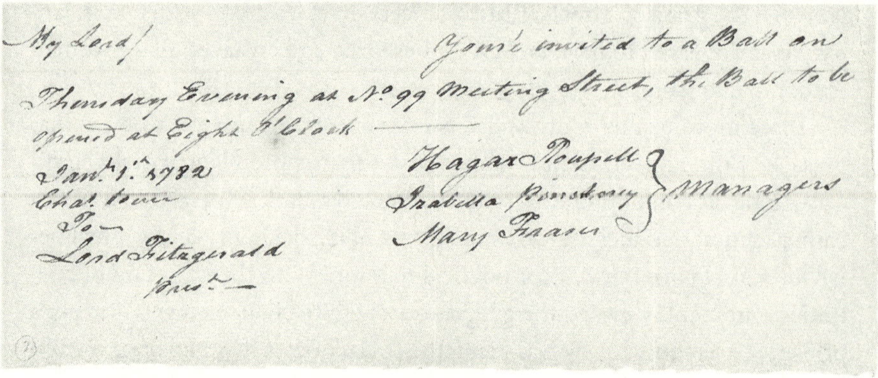

My Lord!
You're invited to a Ball on Thursday Evening at No. 99 Meeting Street, the Ball to be opened at Eight O'Clock —

Jan.ry 1st 1782
Chas. town
To —
Lord Fitzgerald
Present —

Hagar Poupell
Isabella [illegible]
Mary Fraser
} Managers

FIGURE 23 Copy of Ticket to the Ethiopian Ball, enclosed in Daniel Stevens to John Wendall, Feb. 20, 1782. MS Am 1907. Courtesy of Houghton Library, Harvard University, Cambridge, Mass.

Occupation enhanced the power of Black women to shape these spaces and the entertainments that occurred in them. But their ability to do so was not entirely unprecedented. For example, on his 1778 tour of South Carolina, Ebenezer Hazard remarked on the "peculiarity" of "black dances" in the state, noting that "Negro and Mullatto women" hosted elegant dances for "many of the first [white] gentlemen" in the region. Although Hazard recorded the hostesses' elegant dress and "polite behavior," he was silent as to whether they were enslaved or free. His observation that the women were "generally in keeping," implying that they were gentlemen's mistresses, is nevertheless reminiscent of *plaçage* and quadroon balls in New Orleans. Another observer reported in 1772 that at private dances, Charleston's Black community danced, socialized, and mocked their enslavers by imitating their manners. These "nocturnal rendezvouses" took place in the homes of free Black people, apartments rented to slaves, or, notably, in "the *kitchens* of such Gentlemen as frequently retire, with their families, into the country." Charleston's enslaved community, therefore, had a tradition of appropriating the manners, rituals, and homes of their enslavers for their own entertainment, but the January 1782 ball boldly moved such interactions out of the kitchen, a largely Black space, into the predominantly white rooms of 99 Meeting Street. The tradition of "black dances," moreover, raises provocative questions about the relationship between the ball attendees and the officers who escorted them: were these women, too, "in keeping"? By claiming these traditions, were they assuming a role usually reserved for free Black women, asserting both freedom and authority through social ritual? Or had the hostesses and attendees previously participated in similar entertainments and simply exchanged white Charlestonians for British officers?[73]

In addition to the city's precedents, Afro-Caribbean traditions from the British colony of Jamaica, where enslaved laborers regularly held balls dressed in European finery, might have influenced the event. In particular, the ball might have had ties to the Anglo-Caribbean and African-derived festival of Jonkannu, which, as it evolved throughout the seventeenth and eighteenth centuries, merged creole-African carnivalesque traditions with the Anglican Christmas holiday. Jonkannu took place on Boxing Day, December 26, when families donated Christmas leftovers to the poor. Slaveowners in Jamaica and other British-controlled Caribbean islands were often without their European families, and so they instead spent the day alongside the people that they enslaved. Jonkannu's practices varied among plantations, but contemporary accounts describe enslaved people attired in masks and lavish clothing, accompanied by the whiteface character of "John Canoe," dancing through the streets to the beat of drums in a festive inversion and mimicry of the plantation hierarchy. After 1790, this tradition evolved to include "Set Girl" dancing entertainments in which slaveowners "provid[ed] luxurious, European-style costumes to young African-descended women chosen for their beauty and light skin color." The dance itself was "a caricature of a vain, fine lady," with the "Set girls pranc[ing] on the balls of their feet and swing[ing] their hips provocatively."[74]

The supposed January 1782 ball involving enslaved Charleston women and British officers is reminiscent of these island practices. The event predates the "Set Girl" dances, yet the longer Caribbean traditions of interracial socialization and Jonkannu, particularly the timing of the latter (in late December), are suggestive of the influence of these Anglo-Afro-Caribbean traditions on the Charleston event—a sign not only of the British military presence in colonial Jamaica, including earlier in the American war, but also of the city's Caribbean roots. Charleston's deeply racialized and hierarchical plantation society, like Britain's Caribbean colonies, had a long history of interracial sex and socialization that occurred along a spectrum of coercion.[75]

The Charleston ball echoed these broader patterns of socialization, yet the wartime context transformed the significance of these practices. That the ball's organizers were probably enslaved prior to the occupation gestures to the leverage that Black Charlestonians possessed in the occupied city and suggests that some female attendees were probably willing participants in the event. Many enslaved people avoided unnecessary gambles during the American Revolution, and women's choices to align themselves with British

FIGURE 24 Isaac Mendes Belisario, *Red Set Girls, and Jack-in-the-Green*, 1837. From I. M. Belisario, *Sketches of Character, in Illustration of the Habits, Occupation, and Costume of the Negro Population, in the Island of Jamaica* . . . (Kingston, Jamaica, 1837). Courtesy of Yale Center for British Art, New Haven, Conn.

officers might have been strategic, relatively low-risk decisions that promised protection, food, and potentially freedom. Even so, these choices were not risk free. Slavery and slave sales persisted throughout the occupation, and contemporary accounts suggest that elite Charlestonians leased enslaved women to British officers. Some of these women might also have been in attendance. There is no way to know for certain why the women attended the ball or whether they were voluntary participants.[76]

The Charleston ball nevertheless reinforces the importance of sociability as a site of wartime power contests that were deeply tethered to prevailing notions of patriarchy and paternalism. Just as they did at the Meschianza, the British officers at Charleston's "Ethiopian Ball" performed power and challenged the authority of American men through their interactions with civilian women. The ball was not an anomaly in the city's race relations so much as a rejection of white male Charlestonians' mastery. From a legal standpoint, white Carolina slaveholders owned enslaved women's bodies, including the use of their labors and sexuality. British officers' socialization with enslaved women undercut these rights. The control of enslaved women's bodies thus became a metaphor for the broader military conflict; it was a demonstration of the virility of British officers and the enfeebled authority of male revolutionaries.[77]

Yet, even if the ball was simply a piece of propaganda, it still gestures to the widely held perception, one undoubtedly based in fact, about the new liberties and self-possession that Black women enjoyed behind British lines. And revolutionaries' outrage at their actions was very real. Indeed, if the ball was invented, the fact that the author, Daniel Stevens, an American merchant and lieutenant in the Charleston Artillery, invoked socialization between Black women and British officers is, in itself, a revealing choice. Black women's self-possession and their status as desirable social (and implied sexual) companions for British officers exposed the fragility of the racial order that undergirded enslavers' social authority and domestic power. Such a direct affront to the patriarchal ideal of the slaveholding household offered a potent, widely legible illustration of British tyranny.

Three weeks after the supposed ball, writing from Continental headquarters outside Charleston, Daniel Stevens penned a letter to a friend in which he recounted the event and stridently condemned British officers' interactions with "our female Slaves." Omitting any mention of the city's precedents for the ball, Stevens proclaimed a general white American male ownership of enslaved women's bodies and denounced the event as an example of British barbarity. His account repeatedly criticized officers' failure to interact appropriately with enslaved women, condemning "these chaps who call themselves Gentlemen" as "shameless brutes" and "tyrants." The damning nature of these interactions was amplified because of the social space in which these exchanges occurred, a private home—the literal seat of white men's authority as masters and patriarchs.[78]

It is notable, therefore, that Stevens excluded male enslavers from his tale. Whether because of their actual absence or an unwillingness to concede the diminished reach of their power, Stevens focused instead on Charleston's slaveholding women, asserting, "Many of these wretches were taken out of houses before their mistresses faces." This was not only an affront to female enslavers, whom British officers had overlooked in preference for their slaves, it also challenged their authority and revealed their inability to control enslaved women. Enslaved women's departure upended racial power relations; white women remained at home while the Black women they enslaved departed for a ball on the arms of gentlemen. The ball temporarily altered the racialized meanings embedded in Charleston's private homes, which had long been places of Black labor and white socialization, owned by men but presided over by women. In appropriating these spaces for their own entertainment, enslaved women and British officers denied white Charlestonians' exclusive right to private homes as places of leisure.[79]

Significantly, Stevens denounced the ball alongside another British transgression: that "the British tyrants . . . have arm'd our Slaves, against us." The juxtaposition of these two issues suggests that for elite Charlestonians, both actions were menacing, albeit in gendered ways. An armed male slave and a female ball attendee threatened male property rights and removed enslaved people from their proper place in the social hierarchy of revolutionary Charleston. Both situations enabled Black men and women to assert an element of personhood previously denied them. Weapons remained the prerogative of free men across social ranks; attending fancy balls was the privilege of free women. Broadly speaking, then, enslaved people's participation in these previously forbidden practices transformed them into men and ladies, an affront to Charleston's racial order. Stevens asserted that the arming of enslaved men indicated that British officers were "lost to all sense of honour," and their participation in the ball proved that "they are likewise to that of shame." Both, he made clear, degraded officers' masculinity and honor.[80]

The ball thus proved a useful tool for Stevens to impugn the masculinity and authority of British officers. Criticizing the "shame and perfidy [of] the Officers of that once great Nation," Stevens decried the exorbitant cost and late hour of the festivities and, most egregiously, British officers' socialization with "Negro Wenches." Enslaved women's presence at the ball subverted Charleston's social order in a distinctly gendered and racialized fashion. Rather than serving others, female slaves were waited on by British officers. The ball attendees dressed in a manner befitting Charleston's elite and partook in activities reserved for the slaveowning class. In performing the role of ladies, these women donned the material trappings of elite womanhood—silk dresses, hair rolls, and powder. They traveled in carriages, danced with white men, and used calling cards, all under the purview of white men who were not their enslavers. Invading the spaces of Charleston's elite homes, these women performed personhood and laid claim to the rituals and materiality of Anglicized womanhood. In their misuse of enslaved property, Stevens insisted, British officers had demonstrated ill-judgement and proven their unsuitability for governance in both polite society and politics.[81]

Even if the ball was a fabrication, the very possibility that the "Ethiopian Ball" *could* have occurred behind British lines signals how British occupation and the possibilities it afforded enslaved and self-emancipated women proved deeply threatening in the imagination of white enslavers because of how it removed these women from their control. Similar to the discourse around the Meschianza, Daniel Stevens's account of the supposed "Ethiopian Ball" suggests that Britain's courtship of young women felt deeply personal to revolutionaries because of how fully it destabilized the norms and power relations of revolutionary households by eroding men's control over the unmarried women of all races who resided in their households. In Stevens's telling, the ball functioned, above all, as an affront to white men's mastery: it revealed their slipping grasp on authority and their inability to assert both the power and the privileges of their position. Through their control of enslaved women's bodies, British officers usurped American men's prerogative to be the sole masters and beneficiaries of their enslaved property. And they did so within the very houses that epitomized that authority. Failing to acknowledge enslaved (or formerly enslaved) women's agency in both organizing and attending the ball, Stevens deliberately obscured the extent to which these women challenged male revolutionaries' mastery by denying enslavers' exclusive right to their bodies—a rejection of both slaveholders' authority and their masculinity. By framing the event as an example of British perfidy, implying that it was British officers—not Black women—who challenged white men's authority, who had the audacity to claim revolutionaries' property and subvert social spaces for their own use, Stevens minimized the ball's dangerous ramifications for the city's racial and gender order. Such threats, he implied, would vanish with the army's removal.

Sociability between unmarried women and British officers emerged as a gendered site of political contest precisely because social interaction was about personal conquest. The gendered and raced implications of these relationships were deeply entangled with the patriarchal power embedded within the same domestic spaces where sociability occurred. Young unmarried women, both white and Black, wielded unprecedented levels of social power in British garrisons. This influence, which had real implications for women's lives, also proved acutely concerning to revolutionaries because of how these relationships destabilized the patriarchal racial and gender relations that grounded the domestic prerogatives of American men.

That men on both sides of the conflict sexualized young women's relationships with British officers is perhaps unsurprising; again and again throughout history, women's sexuality has been invoked to defuse their power, undermine their actions, and reassert patriarchal control. Nor is it surprising that revolutionaries embraced the language of infidelity to condemn these relationships; charges of political and sexual promiscuity offered a fitting contrast to revolutionaries' calls for patriotic virtue.

What *is* noteworthy, however, is white revolutionaries' rapid scramble in the aftermath of British occupation to reinscribe perceived sexual and social transgressions onto the bodies of Black women. In the parading of a sex worker through the streets of Philadelphia and in the refusal to recognize Black women's agency or acknowledge the logic behind their wartime choices, revolutionaries relegated these women instead to the status of paramours and pawns of British officers. Such racialized reimagining of wartime socialization endeavored to redeem the soiled virtue of young white women by framing their wartime social power as fanciful, youthful ignorance and relocating social and sexual transgression onto the bodies of Black women. This rhetorical displacement reinforced racial stereotypes about Black women's sexual availability and reasserted slaveholders' control of the bodies and sexuality of the women they enslaved. Reducing Black women's wartime actions and their alliance with British officers to a sexual arrangement, enslavers refused to accept the revolutionary nature of Black women's wartime actions. Such assumptions also, crucially, erased Black women's kinship ties and their deliberate pursuit of liberty behind British lines alongside their husbands, children, and other kin. For, as enslaved people's wartime flight to occupied cities reveals, freedom was, for many people, a family endeavor.

CHAPTER SIX

Went Off with the King's People

Venus slipped into the street, quietly closing the door behind her. Steadying herself, she took a deep breath before walking away from the house, casually, as if on an errand. Venus and her husband had toiled, scrimped, and saved for months to earn enough money to purchase her freedom. Owing to wartime labor shortages, there was an abundance of work in the British Army's New York headquarters. Soldiers required washing and ironing. Officers sought manservants. White women required help managing their households. Taverns and coffeehouses were frequently in need of assistance. And there was always the opportunity to sell biscuits or hawk goods in the city market. Laboring at odd jobs in their spare time, Venus and her husband had slowly but surely added their earnings—forty pounds in all—to the ten pounds that Venus's previous enslaver had placed in trust for her when he sold her to Charles Boardwine. But now, despite his promises, Charles Boardwine refused to give Venus her freedom—or the money. So, taking matters into their own hands, Venus and her husband concocted a new plan: if she could not earn her freedom, she would take it.[1]

Two days later, Charles Boardwine placed a notice advertising Venus's escape and offering a reward for her return. It was conventional, as runaway ads go, and sparse on details. But, later that week, an extraordinary response appeared in the *New-York Mercury, or General Advertiser:*

> MASSA, me see in a newspaper, Mr. B[oar]d[win]e advertise poor VENUS for run-away. . . . I had ten pounds that was given by my old Massa to Mr. B[oar]d[win]e to keep for me. Massa tell me, "Venus, you work, get more money to buy yourself free." My husband and me get forty pounds by working very hard; me give all to Mr. B[oar]d[win]e; me ask Mr. B[oar]d[win]e, "Me be free."—- No, you black deel [devil], you get no money."—- Me tink no right for a French gentleman to cheat poor Negro.
>
> Now, Mr. B[oar]d[win]e, as you a French gentleman, please give back the money to my poor husband, then me come home again.[2]

Written in Venus's voice, the ad is remarkable. Taking to the newspaper—the very space where slaveholders advertised for fugitives and sold enslaved people as commodities—to declare that she had been wronged, Venus endeavored to enforce the verbal contract that she had made with her enslaver. Recounting how she had earned the money to purchase herself and paid that money to her enslaver, Venus asserted possession of herself and proclaimed Charles Boardwine's treachery to the entire city. The boldness of this approach suggests that Venus had a protector in the occupied city, likely a white person, given the ad's stereotypical mimicry of enslaved vernacular. In the British Army's North American headquarters, such a person was almost certainly an officer; perhaps Venus's husband was employed among the troops and found someone willing to assist them. Seizing the opportunity, Venus published a rebuttal to her enslaver's ad that asserted, unequivocally, that she was not a fugitive, that she had earned her freedom, and that she wanted her money back.[3]

Although articulated through layers of intermediaries, Venus's advertisement offers a powerful example of how British occupation created circumstances in which enslaved men and women could not only challenge the racial hierarchies and labor norms of slaveholding households but do so in ways that allowed them to lay claim to and protect their kin. Asserting possession of herself and detailing the labors of love that facilitated her flight from bondage, Venus's narrative of freedom seeking proved the ideological

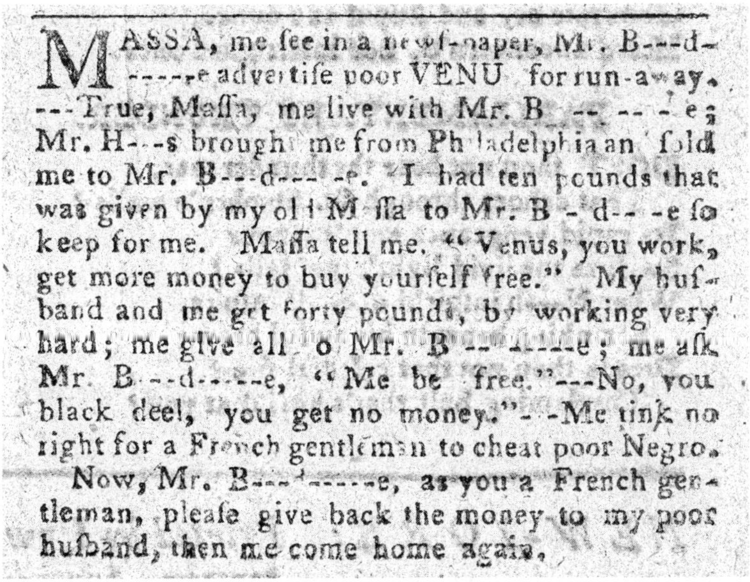

MASSA, me ſee in a news-paper, Mr. B---d-----e advertiſe poor VENU for run-away. ---True, Maſſa, me live with Mr. B---- -- -e; Mr. H---s brought me from Philadelphia an' ſold me to Mr. B---d-----e. I had ten pounds that was given by my old Maſſa to Mr. B--d-- -e ſo keep for me. Maſſa tell me, "Venus, you work, get more money to buy yourſelf free." My huſband and me get forty pounds, by working very hard; me give all to Mr. B---d----e; me aſk Mr. B---d-----e, "Me be free."---No, you black deel, you get no money."- -Me tink no right for a French gentleman to cheat poor Negro.

Now, Mr. B---d------e, as you a French gentleman, pleaſe give back the money to my poor huſband, then me come home again.

FIGURE 25 "Massa, Me See in a News-Paper," *New-York Mercury, or General Advertiser,* July 5, 1782. Courtesy of the American Antiquarian Society, Worcester, Mass.

fallacy of the legal, economic, and social apparatus of early American slavery, which situated the family ties of African and African-descended people squarely in the realm of capital. As historian Jennifer L. Morgan has argued, the legal doctrine of *partus sequitur ventrem,* in which Black children inherited the free or enslaved status of their mother, "rendered black women's bodies as economic rather than domestic spaces," defining their offspring, not as children or as kin, but as capital that could be valued and sold in the marketplace. Such laws, Morgan concludes, "structurally denied African people the place of family." Yet occupation and its emancipatory potential destabilized slaveholding in vital ways, providing enslaved men and women a brief opportunity to safeguard their loved ones behind British lines—an opportunity that thousands of men, women, and children took advantage of. In so doing, their actions forcefully exposed the weaknesses of a labor system premised on the disavowal of Black kinship.[4]

Under colonial legal regimes, enslaved laborers were integral to the security, stability, and functioning of slaveholding households. Enslaved people built the residences where enslaving families dwelled. They washed the floors, cooked meals, laundered clothes, nursed white infants, and undertook the daily labor of caring for white men, women, and children. They shaped how white families inhabited their houses and their comfort within them. Enslaved bodies and labor undergirded enslavers' wealth. Enslaved women were the embodied foundation, the lynchpin of this entire system, their productive and reproductive labors commandeered to perpetuate the institution. These legal and social practices coded households and their attendant protections as the privileges of whiteness, implicitly denying the same legal recognition and domestic security to Black families. Enslaved people nevertheless maintained their own understandings of family life that existed within, outside, and beyond the walls of white patriarchal households. Often rooted in African kinship structures and new connections forged both during and after the Middle Passage, these expansive networks were defined, at times, by blood but also by culture, choice, and love, forming bonds that crisscrossed city blocks, transcended state lines and national boundaries, and even reached across oceans.[5]

By weakening the white households that undergirded enslavement and providing new destinations of refuge behind British lines, occupation destabilized slaveholding throughout the colonies, creating an environment in which the protection of Black kin was more achievable and family freedom more plausible. Reading these altered dynamics and trusting British promises of emancipation, tens of thousands of enslaved refugees and their kin fled to occupied cities during the Revolution. This wartime surge in family freedom seeking suggests that British emancipatory policies, officers' (somewhat erratic) protection of self-liberated refugees, and the proximity of British lines fueled flight in the regions surrounding the army's urban garrisons. Occupied cities were often not the sanctuaries that enslaved families hoped: disease, starvation, violence, and the threat of reenslavement flourished in military encampments. Still, through their collective flight, husbands and wives, parents and children, siblings, grandparents, aunts and uncles, and fictive (chosen) kin endeavored to reclaim the autonomy and control over their loved ones that the laws, customs, and language of enslavement sought to erase and deprive them of.[6]

Although enslaved people had their own understandings of family, they existed within a Eurocentric world that conceptualized the household as a legal entity that allocated control over kin, labor, and wealth, the very things enslavement denied enslaved people by categorizing them as outside its protections. Occupation, however, altered these dynamics, creating an unprecedented moment of possibility that many enslaved people leveraged to protect their loved ones and gain recognition of their right to claim their kin as their own—or, in other words, to secure their own households. These aspirational

Black households that emerged in British-occupied cities—households whose very existence had previously been denied under prevailing racial and legal regimes—encompassed a broad array of kin and endeavored to make these expansive kinship ties legible to occupation authorities. Behind British lines, households thus functioned as a vital tool by which enslaved refugees endeavored to bolster the legal and social recognition of their kinship relations and to secure freedom for themselves and their loved ones.

The implications of these actions resonated far beyond British lines. In acting to protect and liberate their loved ones, enslaved people—enslaved women in particular because of how racial meanings were concretized and perpetuated through their bodies—upended the lives, assumptions, and financial security of slaveholders on both sides of the conflict. Posing a potent threat to the comfort and safety of those that held them in bondage, enslaved people's efforts to secure their households endangered the financial and ideological underpinnings of the very households that many American revolutionaries were coming to associate with their own independence.

GEOGRAPHIES OF SLAVERY AND FREEDOM IN OCCUPIED REGIONS

From the moment that John Murray, fourth earl of Dunmore and royal governor of Virginia, issued his November 1775 proclamation freeing all indentured and enslaved men who aided his efforts in crushing the incipient rebellion, the British Army became a destination for enslaved freedom seekers throughout British North America. Approximately 1,500 people, including not only men but also women and children, answered Dunmore's call. Although the British planned only to emancipate men, enslaved families' insistence on fleeing together forced the British Army to amend its policies and accept a more diverse refugee population. The following year, Sir William Howe reinforced this position, promising protection to any enslaved person belonging to rebels. Finally, in 1779, as Britain embarked on the Southern Campaign, Sir Henry Clinton expanded the army's emancipatory policies by issuing the Philipsburg Proclamation, which promised freedom "to every NEGROE Who shall desert the Rebel Standard." Like earlier policies, the Philipsburg Proclamation only applied to those people—ideally, men—enslaved by revolutionaries; those enslaved by loyalists were excluded from the British Army's promises of freedom and sanctuary. This prerequisite was, however, difficult to enforce and easy to circumvent. For the remainder of the war, families enslaved by both loyalists and revolutionaries flocked to British garrisons in pursuit of tenuous, though realistic, promises of security for themselves and their loved ones. So enticing was this prospect that wherever the British established themselves, "all the negroes, men, women, and children, upon the approach of any detachment of the King's troops, thought themselves absolved from all respect to their American masters, and entirely released from servitude," Lieutenant Colonel Banastre Tarleton recalled in his memoirs of the American Revolution. By war's end, nearly 20,000 enslaved Africans and African-Americans found freedom behind British lines.[7]

Word of the British Army's emancipatory policies spread rapidly through enslaved communities in British North America. On hearing news of Lord Dunmore's proclamation, perhaps through one such network, a Black Philadelphia man was emboldened to challenge a white woman who "reprimand[ed]" him for refusing to get out of her path. Calling the woman a "d[amne]d white bitch," he warned her of impending retribution when "Lord Dunmore and his black regiment come." For enslaved communities in and around occupied cities, the arrival of Black refugees and soldiers alongside British forces proved the truth of these rumors. Accompanying a party of British dragoons on a raid of revolutionary John Postell's South Carolina plantation, three Black men "invited" those enslaved there to accompany them to the British stronghold in Camden, "promising them rewards if they would, and that [Postell] should never get them again." Seizing the opportunity, several people departed with the soldiers. "In a few days I had scarcely a negro left to cut me a stick of Wood," Postell complained.[8]

Throughout occupied regions, the presence of the British Army and its emancipatory policies introduced new opportunities, choices, and destinations of freedom into the lives of enslaved laborers. These circumstances allow us to glimpse enslaved people's varied responses to the disruption that occupation introduced into the households that enslaved them. For many people, such as enslaved Georgians Flora, Sandy, and Cooper, autonomy and reunification with their spouses were their primary aims. Nineteen-year-old Charity and her two-year-old son, Peter, who had been sold away from their family ten months prior, were similarly "anxious to get back" to their loved ones. Some took actions more akin to truancy, seeking out nearby family and simply enjoying the momentary lack of oversight over their labors and their bodies. Others, conversely, made concerted bids to escape bondage. Phoebe, an enslaved woman in New York, slipped away "in the night." Bina, Elsey, Jude, and York disappeared into garrison refugee populations, hiding in plain sight amid the crowds of self-emancipated people who followed the British Army. Some people, like twenty-one-year-old New Yorker Prussia, "go[t] on board the first ship that would take" them and found liberation by sea, boarding British transports and merchant ships to distant ports. Others absconded to swamps or maroon camps located on islands in the Savannah River that bordered both South Carolina and Georgia. A few people sought shelter among Native tribes in the interior. Still others, like Sylvia, who carried approximately twenty pounds of wearing apparel with her, left bondage escorted by British troops. Behind British lines, men and women alike often found employment in officers' retinues. Those like Cato, who was "a handy fellow about a house, and a good waiter" as well as a musician, were especially in demand. For men, military employment offered an alternative route to freedom. James Richard and Harry Robbins "entered into his Majesty's service as waggon drivers"; others, like Robert Kupperth, became drummers for Hessian regiments.[9]

The nature, practice, and meaning of bondspeople's wartime pursuit of freedom was as varied as enslaved populations themselves. Freedom, as Neil Roberts has theorized, "is not a place; it is a state of being," one that is "multidimensional, constant, and never static." In other words, freedom was more multifaceted than a legal status, more convoluted than simply arriving at a destination. Enslaved people defined their own meaning and practices of freedom as they navigated the upheaval of the American Revolution. But British occupation facilitated these efforts in vital ways. In occupied regions, seizing freedom was still dangerous, still precarious, yet the circumstances created by war also offered a more promising path to self-liberation than almost any previous context.[10]

Within these new wartime geographies, British-occupied cities were a common destination for enslaved freedom seekers, many of whom trusted in the army's promises of emancipation and protection. Exemplifying this faith, seventeen-year-old Quamina mocked his loyalist enslaver "to [his] face" before disappearing into the anonymity of the Charleston garrison. Quamina forcefully scorned the man's authority to hold him in bondage and, according to his enslaver, taunted that "he can go when he pleases, and I can do nothing to him, nor shall ever get a topper for him." Quamina was not alone in believing so. Arriving in occupied Savannah in 1779, royal governor James Wright was astonished by the number of Black refugees in the city. "I may venture to say some or several Thousands" have flocked to the city, he estimated; he included in this number people captured by Native allies and on military raids along with the "vast Many" who "Come over of themselves."[11]

Around occupied cities, the movement of British troops could facilitate enslaved people's flight to British lines. Enslaved guides, such as Quamino

Dolly, who led British troops to Savannah along a hidden path frequented by slaves, found their way to occupied cities at the head of these expeditions, earning their freedom in exchange for conducting troops through unfamiliar territory. Foraging expeditions and other raids routinely targeted plantations; British naval galleys offered safe passage to garrisons. At Van Cortlandt Manor, north of New York City, Brigit helped Jin conceal herself in the garret above the kitchen for nearly a month as the women, along with others on the property, awaited the arrival of a British galley that they hoped would carry them to freedom. Brigit was seemingly the leader of this scheme; when two women expressed hesitation, "brigit Maid it her buisiness" to advise them against leaving the property with their enslaver. Instead, she instructed, the women should "come to her as soon as they heard the regulars where come again," and "thay where all to go off with" the British, who would then set the house ablaze "when thay where gone."[12]

Proximity to British lines facilitated enslaved people's wartime flight, but regional geography mattered, too. In New England, where enslaved populations were comparatively smaller and where much of the fighting occurred before British emancipatory policies were firmly established, flight was more infrequent. Then, in 1778, the formation of the all-Black First Rhode Island Regiment offered bounties to slaveholders who enlisted their slaves in the Continental army. Seeking to avoid forced conscription, enslaved men and their families flocked to British lines "for protection," as British major general Robert Pigot reported from the Newport garrison in August 1778. Conversely, in New York, where the enslaved population was more fragmented, it was more common for individuals to slip away. In the south, especially Georgia and South Carolina, where there were larger, more established slave communities, group flight was more prevalent. But it was not exclusive to the region. Outside of Philadelphia, Moses, true to his biblical namesake, recruited a contingent from his "neighbourhood to go with him and join the ministerial army."[13]

As British occupation unsettled systems of household oversight in and around garrisoned cities, enslaved people, even those who chose not to join the British, were able to exploit this moment to alter their conditions or to secure the safety of their kin. Throughout occupied regions, a pervasive awareness of the new, alternative life available to enslaved people behind British lines and slaveholders' frequent need to make quick decisions in response to troop movements enhanced enslaved people's ability to turn these circumstance to their advantage—often, by simply refusing to cooperate with enslavers' plans at a moment when expediency was essential. One enslaved New York woman, a cook and laundress, was offered for sale in October

1782 and "sold for no other reason but that she is averse to being carried" to the Caribbean, where her enslaver was relocating. In Charleston, similarly, an unnamed woman manipulated her value as a laborer to ensure that she would not be separated from her son. Detailing a relative's plans to leave the Charleston garrison, Anne Hart lamented that she had been forced to relinquish one of her own slaves, a young boy. "Mrs. Harts determination to carry her Wench, and her refusing to go without her Child is the cause of his going," she explained. Making their intentions and preferences known, bondspeople occasionally succeeded in securing working assignments or sales that kept them near their kin.[14]

These altered dynamics are also evident among people enslaved by revolutionaries who successfully escaped to British lines, where their newly freed status granted them substantial sway in their dealings with their former enslavers. Once refugees had reached the safety of British lines and claimed their rights under British emancipatory policies, revolutionary slaveholders had no power to forcibly reenslave these people; if they wanted to recover their enslaved people, they had to negotiate with them. Writing from South Carolina in June 1780, mere weeks after the British capture of Charleston, Samuel Massey, Henry Laurens's enslaved chief builder, informed him that several enslaved families from Laurens's Smalls Field plantation had fled to British lines to escape Andrew Campbell, an overseer that they despised. "Most of them can hardly be purSwaided to Stay," he reported. Later that month, James Custer, another of Laurens's employees located some of the fugitives in the Charleston garrison, where they informed him they were "willing to go home[,] provided I would promise them not to be under Campbell again." Stipulating this as a condition of their return, these people exploited their value as property and laborers to gain a measure of control over their workplace and their kin. Powerless to force them back to bondage—as people enslaved by a rebel, the fugitives were protected by the 1779 Philipsburg Proclamation—Custer was "obliged" to concede their ultimatum and offered them their choice of Laurens's other plantations. Although certainly not legal freedom, such arrangements had the potential to unify kin while also serving slaveowners' interests. As Massachusetts slaveholder Christian Barnes reflected after her family's purchase of Prince, the son of their enslaved woman, "Daphney appears to be much better reconciled to a state of Slavery since her sons arrival—upon the whole I do not believe there is a happier set of Negros in any kitchen in the Province."[15]

Crucially, however, these new geographies of freedom excluded one significant group of people in occupied regions: those enslaved by loyalists. For these families, British occupation did not disrupt the everyday practice or transactions of the slave system. Even in British garrisons, with their large refugee communities of freed people, sales of enslaved people persisted. Children were torn from their parents; spouses were separated from one another. The British were committed to protecting the property, including slaves, of white British subjects. Thus, while commanding officers deployed emancipation as a military measure and, ultimately, upheld their promise when they evacuated the country in 1783—an act that one historian has termed "the most significant act of emancipation in early American history"—they never intended to fight a war to end slavery. For many enslaved families, consequently, British occupation did not alleviate the pain of separation. It exacerbated it.[16]

When the loyalist Winslow family evacuated Boston alongside the British Army and relocated to Halifax in March 1776, Rose—who, according to the recollections of Isaac Winslow, was five or six years old at the time—was gifted to the departing Mary Winslow by her father. Rose's youth indicates that she might have been intended less as a maidservant and more as a transportable form of capital; because of space constraints, loyalist refugees were permitted to carry "only the smallest possible quantity of absolute necessaries" aboard the British fleet.[17]

As they abandoned their houses, furniture, silver, and other valuable possessions, the future security of white loyalist families like the Winslows depended on the wealth embodied in those people that they enslaved, with little consideration for the Black families affected by these decisions. Rose's parents and her sister Cinna remained in Boston while she accompanied the Winslows first to Halifax and then to the New York garrison. Rose was an ebullient child—Isaac Winslow, for whom Rose served as a playmate, remembered her "mischievous disposition" and "wild pranks"—but she missed her family and yearned to see them. "She used often to expect them . . . to visit her," Isaac recalled, recounting one instance "when there was general salutes from the ships of war and batteries for the occasion of some British victory . . . Rose came in delighted to my mother saying 'Oh Missis, the guns are firing—father's a coming.'"[18]

Rose's disappointment on that occasion must have only been matched by her joy in learning in June 1784 that her enslaver had bumped into her sister Cinna on the street in Boston. "I saw a Negro Girl there who looked so much like Rose that I asked her if her name was not Cinna," Isaac Winslow (father of the earlier Isaac) recounted to his wife; "on her telling me it was, I conversed about her Sister." Slaveholders were often intimately aware of the familial dynamics of those that they enslaved; nevertheless, for Isaac to recall

Cinna's name—a woman who resided outside of his household, eight years after he last saw her—hints at the frequency with which Rose might have talked about her sister and the family she left behind in Boston. For their part, Rose's family must have been both simultaneously relieved to learn that the girl had survived the war and also pained that she remained in bondage; forcibly transported out of Massachusetts as a child, Rose had not benefited from the state's abolition of slavery the previous year. Still, after years of hoping and waiting, Rose must have been gratified to have news of her family. She sent a simple, heartfelt message that Mary Winslow transcribed on the back of her response to her husband: "Rose says remember my love to Father and Mother and Sister Cinna." Two months later, the Winslows returned to Boston, bringing Rose with them. They manumitted her that same year in accordance with the state's new antislavery laws, nearly eight years after she was wrested away from her family aboard a British transport ship. For Rose, the upheaval that occupation introduced into the loyalist household where she was enslaved meant that she spent the entirety of the war in bondage behind British lines, residing far from her kin in the same occupied cities that were destinations of freedom and household autonomy for enslaved refugees throughout the colonies.[19]

Still, as other examples from occupied cities suggest, although people enslaved by loyalists faced additional hurdles, many of them succeeded in circumventing the stated limitations of British emancipatory policies. Recognizing the unparalleled potential of this moment, many enslaved individuals leveraged the chaos that occupation introduced into urban life to pursue the possibility of households and security for their loved ones. Some elected to remain in the cities where they resided, endeavoring to blend in among the refugees crowding British garrisons. Others fled aboard military vessels, using British ships to transport themselves to places where they and the identities of their enslavers were unknown. This might have been the case for Cato and Chloe, an enslaved couple who were eager to return to Jamaica, where they had previously resided before being sold to a loyalist in the Charleston garrison. There, they lodged on Bay Street, within view of the ships arriving and departing in Charleston harbor. In February 1782, the couple might have seen an opportunity to return to the island. Carrying their two-year-old daughter, Jenny, Chloe and Cato absconded into the garrison, where possibly they tried to board one of the British naval ships heading toward the Caribbean.[20]

As this suggests, enslaved people throughout the colonies recognized British occupation as a moment of immense possibility. Slaveholders' diminished power and the promise of protection, and possibly emancipation, behind British lines offered an unprecedented opportunity for bondspeople to safeguard their kin and secure their households. Yet wartime scarcities, duplicitous soldiers, and inconsistent policies meant that the attainment of these goals was uncertain and frequently illusory. Enslaved people were not unaware of these risks. But their efforts to realize the possibilities of this moment reveal their keen awareness of the life-altering potential awaiting them behind British lines.

BEHIND BRITISH LINES

Many enslaved refugees who fled to occupied cities calculated that, whatever unknown dangers lay behind British lines, the potential of claiming their own kin and households made flight to occupied cities a risk worth taking. These strategic choices were possible, in large measure, because of the confluence between the British Army's tactical objectives to deprive rebels of their enslaved property and a corresponding demand among both individual officers and the larger military establishment for laborers. Collectively, these military priorities eroded the abilities of slaveholders in occupied regions to command enslaved bodies and labor in ways that could grant enslaved refugees a degree of provisional freedom behind British lines. Yet this tenuous liberty was deeply contingent on the continued support of military patrons.

Occupied cities offered both official and makeshift employment for enslaved refugees. They labored on public works, served as guides, and toiled as officers' servants, cooks, and laundresses. In return, the British Army provided both men and women with wages and rations. Waged labor, although preferable to slavery, was nevertheless typically dirty, hard work in jobs that white inhabitants refused to do. Black refugees cleaned the streets, performed manual labor, and built fortifications. After 1776, the Black Pioneers, a noncombatant unit comprised of Black refugees and the remnants of Lord Dunmore's disbanded "Ethiopian Regiment," was responsible for much of this work. But the army also needed men such as twenty-year-old Tom, an enslaved refugee from Pennsylvania, who was "a tolerable good" fifer. Shoemakers like Quash, Peter, and Amery, who found work in occupied Charleston, were likewise in high demand. Officers sought personal servants, such as Anthony, a hairdresser, who hired himself out in the Savannah garrison. Officers' wives were also eager for help. Lois, a Massachusetts woman, left "with an English Lady" and accompanied her to London. Women like Jean, "a compleat washer and ironer" from South Carolina, also found ready

FIGURE 26 [John Rose?], *Miss Breme Jones*, circa 1785–1787. Watercolor and ink on wove paper. Accession no. 2008.300.1. Colonial Williamsburg Foundation Museum Purchase, The Friends of Colonial Williamsburg Collections Fund, Williamsburg, Va.

Behind British lines, self-emancipated women often found work as laundresses, cooks, or officers' servants.

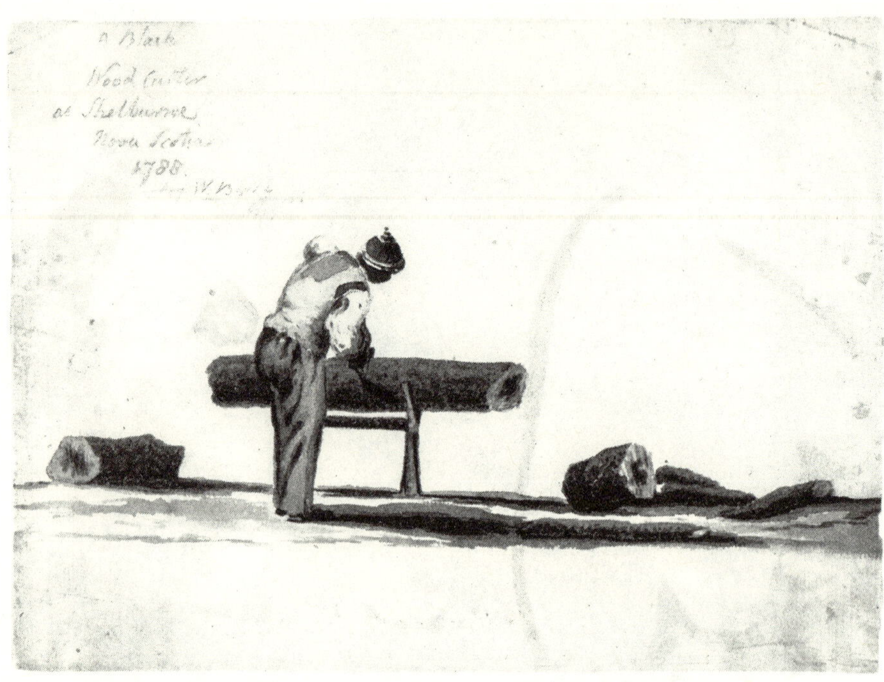

FIGURE 27 [William Booth], *A Black Canadian Wood Cutter at Shelburne, Nova Scotia*, 1788. W. H. Coverdale Collection of Canadiana, Manoir Richelieu Collection/e008438313. Courtesy of Library and Archives Canada

A depiction of a man who evacuated with the British Army and made his way to Nova Scotia after the Revolution, this watercolor also portrays the manual labor that many self-emancipated men performed behind British lines.

employment in occupied cities. Describing one Hessian corps in 1781, Captain Johann Ewald observed, "Every officer had . . . three or four Negroes, as well as one or two Negresses for cook and maid. Every soldier's woman was mounted and also had a Negro and Negress on horseback for her servants."[21]

Officers and their wives not only offered employment, they also functioned as critical shields for Black refugees in British garrisons. Despite military proclamations promising emancipation, in practice, implementation depended on individuals. Proximity to Black refugees helped foster these protective sentiments. Surprised by "a pleasing Conversation" he had with a Black man in New York, Ambrose Serle, secretary to Admiral Lord Richard Howe, confessed, "I did not expect to find half his Sense or Sensibility in any of his Complexion." Contemplating the widespread practice of slavery in the colonies, Serle denounced Americans for "bawling about the Rights of *human Nature*" while continuing to enslave African and African-descended people. Many officers, motivated by a combination of self-interest, abolitionist sentiments, or a desire to inflict injury on rebellious slaveholders, shielded fugitives within the lines. "They pretend them Spys, or Guides . . . or under promises of freedom from . . . [an] Officer of Rank or free by proclamation," General Alexander Leslie explained.[22]

The frequency with which fugitives appeared in public alongside officers in occupied regions attests to the security that these arrangements conferred—much to slaveholders' frustration. Luke, his former enslaver grumbled, had been "seen attending on an officer or serjeant in the market, to whom he had hired himself." Meanwhile, in Philadelphia, Toney "was protected from his master by a Capt. Averne of the British grenadiers, on whom he waited last winter, and since by Capt. Cannon, of the 57th, grenadiers." Captain James Moncrieff of the Royal Engineers summed up the feelings of many British officers who protected Black refugees within the lines. Having "offer[ed] them every Assurance of not being obliged to return to their former Masters," he explained, "I cannot help considering myself bound in duty and humanity, to render ever assistance in my power to their relief." To forsake his promises, Moncrieff avowed, "would be the height of Injustice and inhumanity."[23]

Nevertheless, officers and their families rarely shielded Black refugees out of pure compassion; most did so because they stood to benefit from their labor. Consequently, when safeguarding refugees became too costly, or inconvenient, they frequently abandoned the enslaved people under their protection. In July 1781, when a white slaveholder delayed the departure from New York of General Friedrich von Riedesel and his wife, Baroness Frederika von Riedesel, by claiming their self-emancipated Black servants as his slaves, the couple attempted to purchase the family's freedom, but, on hearing the man's exorbitant price, they relinquished them. "Had all this not happened at the moment of our departure, I believe that we yet would have kept them," Frederika reflected. She came to regret the decision, not on principle, but because of the inconvenience. "Maidservants in Canada are poor and especially difficult to find," she complained.[24]

Such casual indifference to the plight of Black refugees was compounded by duplicitous actors in occupied cities who sought to profit by trafficking in self-emancipated people, either to be their own personal servants or for their potential sales revenue. Even behind the alleged safety of British lines, where the daily lives of enslaved refugees could resemble a state of freedom, their status remained precarious. Liberty could be revoked at any moment by the actions of unscrupulous actors, pragmatic officers, or relentless slaveholders.

In South Carolina, for instance, a Captain Lewes tricked Boston King into accompanying him into the countryside on the pretext of reuniting him with the officer who employed him. Two hours into their journey, Lewes revealed that he was, in fact, deserting and claimed Boston King as his slave. "If you do not behave well, I will put you in irons, and give you a dozen stripes every morning," Lewes warned. Boston King, fortunately, managed to escape and return to his regiment, but his experience is nevertheless indicative of the vulnerability of Black refugees behind British lines.[25]

Deceitful officers were not the only dangers Black refugees faced in occupied cities. British emancipatory policies loosened but did not fundamentally upend racial hierarchies. Slavery and racial prejudice persisted behind British lines. White officers and inhabitants assaulted Black refugees in the streets. Presumptions of Black criminality meant that refugees were under constant surveillance; white inhabitants commonly appropriated goods from people they suspected of theft. Other forms of violence and assault persisted throughout the war. Military officials distributed enslaved people among officers as "booty" and conscripted them as laborers for public works projects, where many workers perished. Women were vulnerable to sexual abuse. And, as the war progressed, the army also sold enslaved people to purchase military supplies. Thus, although nominally free behind British lines, refugees endured overcrowding, uncertainty, forced labor, violence, and a constant threat to their liberty.[26]

Clustered together in the poorer areas where white loyalist refugees did not want to reside—in what one New Yorker termed "the Negro houses"—Black refugees faced worse conditions than their white counterparts, who were allotted housing by British officials. Writing of these impoverished New York neighborhoods, loyalist Nicholas Cresswell painted a bleak picture. On nearly every street, there was "stagnate water . . . and filth of every kind. Noisome vapours arise from the mud left in the docks and slips at low water, and unwholesome smells are occasioned by such a number of people being crowded together in so small a compass almost like herrings in a barrel, most of them very dirty and not a small number sick of some disease, the Itch, Pox, Fever, or Flux." Describing the situation of enslaved refugees in occupied New York, Adjutant General Major Carl Leopold Baurmeister estimated that "Half of them are no longer alive." Racial biases also shaped white inhabitants' perceptions of these crowded refugee camps by enhancing white inhabitants' fears of disease, thereby contributing to inadequate medical care and the occasional sequestration or outright abandonment of Black refugees. Writing of a "malignant fever" spreading through the Charleston garrison, loyalist James

Simpson speculated on racial health disparities, suggesting that inherent differences between the races accounted for the disease's prevalence among the garrison's Black refugee community. "It is [a] matter of no small consolation" that the fever "hath not as yet Communicated itself to any White people," he confided to Sir Henry Clinton.[27]

Taking refuge behind British lines was thus a gamble—one that could result in tragedy but that also had the potential to bring about positive, life-altering change. Strategically assessing these risks, many enslaved families calculated that British lines offered the potential of a different future—one where they could possess themselves and regain autonomy over their family life, where they could protect their loved ones, establish households, and embark on a new chapter. As a bewildered British official recounted in New York, enslaved men "hav[e] no Property not even in ~~themselves~~ their Wives or Children." For many enslaved kin, the promise of establishing their own households beyond the confines of slavery was a risk worth taking.[28]

FAMILY FLIGHT

Hoisting the squirming toddler higher on her hip, Rose winced as she felt Rynah grab a lock of hair. She reached up to disentangle the curls from her daughter's fingers but then thought better of it; perhaps it would keep her busy. Instead, Rose reached down to grasp the hand of six-year-old Judy walking beside her, the girl's abundant curls a mirror reflection of her own. Giving Judy a reassuring smile, Rose led her girls through Charleston's crowded streets. Born into slavery in the Carolina Lowcountry, Rose was deeply aware of the dangers, predations, and heartbreak that enslaved African-descended women endured on a routine basis. She did not want that future for Judy and Rynah. Since British troops had captured Charleston nearly two years earlier, thousands of Black refugees had poured into the city. As she went about her daily errands, Rose had slowly gathered information, made acquaintances, and concocted a plan to bring her daughters to freedom among the refugee communities residing within the British lines. With luck, Rose, Judy, and Rynah would be able to hide in plain sight.[29]

Like Rose and her daughters, many enslaved people who lived in and around occupied cities pursued freedom as a collective endeavor alongside their husbands and wives, parents and children, siblings, friends, and kin. British occupation created conditions that allowed for the possibility of reconstructing kinship ties and securing households that might protect these relationships. The collective flight of kin, whether to British lines, other plantations, or the backwoods interior, both inflicted financial losses on slaveholders and unequivocally asserted the primacy of Black kinship over slaveholders' economic aims. Collaborating with their loved ones, many enslaved people recognized that British occupation created a moment of possibility to achieve these aims for themselves and future generations.

Runaway ads and other correspondence documenting the self-liberation of enslaved people offer a glimpse into the kinship relations that informed these decisions. Given the fragmentary nature of sources, sometimes these kinship relations are submerged or emerge out of only partial, momentary glimpses of individual lives. Despite these archival limitations, it is clear that by weakening systems of oversight and demarcating new and perhaps more accessible safe havens, British occupation facilitated family flight. At James Smyth's plantation outside of Charleston, for instance, a group comprised of several, possibly related, families escaped together as the British approached the city in April 1780: "ADAM, MYRTILLA his wife, and two children; TOM, CLOE his wife, and three children; CYRUS, MARIA his wife, and one child." Tamar, a fifty-year-old man, and Lucy, a sixteen-year-old girl, accompanied the three families. Similarly, at Henry Laurens's Smalls Field plantation, those that "whent of[f] with the kings people" tended to do so in family groups—a stark deviation from the previous decade, in which most fugitives from Laurens's plantations were single, male, and recently enslaved.[30]

For many kin groups who had been separated by sales and other slaving practices, familial reunification was the first step toward freedom in occupied regions. Such was the case for Charlotte and Dick, who were enslaved in Sunbury, Georgia, approximately forty miles south of Savannah. Charlotte, "a stout young" woman, might have been one of the "handy house wenches" advertised on the property. Dick was probably African. The couple was expecting a child, but they were separated before her birth. After the death of their enslaver in the fall or winter of 1780–1781, Jacob Bühler, a loyalist tavern keeper from Ebenezer, Georgia, purchased Dick and moved him approximately sixty miles away from his pregnant wife. In January 1781, just as Charlotte was preparing to give birth, the *Royal Georgia Gazette* advertised an auction of the remaining estate on the plantation where she was enslaved. Whether motivated by knowledge of the impending auction, his wife's imminent labor, or both, Dick escaped from the plantation where he had been sold and traveled sixty miles across war-torn Georgia in order to return to Charlotte's side, possibly in time to witness the birth of their daughter, Mary, in early February.[31]

Shortly thereafter, the family fled. They might have made their way to the Savannah garrison; Dick was described at one point as wearing "yellow cloth soldiers breeches with a number on the buttons," so possibly he had connections among the occupying troops. Traveling with an infant was nevertheless difficult. Charlotte was probably not fully recovered from childbirth. Both circumstances would have slowed their journey. The family was recaptured at some point that spring or summer. However, they seemingly managed to convince Dick's enslaver to purchase Charlotte and Mary, because, by late October 1781, when the family made their second attempt at escape, Jacob Bühler claimed all three of them as his property. This time, Charlotte, Dick, and Mary carried "a large bundle of cloaths" that would allow them to alter their appearance and avoid detection; quite unusually, they also carried "a green rug" that they perhaps hoped to sell or barter.[32]

Extended and fictive kinship relationships, which were not typically documented by enslavers, are more difficult to trace, yet runaway ads provide tantalizing glimpses of the more expansive kinship networks that shaped bondspeople's flight in occupied regions as they endeavored to secure their own households. For instance, in May 1781, Will, Peter, and Duke—three African men bearing identical tribal marks, "three . . . on each side the temple, and one between the eyes"—made their escape together in New York. Further south, Sarah, Renah, Rose, Butcher, Prince, and Mousa, "all of the Guinea country," escaped together from Purysburgh, South Carolina, "and went into Georgia" in March 1781. Later that same year, a group consisting of two nuclear families and another forty-five-year-old man absconded from Beaulieu, Georgia, by commandeering a twenty-foot yawl and sailing toward the Altamaha River, which led inland to a swampy region inhabited by both maroons and Creeks. The nature of the group's relationships is impossible to know with certainty, but Hercules (who fled with his wife and their two children) and Jack were "of the Angola country"; Auba (who absconded with her husband and their two children) was not identified by her ethnicity, but her name indicates that she was also African. Collective flight encompassed not only those related by blood but also by kinship, shared circumstances, affection, or some combination thereof.[33]

Sporadic examples, such as these, that explicitly identify the tribal markings or ethnic affiliation of enslaved people hint that the pursuit of freedom alongside kin was pervasive throughout the war. In advertising for the return of self-liberated people, enslavers identified only the most obvious familial connections, publicizing identifying characteristics that they hoped would aid in recapture. That such ads failed to document—perhaps failed to notice—the more expansive, nuanced connections of kinship that linked enslaved people is unsurprising; the erasure of enslaved people's familial ties was critical to the system of slavery itself. Yet those examples that do surface in slavery's archive attest to the broader network of tribal affiliation, fictive kinship, and familial relationships that informed and shaped bondspeople's wartime pursuit of freedom as a collective practice based in love, affection, and community.[34]

Enslaved women were critical to bids to safeguard kin and households through flight to occupied cities. The notion of "black femme freedom," as theorized by historian Jessica Marie Johnson, suggests that "black women exploited every tool at their disposal on behalf of themselves and their kin." Rooted in love and self-possession, Black women's "audacity to challenge those who presumed mastery" over them, Johnson argues, was central to the practice of freedom and helped construct "a life-sustaining definition of blackness [that] emerged out of black women's survival, the survival of their children, the creation of self-sustaining communities across African origins, racial nomenclatures, and the precarity of bondage." These efforts are exemplified by "Old Rose, a short black Ebo" woman in her mid-fifties and the matriarch of a large, extended South Carolina family, who led her family to freedom in January 1781, during the British occupation of Charleston. Among the group were Rose's daughters Celia (36), Sue (32), her son Dick (approximately 22), Celia's "elderly" husband Cato, and Rose's granddaughter Elsey (6). Four others—Scipio (36), an Angolan woman named Kate, "Town Sue" (35), and Will, a waiting boy—also accompanied the group. Although not identified as family, possibly Scipio, Kate, Town Sue, and Will were kin. Reconstituted kin groups, united by blood, trauma, or choice, were widespread throughout the American south.[35]

The critical role of Black women in shaping family freedom is most visible in instances of pregnancy or the birth of a child. British emancipatory policies made occupied cities destinations for expectant mothers throughout the colonies; any child born within British lines would be free. Reflecting concerted bids to bequeath freedom to their unborn children, many pregnant women strategically timed their flights to ensure that their child would be born behind British lines. In so doing, self-emancipated mothers endeavored to make their kinship ties legible to occupation authorities, a strategy that could protect their children by enhancing mothers' ability to lay claim to both their kin and their collective freedom.

Particularly for women who were advanced in their pregnancies, proximity to British lines facilitated escape. Thirty-year-old Rachel was "great with child" when she fled to the New York garrison in January 1780. Forced

RAN AWAY ſome time ago from Mrs. Mary Thomas's plantati-on in South Carolina, the following

Negroes:

Old Roſe, a ſhort black Ebo wench, about 56 years old;—Celia, a ſhort wench, (daughter to the above Old Roſe) about 36 years old;—Elſey, thick and chubbed, (a grand daughter of ſaid Roſe) about ſix years old;—Cato, an elderly fellow, of a yellow complexion, and huſband of the above Celia, but perhaps changed;—Kate, a middle ſized wench, with her country marks about her face, ſpeaks bad Engliſh, of the Angola country;—Scipio, a middle ſized well ſet fellow, 36 years old;—Dick, a middle ſized well ſet fellow, and ſon to Old Roſe, he is above 22 years old;—Town Sue, a ſhort wench with a caſt in one eye, ſpeaks very good Engliſh, is ſmart and ſenſible, and about 35 years old;—Will, a ſmart waiting boy, tall, long viſaged, with two large fore teeth, which are continually ſhewn by his mouth being ſeldom ſhut, had on a green coat trimmed with livery lace, which was his waiting dreſs;—Country Sue, a middle ſized wench, but rather inclined to tall, a ſiſter to Celia, and daughter of Old Roſe, 32 years old.

Whoever delivers the above Negroes to Mrs. Thomas in Charleſtown, or the ſubſcriber in Savannah, ſhall be handſomely rewarded; and whoever harbours, conceals, or carries them off, may depend upon being proſecuted to the utmoſt rigour of the law. D. ZUBLY jun.

FIGURE 28 "Ran Away Some Time Ago from Mrs. Mary Thomas's Plantation," *Royal Georgia Gazette* (Savannah, Ga.), Jan. 4, 1781, [1]

to work long hours while pregnant, enslaved mothers were accustomed to taxing physical activity and the mental stamina necessary to make the flight. Nevertheless, doing so was undoubtedly uncomfortable, cumbersome, and slow. It was also a gamble. Within enslaved communities, many women had networks of kin and trusted, experienced midwives to assist them with childbirth; there was no guarantee of similar support behind British lines. For some women, such as Jenny, who was "big with child" when she disappeared into the Savannah garrison in June 1781, possibly reuniting with her mother, the presence of kin behind British lines might have motivated their flight. Yet many other expectant mothers escaped late in their pregnancies, despite the uncertainty or unknowability of maternal care and community networks behind British lines—perhaps to the detriment of their own health. Dinah, for instance, a twenty-year-old enslaved woman in Philadelphia, escaped to British lines in June 1778, just as the British Army was preparing to evacuate the city. "Big with child, and near the time of her lying in" when she absconded, Dinah could not afford to wait until after giving birth to make her way to the army—to postpone her flight might have caused her to miss her chance. Hazarding an escape during the final weeks of her pregnancy, Dinah made a concerted, strategic choice. Giving birth behind British lines not only secured her own freedom, it ensured that her child would be born free and that Dinah would be able to mother her child as she saw fit, free from fear and beyond the reaches of the slave trade.[36]

Expectant mothers' flights to British lines indicate the hope that these women placed in the British Army to secure their children's futures, but their efforts also held deeper meaning. Enslaved women were deeply aware of how the system of hereditary racial slavery was premised on their bodies and reproduction. Enslavers' coopting of enslaved women's reproductive lives and labors made Black women astute "theorists of power" who were adept at reading social and political landscapes in order to "carve out spaces of safety and surety for themselves or their children." For enslaved women, who understood that their wombs could birth both bondage and freedom, new wartime geographies and the proximity of freedom behind British lines offered an unprecedented moment to alter the trajectory of their lives and those of their children. In colonies under revolutionary control, laws assigning the status of the mother to the child persisted; the offspring of an enslaved woman would be born a slave. But that was not the case in regions under British control. Expectant mothers' efforts to reach British lines, therefore, were not simply intended to secure freedom for themselves. Behind British lines, their wombs—which elsewhere in the colonies condemned their children to a life of slavery—could instead bequeath freedom. The "Book of Negroes," the register of self-emancipated people who evacuated with the British at the end of the war, records sixty-six children who were "Born within the British Lines" and evacuated the garrison in 1783. Certainly there were more that went unrecorded. Notably, then, expectant mother's efforts to give birth behind British lines signaled a reclaiming of their own bodies and reproductive capacities. There, they could birth kin—children that they possessed as their own, children defined solely by their familial lineages, rather than the economic aims of white slaveholders. Occupation, in other words, facilitated these women's abilities to secure the future of their households.[37]

Making similar calculations, enslaved mothers in and around British lines absconded with young children in comparatively higher numbers than peacetime. Not surprisingly, given the difficulties of travel with infants and toddlers, women who arrived inside British lines with children tended to travel shorter distances and often hailed from neighboring regions. In August 1781, Cumba traveled to Savannah from the Great Ogeechee River region, bringing her three-year-old daughter with her. Isabella, a seamstress, escaped to Charleston in November 1780 from a plantation on John's Island accompanied by her two children, six-year-old Jack and an unnamed three-month-old baby girl. On the outskirts of New York City, according to General James Pattison, great numbers of "Female Negroes with Children" entered the garrison by crossing the Hudson River from New Jersey. These women faced daunting journeys: evading white inhabitants and soldiers who might inflict violence or return them to bondage, traversing swamps and rivers, navigating war-torn farms and ravaged countryside, in both sweltering heat and frigid cold—all while carrying children in their arms and keeping them from crying out and giving them away. Given these obstacles, some mothers chose—although, of course, many others were forced—to leave with raiding parties of British troops. An unnamed South Carolina woman enslaved by Elizabeth Thompson, for instance, "went away with a British Regiment with her own consent" and brought her child with her. These decisions were not without danger. Unknown soldiers might be violent; there was no guarantee that they would uphold their promises of freedom. Yet they also offered an armed escort to the security of British lines, which, for women with young children, was a comparatively safer and easier journey.[38]

Women enslaved by loyalists and others that resided within British garrisons faced related, but distinct, challenges. They, too, had to plan carefully. They, too, carried sleeping children and quieted tearful infants as they pursued freedom in occupied cities. But they also had the benefit of local knowledge; they did not have as far to travel and probably had support networks nearby. Illustrative of these dynamics, twenty-six-year-old Lucy, who was born in Charleston, relied on her knowledge of the occupied city to successfully escape with four young children, all under the age of eight. People enslaved locally were, nevertheless, more likely to be owned by loyalists—and therefore ineligible for British proclamations. Even as they concealed themselves within garrison refugee communities, they were more likely to be recognized. Many of them had previously worked in city markets or hired themselves out; they were "well known" about town. They did not have the security of anonymity. Perhaps this is why, in December 1779, Dinah, an enslaved Brooklyn woman, took her infant son Jack and hopped "on board the fleet," embarking for Charleston, South Carolina. A similar desire to avoid recognition might account for Violet's decision to "cut short" the hair of her two sons, Willis (7) and Joe (2), before the three of them disappeared into garrisoned New York, possibly intending to board one of the transport ships carrying British troops from the city. Violet might have had additional motives. Her toddler, Joe, was described of being "rather of a yellow complexion," suggesting that his father might have been a white man. Possibly Joe's father was David Campbell, who advertised for their return. Perhaps she sought to escape him. Or maybe he was another man in the garrison, a soldier perhaps, who was willing to shield her and her sons.[39]

It is worth noting that many enslaved fathers throughout occupied regions made choices similar to those of enslaved mothers, but slavery's linguistic and administrative practices frequently curtail our ability to see these efforts. Because of how slavery both defined and erased parenthood along gendered lines, children who escaped to British lines were most likely to be identified by their attachment to their mother. Even in instances where men were recorded along with their family, such as Hercules, an Angolan man enslaved in Georgia who absconded in October 1781 with his wife, Betty, and their children, Peter and Winter, their enslaver referred to them as "her children." Unusually, a revised notice the following week clarified that Peter and Winter were "both their children." This convention is unsurprising given that, legally, children inherited their mother's enslaved or free status and that men were more likely to be sold away from their families. In the eyes of enslavers, paternal connections meant little by way of profit, and, thus, there was less incentive for enslavers to record them. Yet these record-keeping practices obscure the actions of fathers who collaborated with their wives to safeguard their households, such as Abraham, who along with his wife, Moll, carefully planned their escape around shifting troop movements, the frigid New York winter, and Moll's advancing pregnancy, waiting until she had recovered from childbirth and their infant daughter was sturdy enough to travel before they carried the five-month-old and her three-year-old brother to British lines on Long Island in April 1777. Slavery's linguistic conventions also efface the actions of the many fathers like Will, a fifty-year-old African man who escaped with his son Casey in the Savannah garrison.[40]

In carrying their children to British lines, enslaved parents asserted the parental rights that slavery sought to deny them, retrieving their children from the clutches of slaveholders and repossessing them as parents, redefining them solely as kin—not property. In so doing, enslaved parents rejected slaveholders' right to define their family life and their relationship to their kin. The ability to establish their own, autonomous households was therefore integral to the conditional freedom that self-emancipated people found in occupied cities. Behind British lines, the capacity to claim kin—to claim their households—remained central to how enslaved people embodied, practiced, and defended the provisionally free status of themselves and their loved ones.

CLAIMING FREEDOM, CLAIMING KIN

In July 1780, an eighteen-year-old enslaved woman absconded from her enslaver in the New York garrison. "Says she is a free Negro, tho' born in my family," Reverend John Agnew, a Virginia loyalist and chaplain for the Queen's American Rangers, complained as he advertised the woman's escape. Her name was Pamela, he noted, but she "often calls herself MIRA, after her sister." We know very little about Mira, as she called herself. Mira was "very lusty and likely." She smiled when she spoke and when people spoke to her. Her enslaver felt that her smiles were insincere; she "is very deceitful and given to lying," Agnew cautioned.[41]

Before arriving in New York, Mira resided on a plantation in Suffolk Parish, Virginia, where John Agnew enslaved fifty-one people. But, as the rebellion mounted, his loyalism made him a target, and he fled to the British Army's New York headquarters in August 1777. Mira, meanwhile, remained in Virginia nursing Agnew's ailing wife until May 1779, when the woman was well enough to join her husband. Traveling aboard a British naval vessel, Mira accompanied her enslaver to the British garrison, where, the following year, she would escape from bondage.[42]

Between these bare outlines of Mira's personal history, the advertisement publicizing her escape reveals one other significant detail of her life: claiming kin was central to how Mira conceived of freedom as she pursued liberty behind British lines. When Mira disappeared into the New York garrison, she severed her ties to the Agnew household and created her own, remaking herself as a free Black woman. As she did so, she adopted a new name—her sister's. Practically, altering her name shielded Mira from detection. But it also, significantly, affirmed the kinship ties that the system of slavery devalued and tried to erase. In adopting her sister's name, Mira followed a customary African tradition of taking on an additional name "to mark important life transitions." In doing so, she asserted her kinship ties as a central feature of how she identified herself and her household in occupied New York.[43]

Within occupied cities, household and community formation and the kinship ties they sheltered were vital to how self-emancipated people conceived of, enacted, and defended their newfound, if conditional, freedom behind British lines. The claiming of kin was both a central performance of freedom and a critical strategy of securing it in occupied cities. Military records and officers' correspondence showcase Black refugees' persistent demands for security for themselves and their kin, including women, children, and the elderly who could not enlist. Indicative of the extent to which self-liberated people conceived of freedom as a collective practice, British general Alexander Leslie discovered that, contrary to the army's preparations for the evacuation of Charleston in the autumn of 1782, Black men who had claimed British protection "expect[ed] to be brought off, including their Wifes and children." Those who had been formerly enslaved had a distinctive awareness of how the ability to claim their kin as their own was linked to the practice of freedom. Through assertions of kinship, refugees claimed possession of themselves and their loved ones, a right that they, in the words of historian Marisa J. Fuentes, had been "dispossessed" of under slavery. Households and the claims of kin that they represented were integral to how Black refugees embodied and proclaimed their new, albeit tenuous, freedom behind British lines.[44]

Claiming kin was a central practice of freedom in occupied cities, but it also required that enslaved refugees establish their free status. They adopted various strategies to do so. Flora, a South Carolinian who "ha[d] a slow mild way of talking," obtained a pass in Charleston attesting to her free status that she continued to carry with her in the New York garrison. Meanwhile, Duke, who escaped from his loyalist enslaver in 1779, might have spent time in both the Philadelphia and Newport garrisons prior to his arrival in New York, for he "talk[ed] much" of his time in both of those cities, an indication that he might have been influenced by the communities of refugees that he witnessed there, performing and proclaiming their own freedom. Some, like Venus, who opened this chapter, took to public venues such as newspapers and hearings to proclaim their free status. Others did so in more quotidian ways—in how they carried their bodies, in how they spoke, in how they addressed others. Grace, a so-called Coromantee woman enslaved in New York, loudly rejected her state of bondage even though she had not yet mastered the English language—but she knew enough to assert her freedom. "She tells people that she is free," her disgruntled enslaver complained. Assertions of free status, a useful defense for people pursued by slaveholders, were nevertheless more than a means of disguise or a method of self-preservation. Such daily "performances of freedom," as Simone Browne has argued in her study of Black surveillance in colonial New York, were profound statements of self-possession that "constitute[ed] the black subject not as slave or fugitive, nor commodity but as human."[45]

Clothing was critical to how self-liberated people signaled, performed, and inhabited their freed status behind British lines. Practically, changes of clothing assisted self-liberated people in evading enslavers. Runaway ads enumerated the outfits that enslaved people wore when they fled and additional attire they carried, details, enslavers hoped, that would identify fugitives. Anticipating this, some people, such as Rachael, foiled enslavers' efforts by carrying multiple changes of clothing. "Her dress cannot be described, as she has taken all her cloaths with her," Rachael's enslaver lamented in occupied New York City. Military dress, a uniquely masculine form, also signaled free status and proclaimed the martial contributions that men had committed in exchange for their freedom. Uniforms could also, however, be a clever disguise, providing men with a passport to move freely under the auspices of military employment. In addition to facilitating escape and enabling movement, clothing was one of the few forms of property that enslaved people could own, by custom if not statute, making textiles a crucial resource that could be traded, sold, bartered, or pawned within British garrisons. These multiple facets of sartorial performance were on full display behind British lines.[46]

Observing self-liberated refugees, Hessian captain Johann Ewald was particularly struck by their attire. "They had plundered the wardrobes of their masters and mistresses, divided the loot, and clothed themselves piecemeal with it," he described. One man went shirtless but wore silk breeches; another donned a vibrantly dyed coat. Among the women, Ewald spied silk bodices, corsets, skirts, and "a lounging robe with a long train." He also saw wigs and "all different styles of hats and coiffures." "When I first beheld this train I could not grasp it," he confessed, "and I wondered as much about the indulgent character of Lord Cornwallis as I admired him for his military abilities."[47]

Beneath Captain Ewald's condescension, however, is an alternative reading of this scene, in which the vibrant, colorful attire shared among the Black refugees signaled the joy and community they found behind British lines. Clothing was an integral component of the enslaved tradition of pleasure as resistance, in which bondspeople throughout the American south donned special, ornamental dress for dances and other celebratory events, resisting their enslavement by using their bodies for joy and community building. The continuation of these practices is evident in Ewald's account of self-liberated people's mismatched, incongruous dress, which he interpreted as evidence of Black inferiority and ignorance of the standards of white Euro-American taste. To the contrary, these sartorial practices reveal a jubilant communal ethos, a desire to share their newfound, material rewards and visible markers of freedom. Unlike those men whose jobs with the British Army entitled them to wear military dress, most newly liberated people lacked a uniform that proclaimed their free status. So, they made their own. Rejecting the coarse, drab, ill-fitting garb of their enslavement, they donned rich silks, wigs, and dressing gowns, dividing these garments among themselves as badges of freedom.[48]

Clothing, however, not only signified "the pleasures of resistance" and the communal ethos behind British lines, it could also be a way to signal household and kinship ties, particularly in moments of grief. In occupied Charleston, Isabella, a seamstress who was "very fond of dressing well . . . appeared lately in mourning cloaths for the death of her mother." A simple act, Isabella's choice to don mourning upon her mother's death might have been an option that would have been previously unavailable to her. Throughout the Atlantic world, the enslaved honored their dead with ceremonial feasts and raucous processions that included call-and-response singing, dancing to the music of drums and rattles, and rites such as animal sacrifice and "supernatural inquests," rituals originating in Africa that took on new, creolized forms in the Americas. But mourning clothing would have been prohibitively expensive for most enslaved people. Urban slaves could hire themselves out for wages and perhaps purchased mourning attire, either new or secondhand. Still, it was an investment that delayed many people's aims to purchase freedom. Alternatively, in their wills, some slaveholders, such as New Yorker William Brownejohn, stipulated that their slaves be provided with "decent mourning" attire on their death. Within the broader context of American slavery, then, black attire on an enslaved body functioned less as a mark of personal grief than as a performative ritual intended for a white audience, signifying a white family's loss and reinforcing narratives about enslaved people's affections for their enslavers.[49]

This context underscores the significance of Isabella's mourning attire. Free to mourn her mother as she chose, Isabella elected to partake in a sartorial ritual that broadcast her kinship ties by publicly signaling her grief at her mother's death. As a seamstress, Isabella presumably fashioned the clothing herself, a labor of love in which she exerted her skills on behalf of her own household to honor her mother. In so doing, Isabella participated in a ritual that was largely the province of white colonists, making a public profession of her grief and familial ties in a way that was legible to all inhabitants of the garrison, both Black and white. Isabella's mourning attire was also, however, a powerful assertion of kinship. Her children, six-year-old Jack and a three-month-old infant girl, whom she carried with her to British lines, probably also donned mourning clothes for their grandmother. The household's mourning attire therefore proudly signaled kinship ties that spanned generations—a proclamation of family and freedom that challenged the very logic of enslavement.

Behind the safety of British lines, self-liberated refugees not only reinforced existing kin connections, they forged new communities and households to replace those that they had left behind. Entries in the "Book of Negroes," a register of enslaved people who evacuated New York with the British Army in 1783, make clear that men and women fell in love and created families behind British lines. Indeed, the organization of the document reinforces these household units, often listing husbands, wives, and their children together. John Prison, who escaped from slavery in South Carolina and served in the Engineer's Department, married Catherine, a free Black woman who had been indentured on Long Island. Boston King, the self-liberated South Carolina man who narrowly avoided reenslavement by a devious officer, similarly found love and community behind British lines, marrying a woman named Voilet who had liberated herself from a plantation in North Carolina. "Altho' I was much grieved at first, to be obliged to leave my friends, and reside among strangers," he recalled, "I began to feel the happiness of liberty, of which I knew nothing before."[50]

Examples throughout British garrisons illustrate both the bonds that united refugees and how these communities safeguarded their tenuous liberty by sharing strategies and information that helped individuals evade recapture and secure the safety of their kin and households. The pursuit of freedom was both an individual practice and a communal ethos. Stephen, his South Carolina enslaver complained, had become "very specious and knowing, having been some time with the British army." Gesturing to the pervasiveness of these networks and the troubles that they posed for enslavers, one New Yorker touted as a benefit that a woman he offered for sale "has been kept close from getting any acquaintance in town." Networks such as these are likely why Peg, who stole herself to freedom in occupied New York, knew to carry what her enslaver suspected was "a forged freedom pass" that permitted her to move freely about the garrison. Behind British lines, collective and individual resistance was intermingled, rooted in both existing and newfound community connections.[51]

Ranging from daily, quotidian acts to more visible, violent defenses of family and kin, self-liberated people within the British lines fiercely proclaimed and protected the freedom of individuals, their reconstituted communities, and their newly forged households. Frustrated enslavers grumbled about the numbers of self-liberated people "lurking about" British garrisons who were "conceal'd," "secreted," and "harboured" by refugee communities. Beck, for instance, who resided "behind the old Church" in Charleston, shielded her seventeen-year-old daughter Harriet when she escaped from her enslaver in December 1780. In Savannah, self-liberated refugees' fierce defense of their freedom led the city's white inhabitants to decry what they termed a "dangerous tendency": "the number of Negroes . . . who harbour, and even protect with fire arms, Negroes run away from their owners."[52]

For many self-liberated people behind British lines, the pursuit of household autonomy and the defense of kin were integral to their pursuit of freedom in occupied cities. In slavery, Black kin were subject to the whims and abuses of capricious slaveowners. Physical and psychological abuse were routine; neither was Black family life protected. Sales separated families; slaveholders raped and sexually abused enslaved women. Intended to instill fear, these gruesome practices rippled throughout enslaved communities, spreading dread and stoking resentment among those unable to protect their kin. Marriage and family life freed from these malicious intrusions became a critical element of the nineteenth-century abolition movement and an important feature of emancipated people's new, free lives. Behind British lines, these aspirations of familial and household autonomy became more accessible to those people who stole themselves and their kin to freedom.[53]

The example of Pompey Rumsey exemplifies these trends. A free Black man employed in the New York household of Sir Guy Carleton, the commander in chief of British forces in North America, Pompey acted to avoid being separated from his wife, Cairo. Cairo was enslaved by a New York loyalist who intended to evacuate to Canada. Learning of these plans, Pompey approached his wife's enslaver and "expressed a desire of going with his Wife," a conversation which subsequently led to Sir Guy Carleton releasing Pompey from his service and issuing him a passport permitting him to depart New York. In October 1783, Cairo and Pompey boarded a ship to New Brunswick. Although Cairo, regrettably, was never freed, the Rumseys' strategy to protect their household worked. In New Brunswick, they built a life together that spanned at least four decades, and local baptismal records gesture to the community that they found there: in 1822, Richard and Sarah Hopewell, a Black couple, named their firstborn daughter Cairo Rumsey Hopewell; her brother, John Pompey Rumsey Hopewell, was born the following year.[54]

Unsurprisingly, white inhabitants of British garrisons were often resistant to self-liberated people's assertions of familial autonomy and self-possession. Throughout occupied cities, slaveholders endeavored to reassert the institutions, policies, and power relations of slavery. Racialized fears about enslaved people's potential vengeance and the perceived indolence of self-emancipated refugees led civilian enslavers to petition occupying authorities for greater control of Black labor and bodies. Attempting to force refugees back into restrictive systems of control, slaveholders sought to reinscribe captivity and labor onto Black bodies, a frantic reassertion of oppressive legal and labor systems that indicates how fully self-liberated families behind British lines succeeded in inverting slavery's calculation of capital over Black kinship.

At times, these confrontations ended in violence. In August 1781, for instance, James Aske, a Black waggoner in the Quarter Master General's Department in New York, confronted James Guffie, a white conductor who oversaw the unit, after learning that the man had slept with his wife. James Guffie denied the charge. We can only speculate as to why James Aske believed that his supervisor had slept with his wife. Perhaps she told him. Maybe she was pregnant. Possibly she contracted a venereal disease. Whatever the reason, according to eyewitnesses, James Aske confronted the white man, accused him of "laying with his Wife," and announced his intention to resign, declaring that "he would not stay with such a Rascal as [Guffie]." Proclaiming his spousal rights, James Aske challenged both military and racial hierarchies to claim his wife as his own, making clear that he was unwilling to tolerate a continuation of the dynamics of enslavement in which his wife's body was available to the predations of white men. It is impossible to know his wife's feelings about the matter; we can only guess at her pain and the violation she felt, as she did not testify in the subsequent court-martial, and the court did not even record her name. But what is strikingly clear is that when British troops trespassed on his household, James Aske—not unlike white male householders throughout occupied regions who fiercely contested the varied ways that occupation undermined their patriarchal rights—asserted his right as a head of household to protect his wife, his familial autonomy, and his marital intimacy. This bold proclamation of patriarchal rights, however, enraged James Aske's supervisor. James Guffie responded to these accusations by bludgeoning the man to death with a stick of firewood, defending his actions as an extension of his "Authority to correct the Negroe, whenever he behaved insolent or any way improper."[55]

In addition to such interpersonal violence, these dynamics also occurred at an administrative level. Civilian governing boards throughout occupied regions instituted policies intended to restrict the liberties of Black refugees. In Charleston, for instance, local occupation authorities mandated identification tickets for any Black inhabitant unaffiliated with the military (the army provided its own documentation to enlisted laborers) and confined those people identified in public without them in the sugar house. They attempted to prevent dram shops from selling liquor to Black refugees, insisting that alcohol "encourage[s] them to commit thefts and other enormities." Framing the need to control and surveil Black refugees as a public good that could ameliorate declining crop production, the city's civilian board of police warned the British commandant that "the Negroes would be very apt to contract bad Habits; and such as might be dangerous to the Community hereafter, if they were suffered to remain in a state of Idleness." The solution, they advocated, was to restore the pre-occupation labor system and return self-liberated refugees to planation labor.[56]

In Georgia, the only colony to revert to British civil governance during the war, civilian administrators went one step further toward reinstating prewar racial hierarchies. In March 1781, the *Royal Georgia Gazette* reprinted copies of colonial laws intended to regulate Black bodies and restrict their movements. Dating from the 1760s, the enumerated measures included, among others, curfews, mandatory passes, and the formation of slave patrols authorized to physically "correct every such slave . . . by whipping." The patrols were also empowered to search Black homes and seize both ammunition and guns from those without written permission from their enslavers to possess such arms. Unwilling to tolerate self-liberated peoples' overt practices of freedom, white enslavers throughout British garrisons scrambled to reassert control over Black people's lives and bodies by resurrecting restrictive laws and reinstating oppressive systems of labor and surveillance.[57]

These efforts only intensified after the signing of the Treaty of Paris in 1783. Article VII of the treaty stipulated that "his Britannic Majesty shall with all convenient speed, and without causing any Destruction, or carrying away any Negroes or other Property of the American Inhabitants, withdraw all his Armies, Garrisons and Fleets from the said United States." In other words, the article mandated that the British Army return the self-emancipated people behind their lines to American slaveowners. When news of the treaty reached British headquarters in New York, Boston King recalled the "inexpressible anguish and terror" among the garrison's enslaved community on hearing "that all the slaves . . . were to be delivered up to their masters."

Shortly thereafter, the arrival of enslavers "from Virginia, North-Carolina, and other parts, and seizing upon their slaves in the streets of New-York, or even dragging them out of their beds," exacerbated these fears. After having lived many months and years in relative freedom alongside their families, the prospect of reenslavement "embittered life to" many of the self-liberated people within the garrison's refugee community, Boston King recalled, and "for some days we lost our appetite for food, and sleep departed from our eyes."[58]

And yet, Black refugee families refused to quietly surrender to this fate. As slaveholders descended upon the British Army's New York headquarters in the spring of 1783, Black refugees continued to assert their self-possession and that of their kin by resurrecting the strategies that had safeguarded their households throughout the occupation. "They insist on their rights under the proclamation," Hessian adjutant general Carl Leopold Baurmeister recounted, and "refuse to be delivered in so unwarrantable a manner." In response to this outpouring of resistance, the British Army committed to upholding their promises of sanctuary, maintaining that the treaty did not apply to those who had sought refuge behind British lines before it was signed. As Sir Guy Carleton explained to an exasperated George Washington, despite the treaty provisions, he was unable to rescind previous British emancipatory declarations and "had no right to deprive [Black refugees] of that liberty I found them possessed of" when he assumed command of the British Army in 1782. Moreover, Carleton acknowledged, in a testament to the determined efforts of self-liberated refugees, even had he been inclined to comply with the treaty, "they would, in spite of every means to prevent it, have found various methods of quitting this place, so that the former owner would no longer have been able to trace them." By all accounts, Carleton acted out of a sense of obligation to the self-emancipated people who had responded to British proclamations. That the measure happened to inflict financial losses on the upstart American rebels who had defeated his army on the battlefield was an added bonus.[59]

To ensure the protection of Black refugees, in the spring of 1783 the British distributed what came to be known as Birch certificates, after Brigadier General Samuel Birch, the British commandant of New York City, who spearheaded the effort. These passports certified the freed status of refugees who liberated themselves by responding to British military proclamations or through service to the army and who were therefore authorized to evacuate the garrison aboard British transport ships. Only those refugees who had voluntarily resided behind British lines before the signing of the provisional peace treaty on November 30, 1782, qualified for a certificate. To appease

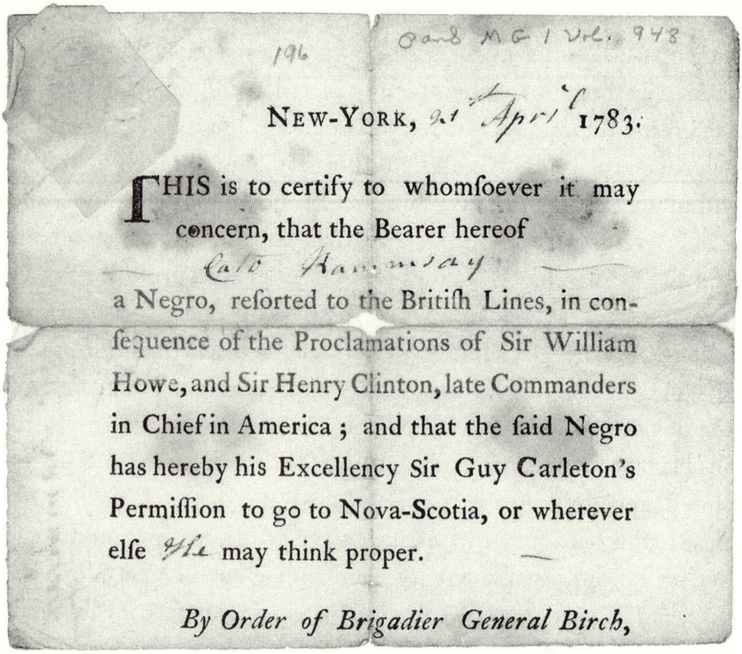

196

Gand MG 1 Vol. 948

NEW-YORK, 21st April 1783.

THIS is to certify to whomſoever it may concern, that the Bearer hereof

Cato Ramsay

a Negro, reſorted to the Britiſh Lines, in conſequence of the Proclamations of Sir William Howe, and Sir Henry Clinton, late Commanders in Chief in America; and that the ſaid Negro has hereby his Excellency Sir Guy Carleton's Permiſſion to go to Nova-Scotia, or wherever elſe He may think proper.

By Order of Brigadier General Birch,

FIGURE 29 Cato Ramsay's Birch Certificate of Freedom, 1783. Courtesy of Nova Scotia Archives, Halifax

American officials, the British recorded the name, status, and previous enslaver of every Black person, free, freed, and enslaved, who embarked from the garrison so that, if necessary, there would be a record to compensate American slaveowners. But, in the chaos of these final months, the British Army also took an unprecedented step in collaboration with American officials: it formed a board of inquiry to adjudicate disputed claims about the status of Black people evacuating the garrison aboard British ships. Although the outcome of these hearings was far from certain, their very existence underscores how the circumstances of occupation presented enslaved people with an unparalleled moment to seize freedom and gain recognition of their claims, both during the war and in its chaotic aftermath, as the British prepared to evacuate the colonies.[60]

BEFORE THE BOARD OF INQUIRY

Held at the Fraunces Tavern in New York between May and November 1783, the arbitration hearings before the board of inquiry—eleven cases that determined the fate of fourteen individuals—offer an unparalleled view of how self-liberated people behind British lines defended their families and argued for their possession of themselves and their kin. At the hearings, both white enslavers and self-liberated Black refugees testified before a committee of British and American representatives; their testimonies bring into sharp relief the competing, contradictory visions of liberty that existed between enslaved people and those that sought to keep them in bondage. Unlike the glimpses of self-liberated people's practices and proclamations of freedom filtered through runaway ads and other sources created by enslavers, the transcripts of the arbitration hearings allow us to hear the voices of self-liberated people, as close as we can come to their own words, as they proclaimed ownership of themselves and argued for their continued freedom and that of their kin.[61]

Most of the Black litigants who appeared in front of the board were pulled off departing British transport ships as the British evacuated New York City—the last of their coastal garrisons—in March 1783. Their freedom was cruelly thrown into question at the very moment when, after years of conditional freedom behind British lines, they might have finally thought themselves safe, finally allowed themselves to feel relief and excitement. Recounting a similar instance that occurred during her own departure from the New York garrison in July 1781, Baroness Frederika von Riedesel, the wife of a Hessian general, witnessed the agony of a family of Black refugees whose freedom was snatched away just as they were on the cusp of securing it. After "the signal for departure was given," the ship was halted and a white inhabitant—a newly professed loyalist who had previously supported the rebellion—came on board and claimed the refugees as his property. "The horror and lamentation of these poor people were extremely great," Frederika recounted. Faced with an imminent return to bondage under "an evil master, who had treated them badly," Phyllis, a young woman, fainted. "When she regained her senses," the baroness related, "she threw herself at my feet, and, clutching, had to be withdrawn by force."[62]

From the outset, the decks were stacked against Black litigants who appeared before the board of inquiry; the very existence of these hearings signaled the imminent return of racial labor systems and hierarchies as the British prepared to evacuate the continent. Racial prejudices, legal hurdles, and other obstacles tilted the board's sympathies toward the claims of white enslavers—with one caveat: cases where loyalist claimants petitioned for ownership of Black refugees who had previously met the requirements of British proclamations were typically referred to Sir Guy Carleton, who proved likely to rule in refugees' favor. This avenue was nevertheless uncertain; as they testified before the board, Black litigants fought for themselves, their kin, and the continued freedom of their households.

In August 1783, Mercy and her three children were pulled off a ship departing for Nova Scotia and hauled before the board of inquiry. The family had previously been enslaved in Westchester County, New York, by Gabriel Legget, a revolutionary whose wartime allegiance—like that of many white colonists—was flexible. To retain possession of his farm within the British lines, Legget professed loyalty to the crown in 1776; he remained in residence until October 1779, when he was unceremoniously evicted to accommodate a British officer who required quarters. Having fled to garrisoned Long Island prior to Legget's eviction, Mercy worked at the Brooklyn ferry to support her family. At some point between 1779 and 1783, she returned to Westchester, perhaps to reconnect with kin and other members of her community; she might have obtained employment among the British officers quartered on the Legget farm. When British forces evacuated the region in May 1783, Mercy and her children accompanied them to New York City. The following month, she obtained a Birch certificate, and, in July, the family boarded a ship to Nova Scotia—before being pulled ashore and brought before the board of inquiry sitting in Fraunces Tavern.[63]

Mercy arrived at the hearing prepared to refute Gabriel Legget's claims to herself and her children. Perhaps anticipating this day, in the months since she and her children had seized their freedom, Mercy had carefully collected documentary evidence to prove the free status of her household. Proffering her Birch certificate, she testified about living in relative freedom after Legget was ousted from his farm. She noted, in particular, that she obtained the certificate on the recommendation of Dr. Peter Huggeford, a surgeon in the Loyal American Regiment, who also hailed from Westchester County. Dr. Huggeford's recognition of Mercy's freedom and his efforts on her behalf bolstered her case by signaling her connections within the British military establishment and demonstrating that neighbors understood her and her children to be free. Significantly, Mercy also produced General Wilhelm von Knyphausen's order of eviction, which cited Gabriel Legget's "bad character"—meaning his rebel politics and possibly a betrayal of his loyalty oath—as rationale for his expulsion. In short, she established herself as a model Black refugee while simultaneously undermining the credibility of her enslaver.[64]

Mercy almost succeeded. Her case hinged on a technicality: while Gabriel Legget claimed British protection, the people he enslaved were excluded from emancipatory proclamations; they became eligible once he was expelled from British lines in 1779. But, because Mercy parted ways with Legget before his eviction, "she was not sent out of the Lines with him" and, thus, the board concluded, "never became entitled to the Benefit of those Proclamations." In other words, having never resided outside of British lines, Mercy had not, technically, come within them to seek protection. The decision must have felt arbitrary and cruel. The disruption of occupation and the new geographies it created had allowed Mercy's household to live, for years, in relative freedom. But it had been illusory. The very proximity to British lines that facilitated her escape with three small children now barred her from its promises.[65]

Samuel Doson and his two children, Peter and Elizabeth, were also among those examined before the board of inquiry. A self-liberated man who had been enslaved by Westchester revolutionary Luke Teller, Samuel Doson was involved in two separate hearings—one in regard to his own freedom and another about that of his children. Appearing before the board of inquiry in July 1783, Samuel attested that he came within the British lines in April 1778 "with Consent of" Aaltje Teller, his enslaver's mother, who seemingly assumed responsibility for Samuel during her son's militia service. During that time, Aaltje might have instructed Samuel to help her loyalist son Abraham flee to New York City; as Samuel explained to the board, his rumored involvement in Abraham's flight caused him to be "ill used by the continental People in the Country and that was that Reason of his determining to come within the British lines." Before doing so, however, Samuel traveled to Westchester to retrieve his children, Peter and Elizabeth, who were enslaved by Cornelia Beekman, the daughter of the revolutionary New York lieutenant governor Pierre Van Cortlandt. "In April 1778," Samuel "took [his children] from the House . . . and brought them to the City of New York where they have remained ever since." For reasons that are unclear, the children's mother, who was also enslaved by the Beekmans, did not accompany her family when they boarded a British galley and sailed downriver to occupied New York, where Samuel, Peter, and Elizabeth resided together behind the provisional safety of British lines for more than five years. In May 1783, Samuel obtained a Birch certificate that guaranteed him passage out of the garrison; two months later, he and his children boarded a ship to Nova Scotia from which they were promptly removed when Abraham Teller claimed Samuel Doson, his brother's slave, as his property.[66]

Samuel Doson's testimony offers a glimpse into how enslaved refugees carefully narrated their journeys to British lines in ways that bolstered both their own and their kin's claims to freedom. His Birch certificate clearly identified him as having been enslaved by a rebel—an unequivocal indicator that he qualified for British proclamations. And yet, in narrating his journey to British lines, Samuel Doson did more than simply counter Abraham Teller's claims of ownership; he implicitly argued for his children's liberty by recounting his journey to British lines as a family endeavor. Underscoring the timing of the family's escape in April 1778, he clarified that Peter and Elizabeth, who were also enslaved by a rebel, indisputably fell within the parameters of British proclamations and had arrived within British lines well before the 1782 provisional peace treaty and thus were entitled to the benefits of British protection. Of particular note in these brief testimonies was Samuel's use of active language—he "determin[ed] to" escape; he "took" his children and "brought them to" the garrison. It was an assertion of his kinship claims and his right to make decisions regarding his household and the welfare of his children.[67]

The board of inquiry referred the matter to the commandant and board of police, who declared Samuel Doson free. It was, however, a bittersweet victory. Peter and Elizabeth's case, the board felt, was more straightforward. Gerard G. Beekman, the husband of their enslaver Cornelia Beekman, produced a certificate of ownership for the children and their mother. Gender conventions are integral to understanding Peter and Elizabeth's fate. Even though their father had been declared free, they were born to an enslaved mother, and, in accordance with colonial slave codes, they followed her status. Moreover, even though Elizabeth and Peter Doson qualified for British protection by virtue of their flight from a rebel slaveholder, that they were owned by Cornelia Beekman—not her husband—might have thwarted this line of defense. As a married woman and, theoretically, apolitical actor, Beekman could conceivably argue that her enslaved property should be excluded from punitive measures aimed at American rebels. Racialized and gendered definitions of property, motherhood, and lineage thus allowed the board to justify their denial of Samuel Doson's fatherhood, erasing his paternal claims to his children and his household by reasserting the grammar and laws of slavery in which white authorities had the power to determine the shape of Black kin networks and households.[68]

Despite the odds stacked against them, self-liberated people testifying before the board of inquiry occasionally prevailed in wresting control of their families from white enslavers. A. [Toney] Bartram brought his daughters Nancy and Flora with him when he escaped from Connecticut to British lines in New York in July 1779. There, the family obtained certificates of freedom—certificates that proved critical to Toney's ability to keep his daughters safe. In May 1783, Nancy was "detained" by a white man who intended "to send her to her former Master in Connecticut." Like Samuel Doson, Toney Bartram used active language to argue for his paternal rights and to claim his daughters as part of his household. "Complain[ing]" to the board, he "demand[ed] his Daughter Nancy" be returned to him, "as she came with him into the British Lines" in 1779, thus entitling her to protection. Because the white man who had abducted her "could not produce any Authority" for the child, Nancy was "ordered . . . to be set at Liberty" and not to be "detain[ed] . . . any longer contrary to her inclinations."[69]

The extraordinary nature of Black refugees' defense of their households and their assertions of their right to possess themselves and their kin become even clearer when juxtaposed with the testimonies of enslaved people brought before other occupation governing bodies. In February 1779, following the murder of a white overseer, three enslaved people—Louie, Tina, and Diana—were forced to testify before the civilian board of police in occupied Savannah. These testimonies, given under duress and with the certainty of harsh punishments if witnesses were found to be accomplices to the crime, expose the complicated matrix of power relations that enslaved people inhabited in British garrisons. Presenting himself as nonthreatening, Louie lied and claimed ignorance, even though he had a prolonged conversation with the suspected murderer. Diana insisted that she had been "lying sick in Bed" and had overheard the planning but not participated in it. Tina admitted to joining the conversation but, emphasizing her piety, testified that she had refused to become involved because "it was a sin to kill any Body." Both women attempted to protect Louie with their testimonies. According to Tina, Louie had argued against killing Joseph Weatherly because the overseer "was a good Man"; Diana attested that Louie attempted to dissuade the suspected murderer from his plans and to appease Charles's resentment at having to move frequently between plantations by telling him "he could not help it that they belong'd to the white people and that if they were Order'd they must go."[70]

To the best of their ability, Tina, Diana, and Louie tried to protect one another as they told white officials what they wanted to hear: that enslaved people feared and esteemed those who enslaved them, that they blithely accepted the constraints on their autonomy, and that they had no interest in challenging slaveholders' authority. Juxtaposed with the 1783 hearings before the board of inquiry, these testimonies indicate how fully occupation unsettled racial hierarchies and labor systems. Freed from the constraints of bondage and shielded, they hoped, by the British Army, in making their cases before the board of inquiry Black refugees removed the masks of docility and subservience that enslavers expected to see, exposing their fierce defiance, their love of their kin, and their preparedness to defend the liberty of themselves and their households—with little regard for the lives, well-being, or livelihoods of white enslavers. For slaveholders throughout the colonies, this realization and its implications were deeply unnerving.

THE VIEW FROM SLAVEHOLDING HOUSEHOLDS

The widespread flight of enslaved laborers in and around British garrisons unsettled white households on multiple levels: it troubled enslavers' delusions of happy and affectionate slaves; it overturned racist rhetoric that diminished the value of Black kin; it damaged slaveholders' finances, disrupted labor arrangements, and upended household dynamics. Many slaveowners were unprepared for the extent of this domestic disruption and how it altered their daily routines and comforts. So troubling was the loss of enslaved laborers, John Andrews reported from occupied Boston in 1775, that many inhabitants, contrary to their inclinations, remained in the city because of prohibitions on carrying personal property, particularly enslaved laborers, across the lines. "In regard to slaves [the army's] actions have . . . influence[d] many to stay, who would otherways have gone," he related. British occupation and enslaved people's pursuit of freedom and familial autonomy during the American Revolution dislodged critical ideological pillars that undergirded American slavery by demonstrating to enslavers the fragility of their system and adding increased discomfort and uncertainty to their daily lives.[71]

After the fall of Charleston to the British Army in 1780, a woman named Rynah absconded from the South Carolina household where she was enslaved to be with her husband, Will, who worked as a waiting man for Lieutenant Andrew Durnford of the Royal Engineers. The couple accompanied the lieutenant to the Savannah garrison, where he served as the deputy-assistant quartermaster general, and remained there for approximately two years until the British Army abandoned the city in July 1782. Described as "a very valuable House Servant," Rynah was probably a welcome addition to Lieutenant Durnford's household. She likely cleaned for him, sewed, perhaps did his laundry or cooked. Having labored for years among the South Carolina urban elite, Rynah was probably knowledgeable about entertaining and experienced in the management of a genteel southern residence—invaluable skills for a high-ranking officer seeking to impress both his comrades and civilian inhabitants. For Rynah however, Lieutenant Durnford was also a valuable asset: by shielding Rynah from her enslaver, his protection enabled Rynah and Will to establish their own household behind British lines.[72]

Following the evacuation of Savannah, in August 1782 the Royal Engineers briefly stopped in Charleston en route to British headquarters in New York City. Anticipating their arrival, Rynah's previous enslaver, Rawlins Lowndes, a former supporter of the revolutionary cause who had opposed independence and later in the war took British protection, applied to commanding officers in the Charleston garrison and received "assurances" that Rynah would not be allowed to continue on to New York. But, while the Royal Engineers docked in Charleston, Lieutenant Durnford, likely in collaboration with Rynah and Will, "did not permit [Rynah] to come on Shore." Perhaps he simply sought to aid the couple. Or perhaps Rynah had made him aware that Rawlins Lowndes, a member of the state's provincial congresses, former revolutionary president of South Carolina, and current member of the state senate, was not the ardent loyalist that he presented himself to be. The following day, the Royal Engineers—and Rynah along with them—left for New York.[73]

British occupation, Rawlins Lowndes was frustrated to discover, obstructed his ability to claim Rynah, now organized into her own household, as his property or to compel her labor. He elevated his appeal to Sir Guy Carleton, commander in chief of the British forces in North America. Situating Rynah's flight as part of the broader erosion of slaveholders' power and property in occupied Charleston, Lowndes insisted that "the Continual Deprivation of Property, which I daily suffer," was "neither Warranted by any Principle of War or Policy." His misfortunes, he alleged, were symptomatic of a larger issue within the Charleston garrison: "the prevalent practise of carrying off Negroes." "Scarcely a Vessel Sails, but some of the Inhabitants lose this kind of property," he complained. Yet, even as Lowndes framed his request as that of an aggrieved property owner, it is clear that his campaign to reenslave Rynah was not just financial, nor was it simply about reasserting his mastery. Rather, it was rooted in his obligations as a head of household. "I could not have prevailed upon my self so far as to have made this Representation, were it not for the Repeated Solicitation of my Family," he explained to General Carleton. But his family was "particularly attached to" Rynah, especially his children, whom she had "nursed . . . and had the Care of their Infancy." In fleeing bondage to establish her own household, Rynah had upset the balance of that of her enslaver.[74]

Framed in the guise of an indulgent patriarch making an appeal on behalf of his distraught children, Rawlins Lowndes's efforts to recapture Rynah nevertheless reflect the disarray that her absence introduced into the Lowndes household. Rawlins's wife, Sarah, had recently given birth, and the family was sorely in need of the childcare and labor that Rynah had provided to his surviving seven children by his previous wives. Perhaps it was at Sarah's urging that Rawlins pursued Rynah. Sarah was only sixteen when she wed the fifty-two-year-old Rawlins in 1773. The couple's first two children died in the summer of 1778, sending her into a deep depression. William's healthy birth in February 1782 must have been a relief but also reignited the couples' fears about their earlier losses. The extent to which Sarah Lowndes relied on Rynah's knowledge and experienced care—and to which Rawlins entrusted her as a caretaker for both his young wife and newborn child—is reflected in Lowndes's frantic pursuit of Rynah, even as he seemingly accepted the losses of seventy-four other slaves as casualties of war.[75]

At issue here, were two irreconcilable notions of households and Rynah's place within each of them. In fleeing the Lowndes household to establish her own, Rynah achieved a level of autonomy over her family life and her kin, the ability to build a life far from the household where she had been held in bondage. These were the same objectives that motivated enslaved people throughout the colonies to flee to British garrisons. In contrast, Rawlins Lowndes felt that Rynah's pursuit of freedom had compromised his own household. It deprived him of labor, depleted his finances, and exposed his weakened authority.

Laying bare the nexus of household power dynamics, racial and labor hierarchies, and emotional attachments that motivated his actions, Rawlins Lowndes turned to the language of seduction to convey the injury inflicted on his household. "This Wench was Seduced away from me, by her Husband," he groused. By invoking this rhetorical framing, he studiously ignored Rynah's active pursuit of family and freedom, insisting that she had been falsely duped (by her own husband, nonetheless) into prioritizing her own household, her own kin above those of her enslaver. In so doing, he attempted to reinstate the pre-occupation norms that valued enslavers' desires, finances, and ease over Black kinship and family life. It was a deliberate move. For as enslavers like Rawlins Lowndes well understood, enslaved women's wartime claiming of their kin and their reproductive capacities had the potential to topple the entire slave system. Hence, these choices, these relationships, these households could not be afforded validity. Moreover, by rejecting the legitimacy of Rynah's household and marriage, Lowndes endeavored to restore some semblance of balance to his disordered household, which had suffered severe setbacks under British occupation and enslaved people's responses to it. Rynah's presence would facilitate this transformation, enriching his comfort, his peace of mind, his identity as a southern patriarch, and the equanimity of his own household.[76]

Throughout the American Revolution, slaveowners across the colonies similarly invoked the rhetoric of seduction to describe enslaved people's decisions to pursue liberty and claim freedom during the war, insisting that enslaved people were being "decoyed," "seduced," and "deluded away" from their rightful allegiance to white households by nefarious actors who were twisting British emancipatory policies for their own personal gain. That enslavers understood enslaved people's pursuit of family freedom as transgressive reveals how fully those people who stole themselves and their kin to freedom undermined the rhetoric and practice of enslavement. Indeed, refusing to recognize the kinship bonds, motivations, and agency of those people that they enslaved or to grant legitimacy to enslaved kin's conceptions of households, obstinate slaveowners instead frequently framed enslaved people's flight as a personal affront. Writing to his father of Will's successful escape in January 1778, Philadelphian Benjamin Chew, Jr., declared, "The Hardships he must experience from a different way of living than that in your Employ, will sufficiently furnish his Ingratitude."[77]

Even when confronted with enslaved people's rejection of bondage, many enslavers stubbornly professed their expectation that enslaved people's flight was temporary, believing that fugitives' emotional attachments to slaveholders might convince them to return from British lines. While her son Thomas, a paroled Continental officer, was recovering from his injury near Camden, South Carolina, in September 1780, Eliza Lucas Pinckney advised him to seek out Flora, a washerwoman who had been enslaved by Eliza's daughter Harriot Horry and who fled to the British camp at Camden when Charleston fell to the British Army in May 1780. Praising Flora as "very handy," Eliza advised her son that the enslaved woman would "be of great service to you, if you can prevail with her to be with you." Expecting that Flora retained a sense of loyalty to the Pinckney family, Eliza's choice of words—"prevail"—is nevertheless revealing. She recognized that she and her children could no longer compel Flora's service; it would have to be freely given and the terms negotiated. Nevertheless, the Pinckneys were optimistic that Flora would agree to assist Thomas—that, despite evidence to the contrary, Flora would be willing to prioritize her former enslavers' needs over those of her own as well as those of her loved ones and the business connections she had built behind British lines. Revealing the dual motivation behind her advice, Eliza Pinckney directed Thomas, "Your Sister wishes you will imploy her." If Flora could be located and returned to family custody, the Pinckeys hoped, then she could also be returned to bondage in their household.[78]

Slaveholders' insistence on the supposed devotion of the enslaved masked their own dependence upon those they held in bondage. Writing of Thomas, a man that her family enslaved, New Yorker Helen Kortright Brasher recalled, "On him in the absence of his master we relyed." As the family's only male servant, Thomas became the man of the Brasher household during the war, providing food, firewood, and protection for Helen and her children during her husband's extended sojourns to the New York Provincial Congress. Thomas's sudden death from natural causes during the war was thus "an irreparable loss" Helen recalled, and "the children grieved for their beloved Thomas as if they had lost a father." Believing that Thomas reciprocated these affections and was "cheerful, [and] happy" in bondage, in her 1802 memoir Helen went so far as to deny her own coercive role in his enslavement. "Slave he was not," she insisted, "for he might have taken his liberty if he chose it as others had done, but he chose to remain with his mistress and children whom he truly loved and faithfully served." Willfully ignoring factors such as age, illness, fear, or family ties that might have dissuaded Thomas from pursuing freedom behind British lines, Helen insisted that Thomas's affection for his enslavers and their safety trumped his own desire for liberty—a convenient fiction that bolstered her own self-image as a benevolent enslaver and that tempered her startling admission of her family's dependence on Thomas as a "provider" and father figure during the war.[79]

Still, even as obstinate slaveholders insisted on the devotion of those they enslaved, they were conscious of how occupation accelerated and emboldened enslaved people's resistance to bondage. These circumstances intensified fears of violence and reinvigorated long-standing concerns about enslaved rebellion. Simply put, white enslavers, especially those who resided in proximity to British lines, no longer felt safe in their houses. In occupied New York, where the streets were flooded with enslaved refugees, Elizabeth Shipton awoke in terror from a nightmare in which she dreamed her fiancé was "assassinated by one of our own servants." Writing to make sure that he was indeed "safe and well," she recounted the lingering unease that the dream had evoked about the enslaved people within her own household. "It may betray a weakness of Mind," she admitted, "but the Idea hangs about me still, I cannot forget it." Regarding those they enslaved with wary eyes, white enslavers across the political spectrum worried about how British policies could embolden enslaved people to take freedom by force. "There is no knowing a Slave," South Carolina enslaver James H. Thomson cautioned.[80]

In some instances, these fears came to fruition. Outside the Boston garrison in the spring of 1775, during the tumultuous weeks that followed the Battles of Lexington and Concord, an enslaved man named Job informed local revolutionaries that his enslaver, shopkeeper Elizabeth Inman, was a loyalist. The militia's unusually fierce response—especially toward an elite, well-connected woman—suggests that Job accused Elizabeth of more serious activities than harboring British sympathies; he might have implied that she was actively supporting the besieged Boston garrison or aiding the British war effort. Possibly, she was. Accusations of espionage haunted Elizabeth Inman throughout the war, and, on at least one occasion in 1777, she smuggled information to an imprisoned British officer by hiding notes in hair powder. And an enslaved person—someone whose constant yet invisible presence in household spaces meant that they were often forgotten or taken for granted, whose discretion, whether because of fear or loyalty, was assumed—was in a good position to know. In an incident that Elizabeth described as "too serious" to commit to paper, revolutionary militia surrounded her home; in her estimation, the event was "like to have proved fatal" if she "had not been roused beyond reason to have acted an uncommon part I mean calling Gentlemen to turn away men who had done nothing but thier [*sic*] duty considering the story Job told them." "Job has render'd this place useless to you and very disagreeable for any of your family to live at," a "desgusted" Elizabeth informed her husband.[81]

As "Job's affair" suggests, enslaved laborers actively shaped the spaces that slaveholders inhabited—a reality that became terrifyingly obvious amid the disruption of war and British occupation. In April 1782, a self-emancipated South Carolina man led a party of Black dragoons, an all-Black cavalry unit organized by the British Army in 1782, to the plantation where he had been enslaved. He was well-known among the neighborhood and might have intended to foment revolt or to liberate his connections. Wielding arms, the group of Black men surrounded the house of his former enslaver, William Matthews, demanding that he come outside. Upon his refusal, the men "threaten'd to hack in by force" but decided against the tactic. Instead, they requested refreshments from enslaved people on the property, "swearing" to them that if William Matthews had "not been an Invalid they would have fired the House and cut [him] in peices [*sic*]." In sparing Matthews, the group's clemency functioned as an assertion of power—of their right to inflict and withhold violence, with the implicit threat of future reprisal if so inclined. Backed by the might of the British Army, these men had not only severed their own chains of bondage, they exacted retribution by destroying the residences that embodied slaveholders' authority and status, wreaking terror on the enslavers who had long terrorized Carolina's Black community. Subjecting white households to invasion, violence, and fear reminiscent of that which enslaved families endured, these incidents exposed the fragility of the households that underwrote the privileges and mastery of the slaveholding elite. William Matthews believed that the incident, which he described as "a most atrocious attempt on my Person and effects by a run-away slave," was motivated by personal vengeance. "I cannot think myself safe a single Night without this Offender punished," he confessed to a friend.[82]

British occupation, as William Matthews feared, provided opportunities for enslaved people to enact vengeance on their enslavers. Charles, a man enslaved by the family of Georgia governor Sir James Wright and his son Alexander, seized on the British occupation of the city to murder Joseph Weatherly, the overseer of various Wright family plantations. Escaping from Alexander Wright's Richmond and Kew plantation located on the border of South Carolina, Charles made his way to another Wright plantation near Savannah. Sheltering among the enslaved community there, Charles hoped to recruit them to join his cause. He shared his experiences being dragged between the Wrights' various plantations and his expectations that they, too, might share his fate. Frustrated by his nomadic existence and feeling that Joseph Weatherly was unfairly "troubling him," Charles saw the British occupation of the city as a moment to gain control of his life. "If the rest of the Negroes had as good a heart as he had they would go to Ogechee and Kill Mr. Weatherly, by hiding themselves in the Bushes and shooting him as he rode along," Charles proclaimed. Shortly thereafter, Joseph Weatherly was murdered by two men, one of whom matched Charles's description.[83]

Outside of British garrisons, revolutionaries decried Britain's emancipatory policies as an attack on American households and liberties. "Hell itself could not have vomitted any thing more black than [Dunmore's] design of emancipating our slaves," one Philadelphian declared in 1776, cautioning, "we know not how far the contagion may spread." Among white colonists, British emancipatory policies exacerbated deep-rooted white fears about enslaved rebellion, particularly among the slaveholding communities of the southern colonies. While traveling through North Carolina in 1775, Janet Schaw heard rumors that the British were "promising every Negro that would murder his Master and family that he should have his Master's plantation." Dismissing the story as revolutionary propaganda, Schaw suspected that the revolutionaries would "pay for" their fearmongering. "The Negroes have got it amongst them and believe it to be true. Tis ten to one they may try the experiment," she mused. Such fears reverberated in slaveholding households throughout the colonies.[84]

Fearing the consequences of emancipation for white households, revolutionary propaganda sought to reinforce the notion that the breakdown of the household—and, thus, the broader social order—was the intended aim of British policies. As one South Carolina revolutionary lamented in 1780, "My affairs are left entirely at the mercy of Negroes. and an insatiable enemy." Indeed, so pervasive was the conflation of the British Army with enslaved freedom that, in 1781, one Rhode Island newspaper published an imagined conversation between two Black men: Toney, a veteran who supported the rebellion, and Cuffee, who celebrated Britain's emancipatory policies. The revolutionary Toney warned Cuffee to be skeptical of Britain's promises of freedom. "Brittain he no make slave, ha! ha! ha! Who make all he rum, all he sugar, all he molasses[?] . . . O Cuffee you go West Indies, you see Brittan slave[s] . . . you see um haft tarve, he whip, he hang um by de rib; he kill sixteen tousand ebbery year at Jamaica." "Merica no kill Negro, no tarve um," Toney gravely asserted. Underscoring Britain's hypocrisy to a sympathetic revolutionary readership, the imagined conversation was not intended to convert the enslaved to the revolutionary cause. To the contrary, fearmongering propaganda about the threat that British policies posed to the households that undergirded the social order was far more effective at uniting white colonists in opposition to Britain than it was in dissuading enslaved people from pursuing the promise of freedom and family behind British lines.[85]

After the war's conclusion in 1783, enslaved people continued to testify about their self-possession; articulations that drew on and were deeply entwined with their wartime experiences in occupied cities. In 1784, a full year after the British evacuation of New York, Molly, a seventeen-year-old woman whom Connecticut loyalist Samuel Jarvis, Jr., claimed as his property, insisted "that she was taken from South Carolina by the British Army" and was being wrongfully enslaved. Like countless Black refugees had throughout the war, Molly proclaimed her free status as a result of British occupation, but, without the backing of the British Army, she had lost the leverage that had made these techniques so successful in and around occupied cities. Still, she refused to quietly return to bondage. The man who held Molly captive, Samuel Jarvis, Jr.—whether genuinely or selfishly—rebutted her claims. "She pretends," he insisted, as he attempted to overwrite Molly's narrative with his own.[86]

Molly and Samuel Jarvis, Jr.'s, competing wartime narratives were not unusual. In the years and decades after the Revolution, Black Americans like Molly continued to proclaim their freedom and their kinship ties. In sharing their stories of how they navigated the upheaval of the Revolution and its meaning for Black households and communities, these people planted seeds of resistance and hope for future possibilities.[87]

Yet, even as they did so, many white Americans, like Samuel Jarvis, Jr., attempted to erase the liberatory potential of the war years for the many enslaved people who seized on wartime disruption and British occupation to claim their own kin and establish households that could protect them. Drowning out alternative perspectives, they embraced a single, national founding mythology that lauded the wartime valor of white male revolutionaries, the virtue of their wives and daughters, and their collective commitment to defending white Americans' property, families, and liberty. Enslaved laborers appeared in this narrative, not on their own terms—not as pursuing the same goals of family, household, and liberty—but as proxies (often portrayed alongside Britain's Native allies) that proved the ferocity and violence of British tyranny. Positioning these groups as oppositional to white revolutionaries, these tropes cemented a unifying narrative of white revolutionaries' triumph over the wartime dangers to their households, property, and families. These narratives distilled enslaved people's complex wartime actions into a flat, discriminatory trope that served the political, cultural, and economic interests of the new nation by uniting the fragmented and fragile union around shared experience and national aspirations of white householders.[88]

To acknowledge the multifaceted nature of Black wartime freedom would be to contradict white revolutionaries' understanding of themselves as defenders of liberty, standing firm against British tyranny—as well as their aim for the nation's future prosperity. As Georgia revolutionary and Continental Congress delegate Joseph Clay explained in 1784, "The Negro business . . . it is to the Trade of this Country, as the Soul to the Body, and without it no House can gain a proper Stability." Black people's wartime efforts to reclaim family and freedom were incompatible with the story that white Americans wanted to tell about the birth of the nation. Instead, as white revolutionaries narrated the war and its consequences, they recast Black freedom seekers' pursuit of liberty and family as evidence of British tyranny and antithetical to national priorities. These stories would prove remarkably enduring, shaping the cultural memory of the war and its consequences in the early decades of the new nation.[89]

EPILOGUE

To Set under Our Own Vines in Peace, Liberty, and Safety

Writing from Philadelphia in April 1777 in the midst of the American Revolution, John Adams pondered how to bolster support for the revolutionary cause among Pennsylvanians. The invasion of the British Army, he mused, would be an effective catalyst. "Nothing quickens and determines People so much, as a little Smart," he speculated; "a few Houses and Plantations plundered, as many would be, if [General] Howe should come here, would set them all on Fire. Nothing would unite and determine Pensilvania so effectually." Indeed, as revolutionaries like Adams recognized, the British Army's threat to households and property was a compelling tool to unite colonists against a common enemy: invasion, urban warfare, property damage, and the ensuing disruption to household routines and labor regimes unsettled both patriarchal models of household governance and colonists' nascent domestic identities, imperiling the security, both emotional and financial, that many white Americans derived from their households.[1]

Contrary to colonists' fervent rallying cries in the 1760s and 1770s about the sanctity of property rights, the British Army repeatedly proved throughout the war that American households were not castles. As a 1777 Congressional investigation concluded, the British were "barbarous ravagers" who left a wake of "desolation" in their tracks, as evidenced by troops' mistreatment of Continental soldiers and prisoners of war, the sexual violation of American women, and widespread property destruction, including "fences destroyed, houses deserted, pulled in pieces, or consumed by fire, and the general face of waste and devastation spread over a rich and once well cultivated and well inhabited country." Indeed, war demonstrated that Americans were ill-prepared to defend their property and families against the British Army's abuses.[2]

Occupied regions offered undeniable evidence of the threat that the British Army posed to American households. Battles destroyed residences and crops. Robbers pilfered cherished valuables. Officers quartered themselves on families, usurping household space. Domestic servants disappeared with soldiers, leaving white families to fend for themselves. Enslaved kin absconded to British lines in pursuit of freedom. Wives and daughters refused to obey their husbands and fathers, instead charting their own paths through the war. Condemning invaded and endangered households as evidence of British tyranny, revolutionaries' accounts of property destruction, overrun residences, recalcitrant servants, vengeful slaves, and endangered wives and daughters resonated across revolutionary society. The symbolic function of the household as a representation of American and masculine independence—as a representation of the very rights and freedoms that Americans fought to protect—meant that the ways in which British occupation destabilized households and exposed the fragility of the patriarchal norms that grounded revolutionary society reverberated throughout the colonies, even among those who did not experience it directly. These tales of life under occupation not only bolstered enthusiasm for the rebellion, they also served to unite American colonists, particularly urban Anglo-Americans of upper and middling status, into a common, aggrieved American population, bound by shared emotional distress, empathy, domestic disorder, and a profound sense of violation at the hands of the British Army.

By invoking the shared trauma of the British Army's domestic warfare—of the wartime threat to property, the resulting disturbance of the social order, and householders' desires for normalcy—revolutionaries forged critical connections among white colonists. Such propaganda efforts were, however, not only about the waging of war, they were also deeply entangled with the making of national origin stories; reports of British abuses laid the foundation for some of the earliest articulations of an emergent national identity. "Not only History should perform her Office, but Painting, Sculpture, Statuary, <*Medalling?*> and Poetry ought to assist in publishing to the World, and perpetuating to Posterity, the horrid deeds of our Enemies," John Adams proclaimed in 1777. Such undertakings, he reasoned, "will shew the Persecution, We suffer, in defence of our Rights—it will shew the Fortitude, Patience, Perseverance and Magnanimity of Americans, in as strong a Light, as the Barbarity and Impiety of Britons, in this persecuting War." Or, as he put it earlier in the conflict: "Posterity must hear a Story that shall make their Ears to Tingle."[3]

Exemplifying these early efforts to shape the memory of the war, in 1779, Congress tasked Benjamin Franklin with creating "a school Book" to "Illustrate British Cruelties" and "impress [children's] minds . . . with a deep sense of [Britain's] bloody and insatiable Malice and Wickedness." A printer by trade, Franklin was enthusiastic about the assignment and invited the Marquis de Lafayette to collaborate with him on the project. Lafayette was similarly taken with the idea, declaring that Britain's wartime abuses "Must be known By the future American posterity." Together, the pair developed plans for twenty-six prints that portrayed a range of misdeeds, including British troops' disrespect for American troops and their cruelty toward prisoners of war; their destruction of property and burning of American cities; their encouragement of Native allies to slaughter white families; their enticement of enslaved laborers to rebel, even condoning the murder and rape of slaveholders; and their raids on American households, in which lascivious British officers climbed into the beds of sleeping American women and assaulted them at the point of a bayonet. Undeniably effective political messaging, the schoolbook espoused a tale of violent, forcible violation at the hands of a rapacious enemy, contributing to an emergent national dialogue about the triumph of American independence over Britain's tyrannical despotism. Although the schoolbook was never published—Lafayette's return to the battlefield in March 1780 slowed the project, and the American victory at Yorktown in October 1781 might have halted the endeavor entirely—their framing of the conflict would remain integral to an ongoing project of national identity formation that lasted throughout the war and into the early years of the Republic.[4]

Revolutionaries' project to catalog British abuses was a calculated political strategy, yet their efforts were successful because they were based in truth, reflecting the genuine trauma, violence, and devastation that many civilians personally experienced as a result of war and occupation. The Revolution introduced terror, instability, and fear into the lives of people throughout the colonies. Family separation, loss, and hardship were commonplace during the war. For many people, British occupation exposed the tenuousness of societal foundations, accentuating the vulnerability of their households and the fragility of property. "Oh! how changed did everything appear," a shocked Helen Kortright Brasher declared on returning to New York City at the end of the war. In the aftermath of seven years of conflict and British occupation, her house appeared "racked, abused and filthy," her neighbors nearly unrecognizable. The emotional and financial damages that accompanied the transformation of American households into literal and metaphorical battlefields underscores the importance of domestic warfare to how white Americans—especially those of elite and middling status—withstood, conceptualized, and processed the experience of living through the American Revolution.[5]

FINALLY OVER

In December 1777, Philadelphian Christopher Marshall reflected on the upheaval that British occupation had wrought on his life. "Our City," he bemoaned, was "in the hands of cruel taskmasters; the country around ravaged, stripped and destroyed, with houses, barns, etc., burnt and levelled with the ground." Most distressing, however, was the precarious situation of his children and their families, who continued to reside within city limits, unlike Christopher and his wife, who had taken refuge in the Pennsylvania countryside. "The thoughts of these things, and having my children with their lovely offspring in the very jaws of these enemies, afflict me sorely, break my peace and disturb my rest," he confessed. For the next six months, Christopher—restless, worried, and sleepless—anxiously awaited letters from his children that assured him of their safety and recounted the state of affairs within the Philadelphia garrison.[6]

When the British finally abandoned Philadelphia in June 1778, Christopher Marshall returned to the city to survey the damage for himself. He was stunned. "Grief seized me in beholding the ruins, viz., houses quite demolished," he recounted. The Marshall residence had fared better than most, but the family's other properties had not escaped the destruction. One building near the almshouse "[was] quite gone with the brick-walls, chimneys, etc., the doors, cases, windows and cases, etc., either destroyed or carried away entirely." And the family's country retreat near the barracks was likewise laid to waste. "My mind was so pained" by the realization that "our once rural, beautiful place . . . [was] now nothing but wanton desolation and destruction," Christopher wrote in anguish, that he was forced to abandon his survey of the damage and "returned into the city" to mourn his losses.[7]

War left unmistakable scars on civilian communities. Ravaged fields and broken stumps. Ruined fences. Unpaved streets with crumbling houses and broken windows. Damaged mantlepieces and curtains slashed to shreds. Bayonet holes in family portraits. Empty chairs. Nor were all scars visible. "The late revolution was . . . like an earthquake making mighty changes as well as among nations so among individuals," Isaac Winslow reflected from postwar Boston. For eight long years, civilians had endured fear, uncertainty, loss, and grief. Wartime opportunities for enslaved kin to seize freedom, for domestic servants to chart new lives, and for young unmarried women to pursue entertainment and social power contributed to a sense of perilousness and uncertainty that seeped into the most intimate spaces of American life. Such anxieties were not constant throughout the war, but they were persistent, ebbing and flowing as armies circulated through civilian communities and new fields of battle emerged. One Philadelphia woman, according to poet Hannah Griffitts, died of "a Violent Nervous Disorder, occasion'd by the Distress she suffer'd in the Late Distracted Times." As much as relieved civilians might have celebrated news of peace in 1783, they would not easily forget the experience of war and its consequences for their families.[8]

It is unsurprising in the wake of a devastating war that many people simply wanted to be safe with their families and secure in their households. This was true for families of all races and states of freedom, but the documentary record tilts heavily toward elite and middling white families—those who would shape the politics and culture of the new nation. "I would give the World to be with you Tomorrow," John Adams fervently professed to Abigail as he relayed the long-awaited news that preliminary peace articles had been signed in January 1783. "I have lived too long without my Family," he declared; *"J'ai besoin d'être Pere"* (I need to be a Father). "Need I add how earnestly I long for the day when Heaven will again bless us in the Society of each other," Abigail responded, envisioning the joy their reunion would bring, the domestic bliss, and the meals that she would prepare when John returned home. "Come and give happiness to her to who know[s] not either solid pleasure or real felicity seperated from you," Abigail implored. "I wonder whether any body but you would believe me Sincere if I were to Say how much I love you, and wish to be with you and never to be Seperated more?" John vowed.[9]

As the war drew to a close, scattered families gathered in long-anticipated reunions and embraced their loved ones, perhaps for the first time in months, if not years. In muddy trenches and frigid campsites, men had dreamed of holding their wives and kissing their children. They had pictured how their children had grown since they had last seen them. They had carried on "imaginary conversation[s]" with their loved ones to drive out dark thoughts. "I am often in Idea present with thee round a social Fire Side . . . and can Frequently carry on a Conversation of some length . . . while thy attention is in some manner taken off by the necessary care of the little Stranger, and others by the half known language of our dear little Joshua, who I make no doubt is growing more interesting daily," an exiled Thomas Fisher wrote to his, wife, Sarah, in December 1777. Rosy, idealized visions of home and family sustained many men throughout the conflict.[10]

For many people, the experience of living through the Revolution was a deeply distressing, traumatic ordeal, one wracked by inner turmoil, fear, and insecurity. These emotions manifested most palpably in domestic life. Unable to shield their families against the violence of war and occupation, many men worried that their own actions had endangered their families. "Twas Death to leave you, twas worse to stay," Massachusetts loyalist Benjamin Pickman wrote to his wife in July 1775; still, he confessed, "I some Times blame myself for having left you and my Family." Pained by his family's situation in the Philadelphia garrison, Henry Drinker worried how they managed in his absence, particularly his wife. "I should think it my duty and business to have inserted my mean capacity and weak abilities to ease and soften thy anxieties and cares . . . had I been permitted to have remain'd with my dear Family," he professed. Letters from home detailing wartime hardship only exacerbated these concerns, causing many men to feel frustrated and helpless as their families suffered. They longed to return home, if only to relieve their wives' burdens and soothe their children's fears. "It would be a Joy to me to fly home, even to share with you your Burdens and Misfortunes. Surely, if I were with you, it would be my Study to allay your Griefs, to mitigate your Pains," one Massachusetts man professed to his wife during the British occupation of Boston.[11]

Shouldering sole responsibility for childcare, subsistence, and the welfare of their households and family businesses amid the chaos and uncertainty of war—at times with British officers quartered in their residences—many white women also experienced the Revolution as a prolonged period of anxiety and emotional distress. "Tedious days Melancholly nights," Mary Gould Almy lamented from Newport in 1778; "I wonder what keeps me alive." By lonely firesides, women gathered their children in their laps as cannons echoed overhead and windowpanes rattled around them. Burying their own apprehensions, they reassured anxious daughters and sons that their fathers would be home soon—even as they increasingly referred to themselves as widows in their own minds. Separation, Sarah Redwood Fisher admitted, was "very hard to bare." Crying into their pillows, women dreamed of embracing their husbands and fervently wished for the safe return of their partners. Letters offered momentary consolation, but they were "a cold comfort in a winters Night," especially as letters were often guarded, constrained by the knowledge that correspondence was carried unsealed across military lines and open to prying eyes. "The open manner in which our letters are sent, prevents the feelings of the Heart being properly express'd," Elizabeth Drinker regretted during her husband Henry's exile. Still, the couple's children treasured these stilted communications. Seven-year-old Henry memorized the letter his father wrote to him. And three-year-old Molly, after listening attentively to the parts of her father's missive addressed to her, went up to her mother "without speaking, with her mouth held up by way of demanding the Kiss [her father] sent her."[12]

The end of the war meant that, at long last, these desires for reunification could be made real. Peace promised an end to uncertainty and separation, to loneliness and fear—for white families, at least. It meant that they no longer worried about soldiers knocking at their door to request quarters or being awakened in the middle of the night by armed men ransacking their homes. It meant an easing of the daily hardship of subsistence and survival, a return to bustling markets and abundant crops. For women of all races, peace lessened—though certainly did not alleviate—the threat of rape and violence that shaped the way they moved through their neighborhoods as they navigated life under military occupation. Nearly six months to the day after the British evacuated Philadelphia—having spent much of the previous year pregnant, caring for an infant and a toddler while separated from her husband—Sarah Logan Fisher enjoyed a contented evening at home with her "beloved" husband and "our sweet Children." "May we be sensible of the Blessing and favour of being united together and having two such sweet pledges of our mutual Love," she reflected in her diary; "it seems a Happiness almost too exquisite to last."[13]

For white men and women alike, peace promised the one thing that many families had longed for during the war: "domestic Happiness." In the postwar years, Americans embraced their families with vigor. Some elite white women, especially those of the younger generation, like Lucy Knox, wife of Continental major general Henry Knox, were nevertheless reluctant to relinquish the domestic power they had wielded during the war. "I hope you will not consider yourself as commander in chief of our own house," Lucy insisted, declaring, "There is such a thing as equal command." But such women were, in many ways, outliers. War had exposed the fault lines in traditional household arrangements and left many women vulnerable. Eager for a return to normalcy, many white women were happy to retreat from the position of household head on their husbands' return. After all, they realized, there was protection in dependence. "All my desires and all my ambition is to be Esteemed and Loved by my Partner, to join with him in the Education and instruction of our Little ones, to set under our own vines in Peace, Liberty and Safety," Abigail Adams avowed. Family life, free from the burdens and fears of war, was an alluring prospect after years of separation, hardship, and anxiety. Writing to his wife, Mary, from whom he was separated for nearly a decade, Benjamin Pickman expressed his desire to "pass my Days in Tranquility at Home" with his family. "For the remaining Part of my Life I shall be only a Spectator," he promised; "I am determined to preserve my Mind unruffled should I see the Whole Fabrick of Nations crumbling to Pieces." The fruits of liberty were to be found in domestic tranquility.[14]

Indeed, in the introductory preface to her 1805 *History of the Rise, Progress, and Termination of the American Revolution,* historian Mercy Otis Warren invoked these shared remembrances of domestic warfare to soften readers' prejudices toward a history of war authored by a woman. "Doubtless it is the more peculiar province . . . of manly eloquence, to describe the blood-stained field, and relate the story of slaughtered armies," she acknowledged. Yet, she argued, the warfare of the American Revolution had not been limited to "the blood-stained field." It had been a war waged on city streets, among civilian communities, and within American households. "The horrors of civil war rushing to habitations not inured to scenes of rapine and misery; even to the quiet cottage, where only concord and affection had reigned; stimulated to observation a mind that had not yielded to the assertion, that all political attentions lay out of the road of female life," she explained. The war's intrusion into the most intimate domains of American households affected men and women alike. Foregrounding this perspective, she hoped, would resonate among readers. For as Mercy Otis Warren acutely understood, for many citizens of the new United States, the trauma of the American Revolution was fundamentally entwined with domestic life.[15]

Both during and after the Revolution, white Americans invoked the biblical image of the vine and fig tree to express their hopes for peace, domestic bliss, and freedom from fear in the new nation. Derived from Micah 4:4—"Every man under his vine and under his fig tree; and none shall make them afraid"—the metaphor was not new in revolutionary circles. As early as 1769, colonists adopted the phrase to draw explicit connections between revolutionaries' efforts to secure political liberty and the sanctity of their domestic lives. During the early years of the imperial crisis, the metaphor conveyed the invasive nature of taxes and fears of search and seizure, but the experience of war and British occupation gave new awareness to the meaning and consequences of domestic invasion. After the outbreak of war, the notion of a secure domestic refuge became both a distant memory and a hope for the future that conveyed both long-awaited familial reunions and the promised blessings of liberty. As Virginia delegate to the Continental Congress George Mason fervently wished in 1776 amid the throes of war, "May God grant us a Return of those halcyon Days; when every Man may sit down at his Ease under the Shade of his own Vine, and his own fig-tree, and enjoy the Sweets of domestic Life!"[16]

Perhaps no American revolutionary invoked the imagery of the vine and fig tree more frequently than George Washington. The metaphor is pervasive throughout the general's personal correspondence, especially as the war drew to a close. Awaiting word of the final peace treaty in October 1783, he expressed his "a[n]xious desire to quit the walks of public life, and under the shadow of my own vine, and my own Fig-tree, to seek those enjoyments, and that relaxation, which a mind that has been constantly upon the stretch for more than eight years, stands so much in need of."[17]

Aligning with many peoples' own desires for domestic tranquility, Washington's well-known love of private life and his long-desired homecoming endowed his beloved Mount Vernon with outsized significance in the young Republic. Throughout the country, Americans celebrated General Washington's triumphant return to his plantation, heralding him as the American Cincinnatus, an allusion to the Roman general who relinquished power and retired to his farm after defeating a tyrant. "Without Mount Vernon, the comparison to Cincinnatus would not work," one Washington scholar has argued; "the public had to understand the private world Washington left and returned to in order to appreciate his sacrifice." Symbolizing George Washington's long-awaited retirement, Mount Vernon loomed large in the popular imagination as a peaceful retreat where the conquering hero returned home to reap the fruits of his sacrifices to the nation. The plantation, scholars have argued, was "the tangible embodiment of his independence," both as an autonomous landholder and a citizen of the new United States; the hero's return to his safe, protected household symbolized both the sacrifices of war and the hopes of the nation. War and British occupation had demolished colonists' conception of houses as castles; but, in the aftermath of the Revolution, Mount Vernon provided a new symbol for the nation to rally around: the tranquil, independent household as the reward for white Americans' wartime sacrifices and patriotism—without the troublesome monarchical metaphor.[18]

Enshrining domestic life as a critical pillar of American independence, the public veneration of Mount Vernon signified the emergence of an incipient "secular American culture and identity" centered around the private home. Reflecting many Americans' own desires for domestic tranquility in the aftermath of civil war, the Washingtons' private retreat became a public spectacle in the early years of the Republic. Visitors made pilgrimages to Mount Vernon to observe the victorious general and partake in the fruits of his victory. As the Washingtons and their numerous enslaved laborers entertained these visitors, they performed republican independence and American domesticity for an eager public. These enactments, which were also circulated in print form, notably Edward Savage's depictions of George Washington—clad in his military uniform, strolling on the west lawn of Mount Vernon, and gathered around the table with his family (with enslaved laborers in both images hovering near the edges of the frame)—lauded both the general's domestic retirement and the idealized postwar household (Figures 30 and 31).[19]

This public obsession with Mount Vernon helped cement the relationship between private domesticity and American independence in the national consciousness. Mount Vernon, with its classically inspired, republican simplicity—that maintained the racial and gender hierarchies of the plantation household—offered a model of American architecture and American households at a time when most other publicly identifiable buildings were vestiges of British rule. George Washington's unique position as the general who won American independence, as the nation's first president—as the father of the country—meant that Mount Vernon also came to be the nation's home, a widely recognizable, uniquely American symbol that united the nascent Republic. Printmakers and engravers throughout the nation reproduced Savage's images of Mount Vernon, circulating them for popular consumption. By the end of the eighteenth century, these images of Mount Vernon proliferated to

FIGURE 30 Edward Savage, *A View of Mount Vernon*, 1792 or after. Oil on canvas. 23 in. x 35 1/8 in. (58.4 c.m. x 89.2 c.m.). Gift of Edgar William and Bernice Chrysler Garbisch. Accession no. 1953.5.89. Courtesy of the National Gallery of Art, Washington, D.C.

an unprecedented degree, appearing on mass-produced clocks and ceramics. In purchasing these items, American citizens could bring Mount Vernon into their own households, emulating the general's domestic felicity beneath their own vines and fig trees. Within the popular imagination, Mount Vernon not only came to symbolize the fruits of victory, it actively modeled the practice of independence in the new Republic.[20]

And so, perhaps it is unsurprising that, in the years after the war, white American men reclaimed their households, where they, like Washington, planned to enjoy the fruits of independence under their own vines and fig trees, surrounded by their families and "enjoy[ing], without molestation, the sweets of Peace and domestic happiness." The resumption of domestic life, free from fear, was integral to how many white Americans envisioned their newfound independence. After eight long years of war, familial separation, and hardship, revolutionaries reveled in their hard-won domestic tranquility, secure in the belief that their residences were safe from the invasions and violations of the war years. As officials in Schenectady, New York, proclaimed in June 1782, "We anticipate the glorious period when the Voice of War shall be

FIGURE 31 Edward Savage, *The Washington Family*, circa 1789–1796. Oil on canvas. 84 1/8 in. x 111 7/8 in. (213.6 c.m. x 284.2 c.m.). Andrew W. Mellon Collection. Accession no. 1940.1.2. Courtesy of the National Gallery of Art, Washington, D.C.

at an end, when the Inhabitants of our Bleeding Country, shall be enabled to sit under their Vines and Fig-Trees, and no savage foe to disturb their Rest."[21]

Indeed, during the 1780s and 1790s, domestic life found its way into national politics as a symbol for American independence precisely because it resonated among a war-weary populace—many of whom had already embraced domestic tranquility as their reward for wartime hardship. "There is no part of the earth where so much" domestic happiness "is enjoyed as in America," Thomas Jefferson enthused in 1788. Domestic felicity, Americans agreed, was uniquely entwined with the character of the new nation. No other country, Abigail Adams proudly proclaimed, "Boast[ed] that first of Blessings, the Glory of Humane Nature; the inestimable privelege of setting down under their vines; and fig trees, enjoying in peace and security what ever Heaven has lent them; having none to make them affraid."[22]

FIGURE 32 "The Sower" Indian peace medal (Seasons medal). 1796. Designed by John Trumbull. Engraved by Conrad Heinrich. Medal, copper, 46 g, 12:00. Transfer from the Yale University Library, Numismatic Collection, 2001, Bequest of the Charles Wyllys Betts, B.A. 1867, M.A. 1871, Collection. Accession no. 2001.87.3433. Courtesy of Yale University Art Gallery, New Haven, Conn.

So pervasive was this association of domestic tranquility with the American nation and the American character that, by 1797, as American officials drew up plans for new peace medals to be distributed in diplomatic exchanges with Indigenous nations, they chose scenes representing domestic life. Designed by Continental veteran John Trumbull, the three medals, collectively known as the "Season Medals," were struck in 1798 to commemorate Washington's second presidential term. Trumbull's motifs depict idealized domestic scenes: a farmer sowing his fields with a rustic cabin in the background; a shepherd overseeing his herds; a woman spinning by the hearth with her children—one in a cradle, one playing at her feet—and another woman, weaving in the background, while a teakettle boils (Figures 32, 33, 34). Intended to both encourage assimilation and to convey the authority and power of the new nation, the peace medals were proclamations of identity.

FIGURE 33 "The Shepherd" Indian peace medal (Seasons medal). 1796. Designed by John Trumbull. Engraved by Conrad Heinrich. Medal, silver, 20.265 g, 12:00, 48mm. Transfer from the Yale University Library, Numismatic Collection, 2001, Bequest of the Charles Wyllys Betts, B.A. 1867, M.A. 1871, Collection. Accession no. 2001.87.3432. Courtesy of Yale University Art Gallery, New Haven, Conn.

Domestic life, they made clear, was vital to the practice of independence, to American nationalism, and to projections of state power.[23]

REIMAGINING OCCUPATION IN THE EARLY REPUBLIC

Professions of domestic tranquility nevertheless masked lingering anxieties about how the Revolution's domestic warfare, and particularly British occupation, had exposed the tenuousness of the gendered, racialized, and societal bedrocks that structured colonial society and that were vested within the household. War had fundamentally, if fleetingly, altered the power dynamics of revolutionary households. Throughout the colonies, enslaved kin had seized on this moment to pursue freedom and secure their own

FIGURE 34 "The Family" Indian peace medal (Seasons medal). 1796. Designed by John Trumbull. Engraved by Conrad Heinrich. Medal, silver, 46 g, 12:00, 48 mm. Mabel Brady Garvan Collection. Accession no. 1932.105. Courtesy of Yale University Art Gallery, New Haven, Conn.

households; others resisted their enslavement through violence, leveraging the arms and allies that occupation granted them to enact vengeance on slaveholders. Young women of various races and statuses had rejected mechanisms of patriarchal oversight and revolutionaries' calls for austere domestic solitude, instead pursuing entertainment, romance, sex, and occasionally marriage with British soldiers. But they were not the only ones who chafed against patriarchal models of governance. In households throughout occupied regions, white women of the upper ranks frequently clashed with their husbands about the best way to secure their property and care for their families, sometimes choosing to chart their own path, rather than follow the lead of their male relatives. Such occurrences were widespread throughout occupied regions. But even those who had not personally experienced these disruptions had heard stories—indeed, these stories had been a critical aspect of revolutionaries' tactics to garner wartime support.[24]

Thus, even after peace had been secured, lingering concerns about the security of households and the social order that they supported persisted, in large measure because the root cause of wartime fissures remained essentially unchanged. White Americans' successful reclamation of their households, their ability to sit in peace under their vines and fig trees, hinged on a reimagining of the wartime home front that neutralized these internal sources of instability by confining them to the war years. Wartime depictions of occupation—like Franklin and Lafayette's "little Book"—frequently summoned violent imagery of invasion and rape to signal the dangers that British rule posed to colonists' rights and security. Endeavoring to garner support for the rebellion, these narratives functioned as cautionary tales that villainized the British whilst also exhibiting the dire consequences of toppling racial relations and constraining the power of household heads in occupied regions. It was a useful wartime propaganda technique, but one that sat uneasily with Americans' postwar desire for domestic tranquility.[25]

In the early years of the Republic, a proliferation of cultural depictions, including art, novels, and founding mythologies, spoke directly to these postwar apprehensions, proactively projecting a tranquil vision of the nation and the household that soothed lingering anxieties resulting from wartime traumas. A careful renarration of British occupation in both popular culture and popular memory was essential to making plausible the realization of domestic tranquility that defined the very meaning of American independence. Reframing the messy, chaotic home fronts of the war years, early national portrayals of occupation frequently depicted household instability as emerging from British tyranny, rather than acknowledging how occupation had exposed preexisting fissures endemic to the household itself. Or, to put it another way: in the hands of early national authors and artists, British occupation primarily functioned as a vehicle to reify the patriarchal household and conceal its instabilities. Draining the home front of its complexity and nuance, such portrayals bolstered the honor, dignity, and power of American men and reinforced the need to protect vulnerable domestic domains and the liberties enshrined therein.[26]

To this end, early national literary representations—such as *Amelia; or, The Faithless Briton* (1787), the first novel written about the Revolution—frequently reimagined occupation as whitewashed, caricatured tales of seduction, in which untrustworthy British officers, who often gained entry to domestic spaces through quartering, seduced virtuous American daughters away from their duties to their fathers and to the revolutionary cause. It was a shrewd substitution. A clear metaphor for the political contest, billeted British officers jeopardized the patriarchal power, liberty, and happiness of male heads of household; but, because of their whiteness and their gentlemanliness, they did not overtly challenge class or racial hierarchies. Seduction plots effectively expunged occupied regions of enslaved rebellion, violence, and women of all races who voluntarily pursued entertainment or employment within British lines. In so doing, early national authors firmly reasserted a model of patriarchal household governance in which the primary threat to household stability—predatory British officers—was conveniently neutralized when British troops departed North America at war's end.[27]

The visual arts also contributed to these efforts to tame wartime home fronts, rebranding tumultuous wartime households as idealized symbols of the freedoms for which the war had been fought and won. South Carolina artist John Blake White's painting *Mrs. Motte Directing Generals Marion and Lee to Burn Her Mansion to Dislodge the British* (circa 1811) is emblematic of these undertakings (Figure 35). The painting depicts the 1781 act that earned South Carolinian Rebecca Motte lasting fame in which she provided Continental lieutenant colonel Henry Lee with a case of East Indian arrows to set her house ablaze and force the British troops entrenched there to surrender. Motte herself took great pride in her contribution to the battle; in 1855, her longtime acquaintance Harriot P. Rutledge remembered that Motte relished telling the story to young children. "She has painted this scene to me so often," Rutledge recalled, "that I seem to see her standing as she described herself on a low stool before her wardrobe looking eagerly for the arrows" that she kept concealed on the top shelf. For the remainder of her life, Rebecca Motte used the arrow case as a knitting needle case, proudly displaying the weapons that she had willingly deployed against her own house. Yet, in artistic form, White's painting immortalized her, not as a revolutionary, but as the embodiment of the principles for which revolutionaries fought and bled. Reminiscent of contemporary depictions of Liberty, White portrayed Motte in a simple white dress with flowing hair, a red cloth on the table beside her, her arms extended in apparent supplication to the heroic Continental officers who would oust the British from her residence. In White's rendering, Rebecca Motte, standing at the domestic threshold atop a literal pedestal, enshrined American liberty and civic virtue within the household.[28]

Suggesting that American independence was exemplified by white householders' wartime defense of their families, their triumph over their enemies, and their postwar reclamation of their property, these artistic and literary

FIGURE 35 John Blake White, *Mrs. Motte Directing Generals Marion and Lee to Burn Her Mansion to Dislodge the British*, [circa 1811]. Oil on Canvas, 24.5 in. x 29.625 in. (62.23 c.m. x 75.2475 c.m.). Accession no. 33.00001.000. Courtesy of the United States Senate Collection, Washington, D.C.

undertakings were deeply interwoven with the reassertion of patriarchal household structures. In many ways, these endeavors were aspirational, an attempt to fortify a vision of patriarchal governance that had always been firmer in ideology than in practice. Nevertheless, such efforts not only aligned with the personal desires of white property-owning Americans, they successfully tethered these aspirations to national independence, entwining domestic life with the very founding of the nation. By erasing the revolutionary potential of the wartime years—in essence, by obscuring the nuanced interactions between the military and civilians of all races, genders, and states of freedom that defined the experience of war in occupied regions—these postwar narrations reduced the complex experience of life under military occupation to a simplified and gendered narrative of violation that reinforced white

FIGURE 36 Edward Savage, *Liberty: In the Form of the Goddess of Youth, Giving Support to the Bald Eagle*, 1796. Stipple engraving printed in colors, 25 in. x 16 3/8 in. (63.5 cm x 41.59 cm). Mabel Brady Garvan Collection. Accession no. 1946.9.344. Courtesy of Yale University Art Gallery, New Haven, Conn.

FIGURE 37 Samuel Jennings, *Liberty Displaying the Arts and Sciences, or the Genius of America Encouraging the Emancipation of the Blacks*, 1792. Oil on canvas, 60.25 in. x 74 in., OBJ 250. Courtesy of the Library Company of Philadelphia

revolutionaries' wartime sacrifices and reconfigured white households as symbols of the nation and its ideals.[29]

SECURING DOMESTIC TRANQUILITY IN THE NEW NATION

Yet, for many citizens in the new nation, this idealized vision of domestic tranquility was nevertheless complicated by the effects of eight years of war and British occupation. Many houses were damaged or destroyed during the war; years of absence had wreaked havoc on domestic finances and labor arrangements. Poor families of all races struggled to rebuild their lives and credit after years of warfare—circumstances that complicated their dreams of independent property ownership. Many returning veterans struggled in the postwar years, hampered by a combination of delinquent military backpay and rising postwar inflation that inhibited men's ability to repay their debts. In western Massachusetts, these circumstances spiraled into a full-scale revolt against the state government in 1786, led by a group of white veterans who felt that they were being wrongfully deprived of their property. As one supporter of the insurgents expounded, many of the rebels "have Served in the army Dureing the whole course of the War, for Little or no Wages," and now were "Left Destitute of the means of Cultivating their Little hard farms, and of Milk to Nourish their Little ones."[30]

During the 1780s, the federal and state governments across the nation crafted ameliorative policies that rewarded veterans' wartime service with land on which to cultivate their own vines and fig trees. American officials dreamed of a nation stretching from coast to coast, populated by white families who resided on their own property in peace and liberty. A desire to create stable white households supported by individual property ownership drove expansion into the west. During the Revolution, Congress and various states had offered enlistment bounties, usually land or enslaved laborers, to men who fought in state and Continental forces, but, in 1788, Congress redoubled these efforts by passing legislation that granted western land bounties to Continental veterans. Veterans' bounties thus provided a foundation for individual citizens to begin their lives anew while also tethering their interests to the federal government. Lauding "the fostering influence of the new government," George Washington prophesied that the spread of independent white households across the continent would ameliorate "the burdens of the war"; then, he predicted, "Every one (under his own vine and fig-tree) shall begin to taste the fruits of freedom."[31]

As Americans sought to rebuild their lives and build a nation in the postwar years, the mutual expansion of households and the federal government facilitated these efforts. In addition to state-financed bounties, joint venture speculation companies throughout the nation invested in Indigenous lands on the western and northern frontiers of the nascent American states, reaping astounding profits when they resold these plots to eager settlers who desired to establish their own stable households supported by property ownership. These speculative markets linked the economic and governmental interests of diverse states, uniting the young nation across state boundaries. Moreover, the proliferation of white households across the continent both served the interests of individual families and state and federal governments by solidifying land claims and establishing the boundaries of the new nation. White women and children were essential to these ventures, their presence signifying the domestication of supposedly unclaimed, wild lands and the expanding threshold of the American empire. When Native nations resisted settlers' incursions, sensational stories of the murder of white families and calls to defend American women, children, and households justified the use of military force to defend stolen territories. Indeed, settlers and speculators helped bolster the authority of the new federal government by clamoring for a centralized authority to enforce and secure their land claims.[32]

Veterans' bounties and speculative endeavors, which allowed white revolutionaries to realize their dreams of domestic tranquility, often came at the expense of those on the margins of the new Republic. The burgeoning American empire presaged conflict and dispossession for Indigenous families. Native nations continued to assert their sovereignty in diplomatic overtures to the new United States, but, without the support of their British allies, many tribes faced an onslaught of eager, westward-moving white settler families who were willing to defend their claims with violence, to the detriment of Indigenous communities. In a different iteration of land confiscation, white loyalists found their land, property, and slaves seized as punishment for their allegiances—despite prohibitions in the 1783 Treaty of Paris—and bestowed on Continental veterans (typically officers) or auctioned off to generate state revenue. These land policies were imbricated with the process of state making, drawing clear distinctions between those citizens entitled to the benefits and protections of property and those noncitizens whose property was liable to seizure for the reward of those who had sacrificed for the revolutionary cause.[33]

Likewise, the postwar domestic life of enslaved families—even among those fortunate enough to reside together—existed in stark contrast to that of white families. Black kinship continued to be seen as expendable for white profit. As such, the houses of the enslaved were never conceived of as private, protected spaces. To the contrary, enslavers constructed dwellings to maximize surveillance and facilitate oversight of Black kin. Enslaved people knew that overseers and slaveholders might enter their cabins at any hour of the day or night, that, at any moment, their loved ones could be violently seized and sold to distant plantations. The military conflict might have receded, but Black families' war against bondage only intensified as they continued to fight for the liberty and familial autonomy promised by revolutionary ideology.[34]

In the years after the war, hardening racial boundaries thus not only defined the racialized contours of citizenship but contributed to a growing consensus that security in one's property and family—the promised rewards for wartime hardship and the defining features of American independence—was contingent on whiteness. Coded white in the popular imagination, the newly independent American household was interwoven with racialized conceptions of citizenship and property rights that were increasingly understood as central to the creation of the new nation and Americans' pursuits of happiness. The secure, private home, in other words, came to symbolize the power of elite and middling white families who would shape the new nation.[35]

Lawmakers in the early Republic idealized a household model where control was vested firmly—and exclusively—in the hands of (white male) property owners and safeguarded by legal protections. The Bill of Rights—drafted in 1789 and ratified in 1791 as part of the new federal Constitution—further concretized the relationship between domestic tranquility, independent households, and the nascent American state by erecting legal protections that reinforced the authority of (typically male, white) heads of household over their property and dependents. Protecting against the future billeting of troops, the Third Amendment prohibited peacetime quartering "without the consent of the Owner, nor in time of war, but in a manner to be prescribed by law." The Fourth Amendment forbade unlawful search and seizure, proclaiming "the right of the people to be secure in their persons, houses, papers, and effects." And the Fifth Amendment ensured that no person would "be deprived of life, liberty, or property, without due process of law; nor shall private property be taken for public use, without just compensation."[36]

Lawmakers and politicians envisioned an inviolable household—one whose threshold would not be crossed without legal permission granted by representatives of the people or the owner's consent. Vesting authority over the household in property owners and their political representatives—both of whom were overwhelmingly white and male—these visions of domestic security reasserted white men's control over their households and property in the wake of a conflict in which such authority had been destabilized by the combined effects of British occupation, military conflict, and the wartime actions of their own household dependents. British officers, or so revolutionary propaganda implied, had invaded American homes, destroyed family heirlooms, confiscated much-needed supplies, corrupted young women, and seduced domestic servants and enslaved laborers away from their duties. Such allegations were, of course, overblown; the reality of life in British garrisons was far more nuanced. Nevertheless, occupied households had exhibited an alternative model of household governance in which, for various reasons, the authority of male heads of households was radically diminished.

Men's undisputed authority over their households and property was thus an integral pillar of the new federal government and the country that lawmakers sought to create for the new, independent citizenry. Such notions, of course, were not new. Rather, it is the reassertion of these household hierarchies in this moment—at a time when they had been so fully destabilized and undermined by war—that clarifies how American revolutionaries and lawmakers viewed the independent household and its role in the new nation. The independent, private household thus not only had cultural resonance as the symbol of American independence, it was crystallized in the laws of the early Republic as a central component of the rights of American citizens.

The reassertion of these patriarchal norms, broadly speaking, perpetuated gender inequalities within the new nation. Vesting power in the household served to reinforce men's authority over their legal dependents, including wives, children, domestic servants, and enslaved laborers. Yet emergent idealizations of domesticity and legal protections that ensured the privacy and power of property owners also had the potential to enhance the standing of individual white women of the middling and elite classes by shoring up the financial and legal power of their male relatives and investing their domestic roles with national significance. The cultivation of republican virtue—virtue that was increasingly defined, like the households that nurtured it, as white, upper-class, and feminized—would begin at home. In idealized republican households, virtuous white women, rechristened as republican wives and mothers, served as guardians of the virtue of their husbands and children.[37]

Collectively, the postwar veneration and legal protections instated around white family life and property indicate how the war accelerated the rise of private domesticity in the early American Republic. Such ideas, certainly, were already circulating throughout the Atlantic world in the late eighteenth century. But they took on new immediacy and relevance in the aftermath of a destructive war in which elite and middling white property owners had experienced a sweeping assault on their ability to govern their property, households, domestic laborers, and enslaved populations. The ideology of domesticity and the private home was a critical facet of white property owners' efforts at class consolidation and bolstering their own power after the unprecedented challenges of the war years.

Reorienting the history of the American Revolution around the household reveals the extent to which Americans' reverence of domestic life in the early decades of the Republic arose, at least, in part, from the experience and memory of warfare and British occupation and its assault on the idealization and material security of white households. White Americans emerged from the Revolution deeply anguished and shaken by the wartime threats to their property, security, and power. These experiences offer vital context for understanding incipient legal protections around property, nascent ideas about privacy, the emergence of the cult of domesticity, and a burgeoning national identity that was deeply tethered to the household. In the years after the American Revolution, the private household—an idealization that was available, for the most part, to upper-class white families—assumed new prominence in American life and culture: it was a place of family gathering, the emblem of patriarchal power, and the embodiment of the liberty for which men had sacrificed their lives. Nestling these ideals within the household had the effect of reasserting patriarchal control, enshrining white male revolutionaries' reclamation of domestic authority and their enjoyment of their property and families as the fruits of victory. After the turmoil and the invasions of the war years, white American men were, at last, secure in their right to home rule—both political and domestic. And none could make them afraid.

ACKNOWLEDGMENTS

It is a privilege to be able to thank the many people who contributed to the making of this book and who supported me along the way. This book began at American University, where, as a graduate student, I benefited in countless ways from the warm intellectual community and exceptional professors who welcomed me into the world of professional historians. First and foremost, my graduate advisor, Kate Haulman, deserves special thanks. As a historian, a teacher, a mentor, and a scholar of early American women's and gender history, Kate is an inspiration, and I am fortunate to have continued to benefit from her wisdom and friendship in the years since graduate school. Her kindness, humor, grace, and intellectual generosity have invaluably shaped my own professional trajectory, and it is difficult to convey the depth of my gratitude for her mentorship, her steadfast support, and her encouragement of both me and this project over the years. At American University, I also had the privilege of working closely with Gautham Rao, who, from the moment I entered my first graduate seminar, has been an invaluable source of advice, encouragement, inspiration, and collegiality. Unfailingly generous with his time and his support, Gautham has always believed in me and in the importance of this book, for which I am exceedingly grateful. In addition, Eileen Findlay, Kathy Franz, Max Paul Friedman, and April Shelford all helped me to orient myself in this profession by modeling excellence in their own teaching and scholarship. I would also be remiss if I failed to acknowledge my undergraduate advisor at Colby College, Jason Opal, who sparked my interest in family history and who sent me on my very first archival research trip—an experience that set me on this path and is, in no small measure, why you have this book in front of you today.

I feel incredibly fortunate that *The Home Front* landed at the Omohundro Institute (OI), whose books I have long admired. From my earliest conversations with her, Cathy Kelly believed in this book and its potential, supporting my vision and encouraging me to pursue the most ambitious version of this project. Emily Suth has been an unflagging source of support, advice, and encouragement throughout the editorial process, for which I am deeply appreciative. During my time writing this book, Nick Popper took over editorial duties at the OI, and his shrewd critiques and adept guidance helped shepherd it to completion. Kaylan Stevenson's meticulous copyediting sharpened my prose, and I am grateful to her for her efforts and her patience with my many questions. Ellen Hartigan-O'Connor and Donald Johnson provided thoughtful, incisive feedback that strengthened the manuscript and helped to shape this book into what it is today. My thanks also go to Meridith Murray for completing the index in such a thoughtful and expert manner.

As I worked on this project, I was fortunate to have the opportunity to do so at various scholarly institutions where I benefited from both financial support and the kindness and wisdom of other scholars. The McNeil Center for Early American Studies truly is a special place, and I am deeply grateful to Dan Richter for the community he has created there and for his efforts to support junior scholars and introduce them to the profession; my time at the McNeil Center was truly life changing, both professionally and personally. Since its inception, this project also benefited from generous financial support from the Department of History and the College of Arts and Sciences at American University, the David Library of the American Revolution (now the David Center for the American Revolution at the American Philosophical Society), the New York Public Library, the New-York Historical Society, and a joint fellowship from the Massachusetts Historical Society (MHS) and the National Endowment for the Humanities (NEH) (any views, findings, conclusions, or recommendations expressed in this book do not necessarily reflect those of the NEH). Special thanks go to Kid Wongsrichanalai, Dan Hinchen, and the rest of the MHS staff, who truly went above and beyond to ensure that I could access their archives amidst a global pandemic. I put the finishing touches on this book while on fellowship at the Karsh Institute of Democracy at the University of Virginia, where Laurent Dubois, Jessica Kimpell Johnson, and the welcoming community of early Americanists in

Charlottesville have made the process of concluding this book a truly delightful experience.

Much of this book was written while at the University of Oklahoma (OU). I feel extraordinarily lucky to have landed at OU, where I have found wonderful, supportive colleagues and good friends—all of which became even more essential as my first few years in Oklahoma unfolded in the midst of the COVID-19 pandemic. My thanks to Jamie Hart, my former department chair, for his support of my research early on at my time at OU, and to Elyssa Faison, my current chair, who has been a constant source of support and a tireless advocate for me and this project. Kathy Brosnan, Lizzie Grennan Browning, Lois Coleman Carpenter, Jennifer Davis, Sarah Hines, Anne Hyde, Adam Malka, Cori Simon, Melissa Stockdale, Traci Brynne Voyles, and Jane Wickersham, along with the members of Committee G and my colleagues in the Department of History, have provided invaluable support, advice, and encouragement since arriving at OU. Yoga and coffee with Ronnie Grinberg and Jenn Holland offered humor and much-needed breaks from the writing process, as did weekly trivia nights with Lewis Eliot, Cece McTighe, and Allison Becker. In addition to my community at OU, the Department of History, along with the Office of the Vice President for Research and Partnerships and the Office of the Provost at the University of Oklahoma, provided generous financial support that enabled me to complete the research and writing of this book. And my sincere thanks to Teresa Rodriguez for her help organizing images, as well as to Janie Adkins, Danni McCutchen, and Christa Seedorf, who provided invaluable administrative support at various stages throughout this project.

I am also grateful for the generosity of numerous scholars who commented on various drafts and conference papers as this project developed. I am especially indebted to Kimberly Marshall and the University of Oklahoma Arts and Humanities Forum for its support in hosting a manuscript workshop. My deepest thanks go to my workshop readers, Kathleen Brown, Jennifer Davis, Traci Brynne Voyles, and Rosemarie Zagarri, for their discerning feedback and astute comments and our generative conversation—all of which not only made for an extraordinary day but also contributed to the making of this book in vital ways. Over the course of working on this project, I also presented chapters at the McNeil Center for Early American Studies, the Helmerich Center for American Research at the Gilcrease Museum and the University of Tulsa, and the Pauline Maier Seminar in Early American History at the MHS; I am grateful to all of the seminar attendees for their stimulating conversations and close engagement with my work. Additionally, my writing group, Kristen Beales, Jacqueline Beatty, and Shira Lurie, were an unflagging source of support throughout the writing process, and their insights helped to shape the book from its earliest stages. Kathy Brosnan, Benjamin Carp, Carolyn Eastman, Lewis Eliot, Emma Hart, Kate Haulman, Sandie Holguín, Donald Johnson, Cole Jones, Lindsay Keiter, Ben Keppel, Charlene Boyer Lewis, Adam Malka, Holly Mayer, Hayley Negrin, Mary Beth Norton, Gautham Rao, Alec Zuercher Reichardt, Cori Simon, Melissa Stockdale, Alisa Wade, Rachel Walker, and Serena Zabin all also offered valuable feedback on early drafts of various chapters.

I also want to thank the many friends and colleagues who make it such a delight to work in the field of early American history. Nora Slonimsky is truly one of the kindest and most thoughtful people that I know, and I have benefited from her friendship and her brilliance in innumerable ways. Jacqueline Beatty, Mark Boonshoft, Elizabeth Ellis, Alec Zuercher Reichardt, and Rachel Walker have brought laughter to my life, as well as to numerous conferences. Serena Zabin, Charlene Boyer Lewis, and Jessica Choppin Roney have been models of scholarly and personal generosity, always eager to laugh, to chat about history, or to lend a listening ear. I will forever be grateful that my time at American University brought Meghan Kelley and Mattea Sanders into my life; I feel extremely fortunate to have found my kindred spirits. Our friendship has been such a joy, and my life is richer for it. Cassie Caplan has been listening to me talk about history since we were in elementary school; I am beyond grateful for her friendship and her willingness to host me during research trips to New York. So many others have provided fun, laughter, kindness, and camaraderie over the years that I have toiled away on this book; it is nearly impossible to thank all of them individually, but I am incredibly grateful for each of you.

I also owe a profound debt of gratitude to my family, who has cheered me on at every step of the way and whose love and encouragement have supported me over the years. My parents, Allyson and Jim Duval, have been an unwavering source of love and support, and, from an early age, they always encouraged me to pursue my passions. My siblings, Bill Duval and Katie Hookailo, have helped me in innumerable ways, as have their spouses, Danielle Duval and Dan Hookailo, and I am so grateful for our adventures together. Lori and Steve Bird have always treated me like a daughter, and they, along with Eric and Deirdre Bird, have supported and encouraged me along the way. I feel incredibly lucky to have married into the extended

Bird/Weyers family, who have warmly welcomed me into the fold and enthusiastically (and patiently!) inquired about my progress on this book over the years.

Finally, my deepest gratitude goes to my husband, Kevin Bird. His love has brought so much joy to my life. His encouragement and unwavering support have sustained me through graduate school, the ups and downs of the academic job market, and the writing of this book. Through it all, we have called many different places home, and, without hesitation, he has accompanied me on every step of this journey, enriching my life immeasurably along the way. It feels fitting that our daughter Nelle arrived shortly after I submitted the final copyedits for this book, bringing an abundance of joy and sweetness into our lives as we embark on this new chapter together. Kevin and Nelle, this book is for you.

NOTES

ABBREVIATIONS

Adams Family Papers
: Adams Family Papers: An Electronic Archive, Massachusetts Historical Society, Boston, https://www.masshist.org/digitaladams/archive/

AHR — *American Historical Review*

APS — American Philosophical Society, Philadelphia

BOP — Charleston Board of Police Records, Library of Congress, Washington, D.C.

Cornwallis Papers
: Ian Saberton, ed., *The Cornwallis Papers: The Campaigns of 1780 and 1781 in the Southern Theatre of the American Revolutionary War*, 6 vols. (East Sussex, U.K., 2010)

DLAR — David Library of the American Revolution, Washington Crossing, Pa. (as of 2020, the David Center for the American Revolution, American Philosophical Society, Philadelphia)

EAS — *Early American Studies: An Interdisciplinary Journal*

ELP and HPH Digital Papers
: Constance Schulz, ed., *The Papers of Eliza Lucas Pinckney and Harriott Pinckney Horry Digital Edition* (Charlottesville, Va., 2012)

FO — Founders Online, The National Archives and Records Administration, Washington, D.C., http://www.founders.archives.gov

GCM — Judge Advocate General's Office: Courts-Martial Proceedings and Board of General Officers' Minutes

GHS — Georgia Historical Society, Savannah, Ga.

GHQ — *Georgia Historical Quarterly*

HCQSC — Quaker and Special Collections, Haverford College, Haverford, Pa.

HSP	Historical Society of Pennsylvania, Philadelphia
ISM	Independence Seaport Museum, Philadelphia
JAH	*Journal of American History*
JER	*Journal of the Early Republic*
LCP	The Library Company of Philadelphia
LOC	Library of Congress, Washington, D.C.
MHS	Massachusetts Historical Society, Boston
NARA	The National Archives and Records Administration, Washington, D.C.
NHS	Newport Historical Society, Newport, R.I.
NYHS	The New-York Historical Society, New York
NYPL	The New York Public Library, New York
"Pattison Letters"	"Official Letters of Major General James Pattison," in New-York Historical Society, *Collections*, VIII (New York, 1876)
PMHB	*Pennsylvania Magazine of History and Biography*
PMHS	Massachusetts Historical Society, *Proceedings*
RIHS	The Rhode Island Historical Society, Providence, R.I.
RLA	Redwood Library and Athenaeum, Newport, R.I.
SCDAH	South Carolina Department of Archives and History, Columbia, S.C.
SCHGM	*South Carolina Historical and Genealogical Magazine*
SCHS	South Carolina Historical Society, Charleston, S.C.
SCL	South Caroliniana Library, University of South Carolina, Columbia, S.C.
SHC	Southern Historical Collection, Wilson Library, University of North Carolina, Chapel Hill, N.C.
TNA	The National Archives, Kew, Richmond, U.K.
WCL	William L. Clements Library, University of Michigan, Ann Arbor, Mich.
WMQ	*William and Mary Quarterly*

PROLOGUE

1. Reimagined from Mary King's perspective, this narration is derived from Richard King's testimony about that evening; see [Richard] King to Silas Burbank, May 31, 1773, FO, https://founders.archives.gov/documents/Adams/05-01-02-0003-0002-0006 ("no humain," "Dashing," "Scarce," "Father," "Convey[ed]"), Adams' Minutes of the Review: Cumberland Superior Court, July 1774, https://founders.archives.gov/documents/Adams/05-01-02-0003-0002-0014 ("Thumping"), King's Petition to the General Court, Jan. 4, 1768, https://founders.archives.gov/documents/Adams/05-01-02-0003-0002-0002, Deposition of Silas Burbank, June 28, 1773, https://founders.archives.gov/documents/Adams/05-01-02-0003-0002-0008.

2. Adams' Minutes of the Review, July 1774, FO ("Lord," "hacked"), Writ of Review—Stewart et al. v. King: Cumberland Superior Court, June 1774, https://founders.archives.gov/documents/Adams/05-01-02-0003-0002-0004 ("defaced," "broke," "bruised," "burnt"), King's Petition to the General Court, Jan. 4, 1768. The family left one of the marks intact, handing the story of that terrifying evening down through the generations; see Augustus

F. Moulton, *Grandfather Tales of Scarborough* (Augusta, Maine, 1925), 66–68. According to local folklore, Richard King survived the raid by concealing himself under the bed of a sick enslaved laborer—but, if true, he omitted this fact from the court documents. The legend's existence, nevertheless, gestures to how fully invasion overturned household dynamics and challenged householders' prerogatives of mastery. See William S. Southgate, *The History of Scarborough from 1633 to 1783*, Maine Historical Society, *Collections*, III (Portland, Maine, 1853), 183. I am grateful to Dave Gary for pointing me to this source.

3. King's Petition to the General Court, Jan. 4, 1768, FO ("on account," "haveing," "lately," "best"), Deposition of Silas Burbank, June 28, 1773 ("[hung]"), [Richard] King to Silas Burbank, May 31, 1773 ("a frish," "flee wheather," "Devowerers").

4. Deposition of Silas Burbank, June 28, 1773, FO ("favourer"), Adams' Minutes of the Review, July 1774 ("he deservd"); Moulton, *Grandfather Tales*, 65, 68. Richard King died before the war began, so he was never forced to choose a side.

5. King's Petition to the General Court, Jan. 4, 1768, FO. See also Writ of Review—Stewart et al. v. King, June 1774, ibid. For an overview of Adams's involvement in the trial, see "Editorial Note," FO, https://founders.archives.gov/documents/Adams/05-01-02-0002-0001-0001. For more on John Adams and the Boston Massacre, see John Phillip Reid, "A Lawyer Acquitted: John Adams and the Boston Massacre Trials," *American Journal of Legal History*, XVIII (1974), 189–207.

6. John Adams to Abigail Adams, July 7, 1774, FO, https://founders.archives.gov/documents/Adams/04-01-02-0088.

7. "Autobiography of John Adams, Part 1, 'John Adams,' through 1776," Adams Family Papers, sheet 12 ("surveyed," "apprehensive," "incurr[ed]," "Suspicions"), sheet 13 ("family"). For Adams's election to the state legislature, see "Editorial Note," FO. For the importance of families to the massacre, see Serena Zabin, *The Boston Massacre: A Family History* (Boston, 2020).

8. John Adams, Diary, June 25, 1774, FO, https://founders.archives.gov/documents/Adams/01-02-02-0004-0004-0002 ("I feel"), John Adams to Abigail Adams, July 3, 1774, https://founders.archives.gov/documents/Adams/04-01-02-0084 ("I am much concerned"). For 1774 as a turning point, see Mary Beth Norton, *1774: The Long Year of Revolution* (New York, 2020).

9. Adams' Minutes of the Review, July 1774, FO (quotations). For the legislative and historical roots of the castle precedent, see Amanda Vickery, "An Englishman's Home Is His Castle? Thresholds, Boundaries, and Privacies in the Eighteenth-Century London House," *Past and Present*, no. 199 (May 2008), 154–156; and William Cuddihy and B. Carmon Hardy, "A Man's House Was Not His Castle: Origins of the Fourth Amendment to the United States Constitution," *WMQ*, 3d Ser., XXXVII (1980), 371–400. For Massachusetts law, which more so than other colonies "nearly embodied the house-as-castle ideal," see ibid., 392–398 (quotation, 392). For more on British troops in Boston, see Richard Archer, *As If an Enemy's Country: The British Occupation of Boston and the Origins of Revolution* (Oxford, 2010); Eric Hinderaker, *Boston's Massacre* (Cambridge, Mass., 2017); Donald F. Johnson, *Occupied America: British Military Rule and the Experience of Revolution* (Philadelphia, 2020), 18–20; Zabin, *Boston Massacre;* and John Gilbert McCurdy, *Quarters: The Accommodation of the British Army and the Coming of the American Revolution* (Ithaca, N.Y., 2019), 166–167, 178–193, 196–200, 218–231. For John Adams's relationship with military service, see John E. Ferling,

"'Oh That I Was a Soldier': John Adams and the Anguish of War," *American Quarterly,* XXXVI (1984), 258–275. For the slavery metaphor, see Peter A. Dorsey, "To 'Corroborate Our Own Claims': Public Positioning and the Slavery Metaphor in Revolutionary America," *American Quarterly,* LV (2003), 353–386.

10. Adams' Minutes of the Review, July 1774, FO (emphasis mine).

11. Ibid. (quotations), n.29, n.30 (emphasis mine). See also [Richard] King to Silas Burbank, May 31, 1773, FO.

12. Adams' Minutes of the Review, July 1774, FO.

13. Ibid. (quotations). For emotion and the American Revolution, see Nicole Eustace, *Passion Is the Gale: Emotion, Power, and the Coming of the American Revolution* (Williamsburg, Va., and Chapel Hill, N.C., 2008).

14. Vickery, "An Englishman's Home," *Past and Present,* no. 199 (May 2008), 152 ("threshold"), 156; L. Kinvin Wroth and Hiller B. Zobel, ed., *Legal Papers of John Adams,* II (Cambridge, Mass., 1965), 142 ("One of the most"). For castle doctrine, see Cuddihy and Hardy, "A Man's House Was Not His Castle," *WMQ,* 3d Ser., XXXVII (1980), 371–400, esp. 371–372; and Carole Shammas, *A History of Household Government in America* (Charlottesville, Va., 2002), 24–52. For the colonial household, see John Demos, *A Little Commonwealth: Family Life in Plymouth Colony* (New York, 1970); Mary Beth Norton, *Liberty's Daughters: The Revolutionary Experience of American Women, 1750–1800* (Boston, 1980), 3–39; Barry Levy, *Quakers and the American Family: British Settlement in the Delaware Valley* (New York, 1988); Kathleen M. Brown, *Good Wives, Nasty Wenches, and Anxious Patriarchs: Gender, Race, and Power in Colonial Virginia* (Williamsburg, Va., and Chapel Hill, N.C., 1996), esp. 15–17, 24–27, 247–373; Mary Beth Norton, *Founding Mothers and Fathers: Gendered Power and the Forming of American Society* (New York, 1996), 38–180; Cynthia A. Kierner, *Beyond the Household: Women's Place in the Early South, 1700–1835* (Ithaca, N.Y., 1998), 9–67; Lisa Wilson, *Ye Heart of a Man: The Domestic Life of Men in Colonial New England* (New Haven, Conn., 1999); Karin Wulf, *Not All Wives: Women of Colonial Philadelphia* (Ithaca, N.Y., 2000), 85–117; Shammas, *History of Household Government,* 23–52; Holly Brewer, "The Transformation of Domestic Law," in Michael Grossberg and Christopher Tomlins, eds., *The Cambridge History of Law in America,* I (Cambridge, 2008), 288–323; and M. Michelle Jarrett Morris, *Under Household Government: Sex and Family in Puritan Massachusetts* (Cambridge, Mass., 2013). For comparative English analyses, see Naomi Tadmor, *Family and Friends in Eighteenth-Century England: Household, Kinship, and Patronage* (Cambridge, 2001); Vickery, "An Englishman's Home," *Past and Present,* no. 199 (May 2008), 147–173; Vickery, *Behind Closed Doors: At Home in Georgian England* (New Haven, Conn., 2009); and Karen Harvey, *The Little Republic: Masculinity and Domestic Authority in Eighteenth-Century Britain* (Oxford, 2012).

15. "Letter IX," in [John Dickinson], *Letters from a Farmer in Pennsylvania, to the Inhabitants of the British Colonies* (Philadelphia, 1774), 89 ("place," "utterly"); Abigail Adams to Mercy Otis Warren, Feb. 3, 1775, FO, https://founders.archives.gov/documents/Adams/04-01-02-0122 ("admired," "these Truths," "cannot be happy," "We know too well"); for original quote, see "Letter XII," in [Dickinson], *Letters from a Farmer,* 129.

16. U.S. Const., preamble (quotation); John Adams to Rufus King, Dec. 23, 1785, FO, n. 2, https://founders.archives.gov/documents/Adams/06-18-02-0031. According to Rufus King's biographer, he never mentioned the attack in his surviving writings—an omission that Robert Ernst attributes to "youthful resiliency or a subconscious urge to forget" but that

also suggests that the incident "may have fostered his deep-rooted concern as an adult for protection against turbulence and lawlessness"; see Ernst, *Rufus King: American Federalist* (Williamsburg, Va., and Chapel Hill, N.C., 1968), 11.

INTRODUCTION

1. Hannah Winthrop to Mercy Otis Warren, circa May 1775, Correspondence with Mercy Otis Warren, 1752–1789, MHS (quotations).

2. Ibid. ("mangled," "roads," "Some"); Sarah Winslow Deming Journal, 1775, MHS, Collections Online, https://www.masshist.org/database/viewer.php?item_id=1090 ("We had," "did not").

3. Hannah Winthrop to Mercy Otis Warren, circa May 1775, Correspondence with Mercy Otis Warren.

4. Ibid.

5. Mercy Otis Warren to Hannah Winthrop, June 3, 1775, Correspondence with Mercy Otis Warren.

6. Abigail Adams to Mercy Otis Warren, May 2, 1775, FO, https://founders.archives.gov/documents/Adams/04-01-02-0126 (quotation). For other scholarship in this vein, see T. H. Breen, *The Will of the People: The Revolutionary Birth of America* (Cambridge, Mass., 2020); Holger Hoock, *Scars of Independence: America's Violent Birth* (New York, 2017); T. Cole Jones, *Captives of Liberty: Prisoners of War and the Politics of Vengeance in the American Revolution* (Philadelphia, 2019); Donald F. Johnson, *Occupied America: British Military Rule and the Experience of Revolution* (Philadelphia, 2020); Matthew P. Dziennik, "New York's Refugees and Political Authority in Revolutionary America," *WMQ*, 3d Ser., LXXVII (2020), 65–96; and Serena Zabin, *The Boston Massacre: A Family History* (Boston, 2020).

7. This study builds on long-standing debates about how revolutionary the war was, who benefited from it, and whose experiences we center in that telling. For an overview of scholarship that has embraced that there was, not one, but many revolutions, see Alfred F. Young and Gregory H. Nobles, *Whose American Revolution Was It? Historians Interpret the Founding* (New York, 2011); and Alan Taylor, *American Revolutions: A Continental History, 1750–1804* (New York, 2016). For the gendered dimensions of these debates, see Rosemarie Zagarri, "Introduction," in Barbara B. Oberg, ed., *Women in the American Revolution: Gender, Politics, and the Domestic World* (Charlottesville, Va., 2019), 1–15, esp. 3; and Holly A. Mayer, "Introduction," in Mayer, ed., *Women Waging War in the American Revolution* (Charlottesville, Va., 2022), 1–21. For an example of this multifaceted approach, see Woody Holton, *Liberty Is Sweet: The Hidden History of the American Revolution* (New York, 2021). For a conversation about the state of the field, see T. H. Breen et al., "The Revolution at 250: A Conversation," *JER*, XLIV (2024), 513–579.

8. *The Home Front* takes inspiration from John Shy's call to integrate the cultural, social, and military histories of the American Revolution and consider the war as "a political education conducted by military means"; see Shy, "The American Revolution: The Military Conflict Considered as a Revolutionary War," in Stephen G. Kurtz and James H. Hutson, eds., *Essays on the American Revolution* (Williamsburg, Va., and Chapel Hill, N.C., 1973), 147. How we narrate war has the potential to both uncover previously unrecognized aspects

of warfare and to illuminate the broader power dynamics that shape the meanings derived from war; see Jill Lepore, *The Name of War: King Philip's War and the Origins of American Identity* (New York, 1998); and Lisa Brooks, *Our Beloved Kin: A New History of King Philip's War* (New Haven, Conn., 2018).

9. Mary Beth Norton, *Founding Mothers and Fathers: Gendered Power and the Forming of American Society* (New York, 1996), 96 ("little"), 137; Freya Gowrley, *Domestic Space in Britain, 1750–1840: Materiality, Sociability, and Emotion* (London, 2022), 223, 225 ("site"); see also Carole Shammas, "Anglo-American Household Government in Comparative Perspective," *WMQ*, 3d Ser., LII (1995), 128. In 1774, 80 percent of people residing in the American colonies were legal dependents; see Carole Shammas, *A History of Household Government in America* (Charlottesville, Va., 2002), 32.

For households and social order, see Christine Stansell, *City of Women: Sex and Class in New York, 1789–1860* (Urbana, Ill., 1982); Stephanie McCurry, *Masters of Small Worlds: Yeoman Households, Gender Relations, and the Political Culture of the Antebellum South Carolina Low Country* (New York, 1995); Shammas, "Anglo-American Household Government," *WMQ*, 3d Ser., LII (1995), 104–144; Norton, *Founding Mothers and Fathers;* Shammas, *History of Household Government;* Holly Brewer, "The Transformation of Domestic Law," in Michael Grossberg and Christopher Tomlins, eds., *The Cambridge History of Law in America,* I (Cambridge, 2008), 288–323; Karen Harvey, *The Little Republic: Masculinity and Domestic Authority in Eighteenth-Century Britain* (Oxford, 2012); Maile Arvin, Eve Tuck, and Angie Morrill, "Decolonizing Feminism: Challenging Connections between Settler Colonialism and Heteropatriarchy," *Feminist Formations,* XXV, no. 1 (Spring 2013), 8–34; Honor Sachs, *Home Rule: Households, Manhood, and National Expansion on the Eighteenth-Century Kentucky Frontier* (New Haven, Conn., 2015); Laurel Clark Shire, *The Threshold of Manifest Destiny: Gender and National Expansion in Florida* (Philadelphia, 2016); Toby L. Ditz, "Manhood and the US Republican Empire," in Ellen Hartigan-O'Connor and Lisa G. Masterson, eds., *The Oxford Handbook of American Women's and Gender History* (Oxford, 2018), 43–69; Kathryn Kish Sklar, "Reconsidering Domesticity through the Lens of Empire and Settler Society in North America," *AHR,* CXXIV (2019), 1249–1266; and Jacqueline Beatty, *In Dependence: Women and the Patriarchal State in Revolutionary America* (New York, 2023). For theorizations of household power, see Ann Laura Stoler, *Carnal Knowledge and Imperial Power: Race and the Intimate in Colonial Rule* (Berkeley, Calif., 2002); Mary S. Hartman, *The Household and the Making of History: A Subversive View of the Western Past* (Cambridge, 2004); and Arvin, Tuck, and Morrill, "Decolonizing Feminism," *Feminist Formations,* XXV, no. 1 (Spring 2013), 8–34.

For scholarly conversations about the household and domesticity, see "Men at Home: Domesticities, Authority, Emotions, and Work," special issue, *Gender and History,* XXVII, no. 3 (2015); and the *AHR* roundtable "Unsettling Domesticities: New Histories of Home in Global Contexts," *AHR,* CXXIV (2019), 1246–1336. For more on households and Anglo-American identity, see Richard L. Bushman, *The Refinement of America: Persons, Houses, Cities* (New York, 1992); Bernard L. Herman, *Town House: Architecture and Material Life in the Early American City, 1780–1830* (Williamsburg, Va., and Chapel Hill, N.C., 2005); Onni Gust, *Unhomely Empire: Whiteness and Belonging, c. 1760–1830* (London, 2021); and Gowrley, *Domestic Space in Britain.* For more on household scholarship, see note 26, note 27, and note 29, below.

10. Households are not inert structures; they are dynamic spaces whose social, cultural, and political meanings are continuously renegotiated in response to fluctuating social relations and their accompanying power dynamics; see Doreen Massey, *Space, Place, and Gender* (Minneapolis, Minn., 1994), 154–155.

11. John Adams to Abigail Adams, Apr. 14, 1776, FO, https://founders.archives.gov/documents/Adams/04-01-02-0248.

12. "After 1783," historian James L. Abrahamson asserts, "Americans . . . made Liberty their goddess and their Country an object of worship"; see Abrahamson, *The American Home Front: Revolutionary War, Civil War, World War I, World War II* (Washington, D.C., 1983), 16.

13. Onni Gust argues that alienation from domestic spaces and a sense of "belonging" remade notions of home among Britons living abroad during this period; Serena Zabin's analysis of discourses about the imperial family also suggests the importance of home and family to conceptions of national belonging; see Gust, *Unhomely Empire;* and Zabin, *Boston Massacre,* 18–19, 222–228. Donald F. Johnson has similarly noted how living under British occupation governments alienated many from the crown; see Johnson, *Occupied America,* 6. For more on the United States as a postcolonial nation, see Kariann Akemi Yokota, *Unbecoming British: How Revolutionary America Became a Postcolonial Nation* (Oxford, 2011).

14. The most comprehensive studies of occupation are Johnson, *Occupied America;* and John D. Roche, "'[America] May Be Conquered with More Ease than Governed': The Evolution of British Occupation Policy during the American Revolution" (Ph.D. diss., University of North Carolina, 2015). For Boston, see Richard Archer, *As If an Enemy's Country: The British Occupation of Boston and the Origins of Revolution* (Oxford, 2010); and Zabin, *Boston Massacre.* For New York, see Judith Van Buskirk, "Crossing the Lines: African-Americans in the New York City Region during the British Occupation, 1776–1783," *Pennsylvania History: A Journal of Mid-Atlantic Studies,* in "Explorations in Early American Culture," eds. William Pencak and George W. Boudreau, special issue, LXV (1998), 74–100; Van Buskirk, *Generous Enemies: Patriots and Loyalists in Revolutionary New York* (Philadelphia, 2002); and Ruma Chopra, *Unnatural Rebellion: Loyalists in New York City during the Revolution* (Charlottesville, Va., 2011). For Newport, see Walter K. Schroder, *The Hessian Occupation of Newport and Rhode Island, 1776–1779* (Westminster, Md., 2005); and Travis Glasson, "The Intimacies of Occupation: Loyalties, Compromise, and Betrayal in Revolutionary-Era Newport," in Patrick Spero and Michael Zuckerman, eds., *The American Revolution Reborn* (Philadelphia, 2016), 29–47. For Philadelphia, see Willard O. Mishoff, "Business in Philadelphia during the British Occupation, 1777–1778," *PMHB,* LXI (1937), 165–181; John W. Jackson, *With the British Army in Philadelphia, 1777–1778* (San Rafael, Calif., 1979); Darlene Emmert Fisher, "Social Life in Philadelphia during the British Occupation," *Pennsylvania History,* XXXVII (1970), 237–260; Aaron Sullivan, *The Disaffected: Britain's Occupation of Philadelphia during the American Revolution* (Philadelphia, 2019); and Judith Van Buskirk, "They Didn't Join the Band: Disaffected Women in Revolutionary Philadelphia," *Pennsylvania History,* LXII (1995), 306–329. For Charleston, see Walter J. Fraser, Jr., *Patriots, Pistols, and Petticoats: "Poor Sinful Charles Town" during the American Revolution* (Charleston, S.C., 1976); George Smith McCowen, *The British Occupation of Charleston, 1780–82* (Columbia, S.C., 1972); and Lauren Duval, "Mastering Charleston: Property and Patriarchy in British-Occupied Charleston, 1780–82," *WMQ,* 3d Ser., LXXV (2018), 589–622. For Savannah, see Alexander A. Lawrence,

Storm over Savannah: The Story of Count D'Estaing and the Siege of the Town in 1779 (Athens, Ga., 1951); Martha Condray Searcy, "1779: The First Year of the British Occupation of Georgia," *Georgia Historical Quarterly*, LXVII (1983), 168–188; Leslie Hall, *Land and Allegiance in Revolutionary Georgia* (Athens, Ga., 2001); Greg Brooking, "'Of Material Importance': Governor James Wright and the Siege of Savannah," *Georgia Historical Quarterly*, XCVIII (2014), 251–299; and Timothy Lockley, "'The King of England's Soldiers': Armed Blacks in Savannah and Its Hinterlands during the Revolutionary War Era, 1778–1787," in Leslie M. Harris and Daina Ramey Berry, eds., *Slavery and Freedom in Savannah* (Athens, Ga., 2014), 26–41.

15. Carl Bridenbaugh, *Cities in Revolt: Urban Life in America, 1743–1776* (New York, 1955), 215–217; Barratt Wilkins, "A View of Savannah on the Eve of the Revolution," *Georgia Historical Quarterly*, LIV (1970), 578; Benjamin L. Carp, *Rebels Rising: Cities and the American Revolution* (New York, 2007), 225; Taylor, *American Revolutions*, 23. For studies of the Revolution with similar urban framings, see Bridenbaugh, *Cities in Revolt;* Gary B. Nash, *The Urban Crucible: The Northern Seaports and the Origins of the American Revolution* (Cambridge, Mass., 1986); Carp, *Rebels Rising;* Kate Haulman, *The Politics of Fashion in Eighteenth-Century America* (Chapel Hill, N.C., 2011); and Johnson, *Occupied America.*

16. Hesse-Kassel (Electorate), Platte Grenadier Battalion, Journal, June 4, 1780, LOC (quotation). For refinement, see Bushman, *Refinement of America;* T. H. Breen, *The Marketplace of Revolution: How Consumer Politics Shaped American Independence* (Oxford, 2004); Herman, *Town House;* Serena R. Zabin, *Dangerous Economies: Status and Commerce in Imperial New York* (Philadelphia, 2009), 6–9, 65–70; and Jennifer L. Anderson, *Mahogany: The Costs of Luxury in Early America* (Cambridge, Mass., 2012). For households and family life, see Nancy F. Cott, *The Bonds of Womanhood: "Woman's Sphere" in New England, 1780–1835* (New Haven, Conn., 1977); Mary Beth Norton, *Liberty's Daughters: The Revolutionary Experience of American Women, 1750–1800* (Boston, 1980), 3–151; Jan Lewis, *The Pursuit of Happiness: Family and Values in Jefferson's Virginia* (Cambridge, 1983); Barry Levy, *Quakers and the American Family: British Settlement in the Delaware Valley* (Oxford, 1988); Lisa Wilson, *Ye Heart of a Man: The Domestic Life of Men in Colonial New England* (New Haven, Conn., 1999); and Lorri Glover, *Founders as Fathers: The Private Lives and Politics of the American Revolutionaries* (New Haven, Conn., 2014). For labor and enslavement, see Jeanne Boydston, *Home and Work: Housework, Wages, and the Ideology of Labor in the Early Republic* (Oxford, 1990); Bernard L. Herman, "The Embedded Landscapes of the Charleston Single House, 1780–1820," *Perspectives in Vernacular Architecture*, VII (1997), 41–57; Stephanie M. H. Camp, *Closer to Freedom: Enslaved Women and Everyday Resistance in the Plantation South* (Chapel Hill, N.C., 2004); Thavolia Glymph, *Out of the House of Bondage: The Transformation of the Plantation Household* (Cambridge, 2008); Wendy Anne Warren, "'The Cause of Her Grief': The Rape of a Slave in Early New England," *JAH*, XCIII (2007), 1031–1049; Terri L. Snyder, "'To Seeke for Justice': Gender, Servitude, and Household Governance in the Early Modern Chesapeake," in Douglas Bradburn and John C. Coombs, eds., *Early Modern Virginia: Reconsidering the Old Dominion* (Charlottesville, Va., 2011), 128–157; Andrea C. Mosterman, *Spaces of Enslavement: A History of Slavery and Resistance in Dutch New York* (Ithaca, N.Y., 2021), 78–102; Caylin Carbonell, "Fraught Labor, Fragile Authority: Households in Motion in Early New England" (Ph.D. diss., The College of William and Mary, 2020); and Whitney Nell Stewart, *This Is Our Home: Slavery and Struggle on Southern Plantations* (Chapel Hill, N.C., 2023). For family finances, see J. M. Opal, *Beyond the Farm: National Ambitions in*

Rural New England (Philadelphia, 2008); Ellen Hartigan-O'Connor, *The Ties That Buy: Women and Commerce in Revolutionary America* (Philadelphia, 2009), esp. 13–38; and Sara T. Damiano, *To Her Credit: Women, Finance, and the Law in Eighteenth-Century New England Cities* (Baltimore, Md., 2021).

17. For households and identity, see Bushman, *Refinement of America,* xviii, 100–138; Susan M. Stabile, *Memory's Daughters: The Material Culture of Remembrance in Eighteenth-Century America* (Ithaca, N.Y., 2004); Herman, *Town House,* esp. 33–76; Amanda Vickery, *Behind Closed Doors: At Home in Georgian England* (New Haven, Conn., 2009); Gust, *Unhomely Empire;* and Gowrley, *Domestic Space in Britain.* For slavery, see Anderson, *Mahogany,* 29, 50–54; and Jared Ross Hardesty, *Unfreedom: Slavery and Dependence in Eighteenth-Century Boston* (New York, 2016), 49.

18. Memorial of Scipio Handley, AO 12/47, 118–120 ("furniture," 120), TNA; Hesse-Kassel (Electorate), Platte Grenadier Battalion Journal, June 4, 1780 ("Wretched"); Bernard L. Herman, "Slave and Servant Housing in Charleston, 1770–1820," *Historical Archaeology,* XXXIII, no. 3 (1999), 90–91. For impoverished neighborhoods, see Hartigan-O'Connor, *Ties That Buy,* 13–38; see also Stansell, *City of Women,* 41–62. For enslaved homemaking, see Dylan C. Penningroth, *The Claims of Kinfolk: African American Property and Community in the Nineteenth-Century South* (Chapel Hill, N.C., 2003); Anthony E. Kaye, *Joining Places: Slave Neighborhoods in the Old South* (Chapel Hill, N.C., 2007); and Stewart, *This Is Our Home.*

19. John Gilbert McCurdy, *Quarters: The Accommodation of the British Army and the Coming of the American Revolution* (Ithaca, N.Y., 2019), 165–200, esp. 166–167, 174. For imperial ties, see Zabin, *Dangerous Economies.*

20. For urban barracks and peacekeeping, see Molly Perry, "Buried Liberties and Hanging Effigies: Imperial Persuasion, Intimidation, and Performance during the Stamp Act Crisis," in Zachary McLeod Hutchins, ed., *Community without Consent: New Perspectives on the Stamp Act* (Hanover, N.H., 2016), 36–66; McCurdy, *Quarters,* 165–174, 178; and Zabin, *Boston Massacre,* 23–26, 141–150. For the Boston Massacre, see Zabin, *Boston Massacre,* 52; and McCurdy, *Quarters,* 89–126, 180–183. For more on prewar Boston, see John W. Shy, *Toward Lexington: The Role of the British Army in the Coming of the American Revolution* (Princeton, N.J., 1965); and Archer, *As If an Enemy's Country.*

21. Isaac Smith, Sr., to Isaac Smith, Jr., June 30, 1775, Smith-Carter Family Papers, 1669–1880, reel 2, box 2, folder 13, June–December 1775, image 4–6, MHS, Digitized Collections, https://www.masshist.org/collection-guides/digitized/fa0540/b02-f13#4 ("marshall"), postscript, July 1, 1775 ("There is," "standing"). For more on the castle metaphor, see William Cuddihy and B. Carmon Hardy, "A Man's House Was Not His Castle: Origins of the Fourth Amendment to the United States Constitution," *WMQ,* 3d Ser., XXXVII (1980), 371–400.

22. [Emer] de Vattel, *The Law of Nations; or, Principles of the Law of Nature; Applied to the Conduct and Affairs of Nations and Sovereigns,* II (London, 1759), 51–53, 59 (quotations), 61–66; Stephen Conway, "The British Army, 'Military Europe,' and the American War of Independence," *WMQ,* 3d Ser., LXVII (2010), 69–100. For occupation policy specifically, see Horst Carl, "Restricted Violence? Military Occupation during the Eighteenth Century," in Erica Charters, Eve Rosenhaft, and Hannah Smith, eds., *Civilians and War in Europe, 1618–1815,* I (Liverpool, U.K., 2012), 118–128.

23. Vattel, *Law of Nations,* II, 51–53 ("enemies," 51, "politeness," 53, "in itself," 53), 64–66.

24. Edward H. Tatum, Jr., ed., *The American Journal of Ambrose Serle, Secretary to Lord Howe, 1776–1778* (San Marino, Calif., 1940), Nov. 24, 1777, 265.

25. Molly Pemberton to Israel Pemberton, Feb. 2, 1778, Pemberton Family Papers, 1641–1880, XXXI, 101, HSP.

26. [Alexander Hamilton], "A Full Vindication of the Measures of the Congress, etc.," [Dec. 15], 1774, FO, https://founders.archives.gov/documents/Hamilton/01-01-02-0054 (quotations); see also [John Dickinson], *Letters from a Farmer in Pennsylvania, to the Inhabitants of the British Colonies* (Philadelphia, 1774), 48. Gesturing to these dynamics, historian Carl Lotus Becker famously asserted that two fundamental issues underlay revolutionary politics: "the question of home rule" and "of who should rule at home," meaning, who would wield political power. Yet, even as it invoked domestic metaphors, Becker's analysis remained rooted in the political realm, sidestepping both the military conflict and the lived experience of American households; see Becker, *The History of Political Parties in the Province of New York, 1760–1776* (Madison, Wisc., 1909), 22 (quotations); Jan Lewis and Honor Sachs have likewise invoked Becker to frame questions about gender and revolutionary households; see Jan Lewis, "Women and the American Revolution," *OAH Magazine of History*, VIII, no. 4 (Summer 1994), 23–26; and Sachs, *Home Rule*, 6–7. For the entwined nature of gender, family, and households in the politics of the early Republic, see Lewis, *The Pursuit of Happiness;* Mark E. Kann, *A Republic of Men: The American Founders, Gendered Language, and Patriarchal Politics* (New York, 1998); Shammas, *History of Household Government;* Glover, *Founders as Fathers;* Sachs, *Home Rule;* Shire, *Threshold of Manifest Destiny;* Ditz, "Manhood and the US Republican Empire," in Hartigan-O'Connor and Masterson, eds., *Oxford Handbook of American Women's and Gender History*, 43–70; and Barry Bienstock, Annette Gordon-Reed, and Peter S. Onuf, eds., *Family, Slavery, and Love in the Early American Republic: The Essays of Jan Ellen Lewis* (Williamsburg, Va., and Chapel Hill, N.C., 2021).

For more on property in revolutionary politics, see Stanley N. Katz, "Thomas Jefferson and the Right to Property in Revolutionary America," *Journal of Law and Economics*, XIX (1976), 467–488; Cuddihy and Hardy, "A Man's House Was Not His Castle," *WMQ*, 3d Ser., XXXVII (1980), 371–400; David Schultz, "The Locke Republican Debate and the Paradox of Property Rights in Early American Jurisprudence," *Western New England Law Review*, XIII (1991), 155–187; and Schultz, "Political Theory and Legal History: Conflicting Depictions of Property in the American Political Founding," *American Journal of Legal History*, XXXVII (1993), 464–495; for more on property in revolutionary historiography, see note 27, below.

For consumer goods and the imperial crisis, see T. H. Breen, "'Baubles of Britain': The American and Consumer Revolutions of the Eighteenth Century," *Past and Present*, no. 119 (May 1988), 93–103; Breen, *Marketplace of Revolution;* Michael Zakim, "Sartorial Ideologies: From Homespun to Ready-Made," *AHR*, CVI (2001), 1553–1565; Cynthia A. Kierner, *Beyond the Household: Women's Place in the Early South, 1700–1835* (Ithaca, N.Y., 1998), 76; Kate Haulman, "Fashion and the Culture Wars of Revolutionary Philadelphia," *WMQ*, 3d Ser., LXII (2005), 625–662; and Haulman, *Politics of Fashion.*

For the importance of domestic life in shaping worldviews, see Naomi Tadmor, *Family and Friends in Eighteenth-Century England: Household, Kinship, and Patronage* (Cambridge, 2001); Herman, *Town House*, 1; Vickery, *Behind Closed Doors;* Harvey, *Little Republic;* Gust, *Unhomely Empire;* and Gowrley, *Domestic Space in Britain.*

27. Studies of property during the Revolution have focused on legal arguments and political rhetoric, rather than considering how lived experience and emotional connections to household space shaped political action and priorities. For a good overview of this scholarship, see Schultz, "Political Theory and Legal History," *American Journal of Legal History,* XXXVII (1993), 464–495; and Schultz, "The Locke Republican Debate," *Western New England Law Review,* XIII (1991), 155–187. For examples of studies that center questions of property, see Charles A. Beard, *An Economic Interpretation of the Constitution of the United States* (New York, 1913); Marc Egnal and Joseph A. Ernst, "An Economic Interpretation of the American Revolution," *WMQ,* 3d Ser., XXIX (1972), 3–32; Katz, "Thomas Jefferson and the Right to Property," *Journal of Law and Economics,* XIX (1976), 467–488; Robert S. Lambert, "The Confiscation of Loyalist Property in Georgia, 1782–1786," *WMQ,* 3d Ser., XX (1963), 80–94; Woody Holton, *Forced Founders: Indians, Debtors, Slaves, and the Making of the American Revolution in Virginia* (Williamsburg, Va., and Chapel Hill, N.C., 1999); Hall, *Land and Allegiance in Revolutionary Georgia;* Michael A. McDonnell, *The Politics of War: Race, Class, and Conflict in Revolutionary Virginia* (Williamsburg, Va., and Chapel Hill, N.C., 2007); Rebecca Brannon, *From Revolution to Reunion: The Reintegration of the South Carolina Loyalists* (Columbia, S.C., 2016); Kimberly M. Nath, "The British Are Coming, Again: Loyalists, Property Confiscation, and Reintegration in the Mid-Atlantic, 1777–1800" (Ph.D., diss., University of Delaware, 2016); Tom Cutterham, *Gentlemen Revolutionaries: Power and Justice in the New American Republic* (Princeton, N.J., 2017); Justin du Rivage, *Revolution against Empire: Taxes, Politics, and the Origins of American Independence* (New Haven, Conn., 2017); and Marcus Gallo, "Property Rights, Citizenship, Corruption, and Inequality: Confiscating Loyalist Estates during the American Revolution," *Pennsylvania History,* LXXXVI (2019), 474–510.

The Revolution, Linda K. Kerber, Mary Beth Norton, and Jeanne Boydston have independently argued, politicized households and women's domestic labor; see Kerber, *Women of the Republic: Intellect and Ideology in Revolutionary America* (Williamsburg, Va., and Chapel Hill, N.C., 1980), 41–67, 285–288; Norton, *Liberty's Daughters,* 3–151; and Boydston, *Home and Work,* 30–32. For other exemplary studies of gender and households in early America, see Cott, *Bonds of Womanhood;* McCurry, *Masters of Small Worlds;* Kathleen M. Brown, *Good Wives, Nasty Wenches, and Anxious Patriarchs: Gender, Race, and Power in Colonial Virginia* (Williamsburg, Va., and Chapel Hill, N.C., 1996); Laura F. Edwards, *Gendered Strife and Confusion: The Political Culture of Reconstruction* (Urbana, Ill., 1997); Kierner, *Beyond the Household;* Glymph, *Out of the House of Bondage;* Thavolia Glymph, *The Women's Fight: The Civil War's Battles for Home, Freedom, and Nation* (Chapel Hill, N.C., 2020); Shammas, *History of Household Government;* Hartigan-O'Connor, *Ties That Buy;* Glover, *Founders as Fathers;* Sachs, *Home Rule;* Shire, *Threshold of Manifest Destiny;* Carbonell, "Fraught Labor, Fragile Authority"; Damiano, *To Her Credit;* and Stewart, *This Is Our Home.*

Notable examples that bridge this divide include Holly A. Mayer, *Belonging to the Army: Camp Followers and Community during the American Revolution* (Columbia, S.C., 1996); Ami Pflugrad-Jackisch, "'What Am I but an American': Mary Willing Byrd and Westover Plantation during the American Revolution," in Oberg, ed., *Women in the American Revolution,* 171–191; Zabin, *Boston Massacre;* and Karen Cook Bell, *Running from Bondage: Enslaved Women and Their Remarkable Fight for Freedom in Revolutionary America* (Cambridge, 2021); for more on this dichotomy between social and military history, see Dillon L. Streifeneder,

"American Revolution or Revolutionary War?" *Panorama*, Jan. 21, 2025, https://thepanorama.shear.org/2025/01/21/american-revolution-or-revolutionary-war/. Scholars of slavery have been most attuned to how the Revolution's warfare destabilized social hierarchies and institutions, creating opportunities for the enslaved; see Sylvia R. Frey, *Water from the Rock: Black Resistance in a Revolutionary Age* (Princeton, N.J., 1991); Robert Olwell, *Masters, Slaves, and Subjects: The Culture of Power in the South Carolina Low Country, 1740–1790* (Ithaca, N.Y., 1998); Van Buskirk, "Crossing the Lines," in "Explorations in Early American Culture," eds. Pencak and Boudreau, special issue, *Pennsylvania History*, LXV (1998), 74–100; Cassandra Pybus, *Epic Journeys of Freedom: Runaway Slaves of the American Revolution and Their Global Quest for Liberty* (Boston, 2006); Gerald Horne, *The Counter-Revolution of 1776: Slave Resistance and the Origins of the United States of America* (New York, 2014); and Sean Gallagher, "Black Refugees and the Legal Fiction of Military Manumission in the American Revolution," *Slavery and Abolition*, XLIII (2022), 140–159.

28. Historians, John Shy has argued, must examine the American Revolution from the perspective of those who lived through it: "as a process, which entangled large numbers of people for a long period of time in experiences of remarkable intensity"; see Shy, "The American Revolution," in Kurtz and Hutson, eds., *Essays on the American Revolution*, 124 (quotation); for the American Revolution as a civil war, see ibid., 121–156; and Mayer, "Introduction," in Mayer, ed., *Women Waging War*, 1–8; see also Norton, *Liberty's Daughters*, 195; and Abrahamson, *American Home Front*, 5–6.

29. Kerber, *Women of the Republic*, 8–12 ("Republican Motherhood," 11), 33–67, esp. 265–288; Jan Lewis, "The Republican Wife: Virtue and Seduction in the Early Republic," *WMQ*, 3d Ser., XLIV (1987), 689–721; Zagarri, "Introduction," in Oberg., ed., *Women in the American Revolution*, 2 ("ripple"); and Norton, *Liberty's Daughters*, 195–242. For the politicization of the domestic, see ibid., 55–66, 176–177; Lewis, "The Republican Wife," *WMQ*, 3d Ser., XLIV (1987), 689–721; Zagarri, "Introduction," in Oberg., ed., *Women in the American Revolution*, 1–15; Joan Hoff Wilson, "The Illusion of Change: Women and the American Revolution," in Alfred F. Young, ed., *The American Revolution: Explorations in the History of American Radicalism* (DeKalb, Ill., 1976), 385–431; Joan R. Gundersen, "Independence, Citizenship, and the American Revolution," in "Women and the Political Process in the United States," special issue, *Signs: Journal of Women in Culture and Society*, XIII (1987), 59–77; Linda K. Kerber, "The Paradox of Women's Citizenship in the Early Republic: The Case of Martin vs. Massachusetts, 1805," *AHR*, XCVII (1992), 349–378; Rosemarie Zagarri, "Morals, Manners, and the Republican Mother," *American Quarterly*, XLIV (1992), 192–215; Zagarri, "The Rights of Man and Woman in Post-Revolutionary America," *WMQ*, 3d Ser., LV (1998), 203–230; and Zagarri, *Revolutionary Backlash: Women and Politics in the Early American Republic* (Philadelphia, 2007). For an overview of these scholarly developments, see Mayer, "Introduction," in Mayer, ed., *Women Waging War*, 5–8. For political rights, see Norton, *Liberty's Daughters*, 228–255; Kerber, *Women of the Republic*, 69–136; Susan Branson, *These Fiery Frenchified Dames: Women and Political Culture in Early National Philadelphia* (Philadelphia, 2001); Catherine Allgor, *Parlor Politics: In Which the Ladies of Washington Help Build a City and a Government* (Charlottesville., Va., 2000); Zagarri, *Revolutionary Backlash;* Jan Ellen Lewis, "What Happened to the Three-Fifths Clause: The Relationship between Women and Slaves in Constitutional Thought, 1787–1866," *JER*, XXXVII (2017), 1–46; and Beatty, *In Dependence*. For the gendered nature of virtue, see Lewis, "The Republican Wife,"

WMQ, 3d Ser., XLIV (1987), 689–721; Ruth H. Bloch, "The Gendered Meanings of Virtue in Revolutionary America," in "Women and the Political Process in the United States," special issue, *Signs*, XIII (1987), 37–58; and Clare A. Lyons, *Sex among the Rabble: An Intimate History of Gender and Power in the Age of Revolution, Philadelphia, 1730–1830* (Williamsburg, Va., and Chapel Hill., N.C., 2006), 390–392.

For education and forays into public life, see Cott, *Bonds of Womanhood;* Kerber, *Women of the Republic*, 185–288; Mary P. Ryan, *Cradle of the Middle Class: The Family in Oneida County, New York, 1790–1865* (Cambridge, 1981); Linda K. Kerber et al., "Beyond Roles, Beyond Spheres: Thinking about Gender in the Early Republic," *WMQ*, 3d Ser., XLVI (1989), 565–585; Margaret A. Nash, "Rethinking Republican Motherhood: Benjamin Rush and the Young Ladies' Academy of Philadelphia," *JER*, XVII (1997), 171–191; Mary Kelley, *Learning to Stand and Speak: Women, Education, and Public Life in America's Republic* (Williamsburg, Va., and Chapel Hill, N.C., 2006); Lucia McMahon, *Mere Equals: The Paradox of Educated Women in the Early American Republic* (Ithaca, N.Y., 2012); Sarah Knott, "Female Liberty? Sentimental Gallantry, Republican Womanhood, and Rights Feminism in the Age of Revolutions," *WMQ*, 3d Ser., LXXI (2014), 425–456; and Mary Sarah Bilder, *Female Genius: Eliza Harriot and George Washington at the Dawn of the Constitution* (Charlottesville, Va., 2022).

For reproduction, see Susan E. Klepp, *Revolutionary Conceptions: Women, Fertility, and Family Limitation in America, 1760–1820* (Williamsburg, Va., and Chapel Hill, N.C., 2009); for the racialized aspects of motherhood, see Nora Doyle, *Maternal Bodies: Redefining Motherhood in Early America* (Chapel Hill, N.C., 2018). For coverture, see Kerber, *Women of the Republic*, 137–155; Marylynn Salmon, *Women and the Law of Property in Early America* (Chapel Hill, N.C., 1986); and Lewis, "The Republican Wife," *WMQ*, 3d Ser., XLIV (1987), 689–721. For marriage, see Nancy F. Cott, "Divorce and the Changing Status of Women in Eighteenth-Century Massachusetts," *WMQ*, 3d Ser., XXXIII (1976), 586–614; Cott, "Marriage and Women's Citizenship in the United States, 1830–1934," *AHR*, CIII (1998), 1440–1474; Kerber, *Women of the Republic*, 115–184; Anya Jabour, *Marriage in the Early Republic: Elizabeth and William Wirt and the Companionate Ideal* (Baltimore, Md., 1998); Ruth H. Bloch, "The American Revolution, Wife Beating, and the Emergent Value of Privacy," *EAS*, V (2007), 223–251; and Brewer, "Transformation of Domestic Law," in Grossberg and Tomlins, eds., *Cambridge History of Law in America*, I, 288–323. For finances and working women, see Stansell, *City of Women;* Woody Holton, "Abigail Adams, Bond Speculator," *WMQ*, 3d Ser., LXIV (2007), 821–838; Hartigan-O'Connor, *Ties That Buy;* Susan Brandt, "'Getting into a Little Business': Margaret Hill Morris and Women's Medical Entrepreneurship during the American Revolution," *EAS*, XIII (2015), 774–807; Sara T. Damiano, "Writing Women's History through the Revolution: Family Finances, Letter Writing, and Conceptions of Marriage," in "Writing to and from the Revolution: A Joint Issue with the *Journal of the Early Republic*," special issue, *WMQ*, 3d Ser., LXXIV (2017), 697–728; and Damiano, *To Her Credit*.

Such scholarship largely focuses on white middling and elite women; for studies of enslaved women in this same period, see Erica Armstrong Dunbar, *Never Caught: The Washingtons' Relentless Pursuit of Their Runaway Slave, Ona Judge* (New York, 2017); and Bell, *Running from Bondage*.

30. Antoinette Burton, "Toward Unsettling Histories of Domesticity," *AHR*, CXXIV (2019), 1333 (quotation). Calling for scholars to invert "ingrained" historical frameworks that dismiss the household as a venue of meaningful "historical action," Mary S. Hartman

argues that "marriage and household system" have been driving forces of western history and suggests that historians reorient major historical events around the household in order to understand the role of both men and women in "generating some novel gender and power arrangements within those households but also for shaping major developments beyond them." Such a framing, as she explains, necessarily moves beyond "judging" whether events (in her analysis, the Reformation) were "either positive or negative for women" because such questions ultimately "miss the point" and ignore "underlying household and community context[s]." Instead, she advocates for scholars to consider "the distinctive circumstances of subjects, women and men alike, who were engaged together in a larger contest over the exercise of authority . . . that involved a major gender dimension but many other intersecting features as well"; see Hartman, *The Household and the Making of History,* 4 ("ingrained," "historical," "marriage," "generating"), 213 ("judging," "either," "miss," "underlying," "distinctive"). For separate spheres, see Ryan, *Cradle of the Middle Class;* Stansell, *City of Women;* Leonore Davidoff and Catherine Hall, *Family Fortunes: Men and Women of the English Middle Class, 1780–1850* (Chicago, Ill., 1987); Linda K. Kerber, "Separate Spheres, Female Worlds, Woman's Place: The Rhetoric of Women's History," *JAH,* LXXV (1988), 9–39; Kerber et al., "Beyond Roles, Beyond Spheres," *WMQ,* 3d Ser., XLVI (1989), 565–585; Amanda Vickery, "Golden Age to Separate Spheres? A Review of the Categories and Chronology of English Women's History," *Historical Journal,* XXXVI (1993), 383–414; Joan B. Landes, "Further Thoughts on the Public/Private Distinction," *Journal of Women's History,* XV, no. 2 (Summer 2003), 28–39; Mary P. Ryan, "The Public and the Private Good: Across the Great Divide in Women's History," *Journal of Women's History,* XV, no. 2 (Summer 2003), 10–27; Glymph, *Out of the House of Bondage;* Hartigan-O'Connor, *Ties That Buy;* Zabin, *Dangerous Economies;* and Mary Beth Norton, *Separated by Their Sex: Women in Public and Private in the Colonial Atlantic World* (Ithaca, N.Y., 2011). The exemplary study of the household, production, and spheres in early America, remains Boydston, *Home and Work;* for more on this historiography, see note 27 and note 29, above.

31. A renewed interest in the Revolution as a military conflict has led to new scholarship on women's wartime experiences, including Oberg, ed., *Women in the American Revolution;* Zabin, *Boston Massacre;* and Mayer, ed., *Women Waging War;* for a general conversation about the state of the field, including women's and gender history, see Breen et al., "The Revolution at 250: A Conversation," *JER,* XLIV (2024), 513–579. Disappointingly, however, women's and gender scholarship frequently remains sidelined within broader scholarly conversations about the Revolution. In 2017, the *WMQ* and the *JER* published a joint issue, "Writing to and from the Revolution," intended to "help us to see the American Revolution in new ways." Alan Taylor's introductory essay offers no substantive engagement with gender scholarship. Indeed, illustrating the issues at the heart of this study, he notes that "none of the authors" in the forum address military history and that only a single author, Sara T. Damiano, in her exploration of wartime family finances, "focuses on the war years—and she limits her examination to the home front." See Catherine E. Kelley and Joshua Piker, "Editors' Note," in "Writing to and from the Revolution," special issue, *WMQ,* 3d Ser., LXXIV (2017), 618 ("help"), Taylor, "Introduction: Expand or Die: The Revolution's New Empire," 619–632 ("none," 621, "focuses," 622), and Damiano, "Writing Women's History," 697–728. Similarly, although admitting that his list "only scratches the surface" of a vast secondary literature, Robert G. Parkinson's "Guide to Further Reading" at the end of *Thirteen Clocks*—intended to help readers further investigate

the American Revolution—makes no mention of women's and gender history; see Parkinson, *Thirteen Clocks: How Race United the Colonies and Made the Declaration of Independence* (Williamsburg, Va., and Chapel Hill, N.C., 2021), 217–222 (quotation, 217).

32. Mayer, "Introduction," in Mayer, ed., *Women Waging War,* 2 (quotation). "Certainly," Gordon S. Wood has asserted, the Revolution "does not appear to resemble the revolutions of other nations in which people were killed, property was destroyed, and everything was turned upside down"—this is, in fact, precisely what happened in the six cities that the British Army occupied during the war; see Wood, *The Radicalism of the American Revolution* (New York, 1991), 3 (quotations). For other studies of the revolutionary home front, see Kerber, *Women of the Republic,* 35–67; Norton, *Liberty's Daughters,* 195–227; Abrahamson, *American Home Front,* 5–41; John Phillips Resch and Walter Sargent, eds., *War and Society in the American Revolution: Mobilization and Home Fronts* (DeKalb, Ill., 2007); Holly A. Mayer, "Bearing Arms, Bearing Burdens: Women Warriors, Camp Followers, and Home-Front Heroines of the American Revolution," in Karen Hagemann, Gisela Mettele, and Jane Rendall, eds., *Gender, War, and Politics: Transatlantic Perspectives, 1775–1820* (Basingstoke, U.K., 2010), 180–183; Pflugrad-Jackisch, "'What Am I but an American,'" in Oberg, ed., *Women in the American Revolution,* 171–191; and Mayer, ed., *Women Waging War,* esp. Mayer, "Introduction," 1–22, Lauren Duval, "'A Shocking Thing to Tell Of': Female Civilians, Violence, and Rape under British Military Rule," 76–97, Steven Elliott, "Neighbors, Land Ladies, and Consorts: New Jersey Women in the Midst of the Continental Army," 98–113, and Lorri Glover, "Eliza Lucas Pinckney: Female Fortitude and the Revolutionary War," 172–194. For more on how gender and the language of domesticity constitute nationalism, see Anne McClintock, "Family Feuds: Gender, Nationalism, and the Family," *Feminist Review,* no. 44 (Summer 1993), esp. 61–65; Sachs, *Home Rule;* and Shire, *Threshold of Manifest Destiny.*

33. Here, I build on Mary Beth Norton's call to understand the American Revolution as a civil war that unsettled "normal patterns of life"; see Norton, *Liberty's Daughters,* 195. For examples of scholarship that include women's experiences but no substantive analysis of gender, see Sullivan, *The Disaffected;* and Johnson, *Occupied America.* Judith Van Buskirk's *Generous Enemies* and Serena Zabin's *Boston Massacre* are notable exceptions to this trend, although both focus on only a single city. Moreover, because Zabin's subject is the 1770 massacre, she does not consider wartime occupation. Yet, as scholarship in the vein of the new military history in other conflicts shows, a gendered approach to occupation has the potential to reshape our narratives of warfare and civilian-military relationships. For occupation as "a gender war," see LeeAnn Whites and Alecia P. Long, *Occupied Women: Gender, Military Occupation, and the American Civil War* (Baton Rouge, La., 2009), 8–9 (quotation, 9); see also Elaine Tyler May, *Homeward Bound: American Families in the Cold War* (New York, 1988); Maria Höhn, *GIs and Fräuleins: The German-American Encounter in 1950s West Germany* (Chapel Hill, N.C., 2002); Mary Louise Roberts, *What Soldiers Do: Sex and the American GI in World War II France* (Chicago, 2013); Stephanie McCurry, *Women's War: Fighting and Surviving the American Civil War* (Cambridge, Mass., 2019); and Glymph, *Women's Fight.* For an overview of the new military history, see Wayne E. Lee, "Mind and Matter—Cultural Analysis in American Military History: A Look at the State of the Field," *JAH,* XCIII (2007), 1116–1142.

34. Thavolia Glymph has observed similar dynamics during the American Civil War; see Glymph, *Women's Fight.*

35. Karin Wulf, *Not All Wives: Women of Colonial Philadelphia* (Ithaca, N.Y., 2000), 116–117 (quotation, 117). For men, patriarchy, and domesticity, see Brown, *Good Wives, Nasty Wenches*, 247–282, 319–366; Norton, *Founding Mothers and Fathers;* Olwell, *Masters, Slaves, and Subjects*, 181–219; Wilson, *Ye Heart of a Man;* Tadmor, *Family and Friends;* Shammas, *History of Household Government*, 24–82; Toby L. Ditz, "The New Men's History and the Peculiar Absence of Gendered Power: Some Remedies from Early American Gender History," *Gender and History*, XVI (2004), 1–35; Karen Harvey, "The History of Masculinity, circa 1650–1800," *Journal of British Studies*, XLIV (2005), 296–311, esp. 308–311; Harvey, *The Little Republic;* Vickery, *Behind Closed Doors;* Glover, *Founders as Fathers;* Raffaella Sarti, "Men at Home: Domesticities, Authority, Emotions, and Work (Thirteenth–Twentieth Centuries)," in "Men at Home," special issue, *Gender and History*, XXVII (2015), 521–558; Sachs, *Home Rule;* and Gust, *Unhomely Empire.*

36. Consequently, *The Home Front* builds on Michael Grossberg's and Honor Sachs's insights that the American household evolved alongside the state in the postrevolutionary era; see Grossberg, *Governing the Hearth: Law and the Family in Nineteenth-Century America* (Chapel Hill, N.C., 1985), 3–30; and Sachs, *Home Rule.* For continuities, see Jack P. Greene, "The Limits of the American Revolution," in Greene, *Understanding the American Revolution: Issues and Actors* (Charlottesville, Va., 1995), 365, 367–370; and Shammas, *History of Household Government.* For the desire to strengthen households and patriarchal power, see Lewis, *The Pursuit of Happiness;* Kann, *A Republic of Men;* Bloch, "The American Revolution, Wife Beating, and the Emergent Value of Privacy," *EAS*, V (2007), 223–251; Zagarri, *Revolutionary Backlash;* and John Gilbert McCurdy, *Citizen Bachelors: Manhood and the Creation of the United States* (Ithaca, N.Y., 2009). For more on republican virtue, see Gordon S. Wood, *The Creation of the American Republic, 1776–1787* (Williamsburg, Va., and Chapel Hill, N.C., 1969); Linda Kerber, "The Republican Mother: Women and the Enlightenment—An American Perspective," *American Quarterly*, XXVIII (1976), 187–205; Bloch, "The Gendered Meanings of Virtue," in "Women and the Political Process in the United States," special issue, *Signs*, XIII (1987), 37–58; Lewis, "The Republican Wife," *WMQ*, 3d Ser., XLIV (1987), 689–721; Zagarri, "Morals, Manners, and the Republican Mother," *American Quarterly*, XLIV (1992), 192–215; and Craig Bruce Smith, *American Honor: The Creation of the Nation's Ideals during the Revolutionary Era* (Chapel Hill, N.C., 2018).

37. Peter N. Stearns and Jan Lewis, "Introduction" in Stearns and Lewis, eds., *An Emotional History of the United States* (New York, 1998), 1–2 (quotation, 1).

38. For more on material objects, loss, and sense of self, particularly in regard to domestic spaces, see Leora Auslander, "Beyond Words," *AHR*, CX (2005), 1015–1045; and Gowrley, *Domestic Space in Britain*, 221–233.

39. For examining archival biases, see Marisa J. Fuentes, *Dispossessed Lives: Enslaved Women, Violence, and the Archive* (Philadelphia, 2016), 7–8 (quotation, 7), 153 n.16; Saidiya Hartman, "Venus in Two Acts," *Small Axe*, XII, no. 2 (June 2008), 12–14; and Ann Laura Stoler, *Along the Archival Grain: Epistemic Anxieties and Colonial Common Sense* (Princeton, N.J., 2009). For Lucinda, see Sarah Winslow Deming Journal, 1775; and Alice Morse Earle, ed., *The Diary of Anna Green Winslow: A Boston School Girl of 1771* (Boston, 1894), 7, 87 n.14.

40. Sarah Winslow Deming Journal, 1775 (quotation); Sarah Winslow Deming to Joshua Winslow, June 5, 1775, William H. B. Thomas Collection of Winslow and Thomas Family Papers, 1697–1853, folder 5, MHS.

41. Sarah Winslow Deming Journal, 1775. For Boston's Black community, see Elise Lemire, *Black Walden: Slavery and Its Aftermath in Concord, Massachusetts* (Philadelphia, 2009); Hardesty, *Unfreedom,* 71–103; Jared Hardesty, *Black Lives, Native Lands, White Worlds: A History of Slavery in New England* (Amherst, Mass., 2019), 93–117; and David Waldstreicher, *The Odyssey of Phillis Wheatley: A Poet's Journeys through American Slavery and Independence* (New York, 2023), 106–114. For enslaved women's friendships, see Tara A. Bynum, *Reading Pleasures: Everyday Black Living in Early America* (Urbana., Ill., 2023), 41–47. For the Twenty-Ninth Regiment, see Zabin, *Boston Massacre,* 61–64; Waldstreicher, *Odyssey of Phillis Wheatley,* 93; and Lemire, *Black Walden,* 71–72.

42. Because of my focus on patriarchal Anglo-American households, Native nations largely fall outside the scope of this study. Although by no means exhaustive, for an overview of Indigenous involvement in the Revolution, see Taylor, *American Revolutions,* 251–278; Kathleen DuVal, *Independence Lost: Lives on the Edge of the American Revolution* (New York, 2015); and Maeve Kane, "'She Did Not Open Her Mouth Further': Haudenosaunee Women as Military and Political Targets during and after the American Revolution," in Oberg, ed., *Women in the American Revolution,* 83–102. For propaganda and the specter of Native violence in this period, see Robert G. Parkinson, *The Common Cause: Creating Race and Nation in the American Revolution* (Williamsburg, Va., and Chapel Hill, N.C., 2016); Sachs, *Home Rule;* and Shire, *Threshold of Manifest Destiny.*

43. For more on the value of this gendered approach, see Serena R. Zabin, "Conclusion: Writing to and from the Revolution," in "Writing to and from the Revolution," special issue, *WMQ,* 3d Ser., LXXIV (2017), 754–755, 759–761.

CHAPTER 1

1. Abigail Adams to John Adams, July 21, 1776, FO, https://founders.archives.gov/documents/Adams/04-02-02-0033 ("God"); Elizabeth Murray to Catherine, Aug. 12, 1776, Murray-Robbins Family Papers, 1658–1944, box 1, folder 5, MHS ("Gentlemen"), Elizabeth Murray to Dorothy Forbes, June 11, 1776, I ("high heeled"); Nina Moore Tiffany and Susan I. Lesley, eds., *Letters of James Murray, Loyalist* (Boston, 1901), 255. The Massachusetts Provincial Congress ordered the Declaration to be read after services that day; see Abigail Adams to John Adams, Aug. 14, 1776, FO, https://founders.archives.gov/documents/Adams/04-02-02-0057. For Betsy Murray's decision to remain in Massachusetts, see James Murray to Dorothy Forbes and Betsy Murray, Oct. 2, 1775, James Murray Robbins Family Papers, 1638–1899, box 2, MHS.

2. Elizabeth Murray to Catherine, Aug. 12, 1776, Murray-Robbins Family Papers, box 1, folder 5 (quotations). For more on the garden, see James Murray to Dorothy Forbes and Betsy Murray, Oct. 2, 1775, James Murray Robbins Family Papers, box 2.

3. During Bacon's Rebellion, King Charles II dispatched one thousand troops to Virginia to aid Governor William Berkeley's forces, but they arrived after the fighting had concluded and primarily served to intimidate colonists and restore order—not unlike the four regiments deployed to Boston in the 1760s and early 1770s amid the Stamp Act crisis and subsequent colonial resistance movements; see Stephen Saunders Webb, *The Governors-General: The English Army and the Definition of the Empire, 1569–1681* (Williamsburg, Va., and Chapel Hill,

N.C., 1979), 349–371; and John Gilbert McCurdy, *Quarters: The Accommodation of the British Army and the Coming of the American Revolution* (Ithaca, N.Y., 2019), 179–180. Of course, it was not only the British that wrought havoc on American communities. For an example of violence perpetrated by the Continental army, see Thomas Goldthwaite to his daughter, Aug. 20, 1779, James Murray Robbins Family Papers, box 3. For relations between Continental soldiers and civilians, see John A. Ruddiman, *Becoming Men of Some Consequence: Youth and Military Service in the Revolutionary War* (Charlottesville, Va., 2014), 90–116; see also Holger Hoock, *Scars of Independence: America's Violent Birth* (New York, 2017), 127–147.

4. In the words of historian Karin Wulf, urban "community was generated by the interaction among households"; see Wulf, *Not All Wives: Women of Colonial Philadelphia* (Ithaca, N.Y., 2000), 121. For more on colonial cities, see Bernard Herman, "Space in the Early American City," in John Lauritz Larson and Michael A. Morrison, eds., *Whither the Early Republic: A Forum on the Future of the Field* (Philadelphia, 2005), 169–176; Dell Upton, *Another City: Urban Life and Urban Spaces in the New American Republic* (New Haven, Conn., 2008); Emma Hart, *Building Charleston: Town and Society in the Eighteenth-Century British Atlantic World* (Charlottesville, Va., 2010); Ellen Hartigan-O'Connor, *The Ties That Buy: Women and Commerce in Revolutionary America* (Philadelphia, 2009), 2–5, 11, 15–34; Serena R. Zabin, *Dangerous Economies: Status and Commerce in Imperial New York* (Philadelphia, 2009), 57–80; Barbara Clark Smith, *The Freedoms We Lost: Consent and Resistance in Revolutionary America* (New York, 2010), 56–133; and Jessica Choppin Roney, "Introduction: Street and Global Perspectives on the City," in "Cities," special issue, *Eighteenth-Century Studies*, L (2017), 141–153.

5. Narrative of Mrs. Abraham Brasher (Helen Kortright) Giving an Account of Her Experiences in the Revolutionary War, 1802, 31, VF Women, DLAR (quotation). For empathy, see Mary Ellery to Isabel Marchant, May 30, 1775, Ellery in the Vernon Papers, box 62, NHS; and "Letter I," 1782, in Caroline Gilman, ed., *Letters of Eliza Wilkinson, during the Invasion and Possession of Charlestown, S.C., by the British in the Revolutionary War* (New York, 1839), 10–11.

6. Ravaud Kearney Diary, May 12, 15, 1778, June 15, 1778, Mar. 15, 1779, Apr. 4, 1779, July 22, 1779, Manuscripts and Archives Division, NYPL. For Kearney's background, see W. Woodford Clayton, ed., *History of Union and Middlesex Counties, New Jersey, with Biographical Sketches of Many of Their Pioneers and Prominent Men* (Philadelphia, 1882), 498.

7. Andrew Eliot to Isaac Smith, Jr., June 19, 1775, in "September Meeting, 1878," *PMHS*, XVI (Boston, 1879), 288 (quotation). For anxiety, see Elaine Forman Crane, ed., *The Diary of Elizabeth Drinker*, I (Boston, 1991), Sept. 22, 1777, 233, Nov. 21, 1777, 255–256; Timothy Newell, "A Journal Kept during the Time That Boston Was Shut Up in 1775–6," Massachusetts Historical Society, *Collections*, 4th Ser., I (Boston, 1852), Feb. 25, 1776, 271, Mar. 4, 1776, 272, Mar. 9, 1776, 274; and John Andrews to William Barrell, Sept. 15, 1774, Andrews-Eliot Correspondence, 1715–1814, box 1, 44, MHS. For colonial military geographies, see McCurdy, *Quarters*, 165–200, esp. 166–167.

8. Sarah Logan Fisher Diary, III, Sept. 21, 1777, [44], Sarah Logan Fisher Diaries, HSP, in The Revolutionary City: A Portal to the Nation's Founding, https://therevolutionarycity.org/islandora/fisher-sarah-logan-diary-volume-3 ("Waggons); "Mrs. Mary [Gould] Almy's Account of the Cannonading of the French Fleet in Newport," Aug. 7, 1778, RLA ("continually," "shrieking," "chilldren"); Sarah Winslow Deming to Joshua Winslow, June 5, 1775, William H. B. Thomas Collection of Winslow and Thomas Family Papers, 1697–1853, folder

5, MHS ("Not knowing"). For fleeing cities, see Henry Knox to Lucy Flucker Knox, July 8, 1776, in Philip Hamilton, ed., *The Revolutionary War Lives and Letters of Lucy and Henry Knox* (Baltimore, Md., 2017), 38; and Sarah Winslow Deming Journal, 1775, MHS, Collections Online, https://www.masshist.org/database/viewer.php?item_id=1898.

9. John Andrews to William Barrell, Apr. 11, 1775, Andrews-Eliot Correspondence, box 1, 51 ("either"), Andrews to Barrell, Apr. 24, 1775, 53 ("If I can escape"). For Andrews's decision to remain, see Andrews to Barrell, Apr. 24, 1775, ibid., 53, Andrews to Barrell, Apr. 25, 1775, 54, and Andrews to Barrell, May 6, 1776, 55.

10. Edward H. Tatum, Jr., ed., *The American Journal of Ambrose Serle, Secretary to Lord Howe, 1776–1778* (San Marino, Calif., 1940), Sept. 15, 1776, 104 ("trampl[ed]"), Sept. 16, 1776, 106, Crane, ed., *Diary of Elizabeth Drinker*, I, Dec. 19, 1777, 167 ("Gen. Howe," "I hope"). For sentiments similar to Drinker's, see Sarah Winslow Deming Journal, 1775. For more on disaffected populations, see Judith Van Buskirk, "They Didn't Join the Band: Disaffected Women in Revolutionary Philadelphia," *Pennsylvania History: A Journal of Mid-Atlantic Studies*, LXII (1995), 306–329; and Aaron Sullivan, *The Disaffected: Britain's Occupation of Philadelphia during the American Revolution* (Philadelphia, 2019).

11. For Prévost, see Elizabeth Lichtenstein Johnston, *Recollections of a Georgia Loyalist*, ed. Arthur Wentworth Eaton (New York, 1901), 58 (quotation), 59. For attempts to safeguard property, see Memorial of Joseph Galloway, AO 12/38, 85, TNA; Margaret Hill Morris Diary, Dec. 20, 1776, HCQSC; Diary Kept by an Unknown Person in the British Garrison at Newport, R.I., 1778, Aug. 1, 1778, Manuscripts and Archives Division, NYPL; and Joseph Clay to John Gibson, June 9, 1779, in "Letters of Joseph Clay Merchant of Savannah, 1776–1793," Georgia Historical Society, *Collections*, VIII (Savannah, Ga., 1913), 140. For the Siege of Savannah, see Johnston, *Recollections of a Georgia Loyalist*, ed. Eaton, 63; Alexander A. Lawrence, *Storm over Savannah: The Story of Count D'Estaing and the Siege of the Town in 1779* (Athens, Ga., 1951), 81; and Friederike Baer, *Hessians: German Soldiers in the American Revolutionary War* (New York, 2022), 317. Civilians' efforts to seek cover were nevertheless often futile: "Even [in the cellars] they do not escape the fury of our bombs," one Continental officer sorrowfully reported after hearing of gruesome civilian casualties in Savannah; see John Jones to Polly Jones, Oct. 7, 1779, in George White, *Historical Collections of Georgia* (New York, 1854), 536. Although slaveholders in Georgia and South Carolina initially resisted arming enslaved men during the Revolution, such multiracial defenses were common in the colonial period; see Watson W. Jennison, *Cultivating Race: The Expansion of Slavery in Georgia, 1750–1860* (Lexington, Ky., 2012), 44–46. For more on enslaved people in revolutionary Savannah, see Sylvia R. Frey, *Water from the Rock: Black Resistance in a Revolutionary Age* (Princeton, N.J., 1991), 81–107; and Timothy J. Lockley, "'The King of England's Soldiers': Armed Blacks in Savannah and Its Hinterlands during the Revolutionary War Era, 1778–1787," in Leslie M. Harris and Daina Ramey Berry, eds., *Slavery and Freedom in Savannah* (Athens, Ga., 2014), 26–41. For Indigenous involvement in the southern theater, see Joshua S. Haynes, *Patrolling the Border: Theft and Violence on the Creek-Georgia Frontier, 1770–1796* (Athens, Ga., 2018), 63–83; James MacDonald, "Caught between Two Fires: The Catawba and the Cherokee Choose Sides in the American Revolution," in Jeff Broadwater and Troy L. Kickler, eds., *North Carolina's Revolutionary Founders* (Chapel Hill, N.C., 2019), 67–87; and Kathleen DuVal, *Independence Lost: Lives on the Edge of the American Revolution* (New York, 2015), esp. 75–99, 165–166, 177–185, 236–269, 292–312, 324–332.

12. Crane, ed., *Diary of Elizabeth Drinker,* I, Oct. 23, 1777, 248 ("like an Earth Quake"), Nov. 11, 12, 1777, 252, Nov. 15, 1777, 253 ("like thunder"), Nov. 21, 1777, 255; Francis Sheftall to Mordecai Sheftall, July 20, 1780, in Jacob R. Marcus, *The American Jewish Woman: A Documentary History* (New York, 1981), 30 ("like haile"); Johnston, *Recollections of a Georgia Loyalist,* ed. Eaton, 63 ("houses"); Newell, "A Journal Kept during the Time That Boston Was Shut Up," Massachusetts Historical Society, *Collections,* July 2, 14, 1775, 264, Aug. 1, 15, 16, 20, 27, 1775, 265, Aug. 29–30, 1775, 266, Sept. 14, 1775, 268, Oct. 17, 1775, 269, Dec. 17, 1775, 270, Feb. 2, 1776, 271; "William Cheever's Diary, 1775–1776," in "January Meeting, 1927," *PMHS,* LX (Boston, 1927), July 7, 1775, 92, Aug. 2, 1775, 93, Aug. 27, 30, and Sept. 22, 1775, 94, Mar. 3, 1776, 96, Mar. 5, 1776, 97; John Rowe Diary, Mar. 3, 4, 1776, P–786, reel 2, MHS; Mary Heriot to Robert Heriot, May 23, 1781, Robert Heriot Correspondence, 1781, SCHS; Josiah Smith to M. Hodsten, Aug. 5, 1780, Josiah Smith Letter book, 1771–1784, M-3018, 396–397, SHC. For rumors of arson, see James Murray to Elizabeth Inman, May 23, 1775, James Murray Robbins Family Papers, box 2; James Grant to Richard Rigby, May 12, 1776, James Grant of Ballindalloch Papers, 1740–1819, Army Career Series (1740–1805), reel 28, DLAR; Crane, ed., *Diary of Elizabeth Drinker,* I, Sept. 24, 1777, 234, Sept. 25, 1777, 235, Sept. 26, 1777, 235–236; John Bowater to Basil Feilding, sixth earl of Denbigh, Sept. 26, 1776, in Marion Balderston and David Syrett, eds., *The Lost War: Letters from British Officers during the American Revolution* (New York, 1975), 101; and Ira D. Gruber, ed., *John Peebles' American War: The Diary of a Scottish Grenadier* (Mechanicsburg, Pa., 1998), Sept. 26, 1777, 138, Aug. 3, 1778, 206. For loyalist patrols, see Memorial of Jonathan Adams, AO 12/42, 185–186, TNA, and Memorial of Thomas Banks, AO 12/38, 380–381. For the 1776 New York fire, see Tatum, ed., *American Journal of Ambrose Serle,* Sept. 21, 1776, 110–111; *The Diary of Frederick Mackenzie, Giving a Daily Narrative of His Military Service as an Officer of the Regiment of Royal Welch Fusiliers during the Years 1775–1781, in Massachusetts, Rhode Island, and New York,* I (Cambridge, Mass., 1930), Sept. 20, 1776, 58–60; Maya Jasanoff, *Liberty's Exiles: American Loyalists in the Revolutionary World* (New York, 2011), 32; and Benjamin L. Carp, *The Great New York Fire of 1776: A Lost Story of the American Revolution* (New Haven, Conn., 2023).

13. Sarah Winslow Deming Journal, 1775 (quotations). For more on disease, see Paul E. Kopperman, "The Medical Dimension in Cornwallis's Army, 1780–1781," *North Carolina Historical Review,* LXXXIX (2012), 367–398; Serena Zabin, *The Boston Massacre: A Family History* (Boston, 2020), 74–78; and Elizabeth A. Fenn, *Pox Americana: The Great Smallpox Epidemic of 1775–82* (New York, 2001), esp. 44–134.

14. Deborah Norris Logan to [Alexander] Garden, Sept. 26, 1822, John F. Watson Historical Collection, box 4, HSP; Diary of Robert Morton, Oct. 5, 1777, Nov. 18, 1777, Nov. 22, 1777, ISM; Crane, ed., *Diary of Elizabeth Drinker,* I, Sept. 27, 1777, 236, Oct. 23, 1777, 248, Nov. 22, 1777, 256–257; Loftus Cliffe to Jack Cliffe, Oct. 24, 1777, Loftus Cliffe Papers, 1769–1784, WCL. Mary Beth Norton has speculated that Washington's 1776 successful escape from Manhattan might have spurred retaliatory violence and a "rampage of rape" against civilians in New Jersey; see Norton, *Liberty's Daughters: The Revolutionary Experience of American Women, 1750–1800* (Boston, 1980), 202. For more on the war in New Jersey, see James J. Gigantino, II, ed., *The American Revolution in New Jersey: Where the Battlefront Meets the Home Front* (Rutgers, N.J., 2015).

15. Unknown to Elizabeth Murray [Robbins], [Nov. 28, 1779], James Murray Robbins Family Papers, box 3 ("banished," "unwell"); Molly Pemberton to James Pemberton, Nov.

24, 1777, Pemberton Family Papers, 1641–1880, XXXI, 46, HSP ("so frighted"), Molly Pemberton to James Pemberton, Nov. 17, 1777, 28; Abigail Adams to John Adams, June 18–20, 1775, Adams Family Papers ("constant"), Abigail Adams to John Adams, May 24, 1775 ("We know not what"), Abigail Adams to John Adams, Mar. 2–10, 1776 ("I went to Bed"); Theodore Foster Diary, June 7, Aug. 10, 1778, Theodore Foster Papers, circa 1640s–1820s, Ser. 2, box 5, RIHS.

16. Sarah Winslow Deming to Joshua Winslow, June 5, 1775, William H. B. Thomas Collection of Winslow and Thomas Family Papers, folder 5 ("terror"); "Mrs. Mary [Gould] Almy's Account," Aug. 7, 1778 ("6 children," "cut"), Aug. 8, 1778 ("Nothing," "Attempt").

17. Although the British government promised to compensate property owners, claims for restitution often dragged on for years after the war's conclusion, and families were rarely reimbursed for the entirety of their losses. For compensation, see Maya Jasanoff, "The Other Side of Revolution: Loyalists in the British Empire," *WMQ*, 3d Ser., LXV (2008), 216. In the meantime, many civilians suffered as the British Army garrisoned their cities. For Philadelphia, see Johann Ewald, *Diary of the American War: A Hessian Journal*, ed. and trans. Joseph P. Tustin (New Haven, Conn., 1979), Sept. 26, 1777, 92; see also G. D. Scull, ed., "Journal of Captain John Montrésor, July 1, 1777, to July 1, 1778, . . . (Continued . . .)," *PMHB*, VI (1882), Sept. 26, 1777, 42. For Charleston, see Frey, *Water from the Rock*, 121–127. The British also attempted, often unsuccessfully, to conscript free laborers; see Scull, ed., "Journal of Captain John Montrésor," *PMHB*, VI (1882), Oct. 2, 1777, 44–45, Oct. 3, 1777, 45, Oct. 13, 1777, 48; *Diary of Frederick Mackenzie*, I, Sept. 13, 15, 1777, 177–178; and [Fleet Greene], "Newport in the Hands of the British: A Diary of the Revolution . . . ," *Historical Magazine . . .*, IV (1860), Oct. 17, 1777, 34, and Oct. 22, 1777, 35. For loyalists, see Memorial of Thomas Banister, AO 13/59, 24–25, TNA.

18. Paul Revere to Rachel Revere, August 1778, Revere Family Papers II, 1775–1864, MHS ("It does not," "some"); E. A. Benians, [ed.], *A Journal by Tho: Hughes . . . (1778–1779)* (Cambridge, 1947), Oct. 6, 1778, 46 ("picture"). For razing, see Robert Pigot to Sir Henry Clinton (copy), Aug. 31, 1778, CO 5/96: Military despatches, 1778, TNA; and Johann Conrad Döhla, *A Hessian Diary of the American Revolution*, ed. and trans. Bruce E. Burgoyne (Norman, Okla., 1990), Dec. 31, 1778, 96. For more on the physical devastation the war inflicted on urban ports, see Hartigan-O'Connor, *Ties That Buy*, 35–36.

19. Margaret Hill Morris Diary, Dec. 20, 1776 ("Noise"); Molly Pemberton to Israel Pemberton, Feb. 2, 1778, Pemberton Family Papers, XXXI, 101 ("thickly"); BOP, Jan. 5, 1781, reel 520 ("heaps," "owing"); Grand Jury Presentments, [June 1780], Stanford Brown Collection of Revolutionary War and Early Nineteenth Century Records, 1776–1878, folder 1, GHS ("filth," "indecent"). See also BOP, Apr. 18, 1782, May 14, 1782, reel 525. For encampments and parades, see Royal Artillery, Brigade Orders, Dec. 9, 1777, James Pattison Papers, 1777–1781, film 47, DLAR, James Pattison to Lord Amherst, Jan. 23, 1778; and John F. Watson, *Annals of Philadelphia . . .* (Philadelphia, 1830), 684–685. For soldiers camped on Boston Common, see Zabin, *Boston Massacre*, 55; and John Andrews to William Barrell, Sept. 25, 1774, Andrews-Eliot Correspondence, box 1, 45a, 45b. For soldiers bathing in Newport, see General Orders, Rhode Island, June 8, 1777, WO 36/2, TNA.

20. Newell, "A Journal Kept during the Time That Boston Was Shut Up in 1775–6," Massachusetts Historical Society, *Collections*, Oct. 10, 1775, 268 ("wheeling"); "Letter XI," July 14, [?], in Gilman, ed., *Letters of Eliza Wilkinson*, 98 ("hooking-arms"); GCM of Thomas Bishop, New York, Nov. 16–24, 1779, WO 71/91, 3, film 675, reel 13, DLAR ("to go about"). For streets,

see John Andrews to William Barrell, Aug. 1, 1774, Andrews-Eliot Correspondence, box 1, 35. For valuables, see Crane, ed., *Diary of Elizabeth Drinker,* I, Dec. 13, 1777, 263, Dec. 26, 1777, 270.

21. Crane, ed., *Diary of Elizabeth Drinker,* I, Dec. 13, 1777, 263 (quotation). For holidays, see ibid., I, Dec. 24, 1777, 269, and Mar. 17, 1778, 289. For soldiers' drunkenness, see Elizabeth Ellery Dana, ed., *The British in Boston: Being the Diary of Lieutenant John Barker of the King's Own Regiment from November 15, 1774, to May 31, 1776 . . .* (Cambridge, Mass., 1924), Jan. 1, 1775, 18; Gruber, ed., *John Peebles' American War,* Oct. 1, 1777, 139–140; Sylvia Frey, *The British Soldier in America: A Social History of Military Life in the Revolutionary Period* (Austin, Tex., 1981), 63–66; and Paul E. Kopperman, "'The Cheapest Pay': Alcohol Abuse in the Eighteenth-Century British Army," *Journal of Military History,* LX (1996), 445–470. For brawls, see John Andrews to William Barrell, Oct. 30, 1774, Andrews-Eliot Correspondence, box 1, 46, Andrews to Barrell, Jan. 2, 1775, 48; and Abigail Adams to Mercy Otis Warren, Jan. 25, 1775, FO, https://founders.archives.gov/documents/Adams/04-01-02-0120. For victory celebrations, see "Valentin Asteroth's Diary of the American War of Independence," 1776, in Bruce E. Burgoyne, ed. and trans., *Diaries of a Hessian Chaplain and the Chaplain's Assistant* (Dover, Del., 1990), Mar. 26–27, 1781, 44–45; and Joseph G. Rosengarten, ed. and trans., "Popp's Journal, 1777–1783," *PMHB,* XXVI (1902), Nov. 19, 1779, 33. For civilians outside city limits, the army's retreat into winter quarters was a welcome respite from the constant plunder they endured the rest of the year; see Narrative of Mrs. Abraham Brasher, 1802, VF Women, 34. Houses were often targets of violence in revolutionary America; see Sarah Logan Fisher Diary, III, July 4, 1777, [14–15]; Crane, ed., *Diary of Elizabeth Drinker,* I, July 4, 1777, 225, July 4, 1778, 314; Robert Gray, "Observations on the War in Carolina," n.d., SCHS; and Edmund S. Morgan, "Thomas Hutchinson and the Stamp Act," *New England Quarterly,* XXI (1948), 459–461.

22. John Andrews to William Barrell, Mar. 18, 1775, Andrews-Eliot Correspondence, box 1, 50 ("Yankee Doodle," "most vile," "scurrilous"), Andrews to Barrell, Apr. 11, 1775, 51 ("childish," "with much greater courage"); John Adams to Abigail Adams, July 6, 1774, FO, https://founders.archives.gov/documents/Adams/04-01-02-0086 ("Are not Riots").

23. Ewald, *Diary of the American War,* ed. and trans. Tustin, June 21, 1781, 305 (quotation). For enslaved refugees, see Betty Wood, "'High Notions of Their Liberty': Women of Color and the American Revolution in Lowcountry Georgia and South Carolina, 1765–1783," in Philip D. Morgan, ed., *African American Life in the Georgia Lowcountry: The Atlantic World and the Gullah Geechee* (Athens, Ga., 2010), 59–60; Frey, *Water from the Rock,* 121–127; Cassandra Pybus, "Jefferson's Faulty Math: The Question of Slave Defections in the American Revolution," *WMQ,* 3d Ser., LXII (2005), 254; and BOP, Aug. 11, Sept. 8, 1780, reel 520. For particularly evocative examples of loyalist refugees, see Memorial of John Philips, AO 12/46, 71–72, TNA, Memorial of George Long, AO 12/49, 41, and Memorial of Richard Pearis, AO 12/49, 307–308. For tensions between neighbors, see T. Cole Jones, *Captives of Liberty: Prisoners of War and the Politics of Vengeance in the American Revolution* (Philadelphia, 2020), 109–123; and T. H. Breen, *The Will of the People: The Revolutionary Birth of America* (Cambridge, Mass., 2019), 86–121. For women in the British military, see Frey, *British Soldier,* 59–62; and Zabin, *Boston Massacre,* 94–104. For merchants, see Willard O. Mishoff, "Business in Philadelphia during the British Occupation, 1777–1778," *PMHB,* LXI (1937), 165–181. For sex workers, see Holly A. Mayer, *Belonging to the Army: Camp Followers and Community during the American Revolution* (Columbia, S.C., 1996), 110–112; and Frey, *British Soldier,* 61–62.

24. Gruber, ed., *John Peebles' American War,* Sept. 26, 1777, 138 ("by all accounts"); John Bowater to Basil Feilding, earl of Denbigh, June 5 and 11, 1777, in Balderston and Syrett, eds., *Lost War,* 131 ("swallow"). For more on the flexibility of allegiance, see Jasanoff, *Liberty's Exiles,* 8–9; Donald F. Johnson, "Ambiguous Allegiances: Urban Loyalties during the American Revolution," *JAH,* CIV (2017), 610–631; Sullivan, *Disaffected;* and Breen, *Will of the People,* 94–95.

25. Captain Wagner to Your Excellency [George Washington], Oct. 16, 1777, Morristown Hessian Documents, Z 110, DLAR (quotation). For loyalist involvement in identification and disarming, see Franklin Bowditch Dexter, ed., *The Literary Diary of Ezra Stiles, D.D., LL.D., President of Yale College,* II (New York, 1901), Dec. 14, 1776, 97; Memorial of Joseph Galloway, AO 12/38, 28, TNA, Memorial of John Parrock, AO 12/10, 138, and Memorial of Edward Bartlett, AO 12/40, 177. For examples of imprisonment, see John Leach Diaries, II, 1775–1776, MHS, Collections Online, https://www.masshist.org/database/6673, Peter Edes Diary, June–October 1775, MHS, Collections Online, https://www.masshist.org/database/1978; and James Allen, "Diary of James Allen, Esq., of Philadelphia, Counsellor-at-Law, 1770–1778 (Continued)," *PMHB,* IX (1885), 291. For demolition, see [Greene], "Newport in the Hands of the British," *Historical Magazine,* IV (1860), Oct. 21, 1777, 35; Matthew Robinson Petition, July [14], 1783, British Headquarters Papers [facsimiles], 1775–1783, MssCol 1209, box 34, 8435, Manuscripts and Archives Division, NYPL; and Benians, [ed.], *Journal by Tho: Hughes,* Oct. 6, 1778, 45–46. Loyalists tended to fare better than their rebel neighbors, but neither were they secure in their property; see General Orders, Rhode Island, Dec. 23, 1776, WO 36/2, TNA, and Memorial of John Davies, AO 12/46, 40. For property confiscation, see James Wright to George Germain, Feb. 10, 1780, James Wright Papers, 1772–1784, folder 3, GHS; and Lauren Duval, "Mastering Charleston: Property and Patriarchy in British-Occupied Charleston, 1780–82," *WMQ,* 3d Ser., LXXV (2018), 589–622.

26. "Letter VIII," n.d., in Gilman, ed., *Letters of Eliza Wilkinson,* 89 ("insulted"), "Letter X," May 19, 1781, 94 ("rebel ladies"); Loftus Cliffe to Bartholomew Cliffe, Nov. 12, 1777, Loftus Cliffe Papers ("ma[de] no Scruple," "all a damned set"). For imprisonment, see [Greene], "Newport in the Hands of the British," *Historical Magazine,* IV (1860), July 4, 5, 1777, 1; William Moultrie, *Memoirs of the American Revolution, So Far as It Related to the States of North and South-Carolina, and Georgia . . . ,* II (New York, 1802), 299–300; and "Diary of Lieut. Anthony Allaire, of Ferguson's Corps; Memorandum of Occurrences during the Campaign of 1780," in Lyman C. Draper, *King's Mountain and Its Heroes: History of the Battle of King's Mountain, October 7th, 1780, and the Events Which Led to It* (Cincinnati, Ohio, 1881), [Apr.] 22, 1780, 492.

27. For urban governance, see William J. Novak, *The People's Welfare: Law and Regulation in Nineteenth-Century America* (Chapel Hill, N.C., 1996); and Smith, *Freedoms We Lost,* 1–46, 62–133. See also Hart, *Building Charleston;* and Jessica Choppin Roney, *Governed by a Spirit of Opposition: The Origins of American Political Practice in Colonial Philadelphia* (Baltimore, Md., 2014). For Committees of Safety, see Christopher F. Minty, "'Of One Hart and One Mind': Local Institutions and Allegiance during the American Revolution," *EAS,* XV (2017), 99–132, esp. 119–127; and Breen, *Will of the People,* 123–126, 130–158.

28. Andrew Eliot to Isaac Smith, Jr., Apr. 9, 1776, Smith-Carter Family Papers, 1669–1880, reel 2, box 2, folder 16, April–October 1776, image 4, MHS, Digitized Collections, https://www.masshist.org/collection-guides/digitized/fa0540/b02-f16#4 ("We have been"); "William

Cheever's Diary, 1775–1776," in "January Meeting, 1927," *PMHS,* LX (Boston, 1927), June 19, 1775, 92 ("usual," "Press-Gangs"), July 21, 1775, 93 ("Provost"); and James Murray to Elizabeth Inman and Dolly Forbes, July 26, 1775, Murray-Robbins Family Papers, box 1, folder 4 ("be Eye"). For movement and passes, see Permit to Pass through British Lines, May 1775, Miscellaneous Bound Manuscripts, 1774–1775, MHS; John Andrews to William Barrell, May 6, 1775, Andrews-Eliot Correspondence, box 1, 55; Abigail Adams to John Adams, May 7, 1775, FO, https://founders.archives.gov/documents/Adams/04-01-02-0130; Crane, ed., *Diary of Elizabeth Drinker,* I, Nov. 24, 1777, 257; Newell, "A Journal Kept during the Time That Boston Was Shut Up," Massachusetts Historical Society, *Collections,* Nov. 4, 1775, 269; Memorial of Ann Carlisle, AO 12/43, 9, TNA; and General Orders, Rhode Island, Dec. 14, 1776, Jan. 7, 1777, May 30, 1777, and June 11, 1777, WO 36/2, TNA. For speculation, see Abigail Adams to Mercy Otis Warren, May 2, 1775, FO, https://founders.archives.gov/documents/Adams/04-01-02-0126; and John Andrews to William Barrell, June 1, 1775, Andrews-Eliot Correspondence, box 1, 56. For military rationale, see Stephen Moylan to Colonel Baldwin, Dec. 4, 1776, Miscellaneous Bound Manuscripts, 1774–1775, MHS; Stephen Payne Adye to Lieutenant Symes, Feb. 12, 1780, in "Pattison Letters," 367, and John L. C. Roome to Thomas Ward, July 20, 1780, 413–414.

29. Daniel Huger Horry, Jr., to Eliza Lucas Pinckney, Apr. 4, 1781, *ELP and HPH Digital Papers* ("been a long time," "Change"); "Diary of Captain Johann Hinrichs," December 1779–June 25, 1780, in Bernhard A. Uhlendorf, ed. and trans., *The Siege of Charleston with an Account of the Province of South Carolina: Diaries and Letters of Hessian Officers from the Von Jungkenn Papers in the William L. Clements Library* (Ann Arbor, Mich., 1938), Mar. 14, 1780, 207 ("very easy"); A. R. Newsome, ed., "A British Orderly Book, 1780–1781: III," *North Carolina Historical Review,* IX (1932), 277, 280. For other examples of enslaved messengers, see Eliza Lucas Pinckney to Elizabeth Motte Pinckney, Sept. 12, 1780, *ELP and HPH Digital Papers,* Eliza Lucas Pinckney to Thomas Pinckney, Sept. 17, 1780, Charles Cotesworth Pinckney to Eliza Lucas Pinckney, Sept. 23, 1780, Charles Cotesworth Pinckney to Eliza Lucas Pinckney, Nov. 13, 1780, Harriott Pinckney Horry to Eliza Lucas Pinckney, Jan. 7, 1781, and Charles Cotesworth Pinckney to Eliza Lucas Pinckney, Jan. 29, 1781. For an examination of enslaved people's opportunity and mobility in the army's New York garrison, see Judith Van Buskirk, "Crossing the Lines: African-Americans in the New York City Region during the British Occupation, 1776–1783," in "Explorations in Early American Culture," eds. William Pencak and George W. Boudreau, special issue, *Pennsylvania History,* LXV (1998), 74–100. For enslaved mobility during the colonial period, see Andrea C. Mosterman, *Spaces of Enslavement: A History of Slavery and Resistance in Dutch New York* (Ithaca, N.Y., 2021); and Philip D. Morgan, *Slave Counterpoint: Black Culture in the Eighteenth-Century Chesapeake and Lowcountry* (Williamsburg, Va., and Chapel Hill, N.C., 1998), 519–530.

30. For women's wartime roles, see Norton, *Liberty's Daughters,* 155–227; Linda K. Kerber, *Women of the Republic: Intellect and Ideology in Revolutionary America* (Williamsburg, Va., and Chapel Hill, N.C., 1980), 35–113; and Carol Berkin, *Revolutionary Mothers: Women in the Struggle for America's Independence* (New York, 2005). For women's roles as "deputy husbands," see Laurel Thatcher Ulrich, *Good Wives: Image and Reality in the Lives of Women in Northern New England, 1650–1750* (New York, 1982), 35–50. For espionage, see Memorial of Ann Bates, Mar. 17, 1785, T 1/611, TNA; Adye to Symes, Feb. 12, 1780, in "Pattison Letters," 367; Ewald, *Diary of the American War,* ed. and trans. Tustin, Feb. 9, 1778, 119; GCM

of Alexander Campbell, Philadelphia, Feb. 27–28, Mar. 2–4, 9–10, 1778, WO 71/85, 318–319, TNA; Bernard A. Uhlendorf, ed. and trans., *Revolution in America: Confidential Letters and Journals, 1776–1784, of Adjutant General Major Baurmeister of the Hessian Forces* (New Brunswick, N.J., 1957), Dec. 16, 1777, 134; Judith L. Van Buskirk, *Generous Enemies: Patriots and Loyalists in Revolutionary New York* (Philadelphia, 2002), 51–57; and Mayer, *Belonging to the Army,* 37–38.

31. GCM of Mary Fygis, Philadelphia, Mar. 24–25, 1778, WO 71/85, 446, TNA ("from the first," "person"); Ondine E. Le Blanc, ed., "The Journal of the 'Rebel Lady': Katharine Farnham Hay's Account of Her Trip to New York City, 1778," *PMHS,* CIX (Boston, 1998), 114 ("very Suspicious"); Ewald, *Diary of the American War,* ed. and trans. Tustin, Feb. 9, 1778, 119 ("One cannot," "for who knows"). Although Fygis later recanted her accusations against a loyalist officer, she might have indeed carried illicit correspondence; a witness alleged that she transmitted letters between George Washington and American officers in occupied Philadelphia; see GCM of Alexander Campbell, Mar. 3, 1778, WO 71/85, 350, TNA. For searches, see also General Orders, Rhode Island, Jan. 8, 1777, WO 36/2, TNA; [Greene], "Newport in the Hands of the British," *Historical Magazine,* IV (1860), July 31, 1777, 2; [Francis] Marion to Peter Horry, Mar. 8, 1782, in R. W. Gibbes, ed., *Documentary History of the Revolution, Consisting of Letters and Papers Relating to the Contest for Liberty, Chiefly in South Carolina, in 1781 and 1782* (Columbia, S.C., 1853), 266; and Alexander Garden, *Anecdotes of the Revolutionary War in America, with Sketches of Character of Persons the Most Distinguished, in the Southern States, for Civil and Military Services* (Charleston, S.C., 1822), 238. In New York, a soldier's wife likewise avoided arrest when caught robbing a house by "pretend[ing] to be in Labour"—a gambit that worked temporarily, although she was later apprehended; see GCM of John Farren, Thomas Agnew, John Purdy, George Fogwell alias Wilson, New York, Jan. 28–Feb. 12, 1779, WO 71/88, 247, film 675, reel 11, DLAR.

32. [William Bayard] to Gentlemen, Nov. 12, 1778, Bayard-Campbell-Pearsall Families Papers, 1659–1898, box 1, folder 2, Manuscripts and Archives Division, NYPL (quotation). For how disguises can reveal urban geographies and racial dynamics, see Marisa J. Fuentes, *Dispossessed Lives: Enslaved Women, Violence, and the Archive* (Philadelphia, 2016), 72–73, 94–99. For policing of the enslaved, see Mosterman, *Spaces of Enslavement,* 52–77; Stephanie M. H. Camp, *Closer to Freedom: Enslaved Women and Everyday Resistance in the Plantation South* (Chapel Hill, N.C., 2004), 12–34; and Walter Johnson, *River of Dark Dreams: Slavery and Empire in the Cotton Kingdom* (Cambridge, Mass., 2013).

33. Sarah Logan Fisher Diary, IV, Oct. 23, 1777, [14], https://therevolutionarycity.org/islandora/fisher-sarah-logan-diary-volume-4 (quotation). For poverty and poor relief in occupied regions, see J. B. Cutling to John Warren, Dec. 17, 1777, John Warren Papers, 1765–1821, MHS; BOP, June 23, 1780, reel 457; James Morton to James Pemberton, Dec. 4, 1777, Pemberton Family Papers, XXXI, 56; Crane, ed., *Diary of Elizabeth Drinker,* I, 289 n.15; General Orders of W[illia]m Howe, Jan. 10, 1778, 257, Ser. G, film 695, reel 2, Montrésor Family Papers, 1775–1800, DLAR; Joseph Galloway, "By Order of His Excellency Sir William Howe K. B. . . . Proclamation," Feb. 11, 1778, PRO 30/55/8, 939, TNA; *Diary of Frederick Mackenzie,* I, July 13, 1778, 309; and [Greene], "Newport in the Hands of the British," *Historical Magazine,* IV (1860), Mar. 2, 1778, 37. Traditional forms of relief were funded by donations or tax assessments, but, under occupation—with the civil government in tatters and civilians' resources strained—donations often halted. As the war progressed, policies by both armies

that restricted relief to their own supporters exacerbated these circumstances; for examples, see Dexter, ed., *Literary Diary of Ezra Stiles,* II, Jan. 4, 1777, 108; [Greene], "Newport in the Hands of the British," *Historical Magazine,* IV (1860), Oct. 27, 1777, 35; and Mabel L. Webber, ed., "Josiah Smith's Diary, 1780–1781 (Continued)," *SCHGM,* XXXIII (1932), 286–287.

34. John Andrews to William Barrell, June 1, 1775, Andrews-Eliot Correspondence, box 1, 56 ("formerly"); Sarah Logan Fisher Diary, IV, Nov. 5, 1777, [22] ("Ship," "sweet," "How little"); Newell, "A Journal Kept during the Time That Boston Was Shut Up," Massachusetts Historical Society, *Collections,* Aug. 1, 1775, 265. "Provisions of all kinds grow daily more scarce," Elizabeth Drinker worried, recording rumors "that it is reported in the Country that 5/- is given here for a Rat: it is bad enough indeed, but far from being so"; see Crane, ed., *Diary of Elizabeth Drinker,* I, Nov. 11, 1777, 252 ("Provisions"), and Nov. 12, 1777, 252–253 ("it is reported"). For family networks, see Donald F. Johnson, *Occupied America: British Military Rule and the Experience of Revolution* (Philadelphia, 2020), 131–132; and Van Buskirk, *Generous Enemies,* 44–72. For gendered dimensions of poverty, see Wulf, *Not All Wives,* 153–179; Ruth Wallis Herndon, "Poor Women and the Boston Almshouse in the Early Republic," *JER,* XXXII (2012), 349–381; and Clare A. Lyons, *Sex among the Rabble: An Intimate History of Gender and Power in the Age of Revolution, Philadelphia, 1730–1830* (Williamsburg, Va., and Chapel Hill, N.C., 2006), esp. 312–392. For more on hunger and "victual warfare" in the American Revolution, see Rachel B. Herrmann, *No Useless Mouth: Waging War and Fighting Hunger in the American Revolution* (Ithaca, N.Y., 2019), 9 (quotation). See also David C. Hsiung, "Food, Fuel, and the New England Environment in the War for Independence, 1775–1776," *New England Quarterly,* LXXX (2007), 614–654; and Barbara Clark Smith, "Food Rioters and the American Revolution," *WMQ,* 3d Ser., LI (1994), 3–38.

35. John Andrews to William Barrell, June 1, 1775, Andrews-Eliot Correspondence, box 1, 56 ("Pork"); Loftus Cliffe to Bartholomew Cliffe, Nov. 12, 1777, Lotus Cliffe Papers ("Starve"). For fresh meat in Boston, see John Leach Diaries, II, Aug. 19, 1775, [19]. Typically, loyalism was proved through signed oaths; see Johnson, *Occupied America,* 153. For starvation in occupied cities, see ibid., 112–137. For bakers in Charleston, see BOP, Mar. 21 and 27, 1782, reel 525. Charleston's bakers, however, largely "refused to comply with the Regulations," causing the board of police to increase its vigilance, inspecting baker's shops in early April 1782 and levying a fine on Nicholas Lafille for baking underweight bread and "rescuing" fifty confiscated loaves; see BOP, Mar. 27, 1782 ("refused"), Apr. 5, 1782, and Apr. 18, 1782 ("rescuing"), reel 525. For typical colonial market practices, see Emma Hart, *Trading Spaces: The Colonial Marketplace and the Foundations of American Capitalism* (Chicago, 2019); and Smith, *Freedoms We Lost,* 59–72.

36. "Mrs. Mary [Gould] Almy's Account," Aug. 12, 1778 (quotation). For officers' predictions, see John Bowater to Basil Feilding, sixth earl of Denbigh, Nov. 5, 1776, in Balderston and Syrett, eds., *Lost War,* 103. For false loyalty, see Alexander Leslie to Sir Henry Clinton, Dec. 27, 1781, British Headquarters Papers [facsimiles], MssCol 1209, box 18, 3991. For more on flexibility of allegiance, see Johnson, "Ambiguous Allegiances," *JAH,* CIV (2017), 610–631.

37. Sir Charles Blagden to Joseph Banks, Sept. 12, 1778, Letters from Sir Charles Blagden to Sir Joseph Banks, 1776–1780, MssCol 312, Manuscripts and Archives Division, NYPL ("large," "esteemed"); Hannah Bancker to Everet Bancker, May 9, 1783, Bancker Family Papers, 1700–1862, box 1, folder 6, Manuscripts and Archives Division, NYPL ("I could not"); Le Blanc, ed., "Journal of the 'Rebel Lady,'" *PMHS,* CIX (Boston, 1998), 117 ("creeping," "Good God,"

"I felt"), 120. For salt provisions, see *Diary of Frederick Mackenzie,* I, Mar. 11, 1778, 255. For class dynamics, see Smith, "Food Rioters and the American Revolution," *WMQ,* 3d Ser., LI (1994), 3–38. For examples of rations, see various Engineering Department Works and Service Payments in James Moncrieff Papers, 1710–1894, box 1, WCL. Fleeing garrisoned cities, however, rarely offered better prospects. After abandoning "a verey good habitation" in Boston, Abigail Brett "ha[d] been forst to sell part of what Littel I brot . . . with me or I and mine must have sufferd." Four months later, "distrest" and destitute, with three children to care for, she begged a local clergyman, if "it is in your power to releve us in som mesear I now Crave your pittey"; see Brett to [David Jeffries, IV], December 1775, Papers of David Jeffries IV, 1758–1785, box 14, XIV, Jeffries Family Papers, 1622–1880, MHS.

38. For examples of plunder and robbery, see GCM of James Power and Isaac Green, Darby, Pa., Dec. 25, 1777, WO 71/85, TNA, GCM of James Hamill, Darby, Pa., Dec. 25, 1777, WO 71/85; GCM of John Farren, Thomas Agnew, John Purdy, George Fogwell alias Wilson, New York, Jan. 28–Feb. 12, 1779, WO 71/88, 247, film 675, reel 11, DLAR; and Robert Mackenzie, "By His Excellency Sir William Howe, K.B.; General and Commander in Chief, . . . Proclamation," Dec. 18, 1777, *Pennsylvania Ledger: or, The Philadelphia Market-Day Advertiser,* Feb. 28, 1778, [1]. For soldiers' wives and illicit trade, see Dana, ed., *British in Boston: Being the Diary of Lieutenant John Barker,* May 8, 1775, 44; and GCM of Murtoch Laughlan, Charles Neal, and Robert Pearce, Newport, R.I., Dec. 22, 1777, WO 71/85, 159–160, TNA. For exchanges between soldiers (and occasionally their wives) and civilians, see GCM of Winifred McCowan, Boston, Sept. 14–19, 1775, WO 71/81, film 65, reel 7, DLAR; GCM of Thomas Edwards, Newport, R.I., Feb. 14, 1777, WO 71/83, 103, TNA, GCM of Michael Finnerty, Philadelphia, Dec. 17, 1777, WO 71/85, and GCM of Edward Riley, West Chester, Pa., Sept. 19, 1777, WO 71/84, 275. For more on illicit markets in occupied regions, see Van Buskirk, *Generous Enemies,* 112–128; and Johnson, *Occupied America,* 134–136. For an overview of informal economies and trade in secondhand and stolen goods in early America, see Hartigan-O'Connor, *Ties That Buy,* 164–167; and Zabin, *Dangerous Economies,* 57–80.

39. General Orders, Feb. 1, 1778, 122, James Pattison Papers, film 47 (quotation). Another copy of the orders indicates that Cuff was sentenced to either a fine or imprisonment; see General Orders of W[illia]m Howe, Feb. 1, 1778, 268, Ser. G, film 695, reel 2, Montrésor Family Papers. For Cuff's family, see [Quakers], "A List of Free Negroes Residing in the Southern District . . . ," July 22, 1782, African American Collection, box 1, WCL. For illegal goods, see John Andrews to William Barrell, Apr. 11, 1776, Andrews-Eliot Correspondence, box 1, 57. Examples of civilians punished for illicit exchanges are also pervasive throughout British courts-martial.

40. John Andrews to William Barrell, Dec. 22, 1774, Andrews-Eliot Correspondence, box 1, 48 ("Shocking"), Andrews to Barrell, Aug. 6, 1774, 37; Dorothy Murray to Elizabeth Murray, Oct. 27, 1768, Murray-Robbins Family Papers, box 1, folder 1 ("poor wretches," "His back"). In South Carolina, where the whipping of enslaved laborers was more commonplace, Eliza Wilkinson was less disconcerted by the violence of military justice. Learning that a solider convicted of plundering had been sentenced to five hundred lashes, she wryly observed, "So here was 'the devil correcting sin'"; see "Letter III," n.d., in Gilman, ed., *Letters of Eliza Wilkinson,* 35. For more on slavery in New England, see Elise Lemire, *Black Walden: Slavery and Its Aftermath in Concord, Massachusetts* (Philadelphia, 2009); Margaret Ellen Newell, *Brethren by Nature: New England Indians, Colonists, and the Origins of American Slavery* (Ithaca, N.Y.,

2015); Jared Ross Hardesty, *Unfreedom: Slavery and Dependence in Eighteenth-Century Boston* (New York, 2016); and Wendy Warren, *New England Bound: Slavery and Colonization in Early America* (New York, 2016). For corporeal punishment, see John Rowe Diary, Jan. 18, 1776, P–786, reel 2; and "Valentin Asteroth's Diary," in Burgoyne, ed. and trans., *Diaries of a Hessian Chaplain and the Chaplain's Assistant,* Nov. 18–19, 1782, 48. For soldiers' wives receiving lashes, see GCM of Winifred McCowan, Boston, Sept. 13, 1775, WO 71/81, 393–400, film 675, reel 7, DLAR, and GCM of May Colethrate and Elizabeth Clarke, Freehold, N.J., June 27, 1778, WO 71/86, 156–158, film 675, reel 10. For examples of civilians and military justice, see GCM of James O'Brian, Philadelphia, Feb. 24, 1778, WO 71/85, 286–289, TNA, and GCM of Mary Fygis, Philadelphia, Mar. 24–25, 1778, WO 71/85, 456–457. For Black inhabitants appearing before courts-martial, see GCM of James Butler, Camden, N.J., May 14, 1778, WO 71/86, 148–150, film 675, reel 10, DLAR; and GCM of James Power and Isaac Green, Darby, Pa., Dec. 25, 1777, WO 71/85, 189, TNA. For the severity of military justice, see Arthur N. Gilbert, "British Military Justice during the American Revolution," *Eighteenth Century,* XX (1979), 36–37; and Zabin, *Boston Massacre,* 111. For a comparative study, see Gilbert, "Military and Civilian Justice in Eighteenth-Century England: An Assessment," *Journal of British Studies,* XVII, no. 2 (Spring 1978), 41–65, esp. 50–55. See also Frederick Bernays Wiener, *Civilians under Military Justice: The British Practice since 1689 Especially in North America* (Chicago, 1967); Sylvia R. Frey, "Courts and Cats: British Military Justice in the Eighteenth Century," *Military Affairs: The Journal of Military History, Including Theory and Technology,* XLIII (1979), 5–11; and Frey, *British Soldier,* 71–93. In prerevolutionary Boston, inhabitants were routinely sentenced to thirty or forty lashes; military courts, in contrast, frequently imposed between five hundred and one thousand; see Alice Morse Earle, ed., *The Diary of Anna Green Winslow: A Boston School Girl of 1771* (Boston, 1894), 111 n.53.

41. Elizabeth Willing Powel to Ann Francis, Apr. 2, 1778, Powel Family Papers, Ser. III, box 4, folder 3, HSP ("Ones own"); Abigail Adams to Mercy Otis Warren, Oct. 19, 1775, FO, https://founders.archives.gov/documents/Adams/04-01-02-0198 ("I feel but little," "I have no son," "I do not fancy"). Throughout the war, many women reiterated that they felt safe as long as danger did not approach their dwelling; for examples, see Elizabeth Drinker to Henry Drinker, Feb. 14, 1778, Henry and Elizabeth Drinker Letters, 1777–1778 (hereafter Drinker Letters), HCQSC; Abigail Adams to John Adams, June 22, 1775, FO, https://founders.archives.gov/documents/Adams/04-01-02-0152; and Mary Heriot to Robert Heriot, May 23, 1781, Robert Heriot Correspondence.

42. For women managing farms, see Abigail Adams to Mercy Otis Warren, Apr. 13, 1776, FO, https://founders.archives.gov/documents/Adams/04-01-02-0246; and Elizabeth Inman to Ralph Inman, June 14, 1775, James Murray Robbins Family Papers, box 2. For more on women managing farms and the home front, see Norton, *Liberty's Daughters,* 212–224; and Berkin, *Revolutionary Mothers,* 33–34.

43. Mary Pemberton to Israel Pemberton, Oct. 3, 1777, Pemberton Family Papers, XXX, 156 ("ha[d] not been over"); Sarah Logan Fisher Diary, III, Sept. 13, 1777, [41] ("what passes"); Elizabeth Drinker to Henry Drinker, Feb. 2, 1778, Drinker Letters ("not spent," "but few"), and Henry Drinker to Elizabeth Drinker, Sept. 20, 1777 ("at Home," "all rude"). For the Quaker exiles, see Paige L. Whidbee, "The Quaker Exiles: 'The Cause of Every Inhabitant,'" *Pennsylvania History,* LXXXIII (2016), 28–57; and Richard Godbeer, *World of Trouble: A Philadelphia Quaker Family's Journey through the American Revolution* (New Haven,

Conn., 2019), 139–153, 176–179, 186–188. For Quaker worries about youthful indulgence, see Godbeer, *World of Trouble*, 78–79; and Philadelphia and New Jersey Yearly Meeting, Men's and Joint Meeting Minutes, Oct. 29, 1777, Extracts from Minutes of Philadelphia Yearly Meeting, 1758–1777, 1250.A1.3, esp. 374–375, 386–387, HCQSC.

44. Letter (draft) from John Quincy Adams to Joseph Sturge, March 1846, Adams Family Papers, MHS, Collections Online, https://www.masshist.org/database/405 ("My mother"); Elizabeth Adams to Samuel Adams, Feb. 12, 1776, Samuel Adams Papers, 1760–1803, Manuscripts and Archives Division, NYPL, https://digitalcollections.nypl.org/items/2f436c20-195d-0134-36d4-00505686a51c ("in Readiness," "a bed"). For Susan Mason, see Norton, *Liberty's Daughters*, 197.

45. Mary Lucia Bull Guerard to Susannah Stoll Garvey, 1779, in "A Woman's Letters in 1779 and 1782," in North American Women's Letters and Diaries (database), 2 ("impossible," "we never went"); Narrative of Mrs. Abraham Brasher, 1802, VF Women, 29 ("This caused," "every night," "almost frightened"), 30 ("two or three"), 37 ("always surprised," "not to sleep," "if the enemy"), 38 ("laughed"). For more on the Brashers' exile, see John U. Rees, "'It Appeared to Me as If Here We Should Live Secure': A Family's Precarious Refuge in Paramus, 1776 to 1780," in Barbara Z. Marchant, ed., *Revolutionary Bergen County: The Road to Independence* (Charleston, S.C., 2009), 31–42. For New York refugees generally, see Matthew P. Dziennik, "New York's Refugees and Political Authority in Revolutionary America," *WMQ*, 3d Ser., LXXVII (2020), 65–96. For the strain of waiting, see Abigail Adams to John Adams, May 24, 1775, Adams Family Papers.

46. "Letter V," n.d., in Gilman, ed., *Letters of Eliza Wilkinson*, 47 ("always," "eyes"), 48, 51, 57 ("O Major," "they really expected"), 58.

47. Margaret Hill Morris Diary, Dec. 16, 1776 (quotation). Neighborly relations often crossed political divides; see James Murray to Elizabeth Inman, May 23, 1775, James Murray Robbins Family Papers, box 2; and Van Buskirk, *Generous Enemies*, esp. 44–72. For women and performative dependence, see Jacqueline Beatty, *In Dependence: Women and the Patriarchal State in Revolutionary America* (New York, 2023).

48. Jones, *Captives of Liberty*, 103 ("creative"); GCM of Rudolph Esling, Edward [George] Spencer, and Charles Gussett, Philadelphia, Nov. 10, 1777, WO 71/84, 434, TNA ("made several"). For examples of plunder, see GCM of James Power and Isaac Green, Darby, Pa., Dec. 25, 1777, WO 71/85, TNA, GCM of James Hamill, Darby, Pa., Dec. 25, 1777, WO 71/85; GCM of John Farren, Thomas Agnew, John Purdy, George Fogwell alias Wilson, New York, Jan. 28–Feb. 12, 1779, WO 71/88, 241–258, film 675, reel 11, DLAR; Diary of Robert Morton, Sept. 28, 29, 30, 1777, Oct. 2, 19, 23, 24, 1777; General Orders, Rhode Island, Aug. 20, 1777, WO 36/2, TNA; Crane, ed., *Diary of Elizabeth Drinker*, I, Nov. 1, 1777, 250, Dec. 23, 1777, 269; Thomas Parke to James Pemberton, Nov. 10, 1777, Pemberton Family Papers, XXXI, 16, and Samuel Rhodes, Jr., "Account of the Damages Done at Evergreen," Mar. 6, 1778, 162. For forcing into houses, see GCM of William Green and Thomas Salem, Long Island, Oct. 20–Nov. 4, 1779, WO 71/90, 376–383, film 675, reel 12, DLAR.

49. GCM of William Gauble, New York, Sept. 11, 1778, WO 71/87, 186–190, film 675, reel 10, DLAR ("much alarmed"); Crane, ed., *Diary of Elizabeth Drinker*, I, Dec. 11, 1777, 263 ("These are sad times," "'tis hardly safe").

50. "Letter VIII," n.d., in Gilman, ed., *Letters of Eliza Wilkinson*, 88 ("Our very doors"); Döhla, *Hessian Diary*, ed. and trans. Burgoyne, Dec. 31, 1778, 96 ("Everday"); General Orders,

Feb. 18, 1778, 152–153, James Pattison Papers, film 47 ("to bring"); John Andrews to William Barrell, Apr. 11, 1776, Andrews-Eliot Correspondence, box 1, 57 ("If you'll believe"). For demolition for firewood, see Crane, ed., *Diary of Elizabeth Drinker,* I, Dec. 9, 1777, 262, and Dec. 23, 1777, 269. For exorbitant costs, see ibid., I, Nov. 12, 1777, 253; Elizabeth Drinker to Henry Drinker, Feb. 26, 1778, Drinker Letters; General Orders of W[illia]m Howe, Jan. 8, 1778, 255, Apr. 4, 1778, 301, Ser. G, film 695, reel 2, Montrésor Family Papers; Memorial of John Forrester, AO 12/45, 12, 14, TNA; John W. Jackson, *With the British Army in Philadelphia, 1777–1778* (San Rafael, Calif., 1979), 25, 190; Orderly Book, Oct. 26–Dec. 17, 1777, Kept by Serj. Major Richards, Nov. 17, 1777, Orders, Returns, Morning Reports, and Accounts of British Troops, 1776–1781, film 9, DLAR; Thomas Gould's Petition, Revolution, box 44A, folder 7-F, NHS; Memorial of Thomas Banister, AO 13/59, TNA, and GCM of John Rowland, Philadelphia, Dec. 17, 1777, WO 71/85. For depletion of natural resources, see Döhla, *Hessian Diary,* ed. and trans. Burgoyne, July 13, 1778, 79. See also Hsiung, "Food, Fuel, and the New England Environment," *New England Quarterly,* LXXX (2007), 614–654. For more on fuel shortages, see Van Buskirk, *Generous Enemies,* 114; and Johnson, *Occupied America,* 123–126.

51. General Orders of W[illia]m Howe, Dec. 18, 1777, 225 ("Shameful," "absolutely repugnant"), Jan. 8, 1778, 255 ("to execute"), Ser. G, film 695, reel 2, Montrésor Family Papers; Jackson, *With the British Army in Philadelphia,* 190. Howe issued similar orders in New York the previous year; see Johnson, *Occupied America,* 120. For class dynamics, see Stephen Conway, "To Subdue America: British Army Officers and the Conduct of the Revolutionary War," *WMQ,* 3d Ser., XLIII (1986), 390; and James Simpson to Henry Clinton, July 1, 1780, Guy Carleton Papers, PRO 30/55/24, 2877, TNA. For guards, see Diary of Robert Morton, Oct. 19, 1777; and GCM of John Walton and John Connell, Germantown, Pa., Sept. 29, 1777, WO 71/84, 318–321, TNA. For punishment for plunder, see courts-martial records in WO 71/82, WO 71/83, WO 71/85, WO 71/87, WO 71/91, TNA. Military justice reinforced the divide between aristocratic officers and enlisted men in ways that both perpetuated hierarchical military culture and affirmed officers' elevated status; see Emily Merrill, "Judging Empire: Masculinity and the Making of the British Imperial Army, 1754–1783" (Ph.D. diss., University of Pennsylvania, 2015), 248; and Michèle Cohen, "'Manners' Make the Man: Politeness, Chivalry, and the Construction of Masculinity, 1750–1830," in "Special Feature on Masculinities," special issue, *Journal of British Studies,* XLIV, no. 2 (2005), 312–329.

52. Tatum, ed., *American Journal of Ambrose Serle,* Sept. 1, 1776, 87 ("Filth"); GCM of John Walton and John Connell, Germantown, Pa., Sept. 29, 1777, WO 71/84, 319, TNA ("thrown," "door"); John Andrews to William Barrell, Apr. 11, 1776, Andrews-Eliot Correspondence, box 1, 57 ("revelling"). For destruction of civilian property, see Oliver Hart to Joseph Hart, July 18, 1779, Oliver Hart Papers, 1741–1961, SCL; Tatum, ed., *American Journal of Ambrose Serle,* Sept. 1, 1776, 86–87; Diary of Robert Morton, Sept. 28, 29, 1777; GCM of William Richards, Philadelphia, Dec. 15, 1777, WO 71/85, 183, TNA; and Johnson, *Occupied America,* 120–121.

53. GCM of John Cummings, Fort Knyphausen, New York, Dec. 3–4, 1777, WO 71/85, 30, film 675, reel 9, DLAR (quotation); Stephen Conway, "'The Great Mischief Complain'd Of': Reflections on the Misconduct of British Soldiers in the Revolutionary War," *WMQ,* 3d Ser., XLVII (1990), 378; see also Stephen Conway, "From Fellow-Nationals to Foreigners: British Perceptions of the Americans, circa 1739–1783," *WMQ,* 3d Ser., LIX (2002), 65–100. American observers hinted at this class disparity as they critiqued soldiers' actions. "I am persuaded these Plunderers never had the Pleasure of ravaging so opulant a Country before,"

Oliver Hart wryly observed; see Oliver Hart to Joseph Hart, July 18, 1779, Oliver Hart Papers. Plunder and the destruction of civilian property were not limited to the British, however. Similar dynamics unfolded when Continental troops invaded Haudenosaunee communities; see Maeve Kane, "'She Did Not Open Her Mouth Further': Haudenosaunee Women as Military and Political Targets during and after the American Revolution," in Barbara B. Oberg, ed., *Women in the American Revolution: Gender, Politics, and the Domestic World* (Charlottesville, Va., 2019), 83–102.

54. Sarah Lowndes to Rawlins Lowndes, May 17, 1780, quoted in Carl J. Vipperman, *The Rise of Rawlins Lowndes, 1721–1800* (Columbia, S.C., 1978), 226 (quotations).

55. GCM of John Ferne, Moses Abraham, Marcus Myers, New York, Oct. 23, 1780, WO 71/92, 385, film 675, reel 14, DLAR ("that she should be"); Deborah Norris Logan to [Alexander] Garden, Sept. 26, 1822, John F. Watson Historical Collection, box 4 ("two such"). For Black women and protection, see Jennifer L. Morgan, "*Partus Sequitur Ventrem:* Law, Race, and Reproduction in Colonial Slavery," *Small Axe,* XXII, no. 1 (March 2018), 1–17; Jessica Marie Johnson, *Wicked Flesh: Black Women, Intimacy, and Freedom in the Atlantic World* (Philadelphia, 2020); and Kellie Carter Jackson, "'Dare You Meet a Woman': Black Women, Abolitionism, and Protective Violence, 1850–1859," *Slavery and Abolition,* XLII (2021), 269–292.

56. A[ndrew] Eliot, Jr., to [John Eliot], Mar. 20, 1781, Eliot Family Papers, 1688–1937, box 1, folder 4, MHS ("Our Situation"), A[ndrew] Eliot to John Eliot, July 9, 1781 ("we are in," "maurading," "we live").

57. GCM of Charles Fraser, Dudley Wells, Henry Hart, and Cornelius Drewry, Philadelphia, Dec. 30, 1777, WO 71/85, 156–158, TNA.

58. "Letter III," n.d., in Gilman, ed., *Letters of Eliza Wilkinson,* 31 ("thoughts"), "Letter V," n.d., 46 ("we could neither," "least noise," "in our clothes"); Christian Barnes to Elizabeth Inman, Apr. 9, [1775], Murray-Robbins Family Papers, I ("blow," "I did not recover," "sound") (an archival note indicates that the letter is misdated; the incident occurred after the Battle of Lexington); Benjamin Chew, Jr., to Benjamin Chew, Dec. 11, 1777, Chew Family Papers, 1659–1986, Ser. IIc, HSP ("Remembrance").

59. Mary Heriot to Robert Heriot, May 23, 1781, Robert Heriot Correspondence.

60. Unknown to Elizabeth Murray [Robbins], [Nov. 28, 1779], James Murray Robbins Family Papers, box 3.

61. Elizabeth Willing Powel to Ann Francis, Apr. 2, 1778, Powel Family Papers, Ser. III, box 4, folder 3.

62. Sharon Block, *Rape and Sexual Power in Early America* (Williamsburg, Va., and Chapel Hill, N.C., 2006), 16–52, 240–241. For how race and class determined men's capacity to coerce sex, see ibid., 4, 63–80, 163–209; see also Block, "Rape in the American Revolution: Process, Reaction, and Public Re-Creation," in Elizabeth D. Heineman, ed., *Sexual Violence in Conflict Zones: From the Ancient World to the Era of Human Rights* (Philadelphia, 2011), 25–29. I have also written about how occupation altered women's notions of space and safety; see Lauren Duval, "'A Shocking Thing to Tell Of': Female Civilians, Violence, and Rape under British Military Rule," in Holly A. Mayer, ed., *Women Waging War in the American Revolution* (Charlottesville, Va., 2022), 76–97.

63. [Emer] de Vattel, *The Law of Nations; or, Principles of the Law of Nature, Applied to the Conduct and Affairs of Nations and Sovereigns,* II (London, 1759), 51–53 (quotation, 52).

For errands, see Sarah Logan Fisher Diary, V, Jan. 31, 1778, [4], https://therevolutionarycity.org/islandora/fisher-sarah-logan-diary-volume-5; and Crane, ed., *Diary of Elizabeth Drinker,* I, Oct. 9–11, 1777, 241–242, Oct. 18, 1777, 246. For honor, see Arthur N. Gilbert, "Law and Honour among Eighteenth-Century British Army Officers," *Historical Journal,* XIX (1976), 75–87; and Robert Shoemaker, "Male Honour and the Decline of Public Violence in Eighteenth-Century London," *Social History,* XXVI, no. 2 (2001), 190–208.

64. GCM of Robert Brown and John Dillon, Philadelphia, Jan. 7, 1778, WO 71/85, 203 ("dragg'd"), 204 ("Some," "pointed"), 205–209, 211–212 ("ill-using"), TNA. The court proceedings refer to Isabella Mitchell as both Isobel and Isabella; the latter accompanies her own testimony, so I use it here. I have discussed this incident further in Duval, "'A Shocking Thing to Tell Of,'" in Mayer, ed., *Women Waging War in the American Revolution,* 81–83.

65. GCM of Silver Crispin and Mary O'Hara, Philadelphia, Mar. 6, 1778, WO 71/85, 368–369, NUAK ("rebel"); GCM of John Dunn and John Lusty, New Town, Long Island, Sept. 2–9, 1776, WO 71/82, 413, 419–420, film 675, reel 14, DLAR ("yankee whore," "that she was a yankee"). See also Block, "Rape in the American Revolution," in Heineman, ed., *Sexual Violence in Conflict Zones,* 28. For sexual assaults and other mistreatment of loyalist and disaffected women, see Van Buskirk, "They Didn't Join the Band," *Pennsylvania History,* LXII (1995), 320–321; Ruddiman, *Becoming Men of Some Consequence,* 76; and Kacy Dowd Tillman, *Stripped and Script: Loyalist Women Writers of the American Revolution* (Amherst, Mass., 2019).

66. Catherine Dudley to Charles Dudley, Nov. 19, 1775, Dudley Papers, 1768–1837, NHS (quotations). For the Continental army's efforts to regulate troops and prohibit such behavior, see Mayer, *Belonging to the Army,* 33–43; and Ruddiman, *Becoming Men of Some Consequence,* 90–116.

67. Block, "Rape in the American Revolution," in Heineman, ed., *Sexual Violence in Conflict Zones,* 25–30, 32; Holger Hoock, *"Jus in Bello,* Rape, and the British Army in the American Revolutionary War," *Journal of Military Ethics,* XIV (2015), 74–97 (for egregious cases, see 78–84; for officers' discretion, see 79). As Emily Merrill has argued, it was only in rare instances where the interests of officers and civilians "overlapped" that proceedings were initiated and soldiers convicted; see Merrill, "Judging Empire," 247. For more on wartime assault, see Block, "Rape in the American Revolution," in Heineman, ed., *Sexual Violence in Conflict Zones,* 25–30, 32; Norton, *Liberty's Daughters,* 202–204; Kerber, *Women of the Republic,* 46; Hoock, *Scars of Independence,* 164–177; Sharon Block, "Rape without Women: Print Culture and the Politicization of Rape, 1765–1815," *JAH,* LXXXIX (2002), 849–868; and Duval "'A Shocking Thing to Tell Of,'" in Mayer, ed., *Women Waging War in the American Revolution,* 76–97. For Congressional report, see Charles Thomson, "In Congress, April 18, 1777," *Pennsylvania Evening Post* (Philadelphia), Apr. 24, 1777, 229–230. For depositions, see Papers and Affidavits Relating to the Plunderings, Burnings, and Ravages Committed by the British, 1775–1784, Papers of the Continental Congress, M247, roll 66, NARA.

68. GCM of Timothy Spillman, Boston, Dec. 12–28, 1775, WO 71/82, 251 ("taking hold," "her resisting," "prevented," "begg'd"), 252 ("He damned"), 253, 254 ("cruelly beaten"), 255–256 ("a Man's fist," 256), film 675, reel 8, DLAR. Spillman was found guilty and sentenced to receive one thousand lashes (256). For opportunistic assaults, see GCM Robert Brown and John Dillon, Philadelphia, Jan. 7, 1778, WO 71/85, TNA; and John Andrews to William Barrell, Aug. 17, 1774, Andrews-Eliot Papers, box 1, 39.

69. GCM of Thomas Gorman, Brooklyn, N.Y., July 24–Aug. 1, 1778, WO 71/86, 173, film 675, reel 10, DLAR (quotations). Gorman alleged that the two were having an affair, that Sarah "was as willing as he was," that the press-gang deception was Sarah's idea, and that the rape charges arose from her husband's jealousy. His testimony suggests the fine line between coercive sex and sex work, noting that "he once gave her a Dollar and has always been welcome at the house." The court-martial acquitted Gorman and found him not guilty (174). For the Crispins, see GCM of Silver Crispin and Mary O'Hara, Philadelphia, Mar. 6, 1778, WO 71/85, 367–370, TNA. For other examples of bystanders to crime, see GCM of Robert Brown and John Dillon, Philadelphia, Jan. 7, 1778, WO 71/85, 206, TNA; and GCM of John Ferne, Moses Abraham, Marcus Myers, New York, Oct. 23, 1780, WO 71/92, 384, film 675, reel 14, DLAR. For inability to assist, see Affidavits of Elisabeth Cain, Papers and Affidavits Relating to the Plunderings, Burnings, and Ravages Committed by the British, 1775–1784, Papers of the Continental Congress, M247, roll 66, item 53, 29, Affidavit of Abagial Palmer, 31, and Affidavit of Mary Campbell, 33. For more on coercion and consent, see Block, *Rape and Sexual Power,* 27–28.

70. "Letter III," n.d., in Gilman, ed., *Letters of Eliza Wilkinson,* 28, 29 ("making as if"), 30 ("his thumb," "several days," "that they had favored"), 31 ("I seemed," "I cannot," "I trembled"). As members of the Carolina elite, the women's rank and race probably afforded them a small measure of protection, a deterrent that arose less from soldiers' respect for the privileges of status than the fact that elite women's connections with officers made punishment more likely than assaults on laboring and enslaved women. Or perhaps the soldiers were simply in a hurry. For class, deterrence, and relationships with officers, see Watson, *Annals of Philadelphia,* 682–683; and Ray Raphael, *A People's History of the American Revolution: How Common People Shaped the Fight for Independence* (New York, 2001), 132–134.

71. For rape in revolutionary rhetoric, see Block, "Rape without Women," *JAH,* LXXXIX (2002), 852–864; and Block, "Rape in the American Revolution," in Heineman, ed., *Sexual Violence in Conflict Zones,* 34–36. For underreporting of rape and sexual assaults, see Ruddiman, *Becoming Men of Some Consequence,* 93.

72. John Leach Diaries, II, Aug. 11, 1775, [16] ("Provost"), Aug. 12, 1775, [16] ("We are abused"), Aug. 23, 1775, [20] ("G--d Damn"); Peter Edes Diary, Aug. 21, 1775, [13] ("cursed," "most always"); GCM of Silver Crispin and Mary O'Hara, Philadelphia, Mar. 6, 1778, WO 71/85, 368–369 ("was no whore"), TNA. The charges were ultimately dropped as "trifling, and frivolous" (ibid., 370).

73. Abigail Adams to John Adams, May 18, 1777, FO, https://founders.archives.gov/documents/Adams/04-02-02-0188 (quotation). John sent her the report the previous month; see John Adams to Abigail Adams, Apr. 27, 1777, FO, https://founders.archives.gov/documents/Adams/04-02-02-0170. For Abigail's descriptions of herself as cumbersome with child, see Abigail Adams to John Adams, Apr. 17, 1777, FO, https://founders.archives.gov/documents/Adams/04-02-02-0161, Abigail Adams to John Adams, June 1, 1777, https://founders.archives.gov/documents/Adams/04-02-02-0196, Abigail Adams to John Adams, June 8, 1777, https://founders.archives.gov/documents/Adams/04-02-02-0202, and Abigail Adams to John Adams, June 15, 1777, https://founders.archives.gov/documents/Adams/04-02-02-0208.

74. Christian Barnes to Elizabeth Inman, n.d., Murray-Robbins Family Papers, I (quotation). For the cultural significance of houses, see Bernard L. Herman, *Town House:*

Architecture and Material Life in the Early American City, 1780–1830 (Williamsburg, Va., and Chapel Hill, N.C., 2005), esp. 1–76; and Richard L. Bushman, *Refinement of America: Persons, Houses, Cities* (New York, 1992), 100–138.

75. Crane, ed., *Diary of Elizabeth Drinker,* I, Dec. 14, 1777, 264 ("bark[ing]," "I often feel"), Dec. 15, 1777, 264 ("contrive[ed]," "if John," "untye," "large"), Dec. 22, 177, 269 ("Every noise"). For fences and alleys, see ibid., I, Oct. 30, 1777, 249, and Dec. 14, 15, 1777, 264. See also ibid., I, Oct. 30, 1777, 249, Nov. 21, 1777, 256, and Nov. 26, 1777, 259. For women's cries and altercations, see GCM of Silver Crispin and Mary O'Hara, Philadelphia, Mar. 6, 1778, WO 71/85, 369–370, TNA.

76. Memorial of Jeremiah Savage, AO 12/50, 265, TNA ("were all Lost"); Thomas Hill, "Went Off from the Subscriber, at the Time of the British, . . . a Mulatto Wench Named Maria," *South-Carolina Gazette, and General Advertiser* (Charleston, S.C.), Dec. 2–6, 1783, supplement [3] ("WENT OFF"); Robert Bass, "Ran Away the Morning the British Army Left Philadelphia, a Negro Boy Named Tony," *Pennsylvania Evening Post,* July 8, 1778, 226 ("RAN AWAY"); Memorial of Charles Atkins, AO 12/50, 335, TNA ("absconded," "Fleet"); Jane Grove, "Absented Themselves from the Subscriber, and Supposed to Have Followed the Army into Georgia in 1779, the Following Negroes," *Royal Georgia Gazette* (Savannah, Ga.), Jan. 18, 1781, [1] ("followed"). For profit, see Acting Committee Minute Book, 1784–1788, Ser. I, I, 113 (Silve), AmS 0.4, Pennsylvania Abolition Society Papers (Collection 490), 1751–1992, HSP, Pennsylvania Abolition Society Acting Committee Minute Book, 1789–1797, Ser. I, II, 91–93 (Dorcas), AmS .0412. For enlistment bounties, see Memorial of John Orde (cont.), AO 12/46, 420, TNA.

77. "Letter III," n.d., in Gilman, ed., *Letters of Eliza Wilkinson,* 24 ("private"); *Diaries and Letters of William Emerson, 1743–1776 . . . ,* ed. Amelia Forbes Emerson (n.p., 1972), 73, quoted in Lemire, *Black Walden,* 72 ("Red Coats"). For fears of enslaved revolt, see Robert G. Parkinson, *The Common Cause: Creating Race and Nation in the American Revolution* (Williamsburg, Va., and Chapel Hill, N.C., 2016), 100–122, 130–131; and Gerald Horne, *The Counter-Revolution of 1776: Slave Resistance and the Origins of the United States of America* (New York, 2014).

78. For negotiating, see GCM of Michael Finnerty, Philadelphia, Dec. 17, 1777, WO 71/85, 134–135. For partial destruction of fences and sheds, see Major Meltzhaimer to Mr. Brinley, Malbone-Brinley Papers, Ser. III, box 173, folder 1, NHS; and Crane, ed., *Diary of Elizabeth Drinker,* I, Dec. 23, 1777, 269. See also ibid., I, Dec. 25, 1777, 270. For fences and trees, see Thomas Parke to James Pemberton, Nov. 10, 1777, Pemberton Family Papers, XXXI, 16, Phineas Pemberton to James Pemberton, Nov. 18, 1777, 32–33; Sarah Logan Fisher Diary, IV, Nov. 1, 1777, [19]; and Crane, ed., *Diary of Elizabeth Drinker,* I, Oct. 27, 1777, 249; see also Diary of Robert Morton, Oct. 25, 26, 30, 31, and Nov. 1, 1777. For selling furnishings, see Sarah Logan Fisher Diary, IV, Dec. 26, 1777, [31]. For renting out houses, see Eliza Lucas Pinckney to Thomas Pinckney, Dec. 6, 1780, *ELP and HPH Digital Papers.*

CHAPTER 2

1. Elaine Forman Crane, ed., *The Diary of Elizabeth Drinker,* I (Boston, 1991), Dec. 15, 1777, 265 (quotation), Dec. 18–19, 1777, 266. For the Drinker family, see ibid., I, lxxiv. For the

Drinkers' politics, see Richard Godbeer, *World of Trouble: A Philadelphia Quaker Family's Journey through the American Revolution* (New Haven, Conn., 2019), 89–131.

2. Crane, ed., *Diary of Elizabeth Drinker*, I, Dec. 18, 1777, 266 (quotation). For Drinker's rebuffs, see ibid., I, Oct. 6, 1777, 240–241, and Oct. 25, 1777, 248. For Cramond's persistence, see ibid., I, Dec. 18, 19, 1777, 266, and Dec. 29, 1777, 271. Henry Drinker (nephew) began sleeping in the house shortly after his uncle's exile and continued to do so intermittently until his uncle's release, at times with other male neighbors; see ibid., I, Sept. 7, 1777, 227, Sept. 14, 1777, 230, Sept. 25, 1777, 235, Oct. 2, 1777, 238, Oct. 12, 1777, 242, Oct. 30, 1777, 249, Nov. 25, 1777, 259, Dec. 8, 9, 1777, 262, and Dec. 31, 1777, 271. On November 3, 1777, Elizabeth noted her nephew's absence, suggesting that his presence had become a regular thing; see ibid., I, 250. For Henry's age, see Godbeer, *World of Trouble*, 378. Major James Cramond was twenty-six years old at his death in 1781, making him twenty-two or twenty-three when he quartered in the Drinkers' house; see Ira D. Gruber, ed., *John Peebles' American War: The Diary of a Scottish Grenadier* (Mechanicsburg, Pa., 1998), Aug. 30, 1781, 469.

3. For household and identity, see Richard L. Bushman, *The Refinement of America: Persons, Houses, Cities* (New York, 1992), 100–138, 238–279; Lisa Wilson, *Ye Heart of a Man: The Domestic Life of Men in Colonial New England* (New Haven, Conn., 1999); Naomi Tadmor, *Family and Friends in Eighteenth-Century England: Household, Kinship, and Patronage* (Cambridge, 2001); Susan M. Stabile, *Memory's Daughters: The Material Culture of Remembrance in Eighteenth-Century America* (Ithaca, N.Y., 2004); Bernard L. Herman, *Town House: Architecture and Material Life in the Early American City, 1780–1830* (Williamsburg, Va., and Chapel Hill, N.C., 2005); Amanda Vickery, *Behind Closed Doors: At Home in Georgian England* (New Haven, Conn., 2009); Karen Harvey, *The Little Republic: Masculinity and Domestic Authority in Eighteenth-Century Britain* (Oxford, 2012), 134–168; and Onni Gust, *Unhomely Empire: Whiteness and Belonging, c. 1760–1830* (London, 2021).

4. For the gendered nature of the eighteenth-century household, see Stephanie McCurry, *Masters of Small Worlds: Yeoman Households, Gender Relations, and the Political Culture of the Antebellum South Carolina Low Country* (New York, 1995); Mary Beth Norton, *Founding Mothers and Fathers: Gendered Power and the Forming of American Society* (New York, 1996); Robert Olwell, *Masters, Slaves, and Subjects: The Culture of Power in the South Carolina Low Country, 1740–1790* (Ithaca, N.Y., 1998), 181–219; Joanne Bailey, "Favoured or Oppressed? Married Women, Property, and 'Coverture' in England, 1660–1800," *Continuity and Change*, XVII (2002), 351–372; Wilson, *Ye Heart of a Man;* Carole Shammas, *A History of Household Government in America* (Charlottesville, Va., 2002), 24–82; Holly Brewer, "The Transformation of Domestic Law," in Michael Grossberg and Christopher Tomlins, eds., *The Cambridge History of Law in America*, I (Cambridge, 2008), 288–323; Vickery, *Behind Closed Doors;* Lorri Glover, *Founders as Fathers: The Private Lives and Politics of the American Revolutionaries* (New Haven, Conn., 2014); and Harvey, *Little Republic*. For white women's domestic power, see Thavolia Glymph, *Out of the House of Bondage: The Transformation of the Plantation Household* (Cambridge, 2008); Laurel Clark Shire, *The Threshold of Manifest Destiny: Gender and National Expansion in Florida* (Philadelphia, 2016); Stephanie E. Jones-Rogers, *They Were Her Property: White Women as Slave Owners in the American South* (New Haven, Conn., 2019); and Jacqueline Beatty, *In Dependence: Women and the Patriarchal State in Revolutionary America* (New York, 2023).

5. There are few studies of quartering during the American Revolution. John Gilbert McCurdy's *Quarters: The Accommodation of the British Army and the Coming of the American Revolution* (Ithaca, N.Y., 2019) is the most comprehensive examination, but it centers on the prewar years. Most scholarly attention to military-civilian relationships during the Revolution has focused on issues of governance and allegiance, paying minimal attention to the housing of troops and even less to lived, domestic experience. For discussions of quartering, see Ruma Chopra, *Unnatural Rebellion: Loyalists in New York City during the Revolution* (Charlottesville, Va., 2011), 152–158; John D. Roche, "'[America] May Be Conquered with More Ease than Governed': The Evolution of British Occupation Policy during the American Revolution" (Ph.D. diss., University of North Carolina, 2015), 212–218, 229–231; Aaron Sullivan, *The Disaffected: Britain's Occupation of Philadelphia during the American Revolution* (Philadelphia, 2019), 131, 144–146, 165–168; and Donald F. Johnson, *Occupied America: British Military Rule and the Experience of Revolution* (Philadelphia, 2020), 31, 35, 62, 76, 91, 123, 128–130. For the gendered dynamics of occupation, see ibid., 90–96, 100–106; and McCurdy, *Quarters*, esp. 10–49. Women appear in these works in relation to allegiance, but scholarship on gender and quartering remains sparse; see Mary Beth Norton, *Liberty's Daughters: The Revolutionary Experience of American Women, 1750–1800* (Boston, 1980), 204–206; and Ami Pflugrad-Jackisch, "'What Am I but an American?': Mary Willing Byrd and Westover Plantation during the American Revolution," in Barbara B. Oberg, ed., *Women in the American Revolution: Gender, Politics, and the Domestic World* (Charlottesville, Va., 2019), 171–191. Although she does not focus on quartering specifically, Serena Zabin discusses the gendered, domestic impact of the British Army's tenure in prerevolutionary Boston; see Zabin, *The Boston Massacre: A Family History* (Boston, 2020), esp. 49–108. Judith L. Van Buskirk and Travis Glasson have also considered the intimate nature of civilian-military relationships, but quartering is not their primary focus; see Van Buskirk, *Generous Enemies: Patriots and Loyalists in Revolutionary New York* (Philadelphia, 2002); and Glasson, "The Intimacies of Occupation: Loyalties, Compromise, and Betrayal in Revolutionary-Era Newport," in Patrick Spero and Michael Zuckerman, eds., *The American Revolution Reborn* (Philadelphia, 2016), 29–47. For the Continental army, see Steven Elliott, "Neighbors, Land Ladies, and Consorts: New Jersey Women in the Midst of the Continental Army," in Holly A. Mayer, ed., *Women Waging War in the American Revolution* (Charlottesville, Va., 2022), 98–113.

6. Indeed, as Barry Levy has argued, Quaker family life was the model for what came to be understood as "American domesticity" in the 1780s; see Levy, *Quakers and the American Family: British Settlement in the Delaware Valley* (New York, 1988), 191 (quotation), 262–267. See also Emma Jones Lapsansky and Anne A. Verplanck, eds., *Quaker Aesthetics: Reflections on a Quaker Ethic in American Design and Consumption* (Philadelphia, 2003), esp. Bernard L. Herman, "Eighteenth-Century Quaker Houses in the Delaware Valley and the Aesthetics of Practice," ibid., 188–211.

7. The most comprehensive study of the Drinkers' wartime experiences is Godbeer, *World of Trouble*. For more on female heads of household, see Lois Green Carr and Lorena S. Walsh, "The Planter's Wife: The Experience of White Women in Seventeenth-Century Maryland," *WMQ*, 3d Ser., XXXIV (1977), 542–571; Laurel Thatcher Ulrich, *Good Wives: Image and Reality in the Lives of Women in Northern New England, 1650–1750* (New York, 1980), 35–50; Cara Anzilotti, "Autonomy and the Female Planter in Colonial South Carolina," *Journal of Southern History*, LXIII (1997), 239–268; Karin Wulf, *Not All Wives: Women of Colonial Philadelphia*

(Ithaca, N.Y., 2000), 11–20, 85–118; Inge Dornan, “Masterful Women: Colonial Women Slaveholders in the Urban Low Country,” in “British Association for American Studies 50th Anniversary,” special issue, *Journal of American Studies,* XXXIX (2005), 383–402; Kathleen Fawver, “Gender and the Structure of Planter Households in the Eighteenth-Century Chesapeake: Harford County, Maryland, in 1776,” *EAS,* IV (2006), 442–470; Pflugrad-Jackisch, “‘What Am I but an American?’” in Oberg, ed., *Women in the American Revolution,* 171–191; and Lorri Glover, *Eliza Lucas Pinckney: An Independent Woman in the Age of Revolution* (New Haven, Conn., 2020).

8. For how gendered analysis exposes complicated personal relationships with occupying forces, see Zabin, *Boston Massacre.* For coverture and dependency, see Marylynn Salmon, “Equality or Submersion? Feme Covert Status in Early Pennsylvania,” in Carol Ruth Berkin and Mary Beth Norton, eds., *Women of America: A History* (Boston, 1979), 92–113; Linda K. Kerber, “The Meanings of Citizenship,” *JAH,* LXXXIV (1997), 838–841; Rosemarie Zagarri, “The Rights of Man and Woman in Post-Revolutionary America,” *WMQ,* 3d Ser., LV (1998), 203–230; Brewer, “Transformation of Domestic Law,” in Grossberg and Tomlins, eds., *Cambridge History of Law in America,* I, 288–323; and Laura F. Edwards’s contribution to the forum, “Women at the Center,” *JER* (forthcoming). For British martial masculinity, see Robert Shoemaker, “Male Honour and the Decline of Public Violence in Eighteenth-Century London,” *Social History,* XXVI (2001), 190–208; Barbara Taylor, “Feminists versus Gallants: Manners and Morals in Enlightenment Britain,” *Representations,* LXXXVII, no. 1 (Summer 2004), 125–148; Michèle Cohen, “‘Manners’ Make the Man: Politeness, Chivalry, and the Construction of Masculinity, 1750–1830,” *Journal of British Studies,* XLIV (2005), 312–329; Stephen Conway, “The British Army, ‘Military Europe,’ and the American War of Independence,” *WMQ,* 3d Ser., LXVII (2010), 89–94; Emily Merrill, “Judging Empire: Masculinity and the Making of the British Imperial Army, 1754–1783” (Ph.D. diss., University of Pennsylvania, 2015); and Van Buskirk, *Generous Enemies,* 74–76.

9. For gender, courtship, and material life, see Kathleen M. Brown, *Good Wives, Nasty Wenches, and Anxious Patriarchs: Gender, Race, and Power in Colonial Virginia* (Williamsburg, Va., and Chapel Hill, N.C., 1996), 247–282. For more on courtship, see Nicole Eustace, “‘The Cornerstone of a Copious Work’: Love and Power in Eighteenth-Century Courtship,” *Journal of Social History,* XXXIV (2001), 517–546; Ruth H. Bloch, *Gender and Morality in Anglo-American Culture, 1650–1800* (Berkeley, Calif., 2003), 78–101; and Mary Kelley, “‘While Pen, Ink, and Paper Can Be Had’: Reading and Writing in a Time of Revolution,” *EAS,* X (2012), 439–466.

10. For quartering before the Revolution and its importance, see McCurdy, *Quarters,* 165–200; and John Shy, *Toward Lexington: The Role of the British Army in the Coming of the American Revolution* (Princeton, N.J., 1965), 250–258.

11. *The Diary of Frederick Mackenzie Giving a Daily Narrative of His Military Service as an Officer of the Regiment of Royal Welch Fusiliers during the Years, 1775–1781, in Massachusetts, Rhode Island, and New York,* 2 vols. (Cambridge, Mass., 1930), II, Nov. 21, 1778, 423 (quotation). Although the 1689 Mutiny Act prohibited forced quartering in Great Britain, these protections did not extend to the colonies. In colonial North America, quartering was common—and contested by colonial legislatures—however, it was not formalized until the 1765 Quartering Act. For more on the laws and history of quartering in North America, see Tom W. Bell, “The Third Amendment: Forgotten but Not Gone,” *William and Mary Bill*

of Rights Journal, II (1993), 124–126. For the 1765 Mutiny Act, see Great Britain, Parliament, "Quartering Act," May 15, 1765, *The Avalon Project: Documents in Law, History, and Diplomacy*, Yale Law School, 2008, https://avalon.law.yale.edu/18th_century/quartering_act_165.asp; McCurdy, *Quarters*, 92–100, 205; and Shy, *Toward Lexington*, 163–191, 250–258. For the 1774 Quartering Act, see Great Britain, Parliament, "Quartering Act," June 2, 1774, *The Avalon Project: Documents in Law, History, and Diplomacy*, Yale Law School, https://avalon.law.yale.edu/18th_century/quartering_act_1774.asp; McCurdy, *Quarters*, 92–100; and Shy, *Toward Lexington*, 163–191, 250–258. For billeting in private homes, see Andrew Mackillop, "Confrontation, Negotiation, and Accommodation: Garrisoning the Burghs in Post-Union Scotland," *Journal of Early Modern History*, XV (2011), 159–183; Roche, "'[America] May Be Conquered,'" 133; and McCurdy, *Quarters*, 70–77, 82–88, 93–103, 127–164, 214. For officers' implementation of quartering laws, see McCurdy, *Quarters*, 98–100, 220–221; and Roche, "'[America] May Be Conquered,'" 133–134.

12. James Pattison to Captain O'Reilly, Sept. 9, 1779, in "Pattison Letters," 263–264 (quotation). For the evolution and replication of British occupation policy, see Roche, "'[America] May Be Conquered,'" 168–184, 223–236.

13. Bernard A. Uhlendorf, ed. and trans., *Revolution in America: Confidential Letters and Journals, 1776–1784, of Adjutant General Major Baurmeister of the Hessian Forces* (New Brunswick, N.J., 1957), Dec. 16, 1777, 140 ("With so little"); Edward H. Tatum., Jr., ed., *The American Journal of Ambrose Serle, Secretary to Lord Howe, 1776–1778* (San Marino, Calif., 1940), Sept. 19, 1776, 109 ("G.R."); Loftus Cliffe to Bartholemew Cliffe, Feb. 17, 1778, Loftus Cliffe Papers, 1769–1784, WCL ("very good"). For troop numbers, see Johnson, *Occupied America*, 35, 44; and Roche, "'[America] May be Conquered,'" 213–214. For property surveys, see Crane, ed., *Diary of Elizabeth Drinker*, I, Sept. 29, 1777, 237; John W. Jackson, *With the British Army in Philadelphia, 1777–1778* (San Rafael, Calif., 1979), 20–21; [Fleet Greene], "Newport in the Hands of the British: A Diary of the Revolution . . . ," *Historical Magazine . . .*, IV (1860), Jan. 3, 1778, 36, Oct. 1, 1779, 173; and Gruber, ed., *John Peebles' American War*, Nov. 8, 1778, 230. For quarters and storage, see Abigail Adams to John Adams, Sept. 20, 1776, FO, https://founders.archives.gov/documents/Adams/04-02-02-0084. For "G. R.," see also Roche, "'[America] May Be Conquered,'" 215. Although enlisted men could not challenge the barrack master's decisions, officers could appeal to change their quarters; see Gruber, ed., *John Peebles' American War*, Dec. 31, 1777, 157, Nov. 12, 1778, 231, and Nov. 16, 1778, 232.

14. Franklin Bowditch Dexter, ed., *Literary Diary of Ezra Stiles*, II (New York, 1901), Dec. 14, 1776, 97 ("pointing out"); Crane, ed., *Diary of Elizabeth Drinker*, I, Dec. 19, 1777, 266 ("have taken up"). See also Sir Archibald Campbell Revolutionary War letter, Jan. 9, 1779, GHS. For loyalists, see Gruber, ed., *John Peebles' American War*, Nov. 8, 1778, 230; Tatum, ed., *American Journal of Ambrose Serle*, Sept. 19, 1776, 109; Stephen Payne Adye [on behalf of James Pattison] to Joseph Page, Dec. 30, 1779, in "Pattison Letters," 330; and Abigail Adams to John Adams, July 25, 1775, FO, https://founders.archives.gov/documents/Adams/04-01-02-0169. Mistakes happened, however. By late December 1776, the army had confiscated many loyalist homes "upon very vague information that they were the property of Rebels," prompting commanding officers to stipulate that property seizures in Newport required "full proof of the owner's delinquency"; see General Orders, Rhode Island, Dec. 23, 1776, WO 36/2, TNA.

15. James Pattison to Lord Viscount Townshend, Jan. 22, 1778, James Pattison Papers, 1777–1781, film 47, DLAR (quotation), Royal Artillery, Brigade Orders, Feb. 7, 1778. See also

James Pattison to Lord Amherst, Jan. 23, 1778, ibid., and James Pattison to Brigadier Genl. Cleaveland, Jan. 22, 1778. For public buildings, see Molly Pemberton to Israel Pemberton, Feb. 2, 1778, Pemberton Family Papers, 1641–1880, XXXI, 101, HSP; and Diary of Robert Morton, Dec. 8, 1777, ISM. For vacant houses, see Gruber, ed., *John Peebles' American War,* Dec. 17, 1776, 72, Dec. 21, 1776, 73, Mar. 26, 1777, 106; Johann Conrad Döhla, *A Hessian Diary of the American Revolution,* ed. and trans. Bruce E. Burgoyne (Norman, Okla., 1990), Nov. 28, 1778, 91; and Walter K. Schroder, *The Hessian Occupation of Newport and Rhode Island, 1776–1779* (Westminster, Md., 2005), 5. Vacant houses were still cramped; for instance, the entire battalion of the Forty-Second Grenadiers lodged in a single Newport house, while Charleston loyalist Elizabeth Thompson "had 38 Hessians in her House for nine Months"; see Gruber, ed., *John Peebles' American War,* Dec. 21, 1776, 73; and Memorial of Elizabeth Thompson, AO 12/46, TNA. For other accommodations, see John Andrews to William Barrell, Sept. 25, 1774, Andrews-Eliot Correspondence, 1715–1814, box 1, 45a, 45b, MHS, Andrews to Barrell, Nov. 11, 1774, 47; Sarah Logan Fisher Diary, IV, Sept. 26, 1777, [39], Sarah Logan Fisher Diaries, HSP, in The Revolutionary City: A Portal to the Nation's Founding, https://therevolutionarycity.org/islandora/fisher-sarah-logan-diary-volume-4; and Gruber, ed., *John Peebles' American War,* Nov. 8, 1778, 230, Nov. 10, 1778, 231, Nov. 12, 1778, 231, Nov. 16, 1778, 232, Nov. 28, 1778, 234, Aug. 18, 1780, 401, and Oct. 16, 1780, 413. For free civilian labor, see G. D. Scull, ed., "Journal of Captain John Montrésor, July 1, 1777, to July 1, 1778, . . . (Continued . . .)," *PMHB,* VI (1882), Sept. 27, 1777, 43, Oct. 2, 1777, 44, Oct. 3, 1777, 45, Oct. 13, 1777, 48, Oct. 17, 1777, 50, Oct. 21, 1777, 52; *Diary of Frederick Mackenzie,* I, Sept. 13, 1777, 177, Sept. 15, 1777, 178; and [Greene], "Newport in the Hands of the British," *Historical Magazine,* IV (1860), Oct. 17, 1777, 34. For enslaved laborers, see BOP, Aug. 11, Sept. 8, and Nov. 7, 1780, reel 520, and Apr. 18, 1782, reel 525; "Diary of Captain Johann Hinrichs," December 1779–June 25, 1780, in Bernhard A. Uhlendorf, ed. and trans., *The Siege of Charleston with an Account of the Province of South Carolina: Diaries and Letters of Hessian Officers from the Von Jungkenn Papers in the William L. Clements Library* (Ann Arbor, Mich., 1938), May 21, 1780, 301; Johann Ewald, *Diary of the American War: A Hessian Journal,* ed. and trans. Joseph P. Tustin (New Haven, Conn., 1979), Mar. 4, 1780, 203–204; and Sylvia R. Frey, *Water from the Rock: Black Resistance in a Revolutionary Age* (Princeton, N.J., 1991), 121–125. For the Philadelphia State House, see Deborah Norris Logan to [Alexander] Garden, Sept. 26, 1822, John F. Watson Historical Collection, box 4, HSP; and Tatum, ed., *American Journal of Ambrose Serle,* Nov. 24, 1777, 265.

16. Gruber, ed., *John Peebles' American War,* Dec. 17, 1776, 72 ("billited"), Apr. 1, 1777, 107 ("old fellow"), Sept. 1, 1779, 290 ("Big wigs"). For officers' regimental quarters, see ibid., Dec. 31, 1777, 157, Nov. 12, 1778, 231, Nov. 18, 1778, 232, June 20, 1780, 389, and Sept. 29, 1780, 410; for officers' retinues, see ibid., Nov. 18, 1778, 232, and Nov. 5, 1779, 304; see also John Rees, "War as a Waiter: Soldier Servants," *Journal of the American Revolution* (Apr. 28, 2015), https://allthingsliberty.com/2015/04/war-as-a-waiter-soldier-servants/. For officers' wives and children, see George Inman, "George Inman's Narrative of the American Revolution," *PMHB,* VII (1883), 242–245; and Zabin, *Boston Massacre,* 49–108. For examples of high-ranking officers' prime quarters, see John F. Watson, *Annals of Philadelphia . . .* (Philadelphia, 1830), 687.

17. Tatum, ed., *American Journal of Ambrose Serle,* Aug. 7, 1776, 56 ("'Tis a hard"); Ewald, *Diary of the American War,* ed. and trans. Tustin, May 18, 1780, 240 ("beautiful," "extremely"); Loftus Cliffe to Bartholemew Cliffe, Feb. 17, 1778, Loftus Cliffe Papers ("Gentlemen," "Mess"), Loftus Cliffe to Bartholemew Cliffe, Jan. 20, 1778 ("I am myself," "having absolute

Rule"). Such arrangements were common; see Gruber, ed., *John Peebles' American War,* Sept. 11, 1780, 406, June 18, 1781, 453. For more on the importance of messmates and male friendship during the American Revolution, see Rachel Alixandra Engl, "America's First Band of Brothers: Friendship and Camaraderie within the Continental Army during the Revolutionary Era" (Ph.D. diss., Lehigh University, 2019). Officers frequently lodged in the households of the urban elite. In Charleston, for instance, the Motte house (or the Miles Brewton House, as it is now called) served as British headquarters throughout the occupation. It was, according to New Englander Josiah Quincy, Jr., "a most superb house." Pronouncing it "the grandest hall I ever beheld," he went on to describe its furnishings: "azure blue satin window curtains, rich blue paper with gilt, mashee borders, most elegant pictures, excessive grand and costly looking glasses"; see "Journal of Josiah Quincy, Junior, 1773," *PMHS,* XLIX (Boston, 1916), Mar. 7, 1773, 444–445.

18. For distribution of quarters, see Gruber, ed., *John Peebles' American War,* Nov. 10, 1778, 231, Nov. 5, 1779, 304, and Sept. 29, 1780, 410. For repeat billets, see ibid., Nov. 4, 1778, 230, Nov. 5, 1779, 304, Nov. 18, 1781, 494–495, and Nov. 19, 1781, 495. For posting names to the door, see Loftus Cliffe to Bartholemew Cliffe, Feb. 17, 1778, Loftus Cliffe Papers. For the barrack master's list and regulations, see General Orders of W[illia]m Howe, Dec. 14, 1777, 218–219, Jan. 2, 1778, 247, Ser. G, film 695, reel 2, Montrésor Family Papers, 1775–1800, DLAR; John McMahon, "Regulations for the Billet-Office at Charlestown," *South-Carolina and American General Gazette* (Charlest[o]n, S.C.), Dec. 13, 1780, [3]; John McMahon, "Regulations for the Billet-Office, at Charlestown," *Royal Gazette* (Charleston, S.C.), Jan. 16–19, 1782, [1], and McMahon, "The Inhabitants Are Hereby Informed," Mar. 20–23, 1782, [1].

19. Deborah Logan in John F. Watson, *Annals of Philadelphia,* II, 402, M.S. in Historical Society of Pennsylvania, quoted in Darlene Emmert Fisher, "Social Life in Philadelphia during the British Occupation," *Pennsylvania History: A Journal of Mid-Atlantic Studies,* XXXVII (1970), 239 ("as intent"); General Orders of W[illia]m Howe, Jan. 2, 1778, 247, Ser. G, film 695, reel 2, Montrésor Family Papers ("against Officers"). For orders, see General Orders of W[illia]m Howe, Dec. 14, 1777, 218–219, ibid. Howe also issued a similar order on Nov. 2, 1777; see Orderly Book, Oct. 26–Dec. 17, 1777, Kept by Serj. Major Richards, Orders, Returns, Morning Reports, and Accounts of British Troops, 1776–1781, film 9, DLAR. For examples of competition, see Loftus Cliffe to Bartholemew Cliffe, Feb. 17, 1778, Loftus Cliffe Papers; Gruber, ed., *John Peebles' American War,* Nov. 18, 19, 1781, 495; and "XII: From a Hessian in Rhode Island to His Brother," June 24, 1777, in Ray W. Pettengill, ed., *Letters from America, 1776–1779 . . .* (1924; rpt. [Port Washington, N.Y.], 1964), 168. For conditions in barracks, see Sylvia Frey, *The British Soldier in America: A Social History of Military Life in the Revolutionary Period* (Austin, Tex., 1981), 39. For officers' quarters, see ibid., 135. For violence, see Crane, ed., *Diary of Elizabeth Drinker,* I, Dec. 15, 1777, 265, Dec. 18, 1777, 266, and Dec. 19, 1777, 267.

20. For provisions, see Frey, *British Soldier,* 54; and McCurdy, *Quarters,* 188. For rent, see Nisbet Balfour to Henry Clinton, May 5, 1781, Guy Carleton Papers, PRO 30/55/29, 3492, TNA; and Johnson, *Occupied America,* 129. For theft, see GCM of Lieutenant Charles Dalrymple, Newport, R.I., Sept. 2, 1778, WO 71/87, TNA. For more on theft and crime in occupied regions, see Frey, *British Soldier,* 71–93.

21. For fear, see "Sketch of the Life of Elizabeth Henley [Gabeau]," 1838, SCL. For resignation, see Crane, ed., *Diary of Elizabeth Drinker,* I, Dec. 19, 1777, 266; and Elizabeth Drinker to Henry Drinker, Feb. 26, 1778, Henry and Elizabeth Drinker Letters, 1777–1778 (hereafter

Drinker Letters), HCQSC. For repeat billets, see Gruber, ed., *John Peebles' American War,* Nov. 4, 1778, 230, Nov. 5, 1779, 304, Nov. 18, 1781, 494–495, and Nov. 19, 1781, 495.

22. Elizabeth Inman to [Ralph Inman], Apr. 22, 1775, James Murray Robbins Family Papers, 1638–1899, box 2, MHS.

23. Crane, ed., *Diary of Elizabeth Drinker,* I, Dec. 19, 1777, 266 (quotation); Memorial of Joseph Galloway, AO 12/38, 28, TNA; Henry Barry, Permit to William Cornell to Carry a Gun, Feb. 5, 1779, The Sol Feinstone Collection of the American Revolution, reel 1, 078, DLAR. For an example of a soldier defending the house, see "XII: From a Hessian in Rhode Island," June 24, 1777, in Pettengill, ed., *Letters from America,* 168.

24. Unknown to Elizabeth Murray [Robbins], [Nov. 28, 1779], James Murray Robbins Family Papers, box 3 ("sent immediately"); Elizabeth Drinker to Henry Drinker, Feb. 26, 1778, Drinker Letters ("promised"); Crane, ed., *Diary of Elizabeth Drinker,* I, Nov. 13, 1777, 253. When vandals began "taring down the Shed etc." for fuel, Janny Maxel alerted the Drinkers in time for Mary Sandwith to intervene; Sandwith halted the destruction by negotiating a compromise: the men could tear down "the large Gate" in exchange for leaving the house untouched (ibid., I, Dec. 23, 1777, 269, quotations). See also ibid., I, Dec. 25, 1777, 270. For other examples of soldiers' wives and quartering, see Johnson, *Occupied America,* 129–130.

25. Nathanael Greene to Mr. Wallace, July 5, 1779, Sol Feinstone Collection, reel 4, 1888 ("made it a rule"); Nisbet Balfour to Henry Clinton, May 5, 1781, Guy Carleton Papers, PRO 30/55/29, 3492 ("thought it necessary"). Balfour summarized and relayed Cornwallis's position. Finding these practices at odds with revolutionary rhetoric, the Continental army increasingly avoided housing troops near large population centers as the war progressed, preferring instead to utilize existing barracks and public buildings; see Bell, "Third Amendment," *William and Mary Bill of Rights Journal,* II (1993), 127. Billeting regulations requiring compensation, however, were not always adhered to; see Johnson, *Occupied America,* 129.

26. Eliza Lucas Pinckney to Thomas Pinckney, Dec. 6, 1780, *ELP and HPH Digital Papers* ("scheme," "subsist"); Gruber, ed., *John Peebles' American War,* Dec. 19, 1776, 73, Dec. 30, 1776, 75 ("old lady"), Jan. 22, 1777, 82 ("Tho I over paid her"). Pinckney's strategy was not unprecedented; see Ellen Hartigan-O'Connor, *The Ties That Buy: Women and Commerce in Revolutionary America* (Philadelphia, 2009), 25–29. For officers' allowance, see Questions Regarding Lodging [in New York], [December 1777], Guy Carleton Papers, PRO 30/55/7, 799. For renting to the army, see Mabel L. Webber, [ed.], "Josiah Smith's Diary, 1780–1781 (Continued)," *SCHGM,* XXXIII (1932), Feb. 20, 1780, 106; and "A Few Gentlemen Who Can Furnish Their Own Bedding," *South-Carolina and American General Gazette,* Feb. 7, 1781, [1]. For examples of currency depreciation, see Tables of depreciation of South Carolina and Continental currency (1770–1780), George Chalmers Collection, 1606–1817, MssCol 507, Papers Relating to Carolina, box 2, Manuscripts and Archives Division, NYPL. For Wheatley house, see Owners and Occupants of Houses in Newport during the Revolution, box 123, folder 22, NHS. The 1774 Newport census lists a Mary Wheatley who lived with a Black servant. Given that Newport was a center of the Atlantic slave trade, it is likely that he or she was enslaved; see John R. Bartlett, *Census of the Inhabitants of the Colony of Rhode Island and Providence Plantations* (Providence, R.I., 1858), 35; and George Champlin Mason, *Annals of Trinity Church, Newport, Rhode Island. 1698–1821* (Newport, R.I., 1890), 224. For the slave trade in Rhode Island, see Christy Clark-Pujara, *Dark Work: The Business of Slavery in Rhode Island* (New York, 2016).

27. Richard Bache to Benjamin Franklin, July 14, 1778, *The Papers of Benjamin Franklin; Sponsored by the American Philosophical Society and Yale University; Digital Edition by The Packard Humanities Institute,* XXVII ("rapacious," "electric"), https://franklinpapers.org/framedVolumes.jsp; James Lovell to Abigail Adams, July 3, 1778, FO, https://founders.archives.gov/documents/Adams/04-03-02-0047 ("Nothing"), Abigail Adams to John Adams, July 25, 1775 ("raw meat"). "How much better do the Tories fare than the Whigs?" Abigail Adams mused, as she relayed the incident of the raw meat being chopped on the Mahogany table to her husband. "Suppose this worthy good Man was put in with all confidence that nothing should be hurt" (ibid.). For other examples of damages to loyalist property from quartering, see Memorial of Benjamin Wickham, AO 13/80, TNA, Memorial of Major John Forrester, AO 13/59, and Memorial of Elizabeth Thompson, AO 12/46. For the Motte family, see [Sarah Butler] Wister and Agnes Irwin, eds., *Worthy Women of Our First Century* (Philadelphia, 1877), 265–266. For mistreatment of houses, see Abigail Adams to John Adams, Sept. 20, 1776, FO; and James Pattison to the Police, Aug. 4, 1779, in "Pattison Letters," 239. For André, see W. B. R., "Books Taken from Dr. Franklin's Library by Major André.—(From a Memorandum Left by Mrs. Deborah Logan)," in "Notes and Queries," *PMHB,* VIII (1884), 430. For a house returned in good condition, see Thomas Bee to Major Traille, Dec. 16, 1782, Guy Carleton Papers, PRO 30/55/57, 6424.

28. McMahon, "Regulations for the Billet-Office, at Charlestown," *Royal Gazette* (Charleston, S.C.), Jan. 16–19, 1782, [1] ("molest[ing]"), Archibald Lundie, "The Inhabitants of Charlestown Who Have Officers or Soldiers Quartered on Them," June 20–23, 1781, [1] ("not obliged"). For Black inhabitants, see Judith Van Buskirk, "Crossing the Lines: African-Americans in the New York City Region during the British Occupation, 1776–1783," in "Explorations in Early American Culture," eds. William Pencak and George W. Boudreau, special issue, *Pennsylvania History,* LXV (1998), 85–86; see also Johnson, *Occupied America,* 62.

29. Questions Regarding Lodging [in New York], [December 1777], Guy Carleton Papers, PRO 30/55/7, 799 ("settled"); Donald F. Johnson, "Ambiguous Allegiances: Urban Loyalties during the American Revolution," *JAH,* CIV (2017), 610–631 ("powerful," 621); John McMahon, "The Inhabitants Are Hereby Informed," *Royal Gazette* (Charleston, S.C.), Mar. 20–23, 1782, [1]. For unpaid rent, see BOP, July 25, 1780, and Sept. 19, 1780, reel 519. See also George Smith McCowen, *The British Occupation of Charleston, 1780–82* (Columbia, S.C., 1972), 13–42. For examples of petitions to officers, see Memorial of William Blake, Mar. 2, 1782, Guy Carleton Papers, PRO 30/55/36, 4177, Memorial of Eliza Elliot to [Alexander] Leslie, Oct. 11, 1782, PRO 30/55/51, 5487, and Eliza Elliot Petition, Nov. 29, 1782, PRO 30/55/55, 6277. For more on these "collaborator regimes," see Johnson, *Occupied America,* 55–79.

30. Josiah Smith to George Smith, Feb. 28, 1781, Josiah Smith Letter book, 1771–1784, M-3018, 427, SHC (quotation). An October 1777 census in occupied Philadelphia recorded that women accounted for 12,344 of the city's 21,767 inhabitants (57 percent); boys under age eighteen amounted to 4,941; and men between the ages of eighteen and sixty numbered 4,482; see Tatum, ed., *American Journal of Ambrose Serle,* 266n.

31. Ulrich, *Good Wives,* 35 (quotation). For urban economies and gender dynamics, see Wulf, *Not All Wives,* esp. 90–102; Serena R. Zabin, *Dangerous Economies: Status and Commerce in Imperial New York* (Philadelphia, 2009); Hartigan-O'Connor, *Ties That Buy;* Glover, *Eliza Lucas Pinckney;* and Sara T. Damiano, *To Her Credit: Women, Finance, and the Law in*

Eighteenth-Century New England Cities (Baltimore, Md., 2021). For rural areas, see Ulrich, *Good Wives*, 35–50; Laurel Thatcher Ulrich, *A Midwife's Tale: The Life of Martha Ballard, Based on Her Diary, 1785–1812* (New York, 1990); and Cara Anzilotti, *In the Affairs of the World: Women, Patriarchy, and Power in Colonial South Carolina* (Westport, Conn., 2002).

32. Abigail Adams to John Adams, Apr. 7, 1776, FO, https://founders.archives.gov/documents/Adams/04-01-02-0244 *("farmeress[es]")*; Lucy Flucker Knox to Henry Knox, June 3–5, 1777, in Phillip Hamilton, ed., *The Revolutionary War Lives and Letters of Lucy and Henry Knox* (Baltimore, Md., 2017), 106 ("wom[e]n of business"); Sarah Logan Fisher Diary, IV, Nov. 1, 1777, [21] ("I have to think"); Abigail Adams to John Adams, Dec. 10, 1775, FO, https://founders.archives.gov/documents/Adams/04-01-02-0221 ("In these perilous"). For women on the home front, see Norton, *Liberty's Daughters*, 155–227; Linda K. Kerber, *Women of the Republic: Intellect and Ideology in Revolutionary America* (Williamsburg, Va., and Chapel Hill, N.C., 1980), 35–113; Carol Berkin, *Revolutionary Mothers: Women in the Struggle for America's Independence* (New York, 2005); Holly A. Mayer, "Bearing Arms, Bearing Burdens: Women Warriors, Camp Followers, and Home-Front Heroines of the American Revolution," in Karen Hagemann, Gisela Mettele, and Jane Rendall, eds., *Gender, War, and Politics: Transatlantic Perspectives, 1775–1832* (Basingstoke, U.K., 2010), 169–187; Sara T. Damiano, "Writing Women's History through the Revolution: Family Finances, Letter Writing, and Conceptions of Marriage," in "Writing to and from the Revolution: A Joint Issue with the *Journal of the Early Republic*," special issue, *WMQ*, 3d Ser., LXXIV (2017), 697–728; and Oberg, ed., *Women in the American Revolution*. For women's economic activities, see Woody Holton, "Abigail Adams, Bond Speculator," *WMQ*, 3d Ser., LXIV (2007), 821–838; and Susan Brandt, "'Getting into a Little Business': Margaret Hill Morris and Women's Medical Entrepreneurship during the American Revolution," *EAS*, XIII (2015), 774–807. For women's reluctance to fulfill the role of deputy husband, see Narrative of Mrs. Abraham Brasher (Helen Kortright) Giving an Account of Her Experiences in the Revolutionary War, 1802, 24, 26, 34–35, VF Women, DLAR; Abigail Adams to Elizabeth Smith Shaw, March 1778, FO, https://founders.archives.gov/documents/Adams/04-02-02-0323; and Rosemarie Zagarri, *A Woman's Dilemma: Mercy Otis Warren and the American Revolution*, 2d ed. (Chichester, West Sussex, U.K., 2015), 105–114. For children's queries, see Abigail Adams to John Adams, May 27, 1776, FO, https://founders.archives.gov/documents/Adams/04-01-02-0269. For children playing near troops, see Margaret Hill Morris Diary, Dec. 16, 1776, HCQSC; and Watson, *Annals of Philadelphia*, 288. For disease, see Paul E. Kopperman, "The Medical Dimension in Cornwallis's Army, 1780–1781," *North Carolina Historical Review*, LXXXIX (2012), 367–398; and Elizabeth A. Fenn, *Pox Americana: The Great Smallpox Epidemic of 1775–82* (New York, 2001).

33. Benjamin Chew, Jr., and Elizabeth Oswald Chew to Benjamin Chew, Sr., Feb. 3, 1778, Chew Family Papers, 1659–1986, Ser. IIc, box 10, HSP ("daily distresses"); Narrative of Mrs. Abraham Brasher, 1802, 26 ("declaration"), 26–27 ("went to the apartment"), 33–34 ("felt as if God"); Abigail Adams to John Adams, July 12, 1775, FO, https://founders.archives.gov/documents/Adams/04-01-02-0161 ("I want you").

34. Elizabeth Drinker to Henry Drinker, Nov. 17, 1777, Drinker Letters ("women who are but half"), Elizabeth Drinker to Henry Drinker, Nov. 11, 1777 ("distress'd"); Abigail Adams to John Adams, Nov. 12, 1775, FO, https://founders.archives.gov/documents/Adams/04-01-02-0214 ("I have been like a nun"); Alisa Wade, "The 'Widowed State': Women's Labor,

Sacrifice, and Self-Sufficiency in the American Revolution," in Mayer, ed., *Women Waging War,* 245–265, esp. 251; Zagarri, *A Woman's Dilemma,* 78–95.

35. For propaganda denouncing Hessian, Indigenous, and Black British allies, see Robert G. Parkinson, *Thirteen Clocks: How Race United the Colonies and Made the Declaration of Independence* (Williamsburg, Va., and Chapel Hill, N.C., 2021), esp. 82–163.

36. For more on this gendered culture of sensibility, see G. J. Barker-Benfield, *The Culture of Sensibility: Sex and Society in Eighteenth-Century Britain* (Chicago, 1992); and Sarah Knott, *Sensibility and the American Revolution* (Williamsburg, Va., and Chapel Hill, N.C., 2009); see also Taylor, "Feminists versus Gallants," *Representations,* LXXXVII, no. 1 (Summer 2004), 125–148. For gender and occupation, coverture, and British martial masculinity, see note 8, above; for eighteenth-century courtship norms, see note 9, above.

37. For laws of war, see [Emer] de Vattel, *The Law of Nations; or, Principles of the Law of Nature: Applied to the Conduct and Affairs of Nations and Sovereigns,* II (London, 1759), 4, 51–54. Both during and after the war, women's petitions for relief also showcase the manipulation of this gendered language; see Mary Beth Norton, "Eighteenth-Century American Women in Peace and War: The Case of the Loyalists," *WMQ,* 3d Ser., XXXIII (1976), 386–409; Chopra, *Unnatural Rebellion,* 137–139, 182; Johnson, *Occupied America,* 149–150; Jacqueline Beatty, "Complicated Allegiances: Women, Politics, and Property in Post-Occupation Charleston," in Mayer, ed., *Women Waging War,* 227–244, and Todd W. Braisted, "In Reduced Circumstances: Loyalist Women and British Government Assistance, 1779–1783," 212–226. For more on the protections of dependence, see Beatty, *In Dependence.*

38. *Diary of Frederick Mackenzie,* I, Sept. 15, 1777, 178 ("assist[ing]"); Crane, ed., *Diary of Elizabeth Drinker,* I, Oct. 6, 1777, 240–241 ("I put him off," 241), Oct. 25, 1777, 248 ("Number," "be glad," "as I desir'd"), Dec. 19, 1777, 266–267 ("whose Husbands"). For the bed chair, see ibid., I, Oct. 5, 1777, 240 n.44.

39. Watson, *Annals of Philadelphia,* 683 (quotation). The reprieve did not last long, however, and the Norris family was soon required to take in officers of the artillery and two of Lord Howe's secretaries. For the Norris family, see John W. Jordan, *Colonial and Revolutionary Families of Pennsylvania . . . ,* I (Baltimore, Md., 2004), 89. For Mary Pemberton, see Watson, *Annals of Philadelphia,* 684; and Crane, ed., *Diary of Elizabeth Drinker,* I, Dec. 20, 1777, 267–268. The Continental army also quartered in Friends' meetinghouses; see Crane, ed., *Diary of Elizabeth Drinker,* I, July 16, 1776, 218 n.12. For the almshouse, see Diary of Robert Morton, Dec. 8, 1777; and Scull, ed., "Journal of Captain John Montrésor, July 1, 1777, to July 1, 1778, . . . (Continued . . .)," *PMHB,* VI (1882), Sept. 26, 1777, 41. For men's comparative difficulties negotiating with officers, see Diary of Robert Morton, Sept. 30, 1777; John Paul Grimké to J. Bluke, Apr. 27, 1782, John Paul Grimké Letters, 1779–1782, box 1, folder 1, Grimké Family Papers, SCHS, Grimké to Commandant of Charleston, May 3, 1782, Grimké to J. Allen, July 25, 1782, and Allen to Grimké, [1782].

40. For chivalry, see Cohen, "'Manners' Make the Man," *Journal of British Studies,* XLIV (2005), 319–322. Emily Merrill has analyzed these norms in the eighteenth-century British Army; see Merrill, "Judging Empire," esp. 117–118, 243–249. For more on the composition of the British officer corps, see Shy, *Toward Lexington,* 343–358.

41. Mary Lucia Bull Guerard to Susanna Stoll Garvey, 1779, in "A Woman's Letters in 1779 and 1782," North American Women's Letters and Diaries (database), 1.

42. Josiah Smith to Mrs. M. Hodsten, Aug. 5, 1780, Josiah Smith Letter book, M-3018, 397 (quotations). For the Gibbes family, see "Life Sketches of the Revolution," Reminiscences and Sketches, circa 1930? (34/717), 2, 9–10, SCHS. It was nevertheless a nerve-wracking experience that the family characterized as being "prisoners in their own home" (ibid., 10).

43. GCM of Alexander White, New York, May 22, 1780, WO 71/91, 434 ("as she was in distress"), 435 ("She would rather"), film 675, reel 13, DLAR.

44. Crane, ed., *Diary of Elizabeth Drinker,* I, Dec. 15, 1777, 265 (quotations), Dec. 18, 1777, 266.

45. For officers drawing lots for quarters, see Gruber, ed., *John Peebles' American War,* Nov. 10, 1778, 231, Nov. 5, 1779, 304, and Sept. 29, 1780, 410. For the Drinker house, see Fire Insurance Surveys, Henry Drinker, Nov. 6, 1770, Insurance Surveys S01454, S01455, S01456, S01457, The Philadelphia Contributionship Digital Archives, http://www.philadelphiabuildings.org/contributionship/. For Cramond's visits, see Crane, ed., *Diary of Elizabeth Drinker,* I, Dec. 18, 1777, 266, Dec. 19, 1777, 266–267, Dec. 20, 1777, 267–268, and Dec. 29, 1777, 271. For Drinker's earlier success avoiding quartering, see ibid., I, Oct. 6, 1777, 240–241, and Oct. 25, 1777, 248.

46. For deputy husbands, see Ulrich, *Good Wives,* 35–50. For Scots law, see David Armitage, "Making the Empire British: Scotland in the Atlantic World, 1542–1707," *Past and Present,* no. 155 (May 1997), 62. For Scottish quartering practices, see Mackillop, "Confrontation, Negotiation, and Accommodation," *Journal of Early Modern History,* XV (2011), 169. For Scottish women, see Rebecca Mason, "Women, Marital Status, and Law: The Marital Spectrum in Seventeenth-Century Glasgow," in "Women Negotiating the Boundaries of Justice in Britain, 1300–1700," special issue, *Journal of British Studies,* LVIII (2019), 788–794, 800–801, 804. For more on Scots soldiers in the British Army, see Shy, *Toward Lexington,* 352–354; Stephen Conway, "Scots, Britons, and Europeans: Scottish Military Service, c.1739–1783," *Historical Research,* LXXXII (2009), 114–130; Andrew Mackillop, *'More Fruitful Than the Soil': Army, Empire, and the Scottish Highlands, 1715–1815* (East Lothian, Scotland, 2000); and Matthew P. Dziennik, *The Fatal Land: War, Empire, and the Highland Soldier in British America* (New Haven, Conn., 2015). I am grateful for Andrew Mackillop for his insights into Scottish law, quartering, and military practice and for alerting me to the distinctive Scottish legalities that influenced quartering practices.

47. Crane, ed., *Diary of Elizabeth Drinker,* I, Dec. 18, 1777, 266 ("plead off" "a necessary protiction," "to have [a soldier]"), Dec. 19, 1777, 266 ("I expect'd"). For examples of Henry (nephew) sleeping over, see ibid., I, Oct. 2, 1777, 238, Oct. 12, 1777, 242, Oct. 30, 1777, 249, Nov. 3, 1777, 250, Nov. 25, 1777, 259, Dec. 8, 9, 1777, 262, and Dec. 31, 1777, 271. For noises, see ibid., I, Dec. 14, 1777, 264, and Dec. 22, 1777, 269.

48. Crane, ed., *Diary of Elizabeth Drinker,* I, Dec. 19, 1777, 266 (quotations). For the Hessian officer, see ibid., I, Nov. 21, 1777, 256. For Cramond's affiliation, see Elizabeth Drinker to Henry Drinker, Feb. 26, 1778, Drinker Letters; *Diary of Frederick Mackenzie,* II, Aug. 30, 1781, 608; and Max von Eelking, *The German Allied Troops in the North American War of Independence, 1776–1783,* trans. and abr. J[oseph] G[eorge] Rosengarten (Albany, N.Y., 1893), 283.

49. Crane, ed., *Diary of Elizabeth Drinker,* I, Dec. 19, 1777, 266 (quotations). Although she did not mention it, Elizabeth's brief—but forced—experience quartering five Continental soldiers the previous January undoubtedly echoed through her mind; see ibid., I, Jan. 25, 1777, 222; see also ibid., I, 222 n.1.

50. Crane, ed., *Diary of Elizabeth Drinker,* I, Dec. 19, 1777, 266 ("I am straitend," "had their Doors," "had manag'd," "I may be troubld"), Dec. 29, 1777, 271 ("at last agreed"); Elizabeth Drinker to Henry Drinker, Feb. 26, 1778, Drinker Letters ("as our House"). See also Crane, ed., *Diary of Elizabeth Drinker,* I, Dec. 20, 1777, 267.

51. Uhlendorf, ed. and trans., *Revolution in America,* July 4, 1780, 350 ("booty"); "To Be Sold, the Smartest and Most Active Negro Boy in This Town," *New-York Gazette: and the Weekly Mercury,* Apr. 7, 1777, [3] ("smartest"). For Damon, see Crane, ed., *Diary of Elizabeth Drinker,* I, Dec. 30, 1777, 271, and Jan. 1, 1778, 272. For Drinker's omission of Damon, see Elizabeth Drinker to Henry Drinker, Feb. 26, 1778, Drinker Letters. For Henry's abolitionist leanings, see Godbeer, *World of Trouble,* 211–248. For Quaker attitudes toward slavery, see Gary B. Nash and Jean R. Soderlund, *Freedom by Degrees: Emancipation in Pennsylvania and Its Aftermath* (New York, 1991), 41–73, 78–98. For servants and orderlies, see Elizabeth Drinker to Henry Drinker, Feb. 26, 1778, Drinker Letters; and Crane, ed., *Diary of Elizabeth Drinker,* I, Jan. 1, 1778, 272. For livestock, see ibid., I, Dec. 30, 1777, 271. Drinker moved her cow to the washhouse shortly after her husband's exile, following a rash of thefts in neighborhood stables; indeed, she might have preferred that Cramond's livestock occupy the stable because it was an easier target; see ibid., I, Sept. 15, 1777, 230; and Elizabeth Drinker to Henry Drinker, Feb. 26, 1778, Drinker Letters.

52. Crane, ed., *Diary of Elizabeth Drinker,* I, Dec. 29, 1777, 271 (quotation), Dec. 30, 1777, 271, Dec. 31, 1777, 271. Drinker's nephew continued sleeping over for several days; see ibid., I, Jan. 1–3, 1778, 272. Prior to Cramond's arrival, the last time Henry slept in the house was Dec. 9, 1777 (ibid., I, 262).

53. Elizabeth Drinker to Henry Drinker, Feb. 26, 1778, Drinker Letters (quotations). Donald F. Johnson has speculated that Elizabeth might have been motivated by fear; see Johnson, *Occupied America,* 95–96. For more on Quaker women's domestic power, see Levy, *Quakers and the American Family.*

54. Friedrich von der Malsburg, quoted in Schroder, *Hessian Occupation of Newport,* 5 ("People"); Andrews to Barrell, Nov. 11, 1774, Andrews-Eliot Correspondence, box 1, 47 ("You must be sensible").

55. Crane, ed., *Diary of Elizabeth Drinker,* I, Dec. 31, 1777, 271, Jan. 1, 1778, 272, Jan. 5, 1778, 273, Feb. 25, 1778, 286, Mar. 2, 1778, 287 (quotation). For more on disease in military camps, see Kopperman, "Medical Dimension in Cornwallis's Army," *North Carolina Historical Review,* LXXXIX (2012), 367–398.

56. Crane, ed., *Diary of Elizabeth Drinker,* I, July 14, 1771, 162, Dec. 7, 1777, 262, Jan. 8, 1778, 274 (quotation). For Elizabeth's children's ages, see family tree ibid., I, lxxiv.

57. For Elizabeth's discomfort with surveillance, see Elizabeth Drinker to Henry Drinker, Feb. 2, 1778, Drinker Letters (quotations), and Elizabeth Drinker to Henry Drinker, Nov. 5, 1777. For Cramond's access to the house, see Elizabeth Drinker to Henry Drinker, Feb. 26, 1778, ibid. For Henry's desire to hear from the children, see his letters to Elizabeth on Nov. 18, 1777, Dec. 13, and Dec. 27, 1777, ibid. Nevertheless, Henry recognized the need for discretion; see Henry Drinker to Elizabeth Drinker, Jan. 30, 1778, ibid. Elizabeth offered excuses but never promised to make the children write; see her responses to Henry on Nov. 7, 1777, and Jan. 25, 1778, ibid. For Drinker house and noise, see Crane, ed., *Diary of Elizabeth Drinker,* I, Jan. 5, 1778, 273, Feb. 7, 1778, 282, and Nov. 24, 1793, 530. For ceilings, see Fire Insurance Surveys, Henry Drinker, Nov. 6, 1770, Insurance Surveys S01454, S01455, S01456, S01457, The

Philadelphia Contributionship Digital Archives. For Lydia Darragh, see Elizabeth F. Ellet, *The Women of the American Revolution,* I (New York, 1848), 171–177.

58. Elizabeth Drinker to Henry Drinker, Feb. 26, 1778, Drinker Letters (quotations). For an example of officers employing men's wives, see Gruber, ed., *John Peebles' American War,* Nov. 18, 1778, 232, Dec. 19, 1779, 316, 550 n.21.

59. Crane, ed., *Diary of Elizabeth Drinker,* I, Sept. 14, 1777, 230 ("two"), Nov. 8, 1777, 251–252 ("little," 252), Jan. 19, 1778, 276 ("bleu"), Feb. 2, 1794, 544 ("much warmer"). For Henry's office, see ibid., I, Sept. 2, 1777, 226, and Dec. 3, 1793, 532. For front parlor, see ibid., I, Sept. 14, 1777, 230, and Mar. 4, 1792, 476. Every winter, the Drinkers installed a stove in the back parlor, but it was still colder than the front rooms; see Crane, ed., *Diary of Elizabeth Drinker,* I, Nov. 8, 1777, 251–252, Dec. 1, 1778, 336, Nov. 17, 1780, 379, Nov. 15, 1782, 408; and Elizabeth Drinker to Henry Drinker, Nov. 17, 1777, Drinker Letters. As the weather became nicer, Cramond also used the Drinkers' summer house; see Crane, ed., *Diary of Elizabeth Drinker,* I, Mar. 20, 1778, 290. He also occasionally used the other parlor for entertaining; see Elizabeth Drinker to Henry Drinker, Feb. 26, 1778, Drinker Letters.

60. Elizabeth Drinker to Henry Drinker, Feb. 26, 1778, Drinker Letters ("There has not been," "knowing"), Elizabeth Drinker to Henry Drinker, Jan. 1, 1778 ("Our new Guest); Crane, ed., *Diary of Elizabeth Drinker,* I, Feb. 14, 1778, 283 ("I am out of all patience," "he stays out"), Feb. 17, 1778, 284 ("some hints"). Drinker often noted Cramond's hours in her diary. For remarks on his late hours, see ibid., I, Jan. 8, 1778, 274, Jan. 16, 1778, 275, Jan. 29, 1778, 279, Feb. 1, 1778, 280, Feb. 14, 1778, 283, and Feb. 17, 1778, 283–284. For remarks on his early hours, see ibid., I, Feb. 17, 1778, 284, and Mar. 19, 1778, 290.

61. Crane, ed., *Diary of Elizabeth Drinker,* I, Dec. 19, 1777, 267, Dec. 21, 1777, 268 (quotations). Mary Eddy's family's loyalist sympathies might have aided her cause: at least three of her adult sons were prominent loyalist merchants, including Charles, who was among the Quaker exiles. Later in the war, Charles and his brother Thomas relocated to British headquarters in New York; see Ruth Story Devereux Eddy, *The Eddy Family in America . . .* (Boston, 1930), 1186–1188; and Elaine Forman Crane, ed., *The Diary of Elizabeth Drinker: The Life Cycle of an Eighteenth-Century Woman* (Boston, 1994), 317.

62. Phebe Pemberton to Lord William Murray, Feb. 14, 1778, Pemberton Family Papers, XXXI, 122 ("behave[d] himself," "shewn," "several," "enter"), Lowther Pennington to Phebe Pemberton, [Feb. 16], 1778, 133 ("punctually," "settled"); *A List of the General and Staff Officers and of the Officers in the Several Regiments Serving in North-America . . .* (Philadelphia, 1778), 11, 29.

63. Lowther Pennington to Phebe Pemberton, [Feb. 16], 1778, Pemberton Family Papers, XXXI, 133.

64. Phebe Pemberton to Captain Mackenzie, Mar. 26, 1778, Pemberton Family Papers, XXXII, 3 ("House"), Phebe Pemberton to [James] Pattison, Mar. 26, 1778, 4 ("she shall ever," "as Soon is," "depended," "reserv[ing]").

65. Sarah Logan Fisher Diary, III, Sept. 22, 1777, [44–45], https://therevolutionarycity.org/islandora/fisher-sarah-logan-diary-volume-3, IV, Dec. 30, 1777, [32] (quotations); *A List of the General and Staff Officers and of the Officers,* 20. Having been forced to house Continental militiamen in January 1777 after the Pennsylvania Committee of Safety quartered them on inhabitants, particularly targeting Quakers and other "non-associators," Sarah Logan Fisher perhaps worried that Lieutenant Apthorpe, like the other soldiers, would be rude, unruly,

"and so intolerably dirty that even in the cleanest of their houses the stench of their dirt is great enough to cause an infectious sickness." Indeed, although she resented Lieutenant Apthorpe's presence, she was probably relieved to find that he was of a higher rank than the Continental militiamen she previously hosted; see Sarah Logan Fisher and Nicholas B. Wainwright, "'A Diary of Trifling Occurrences': Philadelphia, 1776–1778," *PMHB,* LXXXII (1958), Jan. 23, 1777, 425 ("non-associators"), 426 ("intolerably"). For examples of British officers stealing furniture, see Charles Marshall to Christopher Marshall, Jan. 19, 1778, in T. S., [ed.], "Correspondence of the Children of Christopher Marshall," *PMHB,* XVII (1893), 342; and Jacob E. Cooke, "Tench Coxe: Tory Merchant," *PMHB,* XCVI (1972), 83 n.175.

66. "XV: From Captain Hinrichs, on the Neck near Philadelphia," Jan. 18, 1778, in Pettengill, ed., *Letters from America,* 186 ("abominable," "twelve," "kills"); Gruber, ed., *John Peebles' American War,* Nov. 18, 1778, 232, Jan. 13, 1779, 243 ("Landlady," "some years ago"); Memorial of Jonathan Adams, AO 12/42, 186, TNA ("continually"). Early Americans were deeply interested in the rattlesnake's powers of fascination, which might be what the farmer alluded to here. Or, perhaps it was a political metaphor, as the rattlesnake became a symbol of the revolutionary cause; see Zachary McLeod Hutchins, "Rattlesnakes in the Garden: The Fascinating Serpents of the Early, Edenic Republic," *EAS,* IX (2011), 682–685, 697 n.56 and n.58, 699–700. For the Sackets, see Gruber, ed., *John Peebles' American War,* Nov. 18, 1778, 232; see also ibid., Feb. 17, 1778, 249; and Charles H. Weygant, *The Sacketts of America: Their Ancestors and Descendants, 1630–1907* (Newburgh, N.Y., 1907), 41, 43, 80–86, 90–93. Possibly Peebles referred to Hannah Sacket's mother, Deborah Alsop Simpkins Hazard, who lived with the family and according to Hannah had a "disorder [that] will not permit me to be long absent" (Hannah Sacket to Hannah Sacket, Apr. 23, 1777, ibid., 43). For more on Washington's spy ring, see John A. Nagy, *George Washington's Secret Spy War: The Making of America's First Spymaster* (New York, 2016), 397.

67. Alexander Garden, *Anecdotes of the Revolutionary War in America, with Sketches of Character of Persons the Most Distinguished, in the Southern States, for Civil and Military Services* (Charleston, S.C., 1822), 267 ("introduce[ed]"), 269 ("enemies"). In Long Island, Hanger repeatedly ignored the petitions of Jacobus Cropsey, who alleged that the major "rather insults than helps the oppressed." Elevating his claim to Sir Guy Carleton, Cropsey complained of the "wanton Destruction of his Property and great abuse of his Family" by the British legionnaires lodged in his barn and cellar and detailed their depredations, which included "cruelly and maliciously pulling up the Corn by the Root," stealing poultry, wounding two horses "with their Swords," and killing "his most valuable Horse" to feed their dogs; see Petition of Jacobus Cropsey, Aug. 7, 1782, Guy Carleton Papers, PRO 30/55/46, 5234.

68. Elizabeth Drinker to Henry Drinker, Feb. 26, 1778, Drinker Letters ("We have neither," "I believe"); Crane, ed., *Diary of Elizabeth Drinker,* I, Feb. 17, 1778, 284 ("our major," "they broke up"); Gruber, ed., *John Peebles' American War,* Feb. 17, 1778, 164 ("showy"), Aug. 30, 1781, 469 ("accomplish'd," "pride").

69. Sarah Logan Fisher Diary, V, Jan. 29, 1778, [3], https://therevolutionarycity.org/islandora/fisher-sarah-logan-diary-volume-5 (quotation); Jordan, *Colonial and Revolutionary Families of Pennsylvania,* I, 31–32. For army demographics, see Frey, *British Soldier,* 23; and Eric Robson, "Purchase and Promotion in the British Army in the Eighteenth Century," *History,* XXXVI (1951), 57–72. For honor, see Van Buskirk, *Generous Enemies,* 74–76; see also Merrill, "Judging Empire."

70. Crane, ed., *Diary of Elizabeth Drinker,* I, 152 ("came to live"), 153 ("came to work"), Dec. 31, 1777, 271 ("J. Cramond"), May 8, 10, 1784, 423 ("purchased"), May 28, 1792, 482 ("came to hire"). See also ibid., I, May 3, 1763, 100, Jan. 5, 1774, 190, Dec. 16, 1778, 337, Feb. 10, 1780, 366, Feb. 21, 1782, 396, May 1, 23, 1782, 399, Dec. 8, 1782, 407, Sept. 12, 1783, 415, Aug. 14, 1784, 426, June 27, 1792, 483, June 28, 1792, 484, Sept. 1, 1793, 499, and Dec. 5, 10, 1793, 533. She occasionally used the term *family* to refer to the household as a whole; see ibid., I, June 25, 1771, 159–160, and Dec. 7, 1777, 262. For more on Elizabeth Drinker's relationships with her servants, see Debra M. O'Neal, "Elizabeth Drinker and Her 'Lone' Women: Domestic Service, Debilities and (In) Dependence through the Eyes of a Philadelphia Gentlewoman," in "The World of Elizabeth Drinker: Celebrating the Tenth Anniversary of the Publication of Her Diary," special issue, ed. Elaine Forman Crane, *Pennsylvania History,* LXXVIII (2001), 435–464; and Alison Duncan Hirsch, "Philadelphia Quaker Elizabeth Drinker and Her Servant, Jane Boon: 'Times Are Much Changed, and Maids Are Become Mistresses,'" in Nancy L. Rhoden and Ian K. Steele, eds., *The Human Tradition in the American Revolution* (Wilmington, Del., 2000), 164–166.

71. Crane, ed., *Diary of Elizabeth Drinker,* I, Jan. 5, 1778, 273 ("our Major"), Jan. 19, 1778, 276 ("our officer"), Jan. 20, 1778, 276 ("our Major"), Jan. 29, 1778, 279 ("our Major"); Elizabeth Drinker to Henry Drinker, Dec. 31, 1777, Drinker Letters ("Our Family," "I made many"). Sarah Logan Fisher also referred to Lieutenant Apthorpe as "our lodger"; see Sarah Logan Fisher Diary, V, June 12, 1778, [20].

72. For news, see Crane, ed., *Diary of Elizabeth Drinker,* I, Dec. 31, 1777, 271, Jan. 5, 1778, 273, Feb. 25, 1778, 286, Feb. 27, 1778, 287, and May 8, 1778, 304. For intercession, see discussion of Phebe Pemberton, earlier in this chapter. For resources and social events, see GCM of Alexander Campbell, Philadelphia, Feb. 27–Mar. 10, 1778, WO 71/85, 349, 351, TNA; Eliza Lucas Pinckney to Thomas Pinckney, [September] 1780, *ELP and HPH Digital Papers* [two letters]; and Tatum, ed., *American Journal of Ambrose Serle,* Mar. 2, 1777, 195.

73. "Letter XI," July 14, [?], Caroline Gilman, ed., *Letters of Eliza Wilkinson, during the Invasion and Possession of Charlestown, S.C., by the British in the Revolutionary War* (New York, 1839), 98 ("good-nature[d]"), 99 ("so smilingly"); Watson, *Annals of Philadelphia,* 683 ("living"); Logan in Watson, *Annals of Philadelphia,* II, 402, M.S. in Historical Society of Pennsylvania, quoted in Fisher, "Social Life in Philadelphia," *Pennsylvania History,* XXXVII (1970), 239 ("formed," "blustering," "became").

74. Sarah Logan Fisher Diary, V, Jan. 29, 1778, [3] (quotation); Crane, ed., *Diary of Elizabeth Drinker,* I, Jan. 10, 1778, 274, Mar. 7, 1778, 288, May 19, 1778, 306; Lowther Pennington to Phebe Pemberton, [Feb. 16], 1778, Pemberton Family Papers, XXXI, 133, Lowther Pennington to Phebe Pemberton, February 1778, 150; *A List of the General and Staff Officers and of the Officers,* 11.

75. Crane, ed., *Diary of Elizabeth Drinker,* I, Jan. 5, 1778, 273 ("Most"), June 10, 1778, 310 ("ste[p]"). Instances of Drinker and Cramond's socialization are too numerous to list; see various entries from December 1777 to May 1778. For Cramond accompanying Elizabeth, see ibid., I, June 4, 1778, 309. For Mary Pleasants, see ibid., I, Mar. 2, 1778, 287. For other officers, see ibid., I, May 14, 1778, 305, May 26, 1778, 308, June 8, 1778, 309, June 10, 1778, 310, June 15, 1778, 311, June 16, 1778, 311, and June 17, 1778, 311. For William Ford, who was quartered with Mary (Polly) Pleasants and accompanied her to tea at the Drinkers at least twice, see ibid., I Jan. 3, 1778, 273, May 14, 1778, 305, May 26, 1778, 308, and June 17, 1778, 311. The Captain Ford

referenced could possibly be First Lieutenant William Ford of the Royal Artillery; see *A List of the General and Staff Officers and of the Officers*, 46.

76. Albert Cook Myers, ed., *Sally Wister's Journal: A True Narrative; Being a Quaker Maiden's Account of Her Experiences with Officers of the Continental Army, 1777–1778* (Philadelphia, 1902), Sept. 25, 1777, 66 ("sh[oo]k"), 67 ("My teeth), Nov. 1, 1777, 99 ("miltaryish"); [Deborah Norris] to Sarah Wister, [early April 1778], in Kathryn Zabelle Derounian, "'A Dear Dear Friend': Six Letters from Deborah Norris to Sarah Wister, 1778–1779," in "Notes and Documents," *PMHB*, CVIII (1984), 499, Norris to Wister, [Apr. 18, 1778], 501–505, Norris to Wister, [Dec. 26, 1778], 505–506, [Norris] to Wister, Aug. 6, 1779, 515–516; and Diary of Robert Morton, Oct. 5, 6, 9, 1777. Henry Drinker certainly hoped that his children kept their distance; see Henry Drinker to Elizabeth Drinker, Jan. 30, 1778, Drinker Letters. For gifts, see Uhlendorf, ed. and trans., *Revolution in America*, 25–26. More than fifty years after Hessian major Carl Leopold Baurmeister quartered in David Lewis's house, Rembrandt Peale painted Lewis's portrait wearing a pin he received as a child from the Hessian officer; the pin became a treasured family heirloom.

77. Elizabeth Drinker to Henry Drinker, Feb. 3, 1778, Drinker Letters (quotations), Elizabeth Drinker to Henry Drinker, Feb. 26, 1778; Crane, ed., *Diary of Elizabeth Drinker*, I, Sept. 2, 1777, 226. For Cramond's arrival, see Crane, ed., *Diary of Elizabeth Drinker*, I, Jan. 29, 1778, 279. His servants moved about the house at night, and Elizabeth got a black eye from colliding with Heritta, his stable boy, in a dark hallway; see ibid., I, Feb. 27, 28, 1778, 287. For memories of absent family during the occupation, see Sarah Logan Fisher Diary, V, Jan. 31, 1778, [4].

78. Thomas Fisher to Sarah Logan Fisher, Apr. 14, 1778, Thomas Fisher Letter book, HSP ("I should be glad"), Thomas Fisher to Sarah Logan Fisher, Jan. 12, 1778 ("Officer"), Thomas Fisher to Sarah Logan Fisher, Feb. 3, 1778 ("These things"); Henry Drinker to Elizabeth Drinker, Jan. 30, 1778, Drinker Letters ("Who is it," "strictest," "Did I not").

79. Thomas Fisher to Sarah Logan Fisher, Nov. 18, 1777, Thomas Fisher Letter book ("alleviate," "mitigate"); John Adams to Abigail Adams, Mar. 17, 1776, FO, https://founders.archives.gov/documents/Adams/04-01-02-0234 ("sound"); Miers Fisher to Sarah Redwood Fisher, Apr. 13, 1778, Fisher Family Papers, 1761–1889, Ser. I, box 3, folder 1, HSP ("Does he retain," "or has he forgot"); Henry Drinker to Elizabeth Drinker, Jan. 25, 1778, Drinker Letters.

80. Miers Fisher to Sarah Redwood Fisher, Apr. 13, 1778, Fisher Family Papers, Ser. I, box 3, folder 1 (quotations). For more on merchants, see Willard O. Mishoff, "Business in Philadelphia during the British Occupation, 1777–1778," *PMHB*, LXI (1937), 165–181.

81. Miers Fisher to Sarah Redwood Fisher, Apr. 13, 1778 (quotations), Fisher Family Papers, Ser. I, box 3, folder 1, Sarah Redwood Fisher to Miers Fisher, Nov. 24, 1777.

82. Norton, *Founding Mothers and Fathers*, 96–137 (quotation, 96). For more on the household in Anglo-American political thought, see John Demos, *A Little Commonwealth: Family Life in Plymouth Colony* (New York, 1970); and Olwell, *Masters, Slaves, and Subjects*, 181–219. For limitations of this metaphor, see William Cuddihy and B. Carmon Hardy, "A Man's House Was Not His Castle: Origins of the Fourth Amendment to the United States Constitution," *WMQ*, 3d Ser., XXXVII (1980), 371–400; and Amanda Vickery, "An Englishman's Home Is His Castle? Thresholds, Boundaries, and Privacies in the Eighteenth-Century London House," *Past and Present*, no. 199 (May 2008), 147–173. For an example of this awareness of the destabilizing potential of revolutionary rhetoric, see John Adams to Abigail Adams, Apr. 14, 1776, Adams Family Papers. For more on family separation during the war, see

Damiano, "Writing Women's History through the Revolution," in "Writing to and from the Revolution," special issue, *WMQ*, 3d. Ser., LXXIV (2017), 697–728. For patriarchy, deference, and the Revolution, see Jay Fliegelman, *Prodigals and Pilgrims: The American Revolution against Patriarchal Authority, 1750–1800* (Cambridge, 1982); Alfred F. Young, *The Shoemaker and the Tea Party: Memory and the American Revolution* (Boston, 1999); and Shammas, *History of Household Government*, 53–82.

83. [James] Morton to James Pemberton, Dec. 19, 1777, Pemberton Family Papers, XXXI, 73 ("Soldiery"), Mary [Molly] Smith Pemberton to James Pemberton, Feb. 2, 1778, 102 ("Grandmammy"), John Pemberton to Hannah Pemberton, Feb. 14, 1778, 124–125 ("find"), Hannah Lloyd to James Pemberton, Dec. 29, 1777, 76, James Morton to James Pemberton, Dec. 5, 1777, 58.

84. Elizabeth Drinker to Henry Drinker, Jan. 25, 1778, Drinker Letters ("unless"), Henry Drinker to Elizabeth Drinker, Jan. 30, 1778 ("mention[ed]"), Elizabeth Drinker to Henry Drinker, Feb. 26, 1778 ("our new Guest," "I need not," "some times has").

85. Elizabeth Drinker to Henry Drinker, Feb. 26, 1778, Drinker Letters (quotations), Elizabeth Drinker to Henry Drinker, Jan. 1, 1778.

86. Although Elizabeth Drinker and James Cramond socialized intermittently during his first month in the house, these interactions increased rapidly in February and early March 1778. Even so, aware that her letters were sent unsealed and open to the inquiring eyes of both armies, she had good reason to be circumspect about her relationship with the major, but she also, notably, did not hesitate to voice her condemnation of those "wicked men" who had deprived her of her husband, suggesting that politics was not the only motivation for downplaying their relationship in her letters to Henry. For socialization with Cramond, see various entries from January to March 1778, in Crane, ed., *Diary of Elizabeth Drinker*, I, 280–289. For letters, see Elizabeth Drinker to Henry Drinker, Dec. 8, 1777, Drinker Letters ("wicked"), and Elizabeth Drinker to Henry Drinker, Dec. 27, 1777.

87. Crane, ed., *Diary of Elizabeth Drinker*, I, June 8, 1778, 309, June 9, 1778, 310 ("was very dull," "fine moon-light," "bid"), June 14, 1778, 310 ("wrote"), Dec. 18, 1778, 337, Apr. 27, 1781, 386, Oct. 28, 1781, 392 ("Heard," "young Officer"). For more on Cramond's death, see *Diary of Frederick Mackenzie*, II, Aug. 30, 1781, 608; and "New-York, September 1," *New-York Gazette: and the Weekly Mercury*, Sept. 3, 1781, [2]; see also Gruber, ed., *John Peebles' American War*, Aug. 30, 1781, 469.

88. Crane, ed., *Diary of Elizabeth Drinker*, I, Apr. 30, 1778, 303, May 9, 14, 1778, 305, June 9, 1778, 310, Jan. 25, 1781, 383 (quotations).

89. Henry Drinker to Elizabeth Drinker, Nov. 20, 1777, Drinker Letters.

90. For more on Henry's spiritual resignation, see Godbeer, *World of Trouble*, 168–170, 205, 305, 307.

CHAPTER 3

1. GCM of Silvester Fuller, New York, Aug. 6–12, 1778, WO 71/90, 109–110, 116–117, 124–125, film 675, reel 12, DLAR, GCM of William Demont [sometimes spelled Dumont or Diemont], New York, Oct. 20–Nov. 4, 1779, WO 71/90, 393–394. For more on Demont, see Memorial of William Demont, AO 12/40, 252–256, TNA; and William Paul Deary, "Toward

Disaster at Fort Washington, November 1776" (Ph.D. diss., George Washington University, 1995), 287–328.

2. GCM of Silvester Fuller, Aug. 6–12, 1778, WO 71/90, 115 ("Person"), 124–125 ("domestic," "Quarrel," "sufferance"), film 675, reel 12, DLAR, GCM of William Demont, Oct. 20–Nov. 4, 1779, WO 71/90, 395 ("imposed").

3. GCM of Silvester Fuller, Aug. 6–12, 1778, WO 71/90, 109 ("insulting"), 114 ("be[ing] called," "It was such people"), 117 ("Scoundrel"), 118–119, 124–125 ("equally"), film 675, reel 12, DLAR.

4. Toby L. Ditz, "The New Men's History and the Peculiar Absence of Gendered Power: Some Remedies from Early American Gender History," *Gender and History,* XVI (2004), 12–16 (quotations, 12); see also Carole Shammas, *A History of Household Government in America* (Charlottesville, Va., 2002), 24–82; and Karen Harvey, "The History of Masculinity, circa 1650–1800," *Journal of British Studies,* XLIV (2005), 296–311. For more on patriarchy and domestic life, see Stephanie McCurry, *Masters of Small Worlds: Yeoman Households, Gender Relations, and the Political Culture of the Antebellum South Carolina Low Country* (Oxford, 1995); Kathleen M. Brown, *Good Wives, Nasty Wenches, and Anxious Patriarchs: Gender, Race, and Power in Colonial Virginia* (Williamsburg, Va., and Chapel Hill, N.C., 1996), 247–282, 319–366; Mary Beth Norton, *Founding Mothers and Fathers: Gendered Power and the Forming of American Society* (New York, 1996); Mark E. Kann, *A Republic of Men: The American Founders, Gendered Language, and Patriarchal Politics* (New York, 1998); Robert Olwell, *Masters, Slaves, and Subjects: The Culture of Power in the South Carolina Low Country, 1740–1790* (Ithaca, N.Y., 1998), 181–219; Lisa Wilson, *Ye Heart of a Man: The Domestic Life of Men in Colonial New England* (New Haven, Conn., 1999); Naomi Tadmor, *Family and Friends in Eighteenth-Century England: Household, Kinship, and Patronage* (Cambridge, 2001); Holly Brewer, "The Transformation of Domestic Law," in Michael Grossberg and Christopher Tomlins, eds., *The Cambridge History of Law in America,* I (Cambridge, 2008), 288–323; Karen Harvey, *The Little Republic: Masculinity and Domestic Authority in Eighteenth-Century Britain* (Oxford, 2012); Lorri Glover, *Founders as Fathers: The Private Lives and Politics of the American Revolutionaries* (New Haven, Conn., 2014); Honor Sachs, *Home Rule: Households, Manhood, and National Expansion on the Eighteenth-Century Kentucky Frontier* (New Haven, Conn., 2015); Annette Gordon-Reed and Peter S. Onuf, *"Most Blessed of the Patriarchs": Thomas Jefferson and the Empire of the Imagination* (New York, 2016); Toby Ditz, "Manhood and the US Republican Empire," in Ellen Hartigan-O'Connor and Lisa G. Materson, eds., *The Oxford Handbook of American Women's and Gender History* (Oxford, 2018), 43–69; Lauren Duval, "Mastering Charleston: Property and Patriarchy in British-Occupied Charleston, 1780–82," *WMQ,* 3d Ser., LXXV (2018), 589–622; Freya Gowrley, *Domestic Space in Britain, 1750–1840: Materiality, Sociability, and Emotion* (London, 2022); and Jacqueline Beatty, *In Dependence: Women and the Patriarchal State in Revolutionary America* (New York, 2023).

For honor and British martial masculinity, see Robert Shoemaker, "Male Honour and the Decline of Public Violence in Eighteenth-Century London," *Social History,* XXVI (2001), 190–208; Barbara Taylor, "Feminists versus Gallants: Manners and Morals in Enlightenment Britain," *Representations,* LXXXVII, no. 1 (Summer 2004), 125–148; Michèle Cohen, "'Manners' Make the Man: Politeness, Chivalry, and the Construction of Masculinity, 1750–1830," *Journal of British Studies,* XLIV (2005), 312–329; Stephen Conway, "The British Army, 'Military Europe,' and the American War of Independence," *WMQ,* 3d Ser., LXVII (2010), 89–94;

Emily Merrill, "Judging Empire: Masculinity and the Making of the British Imperial Army, 1754–1783" (Ph.D. diss., University of Pennsylvania, 2015); and Judith L. Van Buskirk, *Generous Enemies: Patriots and Loyalists in Revolutionary New York* (Philadelphia, 2002), 74–76. For honor generally, see Joanne B. Freeman, *Affairs of Honor: National Politics in the New Republic* (New Haven, Conn., 2001); Caroline Cox, *A Proper Sense of Honor: Service and Sacrifice in George Washington's Army* (Chapel Hill, N.C., 2004); and Craig Bruce Smith, *American Honor: The Creation of the Nation's Ideals during the Revolutionary Era* (Chapel Hill, N.C., 2018). For more on British attitudes toward American colonists, see Stephen Conway, "From Fellow-Nationals to Foreigners: British Perceptions of the Americans, circa 1739–1783," *WMQ*, 3d Ser., LIX (2002), 65–100.

5. GCM of Silvester Fuller, Aug. 6–12, 1778, WO 71/90, 114 (quotation), film 675, reel 12, DLAR. For the flexibility of allegiance, see Donald F. Johnson, "Ambiguous Allegiances: Urban Loyalties during the American Revolution," *JAH*, CIV (2017), 610–631.

6. Letter from Matilda Nichols, quoted in Antoinette Forrester Downing and Vincent J. Scully, Jr., *The Architectural Heritage of Newport, Rhode Island: 1640–1915*, 2d ed. (New York, 1967), 434 ("Take it all"); [William Bayard] to Gentleman, Nov. 12, 1778, Bayard-Campbell-Pearsall Families Papers, 1659–1898, box 1, folder 2, Manuscripts and Archives Division, NYPL ("I was long," "unspeakable," "Barns").

7. Narrative of Mrs. Abraham Brasher (Helen Kortright) Giving an Account of Her Experiences in the Revolutionary War, 1802, 24, VF Women, DLAR (quotation). For an articulation of leaving women behind to defend property, see Josiah Smith to George Smith, Feb. 28, 1781, Josiah Smith Letter book, 1771–1784, M-3018, 427, SHC.

8. William Vernon to William Vernon, Jr., Mar. 27, 1777, Vernon Family Papers, 1774–1789, box 49, folder 6, NHS. For slave trading, see Sarah Deutsch, "The Elusive Guineamen: Newport Slavers, 1735–1774," *New England Quarterly*, LV (1982), 229–253.

9. William Vernon to William Vernon, Jr., Mar. 27, 1777, Vernon Family Papers, box 49, folder 6 (quotation); Maud Lyman Stevens, *A History of the Vernon House in Newport, R.I.* (Newport, R.I., 1915), 15–16; Richard A. Harrison, *Princetonians, 1776–1783: A Biographical Dictionary* (Princeton, N.J., 1981), s.v. "William H. Vernon." For more on unmarried sisters in urban households, see Karin Wulf, *Not All Wives: Women of Colonial Philadelphia* (Ithaca, N.Y., 2000), 85–90, 106–110, 115–117.

10. William Vernon to Samuel Vernon, Dec. 8, 1776, quoted in Stevens, *History of the Vernon House*, 20 (quotations). It seems that Esther Vernon might have come to regret her decision, for, in April 1777, William received word that "Aunt Esther is heartily tired of that once pleasant and agreeable Place [Newport]"; see Samuel Sanford to William Vernon, Apr. 3, 1777, Vernon Family Papers, box 79, folder 10.

11. Ralph Inman to Elizabeth Inman, June 13, 1775, James Murray Robbins Family Papers, 1638–1899, box 2, MHS.

12. Elizabeth Inman to Ralph Inman, June 12, 1775, James Murray Robbins Family Papers, box 2 ("worst, "As we have"), Elizabeth Inman to Ralph Inman, June 14, 1775 ("Be assured," "If I did not"), and Elizabeth Inman to Ralph Inman, July 30, 1775.

13. Elizabeth Inman to Ralph Inman, July 30, 1775, James Murray Robbins Family Papers (quotations). Elizabeth eventually traveled to Boston in September 1775, not to join Ralph, but to aid her niece, whose business was floundering. While there, the couple reconciled. But Elizabeth's 1785 will suggests that their marriage remained contentious: she bequeathed

the majority of her estate to her nieces and nephews and allocated only a small conditional annuity to her husband. As one of her nieces reflected after Elizabeth's 1785 death, "Our valued and beloved Aunt was not without her anxieties and perplexities, Mr I[nman']s disposition has given her more trouble than her friends are aware of and his failings were dayly encreasing, his avarice was a source of real misfortune to her." Clearly, the acrimony that emerged during the early years of the war remained a thorn in the Inmans' marriage. See Elizabeth Murray to Mary Murray, June 26, 1785, James Murray Robbins Family Papers, box 4 (quotation); and Patricia Cleary, *Elizabeth Murray: A Woman's Pursuit of Independence in Eighteenth-Century America* (Amherst, Mass., 2000), 187–224.

14. Anne Hart to Oliver Hart, May 14, 1781, Oliver Hart Papers, 1741–1961, Ser. 1, box 1, folder 2, SCL ("Is it worth," "I hardly," "fatigue," "Difficulties," "my family"), Anne Hart to Oliver Hart, Feb. 20, 1781 ("I shoul'd not").

15. Anne Hart to Oliver Hart, May 14, 1781, Oliver Hart Papers, Ser. 1, box 1, folder 2 (quotations). Anne Hart was not alone in embarking on a wartime career; see Woody Holton, "Abigail Adams, Bond Speculator," *WMQ*, 3d Ser., LXIV (2007), 821–838; and Susan Brandt, "'Getting into a Little Business': Margaret Hill Morris and Women's Medical Entrepreneurship during the American Revolution," *EAS*, XIII (2015), 774–807.

16. Oliver Hart to Anne Hart, June 12, 1781, Oliver Hart Papers, Ser. 1, box 1, folder 3 ("I can scarce," "might enjoy," "pretty," "One Thing," "Much rather," "would I"), Oliver Hart to Joseph Hart, Dec. 23, 1780, Oliver Hart Journal, 1779–1780, [June 1], 1780, Ser. 2, box 1 ("could prevail"), Dec. 25, 1780 ("a Home," "if it may"), Apr. 24, 1781 ("No one").

17. Oliver Hart to Anne Hart, June 12, 1781, Oliver Hart Papers, Ser. 1, box 1, folder 3 ("Some evil"), Anne Hart to Oliver Hart, July 19, 1781 ("this same Demon," "for oft"). For Balfour's edict, see Josiah Smith and Mabel L. Webber, "Josiah Smith's Diary, 1780–1781 (Continued)," *SCHGM*, XXXIII (1932), 286–287.

18. Anne Hart to Oliver Hart, July 19, 1781, Oliver Hart Papers, Ser. 1, box 1, folder 3.

19. Ibid. (quotations); Mabel L. Webber, "Descendants of John Jenkins, of St. John's Colleton," *SCHGM*, XX (1919), 235 n.60.

20. "Mrs. Mary [Gould] Almy's Account of the Cannonading of the French Fleet in Newport," Sept. 2, 1778, RLA (quotation); Charles Kingsbury Miller, *Historic Families of America; William Almy of Portsmouth, Rhode Island, 1630, Joris Janssen de Rapaljé, of Fort Orange (Albany), New Amsterdam and Brooklyn, 1623* (Chicago, 1897), 82–83.

21. Memorial of Elizabeth Dores, AO 12/49, 57, TNA ("keen," "fled," "Her Husband"), Memorial of Alexander Bartram, AO 12/40, 108, 115 ("Mrs. Bartram," "she lives"); "The Petition of Jane Bartram, Wife of Alexander Bartram," [to the Supreme Executive Council of . . . Pennsylvania], May 21, 1782, Records of Pennsylvania's Revolutionary Governments (RG-27), microfilm reel 30, frame 89, Pennsylvania State Archives: Pennsylvania Historical and Museum Commission, quoted in Wayne Bodle, "Jane Bartram's 'Application': Her Struggle for Survival, Stability, and Self-Determination in Revolutionary Pennsylvania," *PMHB*, CXV (1991), 195 ("Ever since"); Memorial of H[enry] Hugh Fergusson, AO 12/38, 215–216 ("very Zealous," "Their [*sic*]"), 218 ("quarrel," "originated"), 221, TNA. Elizabeth Dores carried intelligence for the British Army during the war, and, at one point, she was imprisoned for fifteen days on suspicion of spying. As one man attested, "The Americans looked upon her as their bitter foe"; see Memorial of Elizabeth Dores, AO 12/49, 57–58. For the Fergusson's

marriage, see Rodney Mader, "Elizabeth Graeme Fergusson's 'The Deserted Wife,'" *PMHB,* CXXXV (2011), 152.

22. Andrew Eliot to his son, Apr. 23, 1775, Miscellaneous Manuscripts, MHS, Collections Online, https://www.masshist.org/database/viewer.php?item_id=1906 ("This Town," "Everything," "all property"); Andrew Eliot to Thomas Brand Hollis, Apr. 25, 1775, in "Letters of Andrew Eliot," *PMHS,* XVI (Boston, 1879), 281 ("Last week"), 282 ("My heart").

23. "By Major-General Richard Prescott," *Newport Gazette* (R.I.), Mar. 13, 1777, [3].

24. Edward H. Tatum, Jr., ed., *The American Journal of Ambrose Serle, Secretary to Lord Howe, 1776–1778* (San Marino, Calif., 1940), Sept. 2, 1776, 88–89 (quotation). For earlier precedents for this approach, see Christopher O'Riordan, "Popular Exploitation of Enemy Estates in the English Revolution," *History,* LXXVIII (1993), 183–200.

25. Examples of loyalist property losses are pervasive in the records of the Loyalist Claims Commission; see AO 12 and AO 13, TNA.

26. John Leach Diaries, II, 1775–1776, MHS, Collections Online, https://www.masshist.org/database/6673, Dec. 25, 1775, [23] ("to prevent"), Jan. 7, 1776, [25–26] ("I told").

27. Ibid., II, Jan. 7, 1776, [26–27] ("by dint," [26], "[I] stood," [26], "Soldiers," [26 –27], "Rebel," [26], "Cut," [26], "malicious," [27]).

28. For scholarly treatments of the war in South Carolina, see George Smith McCowen, *The British Occupation of Charleston, 1780–82* (Columbia, S.C., 1972); John S. Pancake, *This Destructive War: The British Campaign in the Carolinas, 1780–1782* (Tuscaloosa, Ala., 1985); Sylvia R. Frey, *Water from the Rock: Black Resistance in a Revolutionary Age* (Princeton, N.J., 1991), 108–142; John W. Gordon, *South Carolina and the American Revolution: A Battlefield History* (Columbia, S.C., 2003); and Jim Piecuch, *Three Peoples One King: Loyalists, Indians, and Slaves in the Revolutionary South, 1775–1782* (Columbia, S.C., 2008). For the confiscation of loyalist property, see Robert S. Lambert, "The Confiscation of Loyalist Property in Georgia, 1782–1786," *WMQ,* 3d Ser., XX (1963), 80–94; Rebecca Brannon, *From Revolution to Reunion: The Reintegration of the South Carolina Loyalists* (Columbia, S.C., 2016), 35–96; Kimberly M. Nath, "The British Are Coming, Again: Loyalists, Property Confiscation, and Reintegration in the Mid-Atlantic, 1777–1800" (Ph.D. diss., University of Delaware, 2016); Tom Cutterham, *Gentlemen Revolutionaries: Power and Justice in the New American Republic* (Princeton, N.J., 2017), 70–78; and Marcus Gallo, "Property Rights, Citizenship, Corruption, and Inequality: Confiscating Loyalist Estates during the American Revolution," *Pennsylvania History: A Journal of Mid-Atlantic Studies,* LXXXVI (2019), 474–510.

29. "South-Carolina; By the Right Honourable Charles Earl Cornwallis, Lieutenant General of His Majesty's Forces; . . . a Proclamation," *South-Carolina and American General Gazette* (Charlest[o]n), Oct. 4, 1780, [1] (quotation). For the surrender of Charleston, see [Banastre] Tarleton, *A History of the Campaigns of 1780 and 1781 . . .* (London, 1787), 23; for the Articles of Capitulation, see ibid., 53–54. For an overview of British policies, see McCowen, *British Occupation of Charleston,* 43–79. For paroles, see C. L. Bragg, *Crescent Moon over Carolina: William Moultrie and American Liberty* (Columbia, S.C., 2013), 183–194; Pancake, *This Destructive War,* 66; and Brannon, *From Revolution to Reunion,* 17. For colonial land grants, see Alan Taylor, *American Colonies* (New York, 2001), 146–153, 224–226; see also Edmund S. Morgan, *American Slavery, American Freedom: The Ordeal of Colonial Virginia* (New York, 1975). For Scotland and Ireland, see John D. Roche, "'[America] May Be Conquered with

More Ease than Governed': The Evolution of British Occupation Policy during the American Revolution" (Ph.D. diss., University of North Carolina, 2015), 70–119; and Nicholas Canny, *Kingdom and Colony: Ireland in the Atlantic World, 1560–1800* (Baltimore, Md., 1988), 1–29, 38, 107–133. For English Civil Wars, see O'Riordan, "Popular Exploitation of Enemy Estates," *History,* LXXVIII (1993), 183–200. For property and patriarchal responsibilities, see Jessica Choppin Roney, "'Effective Men' and Early Voluntary Associations in Philadelphia, 1725–1775," in Thomas A. Foster, ed., *New Men: Manliness in Early America* (New York, 2011), 161–162; Sachs, *Home Rule,* 14–16, 31–32; Olwell, *Masters, Slaves, and Subjects,* 181–219; Glover, *Founders as Fathers,* 7–8, 39, 54–55; Philip D. Morgan, *Slave Counterpoint: Black Culture in the Eighteenth-Century Chesapeake and Lowcountry* (Williamsburg, Va., and Chapel Hill, N.C., 1998), 280–285; and Ditz, "New Men's History," *Gender and History,* XVI (2004), 11–12.

30. Olwell, *Masters, Slaves, and Subjects,* 7 ("culture"), 186 ("little"), 198, 199 ("Patriarchs"); see also ibid., 181–219; Marylynn Salmon, *Women and the Law of Property in Early America* (Chapel Hill, N.C., 1986), 10. For South Carolina's slave society, see Olwell, *Masters, Slaves, and Subjects;* Morgan, *Slave Counterpoint,* 95, 100, 257–317; see also Peter H. Wood, *Black Majority: Negroes in Colonial South Carolina from the 1670 through the Stono Rebellion* (New York, 1974); and S. Max Edelson, *Plantation Enterprise in Colonial South Carolina* (Cambridge, Mass., 2006). For contemporary assessments of South Carolina, see "Diary of Captain Johann Hinrichs," December 1779–June 25, 1780, in Bernhard A. Uhlendorf, ed. and trans., *The Siege of Charleston with an Account of the Province of South Carolina: Diaries and Letters of Hessian Officers from the Von Jungkenn Papers in the William L. Clements Library* (Ann Arbor, Mich., 1938), "Part Five or Appendix; Containing a Contribution of Philosophical and Historical Remarks Concerning South Carolina," 319, 327. For more on patriarchal power in South Carolina, see Stephanie McCurry, *Masters of Small Worlds: Yeoman Households, Gender Relations, and the Political Culture of the Antebellum South Carolina Low Country* (New York, 1995); Cara Anzilotti, "Autonomy and the Female Planter in Colonial South Carolina," *Journal of Southern History,* LXIII (1997), 239–268; Inge Dornan, "Masterful Women: Colonial Women Slaveholders in the Urban Low Country," in "British Association for American Studies 50th Anniversary," special issue, *Journal of American Studies,* XXXIX (2005), 383–402; and John Crowley, "Family Relations and Inheritance in Early South Carolina," *Histoire sociale<th>/<th>Social History,* XVII (1984), 35–57. For patriarchal power in early America broadly, see Norton, *Founding Mothers and Fathers;* Mary P. Ryan, *Cradle of the Middle Class: The Family in Oneida County, New York, 1790–1865* (New York, 1981), 31–43; Joan R. Gundersen and Gwen Victor Gampel, "Married Women's Legal Status in Eighteenth-Century New York and Virginia," *WMQ,* 3d Ser., XXXIX (1982), 114–134; and Brewer, "Transformation of Domestic Law," in Grossberg and Tomlins, eds., *Cambridge History of Law in America,* I, 288–323. As Toby L. Ditz argues, men's patriarchal power relied on access to women; see Ditz, "New Men's History," *Gender and History,* XVI (2004), 13–16. For an overview of scholarship on gender and patriarchy, see ibid., 11–27; see also Foster, ed., *New Men.*

31. For Charleston's slaveowning elite, the city and the countryside were linked. They spent summers in town, away from the fevers that swept the Lowcountry; in winter, they retired to plantations adjacent to Charleston. Furnished in the style of English country homes, these retreats manifested affluence and gentility and were sheltered from more labor-intensive inland plantations. The two regions were also entangled economically; on plantations, enslaved laborers produced rice and indigo, which were transferred to Charleston

for shipment. For mobility, see Richard J. Hooker, ed., *A Colonial Plantation Cookbook: The Receipt Book of Harriott Pinckney Horry, 1770* (Columbia, S.C., 1984), 5; and Edelson, *Plantation Enterprise,* 126–165, esp. 151–152; for retreats, see ibid., 141–151, 162–165; for economics, see ibid., 127–141.

32. Charles Cotesworth Pinckney to Eliza Lucas Pinckney, April 1782, *ELP and HPH Digital Papers* ("Since"), Thomas Pinckney to Harriott Pinckney Horry, Sept. 7, 1780 ("If you enquire"), Charles Cotesworth Pinckney to Harriott Pinckney Horry, Oct. 8, 1780, Charles Cotesworth Pinckney to Eliza Lucas Pinckney, Sept. 10, 1780, Eliza Lucas Pinckney to Thomas Pinckney, August 1780. For Charles Cotesworth Pinckney, see Marvin R. Zahniser, *Charles Cotesworth Pinckney: Founding Father* (Williamsburg, Va., and Chapel Hill, N.C., 1967), 65. For prisoners under British occupation, see McCowen, *British Occupation of Charleston,* 62. For paroled officers, see Bragg, *Crescent Moon over Carolina,* 184; see also Betsy Knight, "Prisoner Exchange and Parole in the American Revolution," *WMQ,* 3d. Ser., XLVIII (1991), 201–222. For the flight of servants and enslaved laborers, see James Weymess to Charles Cornwallis, July 22, 1780, in *Cornwallis Papers,* I, 315, Cornwallis to Weymess, July 26, 1780, I, 316; and William Moultrie, *Memoirs of the American Revolution, So Far as It Related to the States of North and South Carolina, and Georgia . . . ,* II (New York, 1802), 118.

33. Henry Clinton to Charles Cornwallis, June 8, 1780, in *Cornwallis Papers,* I, 68 ("indulg[ing]"); Tarleton, *History of the Campaigns,* 71–72 ("pardon," 71, "hinder[ed]," 71, "immediately," 72); Moultrie, *Memoirs,* II, 209–210 ("people," 209, "resistance," 210, "remain[ing]," 210); see also Henry Clinton to Charles Cornwallis, May 29, 1780, in *Cornwallis Papers,* I, 54, and Cornwallis to Clinton, June 2, 1780, I, 55. For the flexibility of allegiance, see Johnson, "Ambiguous Allegiances," *JAH,* CIV (2017), 610–631; and Brannon, *From Revolution to Reunion,* 16–17.

34. Daniel Huger Horry, Jr., Petition, Feb. 3, 1785, *ELP and HPH Digital Papers* ("Nominal"), Thomas Pinckney to Eliza Lucas Pinckney, June 11, 1780 ("Tho' I am sorry," "it can not"); Mabel L. Webber, "Josiah Smith's Diary, 1780–1781," *SCHGM,* XXXIV (1933), Dec. 31, 1781, 78 ("thro' fear," "those Virtuous," "risque[d]"). For flexible allegiances, see McCowen, *British Occupation of Charleston,* 62; and Johnson, "Ambiguous Allegiances" *JAH,* CIV (2017), 610–631.

35. Moultrie, *Memoirs,* II, 210–211 ("pleasing," 210, "remaining," 211).

36. Proclamation, June 3, 1780, in Tarleton, *History of the Campaigns,* 73 ("take), 74 ("considered"); see also ibid., 25–26; William B. Willcox, ed., *The American Rebellion: Sir Henry Clinton's Narrative of His Campaigns, 1775–1782* (New Haven, Conn., 1954), 181, quoted in McCowen, *British Occupation of Charleston,* 54–55 ("every man"); Gabriel Manigault Journal, 1777–1784, Dec. 14, 1782, 34/0648, SCHS ("obliged"). For taking up arms, see Moultrie, *Memoirs,* II, 210; Joseph Johnson, *Traditions and Reminiscences, Chiefly of the American Revolution in the South . . .* (Charleston, S.C., 1851), 164–168; and Brannon, *From Revolution to Reunion,* 18. After victory at Camden in August 1780, Cornwallis decreed that these men "be punished with the greatest rigour . . . imprisoned, and their whole property taken from them or destroyed" and "compensation . . . made out of their effects to the persons who have been *plundered* and oppressed by them"; see Charles Cornwallis to John Harris Cruger, Aug. 18, 1780, in *Cornwallis Papers,* II, 19. For punishments, see Lieutenant John Postell to Provost, June 24, 1781, Transcripts of Letters from Maj. Gen. Nathanael Greene, I, 1780–1782, Records of the Continental Congress, M247, item 172, roll 191, NARA; David Ramsay, *Ramsay's*

History of South Carolina, from Its First Settlement in 1670 to the Year 1808 (Newberry, S.C., 1858), 259–263; and Moultrie, *Memoirs,* II, 240–242. For truancy and enslaved resistance, see Stephanie M. H. Camp, *Closer to Freedom: Enslaved Women and Everyday Resistance in the Plantation South* (Chapel Hill, N.C., 2004), 35–59.

37. "Cruden's Commission," Sept. 16, 1780, in *Cornwallis Papers,* II, 321 ("seizure"), John Cruden to Alexander Stewart, Oct. 28, 1781, VI, 270 ("superintend"), Charles Cornwallis to Marriot Arbuthnot, June 29, 1780, I, 159 ("There is," "and that is"); "Narrative of John Cruden, His Majesty's Commissioner of Sequestered Estates, in South Carolina," 1782, Manuscripts and Archives Division, NYPL ("utmost"). For sequestration guidelines, see "South-Carolina; By the Right Honourable Charles Earl Cornwallis, . . . a Proclamation," *South-Carolina and American General Gazette,* Oct. 4, 1780, [1]; and McCowen, *British Occupation,* 61.

38. Cruden to Stewart, Oct. 28, 1781, in *Cornwallis Papers,* VI, 270 ("many); Robert Gray, "Observations on the War in Carolina," n.d. [circa 1782], SCHS ("and these"); James Simpson to Sir Henry Clinton, July 1, 1780, Guy Carleton Papers, PRO 30/55/24, 2877, TNA ("If he," "I think"). For more on Williamson, see Llewellyn M. Toulmin, "Backcountry Warrior: Brig. Gen. Andrew Williamson: The 'Benedict Arnold of South Carolina' and America's First Major Double Agent," *Journal of Backcountry Studies,* VII (2012), 1–46.

39. "Copy of a Sketch for Embodying Ten Thousand Black Troops in the Province of South Carolina, Presented to the Earl of Dunmore by John Cruden Esq. His Majesty's Commissioner for Forfeited Estates," Jan. 5, 1782, George Chalmers Collection, 1606–1817, MssCol 507, Papers Relating to Carolina, box 2, Manuscripts and Archives Division, NYPL ("Striking," "I would not," "Property"), John Cruden to Earl of Dunmore, Jan. 5, 1782, [Copy] ("little"). See also Sylvia R. Frey, "The British and the Black: A New Perspective," *Historian,* XXXVIII (1976), 225–238; and Philip D. Morgan and Andrew Jackson O'Shaughnessy, "Arming Slaves in the American Revolution," in Christopher Leslie Brown and Morgan, eds., *Arming Slaves: From Classical Times to the Modern Age* (New Haven, Conn., 2006), 180–208.

40. Isaac Winslow and Margaret Catherine Winslow, *Family Memorial: The Winslows of Boston,* ed. Robert Newsom, I (Boston, 1837?–1773?), 216, Winslow Family Memorial, Ms. N-2322, MHS.

41. For scholarship on masculinity and domestic authority, see note 4, above. For domesticity and identity, see Richard L. Bushman, *The Refinement of America: Persons, Houses, Cities* (New York, 1992), 100–138; Susan M. Stabile, *Memory's Daughters: The Material Culture of Remembrance in Eighteenth-Century America* (Ithaca, N.Y., 2004); Bernard L. Herman, *Town House: Architecture and Material Life in the Early American City, 1780–1830* (Williamsburg, Va., and Chapel Hill, N.C., 2005); Amanda Vickery, *Behind Closed Doors: At Home in Georgian England* (New Haven, Conn., 2009); Onni Gust, *Unhomely Empire: Whiteness and Belonging, c. 1760–1830* (London, 2021); and Gowrley, *Domestic Space in Britain.*

42. For legal and cultural precedents, see William Cuddihy and B. Carmon Hardy, "A Man's House Was Not His Castle: Origins of the Fourth Amendment to the United States Constitution," *WMQ,* 3d Ser., XXXVII (1980), 371–400; Norton, *Founding Mothers and Fathers,* 96–137; Olwell, *Masters, Slaves, and Subjects,* 181–219; Amanda Vickery, "An Englishman's Home Is His Castle? Thresholds, Boundaries, and Privacies in the Eighteenth-Century London House," *Past and Present,* no. 199 (May 2008), 147–173; and John Gilbert McCurdy, *Quarters: The Accommodation of the British Army and the Coming of the American Revolution* (Ithaca, N.Y., 2019).

43. Freeman, *Affairs of Honor,* 167–173; see also Cox, *A Proper Sense of Honor;* Cohen, "'Manners' Make the Man," *Journal of British Studies,* XLIV (2005), 312–329; Conway, "British Army, 'Military Europe,' and the American War of Independence," *WMQ,* 3d Ser., LXVII (2010), 69–100; Catriona Kennedy, "John Bull into Battle: Military Masculinity and the British Army Officer during the Napoleonic Wars," in Karen Hagemann, Gisela Mettele, and Jane Rendall, eds., *Gender, War, and Politics: Transatlantic Perspectives, 1775–1820* (Basingstoke, U.K., 2010), 127–146; and Smith, *American Honor.*

44. In the late eighteenth century, the middling sort increasingly sought to emulate the manners of the elite, which was evident in both comportment and in how they regarded domestic spaces; see Bushman, *Refinement of America;* C. Dallett Hemphill, "Middle Class Rising in Revolutionary America: The Evidence from Manners," *Journal of Social History,* XXX (1996), 317–344; Herman, *Town House;* Gust, *Unhomely Empire;* and Gowrley, *Domestic Space in Britain.*

45. E. A. Benians, [ed.], *A Journal by Tho: Hughes . . . (1778–1789)* (Cambridge, 1947), Oct. 25, 1777, 24 ("ignorant"), Oct. 26, 1777, 24 ("people," "servants), Nov. 1, 1777, 25–26 ("neither," 25, "If this," 26, "I wish," 26). For British views of American colonists, see Conway, "From Fellow-Nationals to Foreigners," *WMQ,* 3d Ser., LIX (2002), 65–100; and Serena R. Zabin, *Dangerous Economies: Status and Commerce in Imperial New York* (Philadelphia, 2009), 81–105. For manners and gentlemanliness in Britain, see Taylor, "Feminists versus Gallants," *Representations,* LXXXVII, no. 1 (Summer 2004), 125–148; and Cohen, "'Manners' Make the Man," *Journal of British Studies,* XLIV (2005), 312–329. For manners in North America, see Hemphill, "Middle Class Rising in Revolutionary America," *Journal of Social History,* XXX (1996), 317–344.

46. [Fleet Greene], "Newport in the Hands of the British: A Diary of the Revolution . . . ," *Historical Magazine . . . ,* IV (1860), July 15, 1777, 34 ("for not taking"); John Bowater to Basil Feilding, earl of Denbigh, Apr. 4, 1777, in Marion Balderston and David Syrett, eds., *The Lost War: Letters from British Officers during the American Revolution* (New York, 1975), 122–123 ("such a Levelling," 122, "Thinking him," 122, "told him," 122, "He knew," 122, "Thus it is," 122, "I frequently," 122). For more on Fairchild, see Franklin Bowditch Dexter, ed., *The Literary Diary of Ezra Stiles,* II (New York, 1901), 132; and Sara T. Damiano, "Agents at Home: Wives, Lawyers, and Financial Competence in Eighteenth-Century New England Port Cities," in "Ligaments: Everyday Connections of Colonial Economies," special issue, *EAS,* XIII (2015), 814.

47. Charles Drayton, III, to Mr. Carlisle, 1837, Drayton Family Papers, 1837–1869, SCHS ("slight," "elaborately," "cultivated," "pebbled"); Ira D. Gruber, ed., *John Peebles' American War: The Diary of a Scottish Grenadier* (Mechanicsburg, Pa., 1998), Feb. 28, 1779, 354 ("one of the best").

48. Charles Drayton, III to Mr. Carlisle, 1837, Drayton Family Papers.

49. Ibid.

50. Ibid. (quotations). For eighteenth-century dueling and violence in British masculinity, see Shoemaker, "Male Honour and the Decline of Public Violence," *Social History,* XXVI (2001), 198.

51. For honor culture, see Freeman, *Affairs of Honor;* Shoemaker, "Male Honour and the Decline of Public Violence," *Social History,* XXVI (2001), 190–208; and Smith, *American Honor.* For notions of gentlemanliness, see also Cohen, "'Manners' Make the Man," *Journal of British Studies,* XLIV (2005), 312–329.

52. Thomas Bee to [Peter] Traille, Dec. 16, 1782, Guy Carleton Papers, PRO 30/55/57, 6424 (quotations). For Peg Boden, see Book of Negroes, PRO 30/55/100, 29–30, 10427, TNA. In a similar vein, Hessian officers frequently found connection and community among German populations, who were more likely to agree to quarter German troops. Although there was no one monolithic experience, or even a unified German national identity (people were far more likely to identify with those from their own state), regional proximity could foster collegial relations. This was especially true in Philadelphia, which had a vibrant German community. Captain Johann Ewald, who hailed from the state of Hesse-Kassel, was pleased to find quarters in Philadelphia "with an old Strassburger." Another German officer found quarters and companionship with "an apothecary from Nürnberg," who had immigrated to Philadelphia. Perhaps encouraged by their shared German ancestry, the two men regularly discussed the political situation between Britain and the colonies. Indeed, the apothecary—whom the officer characterized as an "arch-rebel"—was quite persuasive, "prov[ing] to a hair that the King is a tyrant." "He swears I ought to stay in Philadelphia," the officer mused; "as far as I can see, it suits me here very well." See Ewald, *Diary of the American War: A Hessian Journal,* ed. and trans. Joseph P. Tustin (New Haven, Conn., 1979), Dec. 30, 1777, 111 ("Strassburger"); "XVII: From Philadelphia with a Newspaper," May 7, 1778, in Ray W. Pettengill, ed., *Letters from America, 1776–1779* . . . (1924; rpt. [Port Washington, N.Y.], 1964), 191 ("apothecary," "arch-rebel," "prov[ing]," "He swears," "as far as"). For other examples of quartering with Germans, see "Valentin Asteroth's Diary of the American War of Independence," 1776, in Bruce E. Burgoyne, ed., *Diaries of a Hessian Chaplain and the Chaplain's Assistant* (Pennsauken, N.J., 1990), Nov. 25, 1777, 30; Memorial of Justice Walker, AO 12/38, TNA, and Memorial of Margaret Locke, AO 12/38. For quartering generally, see Friederike Baer, *Hessians: German Soldiers in the American Revolutionary War* (New York, 2022), 240–242. For German identity, see Ken Miller, *Dangerous Guests: Enemy Captives and Revolutionary Communities during the War for Independence* (Ithaca, N.Y., 2014), 108–110.

53. GCM of John Cambel, Newport, R.I., Aug. 19, 1777, WO 71/84, 170, 171 (quotation), 172, TNA.

54. GCM of John Cambel, Aug. 19, 1777, WO 71/84, 160 (quotations), 164–166, 169–170, TNA. Donald F. Johnson has argued that this incident was primarily about loyalty, not status; see Johnson, *Occupied America: British Military Rule and the Experience of Revolution* (Philadelphia, 2020), 156.

55. Ibid., 159–160, 161 ("intimate"), 166, 174 ("Nay," "not even," "own").

56. Ibid., 159.

57. Ibid., 162 ("repeatedly," "at any time"), 163 ("As Captain," "Imagined"), 165 ("very improper"). Letters of inquiry were an important first step in dueling culture in which the offended party outlined the insult to his honor and "allow[ed] his recipient an opportunity to explain himself" and potentially resolve the issue before elevating the challenge to violence; see Freeman, *Affairs of Honor,* 176–177 (quotation, 177).

58. GCM of John Cambel, Aug. 19, 1777, WO 71/84, 170–171 ("Charge," 170, "I can hardly," 170, "merely," 170, "presented," 171, "but keeps," 171), 173, TNA. Although he offered little evidence, Cambel accused Tweedy of promoting the revolutionary cause from within the garrison. He might have been correct—at least one member of the Tweedy family was considered a revolutionary; see Dexter, ed., *Literary Diary of Ezra Stiles,* II, 134.

59. GCM of John Cambel, Aug. 19, 1777, WO 71/84, 171 ("Consequence"), 177 ("very improper," "Civil"), TNA. Cambel was reprimanded only for "having taken the Law into his own hands" and "ordered to make public apology to the General" (ibid., 177). In short, he was punished for his disrespect to the general, not his treatment of Tweedy.

60. GCM of John and James Goodrich, New York, July 16, 1781, WO 71/94, 423 ("You Rascal," "with a large," "rendered"), 425 ("John Goodrich"), 426, 428 ("waiting," "first," "coming around"), 429 ("Vile"), 431 ("on [their] own"), 433 ("that he was no Gentleman"), film 675, reel 14, DLAR.

61. GCM of James and John Goodrich, July 16, 1781, WO 71/94, 429 ("Thus provok'd"), 431 ("behavior"), 432 ("What I did"), film 675, reel 14, DLAR.

62. Ibid., 431 (quotation), 436; George M. Curtis, III, "The Goodrich Family and the Revolution in Virginia, 1774–1776," *Virginia Magazine of History and Biography,* LXXXIV (1976), 50, 54–60.

63. GCM of James and John Goodrich, July 16, 1781, WO 71/94, 420, 428, film 675, reel 14, DLAR; Charles Drayton, III, to Mr. Carlisle, 1837, Drayton Family Papers; GCM of John Cambel, Aug. 19, 1777, WO 71/84, 160, 164–166, 169–170, TNA.

64. GCM of Thomas Tomlins Pritchard, New York, July 16, 1779, WO 71/89, 322 ("illused," "[Kendrick]"), 323 ("affraid"), 325, 333, film 675, reel 12, DLAR.

65. Ibid., 333 ("Masters," "This house," "not disturb"), 334, 335 ("Many other," "such as," "laid"), 338 ("Women"). Pritchard insisted that the weapon was for show, that it was unloaded, and that he did not keep cartridges in the house.

66. Ibid., 323 ("heaps"), 333, 334 ("stamping"), 335 ("Similar," "aggravate matters"), 338 ("abuse[d]," "aggravate"). In another instance, Doctor Kendrick "tore up" Lieutenant Pritchard's garden (ibid., 332).

67. Ibid., 328–329 ("one whore," 329), 334 ("very bad"), 335 ("answered").

68. Ibid., 334 ("no more than," "was a Gentleman," "could dine"), 336 ("Shitten"), 337 ("been a common"). In April 1776, Pritchard fled Continental headquarters in New York and went behind British lines as a civilian, where he apparently later enlisted in a provincial regiment; see "Permit Mr Thomas Tomlin Pritchard . . . ," Apr. 18, 1776, in "Notes and Queries," *PMHB,* XV (1891), 123.

69. GCM of Thomas Tomlins Pritchard, July 16, 1779, WO 71/89, 334 ("appropriate"), 338 ("always"), 339 ("for keeping"), film 675, reel 12, DLAR; Allen Robertson, "Methodism among Nova Scotia's Yankee Planters," in Margaret Conrad, ed., *They Planted Well: New England Planters in Maritime Canada* (Fredericton, New Brunswick, 1988), 188.

70. "The Following Is the Opinion and Sentence of a Garrison Court Martial, Held for the Trial of Mr. William Maxwell," *Royal Gazette* (New York), Feb. 9, 1780, [3].

71. Elaine Forman Crane, ed., *The Diary of Elizabeth Drinker,* I, (Boston, 1991), Oct. 28, 1781, 392.

72. For instance, one of Cramond's orderlies deserted on the evacuation of Philadelphia; see ibid., I, Nov. 29, 1795, 756. For temper, see Gruber, ed., *John Peebles' American War,* Aug. 30, 1781, 469.

73. "The Following Is the Opinion and Sentence of a Garrison Court Martial, Held for the Trial of Mr. William Maxwell," *Royal Gazette* (New York), Feb. 9, 1780, [3] (quotations). For board, see Stephen Payne Adye to the Board of Examination, Jan. 11, 1780, in "Pattison

Letters," 341. For unsatisfactory apology, see Stephen Payne Adye to William Maxwell, Feb. 1, 1780, ibid., 359, "To Lieutenant Cramond," 364, and Adye to Maxwell, Feb. 8, 1780, 365.

74. Abigail Adams to John Adams, Oct. 20, 1777, Adams Family Papers (quotation).

75. Letter to George Washington, Aug. 4, 1776, The Sol Feinstone Collection of the American Revolution, reel 3, 1737, DLAR.

76. Ibid. (quotations). For more on this "historical amnesia," see McCurdy, *Quarters,* 237–239 (quotation, 237).

CHAPTER 4

1. For odors from the British camp, see BOP, Jan. 5, 1781, reel 520. For the New York skyline and Saint Michael's blackened steeple, see Louisa Susannah Wells Aikman, "The Journal of a Voyage from Charleston, S.C., to London: Undertaken during the American Revolution," May 28, 1779, 28, North American Women's Letters and Diaries (database). For the city of Charleston, see "Diary of Captain Johann Hinrichs," December 1779–June 25, 1780, in Bernhard A. Uhlendorf, ed. and trans., *The Siege of Charleston with an Account of the Province of South Carolina: Diaries and Letters of Hessian Officers from the Von Jungkenn Papers in the William L. Clements Library* (Ann Arbor, Mich., 1938), "Part Five or Appendix; Containing a Contribution of Philosophical and Historical Remarks Concerning South Carolina," 327. For Charleston's architecture, see Bernard L. Herman, "The Embedded Landscapes of the Charleston Single House, 1780–1820," *Perspectives in Vernacular Architecture,* VII (1997), 42.

2. Elizabeth Anderson Letter to Mrs. Morsey, Aug. 29, 1780, MS 2958.1760, NYHS.

3. Ibid.

4. Sir Guy Carleton, for instance, paid his New York housemaids eight pounds, eight shillings per quarter; the laundry women, three pounds, twelve shillings per month; and the kitchen maid two pounds a month; see Elizabeth Hurley, "Account for Servants' Wages in Sir Guy Carleton's Household," May 16, 1783–Aug. 16, 1783, British Headquarters Papers [facsimiles], 1775–1783, MssCol 1209, box 36, 8868, Manuscripts and Archives Division, NYPL. For an example of wartime currency depreciation, see "Table of Depreciation of South Carolina Currency by Mr. Simpson, 1777–1780," George Chalmers Collection, 1606–1817, MssCol 507, Papers Relating to Carolina, box 2, NYPL, "Scale of Depreciation for South Carolina by Dr. Garden," and "A Table of Depreciation of the Continental Currency and the Value in Specie of One Hundred Dollars in Continental Currency between the 1st of September 1777 and the 18th of March 1780."

5. James Pattison to John Grant, Dec. 21, 1777, Letter Book of Brig. General James Pattison, 1777–1778, James Pattison Papers, 1777–1781, film 47, DLAR ("there can be"); Amelia Taylor to Sir Guy Carleton, Apr. 23, 1783, British Headquarters Papers [facsimiles], MssCol 1209, box 31, 7498 ("camp," "Gentlemen").

6. For exemplary studies of female servants, see Sharon V. Salinger, "'Send No More Women': Female Servants in Eighteenth-Century Philadelphia," *PMHB,* CVII (1983), 29–48; Christine Stansell, *City of Women: Sex and Class in New York, 1789–1860* (Urbana, Ill., 1987); Debra M. O'Neal, "Mistresses and Maids: The Transformation of Women's Domestic Labor and Household Relations in Late Eighteenth-Century Philadelphia" (Ph.D. diss.,

University of California, Riverside, 1994); Alison Duncan Hirsch, "Philadelphia Quaker Elizabeth Drinker and Her Servant, Jane Boon: 'Times Are Much Changed, and Maids Are Become Mistresses,'" in Nancy L. Rhoden and Ian K. Steele, eds., *The Human Tradition in the American Revolution* (Wilmington, Del., 2000), 159–182; Terri L. Snyder, "'To Seeke for Justice': Gender, Servitude, and Household Governance in the Early Modern Chesapeake," in Douglas Bradburn and John C. Coombs, eds., *Early Modern Virginia: Reconsidering the Old Dominion* (Charlottesville, Va., 2011), 128–157; Salinger, *To Serve Well and Faithfully: Labor and Indentured Servants in Pennsylvania, 1682–1800* (Cambridge, 1987), esp. 100–112; and Allison Noelle Madar, "A People Between: Servitude in Colonial Virginia, 1700–1783" (Ph.D. diss., Rice University, 2013), esp. 55–104. For "urban housefuls" and the service industry, see Ellen Hartigan-O'Connor, *The Ties That Buy: Women and Commerce in Revolutionary America* (Philadelphia, 2009), 13–68. For more on domestic labor, see Jeanne Boydston, *Home and Work: Housework, Wages, and the Ideology of Labor in the Early Republic* (New York, 1990); Karin Wulf, *Not All Wives: Women of Colonial Philadelphia* (Ithaca, N.Y., 2000), 135–138; and Mary Beth Norton, *Liberty's Daughters: The Revolutionary Experience of American Women, 1750–1800* (Boston, 1980), 22–23. For domestic servants and cleanliness, see Kathleen M. Brown, *Foul Bodies: Cleanliness in Early America* (New Haven, Conn., 2009), 251–290. For laborers and the Revolution, see J. Franklin Jameson, *The American Revolution Considered as a Social Movement* (Princeton, N.J., 1926); Richard B. Morris, "Class Struggle and the American Revolution," *WMQ*, 3d Ser., XIX (1962), 3–29; Merrill Jensen, "The American People and the American Revolution," *JAH*, LVII (1970), 5–35; Steven Rosswurm, *Arms, Country, and Class: The Philadelphia Militia and "Lower Sort" during the American Revolution* (New Brunswick, N.J., 1989); Gordon S. Wood, *The Radicalism of the American Revolution* (New York, 1991); Billy G. Smith, *The "Lower Sort": Philadelphia's Laboring People, 1750–1800* (Ithaca, N.Y., 1994); Alfred F. Young, *The Shoemaker and the Tea Party: Memory and the American Revolution* (Boston, 1999); and Young, *Liberty Tree: Ordinary People and the American Revolution* (New York, 2006). For examples of errands, see Sarah Logan Fisher Diary, V, Jan. 31, 1778, [4], Sarah Logan Fisher Diaries, HSP, in The Revolutionary City: A Portal to the Nation's Founding, https://therevolutionarycity.org/islandora/fisher-sarah-logan-diary-volume-5; and Elaine Forman Crane, ed., *The Diary of Elizabeth Drinker*, I (Boston, 1991), Oct. 9–11, 1777, 241–242, Oct. 18, 1777, 246.

7. For continuum of violence, see Sharon Block, *Rape and Sexual Power in Early America* (Williamsburg, Va., and Chapel Hill, N.C., 2006), 18–28; see also Madar, "A People Between," 55–164. For examples of assaults on Black women in British courts-martial, see GCM of Cornelius Dunn, Philadelphia, Dec. 19, 1777, WO 71/85, 154–155, TNA, and GCM of Robert Brown and John Dillon, Philadelphia, Jan. 7, 1778, WO 71/85. For more on sexual assault under British occupation, see Block, "Rape in the American Revolution: Process, Reaction, and Public Re-Creation," in Elizabeth D. Heineman, ed., *Sexual Violence in Conflict Zones: From the Ancient World to the Era of Human Rights* (Philadelphia, 2011), 25–38; and Lauren Duval, "'A Shocking Thing to Tell Of': Female Civilians, Violence, and Rape under British Military Rule," in Holly A. Mayer, ed., *Women Waging War in the American Revolution* (Charlottesville, Va., 2022), 76–97.

8. This recreation of Ann Bryan's experiences is based on a description of her actions that evening written by her employer's daughter; see Molly Pemberton to James Pemberton, Nov. 24, 1777, Pemberton Family Papers, 1641–1880, XXXI, 46, HSP (quotations). See also Molly

Pemberton to James Pemberton, Feb. 2, 1778, ibid., 102, and James Pemberton, "A Short Account of My Beloved Son Phineas [. . .]," July 1778," XXXII.

9. Molly Pemberton to James Pemberton, Nov. 24, 1777, Pemberton Family Papers, XXXI, 46.

10. Elizabeth Henley, "Sketch of the Life of Elizabeth Henley," 1838, SCL; Crane, ed., *Diary of Elizabeth Drinker,* I, Dec. 14, 1777, 264, Dec. 22, 1777, 269; Elizabeth Drinker to Henry Drinker, Feb. 26, 1778, Henry and Elizabeth Drinker Letters, 1777–1778 (hereafter Drinker Letters), HCQSC.

11. Isaac Winslow and Margaret Catherine Winslow, *Family Memorial: The Winslows of Boston,* ed. Robert Newsom, I (Boston, 1837?–1873?), 207, Winslow Family Memorial, Ms. N-2322, MHS.

12. GCM of Lieutenant Charles Dalrymple, Newport, R.I., Sept. 2, 1778, WO 71/87, 210 ("speak," "might get me"), 211 ("mentioned"), 215, TNA.

13. Jonathan Willis, "Ran Away on the Morning of the Thirtieth of Dec. Last, . . . an Apprentice Girl Named Margaret Taggart," *Pennsylvania Evening Post* (Philadelphia), Jan. 8, 1778, 11 ("lurking), John Bartram, "Ran Away from Her Master, . . . a Servant Girl Named Ann Powell," Jan. 17, 1778, 27 ("gone"); William Brown to [Isaac Smith], May 26, 1775, Smith-Carter Family Papers, 1669–1880, reel 2, box 2, folder 12, January–May 1775, image 39, MHS, Digitized Collections, https://www.masshist.org/collection-guides/digitized/fa0540/b02-f12#39 ("appeared," "apparently," "without"). For other examples of escaped Philadelphia servants, see Redmond Byrns, "Philadelphia, Dec. 8, 1777; Ran Away Last Night . . . an Irish Servant Girl, Named Ann Orr," *Pennsylvania Evening Post,* Dec. 9, 1777, 571; "Ran-away on Monday Last from the William, Transport, . . . a Boy Named Isaac Tappen," *Pennsylvania Ledger: or, The Philadelphia Market-Day Advertiser,* Mar. 25, 1778, [3], William Statleman, "Run Away from the Subscriber, . . . a Servant Girl Named Polly Sweet," [4], John Bates, "Ran-Away from the Subscriber, . . . a Scotch Servant Girl, Named Jane Clark," Apr. 1, 1778, [1], and Statleman, "Run Away from the Subscriber, . . . a Servant Girl Named Polly Sweet," Apr. 4, 1778, [4]. For more on runaway female servants, see Madar, "A People Between," 165–219. For more on runaway ads during the Revolutionary era, see Jonathan Prude, "To Look upon the 'Lower Sort': Runaway Ads and the Appearance of Unfree Laborers in America, 1750–1800," *JAH,* LXXVIII (1991), 124–159; Simon P. Newman, *Embodied History: The Lives of the Poor in Early Philadelphia* (Philadelphia, 2003), 82–103; and David Waldstreicher, "Reading the Runaways: Self-Fashioning, Print Culture, and Confidence in Slavery in the Eighteenth-Century Mid-Atlantic," *WMQ,* 3d Ser., LVI (1999), 243–272. For unmarried soldiers, see Sylvia Frey, *The British Soldier in America: A Social History of Military Life in the Revolutionary Period* (Austin, Tex., 1981), 59–62. For the most comprehensive analysis of British soldiers' relationships with civilian women, see Serena Zabin, *The Boston Massacre: A Family History* (Boston, 2020), 79–108; and Zabin, "Intimate Ties and the Boston Massacre," in Barbara B. Oberg, ed., *Women in the American Revolution: Gender, Politics, and the Domestic World* (Charlottesville, Va., 2019), 192–210.

14. *Poor Will's Almanack for the Year of Our Lord 1778* (Philadelphia, 1777), [12] ("fewer"); Elizabeth Willing Powel to Mrs. Alexander Wilcocks, Jan. 8, 1781, Powel Family Papers, 1681–1938, Ser. 3, box 4, folder 3, HSP ("an established Maxim," "not to leave"); Mary Pemberton to Israel Pemberton, Oct. 6, 1777, Pemberton Family Papers, XXX, 164.

15. "Wanted to Live with Two Single Gentlemen," *Pennsylvania Evening Post,* Nov. 1, 1777, 527.

16. William Duane, ed., *Extracts from the Diary of Christopher Marshall: Kept in Philadelphia and Lancaster, during the American Revolution, 1774–1781* (Albany, N.Y., 1877), May 2, 1778, 179 ("All the poor"); Crane, ed., *Diary of Elizabeth Drinker,* I, Sept. 10, 1778, 326 ("reduc'd," "Good," "such a time"). For examples of servants leaving with the British, see Sarah Logan Fisher Diary, IV, Dec. 23, 1777, [31], Jan. 4, 1778, [34], https://therevolutionarycity.org/islandora/fisher-sarah-logan-diary-volume-4.

17. For Ann Kelly's employment, see Crane, ed., *Diary of Elizabeth Drinker,* I, Oct. 9, 1775, 211. For her background, see Hirsch, "Philadelphia Quaker Elizabeth Drinker and Her Servant, Jane Boon," in Rhoden and Steele, eds., *Human Tradition in the American Revolution,* 165–167.

18. Elizabeth Drinker to Henry Drinker, Dec. 3, 1777, Drinker Letters (quotation). For relationships between British soldiers and civilian women in prerevolutionary Boston, see Zabin, *Boston Massacre,* 79–108; and Zabin, "Intimate Ties and the Boston Massacre," in Oberg, ed., *Women in the American Revolution,* 192–210.

19. Crane, ed., *Diary of Elizabeth Drinker,* I, Nov. 25, 1777, 258 (quotation); for architecture, see Henry Drinker, "The Philadelphia Contributionship–Cancelled Fire Insurance Surveys," Nov. 6, 1770, Insurance Surveys S01454, S01455, S01456, S01457, The Philadelphia Contributionship Digital Archives, http://www.philadelphiabuildings.org/contributionship/; for servant's quarters, see Richard Godbeer, *World of Trouble: A Philadelphia Quaker Family's Journey through the American Revolution* (New Haven, Conn., 2019), 59. No officer by the name of Tape exists on the British Army's roster. Perhaps the man used a false name; more likely, Elizabeth Drinker misunderstood Ann. Indeed, her diary reveals that she often struggled to discern names spoken in accented English, such as Ann's Irish brogue. The most probable candidate is Captain John Westrop of the Fifth Regiment of Foot. For Drinker's difficulty understanding accents, see Crane, ed., *Diary of Elizabeth Drinker,* I, Dec. 18, 1777, 266. For Westrop, see *A List of the General and Staff Officers and of the Officers in the Several Regiments Serving in North-America . . .* (Philadelphia, 1778), 13.

20. Ira D. Gruber, ed., *John Peebles' American War: The Diary of a Scottish Grenadier* (Mechanicsburg, Pa., 1998), Dec. 31, 1776, 76 ("house"); John Andrews to William Barrell, Aug. 1, 1774, Andrews-Eliot Correspondence, 1715–1814, box 1, 35, MHS ("din'd," "Towards"); Elizabeth Drinker to Henry Drinker, Dec. 3, 1777, Drinker Letters.

21. Johann Conrad Döhla, *A Hessian Diary of the American Revolution,* ed. and trans. Bruce E. Burgoyne (Norman, Okla., 1990), Aug. 11, 1779, 109 ("caught"); "Diary of Lieutenant Heinrich Carl Philipp von Feilitzsch," in Burgoyne, ed. and trans., *Diaries of Two Ansbach Jaegers* (Bowie, Md., 1997), Jan. 4–6, 1778, 33 ("not very pretty," "but she had"). Feilitzsch did not partake of the maid's favors, but he enjoyed causing her male visitors discomfort, admitting, "When the sailors come ashore I amuse myself by watching them. This often annoys them" (ibid., Jan. 4–6, 1778, 33). For soldiers and female civilians generally, see Frey, *British Soldier,* 59–62. For Philadelphia's "pleasure culture," see Clare A. Lyons, *Sex among the Rabble: An Intimate History of Gender and Power in the Age of Revolution, Philadelphia, 1730–1830* (Williamsburg, Va., and Chapel Hill, N.C., 2006), 1 (quotation), 59–114, 186–307. For contemporary attitudes toward prostitution in Philadelphia, see Newman, *Embodied History,* 33–36.

22. Crane, ed., *Diary of Elizabeth Drinker,* I, Nov. 25, 1777, 258.

23. Ibid. (quotations). For swords and their meaning, see T. Cole Jones, *Captives of Liberty: Prisoners of War and the Politics of Vengeance in the American Revolution* (Philadelphia, 2020), 61–62, 214.

24. Crane, ed., *Diary of Elizabeth Drinker,* I, Nov. 25, 1777, 259 (quotation). For other analyses of this incident, see Godbeer, *World of Trouble,* 159–161; Aaron Sullivan, *The Disaffected: Britain's Occupation of Philadelphia during the American Revolution* (Philadelphia, 2019), 124–126; and Donald F. Johnson, *Occupied America: British Military Rule and the Experience of Revolution* (Philadelphia, 2020), 95–96.

25. Crane, ed., *Diary of Elizabeth Drinker,* I, Nov. 25, 1777, 258 ("Children"), Nov. 26, 1777, 259 ("I have not," "have been"), Dec. 19, 1777, 266 ("how I").

26. Crane, ed., *Diary of Elizabeth Drinker,* I, Dec. 1, 1777, 260 ("Buckels"), Dec. 2, 1777, 260 ("desereing," "hir time," "she would," "If you talk"), Dec. 4, 1777, 261. Mary Sandwith saw Ann Kelly on the street later that month, and Ann once again promised to pay for her time; see ibid., I, Dec. 23, 1777, 269.

27. Crane, ed., *Diary of Elizabeth Drinker,* I, Jan. 4, 1778, 273 ("If thee," "officers, "confus'd," "I han't"); Alice Morse Earle, ed., *Diary of Anna Green Winslow: A Boston School Girl of 1771* (Boston, 1894), Feb. 25, [1772], 36 ("No sooner"); John Leach Diaries, II, 1775–1776, MHS, Collections Online, https://www.masshist.org/database/6673,), July 2–17, 1775, [13] ("some of the Vilest"). The Twenty-Ninth Regiment arrived in Boston in September 1768; see Zabin, *Boston Massacre,* 49–55; see also ibid., 79–108. Two Elizabeth Smiths, possibly the same woman, were admitted to the almshouse in August 1769 and another from November 1769 through January 1770; see Records of Admissions and Discharges, Nov. 9, 1758–Apr. 28, 1774, reel 8, 39, Boston Overseers of the Poor Records, 1733–1925, MHS.

28. Eliza Farmar to Jack Halroyd, Dec. 4, 1783, Eliza Farmar Letter book, 1774–1789, HSP ("compleat all," "in the depth"); H[annah] Bancker to Everet Banker, May 9, 1783, Bancker Family Papers, 1700–1862, box 1, folder 6, Manuscripts and Archives Division, NYPL ("I am still," "I have been," "offer[ed]," "See what a poor," "I am at present").

29. Duane, ed., *Extracts from the Diary of Christopher Marshall,* May 16, 1778, 181 ("I and my wife," "that is," "I must"), June 4, 1778, 185 ("Our house," "presence"), July 19, 1778, 193 ("discouraging"), Sept. 18, 1778, 200 ("very ordinary"); see also ibid., Jan. 6, 1778, 157–158, May 17, 1778, 181–182, June 10, 12, 16, 1778, 186–187, and July 27, 30, 1778, 194.

30. Margaret Mascarene Hutchinson to Mrs. Margaret [Holyoke] Mascarene, Apr. 25, 1789, Mascarene Family Papers, 1687–1839, MHS.

31. Crane, ed., *Diary of Elizabeth Drinker,* I, Dec. 18, 1778, 337.

32. For class dynamics, see Judith L. Van Buskirk, *Generous Enemies: Patriots and Loyalists in Revolutionary New York* (Philadelphia, 2002), 75. For mutual agreements, see Frey, *British Soldier,* 61–62; for sex in the eighteenth-century British Army, see Jennine Hurl-Eamon, *Marriage and the British Army in the Long Eighteenth Century: "The Girl I Left Behind Me"* (Oxford, 2014), 127–129.

33. Sarah Logan Fisher Diary, V, Mar. 14, 1778, [11] ("very bad," "licentiousness"); Frey, *British Soldier,* 62 ("marr[y]"); "Church Book of Hesse-Cassel Chaplain Georg C. Coester," in Bruce E. Burgoyne, comp. and trans., *Hessian Chaplains: Their Diaries and Duties* (Berwyn Heights, Md., 2003), 43 ("pleasant," "caused").

34. *The Journal of Nicholas Cresswell, 1774–1777* (New York, 1924), July 2, 1777, 246 ("ammunition"); Margaret Moncrieff Coughlan, *Memoirs of Mrs. Coughlan, Daughter of the Late Major Moncrieffe . . .* (New York, 1864), 43 ("libertines"); Frey, *British Soldier,* 61–62.

35. GCM of Nathaniel Fitzpatrick, Philadelphia, May 29, 1778, WO 71/86, 292 ("Violent"), 294 ("Captain," "kept"), 306–308, TNA.

36. Ibid., 291 ("behaving"), 295, 296 ("Frequently," "throwing"), 299 ("disorder'd"), 304 ("enticed").

37. GCM of Patrick McGuire, New York, Feb. 20, 1781, WO 71/93, 175–176, 180 ("her Bed Gown"), 181 ("much in Liquor"), film 675, reel 14, DLAR.

38. GCM of Nathaniel Fitzpatrick, Philadelphia, May 29, 1778, WO 71/86, 297 ("wish'd"), 304 ("Inveigl[ing]"), TNA.

39. Ibid., 296–298, 308 (quotation).

40. Account Book, Anonymous Financial Records, 1778–1779, HC.MC.975.08.013, HCQSC ("Cohabited," "Poor woman"); *Journal of Nicholas Cresswell,* June 17, 1777, 234 ("declar[ed]"); Johann Ewald, *Diary of the American War: A Hessian Journal,* ed. and trans. Joseph P. Tustin (New Haven, Conn., 1979), Jan. 30, 1778, 118–119 ("These people," 119); Sarah Bancroft to James Bancroft, Dec. 18, 1777, Miscellaneous Bound Manuscripts, 1776–1778, MHS ("We wish"). For Margaret Locke, see Evidence on the Foregoing Memorial of Margaret Locke, AO 12/38, 352, TNA. In 1781, Captain Joshua Locke of the Loyal American Regiment abandoned Margaret and their three-month-old infant (ibid., 350–351).

41. For more on impoverished women and single mothers in early America, see Wulf, *Not All Wives,* 153–179; Kirsten Fischer, *Suspect Relations: Sex, Race, and Resistance in Colonial North Carolina* (Ithaca, N.Y., 2002), 98–130; John Ruston Pagan, *Anne Orthwood's Bastard: Sex and Law in Early Virginia* (Oxford, 2003); Lyons, *Sex among the Rabble,* 59–114, 199, 354–392; Salinger, *To Serve Well and Faithfully,* 109–110; and Cornelia H. Dayton and Sharon V. Salinger, *Robert Love's Warnings: Searching for Strangers in Colonial Boston* (Philadelphia, 2014); see also Cornelia Hughes Dayton, *Women before the Bar: Gender, Law, and Society in Connecticut, 1639–1789* (Williamsburg, Va., and Chapel Hill, N.C., 1995), 157–230. For indentured servants, see Kathleen M. Brown, *Good Wives, Nasty Wenches, and Anxious Patriarchs: Gender, Race, and Power in Colonial Virginia* (Williamsburg, Va., and Chapel Hill, N.C., 1996), 130, 230; and Madar, "A People Between," 59–60. For women's disconnection from natal communities, see Zabin, "Intimate Ties and the Boston Massacre," in Oberg, ed., *Women in the American Revolution,* 198–204.

42. Persifor Frazer, "To Be Sold . . . a Mulatto Wench Named Rachel," *Pennsylvania Packet; or, The General Advertiser* (Philadelphia), Dec. 12, 1778, [3] ("weary"); Debra L. Newman, "Black Women in the Era of the American Revolution in Pennsylvania," *Journal of Negro History,* LXI (1976), 286–287 ("active"); GCM of Mary Basford, Mary Groves, and Elizabeth Jackson, New York, Nov. 25, 1778, WO 71/88, 49–52, film 675, reel 11, DLAR. For an example of Black women as background actors, see GCM of Nathaniel Fitzpatrick, Philadelphia, May 29, 1778, WO 71/86, 295, TNA.

43. Memorial of Elizabeth Thompson, AO 12/46, 80, TNA ("not uncommon"); Paul Dayrell, "Run Away from the Subscriber, a Negro Wench, Named Dinah," *Royal American Gazette,* Dec. 23, 1779, [2] ("supposed," "white cloth"). For Dayrell, see *A List of the General and Staff Officers and of the Officers in the Several Regiments Serving in North-America . . .*

(New York, 1777), 32. Dayrell does not appear in the 1778 register. For more about the lack of records about these relationships, see Betty Wood, "'High Notions of Their Liberty': Women of Color and the American Revolution in Lowcountry Georgia and South Carolina, 1765–1783," in Philip Morgan, ed., *African American Life in the Georgia Lowcountry: The Atlantic World and the Gullah Geechee* (Athens, Ga., 2010), 60.

44. Ewald, *Diary of the American War,* ed. Tustin, June 21, 1781, 305 ("plundered"); Daniel Stevens to John Wendell, Feb. 20, 1782, *PMHS,* XLVIII (Boston, 1915), 342 ("richest"); Memorial of Thompson, AO 12/46, 80. For stopping on the street, see "A Negro Wench Is Detected Wearing a Lutestring Striped Silk Gown," *Royal Gazette* (New York), Mar. 18, 1780, [1]. For enslaved people and the legalities of textiles, see Laura F. Edwards, "James and His Striped Velvet Pantaloons: Textiles, Commerce, and the Law in the New Republic," *JAH,* CVII (2020), 341.

45. "Five Pounds Reward; Run Away, . . . a Negro Wench, Named Kate," *Royal Gazette* (New York), Oct. 18, 1783, [3] ("likely," "her hair," "variety," "Callico"); "Head Quarters, Long Island," June 27, 1778, in William Kelby, ed., *Orderly Book of the Three Battalions of Loyalists Commanded by Brigadier-General Oliver De Lancey, 1776–1778* (New York, 1917), 110 ("Gent[leman]"). For "fancy" enslaved women, see Emily Clark, *The Strange History of the American Quadroon: Free Women of Color in the Revolutionary Atlantic World* (Chapel Hill, N.C., 2013), 161 ("fancy"); and Alexandra J. Finley, *An Intimate Economy: Enslaved Women, Work, and America's Domestic Slave Trade* (Chapel Hill, N.C., 2020).

46. *Journal of Nicholas Cresswell,* July 2, 1777, 246 ("ammunition"); "Five Pounds Reward; Run Away, . . . a Negro Wench, Named Kate," *Royal Gazette* (New York), Oct. 18, 1783, [3] ("great," "shrill"). For more on these military communities, see Frey, *British Soldier,* 62; Holly A. Mayer, *Belonging to the Army: Camp Followers and Community during the American Revolution* (Columbia, S.C., 1996); and Don N. Hagist, "Killed, Imprisoned, Struck by Lightning: Soldiers' Wives on Campaign with the British Army," in Mayer, ed., *Women Waging War in the American Revolution* (Charlottesville, Va., 2022), 132–147. For Boyle in Nova Scotia, see Sir Guy Carleton to Richard Hewlett, Sept. 12, 1783, in William Odbur Raymond Scrapbook, "The Loyalist Regiments Leave New York," Provincial Archives of New Brunswick, https://archives.gnb.ca/exhibits/forthavoc/html/Raymond39.aspx?culture=en-CA; and William Odbur Raymond Scrapbook, "The First English Proprietors of the Parish of Woodstock," Provincial Archives of New Brunswick, https://archives.gnb.ca/exhibits/forthavoc/html/Raymond45.aspx?culture=en-CA.

47. Acting Committee Minute Book, 1789–1797, Ser. I, II, AmS .0412, Pennsylvania Abolition Society Papers (Collection 490), 1751–1992, HSP ("wait," "Sold"); "For the Pennsylvania Packet; It Is Whispered," *Pennsylvania Packet; or, The General Advertiser,* Jan. 26, 1779, [3] ("staid"). These allegations led Phillis's fiancé Pompey to challenge another man to a duel.

48. Zabin, "Intimate Ties and the Boston Massacre," in Oberg, ed., *Women in the American Revolution,* 197–200 (quotation, 198). For more on soldiers' wives, see Paul E. Kopperman, "The British High Command and Soldiers' Wives in America, 1755–1783," *Journal of the Society for Army Historical Research,* LX (1982), 14–34; Frey, *British Soldier,* 62; Holly A. Mayer, "From Forts to Families: Following the Army into Western Pennsylvania, 1758–1766," *PMHB,* CXXX (2006), 5–43; Hurl-Eamon, *Marriage and the British Army;* Hagist, "Killed, Imprisoned, Struck by Lightning," in Mayer, ed., *Women Waging War,* 132–147; and Zabin, *Boston Massacre,* 1–16, 79–108. For the Continental army, see Mayer, *Belonging to the Army.*

Marriages between British or Hessian officers and laboring women were unlikely, but they did, on occasion, occur. Scottish officer John Peebles observed with surprise "a handsome young fellow of good Character and genteel family . . . [who] persist[ed] against all friendly remonstrance to marry a Girl without the least share of beauty, fortune, sense or above Vulgar connexion"; see Gruber., ed., *John Peebles' American War,* Mar. 13, 1778, 169.

49. "Extract of Mr. F letter to Mrs Fn on His First Being Told in a Letter by His Wife of the Accusation," Nov. 12, 1778, quoted in Rodney Mader, "Elizabeth Graeme Fergusson's 'The Deserted Wife,'" *PMHB,* CXXXV (2011), 173 (quotation). Henry Fergusson, who lodged in the Stedman's house during the occupation of Philadelphia, supposedly "diswaded" Jane from the marriage and "told her that he [the soldier] would probably leave her, and that such people in the army Seldom make steady good Husbands" (ibid., 173). Jane later named Fergusson as the father of her bastard child (152). Most officers' servants were soldiers themselves; see John Rees, "War as a Waiter: Soldier Servants," *Journal of the American Revolution* (Apr. 28, 2015), https://allthingsliberty.com/2015/04/war-as-a-waiter-soldier-servants/.

50. Sarah Logan Fisher Diary, V, Feb. 21, 1778, [7], Feb. 28, 1778, [9], and May 29, 1778, [17].

51. "Church Book of Hesse-Cassel Chaplain Georg C. Coester," in Burgoyne, comp. and trans., *Hessian Chaplains,* 44 (quotations); Lyons, *Sex among the Rabble,* 217–225; Ruth H. Bloch, *Gender and Morality in Anglo-American Culture, 1650–1800* (Berkeley, Calif., 2003), 83–90.

52. Kopperman, "British High Command and Soldiers' Wives," *Journal of the Society for Army Historical Research,* LX (1982), 22–24, 26–29.

53. "Church Book of Hesse-Cassel Chaplain Georg C. Coester," in Burgoyne, comp. and trans., *Hessian Chaplains,* 16 (quotations); Kopperman, "British High Command and Soldiers' Wives," *Journal of the Society for Army Historical Research,* LX (1982), 17–22, 33–34.

54. Earle, ed., *Diary of Anna Green Winslow,* Feb. 25, [1772], 37 (quotation). For more on this incident, see note 27, above.

55. Letter G: Knyphausen's Correspondence, Knyphausen to His Serene Highness the Landgrave, Philadelphia, May 23, 1778, 248, Morristown Hessian Documents of the American Revolution, 1776–1783, fiche 57, DLAR ("desertions"); Döhla, *Hessian Diary,* Oct. 25, 1779, 113 ("strictest"). For examples of women causing men to desert, see ibid., June 29, 1779, 106; and Journal of John André, June 17, 1777, Mss.DLAR.film 383, June 11, 1777–Nov. 15, 1778, DLAR.

56. GCM of Mary Jefferies, Brooklyn, N.Y., Aug. 24, 1778, WO 71/86, 174 ("having advised"), 175 ("always," "made their Hut"), 176, film 675, reel 10, DLAR; for the Jeffries' marriage, see Old Swedes Church Gloria Dei: Baptisms, Marriages, 1750–1789, I, Apr. 9, 1778, 569, HSP.

57. Elizabeth Drinker to Henry Drinker, Feb. 26, 1778, Drinker Letters (quotations). For a similar reading of Jane in Elizabeth Drinker's diary, see Hirsch, "Philadelphia Quaker Elizabeth Drinker and Her Servant, Jane Boon," in Rhoden and Steele, eds., *Human Tradition in the American Revolution,* 159–182.

58. Crane, ed., *Diary of Elizabeth Drinker,* I, June 30, 1778, 313 ("unwel"), July 8, 1778, 315 ("vomitting"), July 6–Aug 10, 1778, 314–320, Aug. 19, 1778, 321; see also, Hirsch, "Philadelphia Quaker Elizabeth Drinker and Her Servant, Jane Boon," in Rhoden and Steele, eds., *Human Tradition in the American Revolution,* 175. For Elizabeth's journey, see Crane, ed., *Diary of Elizabeth Drinker,* I, Apr. 5–30, 1778, 296–304. For Sally Brant, see Lyons, *Sex among the Rabble,* 199; and Salinger, *To Serve Well and Faithfully,* 109–110.

59. Crane, ed., *Diary of Elizabeth Drinker,* I, Sept. 7, 1778, 325 ("Jane," "that Janny"), Nov. 29, 1795, 756 ("lived"); for callers, see ibid., I, Sept. 24, 1778, and Oct. 3, 1778, 328–329; for desertion, see ibid., I, Nov. 29, 1795, 756; for subsequent visits, see ibid., I, June 30–July 1, 1781, 389, Sept. 19–24, 1784, 428–429, and Oct. 8, 1785, 440.

CHAPTER 5

1. Ira D. Gruber, ed., *John Peebles' American War: The Diary of a Scottish Grenadier* (Mechanicsburg, Pa., 1998), Mar. 8, 1779, 252 ("clear," "intention"), Mar. 27, 1779, 254 ("young"), Mar. 22, 1781, 433–434 ("sat down," "drank," "remaining"); for Peeble's social activities, see ibid., Feb. 16, 1779, 249, Mar. 31, 1781, 435, Apr. 16, 1781, 438, and May 1, 1781, 441.

2. For colonial precedents, see Serena R. Zabin, *Dangerous Economies: Status and Commerce in Imperial New York* (Philadelphia, 2009), 90–100; Kate Haulman, *The Politics of Fashion in Eighteenth-Century America* (Chapel Hill, N.C., 2011), 34–41; and Haulman, "Rods and Reels: Social Clubs and Political Culture in Early Pennsylvania," *EAS,* XII (2014), 143–173. For the continued political influence of these social gatherings, see the forum in *JER,* XXXV (2015), 165–259, esp. François Furstenberg and David Waldstreicher, eds., "Re-Reintroducing the Republican Court," 165–167; and Samantha Sing Key, "Aristocratic Pretension in Republican Ballrooms: Dance, Etiquette, and Identity in Washington City, 1804," *EAS,* XVI (2018), 460–488.

3. For elite young women's socialization with the British Army, see Darlene Emmert Fisher, "Social Life in Philadelphia during the British Occupation," *Pennsylvania History,* XXXVII (1970), 237–260; John W. Jackson, *With the British Army in Philadelphia, 1777–1778* (San Rafael, Calif., 1979), 209–218; Susan E. Klepp, "Rough Music on Independence Day: Philadelphia, 1778," in William Pencak, Matthew Dennis, and Simon P. Newman, eds., *Riot and Revelry in Early America* (University Park, Penn., 2002), 156–176; Kate Haulman, "Fashion and the Culture Wars of Revolutionary Philadelphia," *WMQ,* 3d Ser., LXII (2005), 625–662; David S. Shields and Fredrika J. Teute, "The Meschianza: Sum of All Fêtes," *JER,* XXXV (2015), 185–214; Serena Zabin, *The Boston Massacre: A Family History* (Boston, 2020), 79–108; and Donald F. Johnson, *Occupied America: British Military Rule and the Experience of Revolution* (Philadelphia, 2020), 80–111; see also Judith L. Van Buskirk, *Generous Enemies: Patriots and Loyalists in Revolutionary New York* (Philadelphia, 2002), 73–105.

4. For Black women in occupied cities, see Debra L. Newman, "Black Women in the Era of the American Revolution in Pennsylvania," *Journal of Negro History,* LXI (1976), 276–289; Betty Wood, "'High Notions of Their Liberty': Women of Color and the American Revolution in Lowcountry Georgia and South Carolina, 1765–1783," in Philip D. Morgan, ed., *African American Life in the Georgia Lowcountry: The Atlantic World and the Gullah Geechee* (Athens, Ga., 2010), 48–76; Lauren Duval, "Mastering Charleston: Property and Patriarchy in British-Occupied Charleston, 1780–82," *WMQ,* 3d Ser., LXXV (2018), 616–622; and Johnson, *Occupied America,* 81–89.

5. I am not the first to highlight the importance of women as cultural arbiters during the war; see Haulman, "Fashion and the Culture Wars," *WMQ,* 3d Ser., LXII (2005), 625–662; and Shields and Teute, "Meschianza," *JER,* XXXV (2015), 193, 198–199.

6. Daniel Stevens to John Wendell, Feb. 20, 1782, *PMHS,* XLVIII (Boston, 1915), 342 (quotation). The Meschianza has been a fixture in the historiography of gender in the American Revolution; see Fisher, "Social Life in Philadelphia," *Pennsylvania History,* XXXVII (1970), 251–253; Randall Fuller, "Theaters of the American Revolution: The Valley Forge *Cato* and the Meschianza in Their Transcultural Contexts," *Early American Literature,* XXXIV (1999), 126–146; Klepp, "Rough Music on Independence Day," in Pencak, Dennis, and Newman, eds., *Riot and Revelry in Early America,* 156–178; Haulman, *Politics of Fashion,* 170–179; and Shields and Teute, "Meschianza," *JER,* XXXV (2015), 185–214. For sexuality, see ibid., 193, 198–199, 203–204, 210; Christian DuComb, *Haunted City: Three Centuries of Racial Impersonation in Philadelphia* (Ann Arbor, Mich., 2017), 26–57; and Johnson, *Occupied America,* 102–103, 170. For the "Ethiopian Ball," see Cynthia M. Kennedy, *Braided Relations, Entwined Lives: The Women of Charleston's Urban Slave Society* (Bloomington, Ind., 2005), 39–40; Wood, "'High Notions of Their Liberty,'" in Morgan, ed., *African American Life in the Georgia Lowcountry,* 64–65; Duval, "Mastering Charleston," *WMQ,* 3d Ser., LXXV (2018), 616–622; and Johnson, *Occupied America,* 81–82.

7. [Deborah Norris] to Sarah Wister, [early April 1778], in Kathryn Zabelle Derounian, "'A Dear Dear Friend': Six Letters from Deborah Norris to Sarah Wister, 1778–1779," in "Notes and Documents," *PMHB,* CVIII (1984), 500 ("they were"); Johann Ewald, *Diary of the American War: A Hessian Journal,* ed. Joseph P. Tustin (New Haven, Conn., 1979), Jan. 30, 1778, 118–119 ("women," "ma[king]"). For the Norris garden, see Deborah Logan, *The Norris House* (Philadelphia, 1867), 1, 5–7. See also Mary Norris Insurance Survey, Mar. 1, 1774, S01760, The Philadelphia Contributionship Digital Archives, www.philadelphiabuildings.org/. For the Royal Artillery's drill schedule, see Royal Artillery, Brigade Orders, Dec. 9, 1777, James Pattison Papers, 1777–1781, film 47, DLAR. For officers' visits, see John F. Watson, *Annals of Philadelphia . . .* (Philadelphia, 1830), 354.

8. Deborah Norris to Sarah Wister, [Apr. 18, 1778], in Derounian, "'A Dear Dear Friend,'" in "Notes and Documents," *PMHB,* CVIII (1984), 500, 503 (quotations). This officer was probably Lieutenant Richard Norris of the Seventeenth Regiment of Foot; see *A List of the General and Staff Officers and of the Officers in the Several Regiments Serving in North-America . . .* (New York, 1778), 18.

9. Elizabeth Murray to Dorothy Forbes, June 11, 1776, Murray-Robbins Family Papers, 1658–1944, I, MHS.

10. "Lady Cathcart to Mrs. Gore," Dec. 4, 1780, in Eugene Devereux, ed., *Chronicles of the Plumsted Family, with Some Family Letters* (Philadelphia, 1887), 46, 78 ("I am sure"); Elizabeth Shipton to Aquila Giles, Monday morning, Giles Family Papers, 1750–1881, box 1, folder 2, NYHS ("Rebellion"). For examples of these gendered social dynamics in other wars, see Elaine Tyler May, *Homeward Bound: American Families in the Cold War Era* (New York, 1988); Maria Höhn, *GIs and Fräuleins: The German-American Encounter in 1950s West Germany* (Chapel Hill, N.C., 2002); and Mary Louise Roberts, *What Soldiers Do: Sex and the American GI in World War II France* (Chicago, 2013).

11. "Letter X," May 19, 1781, in Caroline Gilman, ed., *Letters of Eliza Wilkinson, during the Invasion and Possession of Charlestown, S.C., by the British in the Revolutionary War* (New York, 1839), 94 ("gives"); Mary Clay Letter, circa 1783 [Nov. 9, 1782], no. 925-z, SHC ("patriotic," "horrid"). For fashion and ideology, see "Letter XII," n.d., in Gilman, ed., *Letters of Eliza*

Wilkinson, 104–105; and Haulman, "Fashion and the Culture Wars," *WMQ,* 3d Ser., LXII (2005), 625–662. For examples of socialization across politics, see Fisher, "Social Life in Philadelphia," *Pennsylvania History,* XXXVII (1970), 246–253; Benjamin H. Irvin, *Clothed in Robes of Sovereignty: The Continental Congress and the People Out of Doors* (New York, 2011), 155–159; Samuel W. Ravenel, "The True Story of Katharine Walton," *Southern Bivouac: A Monthly Literary and Historical Magazine,* New Ser., I (1885), 445; and Harriott Horrÿ (Rutledge) Ravenel, *Charleston: The Place and the People* (New York, 1906), 296–299.

12. Samuel Stelle Smith, [ed.], *At General Howe's Side, 1776–1778: The Diary of General William Howe's Aide de Camp, Captain Friedrich von Muenchhausen,* trans. Ernst Kipping (Monmouth Beach, N.J., 1974), Sept. 26, 1777, 36 ("unexpected"); Reinhart J. Pope, trans., *A Hessian Soldier in the American Revolution: The Diary of Stephan Popp* (n.p., 1953), July 16, 1778, 11 ("almost like gods"); Journal of the Von Huyn Regiment, Apr. 1, [1778], quoted in Walter K. Schroder, *The Hessian Occupation of Newport and Rhode Island, 1776–1779* (Westminster, Md., 2005), 117 ("They have," "they side"); Gruber, ed., *John Peebles' American War,* Mar. 25, 1778, 171–172 ("with a party," 171), June 11, 1778, 188; "VIII: Letter from Philadelphia," Feb. 16, 1779, in Ray W. Pettengill, ed., *Letters from America, 1776–1779 . . .* (1924; rpt. [Port Washington, N.Y.], 1964), 258 ("agreeable"). For officers' wives, see Sylvia R. Frey, *British Soldier in America: A Social History of Military Life in the Revolutionary Period* (Austin, Tex., 1981), 20.

13. Loftus Cliffe to Charles Tottenham, July 5, 1778, Loftus Cliffe Papers, 1769–1784, WCL ("I never," "indulged"); Johann Heinriches to the Honourable Counsellor of the Court, H., Jan. 18, 1778, in "Extracts from the Letter-Book of Captain Johann Heinrichs of the Hessian Jäger Corps, 1778–1780," *PMHB,* XXII (1898), 139 ("Assemblies"); Gruber, ed., *John Peebles' American War,* Mar. 16, 1778, 169 ("But most women"). For examples of concerts, dinners, and plays, see "Mrs. Cowley, Most Respectful . . . ," *Newport Gazette* (R.I.), Dec. 1[8], 1777, [3], "Mrs. Cowley, with Her Most Respectful Compli[ments] Humbly Begs Leave," Jan. 1, 1778, [4], "Mrs. Cowley Most Respectfully Begs Leave," Jan. 29, 1778, [3], "New York, January 12; The Theatre Royal in This City Was Opened Last Tuesday Evening," Feb. 5, 1778, [1], "At the Particular Request of a Respectable Gentlemen of the Army," May 21, 1778, [3]; "For the Benefit of Signior Franceschini, There Will Be a Concert of Musick," *South-Carolina and American General Gazette* (Charlest[o]n, S.C.), Feb. 21, 1781, [3]; "By Permission; There Will Be a Concert . . . ," *Royal Gazette* (Charleston, S.C.), Oct. 3–Oct. 6, 1781, [1]; and Gruber, ed., *John Peebles' American War,* Jan. 6, 1778, 161; see also ibid., May 19, 1778, 183.

14. "Mrs. Cowley's Respectful Compliments," *Newport Gazette,* Apr. 24, 1777, [3] ("genteel"); Gruber, ed., *John Peebles' American War,* Jan. 4, 1777, 77 ("ladies"), Jan. 22, 1779, 244 ("none," "handsome," "some," "nothing"); Smith, [ed.], *At General Howe's Side,* trans. Kipping, Jan. 21, 1778, 47 ("from the highest"). For social events, see Fisher, "Social Life in Philadelphia," *Pennsylvania History,* XXXVII (1970), 246; William Howe Orderly Book, Jan. 26, 1778, Mar. 9, 1776–May, 1, 1778, WCL, Digital Collection, https://quod.lib.umich.edu/h/howew/howew.0001.001; "The Gentlemen of the Navy, Army and Town, Are Acquainted, That the Garrison Subscription Balls Will Commence on Friday Evening," *Royal Gazette* (Charleston, S.C.), Jan. 9–12, 1782, [3], "The Second Garrison Subscription Ball," Jan. 26–Jan. 30, 1782, [1], "The Third Garrison Subscription Ball," Feb. 9–13, 1782, [3]; and "Sir William Howe Gave an Elegant Ball and Supper in the Evening," *Newport Gazette,* Jan. 30, 1777, [3], D'Aubant and Maltzburg, "There Is a Subscription Opened for a Ball," [3].

15. Sarah Knott, "Female Liberty? Sentimental Gallantry, Republican Womanhood, and Rights Feminism in the Age of Revolutions," *WMQ*, 3d Ser., LXXI (2014), 428 (quotations), 455–456; Johnson, *Occupied America*, 97–103.

16. "A Letter of Miss Rebecca Franks," 1778, *PMHB*, XVI (1892), 216–217 ("You can have," 216, "rakeing," 217), "Letter of Miss Rebecca Franks," Aug. 10, 1781, *PMHB*, XXIII (1899), 304–305 ("to hear," 305, "single out," 304–305, "'Tis," 304). For libertines, see Clare A. Lyons, *Sex among the Rabble: An Intimate History of Gender and Power in the Age of Revolution, Philadelphia, 1730–1830* (Williamsburg, Va., and Chapel Hill, N.C., 2006), 124–125; and Thomas Foster, "Reconsidering Libertines and Early Modern Heterosexuality: Sex and American Founder Gouverneur Morris," *Journal of the History of Sexuality*, XXII (2013), 65–84, esp. 65–71; see also Jennifer J. Davis, *Bad Subjects: Libertine Lives in the French Atlantic, 1619–1814* (Lincoln, Nebr., 2023).

17. Edward H. Tatum, Jr., ed., *The American Journal of Ambrose Serle, Secretary to Lord Howe, 1776–1778* (San Marino, Calif., 1940), 266n.

18. Mrs. Jauncey to Mrs. Gore, Jan. 27, 1783, in Devereux, ed., *Chronicles of the Plumsted Family*, 87 ("eighty," "Gentlemen"); "A Letter of Miss Rebecca Franks," 1778, *PMHB*, XVI (1892), 217 ("no loss"), "Letter of Miss Rebecca Franks," Aug. 10, 1781, *PMHB*, XXIII (1899), 308 ("Yesterday," "how the girls"). For the duel, see Elizabeth Ellery Dana, [ed.], *The British in Boston: Being the Diary of Lieutenant John Barker of the King's Own Regiment from November 15, 1774, to May 31, 1776 . . .* (Cambridge, Mass., 1924), Nov. 16, 1775, 68.

19. Mrs. Jauncey to Mrs. Gore, Aug. 3, 1783, in Devereux, ed., *Chronicles of the Plumsted Family*, 99 ("and being"), 100 ("awkwardness"), Mrs. Elliot to Mrs. Gore, Sept. 11, 1786, 121 ("all the amusements," "great change); "Letter of Miss Rebecca Franks," Aug. 10, 1781, *PMHB*, XXIII (1899), 305 ("You may imagine," "but so it is").

20. "Letter of Miss Rebecca Franks," Aug. 10, 1781, *PMHB*, XXIII (1899), 304 ("cleverness," "entertain," "decline[d]"); Colonel Stewart to General Wayne, n.d., quoted in Charles J. Stillé, *Major-General Anthony Wayne and the Pennsylvania Line in the Continental Army* (Philadelphia, 1893), 161 ("manners," "They have really").

21. Peter Edes Diary, June–October, 1775, MHS, Collections Online, https://www.masshist.org/database/1978, Sept. 25, 1775, [20–21] (quotation); Gruber, ed., *John Peebles' American War*, Mar. 23, 1778, 171; William Phillips to Elizabeth Shipton Giles, Oct. 19, 1780, Giles Family Papers, box 1, folder 15.

22. "To the Ladies of Rhode-Island," *Newport Gazette*, Apr. 17, 1777, [4] (quotations). For another similar loyalist poem, see Shields and Teute, "Meschianza," *JER*, XXXV (2015), 198–199.

23. E[leanor] Jauncey to Elizabeth Shipton Giles, Mar. 7, 1782, Giles Family Papers, box 1, folder 15 ("This is to be sure"), Elizabeth Shipton to Aquila Giles, n.d., box 1, folder 2 ("among"), Shipton to Giles, Apr. 28, 1780, box 1, folder 1 ("a little Hop"); James Murray to Bessie Smyth, Mar. 5, 1778, in Eric Robson, ed., *Letters from America, 1773–1780; Being the Letters of a Scots Officer James Murray, to His Home during the War for American Independence* (Manchester, U.K., 1951), 52 ("There has been less").

24. Shortly after capturing Newport in December 1779, British and Hessian officers hosted a ball at the Redwood Library; see Diary of Captain Friedrich von der Malsburg, Dec. 30, 1776, quoted in Schroder, *Hessian Occupation of Newport*, 65–67. For colonial precedents, see Zabin, *Dangerous Economies*, 90–100.

25. John Trumbull, *M'Fingal: A Modern Epic Poem* (1776–1820), in *The Poetical Works of John Trumbull . . .*, I (Hartford, Conn.,1820), 139 (quotation), quoted in Robert G. Parkinson, *The Common Cause: Creating Race and Nation in the American Revolution* (Williamsburg, Va., and Chapel Hill, N.C., 2016), 591. For manners, see C. Dallett Hempill, *Bowing to Necessities: A History of Manners in America, 1620–1860* (New York, 1999); Hemphill, "Middle Class Rising in Revolutionary America: The Evidence from Manners," *Journal of Social History*, XXX (1996), 317–344; Rosemarie Zagarri, "Morals, Manners, and the Republican Mother," *American Quarterly*, XLIV (992), 192–215; Barbara Taylor, "Feminists versus Gallants: Manners and Morals in Enlightenment Britain," *Representations*, LXXXVII, no. 1 (Summer 2004), 125–148; Michèle Cohen, "'Manners' Make the Man: Politeness, Chivalry, and the Construction of Masculinity, 1750–1830," *Journal of British Studies*, XLIV (2005), 312–329; and Knott, "Female Liberty?" *WMQ*, 3d Ser., LXXI (2014), 425–456.

26. "Come on My Hearts," Jan. 10, 1781, in Almon W. Lauber, ed., *Orderly Books of the Fourth New York Regiment, 1778–1780, the Second New York Regiment, 1780–1783, by Samuel Tallmadge and Others, with Diaries of Samuel Tallmadge, 1780–1782, and John Barr, 1779–1782* (Albany, N.Y., 1932), 633 ("Sweethearts," "Kiss"), quoted in Charles Royster, *A Revolutionary People at War: The Continental Army and American Character, 1775–1783* (Williamsburg, Va., and Chapel Hill, N.C., 1979), 30, [Wheeler Case], *Poems, Occasioned by Several Circumstances and Occurrencies, in the Present Grand Contest of America for Liberty* (New Haven, Conn., 1778), 6 ("Go act"), quoted ibid., 30; Haulman, "Fashion and the Culture Wars," *WMQ*, 3d Ser., LXII (2005), 648–649; Shields and Teute, "Meschianza," *JER*, XXXV (2015), 190–193, 198–199.

27. Letter V: Journal of the Leib Infantry Regiment, 1776–84, Winter Quarters in R.I., Philadelphia Campaign [English Trans. Fiche 312], 26 (1778), Morristown Hessian Documents of the American Revolution, 1776–1783, fiche 11, DLAR.

28. Richard L. Bushman, *The Refinement of America: Persons, Houses, Cities* (New York, 1992); Zagarri, "Morals, Manners, and the Republican Mother," *American Quarterly*, XLIV (1992), 192–215; Hemphill, *Bowing to Necessities;* Lawrence E. Klein, *Shaftesbury and the Culture of Politeness: Moral Discourse and Cultural Politics in Early Eighteenth-Century England* (Cambridge, 1994); Cohen, "'Manners' Make the Man,'" *Journal of British Studies*, XLIV (2005), 312–329; Stephen Conway, "The British Army, 'Military Europe,' and the American War of Independence," *WMQ*, 3d Ser., LXVII (2010), 69–100.

29. Elizabeth Willing Powel to Anne Francis, Apr. 2, 1778, Powel Family Papers, Ser. III, box 4, folder 3, HSP ("Certainly"); R[ebecca] Coxe to Tench Coxe, February 1778, Coxe Family Papers, 1638–1970, Ser. 2a, box 7, folder 15, HSP ("account," "raised," "we should"); "A Letter of Miss Rebecca Franks," 1778, *PMHB*, XVI (1892), 216–217 ("I know," 217, "more ridiculous," 217, "I've been," 217, "scarce," 216).

30. Sir Archibald Campbell Revolutionary War letter, Jan. 9, 1779, GHS 1581, GHS ("intollerable," "You will please"); Hannah Lawrence Schieffelin, [No. 21], "On the Purpose to Which the Avenue Adjoining Trinity Church Has of Late Been Dedicated," 1779, in "Notebook of Poems," 1774–1794, [48], Manuscripts and Archives Division, NYPL, Digital Collections, https://digitalcollections.nypl.org/items/a3dc5690-c557-0139-c4d3-0242ac110004 ("scene"). For more on revolutionary propaganda, see Parkinson, *Common Cause;* Robert G. Parkinson, *Thirteen Clocks: How Race United the Colonies and Made the Declaration of Independence* (Williamsburg, Va., and Chapel Hill, N.C., 2021); and Joseph M. Adelman,

Revolutionary Networks: The Business and Politics of Printing the News, 1763–1789 (Baltimore, Md., 2019).

31. Johnathan Odell, "Prologue Spoken by Major Robert Chew at the Opening of the Theatre in Philadelphia," Jan. 19, 1778, Accounts of Theatrical Performances for the Entertainment of British Soldiers during the Revolution, 1775–1780, HSP (quotation); Susanna Centlivre, *The Wonder: A Woman Keeps a Secret; A Comedy; As It Is Acted at the Theatre Royal in Drury-Lane . . .* (London, 1714); Fred Lewis Pattee, "The British Theater in Philadelphia in 1778," *American Literature: A Journal of Literary History, Criticism, and Bibliography,* VI (1935), 383; "The Comedy, Called a Wonder or a Woman Keeps a Secret . . . ," *Pennsylvania Ledger: or, The Philadelphia Market-Day Advertiser,* Jan. 3, 1778, [2], "The Comedy, Called a Wonder or a Woman Keeps a Secret . . . ," Jan. 7, 1778, [1]. For martial chivalry in the British Army, see Cohen, "'Manners' Make the Man,'" *Journal of British Studies,* XLIV (2005), 312–329; Conway, "British Army," *WMQ,* LXVII (2010), 69–100; and Catriona Kennedy, "John Bull into Battle: Military Masculinity and the British Army Officer during the Napoleonic Wars," in Karen Hagemann, Gisela Mettele, and Jane Rendall, eds., *Gender, War, and Politics: Transatlantic Perspectives, 1775–1830* (New York, 2010), 127–146.

32. Epilogue to the Tragedy of Gaza by General Burgoyne, Giles Family Papers, box 1, folder 48 ("What is a beau?" "too bold," "to learn"); "Letter of Miss Rebecca Franks," Aug. 10, 1781, *PMHB,* XXIII (1899), 305 ("made the men"). After reading another of Burgoyne's epilogues in April 1776, Abigail Adams quipped, "Burgoine is a Better poet than Soldier"; see Abigail Adams to John Adams, Apr. 14, 1776, FO, https://founders.archives.gov/documents/Adams/04-01-02-0247. For more on the gendered nature of military hierarchies, see Emily Merrill, "Judging Empire: Masculinity and the Making of the British Imperial Army, 1754–1783" (Ph.D. diss., University of Pennsylvania, 2015), 37–66.

33. Tatum, ed., *American Journal of Ambrose Serle,* Aug. 7, 1776, 69 ("If you dont"); [Margaret Coughlan], *Memoirs of Mrs. Coughlan, Daughter of the Late Major Moncrieffe: Written by Herself* (New York, 1864), 31–32, 34, 35 ("*twig,*" "served").

34. Elizabeth Shipton to Aquila Giles, Apr. 28, 1780, Giles Family Papers, box 1, folder 1 ("How," "Sparrow," "Dont"); "An Epilogue Spoke in the Character of a Recruiting Serjeant of the Guards at an Entertainment Given by Mr. Cruden to the Ladies and Gentlemen of Charlestown in Commemoration of the Battle of Guilford Courthouse on the 15th of March 1781," George Chalmers Collection, 1606–1817, MssCol 507, Papers Relating to Carolina, box 1, Manuscripts and Archives Division, NYPL ("Trembling," "Join," "'Tis we enjoy").

35. Elizabeth Oswald Chew to Benjamin Chew, Dec. 15, 1777, Chew Family Papers, 1659–1986, Ser. 2c, box 10, HSP (quotations). For more on officers' gentlemanly manners, see Van Buskirk, *Generous Enemies,* 73–105.

36. Elizabeth Oswald Chew to Benjamin Chew, Dec. 15, 1777, Chew Family Papers, Ser. 2c, box 10.

37. Ondine E. Le Blanc, ed., "The Journal of the 'Rebel Lady': Katharine Farnham Hay's Account of Her Trip to New York City, 1778," *PMHS,* CIX (Boston, 1998), May 11, 1778, 113 ("Rebel"), May 13, 1778, 119 ("chating," "my Gallant," "Next Day"), June 23, 1778, 111 ("truly diverting," "as I had").

38. Hannah Lawrence Schieffelin, [No. 31], "Descend, O Muse, in Deathless Verse," April 1780, in "Notebook of Poems," [74] ("to which the fair," "Of late," "fools," "female size"); Ewald Gustav Schaukirk, "Occupation of New York City by the British," *PMHB,* X (1887),

Aug. 19, 1779, 427 ("military," "lamps," "gentlemen," "walk," "that none"); Johnson, *Occupied America,* 92.

39. "Letter X," May 19, 1781, in Gilman, ed., *Letters of Eliza Wilkinson,* 93 ("I despise"), "Letter XI," July 14, [?], 95 ("quarrel[s]"), "Letter XII," n.d., 104–105 ("concerts," "I would rather"); see also "Letter XI," July 14, [?], ibid., 99.

40. "Letter XI," July 14, [?], ibid., 95–96, 97 ("nothing," "I have often," "for I was"), 98, 99 ("You do not know," "Will you?"), 100; see also Elizabeth Shipton to Aquila Giles, Saturday Afternoon, Giles Family Papers, box 1, folder 2; and Letters between William Tudor and Delia Jarvis, Tudor Family Papers, 1773–1822, MHS. For the gender dynamics of courtship, see Sharon Block, *Rape and Sexual Power in Early America* (Williamsburg, Va., and Chapel Hill, N.C., 2006), 39–50; Nicole Eustace, "'The Cornerstone of a Copious Work': Love and Power in Eighteenth-Century Courtship," *Journal of Social History,* XXXIV (2001), 517–546; and Ruth H. Bloch, *Gender and Morality in Anglo-American Culture, 1650–1800* (Berkeley, Calif., 2003), 78–101; see also Mary Kelley, "'While Pen, Ink, and Paper Can Be Had': Reading and Writing in a Time of Revolution," *EAS,* X (2012), 439–466.

41. Christian Barnes to Elizabeth Murray Smith, [Aug. 7, 1768?], Murray-Robbins Family Papers, I ("great raptures," "whether"); William Rawle to Anna Rawle, n.d. (circa 1779–1780), William Rawle Letter book, 1778–1782, 21–22, WCL ("That female"). For prewar precedents for these civilian-military relationships, see Zabin, *Boston Massacre,* esp. 79–108. For examples of American women who married British and Hessian officers and soldiers, see Max J. Kohler, *Rebecca Franks: An American Jewish Belle of the Last Century* (New York, 1894), 23–27; Don N. Hagist, "Henrietta Overing Auchmuty's Forgotten First Marriage," *Newport History,* LXXXVIII, no. 270 (Spring 2014), 30–41; Andrew Bruce and Henrietta Overing, Marriage Certificate Signed by George Bisset, Newport, Aug. 18, 1778, Guy Carleton Papers, PRO 30/55/11, 1302, TNA; Edward B. Welch, "Joseph Wanton, Junior, an Eighteenth-Century Newport Tragedy," *Newport History,* LXI, no. 208 (Winter 1988), 32–33; Alison Duncan Hirsch, "Philadelphia Quaker Elizabeth Drinker and Her Servant, Jane Boon: 'Times Are Much Changed, and Maids Are Become Mistresses,'" in Nancy L. Rhoden and Ian K. Steele, eds., *The Human Tradition in the American Revolution* (Wilmington, Del., 2000), 174–178; and Travis Glasson, "The Intimacies of Occupation: Loyalties, Compromise, and Betrayal in Revolutionary-Era Newport," in Patrick Spero and Michael Zuckerman, eds., *The American Revolution Reborn* (Philadelphia, 2016), 38–39.

42. Eliza Watson to Mrs. Hutchinson, [June 19], 1787, Hutchinson-Watson Papers, 1766–1903, MHS ("horrid," "pitty"); William Rawle to Anna Rawle, n.d. (circa 1779–1780), William Rawle Letter book, 21 ("pretty Miss Griffiths").

43. Abigail Adams to John Adams, Apr. 7, 1777, FO, https://founders.archives.gov/documents/Adams/04-02-02-0152 ("Stranger," "additional misery"); Abigail Adams, 2d, to Elizabeth Cranch, Feb. 14, 1786, FO, https://founders.archives.gov/documents/Adams/04-07-02-0014 ("delicate"), Abigail Adams, 2d, to Elizabeth Cranch, Dec. 22, 1782, FO, https://founders.archives.gov/documents/Adams/04-05-02-0029 ("I long," "romantick"). Racial prejudices compounded the Boston woman's discovery of her new husband's bigamy; "to add to mortification," Abigail Adams reported, "tis said her [the man's first wife] complexion is not so fair as the American Laidies" (Abigail Adams to John Adams, Apr. 7, 1777, FO). For an overview of married women's rights, see Holly Brewer, "The Transformation of

Domestic Law," in Michael Grossberg and Christopher Tomlins, eds., *The Cambridge History of Law in America,* I (Cambridge, 2008), 288–323.

44. Hannah Lawrence Schieffelin, "A Journal during a Lady's Courtship," 1780 [typescript], [3] ("I am hurried," "I find"), 4–5, Schieffelin Family Papers, Ser. 1, Yale Collection of Western Americana, Beinecke Rare Book and Manuscript Library, Yale University, New Haven, Conn.; Elizabeth Shipton to Aquila Giles, Apr. 26, 1780, Giles Family Papers, box 1, folder 1 ("Hymen," "always"). For more on the Schieffelins, see Van Buskirk, *Generous Enemies,* 68–70; and Johnson, *Occupied America,* 92–93, 142.

45. E[leanor] Jauncey to Elizabeth Shipton Giles, Mar. 7, 1782, Giles Family Papers, box 1, folder 15 ("marrying"); Letter G: Knyphausen's Correspondence, His Serene Highness the Landgrave to Lt Gen v. Knyphausen, June 18, 1778, 229, Morristown Hessian Documents of the American Revolution, fiche 57, DLAR ("I cannot," "hoped for"). The Ansbach-Bayreuth troops permitted eight women per company; some soldiers' wives accompanied the troops from Europe while other men married in North America; see Johann Conrad Döhla, *A Hessian Diary of the American Revolution,* ed. and trans. Bruce E. Burgoyne (Norman, Okla., 1990), 112 n.14.

46. Johann Ewald to Jeannette Van Horne, May 17, 1777, in Ewald, *Diary of the American War,* ed. Tustin, 367 ("It is you"); Elizabeth Shipton to Aquila Giles, Aug. 12, 1780, Giles Family Papers, box 1, folder 1 ("You taste"); Mary Murray to Betsy Murray, July 20, 1775, Murray-Robbins Family Papers, box 1, folder 4 ("I shou'd," "But on the contrary"); Welch, "Joseph Wanton, Junior," *Newport History,* LXI (Winter 1988), 23–24, 32–33.

47. This imagined scene and the recollections that follow draw from both a portrait of Williamina Smith and various descriptions of the roles of young women at the Meschianza; see "Catalogue of Books," Am.3107, HSP ("Meschianza Queen"); Meschianza Dresses, 1778, Watson's Annals Manuscript, Yi2 1609.F.163-166, LCP; Pierre Eugene DuSimitiere, *Pastel Portrait, Probably of Williamina Smith,* DuSimitiere Drawings and Watercolors, Prints and Photographs Division, LCP; John André, "The Meschianza, Humbly Inscribed to Miss Peggy Chew by Her Most Devoted Knight and Servant," June 2, 1778, Cliveden, a Historic Site of the National Trust for Historic Preservation, Philadelphia (hereafter Cliveden); and André, "Particulars of the Mischianza Exhibited in America at the Departure of Gen. Howe; Copy of a Letter from an Officer at Philadelphia to His Correspondent in London," *Gentleman's Magazine and Historical Review,* XLVIII (1778), 355. DuSimitiere painted the portrait after the Meschianza, beginning work in early June 1778. For DuSimitiere's full description of the portrait, see William John Potts, "Du Simitiere, Artist, Antiquary, and Naturalist, Projector of the First American Museum, with Some Extracts from His Note-Book," *PMHB,* XIII (1889), 358–359.

48. André, "The Meschianza, Humbly Inscribed," June 2, 1778, Cliveden ("foremost); "Philadelphia; To the Printer of the Royal Pennsylvania Gazette," *Royal Pennsylvania Gazette* (Philadelphia), May 26, 1778, [3] ("crouding"). For objections, see *Pierre Eugene DuSimitiere: His American Museum 200 Years After . . . ,* exh. cat. (Library Company of Philadelphia, 1985), 2:9. For procession, see André, "Particulars of the Mischianza," *Gentleman's Magazine and Historical Review,* XLVIII (1778), 353; "Philadelphia; To the Printer of the Royal Pennsylvania Gazette," *Royal Pennsylvania Gazette,* May 26, 1778, [3]; Elaine Forman Crane, ed., *The Diary of Elizabeth Drinker,* I (Boston, 1991), May 18, 1778, 306; and "Meschianza Ticket," Henry Clinton Papers, XXXIV, 45–46, WCL.

49. "Some Account of the *Meschianza* by One of the Company, Philadelphia," May 18, 1778, Common Place Book, 1778, Am.005, HSP ("walked"); "Philadelphia; To the Printer of the Royal Pennsylvania Gazette," *Royal Pennsylvania Gazette,* May 26, 1778, [3] ("magnificent"); André, "Particulars of the Mischianza," *Gentleman's Magazine and Historical Review,* XLVIII (1778), 355 ("perfectly"); André, "The Meschianza Humbly Inscribed," June 2, 1778, Cliveden ("blue and white"); Shields and Teute, "Meschianza," *JER,* XXXV (2015), 186–187, 190. For examples of the dresses women wore, see Meschianza Dresses, 1778, Watson's Annals Manuscript, Yi2 1609.F.163–166, John André, [Sketch of a Meschianza Costume], 1778, Yi 2 1069.F.242; DuSimitiere, *Pastel Portrait, Probably of Williamina Smith,* DuSimitiere Drawings and Watercolors; André, "The Meschianza Humbly Inscribed," June 2, 1778, Cliveden; and André, "Particulars of the Mischianza," *Gentleman's Magazine and Historical Review,* XLVIII (1778), 355.

50. DuComb, *Haunted City,* 30–34 ("opulent," 31); Smith, [ed.], *At General Howe's Side,* trans. Kipping, May 18, 1778, 52 ("Everything," "and all"); Shields and Teute, "Meschianza," *JER,* XXXV (2015), 186. For contemporary accounts of the event, see André, "The Meschianza Humbly Inscribed," June 2, 1778, Cliveden; and André, "Particulars of the Mischianza," *Gentleman's Magazine and Historical Review,* XLVIII (1778), 353.

51. Crane, ed., *Diary of Elizabeth Drinker,* I, May 18, 1778, 306 (quotations). The Meschianza was especially elaborate, but charges of frivolity had followed the British Army throughout the war. Writing from Massachusetts in April 1776, Abigail Adams reported, "The officers and Tories have lived a life of Dissipation" in the Boston garrison; see Abigail Adams to John Adams, Apr. 14, 1776, FO.

52. Shields and Teute, "Meschianza," *JER,* XXXV (2015), 190–193 (quotation, 191); DuComb, *Haunted City,* 27–46; for public spectacle, see ibid., 30; and Fuller, "Theaters of the American Revolution," *Early American Literature,* XXXIV (1999), 141. For an example of publication, see André, "Particulars of the Mischianza," *Gentleman's Magazine and Historical Review,* XLVIII (1778), XX.

53. For courtship and submission, see Jan Lewis, "The Republican Wife: Virtue and Seduction in the Early Republic," *WMQ,* 3d. Ser., XLIV (1987), 689–721; Eustace, "'Cornerstone of a Copious Work,'" *Journal of Social History,* XXXIV (2001), 517–546; Bloch, *Gender and Morality in Anglo-American Culture,* 78–101; and Brewer, "Transformation of Domestic Law," in Grossberg and Tomlins, eds., *Cambridge History of Law in America,* I, 288–323.

54. André, "Particulars of the Mischianza," *Gentleman's Magazine and Historical Review,* XLVIII (1778), 354–355 ("No Rival"); Klepp, "Rough Music on Independence Day," in Pencak, Dennis, and Newman, eds., *Riot and Revelry in Early America,* 158 ("sensualized"); Shields and Teute, "Meschianza," *JER,* XXXV (2015), 190–193. Shields and Teute argue that the costumes "symbolized the British/American enmity through gender difference and aestheticized it by substituting court clothes for uniforms and the crusades for the rebellion" (190). They caution, however, against too quickly orientalizing these costumes, given the rage for Turkish dress in the eighteenth century (191). And, as Kate Haulman points out, Philadelphia's women had already embraced the fashions from which André drew his vision; see Haulman, *Politics of Fashion,* 172. For an analysis of the event's racial contours, see DuComb, *Haunted City,* esp. 31–34, 40–42.

55. André, "Particulars of the Mischianza," *Gentleman's Magazine and Historical Review,* XLVIII (1778), 355.

56. "Catalogue of Books" (quotations). For Howe's visits to the Franks house, see Anne Hollingsworth Wharton, *Through Colonial Doorways* (Philadelphia, 1893), 212. A good friend and former schoolmate of Captain John André, one of the event's organizers, Swiss artist Pierre Eugene DuSimitiere (whose portrait of Williamina Smith opened this section), created a similar satirical list in Jamaica in 1762 and likely contributed to the Meschianza's "Catalogue of Books"; see Library Company of Philadelphia, *Pierre Eugene DuSimitiere: His American Museum 200 Years After,* 5:20. Helen Roberta Yalof suggests that the "Catalogue" might have been a type of charades game, with the author having to act out the title; see Yalof, "British Military Theatricals in Philadelphia during the Revolutionary War" (Ph.D. diss., New York University, 1972), 187.

57. Anthony Wayne to Rich[ar]d Peters, July 12, 1778, in Stillé, *Major General Anthony Wayne and the Pennsylvania Line,* 153 (quotations). For similar readings of Wayne's letter that have informed my analysis, see Klepp, "Rough Music on Independence Day," in Pencak, Dennis, and Newman, eds., *Riot and Revelry in Early America,* 163–165; Shields and Teute, "Meschianza," *JER,* XXXV (2015), 200–201; and DuComb, *Haunted City,* 42–44.

58. Wayne to Peters, July 12, 1778, in Stillé, ed., *Major-General Anthony Wayne and the Pennsylvania Line,* 153.

59. William Duane, ed., *Extracts from the Diary of Christopher Marshall: Kept in Philadelphia and Lancaster, during the American Revolution, 1774–1781* (Albany, N.Y., 1877), Dec. 28, 1777, 152 ("our enemies"), Jan. 17, 1778, 161–162 ("revel[ed]," 162).

60. Nathanael Greene to Elihue Greene, n.d., Nathanael Greene Papers, 1770–1798, misc. mss. boxes G, folder 1, AAS.

61. [Hannah Griffitts], "Wrote on Reading Some Paragraphs in the Crisis, April 77," Hannah Griffitts Papers, LCPinHSP.222, 7422.F.52–53, HSP (quotation); Carroll Smith-Rosenberg, "Domesticating 'Virtue': Coquettes and Revolutionaries in Young America," in Elaine Scarry, ed., *Literature and the Body: Essays on Populations and Persons* (Baltimore, Md., 1988), 160–184; Ruth H. Bloch, "The Gendered Meanings of Virtue in Revolutionary America," *Signs: Journal of Women in Culture and Society,* XIII (1987), 37–58; Zagarri, "Morals, Manners, and the Republican Mother," *American Quarterly,* XLIV (1992), 192–215; Haulman, *Politics of Fashion,* 153–180.

62. Shields and Teute, "Meschianza," *JER,* XXXV (2015), 193 (quotation); see also Haulman, *Politics of Fashion,* 153–180.

63. Wayne to Peters, July 12, 1778, in Stillé, ed., *Major-General Anthony Wayne and the Pennsylvania Line,* 153–154. Wayne was decidedly less protective of his wife, advising her in 1780 to garner an introduction to several of Philadelphia's leading revolutionary hostesses "and request them to teach you the secret by which they have become so very fascinating"; see Anthony Wayne to Polly Wayne, June 29, 1780, The Sol Feinstone Collection of the American Revolution, reel 5, 2309, DLAR.

64. Klepp, "Rough Music on Independence Day," in Pencak, Dennis, and Newman, eds., *Riot and Revelry in Early America,* 159, 160, 162–163; Josiah Bartlett to Mary Bartlett, Aug. 24, 1778, in Frank C. Mevers, ed., *The Papers of Josiah Bartlett* (Hanover, N.H., 1979), 214 ("appeared," "Mistresses"). For women's hairstyles and their political significance, see Haulman, *Politics of Fashion,* 156–157, 172–180; and Kate Haulman, "A Short History of the High Roll," *Common-Place,* II, no. 1 (October 2001), http://common-place.org/.

65. Klepp, "Rough Music on Independence Day," in Pencak, Dennis, and Newman, eds., *Riot and Revelry in Early America*, 159 ("corrupted"), 160, 163; John Thaxter to Abigail Adams, July 6, 1778, FO, https://founders.archives.gov/documents/Adams/04-03-02-0048 ("was designed," "end"); Rebecca Franks to Miss Shippen, [Fall 1778], Balch-Shippen Papers, II, 61, HSP ("I'm delighted"). For other analyses of the event, see Haulman, *Politics of Fashion*, 172–174; Irvin, *Clothed in Robes of Sovereignty*, 161–163; and Johnson, *Occupied America*, 170.

66. Unpacking the logic ungirding this transformation, Klepp explains, "a sexualized female could not be simply blackened [i.e. blackface] in the new nation; she must be black. And if black women were sullied, then white women must be virtuous"; see Klepp, "Rough Music on Independence Day," in Pencak, Dennis, and Newman, eds., *Riot and Revelry in Early America*, 169. For the evolution of the event, see John Thaxter to Abigail Adams, July 6, 1778, in L. H. Butterfield and Marc Friedlaender, eds., *Adams Family Correspondence*, III (Cambridge, Mass., 1973), 56 ("noted"), quoted in Klepp, "Rough Music on Independence Day," in Pencak, Dennis, and Newman, eds., *Riot and Revelry in Early America*, 169, Josiah Bartlett to Mary Bartlett, Aug. 24, 1778, in Paul H. Smith et al, eds., *Letters of Delegates to Congress, 1774–1789*, X (Washington, D.C., 1983), 496 ("old"), quoted ibid., 169; and Klepp, "Rough Music on Independence Day," in Pencak, Dennis, and Newman, eds., *Riot and Revelry in Early America*, 165, 169–172, 175 n.50; see also Shields and Teute, "Meschianza," *JER*, XXXV (2015), 200–205; and DuComb, *Haunted City*, 44–46.

67. Hannah Griffitts, "Meschianza; Answer to the Question, 'What Is It?' By a Lady of Philada.," Watson's Annals Manuscript, Yi2 1069.F.241-242, LCP (quotations). As Shields and Teute point out, the veil is also an allusion to the Turkish costumes the women donned at the Meschianza; for further analysis of the poem, see Shields and Teute, "Meschianza," *JER*, XXXV (2015), 187, 195–199.

68. For veils, see Hazel Jones, *Jane Austen and Marriage* (London, 2009), 69–70; Karen K. Hersch, *The Roman Wedding: Ritual and Meaning in Antiquity* (Cambridge, 2010), 95–108; and Merril D. Smith, *Women's Roles in Eighteenth-Century America* (Santa Barbara, Calif., 2010), 8.

69. Watson, *Annals of Philadelphia*, 688, 690–691 (quotations, 691).

70. Griffitts, "Meschianza; Answer to the Question, 'What Is It?' By a Lady of Philada.," Watson's Annals Manuscript, Yi2 1069.F.241-242.

71. For more on the British and enslaved people during the Revolution, see Sylvia R. Frey, *Water from the Rock: Black Resistance in a Revolutionary Age* (Princeton, N.J., 1991); Robert Olwell, *Masters, Slaves, and Subjects: The Culture of Power in the South Carolina Low Country, 1740–1790* (Ithaca, N.Y., 1998); Cassandra Pybus, "Jefferson's Faulty Math: The Question of Slave Defections in the American Revolution," *WMQ*, 3d Ser., LXII (2005), 243–264; Jim Piecuch, *Three Peoples One King: Loyalists, Indians, and Slaves in the Revolutionary South, 1775–1782* (Columbia, S.C., 2008); and Parkinson, *Common Cause*.

72. Daniel Stevens to John Wendell, Feb. 20, 1782, *PMHS*, XLVIII, 342–343 (quotations, 342). Cynthia M. Kennedy and Betty Wood have similarly examined the ball's racial implications, especially as an affront to white Charlestonians; see Kennedy, *Braided Relations, Entwined Lives*, 39–40; and Wood, "'High Notions of Their Liberty,'" in Morgan, ed., *African American Life in the Georgia Lowcountry*, 64–65. The term "Ethiopian Ball" indicates how accounts of the event attempted to disparage Black activities. For the archival construction

of Black women, see Marisa J. Fuentes, *Dispossessed Lives: Enslaved Women, Violence, and the Archive* (Philadelphia, 2016).

73. H. Roy Merrens, "A View of Coastal South Carolina in 1778: The Journal of Ebenezer Hazard," *SCHM,* LXXIII (1972), 177–179, Jan. 18, [1778]–Mar. 5, [1778], 179–193, esp. Feb. 25, [1778], 190 ("peculiarity," "black dances," "Negro," "many," "polite," "generally"); *"Mr. Powell, in My Second Letter," South-Carolina Gazette* (Charleston, S.C.), Sept. 17, 1772, [1] ("nocturnal," *"kitchens"*); Wood, "'High Notions of Their Liberty,'" in Morgan, ed., *African American Life in the Georgia Lowcountry,* 64–65. For *plaçage,* see Emily Clark, *The Strange History of the American Quadroon: Free Women of Color in the Revolutionary Atlantic World* (Chapel Hill, N.C., 2013). For Black uses of space and bodies as sites of resistance and struggle, see Stephanie M. H. Camp, "The Pleasures of Resistance: Enslaved Women and Body Politics in the Plantation South, 1830–1861," *Journal of Southern History,* LXVIII (2002), 533–572.

74. Yvonne Daniel, with Catherine Evleshin, "Parading the Carnivalesque: Masking Circum-Caribbean Demands," in Daniel, *Caribbean and Atlantic Diaspora Dance: Igniting Citizenship* (Urbana, Ill., 2011), 117 ("John Canoe," "Set Girl," "provid[ed]"), 118 (quoting Catherine Evleshin, "caricature," "Set girls pranc[ing]"); for precedents, see ibid., 109–111; for Anglicization and Boxing Day, see ibid., 117; and Kathleen Wilson, "The Performance of Freedom: Maroons and the Colonial Order in Eighteenth-Century Jamaica and the Atlantic Sound," *WMQ,* 3d Ser., LXVI (2009), 45–86, esp. 74–75, 77–80.

75. For Caribbean roots, see Philip D. Morgan, *Slave Counterpoint: Black Culture in the Eighteenth-Century Chesapeake and Lowcountry* (Williamsburg, Va., and Chapel Hill, N.C., 1998), 100. For Atlantic "garrison societies," including Jamaica, see Wilson, "Performance of Freedom," *WMQ,* 3d Ser., LXVI (2009), 72–74 (quotation, 72). For the American Revolution in the Caribbean, see Andrew Jackson O'Shaughnessy, *An Empire Divided: The American Revolution and the British Caribbean* (Philadelphia, 2000). For interracial relationships, see Morgan, *Slave Counterpoint,* 404–409; Richard Godbeer, *Sexual Revolution in Early America* (Baltimore, Md., 2002), 208–213; and Clark, *Strange History of the American Quadroon,* 5–10, 46–48, 64–70.

76. For the labor opportunities available to enslaved women in British military camps, see Wood, "'High Notions of Their Liberty,'" in Morgan, ed., *African American Life in the Georgia Lowcountry,* 59–60. For avoidance of unnecessary risk, see Frey, *Water from the Rock,* 168–169. For leasing, see Memorial of Elizabeth Thompson, AO 12/46, 80, TNA; for sales, see Sylvia R. Frey, "The British and the Black: A New Perspective," *Historian,* XXXVIII (1976), 233–234.

77. For military balls, see Shields and Teute, "Meschianza," *JER,* XXXV (2015), 185–214, esp. 190–193, 198–199. For the "battle of the balls" after the Continental army regained control of Philadelphia, see ibid., 206–210 (quotation, 212).

78. Stevens to Wendell, Feb. 20, 1782, *PMHS,* XLVIII, 342 (quotations).

79. Ibid., 342 (quotation). Private events were more common than public assemblies in Charleston; see Judith Cobau, "The Precarious Life of Thomas Pike, a Colonial Dancing Master in Charleston and Philadelphia," *Dance Chronicle: Studies in Dance and the Related Arts,* XVII (1994), 229–262, esp. 241. For southern households, see Thavolia Glymph, *Out of the House of Bondage: The Transformation of the Plantation Household* (New York, 2008); and Olwell, *Masters, Slaves, and Subjects,* 181–219.

80. Stevens to Wendell, Feb. 20, 1782, *PMHS,* XLVIII, 342 (quotations). For balls and southern genteel culture, see Cynthia A. Kierner, *Beyond the Household: Women's Place in the Early South, 1700–1835* (Ithaca, N.Y., 1998), 43–51.

81. Stevens to Wendell, Feb. 20, 1782, *PMHS,* XLVIII, 342 (quotations).

CHAPTER 6

1. This imagined scene is derived from Venus's published rebuttal to advertisements for her escape, along with the general experiences of enslaved refugees in occupied cities. For Venus's rebuttal to her enslaver, see "Massa, Me See in a News-Paper," *New-York Mercury, or General Advertiser,* July 5, 1782. For enslaved laborers as hired servants in occupied cities, see H. Gaine, "Wanted to Hire, a White Servant Maid, or Negro Wench," *New-York Gazette: and the Weekly Mercury,* Jan. 12, 1778, [4], "Wanted to Hire a Man Servant, of Any Color," Mar. 9, 1778, [3]; "Wanted to Hire or Purchase," *Royal Gazette* (New York), May 8, 1779, [3], and "Wanted to Hire a Sober, Honest, and Industrious Negro Man," Mar. 1, 1780, [3]. For taverns, see "The London Coffee-House Is This Day Opened," *Rivington's New York Loyal Gazette,* Oct. 25, 1777, [1]; and "John Kirk," *Royal Gazette* (New York), Nov. 10, 1781, [3]. For markets, see John Dyckman, "Runaway, a Likely Negro Wench, Named Jane or Gin," *New-York Gazette: and the Weekly Mercury,* May 17, 1779, [3]; and Richard Jenkins, "Four Guineas Reward," *Royal Gazette* (New York), July 27, 1782, [2]. For more on enslaved women in colonial marketplaces, see Robert Olwell, "'Loose, Idle, and Disorderly': Slave Women in the Eighteenth-Century Charleston Marketplace," in David Barry Gaspar and Darlene Clark Hine, eds., *More Than Chattel: Black Women and Slavery in the Americas* (Bloomington, Ind., 1996), 97–110.

2. "Massa, Me See in a News-Paper," *New-York Mercury, or General Advertiser,* July 5, 1782 (quotation). For Boardwine's initial ad, see Charles Boardwine, "Run Away from the Subscriber a Negro Wench Named Venus," *Royal Gazette* (New York), July 3, 1782, [2].

3. Infuriated, the day after Venus's rebuttal appeared, Boardwine advertised a reward equivalent to that for Venus herself "to any person that will inform him of the person" who authored the response; "for I suppose they are the person who decoyed the Wench away," he proclaimed, "and if they are not black in colour they are black in action"; see Charles Boardwine, "Run Away, Monday, the 1st of July, . . . a Negro Wench Named Venus," *Royal Gazette* (New York), July 6, 1782, [2]. For methodological approaches to slave advertisements, see David Waldstreicher, "Reading the Runaways: Self-Fashioning, Print Culture, and Confidence in Slavery in the Eighteenth-Century Mid-Atlantic," *WMQ,* 3d Ser., LVI (1999), 243–272; Antonio T. Bly, "'Indubitable Signs': Reading Silence as Text in New England Runaway Slave Advertisements," *Slavery and Abolition,* XLII (2021), 240–268; and Karen Cook Bell, "Fugitivity and Enslaved Women's Agency in the Age of Revolution," *Journal of Women's History,* XXXIV, no. 4 (Winter 2022), 58–80. I am grateful to Laura F. Edwards for her insights about how Venus's actions reflect concerted legal strategies; for more on people on the margins and legal cultures, see Edwards, *The People and Their Peace: Legal Culture and the Transformation of Inequality in the Post-Revolutionary South* (Chapel Hill, N.C., 2009).

4. Jennifer L. Morgan, *"Partus Sequitur Ventrem:* Law, Race, and Reproduction in Colonial Slavery," *Small Axe,* XXII, no. 1 (March 2018), 14 ("rendered"), 15 ("structurally"); Cassandra

Pybus, "Jefferson's Faulty Math: The Question of Slave Defections in the American Revolution," *WMQ*, 3d Ser., LXII (2005), 243–264. For kinship, reproduction, and slavery, see Morgan, *Laboring Women: Reproduction and Gender in New World Slavery* (Philadelphia, 2004); Morgan, *Reckoning with Slavery: Gender, Kinship, and Capitalism in the Early Black Atlantic* (Durham, N.C., 2021); and Saidiya Hartman, *Lose Your Mother: A Journey along the Atlantic Slave Route* (New York, 2007), 77; see also Stephanie E. Smallwood, *Saltwater Slavery: A Middle Passage from Africa to American Diaspora* (Cambridge, Mass., 2007). For dynamics of slaveholding households, see Eugene D. Genovese, *Roll, Jordan, Roll: The World the Slaves Made* (New York, 1976); Elizabeth Fox-Genovese, *Within the Plantation Household: Black and White Women of the Old South* (Chapel Hill, N.C., 1988); Stephanie McCurry, *Masters of Small Worlds: Yeoman Households, Gender Relations, and the Political Culture of the Antebellum South Carolina Low Country* (New York, 1995); Kathleen M. Brown, *Good Wives, Nasty Wenches, and Anxious Patriarchs: Gender, Race, and Power in Colonial Virginia* (Williamsburg, Va., and Chapel Hill, N.C., 1996); Stephanie M. H. Camp, *Closer to Freedom: Enslaved Women and Everyday Resistance in the Plantation South* (Chapel Hill, N.C., 2004); Thavolia Glymph, *Out of the House of Bondage: The Transformation of the Plantation Household* (Cambridge, 2008); Glymph, *The Women's Fight: The Civil War's Battles for Home, Freedom, and Nation* (Chapel Hill, N.C., 2020), esp. 19–53; Wendy Warren, *New England Bound: Slavery and Colonization in Early America* (New York, 2016); Stephanie E. Jones-Rogers, *They Were Her Property: White Women as Slave Owners in the American South* (New Haven, Conn., 2019); Andrea C. Mosterman, *Spaces of Enslavement: A History of Slavery and Resistance in Dutch New York* (Ithaca, N.Y., 2021); and Whitney Nell Stewart, *This Is Our Home: Slavery and Struggle on Southern Plantations* (Chapel Hill, N.C., 2023).

5. For enslaved women and reproduction, see Deborah G. White, *Ar'n't I a Woman? Female Slaves in the Plantation South* (New York, 1985); Brown, *Good Wives, Nasty Wenches, and Anxious Patriarchs;* Marie Jenkins Schwartz, *Birthing a Slave: Motherhood and Medicine in the Antebellum South* (Cambridge, Mass., 2006); Morgan, *Laboring Women;* and Morgan, "*Partus Sequitur Ventrem,*" *Small Axe,* XXII, no. 1 (March 2018), 1–17; for Black kin and households, see ibid., 12–15; and Turner, *Contested Bodies*. For racial contours of domesticity, see Glymph, *Out of the House of Bondage,* esp. 63–96; Brown, *Good Wives, Nasty Wenches, and Anxious Patriarchs,* 107–136; and McCurry, *Masters of Small Worlds*. For enslaved kin and community, including African precedents, see Genovese, *Roll, Jordan, Roll;* Gwendolyn Midlo Hall, *Africans in Colonial Louisiana: The Development of Afro-Creole Culture in the Eighteenth-Century* (Baton Rouge, La., 1992); Hall, *Slavery and African Ethnicities in the Americas: Restoring the Links* (Chapel Hill, N.C., 2005); Ira Berlin, *Many Thousands Gone: The First Two Centuries of Slavery in North America* (Cambridge, Mass., 1998); Sharla M. Fett, *Working Cures: Healing, Health, and Power on Southern Slave Plantations* (Chapel Hill, N.C., 2002); Jennifer Lyle Morgan, "This Is 'Mines': Slavery and Reproduction in Colonial Barbados and South Carolina," in Jack P. Greene, Rosemary Brana-Shute, and Randy J. Sparks, eds., *Money, Trade, and Power: The Evolution of Colonial South Carolina's Plantation Society* (Columbia, S.C., 2001), 187–216; James H. Sweet, *Recreating Africa: Culture, Kinship, and Religion in the African-Portuguese World, 1441–1770* (Chapel Hill, N.C., 2003); Camp, *Closer to Freedom;* Jessica Millward, *Finding Charity's Folk: Enslaved and Free Black Women in Maryland* (Athens, Ga., 2015), 14–26; Jared Ross Hardesty, *Black Lives, Native Lands, White Worlds: A History of Slavery in New England* (Amherst, Mass., 2019), 93–117; Jessica Marie Johnson, *Wicked Flesh: Black Women,*

Intimacy, and Freedom in the Atlantic World (Philadelphia, 2020); Daina Ramey Berry, "Soul Values and American Slavery," *Slavery and Abolition,* XLII (2021), 201–218; and Morgan, *Reckoning with Slavery.* For more on kinship as a framing, see Ellen Hartigan-O'Connor's contribution to the forum "Women at the Center," *JER* (forthcoming).

Still, as scholars have shown, enslaved families invested care in their homes and endeavored to create comfortable spaces for their loved ones, For enslaved property ownership and homemaking, see Dylan C. Penningroth, *The Claims of Kinfolk: African American Property and Community in the Nineteenth-Century South* (Chapel Hill, N.C., 2003); Laura F. Edwards, "James and His Striped Velvet Pantaloons: Textiles, Commerce, and Law in the New Republic," *JAH,* CVII (2020), 336–361; Mosterman, *Spaces of Enslavement,* 78–102; and Stewart, *This Is Our Home.*

6. During the colonial period, 87 percent of runaways were male, and two-thirds of those made solitary flights; comparatively, during the Revolution, women accounted for one-third of runaways, and more than half of documented freedom seekers fled as groups; see Karen Cook Bell, *Running from Bondage: Enslaved Women and Their Remarkable Fight for Freedom in Revolutionary America* (Cambridge, 2021), 9; see also Mary Beth Norton, *Liberty's Daughters: The Revolutionary Experience of American Women, 1750–1800* (Boston, 1980), 196. In conceptualizing the potential of occupation, I draw from Saidiya V. Hartman's notion of "transient . . . possibilit[ies]"; see Hartman, *Scenes of Subjection: Terror, Slavery, and Self-Making in Nineteenth-Century America* (Oxford, 1997), 12–13. Thavolia Glymph has uncovered similar dynamics during the American Civil War, where the Union Army became a destination of freedom for enslaved women and their families, who "adapt[ed] long-standing strategies of resistance to the revolutionary goal of emancipation"—what she terms "antislavery politics"; see Glymph, *Women's Fight,* 87–123 ("antislavery," 96, "adap[ted]," 106).

7. "By His Excellency Sir Henry Clinton, K.B.," *New-York Gazette: and the Weekly Mercury,* Sept. 6, 1779, supplement [1] ("every NEGROE"); [Banastre] Tarleton, *A History of the Campaigns of 1780 and 1781, in the Southern Provinces of North America* (London, 1787), 89–90 ("all the negroes," 89); see also Sylvia R. Frey, *Water from the Rock: Black Resistance in a Revolutionary Age* (Princeton, N.J., 1991), 86–89, 113–119. For British policies, see Philip D. Morgan and Andrew Jackson O'Shaughnessy, "Arming Slaves in the American Revolution," in Christopher Leslie Brown and Morgan, eds., *Arming Slaves: From Classical Times to the Modern Age* (New Haven, Conn., 2006), 191–192. For Dunmore's proclamation, see Pybus, "Jefferson's Faulty Math," *WMQ,* 3d Ser., LXII (2005), 249–251, 261; for more on enslaved people who ran to the British and their fates, see Frey, *Water from the Rock,* 172–205; Cassandra Pybus, *Epic Journeys of Freedom: Runaway Slaves of the American Revolution and Their Global Quest for Liberty* (Boston, 2006); and Alexander X. Byrd, *Captives and Voyagers: Black Migrants across the Eighteenth-Century British Atlantic World* (Baton Rouge, La., 2008). There is an extensive historiography on slavery in the Revolution; for some particularly influential and relevant works, see Benjamin Quarles, *The Negro in the American Revolution* (Williamsburg, Va., and Chapel Hill, N.C., 1961); Edmund S. Morgan, *American Slavery, American Freedom: The Ordeal of Colonial Virginia* (New York, 1975); Sylvia R. Frey, "The British and the Black: A New Perspective," *Historian,* XXXVIII (1976), 225–238; Judith Van Buskirk, "Crossing the Lines: African-Americans in the New York City Region during the British Occupation, 1776–1783," in "Explorations in Early American Culture," eds. William Pencak and George W. Boudreau, special issue, *Pennsylvania History: A Journal of Mid-Atlantic Studies,* LXV (1998),

74–100; Frey, *Water from the Rock;* Robert Olwell, *Masters, Slaves, and Subjects: The Culture of Power in the South Carolina Low Country, 1740–1790* (Ithaca, N.Y., 1998), 221–270; David Waldstreicher, *Runaway America: Benjamin Franklin, Slavery, and the American Revolution* (New York, 2004); Pybus, *Epic Journeys of Freedom;* Gerald Horne, *The Counter-Revolution of 1776: Slave Resistance and the Origins of the United States of America* (New York, 2014); Robert G. Parkinson, *The Common Cause: Creating Race and Nation in the American Revolution* (Williamsburg, Va., and Chapel Hill, N.C., 2016); Van Buskirk, *Standing in Their Own Light: African American Patriots in the American Revolution* (Norman, Okla., 2017); David Waldstreicher, "Ancients, Moderns, and Africans: Phillis Wheatley and the Politics of Empire and Slavery in the American Revolution," *JER,* XXXVII (2017), 701–733; Robert G. Parkinson, *Thirteen Clocks: How Race United the Colonies and Made the Declaration of Independence* (Williamsburg, Va., and Chapel Hill, N.C., 2021); Bell, *Running from Bondage;* Bell, "Fugitivity and Enslaved Women's Agency," *Journal of Women's History,* XXXIV, no. 4 (Winter 2022), 58–80; and Sean Gallagher, "Black Refugees and the Legal Fiction of Military Manumission in the American Revolution," *Slavery and Abolition,* XLIII (2022), 140–159.

8. "Philadelphia, December 14," *Pennsylvania Evening Post* (Philadelphia), Dec. 14, 1775, 576 ("reprimand[ed]," "d[amne]d," "Lord Dunmore"); Lieut. John Postell to Provost, June 24, 1781, (copy), Transcripts of Letters from Maj. Gen. Nathanael Greene, I, 1780–1782, 247–251 ("invited," 249, "promising," 249, "In a few," 250), Transcripts of Letters from Maj. Gen. Nathaniel Greene, 1780–84, M247, item 172, roll 191, NARA. For enslaved networks, see Anthony E. Kaye, *Joining Places: Slave Neighborhoods in the Old South* (Chapel Hill, N.C., 2007). For more on Black soldiers, see Morgan and O'Shaughnessy, "Arming Slaves in the American Revolution," in Brown and Morgan, eds., *Arming Slaves,* 180–208; George P. Clark, "The Role of the Haitian Volunteers at Savannah in 1779: An Attempt at an Objective View," *Phylon,* XLI (1980), 356–366; George Fenwick Jones, "The Black Hessians: Negroes Recruited by the Hessians in South Carolina and Other Colonies," *South Carolina Historical Magazine,* LXXXIII (1982), 287–302; and Timothy J. Lockley, "'The King of England's Soldiers': Armed Blacks in Savannah and Its Hinterlands during the Revolutionary War Era, 1778–1787," in Leslie M. Harris and Daina Ramey Berry, eds., *Slavery and Freedom in Savannah* (Athens, Ga., 2014), 26–41.

9. For reunification, see Samuel Pearce, "Run Away on Saturday the 21st Inst. a Likely Negro Wench, Named Charity," *New-York Gazette: and the Weekly Mercury,* June 30, 1777, [3] ("anxious"); George Baillie, "Ran Away from the Subscriber, about Ten Days Ago, a Young Negro Man, Named Sandy," *Royal Georgia Gazette* (Savannah, Ga.), May 3, 1781, [2], William Bisset, "Ran Away from the Subscriber on Wilmington Island . . . , a Negro Fellow, Named Cooper," July 19, 1781, [2], and John Murray, "Ran Away from the Subscriber . . . a Tall Stout Well Looking Negro Wench, . . . Named Flora," Aug. 9, 1781, [4]. For hiding in garrisons, see J. Smith, "Run Away, in the Night, . . . a Negro Wench, Named Phoebe," *New-York Gazette: and the Weekly Mercury,* Dec. 16, 1776, [3] ("night"), William Maxwell, "Runaway the Third Instant," Oct. 14, 1776, [3], James Dun, "Five Dollars, Reward; Run Away . . . a Likely Negro Wench, Named Bina," July 26, 1779, [2]; Daniel Larrew, "Thirty Dollars Reward; Ran Away . . . a Negro Wench Named Jude," *Pennsylvania Packet; or, The General Advertiser,* Nov. 3, 1778, [2]; and Andrew Williamson, "Run Away from My Plantation . . . a Negro Woman Named Elsey," *Royal Gazette* (Charleston, S.C.), June 1–5, 1782, [3]. For escaping by ship, see Elizabeth Duncan, "Three Guineas Reward; Run Away . . . a Negro Girl

Named Prussia," *Royal Gazette* (New York), Mar. 21, 1781, [2] ("g[ot] on board"); see also "Run Away a Negro Wench Named Hager," ibid., May 1, 1779, [3], De Keudell, "Deserted on the 25th Inst. from the General Hospital . . . a Negroe, Named Robert Kupperth," Mar. 29, 1780, [2]; "Ten Dollrs Reward; Runaway from His Master on Sunday Morning Last, a Negro Lad Named Minto," *Royal American Gazette* (New York), Nov. 6, 1777, [4], and Paul Dayrell, "Run Away from the Subscriber, a Negro Wench, Named Dinah," Dec. 23, 1779, [2]. For Native tribes, see James Herriot, "Ran Away about Three Weeks Ago, a Tall Slim Slave, Named Hommady," *Royal Georgia Gazette,* Sept. 20, 1781, [2]. For maroons, see Lockley, "'King of England's Soldiers,'" in Harris and Berry, eds., *Slavery and Freedom in Savannah,* 27. For Sylvia, see Memorial of Eliza Moore, AO 13/36, reel 3, GHS. For military employment, see Joseph Mitchell, "Thirty Dollars Reward; Went with the British Army . . . a Negro Man Named Cato," *Pennsylvania Packet; or, The General Advertiser,* Aug. 25, 1778, [1] ("handy"); George Shaw, "Six Pounds Reward; Run-Away on the First Day of June," *New-York Gazette: and the Weekly Mercury,* June 9, 1777, [3] ("entered"); and "Deserted on the 25th Inst. from the General Hospital . . . a Negroe, Named Robert Kupperth," *Royal Gazette* (New York), Mar. 29, 1780, [2].

10. Neil Roberts, *Freedom as Marronage* (Chicago, Ill., 2015), 15 (quotations). For more on the contingency of freedom behind British lines, see Gallagher, "Black Refugees and the Legal Fiction," *Slavery and Abolition,* XLIII (2022), 140–159.

11. John Fisher, "Two Guineas Reward; Run-away a Young Negro Fellow Named Quamina," *South-Carolina and American General Gazette* (Charles[to]n, S.C.), Feb. 24, 1781, supplement [2] ("[his] face," "He can go"); James Wright to George Germain, July 31, 1779, James Wright Papers, 1772–1784, folder 3, GHS ("I may," "vast," "Come over").

12. Cornelia Beekman to Pierre Van Cortlandt, Apr. 12, 1777, in Jacob Judd, ed., *Correspondence of the Van Cortlandt Family of Cortlandt Manor, 1748–1800,* II (Tarrytown, N.Y., 1977), 185–186 ("brigit," 185, "come," 185–186, "thay where," 185, "when thay," 185). For Quamino Dolly, see Lockley, "'King of England's Soldiers,'" in Harris and Berry, eds., *Slavery and Freedom in Savannah,* 26; and Alexander Atkinson Lawrence Papers, 1915–1981, Ser. 4, box 2, folder 42, GHS.

13. Robert Pigot to William Howe, Apr. 10, 1778, British Headquarters Papers [facsimiles], 1775–1783, MssCol 1209, box 5, 1083, Manuscripts and Archives Division, NYPL ("protection"); Charles Read, "Ten Dollars Reward; Ran Away from the Subscriber, . . . a Negro Man Named Moses," *Dunlap's Pennsylvania Packet: or, The General Advertiser* (Philadelphia), Oct. 1, 1776, [1] ("neighbourhood"). For more on the First Rhode Island Regiment, see Van Buskirk, *Standing in Their Own Light,* 95–141.

14. Hugh and Alexander Dean, "Public Aucti[o]n: At 11 O'Clock, on Thursday Next," *Royal Gazette* (New York), Oct. 12, 1782, [2] ("sold"); A. Sealy [Anne Hart] to Mr. Melvill [Oliver Hart?], July 23, 1781, Oliver Hart Papers, 1741–1961, SCL ("Mrs. Harts"). For another example of enslaved people using this moment to ensure their families would be not be separated, see Achsah Chamier, "To Be Sold, a Young Negro Woman, an Excellent Cook," *Royal Gazette* (New York), Feb. 20, 1779, [4]. For sales, see Walter Johnson, *Soul by Soul: Life Inside the Antebellum Slave Market* (Cambridge, Mass., 1999).

15. Samuel Massey to Henry Laurens, June 12, 1780, in David R. Chesnutt and C. James Taylor, eds., *The Papers of Henry Laurens, XV, December 11, 1778–August 31, 1782* (Columbia, S.C., 2000), 305 ("Most"), James Custer to Henry Laurens, June 1780, 303–304 ("willing," 303,

"obliged," 303); Christian Barnes to Elizabeth Murray Smith, Dec. 23, 1769, Murray-Robbins Family Papers, 1658–1944, I, MHS ("Daphney"). Similar negotiations happened throughout Georgia; see Watson W. Jennison, *Cultivating Race: The Expansion of Slavery in Georgia, 1750–1860* (Lexington, Ky., 2012), 46–47.

16. Pybus, "Jefferson's Faulty Math," *WMQ*, 3d Ser., LXII (2005), 264.

17. Isaac Winslow and Margaret Catherine Winslow, *Family Memorial: The Winslows of Boston*, ed. Robert Newsom, I (Boston, 1837?–1773?), 128 (quotation), Winslow Family Memorial, Ms. N-2322, MHS; for Rose, see ibid., 220; for loyalists' financial hardship, see ibid., 131–135.

18. Ibid., I, 220–221 ("mischievous," 220, "wild," 221, "She," 220, "when," 220–221).

19. Isaac Winslow, Sr., to Mary Winslow, June 9, 1784, Winslow Family Papers, 1690–1887, box 2, MHS ("I saw," "on her telling"), Mary Winslow to Isaac Winslow, Sr., June 16, 1784 ("Rose"). For Rose's emancipation, see Winslow and Winslow, *Family Memorial*, ed. Newsom, I, 221, II, C1, XLVI ¾, Winslow Family Memorial. For more on the abolition of slavery in Massachusetts, see Arthur Zilversmit, "Quok Walker, Mumbet, and the Abolition of Slavery in Massachusetts," *WMQ*, 3d Ser., XXV (1968), 614–624; and Gloria McCahon Whiting, "Emancipation without the Courts or Constitution: The Case of Revolutionary Massachusetts," *Slavery and Abolition*, XLI (2020), 458–478.

20. John M'Call, "Run Away from the Subscriber about Ten Days Ago, . . . a Fellow Named Cato, . . . Chloe His Wife, . . . Their Child a Girl about Two Years Old Named Jenny," *Royal Gazette* (Charleston, S.C.), Feb. 16–20, 1782, [3].

21. John Duffield, "Ran Away This Morning from the Subscriber, a Negro Fellow Named Tom," *Pennsylvania Evening Post*, Aug. 30, 1777, 451 ("tolerable"); "Left with the Printer, a Letter Directed as Follows," *Royal Gazette* (New York), Oct. 29, 1783, [2] ("English"); John Waring, "Run-Away from the Subscriber . . . a Tall Black Wench, Named Jean," *South-Carolina and American General Gazette*, Jan. 3, 1781, [3] ("compleat"); Johann Ewald, *Diary of the American War: A Hessian Journal*, trans. and ed. Joseph P. Tustin (New Haven, Conn., 1979), June 21, 1781, 305–306 ("Every," 305); Memorial of James Keith, AO 12/48, 310, 315, TNA; Jacob Deveaux, "Ten Guineas Reward; Ran Away . . . Two Young Negro Men, Named Paris and Anthony," *Royal Georgia Gazette*, June 28, 1781, [2]. For rations and pay, see Instructions for the Office Established to Receive the Pay of Negroes Employed in the Different Departments, 1781, SCL; and Rations Book, July 6, 1781, Chief Engineers Department, Chas. Town, James Moncrieff Papers, 1710–1894, box 4, WCL.

22. Edward H. Tatum, Jr., ed., *American Journal of Ambrose Serle Secretary to Lord Howe, 1776–1778* (San Marino, Calif., 1940), Nov. 19, 1776, 144 ("pleasing," "I did not"), Sept. 8–13, 1777, 249 ("bawling"); Alexander Leslie to Guy Carleton, Oct. 18, 1782, Guy Carleton Papers, PRO 30/55/52, 5924, TNA ("They pretend"). For British policies, see Morgan and O'Shaughnessy, "Arming Slaves in the American Revolution," in Brown and Morgan, eds., *Arming Slaves*, 180–208.

23. Robert Gilmour, "Run Away from [the] Subscriber about Three Months Ago, a Negro Boy Named Luke," *Rivington's New York Loyal Gazette*, Oct. 18, 1777, [4] ("seen attending"); William Ball, "One Hundred Dollars Reward; Ran Away from the Subscriber . . . Three Negro Men," *Pennsylvania Packet; or, The General Advertiser*, Sept. 1, 1778, [3] ("was protected"); James Moncrieff to Alexander Leslie, Sept. 27, 1782, Letter book, Dec. 31, 1780–Oct. 7, 1782, James Moncrieff Papers, box 4 ("offer[ed]," "I cannot," "would be").

24. Marvin L. Brown, Jr., ed. and trans., *Baroness von Riedesel and the American Revolution: Journal and Correspondence of a Tour of Duty, 1776–1783* (Williamsburg, Va., and Chapel Hill, N.C., 1965), July 1781, 113.

25. "Memoirs of the Life of Boston King . . . ," *Methodist Magazine,* VI (1798), 108 (quotation), in Vincent Carretta, ed., *Unchained Voices: An Anthology of Black Authors in the English-Speaking World of the Eighteenth Century,* 2d ed. (Lexington, Ky., 1996), 353–354; for another example, see BOP, Mar. 13, 1781 reel 521.

26. Bernard A. Uhlendorf, ed. and trans., *Revolution in America: Confidential Letters and Journals, 1776–1784, of Adjutant General Major Baurmeister of the Hessian Forces* (New Brunswick, N.J., 1957), July 4, 1780, 350 (quotation). For public works, see BOP, Sept. 8, 1780, reel 520. For sales, see Frey, *Water from the Rock,* 131–132. For sexual abuse, see Cynthia M. Kennedy, *Braided Relations, Entwined Lives: The Women of Charleston's Urban Slave Society* (Bloomington, Ind., 2005), 38–39. For physical assault, see Timothy Newell, "A Journal Kept during the Time That Boston Was Shut Up in 1775–6," Massachusetts Historical Society, *Collections,* 4th Ser., I (Boston, 1852), Oct. 10, 1775, 268; and GCM of Cornelius Dunn, Philadelphia, Dec. 19, 1777, WO 71/85, 154–155, TNA. For confiscation of goods, see "New-York, October 11, 1782; Eight Days Ago There Was a Young Broke Horse . . . Left . . . by a Negro Wench," *Royal Gazette* (New York), Oct. 12, 1782, [3]; "Offered for Sale by a Negro Boy, a Gold Shirt Pin," *Royal Georgia Gazette,* May 31, 1781, [2], "Stopped on Friday Last from a Negro Fellow, a Saddle and Bridle," July 26, 1781, [3]; "Stopped from a Negro, Who Offered It for Sale, a Large Silver Table Spoon," *South-Carolina and American General Gazette,* Aug. 23, 1780, [3], G. Benson, "Charlestown, October 11th, 1780; Whereas It Hath Been Represented unto the Commandant," Oct. 14, 1780, [3], William Hardy, "Stopped from a Negro, a Silver Watch," Oct. 14, 1780, [1], and Daniel Bell, "Stopped from a Negro, a Silver Tumbler," Oct. 18, 1780, [3]. For conditions behind British lines, see Betty Wood, "'High Notions of Their Liberty': Women of Color and the American Revolution in Lowcountry Georgia and South Carolina, 1765–1783," in Philip Morgan, ed., *African American Life in the Georgia Lowcountry: The Atlantic World and the Gullah Geechee* (Athens, Ga., 2010), 55–60; Frey, *Water from the Rock,* 121–128; and Olwell, *Masters, Slaves, and Subjects,* 251–253. For more on conditions for enslaved people in occupied cities, see Van Buskirk, "Crossing the Lines," in "Explorations in Early American Culture," ed. Pencak and Boudreau, special issue, *Pennsylvania History,* LXV (1998), 74–100; and Donald F. Johnson, *Occupied America: British Military Rule and the Experience of Revolution* (Philadelphia, 2020), 80–88, 128, 180–188.

27. Waters Smith, "Four Dollars Reward; Run Away on Tuesday . . . a Negro Wench Named Hester," *New York Gazette: and the Weekly Mercury,* Apr. 20, 1778, [2] ("Negro houses"); *The Journal of Nicholas Cresswell, 1774–1777* (New York, 1924), June 24, 1777, 24 ("stagnate"); Uhlendorf, ed. and trans., *Revolution in America,* June 17, 1783, 569 ("Half"); James Simpson to Henry Clinton, July 16, 1780, Guy Carleton Papers, PRO 30/55/24, 2915 ("malignant," "It is [a] matter," "hath not"). For abandonment, see "Memoirs of the Life of Boston King," *Methodist Magazine,* VI (1798), 107, in Carretta, ed., *Unchained Voices,* 353; and John Andrews to William Barrell, Apr. 11, 1776, Andrews-Eliot Papers, 1715–1814, box 1, 57, MHS.

28. Tatum, Jr., ed., *American Journal of Ambrose Serle,* Sept. 8–13, 1777, 249.

29. This imagined scene is narrated from a collection of advertisements documenting the various escapes of Rose, Rynah, and Judy; see Jacob Sass, "Four Guinea Reward; Run Away . . . a Negro Wench Named Rose, with Two Girls Her Children . . . Named Judy and Rynah,"

Royal Gazette (Charleston, S.C.), Mar. 30–Apr. 3, 1782, [1]; Sass, "Two Guineas Reward; Run-Away . . . a Small Negro Wench Named Rose," *State Gazette of South-Carolina* (Charleston, S.C.), Feb. 6, 1786, [3]; and Sass, "Three Dollars Reward; Ran-Away . . . a Negro Girl Named Juda," *City Gazette and Daily Advertiser* (Charleston, S.C.), July 15, 1794, [4].

30. James Smyth, "Run Away from the Subscriber in April Last, the Following Negroes," *South-Carolina and American General Gazette,* Oct. 21, 1780, [1] ("ADAM"); Massey to Laurens, June 12, 1780, in Chesnutt and Taylor, eds., *Papers of Henry Laurens,* XV, 305–306 ("whent," 305); S. Max Edelson, *Plantation Enterprise in Colonial South Carolina* (Cambridge, Mass., 2006), 250–251. For archival limitations and approaches to documenting the lives of the enslaved, see Marisa J. Fuentes, *Dispossessed Lives: Enslaved Women, Violence, and the Archive* (Philadelphia, 2016); Saidiya Hartman, "Venus in Two Acts," *Small Axe,* no. 26 (June 2008), 1–14; Wendy Anne Warren, "'The Cause of Her Grief': The Rape of a Slave in Early New England," *Journal of American History,* XCIII (2007), 1031–1049; Johnson, *Wicked Flesh;* and Morgan, *Reckoning with Slavery.*

31. Jacob Buhler, "Ran Away Last Thursday, a Negro Fellow, Named Dick," *Royal Georgia Gazette,* Oct. 25, 1781, [2] ("stout"), Joseph Law, "To Be Sold at Publick Vendue," Jan. 18, 1781, [2] ("handy"), Buhler, "Ran Away from the Subscriber the Beginning of February Last, a Negro Fellow, Named Dick," Mar. 8, 1781, [2]. For Jacob Bühler's loyalism, see John Martin, Proclamation, Feb. 20, 1782, Telamon Cuyler Collection, 1609–1942, MS 1170, Ser. 1, Hargrett Rare Book and Manuscript Library, University of Georgia Libraries, Athens, Ga., https://dlg.galileo.usg.edu/data/guan/1170/pdfs/guan_1170_harg1170-038f-015.pdf.

32. Buhler, "Ran Away from the Subscriber the Beginning of February Last, a Negro Fellow, Named Dick," *Royal Georgia Gazette,* Mar. 8, 1781, [2] ("yellow"), Buhler, "Ran Away Last Thursday, a Negro Fellow, Named Dick," Oct. 25, 1781, [2] ("large bundle," "green rug").

33. "Sunday, April 23d. 1781; Run Away from the Ship Euphrates, Three Negro Men, Named Will, Peter, and Duke," *Royal Gazette* (New York), May 12, 1781, [2] ("three"); John Strobhar, "Ran Away from the Subscriber . . . and Went into Georgia, the Following Negroes," *Royal Georgia Gazette,* Mar. 15, 1781, [2] ("all," "went"), John Morel, "Ran Away from the Subscriber on Monday the 8th Instant, the Following Negroes," Oct. 11, 1781, [2] ("Angola"); see also Morel, "Ran Away from the Island of Ossabaw on Monday the 8th Instant, the Following Negroes," *Royal Georgia Gazette,* Oct. 18, 1781, [2]. For Auba, see Jerome S. Handler and JoAnn Jacoby, "Slave Names and Naming in Barbados, 1650–1830," *WMQ,* 3d Ser., LIII (1996), 698.

34. For the erasure of Black kinship in slavery, see Morgan, *Reckoning with Slavery.* For theorizations of slavery's archive, see Hartman, "Venus in Two Acts," *Small Axe,* no. 26 (June 2008), 1–14; and Fuentes, *Dispossessed Lives.*

35. Johnson, *Wicked Flesh,* 14 ("black femme), 173 ("black women," "life-sustaining"), 185 ("audacity"); "Ran Away Some Time Ago from Mrs. Mary Thomas' Plantation," *Royal Georgia Gazette,* Jan. 4, 1781, [1] ("Old Rose," "elderly" "Town Sue").

36. "Run-Away, a Negro Wench Named Rachael," *New-York Gazette: and the Weekly Mercury,* Jan. 24, 1780, [3] ("great with child"); "Ran Away Last Night, a Negro Wench, Named Jenny," *Royal Georgia Gazette,* June 28, 1781, [2] ("big with child"); "Philadelphia, July 6, 1778; Twenty Dollars Reward; Ran Away with the Last of the British Troops . . . a Servant Negro Woman Named Dinah," *Pennsylvania Packet; or, The General Advertiser,* July 16, 1778, [1] ("Big with child, and near"). For enslaved midwives, see Fett, *Working Cures;* and Sara

Collini, "The Labors of Enslaved Midwives in Revolutionary Virginia," in Barbara B. Oberg, ed., *Women in the American Revolution: Gender, Politics, and the Domestic World* (Charlottesville, Va., 2019), 19–39.

37. Morgan, *"Partus Sequitur Ventrem," Small Axe,* XXII, no. 1 (March 2018), 16 ("theorists," "carve"); "The Book of Negroes," PRO 30/55/100, 59 ("Born"), 10427, TNA. Digital images of the "Book of Negroes" are available at the "African Nova Scotians in the Age of Slavery and Abolition," Nova Scotia Archives, https://archives.novascotia.ca/africanns/book-of-negroes/. For more on enslaved women and reproduction, see Morgan, *Laboring Women;* and Morgan, *Reckoning with Slavery.* For more on geographies, see Katherine McKittrick, *Demonic Grounds: Black Women and the Cartographies of Struggle* (Minneapolis, Minn., 2006).

38. James Pattison to Abraham C. Cuyler, May 25, 1780, in "Pattison Letters," 397 ("Female"); Memorial of Elizabeth Thompson, AO 12/46, 78, 80, TNA ("went away"); Absalom Obrey, "Ran Away from the Subscriber at Great Ogechee, . . . a Negro Wench, Named Cumba," *Royal Georgia Gazette,* Aug. 16, 1781, [2]; Thomas Farr, "A Likely Mustee Woman Named Isabella . . . ," *South-Carolina and American General Gazette,* Nov. 4, 1780, [1].

39. Richard Jenkins, "Four Guineas Reward; Run Away from the Subscriber, a Negro Wench, about 24 Years of Age," *Royal Gazette* (New York), July 27, 1782, [2] ("well known"), David Campbell, "Five Guineas Reward; Went Off . . . a Negro Wench, Called Violet," May 24, 1783, [2] ("cut," "rather"); Paul Dayrell, "Run Away from the Subscriber, a Negro Wench, Named Dinah," *Royal American Gazette,* Dec. 23, 1779, [2] ("on board"); "Twenty Guineas Reward," *South-Carolina and American General Gazette,* Aug. 16, 1780, [1]; see also Samuel Livingston, "Ran Away from the Subscriber in March Last, a Negro Wench, Named Eve," *Royal Georgia Gazette,* July 26, 1781, [2]. For connotations of "yellow," see Sharon Block, "Early American Bodies: Creating Race, Sex, and Beauty," in Jennifer Brier, Jim Downs, and Jennifer L. Morgan, eds., *Connexions: Histories of Race and Sex in North America* (Champaign, Ill., 2016), 91–92.

40. John Morel, "Ran Away from the Subscriber on Monday the 8th Instant, the Following Negroes," *Royal Georgia Gazette,* Oct. 11, 1781, [2] ("her"), Morel, "Ran Away from the Island of Ossabaw, the Following Negroes," Oct. 18, 1781, [2] ("both"), Geo[rge] Thomas, "A Guinea Reward; Ran Away . . . Two Negroes, Named Will and Casey," Sept. 13, 1781, [2]; Thomas Pill, "Five Pounds Reward; Run-Away from the Subscriber . . . a Negro Man . . . by the Name of Abraham," *New-York Gazette: and the Weekly Mercury,* June 30, 1777, [3]. For slavery and parenthood, see Hortense J. Spillers, "Mama's Baby, Papa's Maybe: An American Grammar Book," *Diacritics,* XVII, no. 2 (Summer 1987), 65–81.

41. J[ohn] Agnew, "Run Away, a Virginia Negro Woman, Called Pamela," *Royal Gazette* (New York), Aug. 23, 1780, [2].

42. Ibid.; Otto Lohrenz, "Impassioned Virginia Loyalist and New Brunswick Pioneer: The Reverend John Agnew," *Anglican and Episcopal History,* LVI (2007), 29, 37–45. For Agnew's plantation, see Deposition of James Agnew, Aug. 28, 1787, AO 13/27, 92, reel 26, DLAR. In his petition to the Loyalist Claims Commission, Agnew claimed to have sold "Pamela," possibly the same woman, "and her child" along with Mira, whom he described as a "little Girl[]"; see "A List of Negroes Lost by the Revd. John Agnew," AO 13/27, reel 26, DLAR.

43. Handler and Jacoby, "Slave Names and Naming in Barbados," *WMQ,* 3d Ser., LIII (1996), 690 (quotation). For examples of name changes, see Joshua Vaughan, "Sixty Dollars

Reward; Ran Away . . . a Servant Woman Named Mary O'Brian," *Pennsylvania Packet; or the General Advertiser,* May 4, 1779, [1]; "Run Away, on Tuesday the First Inst. a Negro Boy, Named Tom," *New-York Gazette: and the Weekly Mercury,* Aug. 7, 1780, [3]; Frederick Rolfes, "Whereas a Negro Fellow, Formerly Called Peter," *Royal Georgia Gazette,* Mar. 8, 1781, [2], John Strobhar, "Ran Away from the Subscriber, Living near Purysburgh," Mar. 15, 1781, [2], Rolfes, "Whereas a Negro Fellow, Formerly Called Peter," Mar. 15, 1781, [4], and "Hampstead, St. John's River, East Florida, 8th February, 1781; Ran Away . . . a Likely Negro Lad, Named Prince," Mar. 15, 1781, [4]. For examples of supposed passing as free, see Jacob Deveaux, "Ten Guineas Reward; Ran Away . . . Two Young Negro Men, Named Paris and Anthony," *Royal Georgia Gazette,* June 28, 1781, [2]; "Ran Away from His Master in Charlestown, a Few Weeks Ago, a Likely Negro Fellow, Called Stephen," *South-Carolina Gazette and General Advertiser,* Apr. 12, 1783, [2], and "Ran Away from His Master in Charlestown, Some Time Ago, a Likely Negro Fellow, Called Stephen," May 17, 1783, [2]. For more on runaways, see Simon P. Newman, *Embodied History: The Lives of the Poor in Early Philadelphia* (Philadelphia, 2003), 82–103.

44. Alexander Leslie to Guy Carleton, Oct. 18, 1782, Guy Carleton Papers, PRO 30/55/52, 5924 ("expect[ed]"); Fuentes, *Dispossessed Lives;* see also Simone Browne, "Everybody's Got a Little Light under the Sun: Black Luminosity and the Visual Culture of Surveillance," *Cultural Studies,* XXVI (2012), 542–564. Here I also draw from Jessica Marie Johnson's insights on Black women, freedom, and families; see Johnson, *Wicked Flesh,* 10, 172–175.

45. William O'Brien, "Ten Dollars Reward; Run Away the 20th Instant a Negro Wench, Named Flora," *Royal Gazette* (New York), Sept. 21, 1782, [3] ("ha[d] a slow"), Arthur McNeill, "Run Away from the Subscriber . . . a Black Coromantee Negro Wench Named Grace," Dec. 15, 1779, [3] ("She tells"); James Tweed, "Five Dollars, Reward; Run-Away . . . a Negro Man Named Duke," *New-York Gazette: and the Weekly Mercury,* Sept. 6, 1779, [3] ("talk[ed]"); Browne, "Everybody's Got a Little Light under the Sun," *Cultural Studies,* XXVI (2012), 552 ("performances," "constitute[ed]"). For more on Coromantee identity, see Vincent Brown, *Tacky's Revolt: The Story of an Atlantic Slave War* (Cambridge, Mass., 2020), 85–128.

46. David Jones, "Run Away on the 31st Ult. a Likely Negro Wench Named Rachael," *Royal Gazette* (New York), Nov. 20, 1779, [3] (quotation). For military dress, see Tho[ma]s Mills, "Ran Away from the Subscriber on Monday the 19th Inst.; a Negro Fellow, Named Bob," *Royal Georgia Gazette,* Mar. 29, 1781, [4], George Baillie, "Ran Away from the Subscriber, about Ten Days Ago, a Young Negro Man, Named Sandy," May 3, 1781, [2], John G. Williamson, "Five Guineas Reward; Ran Away from the Subscriber . . . the Following Negroes," June 28, 1781, [2]; and Samuel Miller, "Three Pounds Reward; Ran Away . . . a Negro Man Named Jacob," *New-Jersey Gazette* (Trenton, N.J.), Sept. 6, 1784, [3]. For clothing in runaway ads, see Waldstreicher, "Reading the Runaways," *WMQ,* 3d Ser., LVI (1999), 252–254. As Laura F. Edwards as shown, clothing belonged to enslaved people, but "the body that wore them did not"; see Edwards, "James and His Striped Velvet Pantaloons," *JAH,* CVII (2020), 337.

47. Ewald, *Diary of the American War,* ed. and trans. Tustin, June 21, 1781, 305–306 ("They had," 305, "lounging," 305, "all different," 305, "When I first," 305–306, "I wondered," 306).

48. For clothes and celebration, see Stephanie M. H. Camp, "The Pleasures of Resistance: Enslaved Women and Body Politics in the Plantation South, 1830–1861," *Journal of Southern History,* LXVIII (2002), 533–572.

49. Ibid., 533 ("pleasures"); Thomas Farr, "A Likely Mustee Woman Named Isabella," *South-Carolina and American General Gazette,* Nov. 4, 1780, [1] ("very fond"); Vincent Brown, *The Reaper's Garden: Death and Power in the World of Atlantic Slavery* (Cambridge, Mass., 2008), 60–91 ("supernatural," 66); *The New York Genealogical and Biographical Record,* XXXVI (New York, 1905), 174 ("decent"). For the funerary practices of West Africans and enslaved communities throughout the Atlantic, see Brown, *Reaper's Garden,* 60–91; and Erik R. Seeman, *Death in the New World: Cross-Cultural Encounters, 1492–1800* (Philadelphia, 2010), 17–24, 185–231. For mourning attire in early America, see Linda Baumgarten, *What Clothes Reveal: The Language of Clothing in Colonial and Federal America: The Colonial Williamsburg Collection* (New Haven, Conn., 2002), 176–181.

50. "Memoirs of the Life of Boston King," *Methodist Magazine,* VI (1798), 107 (quotations), in Carretta, ed., *Unchained Voices,* 353, 354–356; "Book of Negroes," PRO 30/55/100, 29–30, 70–71.

51. "Ran Away from His Master in Charlestown, a Few Weeks Ago, a Likely Negro Fellow, Called Stephen," *South-Carolina Gazette and General Advertiser,* Apr. 12, 1783, [2] ("very specious"); "At Private Sale; A Bermuda Wench," *Royal American Gazette,* May 13, 1783, [3] ("has been kept"); "Absconded about Three Weeks Past, a Negro Wench, . . . Named Peg," *Royal Gazette* (New York), Apr. 26, 1783, [2] ("forged").

52. James Stobo, "The Following Negroes Have Absented Themselves from Me," *South-Carolina and American General Gazette,* Sept. 6, 1780, [3] ("lurking"), "Run Away Last October, a Young Negro Wench, Well Known in Town by the Name of Harriet," Dec. 6, 1780, [1] ("behind"); "A Negro Wench, Run-Away . . . Is about 22 Years Old, Call'd Betty," *New-York Gazette: and the Weekly Mercury,* Jan. 13, 1777, [4] ("conceal'd"); "One Guinea Reward; Saram, a Mulatto Wench," *Royal Gazette* (New York), Aug. 12, 1778, [3] ("secreted"); Nathaniel Hall, "Ran Away about Three Weeks Ago . . . a Tall Negro Man, Named Paul," *Royal Georgia Gazette,* Aug. 2, 1781, supplement [1] ("harboured"), "Georgia; the Presentments of the Grand Jurors for the Province," Jan. 18, 1781, [1] ("dangerous, "number").

53. For abolition, see Amy Dru Stanley, "Slave Breeding and Free Love: An Antebellum Argument over Slavery, Capitalism, and Personhood," in Michael Zakim and Gary J. Kornblith, eds., *Capitalism Takes Command: The Social Transformation of Nineteenth-Century America* (Chicago, Ill., 2012), 119–144; and Nora Doyle, *Maternal Bodies: Redefining Motherhood in Early America* (Chapel Hill, N.C., 2018), 175–202; see also Tera W. Hunter, *Bound in Wedlock: Slave and Free Black Marriage in the Nineteenth Century* (Cambridge, Mass., 2017).

54. James Peters to Sir Guy Carleton, Oct. 5, 1783, British Headquarters Papers [facsimiles], 1775–1783, MssCol 1209, box 37, 9304 (quotation); "Book of Negroes," PRO 30/55/100, 119–120; James Peters, Will, 1820, Wallace Hale's Early New Brunswick Probate, 1785–1835, Provincial Archives of New Brunswick, https://archives.gnb.ca/. For baptismal registers, see Marianne Grey Otty Database [Gagetown, New Brunswick Anglican church records], University of New Brunswick, Loyalist Collection, https://loyalist.lib.unb.ca/motty. For more on the couple, see "Cairo and Pompey Rumney," *Black Loyalists in New Brunswick,* Atlantic Canada Virtual Archives, https://preserve.lib.unb.ca/wayback/20141205155436/http://atlanticportal.hil.unb.ca/acva/blackloyalists/en/context/biographies/rumney.html; and Stephen Davidson, *Black Loyalists in New Brunswick* (Halifax, 2020), 47–59. The couple's last name is sometimes listed as Rumney, however, I have chosen to use Rumsey, as it is the name used in the baptismal registers of children bearing their names.

55. GCM of James Guffie, New York, Aug. 9, 1781, WO 71/94, 303 ("laying"), 305 ("he would not," "Authority"), film 675, reel 14, DLAR. Possibly, Aske's unnamed wife was Philis, a twenty-two-year-old woman formerly enslaved by Thomas Askin of Charleston who was affiliated with the Wagon Master General Department and evacuated to Nova Scotia in 1783; see "Book of Negroes," PRO 30/55/100, 139–140.

56. Thomas Winstanley, "In Council, September 19, 1780," *South-Carolina and American General Gazette,* Oct. 7, 1780, [3] ("encourage[s]"), "Notice Is Hereby Given . . . ," Sept. 6, 1780, [1]; BOP, June 13, 1780, reel 520 ("Negroes"); Gallagher, "Black Refugees and the Legal Fiction," *Slavery and Abolition,* XLIII (2022), 146–147; see also Frey, *Water from the Rock,* 123–127. After a 1780 fire burned down the Charleston workhouse early in the occupation, the sugar house became the main site of confinement; by the early nineteenth century, it had morphed into an institution exclusively dedicated to the torture and corporeal punishment of disobedient slaves; see Joseph Williams, "Charleston Work House and 'Sugar House,'" *Discovering Our Past: College of Charleston Histories,* https://discovering.cofc.edu/items/show/31.

57. "An Act for the Establishing and Regulating Patrols, and for Preventing Any Person from Purchasing Provisions or Any Other Commodities from, or Selling Such to Any Slave, Unless Such Slave Shall Produce a Ticket from His or Her Owner, Manager, or Employer," Nov. 18, 1765, *Royal Georgia Gazette,* Mar. 29, 1781, [1] (quotation), "An Act to Amend and Continue an Act for the Establishing and Regulating Patrols . . . ," Dec. 24, 1768, ibid., [2]; Johnson, *Occupied America,* 73–75, 86–88, 187–188. For more on Georgia in the revolutionary era, see Leslie Hall, *Land and Allegiance in Revolutionary Georgia* (Athens, Ga., 2001).

58. Treaty of Paris, Sept. 3, 1783, Record Group 11, General Records of the United States Government, 1778–2006, Series, Perfected Treaties, 1778–1945, NARA ("his Britannic"); "Memoirs of the Life of Boston King," *Methodist Magazine,* VI (1798), 157 ("inexpressible," "that all the slaves," "from Virginia," "embittered," "for some days"), in Carretta, ed., *Unchained Voices,* 356. For more on Article VII, see Gallagher, "Black Refugees and the Legal Fiction," *Slavery and Abolition,* XLIII (2022), 150–153.

59. Uhlendorf, ed. and trans., *Revolution in America,* June 17, 1783, 569 ("They insist," "refuse"); Sir Guy Carleton to George Washington, May 12, 1783, FO, https://founders.archives.gov/documents/Washington/99-01-02-11252 ("had no right," "they would"). For Carleton's motivations, see Parkinson, *Common Cause,* 571–572.

60. "Book of Negroes," PRO 30/55/100, 3–15; Pybus, *Epic Journeys of Freedom,* 66. For record of embarkation, see Carleton to Washington, May 12, 1783, FO.

61. For other analyses of these testimonies; see Browne, "Everybody's Got a Little Light under the Sun," *Cultural Studies,* XXVI (2012), 555–558; Simon Schama, *Rough Crossings: Britain, the Slaves, and the American Revolution* (New York, 2006), 150–153; Graham Russell Gao Hodges and Alan Edward Brown, eds., *The Book of Negroes: African Americans in Exile* (New York, 2021), xvii–xix; and Adam McNeil, "Norfolk to Nova Scotia: Judith Jackson's Crooked Road to Freedom," *Colonial Williamsburg,* Mar. 15, 2024, https://www.colonialwilliamsburg.org/learn/deep-dives/norfolk-to-nova-scotia-judith-jacksons-crooked-road-to-freedom/. In 2024, the Fraunces Tavern Museum opened a permanent exhibit about the trials; see "The Birch Trials at Fraunces Tavern," Fraunces Tavern Museum, https://www.frauncestavernmuseum.org/birch-trials-at-fraunces-tavern.

62. Brown, Jr., ed. and trans., *Baroness von Riedesel and the American Revolution,* July 1781, 112–113 ("signal," 112, "horror," 112, "evil," 112, "When," 112, "She threw," 112–113).

63. "Book of Negroes," PRO 30/55/100, 13.

64. Ibid., 13, 15 (quotation).

65. Ibid., 15.

66. Ibid., 7, 8, 9 ("with Consent," "ill used"), 10 ("April," "took"). For Luke Teller's politics, see *New York in the Revolution as Colony and State,* I (Albany, N.Y., 1904), 245. Aaltje Teller appears in the hearing records as Allida Teller, a phonetic spelling of her name. For Teller family genealogy, see Henry A. Stoutenburgh, *A Documentary History of the Dutch Congregation of Oyster Bay, Queens County, Island of Nassau (Now Long Island)* (New York, 1902), 694–696. Some historians have also spelled Samuel Doson's name as Doron; see Winfried Siemerling, *The Black Atlantic Reconsidered: Black Canadian Writing, Cultural History, and the Presence of the Past* (Montreal, 2015), 40–42. Others have spelled it Dobson; see Graham Russell Hodges, ed., *The Black Loyalist Directory: African Americans in Exile after the American Revolution* (New York, 1996), 229.

67. "Book of Negroes," PRO 30/55/100, 9–10 (quotations, 9).

68. Ibid., 10; Thelma Wills Foote, *Black and White Manhattan: The History of Racial Formation in Colonial New York City* (New York, 2004), 224. Peter and Elizabeth were returned to bondage; Samuel Doson did not evacuate the city with the British, so perhaps he continued to reside near his children. See "Book of Negroes," PRO 30/55/100, 10. In a similar instance, when petitioning for the return of confiscated enslaved laborers that she owned on a separate estate, Mary Butler tartly reminded British commander in chief Sir Guy Carleton that, under South Carolina law, "Marriage Settlements were justly held sacred," therefore wives could not be punished for their husbands' politics; see Mary Butler to Sir Guy Carleton, Sept. 16, 1782, British Headquarters Papers [facsimiles], MssCol 1209, box 25, 5604 ("Marriage Settlements"); and Rebecca Brannon, *From Revolution to Reunion: The Reintegration of the South Carolina Loyalists* (Columbia, S.C., 2016), 56, 67–72. For more on separate estates, see Marylynn Salmon, "Women and Property in South Carolina: The Evidence from Marriage Settlements, 1730 to 1830," *WMQ*, 3d Ser., XXXIX (1982), 655–685; see also Salmon, *Women and the Law of Property in Early America* (Chapel Hill, N.C., 1986), 81–140. For loyalist women's separate estates, see Linda K. Kerber, "The Paradox of Women's Citizenship in the Early Republic: The Case of Martin vs. Massachusetts, 1805," *AHR*, XCVII (1992), 349–378. For the grammar of slavery, see Spillers, "Mama's Baby, Papa's Maybe," *Diacritics*, XVII, no. 2 (Summer 1987), 65–81.

69. "Book of Negroes," PRO 30/55/100, 3 (quotations), 150–151. Nancy and Flora, however, did not depart the city with their father.

70. Minute Book of the Board of Police, Feb. 17–19, [1779], Savannah, Ga., item 490, GHS 0793, Telfair Family Papers, 1751–1875, GHS.

71. John Andrews to William Barrell, June 1, 1775, Andrews-Eliot Papers, box 1, 56.

72. Rawlins Lowndes to Sir Guy Carleton, Aug. 8, 1782, Guy Carleton Papers, PRO 30/55/46, 5243 (quotation). For Durnford, see Whitworth Porter, *History of the Corps of Royal Engineers,* II (London, 1889), 400.

73. Rawlins Lowndes to Sir Guy Carleton, Aug. 8, 1782, Guy Carleton Papers, PRO 30/55/46, 5243 (quotations). For Lowndes's politics, see George B. Chase, *Lowndes of South Carolina: An Historical and Genealogical Memoir* (Boston, 1876), 13–16.

74. Rawlins Lowndes to Sir Guy Carleton, Aug. 8, 1782, Guy Carleton Papers, PRO 30/55/46, 5243 (quotations). Thavolia Glymph has traced a similar loss of power among slaveholders during the American Civil War; see Glymph, *Women's Fight,* 34–36.

75. Carl J. Vipperman, *William Lowndes and the Transition of Southern Politics, 1782–1822* (Chapel Hill, N.C., 1989), 1–16; Lowndes to Carleton, Aug. 8, 1782, Guy Carleton Papers, PRO 30/55/46, 5243. For flight from Lowndes's plantation, see Quarles, *Negro in the American Revolution,* 119. Only one of these people, Ben, who worked for a Hessian officer, is recorded in the "Book of Negroes"; see "Book of Negroes," PRO 30/55/100, 96–97.

76. Rawlins Lowndes to Sir Guy Carleton, Aug. 8, 1782, Guy Carleton Papers, PRO 30/55/46, 5243 (quotation); Quarles, *Negro in the American Revolution,* 119. On investigating Lowndes's claim, Carleton returned Rynah to bondage; see Frederick Mackenzie to Rawlins Lowndes, Sept. 9, 1782, Guy Carleton Papers, PRO 30/55/48, 5568, reel 15, DLAR. For Black kinship and capital, see Katherine McKittrick, "Mathematics Black Life," *Black Scholar,* XLIV, no. 2 (Summer 2014), 16–28; and Morgan, *Reckoning with Slavery.*

77. Charles Boardwine, "Run Away, Monday, the 1st of July, from the Subscriber, a Negro Wench Named Venus," *Royal Gazette* (New York), July 6, 1782, [2] ("decoyed"), "Went Away Early on Wednesday Morning . . . a Negro Lad Named Mattis," Aug. 25, 1781, [2] ("seduced"), Robert Cargey, "Run Away Last Saturday, a Negro Boy Named Harry," Aug. 12, 1780, [3] ("deluded"); Benjamin Chew, Jr., to Benjamin Chew, Jan. 19, 1778, Chew Family Papers, 1659–1986, Ser. 2, box 10, folder 7, HSP ("Hardships").

78. Eliza Lucas Pinckney to Thomas Pinckney, Sept. 13, 1780, *ELP and HPH Digital Papers.*

79. Narrative of Mrs. Abraham Brasher (Helen Kortright) Giving an Account of Her Experiences in the Revolutionary War, 1802, 34–35, VF Women, DLAR ("On him," 34, "irreparable," 35, "children," 35, "cheerful," 35, "Slave," 35, "for he might," 35, "provider," 34).

80. Elizabeth Shipton to Aquila Giles, Monday Morning, Giles Family Papers, 1750–1881, box 1, folder 2, NYHS ("assassinated," "safe," "It may betray," "but the Idea"); James H. Thomson to Isaac Harleston, n.d., Isaac Child Harleston Letters, 1780–1936 [typescript], SCHS ("There is").

81. Elizabeth Inman to [Ralph Inman], May 6, 1775, James Murray Robbins Family Papers, 1638–1899, box 2, MHS ("too serious"), Elizabeth Inman to Ralph Inman, May 20, 1775 ("Job has"), Elizabeth Inman to Ralph Inman, June 12, 1775 ("like to have," "not been," "desgusted"). For espionage, see "Transcription from New England Chronicle," July 31, 1777, James Murray Robbins Family Papers, box 3, Archibald Campbell to Elizabeth Inman, Aug. 8, 1777, and Archibald Campbell to Elizabeth Inman, July 19, 1777. See also Patricia Cleary, *Elizabeth Murray: A Woman's Pursuit of Independence in Eighteenth-Century America* (Amherst, Mass., 2000), 184–185, 199–203.

82. Elizabeth Inman to Ralph Inman, June 12, 1775, James Murray Robbins Family Papers, box 2 ("Job's affair"); William Matthews to Gideon White, Apr. 26, 1782, White Family Fonds, film 683, reel 1, no. 130, DLAR ("threaten'd," "swearing," "had not been," "most atrocious," "I cannot"). Possibly this man was Sandy Alexander, who escaped from William Matthews in 1780 at age eighteen and who evacuated with the British Army in 1783; see "Book of Negroes," PRO 30/55/100, 106–107. For more on self-emancipated men in the British Army, see Clark, "Role of the Haitian Volunteers," *Phylon,* XLI (1980), 356–366; Morgan and O'Shaughnessy, "Arming Slaves in the American Revolution," in Brown and Morgan, eds., *Arming Slaves,* 180–208; and Lockley, "'King of England's Soldiers,'" in Harris and Berry, eds., *Slavery and Freedom in Savannah,* 26–41.

83. Minute Book of the Board of Police, Savannah, Ga., Feb. 17–19, [1779] (quotations). The police minutes record James Wright was the sole owner, yet this might be because

Alexander, who purchased the plantation in 1772, was ambivalent about the British cause and later left the colony; possibly he ceded control to his influential father. For more on the plantation, see Georgia Writers' Project, Savannah Unit, Work Projects Administration in Georgia, "Richmond Oakgrove Plantation, Part II," *Georgia Historical Quarterly,* XXIV (1940), 127–130.

84. Margaret Wheeler Willard, ed., *Letters on the American Revolution, 1774–1776* (Boston, 1925), 233 ("Hell," "we know"); [Janet Schaw], *Journal of a Lady of Quality: Being the Narrative of a Journey from Scotland to the West Indies, North Carolina, and Portugal, in the Years 1774 to 1776,* ed. Evangeline Walker Andrews and Charles McLean Andrews (New Haven, Conn., 1921), 199 ("promising," "pay," "Negroes"). Similar fears resonated throughout the colonies; see Elise Lemire, *Black Walden: Slavery and Its Aftermath in Concord, Massachusetts* (Philadelphia, 2009); Parkinson, *Common Cause;* Horne, *Counter-Revolution of 1776;* and Jason T. Sharples, *The World That Fear Made: Slave Revolts and Conspiracy Scares in Early America* (Philadelphia, 2020), 207–241.

85. John Mathews to George Washington, Oct. 14, 1780, FO, https://founders.archives.gov/documents/Washington/03-28-02-0296 ("My affairs"); "A Dialogue between Toney and Cuffee, on State Affairs," *American Journal, and General Advertiser* (Providence, R.I.), Mar. 14, 1781, [2] ("Brittain," "Merica").

86. Samuel Jarvis, "One Guinea Reward; Run Away from the Subscriber . . . a Negro Woman by the Name of Molly," *New-York Journal, and State Gazette,* Nov. 4, 1784, [2].

87. For more on how revolutionary experiences planted the seeds of future resistance, see Gary B. Nash, *Forging Freedom: The Formation of Philadelphia's Black Community, 1720–1840* (Cambridge, Mass., 1988); Frey, *Water from the Rock,* 326–329; and Van Buskirk, *Standing in Their Own Light,* 173–239.

88. For how these racial narratives contributed to the revolutionary cause, see Parkinson, *Common Cause.*

89. Joseph Clay to James Jackson, Feb. 16, 1784, in Georgia Historical Society, *Collections,* VIII (Savannah, Ga., 1913), 194–195 (quotation, 195).

EPILOGUE

1. John Adams to Abigail Adams, Apr. 28, 1777, FO, https://founders.archives.gov/documents/Adams/04-02-02-0171 (quotations). For emotion and the waging of war, see Nicole Eustace, *Passion Is the Gale: Emotion, Power, and the Coming of the American Revolution* (Williamsburg, Va., and Chapel Hill, N.C., 2008); Eustace, *1812: War and the Passions of Patriotism* (Philadelphia, 2012); and T. H. Breen, *The Will of the People: The Revolutionary Birth of America* (Cambridge, Mass., 2019).

2. Charles Thomson, "In Congress, April 18, 1777," *Pennsylvania Evening Post* (Philadelphia), Apr. 24, 1777, 229 (quotations). American diplomats also referenced Congress's 1777 report in communications with France, hoping that King Louis XVI would issue a proclamation against Britain's "barbarous Mode of War"; see John Adams' Draft of the Commissioners to the Comte de Vergennes, Dec. 20, 1778, FO, https://founders.archives.gov/documents/Adams/06-07-02-0196-0002; for more on these diplomatic efforts, see Holger Hoock, "*Jus in Bello,* Rape, and the British Army in the American Revolutionary War," *Journal of Military*

Ethics, XIV (2015), 74–97. For more on the rhetorical function of rape in the Revolution, see Sharon Block, "Rape without Women: Print Culture and the Politicization of Rape, 1765–1815," *JAH,* LXXXIX (2002), 849–868.

3. John Adams to Abigail Adams, Apr. 27, 1777, FO, https://founders.archives.gov/documents/Adams/04-02-02-0170 ("Not only," "will shew"), John Adams to Abigail Adams, Oct. 19, 1775, https://founders.archives.gov/documents/Adams/04-01-02-0199 ("Posterity"). For more on founding origin stories, see Michael A. McDonnell, "War Stories: Remembering and Forgetting the American Revolution," in Patrick Spero and Michael Zuckerman, eds., *The American Revolution Reborn* (Philadelphia, 2016), 9–28; and Michael D. Hattem, *Past and Prologue: Politics and Memory in the American Revolution* (New Haven, Conn., 2020). For the creation of national identity, see David Waldstreicher, *In the Midst of Perpetual Fetes: The Making of American Nationalism, 1776–1820* (Williamsburg, Va., and Chapel Hill, N.C., 1997); Carroll Smith-Rosenberg, *This Violent Empire: The Birth of an American National Identity* (Williamsburg, Va., and Chapel Hill, N.C., 2010); Robert G. Parkinson, *The Common Cause: Creating Race and Nation in the American Revolution* (Williamsburg, Va., and Chapel Hill, N.C., 2016); and Hattem, *Past and Prologue.*

4. Benjamin Franklin to David Hartley, Feb. 2, 1780, FO, https://founders.archives.gov/documents/Franklin/01-31-02-0310 ("school," "impress"), Franklin and Lafayette's List of Prints to Illustrate British Cruelties, [circa May 1779], https://founders.archives.gov/documents/Franklin/01-29-02-0477 ("Illustrate"), Marquis de Lafayette to Benjamin Franklin, May 19, 1779, https://founders.archives.gov/documents/Franklin/01-29-02-0436 ("Must be known"). Franklin supplied ideas for seventeen prints, with Lafayette contributing an additional nine. For the list of prints, see Franklin and Lafayette's List of Prints to Illustrate British Cruelties, [circa May 1779], FO, n.8 ("Of which the first sixteen"); see also Marquis de Lafayette to Benjamin Franklin, July 12, 1779, FO, https://founders.archives.gov/documents/Franklin/01-30-02-0061. For nationalist aims, see Benjamin Franklin to David Hartley, Feb. 2, 1780, FO, and Benjamin Franklin to William Hodgson, June 19, 1780, https://founders.archives.gov/documents/Franklin/01-32-02-0399. Although the book was never published, Franklin commissioned at least one engraving plate and six hundred copies; see Jacques-Donatien Le Ray de Chaumont and Franklin: An Exchange about Accounts, [before Apr. 26, 1782], FO, https://founders.archives.gov/documents/Franklin/01-37-02-0152. Robert Parkinson has persuasively argued that the book was an effort to rile up racial resentment; see Parkinson, *Common Cause,* 400–407. For rape in revolutionary propaganda, see Block, "Rape without Women," *JAH,* LXXXIX (2002), 849–868. For more on civic education in the early Republic, see Mark Boonshoft, *Aristocratic Education and the Making of the American Republic* (Chapel Hill, N.C., 2020); and Mary Sarah Bilder, *Female Genius: Eliza Harriot and George Washington at the Dawn of the Constitution* (Charlottesville, Va., 2021).

5. Narrative of Mrs. Abraham Brasher (Helen Kortright) Giving an Account of Her Experiences in the Revolutionary War, 1802, 47, VF Women, DLAR.

6. William Duane, ed., *Extracts from the Diary of Christopher Marshall: Kept in Philadelphia and Lancaster, during the American Revolution, 1774–1781* (Albany, N.Y., 1877), Dec. 16, 1777, 150 ("Our City," "in the hands"), Dec. 19, 1777, 151 ("thoughts").

7. Ibid., June 25, 1778, 189 ("My mind," "our once," "retur[n]"), June 26, 1778, 190 ("Grief," "[was] quite gone").

8. Isaac Winslow [to Parent(s?)], Aug. 7, 1787, Winslow Family Papers, 1690–1887, box 2, MHS ("late revolution"); [Hannah Griffitts], "Wrote on the Death of a Person Who, Died after a Violent Nervous Disorder, Occasion'd by the Distress She Suffer'd in the Late Distracted Times," April 1780, Hannah Griffitts Papers, LCPinHSP.222, 7422.F.62–69, HSP ("Violent").

9. John Adams to Abigail Adams, Jan. 22, 1783, FO, https://founders.archives.gov/documents/Adams/04-05-02-0040 ("I would give"), John Adams to Abigail Adams, Feb. 26, 1783, https://founders.archives.gov/documents/Adams/04-05-02-0055 ("I have," *"J'ai besoin d'être"*), Abigail Adams to John Adams, Apr. 28, 1783, https://founders.archives.gov/documents/Adams/04-05-02-0076 ("Need I add"), Abigail Adams to John Adams, May 7, 1783, https://founders.archives.gov/documents/Adams/04-05-02-0080 ("Come and give"), John Adams to Abigail Adams, July 26, 1783, https://founders.archives.gov/documents/Adams/04-05-02-0121 ("I wonder").

10. Benjamin Chew, Jr., to Benjamin Chew, Sr., Dec. 17, 1777, Chew Family Papers, 1659–1986, Ser. 2, box 10, folder 7, HSP ("imaginary); Thomas Fisher to Sarah Logan Fisher, Dec. 10, 1777, Logan-Fisher-Fox Papers, 1703–1940, Ser. 4, VIII, HSP ("I am often"); Benjamin Pickman to Thomas and William Pickman, Apr. 18, 1782, Benjamin Pickman Correspondence (photostats), 1775–1787, folder 4, Karolick-Codman Family Papers, 1714–1964, Ms. N-2164, Ser. IV, B.4, box OS 3, MHS.

11. Benjamin Pickman to Mary Pickman, July 21, 1775, Benjamin Pickman Correspondence, folder 1, Karolick-Codman Family Papers ("Twas death," "I some Times"); Henry Drinker to Elizabeth Drinker, Jan. 25, 1778, Henry and Elizabeth Drinker Letters, 1777–1778 (hereafter Drinker Letters), HCQSC ("I should think"); John Adams to Abigail Adams, Oct. 19, 1775, FO ("It would be a Joy"), John Adams to Abigail Adams, July 8, 1777, https://founders.archives.gov/documents/Adams/04-02-02-0218.

12. "Mrs. Mary [Gould] Almy's Account of the Cannonading of the French Fleet in Newport," Aug. 14, 1778, RLA ("Tedious," "I wonder"); Sarah Redwood Fisher to Miers Fisher, Nov. 23, 1777, Fisher Family Papers, 1761–1889, Ser. I, box 3, folder 1, HSP ("very hard"); Abigail Adams to John Adams, Apr. 17, 1777, FO, https://founders.archives.gov/documents/Adams/04-02-02-0161 ("cold comfort"); Elizabeth Drinker to Henry Drinker, Nov. 5, 1777, Drinker Letters ("open manner"), Elizabeth Drinker to Henry Drinker, Feb. 26, 1778 ("without speaking"), and Elizabeth Drinker to Henry Drinker, Jan. 1, 1778. For households and business, see Abigail Adams to John Adams, Apr. 7, 1776, FO, https://founders.archives.gov/documents/Adams/04-01-02-0244, Abigail Adams to John Adams, June 17, 1776, https://founders.archives.gov/documents/Adams/04-02-02-0009; and Sarah Logan Fisher Diary, IV, Nov. 1, 1777, [19–21], Sarah Logan Fisher Diaries, HSP, in The Revolutionary City: A Portal to the Nation's Founding, https://therevolutionarycity.org/islandora/fisher-sarah-logan-diary-volume-4. For missing husbands, see ibid., IV, Dec. 17, 1777, [29]; Abigail Adams to John Adams, Aug. 29, 1776, FO, https://founders.archives.gov/documents/Adams/04-02-02-0071, Abigail Adams to John Adams, Apr. 7, 1776; Hannah Pemberton, Jr., to James Pemberton, Nov. 24, 1777, Pemberton Family Papers, 1641–1880, XXXI, 45, HSP; and "Mrs. Mary [Gould] Almy's Account," Aug. 16, 22, 1778. For widows, see Alisa Wade, "The 'Widowed State': Women's Labor, Sacrifice, and Self-Sufficiency in the American Revolution," in Holly A. Mayer, ed., *Women Waging War in the American Revolution*

(Charlottesville, Va., 2022), 245–265; and Rosemarie Zagarri, *A Woman's Dilemma: Mercy Otis Warren and the American Revolution,* 2d ed. (Chichester, West Sussex, U.K., 2015), 78–95.

13. Sarah Logan Fisher Diary, VI, Dec. 19, 1778, [24], https://therevolutionarycity.org/islandora/fisher-sarah-logan-diary-volume-6.

14. George William Fairfax to George Washington, Dec. 5, 1779, FO, https://founders.archives.gov/documents/Washington/03-23-02-0395 ("domestic"); Lucy Flucker Knox to Henry Knox, Aug. 23, 1777, in Phillip Hamilton, ed., *The Revolutionary War Lives and Letters of Lucy and Henry Knox* (Baltimore, Md., 2017), 119 ("I hope," "There is"); Abigail Adams to John Adams, Aug. 29, 1776, FO ("All my desires"); Benjamin Pickman to Mary Pickman, Aug. 10, 1781, Benjamin Pickman Correspondence, folder 4, Karolick-Codman Family Papers ("pass my Days"), and Benjamin Pickman to Mary Pickman, Feb. 21, 1784, folder 5 ("For the remaining," "I am determined"). For generational differences, see Lucia McMahon, "'Of the Utmost Importance to Our Country': Women, Education, and Society, 1780–1820," *JER,* XXIX (2009), 475–506; Priscilla Mason, "Oration," 1793, in Lisa L. Moore, Joanna Brooks, and Caroline Wigginton, eds., *Transatlantic Feminisms in the Age of Revolutions* (Oxford, 2012), 291–295; and Edith B. Gelles, "Abigail Adams: Domesticity and the American Revolution," *New England Quarterly,* LII (1979), 500–521. For dependence, see Jacqueline Beatty, *In Dependence: Women and the Patriarchal State in Revolutionary America* (New York, 2023).

15. Mercy Otis Warren, *History of the Rise, Progress, and Termination of the American Revolution . . .* (Boston, 1805), iii–iv (quotations, iv).

16. George Mason to George Washington, Apr. 2, 1776, FO, https://founders.archives.gov/documents/Washington/03-04-02-0017 ("May God"). For the metaphor and its significance, see Daniel L. Dreisbach, "The 'Vine and Fig Tree' in George Washington's Letters: Reflections on a Biblical Motif in the Literature of the American Founding Era," *Anglican and Episcopal History,* LXXVI (2007), 299–326. For an overview of these allusions in the revolutionary era, see Gary Shattuck, "Under His Vine and Fig Tree," *Journal of the American Revolution,* June 3, 2014, https://allthingsliberty.com/2014/06/under-his-vine-and-fig-tree/. Woody Holton has argued that this postwar embrace of domestic tranquility was primarily about suppressing rebellion among enslaved people and impoverished farmers, not idealizations of domestic life; see Holton, *Liberty Is Sweet: The Hidden History of the American Revolution* (New York, 2021), 533–534.

17. George Washington to François-Jean de Beauvoir, marquis de Chastellux, Oct. 12, 1783, FO, https://founders.archives.gov/documents/Washington/99-01-02-11929 (quotation); see also George Washington to Lafayette, Feb. 1, 1784, FO, https://founders.archives.gov/documents/Washington/04-01-02-0064.

18. Lydia Mattice Brandt, *First in the Homes of His Countrymen: George Washington's Mount Vernon in the American Imagination* (Charlottesville, Va., 2016), 22–23 ("Without," 22, "public," 22–23); Robert F. Dalzell, Jr., and Lee Baldwin Dalzell, *George Washington's Mount Vernon: At Home in Revolutionary America* (Oxford, 1998), 112 ("tangible"). For Washington as a symbol, see Matthew R. Costello, *The Property of the Nation: George Washington's Tomb, Mount Vernon, and the Memory of the First President* (Lawrence, Kas., 2019), 13–45; and François Furstenberg, *In the Name of the Father: Washington's Legacy, Slavery, and the Making of a Nation* (New York, 2006). For examples of well-wishes, see Elias Dayton to George Washington, Aug. 21, 1783, FO, https://founders.archives.gov/documents/Washington/99-01-02-11726;

Hannah Lawrence Schieffelin, "The Progress of Liberty; Inscribed to General Washington," [1785], in "Notebook of Poems," 1774–1794, [100], Manuscripts and Archives Division, NYPL, Digital Collections, https://digitalcollections.nypl.org/items/a3dc5690-c557-0139-c4d3-0242ac110004; and Annis Boudinot Stockton to George Washington, Aug. 28, 1783, FO, https://founders.archives.gov/documents/Washington/99-01-02-11759.

19. Brandt, *First in the Homes*, 4, 26 (quotation); For pilgrimages, see Dalzell, Jr., and Dalzell, *George Washington's Mount Vernon*, 196–197; and Costello, *Property of the Nation*, 46–81, esp. 48–52.

20. Brandt, *First in the Homes*, 15–21.

21. George Washington to Elias Dayton, Aug. 21, 1783, FO, https://founders.archives.gov/documents/Washington/99-01-02-11727 ("enjoy[ing]"), Frederick Visscher to George Washington, June 30, 1782, https://founders.archives.gov/documents/Washington/99-01-02-08814 ("We anticipate"). Postwar reverence for domestic life is also evident in other wars; see Elaine Tyler May, *Homeward Bound: American Families in the Cold War Era* (New York, 1988); Brooke L. Blower, "V-J Day, 1945, Times Square," in Blower and Mark Philip Bradley, eds., *The Familiar Made Strange: American Icons and Artifacts after the Transnational Turn* (Ithaca, N.Y., 2015), 70–87; and Richard White, *The Republic for Which It Stands: The United States during Reconstruction and the Gilded Age, 1865–1896* (New York, 2017), 136–171.

22. Thomas Jefferson to Anne Willing Bingham, May 11, 1788, FO, https://founders.archives.gov/documents/Jefferson/01-13-02-0076 ("There is no," "is enjoyed"), Abigail Adams to John Quincy Adams, Dec. 26, 1783, https://founders.archives.gov/documents/Adams/04-05-02-0156 ("Boast[ed]"). Washington also viewed domestic happiness as entwined with the Revolution. After a French officer's 1788 marriage, he teased, "Now you are well served for coming to fight in favour of the American Rebels . . . by catching that terrible Contagion—domestic felicity," which, among American men, "commonly lasts . . . his whole life time"; see George Washington to Chastellux, Apr. 25–May 1, 1788, FO, https://founders.archives.gov/documents/Washington/04-06-02-0202.

23. For more on the creation of the medals, see Henry Knox to George Washington, July 7, 1789, FO, https://founders.archives.gov/documents/Washington/05-03-02-0067; and Bauman L. Belden, *Indian Peace Medals Issued in the United States* (New York, 1927), 22–24.

24. As Thavolia Glymph argues in regard to the American Civil War, even though there were no major slave revolts, most enslaved people did not flee, and the majority of white southern residences remained intact, the knowledge that these things happened and "the stories of those who lost their homes, who saw them invaded by enemy soldiers and became refugees fundamentally shaped how Confederate women understood their wartime experience at the time and long after the war had ended"; see Glymph, *The Women's Fight: The Civil War's Battles for Home, Freedom, and Nation* (Chapel Hill, N.C., 2020), 42 (quotation), 43, 50.

25. Marquis de Lafayette to Benjamin Franklin, July 12, 1779, FO (quotation).

26. In their respective books, Donald F. Johnson has argued that "forgetting occupation" was integral to building national unity, and John Gilbert McCurdy has identified the "historical amnesia" around quartering, suggesting that this historiographical oversight is deeply embedded within the historiography of the Revolution and its aftermath; see Johnson, *Occupied America: British Military Rule and the Experience of Revolution* (Philadelphia, 2020), 191; and McCurdy, *Quarters: The Accommodation of the British Army and the Coming of the*

American Revolution (Ithaca, N.Y., 2020), 237; see also McDonnell, "War Stories," in Spero and Zuckerman, eds., *American Revolution Reborn,* 9–28.

27. For British occupation as seduction, see "Amelia: Or the Faithless Briton; An Original Novel, Founded upon Recent Facts," *Columbian Magazine,* I (1787), 677–682, 877–880; Joseph Davenport, "The Seige [*sic*] of Rhode Island, a Play in Seven Acts: Describing the British Occupation of Newport and Narragansett Bay and the Heroic Deeds of Patriotic Rhode Islanders and Their Effort to Rid Their Fair Isle of the Tyrannical Power," 1779[?], 25, Typescript by Jeffrey P. Greene, 1988, RIHS; and James McHenry, *Meredith; or, The Mystery of the Meschianza: A Tale of the American Revolution* (Philadelphia, 1831).The nationalistic intent behind these revisions is made evident by Daniel Wallace, who urged a novelist friend to fictionalize a tragic incident in which a South Carolina man accidentally killed his loyalist sister during a raid on her house. "As fiction will admit some liberties to be taken with the truth," he mused, "you could place her on the Whig side—give her a fictitious name and make her the heroine of the tale, and let her death be by a tory"; see "Incidents of the Revolution in Union, York, and Spartansburg Districts," South Carolina, box 30, folder 17, Miscellaneous Collections: U.S. States and Territories, MssCol 3103, Manuscripts and Archives Division, NYPL. For the role of literature in spreading political ideology and revealing contests over authority, especially in terms of gender, see Linda K. Kerber, *Women of the Republic: Intellect and Ideology in Revolutionary America* (Williamsburg, Va., and Chapel Hill, N.C., 1980), 233–264; Carroll Smith-Rosenberg, "Domesticating 'Virtue': Coquettes and Revolutionaries in Young America," in Elaine Scarry, ed., *Literature and the Body: Essays on Populations and Persons* (Baltimore, Md., 1988), 160–184; Ruth H. Bloch, "The Gendered Meanings of Virtue in Revolutionary America," *Signs: Journal of Women in Culture and Society,* XIII (1987), 37–58; Jan Lewis, "The Republican Wife: Virtue and Seduction in the Early Republic," *WMQ,* 3d Ser., XLIV (1987), 689–721; Cathy N. Davidson, *Revolution and the Word: The Rise of the Novel in America* (New York, 1986), esp. 110–150; Tara Fitzpatrick, "Liberty, Corruption, and Seduction in the Republican Imagination," *Connotations,* IV (1994/1995), 44–66; Jeffrey H. Richards, "The Politics of Seduction: Theater, Sexuality, and National Virtue in the Novels of Hannah Foster," in Della Pollock, ed., *Exceptional Spaces: Essays in Performance and History* (Chapel Hill, N.C., 1998), 238–257; Rodney Hessinger, *Seduced, Abandoned, and Reborn: Visions of Youth in Middle-Class America, 1780–1850* (Philadelphia, 2005), 23–43; Christopher J. Lukasik, *Discerning Characters: The Culture of Appearance in Early America* (Philadelphia, 2011), 73–120; Hugh McIntosh, "Constituting the End of Feeling: Interiority in the Seduction Fiction of the Ratification Era," *Early American Literature,* XLVII (2012), 321–348; and Eve Tavor Bannet, "The Constantias of the 1790s: Tales of Constancy and Republican Daughters," *Early American Literature,* XLIX (2014), 435–466.

28. "Harriott P. Rutledge's Recollections about Mrs. [Rebecca Brewton] Motte," Oct. 9, 1855, Charles C. Pinckney Family Papers, 1855–1945, 43/1096, SCHS (quotations); for more on the arrows, see Alexander Garden, *Anecdotes of the Revolutionary War in America: With Sketches of Character of Persons the Most Distinguished, in the Southern States, for Civil and Military Services* (Charleston, S.C., 1822), 230–232. For early efforts to domesticate Motte and portray her role as passive, see Henry Lee, *Memoirs of the War in the Southern Department of the United States,* II (Philadelphia, 1812), 77; see also Elizabeth F. Ellet, *The Women of the American Revolution,* II (New York, 1848), 72–73. This interpretation has shaped commemorations in intervening centuries; for instance, in 1903, the Rebecca Motte chapter of the

Daughters of the American Revolution erected a tablet honoring Rebecca Motte made from a tabletop from her Charleston residence; see *Tablet to Mrs. Rebecca Motte: Erected by Rebecca Motte Chapter of the Daughters of the American Revolution* (Charleston, S.C., 1903), 7–9, SCHS. For the painting, see William Kloss and Diane K. Skavalia, *United States Senate Catalogue of Fine Art* (Washington, D.C., 2002), 32, 290–293. For a contemporary depiction of Liberty, see Augustin Dupre, *Libertas Americana*, 1782, medal, bronze, 35mm x 47.7 mm, 1 3/8 in. x 1 7/8 in., Accession no. 1991.0009.0563, National Museum of American History, Washington, D.C. For more on the symbol of Liberty, see Yvonne Korshak, "The Liberty Cap as a Revolutionary Symbol in America and France," *Smithsonian Studies in American Art*, I, no. 2 (Fall 1987), 61–62. For the gendered meanings of civic virtue, see Kerber, *Women of the Republic*, 269–288; Lewis, "Republican Wife," *WMQ*, 3d Ser., XLIV (1987), 689–721; Bloch, "Gendered Meanings of Virtue," *Signs*, XIII (1987), 37–58; Rosemarie Zagarri, "Morals, Manners, and the Republican Mother," *American Quarterly*, XLIV (1992), 192–215; and Sarah Knott, "Female Liberty? Sentimental Gallantry, Republican Womanhood, and Rights Feminism in the Age of Revolutions," *WMQ*, 3d Ser, LXXI (2014), 425–456. For more on founding mythologies, see McDonnell, "War Stories," in Spero and Zuckerman, ed., *American Revolution Reborn*, 9–28; and Hattem, *Past and Prologue*.

29. For an overview of efforts to promote simplified narratives of the war years, see Susan E. Klepp, "Rough Music on Independence Day: Philadelphia, 1778," in William Pencak, Matthew Dennis, and Simon P. Newman, eds., *Riot and Revelry in Early America* (Philadelphia, 2002), 163–172; and Benjamin H. Irvin, *Clothed in Robes of Sovereignty: The Continental Congress and the People Out of Doors* (Oxford, 2011) 156–163. For the conservative backlash in the founding era, see Rosemarie Zagarri, *Revolutionary Backlash: Women and Politics in the Early American Republic* (Philadelphia, 2007); and Bilder, *Female Genius*; see also Kerber, *Women of the Republic*, 269–288; and Mary Beth Norton, *Liberty's Daughters: The Revolutionary Experience of American Women, 1750–1800* (Boston, 1980), 295–299.

30. William Whiting, "Some Remarks on the Conduct of the Inhabitants of the Commonwealth of Massachusetts . . . ," in Stephen T. Riley, "Doctor William Whiting and Shays' Rebellion," American Antiquarian Society, *Proceedings*, LXVI (Worcester, Mass., 1957), 144–145 ("have Served," 144, "Left Destitute," 144–145); for more on Shays' Rebellion, see Leonard L. Richards, *Shays's Rebellion: The American Revolution's Final Battle* (Philadelphia, 2002). For domestic finances, see Nathanael Greene to John Martin, Aug. 8, 1782, GHS 0071, Joseph Vallence Bevan Papers, 1733–1826, folder 9, GHS.

31. George Washington to Lafayette, June 18, 1788, FO, https://founders.archives.gov/documents/Washington/04-06-02-0301 (quotations). For enlistment bounties, see *Journals of the Continental Congress, 1774–1789*, XXXIV (Washington, D.C., 1937), July 9, 1788, 306–310. For veterans' bounties, see James L. Abrahamson, *The American Home Front: Revolutionary War, Civil War, World War I, World War II* (Washington, D.C., 1983), 19–21. For households and westward expansion, see Honor Sachs, *Home Rule: Households, Manhood, and National Expansion on the Eighteenth-Century Kentucky Frontier* (New Haven, Conn., 2015); and Laurel Clark Shire, *The Threshold of Manifest Destiny: Gender and National Expansion in Florida* (Philadelphia, 2016).

32. For speculation, see Michael A. Blaakman, "The Marketplace of American Federalism: Land Speculation across State Lines in the Early Republic," *JAH*, CVII (2020), 583–608, esp. 607–608. For white families, see Sachs, *Home Rule*; and Shire, *Threshold of Manifest*

Destiny. For federal government, see Blaakman, "Marketplace of American Federalism," *JAH,* CVII (2020), 583–608; and Jessica Choppin Roney, "Statelessness and State Making in Early Modern North America," conference paper delivered at "Crafting Narratives of Empire: Contested Roots of Revolution in the Long 18th Century," Institute for Thomas Paine Studies, Iona University and the Kinder Institute on Constitutional Democracy at the University of Missouri, New Rochelle, N.Y., Sept. 22–24, 2022.

33. For Native nations, see Kathleen DuVal, *Independence Lost: Lives on the Edge of the American Revolution* (New York, 2015); for resistance to dispossession, see Elizabeth N. Ellis, *The Great Power of Small Nations: Indigenous Diplomacy in the Gulf South* (Philadelphia, 2022), 227–254. During the war, both sides confiscated enemy property—a practice supposedly halted by the 1783 Treaty of Paris. Throughout the 1780s, however, state governments continued to confiscate loyalist property. For confiscation and its significance, see Tom Cutterham, *Gentlemen Revolutionaries: Power and Justice in the New American Republic* (Princeton, N.J., 2017), 66–93; see also Rebecca Brannon, *From Revolution to Reunion: The Reintegration of the South Carolina Loyalists* (Columbia, S.C., 2016). For rewards, see Edmund Randolph to James Madison, June 20, 1782, FO, https://founders.archives.gov/documents/Madison/01-04-02-0164; and "Report of a Committee of the House of Representatives of Georgia," July 29, 1782, GHS 0071, Joseph Vallence Bevan Papers, folder 9.

34. For Black kinship and households under slavery, see Thavolia Glymph, *Out of the House of Bondage: The Transformation of the Plantation Household* (New York, 2008); Dylan C. Penningroth, *The Claims of Kinfolk: African American Property and Community in the Nineteenth-Century South* (Chapel Hill, N.C., 2003); Walter Johnson, *River of Dark Dreams: Slavery and Empire in the Cotton Kingdom* (Cambridge, Mass., 2013); Jennifer L. Morgan, *Reckoning with Slavery: Gender, Kinship, and Capitalism in the Early Black Atlantic* (Durham, N.C., 2021); and Whitney Nell Stewart, *This Is Our Home: Slavery and Struggle on Southern Plantations* (Chapel Hill, N.C., 2023).

35. Honor Sachs argues early national households had racial and national meanings: "As white men conceived of their roles as citizens through the lens of household protection, they bolstered increasingly militant policies against nonwhites as imagined threats to the safety and sanctity of the domestic realm"; see Sachs, *Home Rule,* 147; see also Smith-Rosenberg, *This Violent Empire;* Parkinson, *Common Cause;* and Shire, *Threshold of Manifest Destiny.*

36. U.S. Const., Bill of Rights, amend. III ("without"), IV ("right of the people"), and V ("deprived"). For more on the gendered nature of privacy, see Ruth H. Bloch, "The American Revolution, Wife Beating, and the Emergent Value of Privacy," *EAS,* V (2007), 223–251.

37. For household power, see Bloch, "American Revolution, Wife Beating, and the Emergent Value of Property," *EAS,* V (2007), 226. For virtue, see Bloch, "Gendered Meanings of Virtue," *Signs,* XIII (1987), 55–58; and Clare A. Lyons, *Sex among the Rabble: An Intimate History of Gender and Power in the Age of Revolution, Philadelphia, 1730–1830* (Williamsburg, Va., and Chapel Hill, N.C., 2006), 288–292, 390–392. These ideas about Anglo-American womanhood, historian Rosemarie Zagarri contends, emerged out of Enlightenment discourses and were part of broader eighteenth-century intellectual trends; see Zagarri, "Morals, Manners, and the Republican Mother," *American Quarterly,* XLIV (1992), 208–211. For the gendered construction of the household and idealized domesticity, see Nancy F. Cott, *Bonds of Womanhood: "Women's Sphere" in New England, 1780–1835* (New Haven, Conn., 1977), 63–100; Jeanne Boydston, *Home and Work: Housework, Wages, and the Ideology of Labor in*

the Early Republic (New York, 1990), 43–55, 142–163; Christine Stansell, *City of Women: Sex and Class in New York, 1789–1860* (New York, 1982), 41–75; and Cynthia A. Kierner, *Beyond the Household: Women's Place in the Early South, 1700–1835* (Ithaca, N.Y., 1998), 161–170; for the importance of the symbolic household, see Sachs, *Home Rule,* esp. 10, 150. For more on gender, citizenship, and virtue, see Rosemarie Zagarri, "The Rights of Man and Woman in Post-Revolutionary America," *WMQ,* 3d Ser., LV (1998), 203–230; and Bloch, "Gendered Meanings of Virtue," *Signs,* XIII (1987), 37–58.

INDEX